Global Issues

Global Issues

2005 EDITION

CQ PRESS

A Division of Congressional Quarterly Inc., Washington, D.C.

SELECTIONS FROM **THE CQ RESEARCHER**

CQ Press
1255 22nd Street, N.W., Suite 400
Washington, D.C. 20037

(202) 729-1900; toll-free, 1-866-4CQ-PRESS (1-866-427-7737)
www.cqpress.com

♾ The paper used in this publication exceeds the requirements of the American National Standard for Information Sciences—Permanence of Paper for Printed Library Materials, ANSI Z39.48-1992.

Printed and bound in the United States of America

08 07 06 05 04   5 4 3 2 1

A CQ Press College Division Publication

Director	Brenda Carter
Acquisitions editor	Charisse Kiino
Marketing manager	Bonnie Erickson
Production editor	Joan Gossett
Cover designer	Kimberly Glyder
Composition	Circle Graphics, Inc.
Print buyer	Margot Ziperman
Sales manager	James Headley

Library of Congress Cataloging-in-Publication Data

Global issues : selections from The CQ researcher.
    p. cm.
  Includes bibliographical references.
  ISBN 1-56802-894-6 (pbk. : alk. paper)
  1. Globalization. 2. International relations. 3. Security, International. I. CQ
Press. II. CQ researcher. III. Title.

JZ1318.G558 2005
327—dc22

                                                                                        2004061795

Contents

DEMOCRATIZATION

HUMAN RIGHTS

Annotated Contents

The 16 *CQ Researcher* articles reprinted in this book have been reproduced essentially as they appeared when first published. In a few cases in which important new developments have since occurred, updates are provided in the overviews highlighting the principal issues examined.

CONFLICT, SECURITY AND TERRORISM

Stopping Genocide

Ten years ago, nearly a million ethnic-minority Rwandans died in a government-planned massacre. Political leaders in the United States and the United Nations later admitted they should have intervened and vowed "Never again"—just as they vowed after the Holocaust. But as ethnic killings in western Sudan make tragically clear, genocide still flourishes. The Bush administration supports sanctions against the Khartoum government, but human-rights activists say an international force is needed to protect civilians. With U.S. troops stretched thin in Iraq, however, the United States has been reluctant to act. Some question whether Americans, preoccupied with terrorism, have the appetite for humanitarian military actions. The U.N. has tried to improve its poor record of mobilizing troops by authorizing Western powers to lead forces in recent crises. But many believe the U.N. is politically paralyzed by the competing interests of the five major members of the Security Council, who can veto any military action.

New Defense Priorities

After the Cold War, the Pentagon began downsizing its forces and developing high-tech, mobile weapons designed to deal with "rogue" states like Iraq—less powerful than the Soviet juggernaut but still able to attack the United States and its allies. The Sept. 11, 2001, attacks forced Pentagon planners back to the drawing board to develop new strategies and weapons. President George W. Bush put his new preemptive strike strategy into practice in March 2003 by deposing Iraqi President Saddam Hussein, despite the opposition of most U.S. allies. Defense Secretary Donald H. Rumsfeld continues to transform the military to enable it to counter emerging threats from unconventional forces like al Qaeda.

Re-examining 9/11

After nearly three years, haunting questions remain unanswered about the Sept. 11, 2001, terrorist attacks on the United States: How did the 19 hijackers elude detection to carry out their deadly plot? And why did the government fail to take stronger action against al Qaeda earlier? On July 22, 2004, the independent 9/11 Commission published a long-awaited report on what went wrong on 9/11 and what can be done to prevent future catastrophes. The bipartisan panel's report faulted both the Clinton and Bush administrations for failing to recognize the dangers posed by Osama bin Laden and called for significant changes in U.S. intelligence agencies. But some experts say even major reforms cannot eliminate the danger of future attacks by determined enemies. Indeed, the government continues to warn the public that major terrorist attacks are possible in the United States this year.

Nuclear Proliferation and Terrorism

The discovery of a global black market in nuclear weapons and related technology has intensified concerns that so-called rogue nations and terrorist organizations like Osama bin Laden's al Qaeda network might acquire nuclear bombs. The network run by the "father" of Pakistan's atomic bomb, A.Q. Khan, sold nuclear-weapons materials to Iran and North Korea, which have refused to sign the Nuclear Non-Proliferation Treaty (NPT). Virtually all the other nations of the world are signatories. President George W. Bush responded to the revelations about Khan's network with a plan to strengthen international anti-proliferation efforts, including calling on the U.N. Security Council to require all states to criminalize proliferation of components that could be used to make weapons of mass destruction. While arms experts commended the president for focusing on proliferation, some said his proposals did not go far enough.

The United Nations and Global Security

The United Nations was founded after World War II to promote global security. But following the bitter divisions created in the Security Council in 2003 by the U.S.-led Iraq war, some observers question whether the U.N. can foster global peace and stability. Critics contend that Article 51 of the U.N. charter, which grants nations the right to self-defense, does not allow them to act against rogue states and terrorists. Others say the Security Council lacks credibility because many of today's big powers—like Japan and India—are not permanent members. But U.N. supporters say the charter does allow nations to counter threats, even preemptively, and that the Security Council can effectively promote peace and security.

INTERNATIONAL POLITICAL ECONOMY

Exporting Jobs

The U.S. economy is recovering, but employment continues to lag. Experts blame some of the joblessness on the job-exporting phenomenon known as offshoring. Well-trained, low-wage workers in India, China and other developing countries make exporting American jobs attractive, as does the widespread availability of high-speed Internet connections. In addition, millions of foreign professionals have entered the U.S. work force using temporary visas, while millions more undocumented foreign workers from Mexico and Latin America have found low-wage jobs in the United States thanks to lax immigration and border-control policies. Offshoring proponents say paying lower wages reduces the cost of goods and raises profits, ultimately enabling U.S. companies to create better-paying jobs for Americans. Critics say offshoring simply eliminates good jobs. However, according to a Labor Department report released on June 10, 2004, offshoring was responsible for only a small percentage of U.S. job losses.

Oil Diplomacy

The United States depends on foreign imports to satisfy more than half its voracious appetite for petroleum and petroleum products. Despite efforts to diversify oil suppliers and conserve energy after the 1973 Arab oil embargo, growing energy consumption all but forces the United States to continue relying on Middle Eastern oil. That reliance is likely to continue despite the ongoing occupation of Iraq and growing anti-American sentiment in the region. The Bush administration proposes reducing America's dependence on foreign oil by intensifying domestic production in Alaska and other environmentally sensitive areas. Critics contend that the thirst for oil was behind the administration's plan to invade Iraq as well as its willingness to repeat Cold War mistakes and maintain close relations with dictatorial regimes accused of human-rights abuses.

Japan in Crisis

After years as the economic envy of the world, Japan suffered almost twenty years of a nearly continuous recession. As of July 2002, unemployment, homelessness and crime were on the rise, and the banking system was lurching toward collapse under the weight of a trillion dollars in bad loans. The election in 2001 of Prime Minister Junichiro Koizumi on a radical reform platform had produced little immediate change, owing in part to the power of special-interest politics. Japan also struggled with the economic costs of an increasingly aging population and growing competition from neighboring countries. After the Sept. 11, 2001, attacks on New York City and the Pentagon, the United States pressured Japan to help in the war against terrorism, triggering a debate within the country over its long-standing prohibition against sending troops into overseas combat. While Japan has reversed the downward spiral of recession over the past few years, its economic weaknesses—such as ballooning budget deficits and less-than-expected growth rates—still persist.

DEMOCRATIZATION

Democracy in the Arab World

The monarchs and presidential strongmen who have governed Arab lands since independence in the mid-20th century have been reluctant to share power, allow free elections or permit popular dissent. Following the overthrow of Saddam Hussein, however, President Bush has vowed to establish a working democracy in Iraq—and to promote free elections throughout the region. But

democratization faces daunting obstacles, including the Arab world's limited experience with self-rule, imbalanced economic development and the rise of radical Islamist movements. While some experts see encouraging signs in a few countries, prospects for democracy appear dim in many others, including two major U.S. Arab allies: Egypt and Saudi Arabia.

Trouble in South America

New problems—including the financial collapse of Argentina in 2001—obliterated the past decade of economic growth in South America and pushed the continent into recession. Some economists blame the International Monetary Fund and other multilateral lenders for the decline, arguing they forced South America's fragile economies to adopt free trade and other market-oriented policies without fully considering the consequences. Defenders of the banks' policies blame the economic woes on huge budget deficits and corruption. Meanwhile, leftist guerrillas continue to terrorize Colombia, and political turmoil, especially in Venezuela, has led some experts to worry about the survival of democratic gains made throughout South America in the 1980s and '90s.

Aiding Africa

Liberia's descent into chaos is the latest chapter in the tragic history of sub-Saharan Africa. For decades, the world's poorest region has been battered by famine, AIDS and horrific civil wars that have killed or maimed tens of millions of people. Some Africa-watchers contended in 2003 that the continent's prospects were looking up, and that with increased Western financial help Africa would become more democratic and prosperous in the coming decades. But other experts said that even recent positive steps, like the shift toward democracy in the 1990s, have stalled. Moreover, they warned that sending foreign aid to Africa was a waste of money. The deployment of U.S. troops in war-torn Liberia in 2003 sparked debate over whether America should intervene in nations of questionable strategic importance.

HUMAN RIGHTS

Human Trafficking and Slavery

From the villages of Sudan to the factories, sweatshops and brothels of India and South Asia, slavery and human trafficking still flourish. Some 27 million people world-wide are held in some form of slavery, forced prostitution or bonded labor. Some humanitarian groups buy captives' freedom, but critics say that only encourages slave traders to seize more victims. Meanwhile, nearly a million people are forcibly trafficked across international borders annually and held in captivity. Even in the United States, thousands of women and children from overseas are forced to become sex workers. Congress recently strengthened the Trafficking Victims Protection Act, but critics say it is still not tough enough, and that certain U.S. allies that harbor traffickers are treated with "kid gloves" for political reasons.

Ethics of War

The war on terrorism unleashed by the Sept. 11, 2001, attacks has raised questions about how civilized nations should confront enemies that flout established international humanitarian law. In 2002, Amnesty International and other groups contended the United States was violating the Geneva Convention—which mandates humane treatment of civilians and prisoners of war (POWs)—by holding captives from the war in Afghanistan incommunicado. But the administration said its al Qaeda and Taliban prisoners did not warrant POW status because they did not represent legitimate states. Then in June 2004, the U.S. Supreme Court ruled that the detention of a U.S.-born "enemy combatant" violated the detainee's right to due process. The American-led invasion of Iraq raised similar debates. In early 2003, religious leaders spoke against the U.S. plan to invade Iraq and oust Saddam Hussein's regime. They said attacking Iraq would not constitute a "just war," because Saddam Hussein did not pose an imminent threat. But others said Hussein had to be confronted because he had used weapons of mass destruction before and could do so again.

HEALTH AND THE ENVIRONMENT

Bush and the Environment

Since taking office four years ago, President Bush has sought to reverse an array of regulations and long-standing environmental-protection laws. Administration officials say many of the old rules actually were harming the environment and the economy—such as by permitting delays in removing flammable deadwood from forests or by barring oil and gas production on public land. Bush also repudiated the Kyoto Protocol, an international treaty to slow global warming. Conservationists say such actions jeopardize the progress made in restoring environmental health since the passage of bedrock environmental-protection laws more than 30 years ago. They also contend the president's policies favor the energy industry and others that have long chafed at environmental regulations.

Water Shortages

More than a billion people around the world lack access to safe drinking water, and their numbers are growing. To make matters worse, 40 percent of Earth's inhabitants—nearly 3 billion people—have no sanitation services, often forcing them to sully the little fresh water they have. The drought of 2003 intensified the ongoing struggle between thirsty urban centers in the West and rural communities fighting cities' efforts to tap their pristine rivers. Environmentalists say conservation can alleviate these kinds of water shortages, but others contend privatization of water supplies and more investment in technology offer the most hope.

Fighting SARS

In November 2002, a deadly, new form of pneumonia—severe acute respiratory syndrome (SARS)—broke out in southern China. By the time Chinese authorities acknowledged the SARS outbreak four months later, it had spread beyond China's borders. By June 2003 SARS had afflicted thousands in 32 countries; hundreds had died. Public-health experts around the world were scrambling to eradicate the epidemic and develop vaccines to prevent future outbreaks. In the United States, critics said the outbreak was a wake-up call about underfunding of the public-health system. Meanwhile, some health experts worried that Americans would not be willing to accept quarantines and other strict measures needed to stop a SARS epidemic. They said the World Health Organization should have the power to intervene in any country that fails to take appropriate action.

Preface

In this pivotal era of international policymaking, scholars, students, practitioners and journalists seek solutions to the world's most critical concerns. Is the United Nations doing enough to stop and prevent genocide in the Sudan? How can nations prevent "rogue" states and terrorists from obtaining nuclear weapons? Is democracy taking root in the Arab world because of the U.S.-led occupations of Afghanistan and Iraq? Are nations of the world doing enough to stamp out human trafficking and slavery? To promote viable change and resolution, we must first understand the facts and context of vital global issues.

This 2005 edition of *Global Issues,* the fourth installment of this series, provides comprehensive and unbiased coverage of today's most pressing global problems. It weighs the intricate and at times convoluted dynamics of international issues in order to facilitate sound analysis. *Global Issues* is a compilation of 16 recent reports from *The CQ Researcher,* a weekly policy brief that brings complicated issues into focus. The *Researcher* unpacks difficult concepts and provides balanced coverage of competing perspectives. Each article analyzes past, present and future political maneuvering, and challenges students with questions guaranteed to engage them with problems affecting people worldwide. *Global Issues* is designed to promote in-depth discussion, promote further research and help readers formulate their own positions on crucial international issues.

This collection is organized into five subject areas that span a range of important international policy concerns: conflict, security and terrorism; international political economy; democratization; human rights; and health and the environment. More than half of these reports are new to this edition, which includes two updated reports, "Ethics of War" and "Bush and the Environment." *Global Issues* is an attractive supplement for courses on world affairs in political science, geography, economics and sociology. Interested citizens, journalists and business and government leaders will also turn to it to become better informed on key issues, actors and policy positions.

THE CQ RESEARCHER

The CQ Researcher was founded in 1923 as *Editorial Researcher Reports* and was sold primarily to newspapers as a research tool. The magazine was given its current name and redesign in 1991. While *The CQ Researcher* is still used by hundreds of newspapers, some of which reprint all or part of each issue, high school, college and public libraries are now the main subscribers. Thus, students, not journalists, are now the primary audience for *The CQ Researcher*.

The *Researcher's* staff writers—all highly experienced journalists—sometimes compare the experience of writing a *Researcher* report to drafting a college term paper. Indeed, there are many similarities: Each article is as long as many term papers—about 11,000 words—and is written by one person without any significant outside help. One of the key differences is that the writers interview top experts and government officials for each report. In fact, the *Researcher* won the American Bar Association's coveted Silver Gavel award for magazines in 2002 for a series of nine reports on civil liberties and other legal issues.

Like a student, the staff writer begins the creative process by choosing a topic. Working with the *Researcher's* editors, the writer identifies a subject that has public policy implications and for which there is significant controversy. After a topic is set, the writer embarks on a week or two of intense research. Articles are clipped, books ordered and information gathered from a variety of sources, including interest groups, universities and the government. Once a writer is well informed about the subject, he or she begins interviewing academics, officials, lobbyists and people working in the field. Each piece usually requires a minimum of ten to fifteen interviews, while some especially complicated subjects call for more. After much reading and interviewing, the writer develops a detailed outline. Only then does the writing begin.

CHAPTER FORMAT

Each issue of the *Researcher,* and therefore each selection in this book, has the same structure. They begin with an introductory overview of the topic, which briefly touches on the areas that will be explored in greater detail in the rest of the chapter.

The second section chronicles the most important and current debates in the field. It is structured around a number of key questions, known as "Issue Questions," such as "Should the U.N. Security Council be expanded to include new members?" or "Should Saudi Arabia be held more accountable for its role in the spread of Islamic fundamentalism?" This section is the core of each chapter. The questions raised are often highly controversial and usually the object of much argument among scholars and practitioners. Hence, the answers provided are never conclusive, but detail the range of opinion within the field.

Following "Issue Questions" is the "Background" section, which provides a history of the issue being examined. This retrospective includes important legislative and executive actions and court decisions from the past that inform readers on how current policy evolved.

Next, the "Current Situation" examines important contemporary policy issues, legislation under consideration and legal action being taken. Finally, each selection ends with an "Oulook" section, which gives a sense of what new regulations, court rulings and possible initiatives might happen in the next five to ten years.

Each section contains other regular features that augment the main text: two or three sidebars that examine issues related to the topic; a pro-con debate by two outside experts; a chronology of key dates and events; and an annotated bibliography, detailing major sources used by the writer.

ACKNOWLEDGMENTS

We wish to thank many people for helping to make this collection a reality. Tom Colin, managing editor of *The CQ Researcher,* gave us his enthusiastic support and cooperation as we developed this 2005 edition. He and his talented staff of editors and writers have amassed a first-class collection of *Researcher* articles, and we are fortunate to have access to this rich cache. We also thankfully acknowledge the advice and feedback from current readers and are gratified by their success with the book.

Some readers of this collection may be learning about *The CQ Researcher* for the first time. We expect that many will want regular access to this excellent weekly research tool. Anyone interested in subscription information or a no-obligation free trial of the *Researcher* can contact CQ Press at www.cqpress.com or 1-866-4CQ-Press (1-866-427-7737, toll-free).

We hope that you will be pleased by the 2005 edition of *Global Issues*. We welcome and encourage your feedback and suggestions for future editions. Please direct comments to Charisse Kiino, CQ Press, 1255 22nd Street, N.W., Suite 400, Washington, D.C. 20037; or send e-mail to *ckiino@cqpress.com*.

—The Editors of CQ Press

Contributors

Thomas J. Colin, managing editor of *The CQ Researcher*, has been a magazine and newspaper journalist for more than 30 years. Before joining Congressional Quarterly in 1991, he was a reporter and editor at *The Miami Herald* and *National Geographic* and editor in chief of *Historic Preservation*. He holds a bachelor's degree in English from the College of William and Mary and a bachelor's degree in journalism from the University of Missouri.

Mary H. Cooper specializes in environmental, energy and defense issues. Before joining *The CQ Researcher* as a staff writer in 1983, she was a reporter and Washington correspondent for the Rome daily *l'Unità*. She is the author of *The Business of Drugs* (CQ Press, 1990). She is also a contract translator–interpreter for the U.S. State Department. Cooper graduated from Hollins College with a bachelor's degree in English.

Sarah Glazer specializes in health, education and social-policy issues. Her articles have appeared in *The New York Times, The Washington Post, Glamour, The Public Interest* and *Gender and Work* (a book of essays). Glazer covered energy legislation for the Environmental and Energy Study Conference and reported for United Press International. She holds a bachelor's degree in American history from the University of Chicago.

Benton Ives-Halperin covers the Senate for Congressional Quarterly's online publication *CQ.com*. He is a former *Researcher* assistant editor and graduated from the University of Virginia with a bachelor's degree in English.

Kenneth Jost, associate editor of *The CQ Researcher*, graduated from Harvard College and Georgetown University Law Center, where he is an adjunct professor. He is the author of *The Supreme Court Yearbook* and editor of *The Supreme Court A to Z* (both CQ Press). He was a member of the *Researcher* team that won the 2002 American Bar Association Silver Gavel Award.

Kenneth Lukas, former assistant editor of *The CQ Researcher*, is currently pursuing a master's degree in international relations at the University of Chicago. He graduated Phi Beta Kappa from Rhodes College and received a Fulbright Fellowship to study in Germany.

David Masci, a former writer for *The CQ Researcher*, specialized in social policy, religion and foreign affairs. He is now a senior fellow at the Pew Forum on Religion & Society. He previously was a reporter at CQ's *Daily Monitor* and *CQ Weekly*. He holds a bachelor's degree in medieval history from Syracuse University and a law degree from the George Washington University.

1

Stopping Genocide

Sarah Glazer

Survivors of ethnic violence rest in a refugee camp in western Sudan's embattled Darfur region, where 50,000 people have been killed and a million left homeless. On July 22, the U.S. Congress declared the violence "genocide."

From *The CQ Researcher*, August 27, 2004.

After Arab nomads raided the Sudanese village of Kornei and killed Hatum Atraman Bashir's husband, she fled with her seven children. But when Bashir and a few other mothers crept out one day to find food, the raiders raped them.

"They said, 'You are black women, and you are our slaves,' " she recalled, weeping softly. "One of the women cried, and they killed her. Then they told me, 'If you cry, we will kill you, too.' "

Bashir, already pregnant by one of the rapists when she told this story earlier this summer, was camping in the shade of a tree after stumbling across the border into Chad in search of help from one of the overburdened aid agencies serving Sudanese refugees.[1]

Bashir is part of a wave of more than a million people from the western Darfur region of Sudan left homeless by rampaging nomadic militiamen on horseback, known as the Janjaweed. Since early 2003, the Arab militias have been killing and raping black Africans, who traditionally farm the land, and have burned many of their villages to the ground. The United Nations estimates that violence in Darfur has killed 50,000 and left 2 million short of food and medicine.[2] The Agency for International Development warns that between 300,000 and a million people could die by year's end, depending on how much aid reaches the refugees.[3]

Human-rights groups have accused the Sudanese government of arming the militias in an effort to root out and threaten rebels from Darfur's black African tribal groups. Some villages had been bombed by Sudan's air force and then attacked by Arab militias.[4]

Although the violence began in early 2003, it took until July of this year for the U.S. government and the international community to back up statements of concern with threats of serious action. On

July 30, the United Nations Security Council passed a U.S.-drafted resolution giving the Sudanese government 30 days to disarm and prosecute the Arab militias or face unspecified sanctions.[5]

Congress declared the violence "genocide" on July 22 and urged President Bush to do the same.[6] But as of mid-August, Secretary of State Colin L. Powell studiously avoided using the word "genocide" on the advice of government lawyers, he explained.[7] Under the International Convention on the Prevention and Punishment of the Crime of Genocide, the United States and other participating countries are obliged "to prevent and punish" genocide, although experts say the 1948 treaty is not specific about what that entails. (*See box, p. 4.*)

Even some of the most committed activists have been reluctant to bandy about a word like genocide, concerned that it should be reserved for clear-cut cases. As of mid-August, groups like Amnesty International and Human Rights Watch said they did not have enough information to call the violence in Darfur genocide, even as they called for tougher action by the international community. The African Union also declined to label the situation genocide even as it was sending 150 troops to Darfur to protect its cease-fire monitors and was expressing interest in sending more troops with a broadened mandate to protect civilians.[8]

Complicating the question of whether the situation in Darfur could be called genocide is the fact that some of the victims of the militias are Arab, and not all Arab groups participated in the killings.[9]

Yet critics in Congress and human-rights groups called the response to Darfur too slow and—in some eyes—too weak. They said it bore a disturbing resemblance to the world's inaction 10 years ago, when close to a million Rwandans died in killings now widely described as genocide.[10] In 1994, the Clinton administration also had intentionally avoided describing the Rwanda crisis as genocide because Pentagon lawyers had advised that using the term could commit the United States "to actually do something" under the international genocide convention.[11]

Both former President Bill Clinton and U.N. Secretary-General Kofi Annan have since traveled to Rwanda to express regret over the world's failure to stop the genocide. "We did not act quickly enough after the killing began," Clinton told hundreds of genocide survivors after hearing harrowing eyewitness accounts of the massacre. "We did not immediately call these crimes by their rightful name: genocide."[12]

Two months later, after touring a memorial containing the bones of 3,000 genocide victims, Annan somberly acknowledged, "The world failed Rwanda at that time of evil. The international community and the United Nations could not muster the political will to confront it."[13]

Instead, Clinton officials had urged the Rwandan government to negotiate with rebel militants from the Tutsi ethnic minority—the group the Hutu-led Rwandan government had targeted for killing. An estimated 800,000 minority Tutsi and moderate Hutu's were killed in three months—most hacked to death with machetes. The daily death rate exceeded even Hitler's killing machine. Many observers now agree Rwanda's leaders used their participation at the peace table as a cover for the killings they were planning and executing elsewhere in the country.

Similarly, Bush administration officials have stressed their role in encouraging north-south peace talks between the Sudan government and rebel groups, which want a share of Sudan's oil wealth. (The African rebel groups from Darfur charge they have been largely excluded from those agreements, which is one reason they are rebelling.)

"Once again, the world is turning its back on a defenseless people," said Rep. Tom Lantos, D-Calif., ranking minority member of the House International Relations Committee. He had warned State Department officials earlier this spring that Sudanese government leaders were "masters of manipulating" the international community, even as they engaged in the peace process.[14]

What does it take for a country like the United States to intervene in an ethnically driven massacre abroad—particularly if it puts American soldiers at risk? Increasingly, observers seem to concur with former journalist Samantha Power, a lecturer at Harvard's Kennedy School of Government. Her 2002 book, *A Problem from Hell*, argues that American presidents from Franklin D. Roosevelt to Clinton have been reluctant to intervene unless they perceive it to be in their political interest. And humanitarian intervention is widely viewed as unlikely to be popular with voters.

It's hard to argue for a compelling U.S. interest in far-off Sudan, even if it once harbored al-Qaeda terrorists. But proponents of humanitarian intervention say genocidal countries could indeed threaten the United States because they often become breeding grounds for terrorism and disease.

"Sudan's chaos is destabilizing surrounding countries, especially Chad, which is an increasing source of oil for us," *New York Times* columnist Nicholas D. Kristof recently argued, adding that recent outbreaks of ebola virus and polio in Sudan could also spread to neighboring countries.[15]

In a recent example of how ethnic persecution can spread to surrounding countries, a Hutu rebel faction in Burundi on Aug. 13 shot or hacked to death at least 189 Tutsi refugees from neighboring Congo, who had fled to a refugee camp in Burundi to escape a civil war at home.[16]

Rwandan President Paul Kagame later said the massacre "proves . . . that there have been incidents that are ignored by the international community and the U.N. where people are being killed in eastern Congo, being targeted for who they are."[17]

U.N. officials were investigating whether the killings were perpetrated by Hutu insurgents from neighboring Rwanda, who fled to Congo after participating in the 1994 genocide against Rwanda's minority Tutsi ethnic group.

Some of President Bush's harshest critics have given his administration credit for publicly condemning the killings in Sudan—if late in the game. In early July, Powell visited Sudan and received pledges from Sudanese officials to disarm the militias. The continuing killings in late July spurred the United States to push the Security Council to threaten punitive measures if a 30-day deadline was not met.[18]

Genocide in Sudan

Sudan is Africa's largest country — almost five times the size of France. In the western Darfur region, rampaging Arab militiamen on horseback, known as the Janjaweed, have left more than a million people homeless since early 2003. The militias have been killing and raping black Africans, who traditionally farm the land. The violence has killed some 50,000 and left 2 million short of food and medicine. Aid officials estimate up to a million refugees could die by year's end without sufficient supplies. The violence began in early 2003, but it took until July 2004 for the world community to threaten serious action. Although Congress called the killings "genocide" on July 22, as of mid-August, Secretary of State Colin L. Powell has avoided the word. On July 30, the U.N. Security Council passed a U.S.-drafted resolution giving Sudan 30 days to disarm and prosecute the Arab militias or face unspecified sanctions.

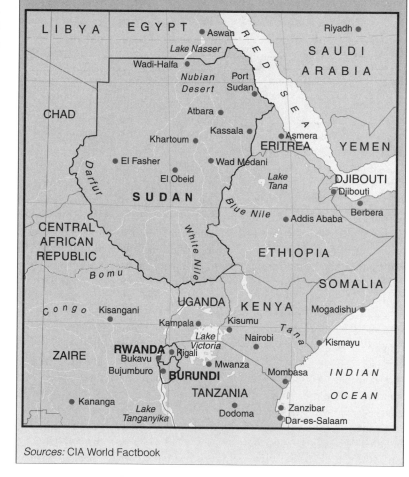

Sources: CIA World Factbook

The Genocide Treaty

The United States and 135 other nations have signed the Convention on the Prevention and Punishment of the Crime of Genocide since the United Nations General Assembly approved it on Dec. 9, 1948. The treaty recognizes that genocide "is contrary to the spirit and aims of the United Nations and condemned by the civilized world" and that "in order to liberate mankind from such an odious scourge, international cooperation is required. . . ."

Key treaty provisions:

- The Contracting Parties confirm that genocide, whether committed in time of peace or in time of war, is a crime under international law which they undertake to prevent and to punish.
- In the present Convention, genocide means any of the following acts committed with intent to destroy, in whole or in part, a national, ethnical, racial or religious group, as such:
  (a) Killing members of the group;
  (b) Causing serious bodily or mental harm to members of the group;
  (c) Deliberately inflicting on the group conditions of life calculated to bring about its physical destruction in whole or in part;
  (d) Imposing measures intended to prevent births within the group;
  (e) Forcibly transferring children of the group to another group.
- The Contracting Parties undertake to enact, in accordance with their respective Constitutions, the necessary legislation to give effect to the provisions of the present Convention, and, in particular, to provide effective penalties for persons guilty of genocide. . . .
- Persons charged with genocide [or attempted genocide or related crimes] . . . shall be tried by a competent tribunal of the State in the territory of which the act was committed, or by such international penal tribunal as may have jurisdiction with respect to those Contracting Parties which shall have accepted its jurisdiction.
- Any Contracting Party may call upon the competent organs of the United Nations to take such action under the Charter of the United Nations as they consider appropriate for the prevention and suppression of acts of genocide. . . .

According to Power, 10,000 peacekeeping troops would be needed to stop the killing.[19] But with its forces stretched thin in Iraq, the United States has so far been unwilling to commit troops to Darfur. In July, the United States was instead urging countries in the African Union and Europe to help, according to Pierre-Richard Prosper, U.S. ambassador-at-large for war crimes issues.[20] "What about the Europeans, Spain—all those people not helping us in Iraq?" he asks. "Why don't they help us? We're pretty locked down in Iraq right now."

American and U.N. reliance on Sudan's government to pacify the same Arab militias they have been charged with arming means "the wolf will guard the henhouse," in the opinion of John Prendergast, who handled African affairs during the Clinton administration. Only an international military force backed by the United States and Europe is likely to succeed, he has suggested.[21]

Complicating matters, the current scandal over American soldiers' abuse of Iraqi prisoners may have fatally undermined the United States' moral credibility if it calls for international military action in Sudan, argues Holly Burkhalter, U.S. policy director for Physicians for Human Rights.

"The U.S. has no authority in the world right now. We couldn't get consensus on a lemonade stand much less United Nations intervention," says Burkhalter, who favors sending troops to protect the delivery of food, medicine and shelter to Sudanese refugees, many of them in unprotected camps inside Sudan.

Some critics blame international inaction on the fact that the Security Council must approve the mobilization of U.N. peacekeepers. Any one of the five permanent members—including nations like Russia and China, which have themselves been accused of human-rights abuses—can veto a resolution. "In this case, it's not the U.S. that's the spoiler as we were with Rwanda," Burkhalter notes.

This time, however, the Security Council has an option that was not available in 1994: It could seek action by the International Criminal Court (ICC) in the Hague, Netherlands, established in 1998 to try crimes against humanity.[22] But such a move would be "difficult for us to even contemplate supporting," Prosper says. Expressing concern that American peacekeepers abroad could be hauled before the court on politically motivated war-crimes charges, the Bush administration has refused to join the court.

Human-rights activists say the administration's opposition to the court reflects its overall disdain for international law. Similarly, some see the administration's choice of an Iraqi-led tribunal to try Saddam Hussein on charges of genocide as just another chance to reject international justice.

"You've got an effort to deliberately hold at arms length international involvement and expertise in the name of an Iraqi-led effort while behind the scenes you have a U.S.-motored effort," says Richard Dicker, director of the International Justice Program at Human Rights Watch.

Bush administration officials counter that the Iraqi court could prove to be an improvement over the tribunals the U.N. set up after the genocides in Rwanda and Yugoslavia in the early 1990s. Those tribunals were criticized for being slow to bring cases to trial and for being held outside the countries where the crimes occurred.

As the United States struggles over its roles in Sudan and Iraq, here are some of the debates taking place in Congress and the international arena:

Is the United States doing enough to stop and prevent genocide?

Sudan may be the test case for determining whether the United States learned any lessons from Rwanda. Some human-rights activists have criticized the United States for doing too little too late, waiting more than a year after the attacks began on Sudanese civilians to consider stronger steps. But as of August, despite continued killing and raping, the administration still was not contemplating military action, despite the urging of some human-rights groups.[23]

Human rights in Darfur started to deteriorate after two rebel groups attacked Sudanese troops in February 2003 over the government's failure to protect civilians

there or to include Darfur in ongoing peace negotiations.[24] Some activists say the Bush administration's slowness to act shows the United States has not learned the main lesson of Rwanda—act early, before crimes escalate to genocide.

"We wouldn't be facing hundreds of thousands of deaths in western Sudan today if we'd learned enough," Burkhalter says.

Yet other analysts say Rwanda has sensitized the administration to the need for earlier action. The United States has taken "the strongest public stance" of any nation against the situation in Darfur, Human Rights Watch declared in May, amid what it called a "shameful" void in international response.[25] In April, Bush called on Sudan to stop the militia attacks.

"I condemn these atrocities, which are displacing hundreds of thousands of civilians, and I have expressed my views directly to President [Omar Hassan Ahmed al] Bashir," Bush said.

Author Power saw Bush's statement as an improvement over Rwanda. "President Bush called Bashir, which is one more phone call than Clinton made to Rwanda in 1994," she said. "At least he's not saying, 'We're not going to send troops, so let's stay mute,' which is what happened before. That's a version of progress."[26]

It's too early to say how much more Bush might be willing to do in Sudan. But some experts say American presidents only risk military intervention if they see some political payoff.

"We don't intervene because the political risks of not acting are less than the political risks of acting," says Jerry Fowler, staff director of the Committee on Conscience, which guides the genocide-prevention activities of the United States Holocaust Memorial Museum. For the first time in its history, the committee declared a "genocide emergency" on July 26, saying that genocide in Sudan "was imminent or actually happening."[27]

Other observers suggest that Americans tend to be far less sympathetic to genocide in remote continents like Africa, where black people are victims, than to similar events in Europe. In 1999, an American-backed NATO bombing campaign to end ethnic killing in Kosovo, in the former Yugoslavia, came after enormous media attention and political pressure, in contrast to scant press attention to Rwanda.[28]

Noting the handful of reporters covering a May 6 hearing on Darfur before the International Relations

AFP Photo/Alessandro Abbonizio

Former Rwandan Prime Minister Jean Kambanda receives a life sentence in September 1998 for his role in the deaths of 800,000 Rwandans in 1994. The special U.N. tribunal in Tanzania was the first international court to convict anyone for genocide and the first to hold a head of government responsible.

Committee, Rep. Donald M. Payne, D-N.J., an African-American, said, "Perhaps if this was in Europe, we'd have TV cameras all over the place. But since it's just another government in Africa, we don't."

The country's attitude toward foreign disasters has also been influenced by the Sept. 11, 2001, terrorist attacks, *New York Times* columnist James Traub argued recently. "One of the consequences of 9/11 may be that vital interests have come to seem so pressing that humanitarianism has become an unaffordable luxury," he suggested.[29]

During his first presidential campaign, President Bush said the "best interests of the United States" would guide his international policies, not the well-being of foreign nations. He indicated he would not send troops if another Rwanda occurred on his watch. In justifying the invasions of Iraq and Afghanistan, however, Bush has recently borrowed the moral arguments used by liberal humanitarian interventionists during the 1990s to push for military action in Rwanda and Bosnia.

Over the summer, Secretary of State Powell came under fire for refusing to call the Sudan killings genocide. "Why would we call it a genocide when the genocide definition has to meet certain legal tests?" he told National Public Radio on June 30. "And based on what we have seen, there were some indicators but there was certainly no full accounting of all indicators that lead to a legal definition of genocide. And that's the advice of my lawyers."[30]

On July 1, the liberal grass-roots group MoveOn.org urged its members to lobby the administration to declare genocide in Darfur: "Formally recognizing the genocide would enable the U.N. Security Council to authorize other countries, like Germany, France, and Spain, which don't have troops in Iraq, to help stop the killing in Sudan."

Contrary to MoveOn's perception, declaring a genocide is not needed to trigger military action by either the United States or the United Nations under the international genocide convention. The U.N. Charter empowers the Security Council to order military forces abroad to protect civilians, under its mission of protecting peace and security, notes Dicker of Human Rights Watch.

However, the international convention does commit participating countries to undertake to "prevent and punish genocide," an obligation weighty enough that administration lawyers have advised presidents against using the term. American presidents mistakenly—and repeatedly—assume their response to genocide must be either military action or nothing at all, Power observes.[31]

President Bush demonstrated that political clout could be exerted in other ways with his call to Sudan's President al Bashir on April 7 to denounce the killings in Darfur. Anxious to have economic sanctions lifted, Sudan announced an immediate cease-fire. When U.S. attention waned, however, the killings resumed.

Often forgotten in the debate over stopping genocide is another obligation of nations under the international convention—to make genocidal leaders accountable for their crimes. Many experts see the International Criminal Court as a crucial ingredient in preventing future genocides.

"By leaving perpetrators of genocide unpunished, we only make genocide more possible, not less," says Juan E. Mendez, the U.N.'s recently appointed special adviser on the prevention of genocide.

But the United States has refused to join the court and has sought exemptions from the court's jurisdiction for U.S. troops and officials, drawing fire from human-rights groups.

"The U.S should be leading the effort to have the Security Council refer the situation in Darfur to the International Criminal Court," Dicker argues. "The court was created to go after those who are behind the Janjaweed and the Sudanese military authorities in their campaign of ethnic cleansing in Darfur."

The Bush administration's opposition to the court makes that unlikely. (*See "At Issue," p. 18.*) Instead, the administration supports setting up ad hoc courts to punish perpetrators as each new genocide arises—as in Rwanda, Yugoslavia and most recently Iraq. But the court's advocates say ad hoc tribunals take too long to establish and are too expensive.

Ambassador Prosper disagrees. "The world has learned over the years and is more efficient in creating those mechanisms," he maintains. He notes that a tribunal set up in about 45 days in Sierra Leone last year indicted those bearing the greatest responsibility for atrocities committed during a civil war that ended in 2002.

The administration also objects to the international court because it does not come under Security Council jurisdiction. If it did, State Department officials argue, the Security Council would prevent politicized prosecutions by the court. Moreover, as an independent entity, the international court doesn't have the political clout to force a state to give up a genocide suspect, Prosper argues.

On June 23, however, the Bush administration backed down from its attempt to get the U.N. to exempt U.S. military personnel serving as U.N. peacekeepers from international court jurisdiction. Secretary-General Annan had criticized the move in light of the accusations that American soldiers in Iraq were torturing prisoners.

"The U.S. is engaging in torture and pretending that it's not," Burkhalter says. "It puts us in a uniquely bad position to be rallying around a moral cause."[32]

Is the U.N. doing enough to stop and prevent genocide?

Annan has spoken out forcefully against the killings in Darfur and sent a special envoy there this summer. The U.N. also surprised some critics on July 30 when the Security Council threatened punitive measures if Sudan did not disarm the Arab militias. But human-rights activists say the U.N. has a weak record on genocide, citing what happened in Rwanda.

Some critics blame the weak record on the structure of the Security Council, the only U.N. organ empowered to authorize military force. Any one of the five permanent members—the United States, England, France, China or Russia—on the 15-member body can block council action. Human-rights groups have accused Russia of genocidal abuses in Chechnya, and China of violating human rights in Tibet.

The qualifications for Security Council membership need to be changed to eliminate members who practice genocide, says William Pace, who heads the Coalition for the International Criminal Court. Likening the council to a fire department, he says: "We shouldn't have pyromaniacs on the Security Council."

The Security Council's makeup has been blamed for the U.N.'s paralysis on several occasions. In June, the council failed to pass a U.S.-backed resolution criticizing Sudan because of opposition from Pakistan and Algeria, the two Muslim countries currently on the council, and China.[33]

When the Clinton administration wanted the Security Council to charge Iraq's Hussein with war crimes, the opposition of a few permanent members—China, Russia and France—blocked any action, according to David J. Scheffer, then-U.S. ambassador-at-large for war-crimes issues. They were more interested in protecting their oil interests in Iraq, he has charged.[34]

In Rwanda, the council responded to the 1994 ethnic killings by reducing its peacekeeping force to just 270 soldiers—one-tenth its original size. Many believe a larger contingent could have saved lives. Author Power has

Modern Genocides vs. the Holocaust

The horrendous death toll from the Nazi Holocaust —6 million Jews and another 5 million Gypsies, homosexuals and communists—prompted U.S. political leaders to vow "Never again."

And yet genocides continue with little effort to stop them. One reason—or excuse—may be that ethnic killings since World War II look very different from the Nazi atrocities. Genocide today usually occurs in the context of wars or armed rebellions, with killing occurring on both sides. This fueled the argument against intervening during the Bosnian war, when Muslims and Serbs were killing each other. "It's been easy to analogize [the Bosnia situation] to the Holocaust," President Bill Clinton's secretary of State, Warren Christopher, told the House Foreign Affairs Committee on May 18, 1993, "but I never heard of any genocide by the Jews against the German people."

Historian Frank Chalk, co-director of the Montreal Institute for Genocide and Human Rights Studies at Concordia University, observes, "The public has in its mind cases like that of the Holocaust, where you could never sustain the argument that the Jewish people were lethal enemies of the Nazis or that the killing was part of military necessity."

But when both the government and the armed opposition are using famine as a weapon to starve civilians on the opposing side, he adds, "It's very hard to tell the public that both sides are doing that, and then mobilize the pressure for intervention."

Rwanda is a case in point. In 1994, the Rwandan government was battling an armed rebellion by the Tutsi Rwandan Patriotic Front at the same time that it was exhorting Hutu mothers and fathers to machete their Tutsi neighbors. But Joyce Leader, the U.S. deputy chief of mission to Rwanda in 1994, says her State Department superiors had enough information to distinguish military from civilian killings.

"That was a clear situation where the violence could have been stopped if there was a show of force by the international community; but the U.S. didn't want to get involved in a civil war—even when the killing of Tutsis was separate from the Tutsi rebel group fighting with government forces," Leader says. "We did inform the higher-ups that different kinds of killings were occurring, but they initially didn't hear it or didn't want to hear it."

---

argued that Annan, who then headed U.N. peacekeeping operations, had so internalized the paralysis governing the veto-prone Security Council that he did not even bother to ask for a council vote in response to an urgent cable from the U.N. troop commander in Rwanda, Romeo Dallaire, warning of an impending massacre. In the cable, Dallaire said he planned to seize arms that he had been informed were being assembled by local Hutu militias to exterminate Tutsi's. Annan's cable rejected the proposed arm raids telling him, "the United States in particular would not support such an aggressive interpretation of his mandate," Power writes.[35]

"We've acknowledged our responsibilities in failing the people of Rwanda," says U.N. spokesman Farhan Haq.

However, Mendez, the special adviser, notes when it comes to genocide, "In the last 10 years there hasn't been a veto on action by any of the permanent five members. I don't see it as having been the main reason the international community failed to act."

Rather, the council's inaction may stem from individual members' desire to avoid a veto, Mendez suggests. In the case of Kosovo, for example, the NATO countries decided not even to seek Security Council authorization for military intervention because they feared a veto, Mendez notes. Instead, they acted on their own, sending in a NATO force in 1999. "It seems to me the U.N. is sometimes scapegoated for the lack of will of some member states: If you don't want to do something, you can argue, 'I can't do it because there will be a veto,'" Mendez says.

The U.N. General Assembly has discussed proposals to abolish the council's veto power, but U.N. spokesman Haq says, "Frankly, I don't think it will be resolved any time quickly."

In April, Annan announced that he wanted his main legacy to be a U.N. better equipped to prevent genocide. Saying regrets over Rwanda had "dominated" his thoughts ever since, Annan announced a plan built around giving early warning of wars and ethnic conflicts that have the potential to escalate into genocide.

"One of the reasons for our failure in Rwanda was that beforehand, we did not face the fact that genocide was a real possibility," he said in Geneva. "And once it started, for too long we could not bring ourselves to recognize it or call it by name."[36]

In that spirit, Annan created a new post this year—special adviser on the prevention of genocide. In July he appointed Mendez, an Argentinean lawyer who was tortured in Argentine prisons as a political prisoner. He will collect information on threats of genocide and recommend action to the Security Council. Human-rights activists have hailed this reform. In the case of Rwanda, for example, information often did not rise to the highest levels of international attention because genocide was not a career priority for either bureaucrats or appointed officials, some argue.

Annan also has called for the use of military force to prevent future genocides. In 1999, he argued for "humanitarian intervention" to protect people subjected to human-rights abuses by their governments. In September 2003 he cited the need for criteria for "coercive" action—an obligation to intervene with force if necessary. However, it usually takes months for the U.N. to gather forces from nations willing to contribute troops. Although the idea of a rapid-reaction force was in the original U.N. Charter, fears about creating a world army blocked its creation. U.N. peacekeepers are only authorized to maintain peace, not stop wars. Humanitarian intervention also sounds similar to the Bush administration's pre-emptive action in Iraq, making some countries nervous that a U.N. intervention could rationalize an act of aggression.[37]

Yet the current system has led to some disasters. The U.N. contingent protecting Srebrenica during the Bosnian war was so small that it was overrun by a Bosnian Serb invasion in 1995. Within days, Bosnian Serbs separated 7,000 Muslim men and boys from their families and executed them.

Following highly critical reports in 1999 highlighting the U.N.'s failures in Srebrenica and Rwanda, Annan appointed a panel of experts to advise the U.N. Led by former Algerian Prime Minister Lakhder Brahimi, it recommended in 2000 the U.N. not enter trouble spots until it could put adequate troops on the ground.[38]

Over the past five years, the Security Council, at Annan's request, has authorized individual nations instead of the U.N. to lead multinational peacekeeping forces in several cases.

For example, last year, in an incident disturbingly reminiscent of Srebrenica, U.N. peacekeepers in Congo's eastern Ituri region found themselves outnumbered, lightly armed and unable to prevent horrifying tribal killings. The Security Council approved a mandate for a French-led multilateral force to restore order with some success. And last year the council authorized a U.S.-led force in Liberia and a French-led force in Ivory Coast. Each time, U.N. troops followed. The council authorized an Australian-led force in East Timor in 1999.

Will the International Criminal Court prevent genocide?

Opponents of the court, including Bush administration officials, argue that any dictator bent on massacring his own people is unlikely to pause at the thought of ICC prosecution.

They note, for example, that in 1995, two years after a U.N. tribunal was created to prosecute genocide in the former Yugoslavia, Bosnian Serb leaders seized Srebrenica and carried out the largest massacre in Europe in 50 years. The commander of the Bosnian Serb army, Ratko Mladic, had the 7,000 Bosnian Muslims executed shortly after it became clear the tribunal was about to indict him.

It's little surprise that "weak tribunals" like the Yugoslavia tribunal "do little to deter potential offenders," writes Gary Bass, an assistant professor of politics and international affairs at Princeton University. But Bass argues that "even more credible efforts" like the Allied military action against Nazi Germany "met with little success when trying to dissuade genocide."[39]

Cornell Professor of Government Jeremy Rabkin says the ICC won't do any better because it has no power to make arrests. "If there are mass atrocities, is it likely the perpetrator is going to stop because people call him names?" he asks. "The ICC has no army, no police."

Supporters of the court answer that a nation's own police force or army is expected to do the physical arresting, much as they do now for the tribunals.

But some of the most likely candidates for genocide prosecution are heads of governments like Sudan that have never ratified the underlying treaty. That means they are not under the court's jurisdiction unless the Security

Council unanimously votes to refer their case to the court. "If you are a butcher, you are not going to ratify it," Rabkin asserts.

If the United States ratified the treaty, it might be inhibited from using force to stop future genocides for fear of being accused of war crimes, Rabkin maintains. Under that scenario, he speculates, "We could have been indicted for attacking Saddam Hussein, but Saddam [who did not ratify the treaty] couldn't have been indicted for butchering his own people."

Brett Schaefer, a fellow at the conservative Heritage Foundation, a Washington think tank, argues that the new court could actually encourage genocidal despots to stay in power indefinitely: "What is the incentive for these folks to step aside if they know they'll be dragged before the ICC and possibly sentenced to life in prison?"

But supporters argue the court is already having a positive effect, such as the ICC prosecutor's announcement in June that he would begin investigating killings in eastern Congo.

"Warlords put down their AK-47s, put on business suits, picked up attaché cases and moved into the Grand Hotel in Kinshasha in hopes of getting jobs in the new transitional government," says Human Rights Watch's Dicker. "I don't want to attribute it all to the ICC, but it was crystal clear to everyone there that the threat of prosecution by this international court had a chilling effect on those associated with the most serious crimes."

History is not necessarily a good guide to whether the prospect of punishment could deter genocidists because it's hardly ever been tried, says historian Ben Kiernan, director of the Yale Genocide Studies Program. The United States didn't even ratify the 1948 international convention against genocide until 1988, he points out. Until the 1990s, he says, most genocidal leaders "didn't even know the genocide convention existed."

Perhaps surprisingly, genocide doesn't just flare up spontaneously during ethnic conflicts but is usually carefully planned and documented. The planning for the Khmer Rouge killings of 2 million people in Cambodia in the late 1970s was revealed in tens of thousands of documents, Kiernan discovered, which he has posted on the Web.[40]

An international court "will hamstring the killing and in a practical sense deter it if [the leaders] know the paperwork can be publicized and used in court against them," Kiernan maintains.

In the United States, however, the heart of the debate is whether the U.S. should bow to an international legal body. The Bush administration believes that ratifying the treaty could put American troops and officials overseas at risk of politicized prosecution. The underlying treaty creates an institution of "unchecked power," and "threatens the sovereignty of the United States" through the court's claim of authority over American citizens, said Undersecretary of State for Political Affairs Marc Grossman.[41]

United States government officials and British Prime Minister Tony Blair have already been accused of war crimes for invading Iraq in communications sent to the court, critics observe. Sally Eberhardt, media liaison at the Coalition for the International Criminal Court (CICC), responds that like any court, the ICC doesn't act on every charge—especially unfounded ones. For example, she notes, the court received 906 communications from individuals and organizations in 85 countries between its opening on July 1, 2002, and June 1, 2004. Of these, the court has publicly announced serious consideration or action in only two cases—Uganda and the Democratic Republic of the Congo.

The court had no jurisdiction over the United States concerning Iraq, according to Eberhardt. But because Britain has ratified the treaty, "Tony Blair could very well be brought up on charges," the Heritage Foundation's Schaefer asserts.

Defenders of the court argue there are enough built-in safeguards to make that unlikely. The ICC only has jurisdiction over a ratifying country if it is unwilling or unable to carry out a prosecution or investigation. The CICC's Pace says the provision is aimed at a country whose court system is a sham. In the case of the United States, "The belief that would ever be a decision of the judges at the ICC is a fantasy," Pace says, because ICC judges are from democratic countries. "These are not [Muammar el] Quaddafi's and Saddam Hussein's judges," he says.

Pace's argument assumes that the United States will agree with the international court over the need to prosecute an American for a given war-related crime. But Johns Hopkins University Professor of International Law Ruth Wedgwood argues the United States could have "good faith differences of opinion in war-making

1900s-1940s
Ottoman Turkey enters World War I and declares intention to empty the country of Christians. In run-up to World War II, Adolf Hitler plans to kill Jews and other "undesirables."

1915-1916 Turks kill 1 million Armenians.

1939-1945 Nazis kill 11 million people.

1945 Allies establish Nuremburg war-crimes tribunal.

1948 U.N. passes a genocide treaty.

1970s
U.S. supports radical regime in Cambodia.

1975-1979 Communist Khmer Rouge regime kills 2 million Cambodians.

1980s
U.S. views Iraq as ally against fundamentalist Muslim Iran; U.S. continues aid as Saddam Hussein kills thousands during Kurdish rebellion.

1987-1988 Hussein uses chemical weapons and execution to kill 100,000 Kurds.

1988 U.S. signs U.N. genocide convention.

1990s
U.S. intervenes in genocide in Bosnia but not Rwanda; genocide trials begin.

1992-1995 An estimated 200,000 predominantly Muslim Bosnians are killed.

1993 Yugoslav genocide tribunal created.

1994 An estimated 800,000 Rwandans are killed by civilians and soldiers.

1995 Bosnian Serbs invade Srebrenica, executing 7,000 Muslims in a day.

1998 U.N. convention agrees to create international genocide court.

March 24, 1999 NATO starts bombing Serbs persecuting Albanians in Kosovo.

May 24, 1999 U.N. tribunal indicts Serbian President Slobodan Milosevic for genocide.

2000s
International tribunals punish Rwandan leaders, stall over Cambodia and Yugoslavia; human-rights groups seek action in Sudan.

May 23, 2002 President Bush withdraws U.S. support for International Criminal Court (ICC).

Aug. 3, 2002 Bush signs American Servicemembers' Protection Act, withholding military aid from countries that refuse to give Americans immunity from ICC.

December 2002 Milosevic trial begins.

2003 U.N. and Cambodian leaders agree to create tribunal to try Khmer Rouge leaders, but political deadlock in Cambodia stalls action. . . . Arab militias begin attacks on black civilians in Sudan.

May 2, 2003 President Bush declares end of U.S. war in Iraq.

April 7, 2004 Bush condemns Sudan killings, urges Sudanese president to act.

June 24, 2004 Bush administration drops attempt in U.N. to exempt U.S. soldiers from International Criminal Court.

June 30, 2004 U.S. hands over Hussein to provisional government of Iraq. . . . Secretary of State Colin L. Powell declines to call Sudan killings "genocide."

July 2004 Iraqi tribunal charges Hussein with war crimes; report finds U.N. has failed to assure Serbian rights in Kosovo; U.N. tribunal convicts 19th Rwandan leader for role in 1994 genocide; Human Rights Watch charges Sudanese government is behind ethnic cleansing in Darfur; Security Council gives Sudan 30 days to disarm and punish the militias operating in Darfur.

Aug. 5, 2004 Preliminary State Department report documents "a consistent and widespread pattern of atrocities" in Darfur, but stops short of terming it genocide.

Aug. 10, 2004 Senate Majority Leader Bill Frist, R-Tenn., calls Darfur killings "genocide."

doctrine" with the court, thereby subjecting it to the court's jurisdiction.

Disagreement would likely arise over the principle of "proportionality," which requires troops to distinguish between military and civilian targets, she predicts. "The U.S. is hardly likely to prosecute its own pilots for faithfully carrying out the air attacks assigned to them," Wedgwood has written.[42]

Still, the prosecution of an American or a Brit remains politically unlikely given the court's dependence on the major democracies for support, says Federico Borello, an international lawyer and senior associate at the International Center for Transitional Justice in New York City. "If the court decides to prosecute Bush, Blair and [France's Jacques] Chiraq, that court is finished," he says.

And finally there are moral arguments. "No criminal-justice system provides perfect deterrence—but it would be astonishing to conclude that we should therefore abandon criminal justice altogether," says Diane F. Orentlicher, a professor of international law at American University's Washington College of Law.

Even Princeton's Bass, a critic of international courts, concludes tribunals are better than the most likely alternative—revenge.

BACKGROUND

Genocide Convention

Historically, the United States has not acted on foreign genocides until domestic political pressure made inaction untenable. Indeed, some historians argue that the United States has never stopped a genocide in progress.

Author Power contends the United States usually had sufficient information that the genocide was occurring but felt intervention would have competed with other national interests.[43]

In 1915, for example, Henry Morgenthau Sr., the U.S. ambassador to Turkey, urged Washington to condemn Turkey's deportation and slaughter of its Armenian minority, but the U.S. refused to act because it wanted to maintain its position of neutrality with the European powers. Some 1 million Armenians were murdered or died of disease and starvation during the genocide.

Government officials dismissed the warnings of Raphael Lemkin, a Polish Jew and international lawyer, who told them about Hitler's extermination plans beginning in the early 1940s. Before and during the United States' entry into the war, the Allies resisted calls to denounce Hitler's atrocities, open their doors to Europe's Jewry or bomb the tracks to Nazi concentration camps. The Germans exterminated 6 million Jews and 5 million other "undesirables," including Jehovah's Witnesses, Poles, gypsies, homosexuals and political opponents during World War II.

Lemkin, haunted by the death of his family under Hitler, coined the word "genocide." Through unrelenting lobbying, he persuaded the fledgling United Nations in 1948 to pass the Convention on the Prevention and Punishment of the Crime of Genocide.

The convention commits participating countries to "prevent and punish" the crime of genocide and empowers them to call upon an organ of the United Nations to take action.

However, "That may mean nothing more than sending a letter to the U.N. Secretary-General," notes the Holocaust museum's Fowler. Just as important, however, may be the political or moral obligations incurred in the public's eyes once the government uses the "genocide" label. "If we call something genocide, we can't be seen not to do anything about it," he says.

The convention includes only two specific legal obligations for participating nations: pass legislation providing effective penalties for persons guilty of genocide and grant extradition of those indicted for genocide. However, because of Senate concerns about threats to U.S. sovereignty, so many conditions were inserted into the convention, Power has contended, "that it carried next to no force" after it was finally ratified by the United States in 1988.[44]

Warnings Ignored

In the 1970s, a few American diplomats and journalists in Cambodia warned of the widespread atrocities being committed in Cambodian villages by radical Maoist communists known as the Khmer Rouge. But America's political left ridiculed such warnings as falling for anti-communist propaganda. For its part, the U. S. government was leery of intervening in Southeast Asia so soon after the trauma of the Vietnam War.

The Khmer Rouge would eventually persecute ethnic Vietnamese, ethnic Chinese, educated citizens, academics and Buddhist monks—anyone seen as a potential political enemy. Between 1975 and 1979, the Khmer

Ethnic Cleansing in Bosnia

Within days after the citizens of Bosnia voted to secede from Yugoslavia in March 1992, Bosnian Serb soldiers and militiamen began rounding up non-Serbs—Muslims and Croats—savagely beating them and often killing them. They also shelled the city of Sarajevo, destroying most Muslim and Croat cultural and religious sites. The Serbs called their actions "ethnic cleansing," a term reminiscent of the Nazi euphemism—"cleansing"—for eliminating the Jews.

Over the next three years, a few State Department diplomats and members of Congress tried to convince the White House to bomb the Serb ethnic cleansers and lift the U.S. arms embargo against the outgunned Bosnian Muslims. Between 1992 and 1995, some 200,000 Bosnians were killed.

Clinton administration officials described the conflict as an ancient, intractable ethnic conflict they were powerless to end. Only when that stance became politically impossible did President Bill Clinton finally intervene, argues journalist Samantha Power, who covered the Bosnian conflict and authored the 2002 book *A Problem from Hell: America and the Age of Genocide.*

On July 11, 1995, Bosnian Serb military leaders seized an area of Srebrenica protected by a small force of U.N. troops, who were unable to resist the invasion. The Bosnians rounded up and slaughtered 7,000 Muslim men and boys.

Sen. Bob Dole of Kansas, then a Republican presidential challenger, pushed legislation through Congress ending the arms embargo. His crusade got editorial support and nightly news coverage, making Clinton's non-interventionist policy politically embarrassing. In a telling scene on the White House putting green, Clinton shouted at his top national security advisers over the mounting political costs: "I'm getting creamed!"[1]

Clinton reversed course, and with his blessings NATO undertook a three-week bombing campaign on Aug. 30, 1995. By then, however, "Bosnia's genocide had been largely completed, and a multiethnic state destroyed," Power writes. Nevertheless, backed by a credible threat of force, the United States convinced the Serbs to stop shelling civilians. That November, the Clinton administration brokered a peace accord between the parties in Dayton, Ohio.

Clinton responded more aggressively when Yugoslav President Slobodan Milosevic began brutalizing ethnic Albanians, mostly Muslims, in the southern Serbian province of Kosovo in the mid-1990s. In 1996, embittered Kosovo Albanians formed the Kosovo Liberation Army, gunning down several Serbian policemen in 1998. The following year, avenging Serbians killed 3,000 Muslims and drove another 300,000 from their homes.

Beginning on March 24, 1999, NATO jets commanded by U.S. General Wesley Clark began a two-and-a-half month bombing campaign. This was "the first time in history the United States or its allies had intervened to head off a potential genocide," Power writes.[2]

She attributes Clinton's decision to bomb to embarrassment over Srebrenica, guilt over Rwanda and fear the fighting could expand into a wider European war.

Two months into NATO's bombing campaign, a U.N. war-crimes tribunal indicted Milosevic for crimes against humanity and war crimes committed in Kosovo. It was the first time a head of state had been charged during a war with violating international law. On June 3, 1999, Milosevic surrendered. On June 9, he signed an agreement forcing Serbian troops to leave Kosovo and permitting 50,000 NATO peacekeepers to enter it.

After numerous delays, Milosevic's trial finally started in February 2002; it is still continuing.

---

[1] Samantha Power, *A Problem from Hell* (2002), pp. 436-437.

[2] *Ibid.*

---

regime of leader Pol Pot killed 2 million people. But the Carter administration maintained diplomatic relations with the regime even after its overthrow, in large part because the United States wanted to maintain good relations with China, Pol Pot's prime backer.

In 1988, Sen. Claiborne Pell, D-R.I., chairman of the Senate Foreign Relations Committee, tried to cut off agri-

cultural and manufacturing credits to Iraq in retaliation for Hussein's attempt in the late 1980s to wipe out Iraq's rural Kurds. A coalition of the Reagan White House and the farm lobby defeated the sanctions package because they wanted to maintain friendly ties with Hussein's regime, then seen as a bulwark against the fundamentalist Muslim government in Iran, and sell wheat and rice to Iraq. As a

Former Yugoslav President Slobodan Milosevic is being tried on charges he masterminded the slaughter of thousands of non-Serb civilians in the 1990s. The U.N. tribunal in The Hague, Netherlands, so far has indicted 101 people for war crimes and convicted 34.

result, Hussein was receiving more that $1 billion in American financial support as his regime was killing 100,000 Kurds.

Three months before the genocide began against Rwanda's minority Tutsis in April 1994, the Canadian commander of the U.N. peacekeeping troops there, Romeo Dallaire, sought permission to round up the Hutu militias' machetes, warning they had built up the capacity to kill "up to 1,000" Tutsi "every 20 minutes."[45]

Denied permission by U.N. headquarters, Dallaire watched the killings helplessly as the United States led the effort to remove most of the troops under his command. Clinton wanted to avoid repeating the country's humiliation in Somalia only eight months before, in October 1993, when 18 American soldiers on a peace-keeping mission had been killed.

The Clinton administration also refused requests from human-rights activists to jam a Hutu radio station that was exhorting Hutus to kill their Tutsi neighbors. A Defense Department memo in May 1994 argued that the jamming would be too expensive— $8,500 per hour—and ineffective compared to military action.[46]

But in the wake of Somalia, the Clinton administration had a firm policy of avoiding humanitarian situations that could lead to military entanglements, and neither the White House nor the Pentagon wanted a

military solution in Rwanda. Just as important was the lack of ringing phones at the White House. "You must make more noise," Clinton foreign policy adviser Anthony Lake told human-rights activists in April 1994, when they asked how they could influence U.S. policy on Rwanda.[47] At the time, Human Rights Watch had not yet developed the grass-roots base to lobby the government, and the press was paying scant attention to Rwanda.

As government-supported radio propaganda warned of a fabricated Tutsi invasion, men and women became killers. An estimated 800,000 Rwandans were killed in 100 days.[48]

The failure of the United States to act in Rwanda has led some scholars to question whether the genocide convention's emphasis on proving genocidal "intent" is counter-productive. Genocide "is absolutely the hardest crime to prove," notes Frank Chalk, co-director of Concordia University's Montreal Institute for Genocide and Human Rights Studies, because the "intent" to destroy a particular group is hard to establish. In addition, he says, "We need to intervene earlier. We can't wait until we have an open-and-shut case."

Chalk is among a group of scholars calling for a broad category of "atrocity crimes" that would carry the international obligation to intervene without carrying such a heavy burden of proof. Former Ambassador Scheffer said that would more likely have produced action in Rwanda and the Balkans, as well as in Iraq.[49]

"Atrocity crimes" would include crimes against humanity and war crimes, which are easier to prove, cover many of the same actions and carry penalties just as great as genocide, Chalk says. Deportations, terror raids and killings, for example, are all considered war crimes and often signal the preliminary stages of a genocide.

CURRENT SITUATION

Punishing Genocide

In November 1994, seven months after the Rwandan genocide started, the Security Council authorized a special tribunal. It handed down its first indictments a few months later, eventually becoming the first international court to convict anyone for genocide and the first to hold a head of government—Prime Minister Jean Kambanda—responsible.

By mid-July, 68 individuals had been arrested for war crimes or genocide in Rwanda, according to the State Department's Office of War Crimes Issues. Of those, 19 had been convicted, including, former Finance Minister Emmanuel Ndindabahizi, who was sentenced to life imprisonment in July.[50]

"It's a good success record," says Alison DesForges, a senior adviser at Human Rights Watch and an expert witness at the Rwanda tribunal. "They've got the real leadership here."

Indeed, the Rwanda tribunal has a far better track record than its counterpart in The Hague, created by the Security Council in 1993 for Yugoslav war crimes. The trial of Slobodan Milosevic, the former Yugoslav president and Serbian leader accused of masterminding the slaughter of non-Serb civilians in the 1990s, did not get started until February 2002 and may not finish. On July 5, Milosevic's poor health prompted judges to postpone the beginning of his defense and to question whether the trial could continue.[51]

The Yugoslav tribunal has indicted 101 people and convicted 34, according to the war-crimes office. However, the government of Serbia-Montenegro has not turned over some of the most important suspects; 21 remain at large, and several reportedly even give media interviews.

NATO has been trying for almost nine years to apprehend the region's most wanted war-crimes suspect, former Bosnian Serb Leader Radovan Karadzic. NATO leaders also have been trying to find former Bosnian Serb army commander Mladic. Both men face accusations that they ordered the Srebrenica slaughter in 1995.[52]

Under congressional legislation conditioning foreign aid on cooperation with the Yugoslav tribunal, Secretary of State Powell told Congress in March that Serbia and Montenegro had not cooperated in apprehending accused war criminals. As a result, aid to the government was halted as of March 31, 2004.[53]

Hussein Tribunal

The world's attention was fixed on Saddam Hussein on July 1, when the former Iraqi leader was charged with war crimes and crimes against humanity in a makeshift courtroom at U.S. military headquarters near the Baghdad airport.

Four days before U.S. soldiers pulled Hussein out of what President Bush called his "spider hole" in December 2003, Iraq's Governing Council had announced that an Iraqi Special Tribunal composed of five-judge panels would hold trials for crimes against humanity, war crimes and genocide committed between July 17, 1968, when Hussein's Baath Party consolidated power, and May 1, 2003, when President Bush declared an end to the war in Iraq.

The starting date for Hussein's trial is uncertain. Ambassador Prosper says there's tension between Iraqis, "who want this done quickly," and the United States, which wants due process preserved. "We don't want to see Iraqis sacrificing quality for speed," he says.

What Iraqis want is "a quick process to judge Saddam guilty and just kill him," said Salem Chalabi, general director of the Special Tribunal.[54]

Human-rights activists fault Iraq for being insufficiently public in forming the tribunal and for not including international lawyers and judges, as in the U.N.'s Yugoslavia and Rwanda tribunals. Some have criticized the heavy involvement of the United States, which has spent years preparing the case against Hussein and is supplying the investigators.[55]

"We're working hard to reduce the active involvement we have," Prosper says. "We'll be there to assist and advise; it needs to be Iraqi, and it needs to be transparent."

As for making the tribunal international, he says, "No one wants a Milosevic trial, which was too long in coming and too long in going—that's a problem with full-blown international tribunals."

The Iraqi tribunal is similar to so-called mixed tribunals, which combine both international and national law. Many human-rights activists consider them a second-best to international tribunals, saying they are too dependent on the whim of a country's leadership. However, it's too early to say how well this relatively new type of tribunal will work.

Another mixed tribunal, which is supposed to try the aging leaders of the Khmer Rouge, has yet to get started. U.N. and Cambodian officials agreed in June 2003 to create the court, but the arrangement requires ratification by the National Assembly. The assembly is basically not functioning because the main political parties remain deadlocked over their roles in the government.

Some human-rights groups have questioned the objectivity of Cambodian judges—who will compose the majority of the tribunal's judges—to try the Khmer Rouge leaders. They note that Prime Minister Hun Sen and other government leaders were themselves once in the Khmer Rouge. Moreover, many of the Khmer Rouge leaders are now in their seventies and could die before the trials get under way.[56]

International Criminal Court

The difficulty of launching tribunals, sometimes years after genocide occurs, spurred support for the ICC. In 1998, 160 nations voted to establish the court. The United States was one of only seven nations voting against the Rome Statute, the treaty creating the court. The other dissenters were China, Iraq, Libya, Yemen, Qatar and Israel.

Although President Clinton signed the treaty, he called it "fundamentally flawed" and did not send it to the Senate for ratification. Currently, 140 countries have signed the treaty and 94 have ratified it.

The Bush administration actively opposes the treaty, arguing that American troops and government officials overseas could be subjected to politically motivated charges. On May 6, 2002, the administration withdrew from the treaty. The administration later negotiated a Security Council resolution providing a one-year exemption from ICC jurisdiction for American troops operating in U.N. peacekeeping operations.

However, the administration recently withdrew its proposal for another one-year exemption following opposition from Secretary-General Annan, who cited the scandal over American soldiers' abuse of Iraqi prisoners and possible violations of the Geneva Convention on torture.[57]

Despite this setback, the Bush administration is pursuing another strategy to avoid the ICC: It is negotiating bilateral agreements with individual allies requiring them not to surrender American citizens to the ICC. As of mid-July, 91 countries had agreed, Ambassador Prosper says.

The Bush administration also has received congressional assistance in enforcing the bilateral treaties. Under the American Servicemembers' Protection Act, signed by Bush on Aug. 3, 2002, the United States must refuse military aid to nations that sign the ICC treaty—unless the administration grants them a waiver. Washington has been using the threat of withdrawing military aid to pressure countries to sign the bilateral agreements, according to human-rights activists.

The legislation also prohibits U.S. participation in peacekeeping activities unless immunity from the ICC is guaranteed for American personnel. It authorizes the president to use "all means necessary and appropriate," presumably including military force, to free Americans detained by the ICC.[58]

Human Rights Watch has charged that the Bush campaign against the ICC has diluted U.S. efforts against genocide, such as leading NATO in its efforts to arrest war criminals in the Balkans or bringing war-crimes charges against Hussein.[59]

Even more disturbing, according to Human Rights Watch Executive Director Kenneth Roth, "A court that exempts the world's superpower risks losing its legitimacy."[60]

For his part, Ambassador Prosper responds that his office has taken a lead role in supporting the tribunals for Yugoslavia, Rwanda, Sierra Leone and Iraq. "Everyone knows we share the same values," he says. "The only difference is the mechanism."

Crisis in Darfur

This summer, aid workers returned to the United States with mounting evidence of genocide in Sudan. On July 17, former Clinton official Prendergast reported seeing mass graves of people who had been killed execution-style, shot in the back of the head. Refugees from Darfur told him their villages had first been bombed by the Sudanese air force and then attacked by Janjaweed militiamen shooting automatic weapons. "There's still mass raping going on," he reported.[61]

On July 30, the Security Council passed a U.S.-drafted resolution threatening sanctions if the Sudanese government failed to disarm and prosecute the marauding Janjaweed militias within 30 days. But in mid-August, with little more than two weeks to go to the Aug. 31 deadline, the violence had deepened amid increasing raids on refugee camps and rapes carried out by Sudanese forces and Arab militamen.[62] Since the beginning of the conflict in 2003, the number of deaths has been estimated at a minimum of 50,000, according to the United Nations, and over a million have fled their homes in Darfur. In the overcrowded refugee camps, epidemics and widespread starvation threatened. Aid officials estimate that up to a million people could die by year's end.[63]

Activists have urged the United States to persuade the Security Council to back up demands for an end to

Healing Rwanda After the Genocide

How does a country heal after ordinary citizens pick up machetes to kill their neighbors by the hundreds of thousands? If the response of Rwanda's increasingly repressive government is any sign, the news is not good.

An international tribunal set up by the United Nations has convicted the leadership of Rwanda's former government of genocide and other war crimes for leading a three-month killing frenzy in 1994. An estimated 800,000 men, women and children from the country's Tutsi minority died at the hands of citizens and soldiers from the majority Hutu ethnic group.

But even though some Tutsi rebel soldiers committed revenge atrocities against Hutu civilians at the time, not one has been arrested or indicted by the international tribunal, because the current Tutsi-backed government refuses to cooperate, according to Alison DesForges, senior adviser to the Africa division of Human Rights Watch.

Rwanda's government, born of the rebel army that stopped the genocide, has also come under criticism for human-rights violations in its efforts to bring other Rwandans to justice for their part in the genocide.

Over the past 10 years, the number of Rwandans held in overcrowded prisons grew to more than 100,000, of which the government has tried fewer than 10,000. Many were arrested in arbitrary sweeps of young Hutu men, according to human-rights activists. Some have remained behind bars the entire time without trial or evidence. "It's enough [simply] for someone to point a finger," says Sara Rakita, a consultant on Africa to the Ford Foundation.

To speed up the trials, the government recently decided to adopt *gacaca*, a traditional form of village justice that deals with minor squabbles, such as the theft of a neighbor's cattle; conventional courts still deal with serious crimes like murder and rape.

But the *gacaca* system has yet to hold a single trial, even though a quarter-million local judges were elected two years ago. Rwanda's rural communities have had trouble gathering the 100-person quorum demanded to attend long hearings held on the open ground in broiling sun or pouring rain.

In addition, the *gacaca* system is aimed solely at Hutu perpetrators. DesForges says many Hutus ask, "Why participate in a system that to them is unbalanced?"

Human-rights activists also question the fairness of the *gacaca* system. DesForges cites a Hutu teacher who was hiding seven Tutsi children in his house during the 1994 massacre. Afraid that his Hutu relatives and neighbors would discover the children, he helped man the roadblock set up to capture and kill Tutsis. Every day, he took a chair to the barrier and read a book. "He didn't hold a weapon. Is that person guilty of genocide?" DesForges asks. Some communities have so defined it; others not, she says.

Personal rivalries and old hatreds may also hold more sway in local courts. "I saw a proceeding where an old man's Hutu sons accused him [of genocidal crimes] because the sons wanted to get the old man's land," DesForges says, even though his Tutsi in-laws defended him.

The government often points to efforts like *gacaca* as an effort to achieve "reconciliation" between Hutu and Tutsis. But it's becoming increasing difficult for citizens of Rwanda to speak freely, according to human-rights groups.

In July, the Rwandan parliament asked the government to dissolve the country's four leading human-rights groups on the grounds that they were harboring "genocidal" ideas.[1] The groups had opposed the government's plans for consolidating land holdings and had asked for justice for victims of the Rwanda Patriotic Front (RPF), the rebel Tutsi group that took power after the genocide in 1994. Last year, the government dissolved the one party that could have successfully contested the RPF in elections. "It's simply an attempt to eliminate dissent," says DesForges.

Ironically, the main lesson Rwanda's ruling party seems to have learned from the U.N.'s failure to stop the 1994 genocide is that the only way to ensure survival of the Tutsis is "to stay in power indefinitely," *The Economist* magazine recently opined. Some of the government's efforts to protect its vulnerable Tutsi minority echo disturbingly of 1994. "It was justified in invading the Congo to disperse [Hutu] genocidaires who were using the place as a base for attacks on Rwanda," the magazine noted, "but it surely did not have to kill 200,000 people in the process."[2]

---

[1] Human Rights Watch press release, "Rwanda: Parliament Seeks to Abolish Rights Group," July 2, 2004.

[2] "Rwanda, remembered: Lessons of a genocide," *The Economist*, March 27, 2004.

Should the U.S. support the International Criminal Court?

YES

William Pace
Convenor, Coalition for the International Criminal Court

Written for *The CQ Researcher*, August 2004

The United States' needless opposition to the International Criminal Court (ICC)—which is supported by nearly 100 democracies—has seriously damaged America's international standing at a time when the U.S. needs to regain the trust of its global partners. The opposition began with the Bush administration's "unsigning" of the court's treaty in May 2002 and continues with the withholding of much-needed aid to economically vulnerable countries that refuse to grant ICC immunity to U.S. personnel.

In light of the many protections built into the ICC treaty, U.S. claims that Americans will be targeted by politically motivated ICC investigations are without merit. Indeed, rather than superceding national jurisdiction, the court's mandate allows it to act *only* where an individual state is unwilling or unable to try alleged criminals itself. As long as the U.S. military and civil judicial systems are functioning, U.S. personnel will *never* face the ICC. Additionally, the ICC has no jurisdiction over acts committed in the U.S. However, U.S. nationals are already prohibited from committing murders, much less war crimes, in other nations. Therefore, to insist that U.S. sovereignty is threatened unless Americans are granted blanket immunity is dangerous nonsense.

Rather than being criticised via unfounded allegations, the ICC should be judged by its track record. In July 2003, the ICC prosecutor announced he would not consider complaints submitted against the United States and United Kingdom's actions in Iraq. The ICC has no jurisdiction over the U.S., and in the case of the U.K,. which is an ICC party, the court would have to first allow for British national jurisdiction to be invoked. Instead, the court has initiated investigations requested by the Democratic Republic of the Congo and Uganda, which have suffered some of the most atrocious human-rights abuses.

By rejecting global consensus on international justice— embodied in effective structures such as the ICC, the U.N. and the Geneva Conventions—the United States has eroded its moral authority and squandered its outstanding legacy of leadership in support of international law. Even when treaty ratification is prolonged, most U.S. administrations sign or engage constructively while new international laws are being tested. Following the revelations of torture at Abu Ghraib prison, U.S. attempts to thwart international law now look all the more unjustifiable.

The ICC provides justice for the victims of the world's greatest atrocities and works to deter future atrocities. At this critical moment in U.S. diplomatic history, the United States should see that rather than the phantom menace it envisions, the ICC can contribute significantly to U.S. national-security interests.

NO

Marc Grossman
Undersecretary of State for Political Affairs

From remarks to the Center for Strategic and International Studies, May 6, 2002

We believe the ICC undermines the role of the United Nations Security Council in maintaining international peace and security.

We believe in checks and balances. The Rome Statute creates a prosecutorial system that is an unchecked power. We believe that in order to be bound by a treaty, a state must be party to that treaty. The ICC asserts jurisdiction over citizens of states that have not ratified the treaty. This threatens U.S. sovereignty.

We believe that the ICC is built on a flawed foundation. These flaws leave it open for exploitation and politically motivated prosecutions.

President Bush has come to the conclusion that the United States can no longer be a party to this process. . . .

Like many of the nations that gathered in Rome in 1998 for the negotiations to create a permanent International Criminal Court, the United States arrived with the firm belief that those who perpetrate genocide, crimes against humanity, and war crimes must be held accountable—and that horrendous deeds must not go unpunished. But the International Criminal Court that emerged from the Rome negotiations . . . will not effectively advance these worthy goals.

First, we believe the ICC is an institution of unchecked power.

Second, the treaty approved in Rome dilutes the authority of the U.N. Security Council and departs from the system that the framers of the U.N. Charter envisioned.

Third, the treaty threatens the sovereignty of the United States. The court, as constituted today, claims the authority to detain and try American citizens, even through our democratically elected representatives have not agreed to be bound by the treaty.

Fourth, the current structure of the International Criminal Court undermines the democratic rights of our people and could erode the fundamental elements of the United Nations Charter, specifically the right to self defense.

Fifth, we believe that by putting U.S. officials, and our men and women in uniform, at risk of politicized prosecutions, the ICC will complicate U.S. military cooperation with many friends and allies who will now have a treaty obligation to hand over U.S. nationals to the court—even over U.S. objections. . . .

We must ensure that our soldiers and government officials are not exposed to the prospect of politicized prosecutions and investigations. Our president is committed to a robust American engagement in the world to defend freedom and defeat terror; we cannot permit the ICC to disrupt that vital mission.

the killing with the threat of U.N. troops, but no such proposal had been made. The Sudanese government was rejecting all proposals for peacekeeping troops to protect civilians and angrily accused the United States of being after its oil and gold. While the African Union was sending a few hundred troops to protect monitors of the cease-fire, it was unclear whether it had either the political power or the practical ability to send more troops to protect civilians.[64]

And some columnists doubted the American public wanted to engage in a humanitarian crusade so soon after the war in Iraq. As *New York Times* writer Traub suggested on July 18, "perhaps the Bush administration's effort to repackage the immensely unpopular war in Iraq as a Wilsonian crusade to free a subject people has discredited the very principle of humanitarian intervention."[65]

Peacekeepers prepare to leave for the troubled Darfur region, in western Sudan, on Aug. 14, 2004. The Rwandan troops are part of a 300-man force being sent by the African Union to restore order following attacks by Arab militiamen on black African villages.

AFP Photo/Gianluigi Guercia

The chaos in Iraq vividly demonstrated the difficulty of rebuilding a country following a military intervention. Another sign of the difficulty came in a report in July that faulted the U.N. and local authorities that have run Kosovo for the past five years for not protecting the province's Serbian minority.[66]

The report appeared four months after thousands of ethnic Albanians—the group Milosevic persecuted in the 1990s—began attacking Serbian communities. The U.N. mission there had been established after Yugoslav and Serbian forces, which had been accused of widespread atrocities, were forced out of Kosovo by the NATO bombing campaign.

OUTLOOK

U.S. Role?

Following genocide, human-rights activists often stress, the international community needs to help rebuild a country's courts and democratic institutions to prevent the kind of revenge violence seen in Kosovo recently. But critics of humanitarian intervention suggest that the United States is not cut out for such ventures, as witnessed by its recent experience in Iraq.

"People may say abstractly, 'Let's do it,'" Cornell University's Rabkin says, "but when they face casualties it's not so pretty. We're not committed enough; we're not willing to shell out what it costs."

Yet humanitarian crises are only likely to proliferate as global struggles over dwindling resources like water and arable land become more desperate. "There are over 200 conflicts around the world. Any of those could be at risk of escalating to mass violence or to genocide," Ambassador Joyce Leader, who was deputy chief of mission in Rwanda during the 1994 genocide, says.

The United States is already involved in 100 peacekeeping operations around the world, according to the State Department, not to mention its major commitment in Iraq. That level of activity raises the question of how many other places the country can afford to send troops.

Other countries have similar problems. "We're all very thin," said Gunther Altenburg, an assistant secretary-general at NATO, which has peacekeeping troops in Afghanistan and Kosovo. Most NATO members are facing budget cuts, he noted. "When the call comes" asking for peacekeeping troops, "maybe they're already in the Balkans or in Afghanistan," he said, and are unwilling or unable to commit more troops.[67]

Practical problems aside, will nations have the political will to stop and punish the next genocide?

After the major genocides of the past century, leaders around the world have publicly pledged "Never again!" repeatedly. That increased consciousness gives some experts hope that this time, the shame over past massacres will mobilize democratic governments around the world. Genocide scholar Chalk notes that Secretary Powell's visit to Darfur this summer is a striking contrast to the U.S. response to Rwanda's massacres in 1994, when not a single prominent government official visited the killing grounds. "I think these guys are really going to do something this time," he says hopefully.

Yale Professor Kiernan sees two conflicting trends in the 1990s. On the one hand, increased world concern about bringing genocidal leaders to justice resulted in concrete solutions—the establishment of tribunals. On the other hand, longstanding ethnic conflicts were exacerbated as the Soviet bloc and Cold War alignments disintegrated—leading to genocide in places like Bosnia. On the negative side, Kiernan suspects that leaders of genocides in countries like Rwanda were encouraged by the slow international response to Bosnia. But on balance, "The story of the '90s is one of increasing awareness of the criminality of genocide and action to punish if not deter it," Kiernan says.

While governments and experts often show great conviction concerning genocides past and future, the Holocaust museum's Fowler notes that "it's very hard to get people to talk about the present"—actual cases in which military power, soldiers' lives and political prestige are at stake.

And it seems likely that there will continue to be despotic leaders who think they can act with impunity, counting on the indecisiveness of the rest of the world—as some experts believe is occurring in Sudan right now.

A reminder of that threat is contained in Adolf Hitler's famous expression of cynicism in August 1939 as he planned his military campaign. Assuring his generals that the Nazis would have the last word in the history books, Hitler said, "Who today still speaks of the massacre of the Armenians?" A week later, he invaded Poland.[68]

NOTES

1. Nicholas D. Kristof, "Magboula's Brush with Genocide," *The New York Times*, June 23, 2004.
2. Reuters, "Factbox: What's Happening in Western Sudan," Aug. 11, 2004.
3. Marc Lacey, "Despite Appeals, Chaos Still Stalks the Sudanese," *The New York Times*, July 18, 2004, p. A1.
4. See Human Rights Watch and Amnesty International Web sites: www.hrw.org and www.amnesty.org.
5. U.N. News Service, "Sudan Must Act on Darfur in 30 Days or Face Measures, Security Council Warns," July 30,2004.
6. The Associated Press, "US Congress Declares Genocide in Sudan," July 23, 2004, at www.cnn.com.
7. *Ibid.*
8. See Reuters, "France Says Peacekeepers May be Needed in Darfur," Aug. 13, 2004, and Reuters, "Sudan Accuses West of Seeking its Oil and Gold," Aug. 12, 2004.
9. Marc Lacey, "In Darfur, Appalling Atrocity, but is That Genocide?" *The New York Times*, July 23, 2004, p. A3.
10. For background on Rwanda, see the following *CQ Researcher* reports by David Masci: "United Nations and Global Security," Feb. 27, 2004, pp. 173-196; "Ethics of War," Dec. 13, 2002, pp. 1013-1037; "Famine in Africa," Nov. 8, 2002, pp. 921-944.
11. Testimony of author Samantha Power before House International Relations Subcommittee on Africa, April 22, 2004.
12. The Associated Press, "Clinton in Africa; Clinton's Painful Words Of Sorrow and Chagrin," *The New York Times*, March 26, 1998, p. A12.
13. James C. McKinley Jr., "Annan Given Cold Shoulder By Officials In Rwanda, *The New York Times*, May 8, 1998, p. A9.
14. House International Relations Committee hearings on Darfur, May 6, 2004.
15. Nicholas D. Kristof, "Dithering as Others Die," *The New York Times*, June 26, 2004.

16. The Associated Press, "At Least 180 Killed in Attack on a Refugee Camp in Burundi," *The New York Times*, Aug. 15, 2004, p. A10.

17. *Ibid.*

18. Warren Hoge, "At UN, U.S. Threatens Penalties on Sudan," *The New York Times*, July 23, 2004.

19. Testimony before House International Relations Committee, April 22, 2004.

20. For background, see Kenneth Jost, "War Crimes," *The CQ Researcher*, July 7, 1995, pp. 585-608.

21. John Prendergast, "Sudan's Ravines of Death," *The New York Times*, July 15, 2004.

22. For background on International Criminal Court, see Masci, "Ethics of War," *op. cit.*; David Masci, "Torture," *The CQ Researcher*, April 18, 2003, pp. 345-368, and Kenneth Jost, "War Crimes," *The CQ Researcher*, July 7, 1995, pp. 585-608.

23. On July 18, Amnesty International blamed the Sudanese government for the Darfur attacks. See "Sudan: Darfur: Rape as a Weapon of War," www.amnestyusa.org.

24. Reuters, "Factbox," *op. cit.*

25. Human Rights Watch, "Too Little, Too Late: Sudanese and International Response 2004," May 2004; www.hrw.org.

26. Maggie Farley, "Annan Calls on Humanity to be Ready to Fight Genocide," *Los Angeles Times*, April 2, 2004.

27. "Holocaust Museum Declares Genocide Emergency," July 26, 2004 at www.ushm.org/conscience/Sudan/Darfur.

28. For background, see Mary H. Cooper, "Future of NATO," *The CQ Researcher*, Feb. 23, 2003, pp. 177-200.

29. James Traub, "Never Again, No Longer?" *The New York Times Magazine*, July 18, 2004, pp. 17-18.

30. Available at www.npr.org.

31. Power testimony, *op. cit.*

32. For background, see Masci, "Torture," *op. cit.*

33. Traub, *op. cit.*, p. 17.

34. Peter Landesman, "Who v. Saddam?" *The New York Times Magazine*, July 11, 2004, p. 34.

35. Power, *op. cit.*, pp. 343-344.

36. Farley, *op. cit.*

37. *Ibid.*

38. U.N. press release, "Report of the Panel on U.N. Peace Operations," Aug. 23, 2000.

39. Gary Bass, *Stay the Hand of Vengeance* (2000), pp. 294-295.

40. See www.yale.edu/gsp.

41. Address to Center for Strategic and International Studies, May 6, 2002.

42. Ruth Wedgwood, "An International Criminal Court is Still a Bad Idea," *The Wall Street Journal*, April 15, 2002.

43. Power, *op. cit.*

44. *Ibid.*, p. xix.

45. Power testimony, *op. cit.*

46. Power, *op. cit.*, pp. 377-378.

47. *Ibid.*, p. 377.

48. James Waller, *Becoming Evil* (2002), pp. 184-185.

49. Doug Saunders, "Is the Brutality in Sudan Genocide?" *Globeandmail.com*, June 19, 2004, p. A1.

50. "World Briefings: Africa: Rwanda: Ex-Minister Jailed for Life," *The New York Times*, July 16, 2004.

51. Reuters, "Poor Health of Milosevic Delays Trial," *The New York Times*, July 6, 2004.

52. Nicholas Wood, "NATO Tries Again, to Capture War Suspect," *The New York Times*, June 22, 2004.

53. State Department press release, "Serbia and Montenegro Certification," March 31, 2004; also see State Department Daily Briefing, March 31, 2004.

54. Landesman, *op. cit.*, p. 36.

55. *Ibid.*

56. Alan Sipress, "Khmer Rouge Trials Stalled by Political Deadlock," *The Washington Post*, May 5, 2004, p. A24.

57. For coverage, see Warren Hoge, "Annan Rebukes U.S. for Move to Give its Troops Immunity," *The New York Times*, June 18, 2004, and Warren Hoge, "US Drops Plan to Exempt GI's from UN Court," *The New York Times*, June 24, 2004, p. A1. Note: "UN Court" is a misnomer; the ICC is an independent entity.

58. See Human Rights Watch, "The United States and the International Criminal Court," www.hrw.org.

59. *Ibid*

60. Remarks to the International Criminal Court Assembly of State Parties, Sept. 9, 2002; www.icc-now.org.

61. "Is Sudan's Crisis a Case of Genocide?" "Weekend Edition," National Public Radio, July 17, 2004, at www.npr.org.

62. Nima Elbagir, "New Violence Deepens Darfur Crisis," Reuters, Aug. 11, 2004.

63. Lacey, *op. cit.*
64. Somini Sengupta, "Crisis in Sudan," *The New York Times*, Aug. 16, 2004, p. A8.
65. Traub, *op. cit.*, pp. 17-18.
66. Nicholas Wood, "Kosovo Report Criticizes Rights Progress by UN and Local Leaders," *The New York Times*, July 14, 2004.
67. The symposium, "The Responsibility to Protect, The Capacity to Prevent and the Capacity to Intervene," was held May 5, 2004, at the Woodrow Wilson International Center for Scholars, Washington, D.C.
68. Quoted in Power, *op. cit.*, p. 23.

BIBLIOGRAPHY

Books

Bass, Gary Jonathan, *Stay the Hand of Vengeance: The Politics of War Crimes Tribunals,* **Princeton University Press, 2000.**
An assistant professor of politics and international affairs at Princeton University finds that war-crimes tribunals—from Napoleon to Milosevic—rarely deter genocide, but are better than the alternative—revenge.

Gourevitch, Philip, *We Wish to Inform You That Tomorrow We Will Be Killed with Our Families,* **Picador, 1998.**
Reporter Gourevitch visits Rwanda in the aftermath of the genocide and in a series of compelling interviews with Rwandans on both sides of the killings explores the themes of guilt, vengeance and responsibility.

Kuperman, Alan J., *The Limits of Humanitarian Intervention: Genocide in Rwanda,* **Brookings Institution Press, 2001.**
Countering the conventional wisdom, an assistant professor of political science at the Johns Hopkins School of Advanced International Studies argues that the Rwandan genocide happened too fast for the West to have prevented it.

Melvern, Linda, *A People Betrayed: The Role of the West in Rwanda's Genocide,* **Zed Books, 2004.**
An investigative journalist details the Rwandan genocide in 1994, the history leading up to it and the role of the Western powers.

Mills, Nicolaus, and Kira Brunner, eds., *The New Killing Fields: Massacre and the Politics of Intervention,* **Basic Books, 2002.**
War reporters and scholars examine why—and why not—the United States has intervened in state-sponsored massacres in Cambodia, Yugoslavia, Rwanda and East Timor.

Power, Samantha, *A Problem from Hell: America and the Age of Genocide,* **Perennial, 2002.**
A former journalist in Bosnia argues that American presidents rarely consider it in their political interest to stop genocides even when they know about them.

Waller, James, *Becoming Evil: How Ordinary People Commit Genocide and Mass Killing,* **Oxford University Press, 2002.**
A psychologist concludes that ordinary people get involved in genocide and do not have to be evil monsters to do so.

Articles

Landesman, Peter, "Who v. Saddam?" *The New York Times Magazine,* **July 11, 2004, pp. 34-39.**
The special court that will try Saddam Hussein and other Iraqis for genocide has come under fire from human-rights activists, who want more international participation, and Iraqis, who want swift justice.

Sengupta, Somini, "Death and Sorrow Stalk Sudanese Across Border," *The New York Times,* **Aug. 20, 2004, p. A1.**
A month after Sudan pledged to crack down on marauding militias, the killings continue and an epidemic threatened to sweep overcrowded refugee camps.

Traub, James, "Never Again, No Longer?" *The New York Times Magazine,* **July 18, 2004.**
The war in Iraq and the Sept. 11, 2001, terrorist attacks have muddied the waters about the legitimacy of intervention, making Americans' vulnerability to terror their prime concern and humanitarian intervention "yesterday's problem."

Reports, Studies and Transcripts

Amnesty International, "Sudan: Darfur: Rape as a Weapon of War," **July 19, 2004; www.amnestyusa.org.**
Rape, abduction and sexual slavery of young girls is being used on a mass scale by Janjaweed Arab militiamen to intimidate black Sudanese, but Amnesty stops short of calling it genocide.

Human Rights Watch, "Darfur Destroyed," May 2004; http://www.hrw.org/reports/2004/sudan0504.
The human-rights group concludes that Sudan has been working hand in glove with the Janjaweed militias attacking villages in Darfur and urges the U.N. to step in.

Human Rights Watch, "Leave No One to Tell the Story: Ten Years Later," April 1, 2004; http://www.hrw.org/reports/1999/rwanda
This update of the Rwandan story 10 years after the genocide describes how ethnic slaughters have spilled into neighboring Burundi and the Congo and how Rwanda's Tutsi-dominated government has become increasingly repressive.

Public Broadcasting Service, "Frontline," "Ghosts of Rwanda," April 9, 2004; www.pbs.org/wgbh/pages/frontline/shows/ghosts.
The transcript of this documentary about the 1994 Rwandan genocide describes the bureaucratic paralysis that seized Washington and the United Nations during the killings; the Web site has links to related interviews and reports.

For More Information

Amnesty International, 322 Eighth Ave., New York, NY 10001; (212) 807-8400; www.amnesty.org. Campaigns for human rights worldwide.

Coalition for the International Criminal Court, 777 U.N. Plaza, New York, NY 10017; (212) 687-2176; www.iccnow.org. A network of 2,000 non-governmental organizations.

Genocide Watch, P.O. Box 809, Washington, DC 20044, (703) 448-0222; www.genocidewatch.org. Coordinates an international campaign to end genocide.

Human Rights Watch, 350 Fifth Ave., 34th Floor, New York, NY 10118-3299; (212) 290-4700; www.humanrightswatch.org. Investigates and exposes human-rights violations around the world.

"Kristof Responds" Web site. *New York Times* columnist Nicholas D. Kristof posts his columns, answers reader e-mail and puts new developments on Darfur here. http://forums.nytimes.com/top/opinion/readersopinions/forums/editorials oped/opedcolumnists/kristofresponds/index.html.

Office of War Crimes Issues, U.S. Department of State; 2201 C St., N.W., Washington, DC 20520; www.state.gov/s/wci. Formulates administration policy in response to atrocities committed around the world.

U.S. Holocaust Memorial Museum Committee on Conscience, 100 Raoul Wallenberg Place, S.W., Washington, DC 20024; www.ushmm.org/conscience. Publicizes present-day threats of genocide.

Yale University Genocide Studies Program, P.O. Box 208206, New Haven, CT 06520-8206; www.yale.edu/gsp. Posts genocide information on its Web site.

2

New Defense Priorities

Mary H. Cooper

Secretary of Defense Donald H. Rumsfeld calls for transforming the military to enable it to counter "asymmetric" threats from unconventional forces like the al Qaeda Islamic terrorist organization. The administration applied some of its new military priorities in the war to oust Iraq's Saddam Hussein, who President Bush said was developing weapons of mass destruction.

From *The CQ Researcher,*
September 13, 2002 (Revised June 2003).

During the Cold War, the U.S. military amassed an arsenal of unprecedented power, including thousands of nuclear weapons, bombers, aircraft carriers, tanks and submarines. But nothing about the Sept. 11 terrorist attacks on New York City and the Pentagon corresponded to the conventional, doomsday war scenarios anticipated by the Pentagon—a Soviet land invasion of Europe or nuclear missile attack against the United States.

Nevertheless, President George W. Bush responded to the attacks in a conventional manner. He declared a "war on terrorism" and sought international support for military action. Then he mounted a U.S.-British offensive against the alleged mastermind of the attacks, Saudi exile Osama bin Laden, his Islamic terrorist organization al Qaeda and its Taliban supporters in Afghanistan.[1]

Although Operation Enduring Freedom used some of the Pentagon's most sophisticated new communications systems and "smart" weapons, many al Qaeda leaders escaped capture. The operation succeeded in toppling the Taliban, but Bush's larger war on terrorism continues amid questions about U.S. preparedness for such unconventional combat.

"As the cliché goes, the generals are always preparing for the last war," said Ranan R. Lurie, a senior associate at the Center for Strategic and International Studies (CSIS). "But there will never be a war that is so different from previous wars as this one is, and we would be extremely irresponsible not to recognize that fact."

But almost two years after Sept. 11, it is still unclear how the attacks will affect U.S. defense policy. In his first effort to adapt strategy and weaponry to a rapidly changing international security environment, Defense Secretary Donald H. Rumsfeld emphasized

U.S. Strength vs. Potential Enemies

The United States far surpasses in manpower and materiel the countries historically identified by the Department of Defense as potential enemies. Moreover, the comparison understates the full military strength of the U.S. because of the higher capability of U.S. weaponry, training and communications, according to the independent Center for Defense Information.

	Active Troops	Reserves	Heavy Tanks	Armored Vehicles	Planes	Helicopters	Warships
U.S.	1,400,000	1,200,000	8,303	24,075	9,030	6,779	200
Iran*	513,000	350,000	1,135	1,145	269	718	8
Iraq	429,000	650,000	2,200	4,400	350	500	--
Libya	76,000	40,000	2,210	2,620	594	202	4
North Korea	1,100,000	4,700,000	3,500	3,060	1,167	320	29
Sudan	104,500	--	170	488	46	28	--
Syria	316,000	396,000	4,850	4,785	640	221	2

*Iran has been historically defined as a potential U.S. enemy, but the Department of Defense removed Iran from the list in March 1999.

Sources: Center for Defense Information, *Military Almanac 2001-2002*, based on data from U.S. Department of Defense and the International Institute for Strategic Studies.

the need to "deter and defeat" unconventional adversaries like bin Laden. He called for a stronger homeland defense and preparations for countering "asymmetric" warfare—unconventional attacks by forces, like al Qaeda, which cannot match the United States' military strength on the battlefield.[2] Indeed, the Sept. 11 hijackers were not regular soldiers, and their commanders acted on behalf of no recognized government.

Since the attacks, Bush has requested, and obtained from Congress, an immediate infusion of money to conduct the war on terrorism. Lawmakers approved a record $382.2 billion military-spending measure for fiscal 2003—a 10 percent, or $34.4 billion, increase over 2002. The Pentagon has requested $399.1 billion for fiscal 2004, a 4.4 percent increase over last year.[3]

Rumsfeld's Pentagon is forging ahead with efforts to build what Rumsfeld says will be a more flexible, mobile military capable of using the latest technology to quash the kinds of asymmetric warfare likely to threaten national security in the future.

"Big institutions aren't swift on their feet," Rumsfeld said on Sept. 3, 2002. "They're ponderous and clumsy and slow." A terrorist organization, meanwhile, "watches how you're behaving and then alters and adjusts at relatively little cost, [in] relatively little time, [with] relatively little training to those incremental changes we make in how we do things."[4]

The solution, Rumsfeld said, is to change the way the U.S. military does things. "Business as usual won't do it," he said.

In the process, Rumsfeld is planning to scuttle some traditional weapons, such as the Crusader, a heavy cannon designed for old-style battlefield combat. Eliminating the $11 billion program—which is already under way—may be the first of several major changes in ongoing weapons systems. The latest "defense planning guidance," which lays out the administration's defense investment priorities for fiscal 2004-2009, calls for the review—and possible elimination—of several other major systems now considered outmoded for future combat scenarios (*see p. 36*).

Aside from the expanded spending bill, however, there are few signs that the attacks have prompted major defense-policy changes. "Although Sept. 11 has created a greater sense of threat and a greater willingness to spend money on national security, the long-term plans of the military establishment's senior policymakers have changed relatively little in response to Sept. 11," said Loren B. Thompson, a defense analyst at the Lexington Institute, a think tank in Arlington, Va. "Judging from the defense planning guidance, what they're trying to achieve and what priorities they plan to pursue are remarkably similar to the goals and terminology used prior to Sept. 11."

Bush's most visible defense-related initiative is the new Department of Homeland Security—a massive, $34.7 billion undertaking to merge some 170,000 federal workers from 22 agencies into a new, Cabinet-level agency dedicated to protecting the United States from terrorist attack.[5]

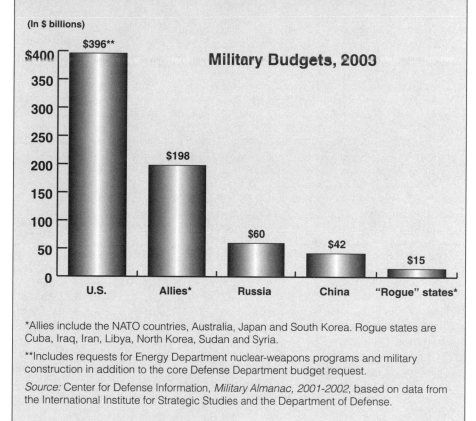

U.S. Military Spending Dwarfs Other Nations'

The proposed U.S. military budget for 2003 exceeds the combined military budgets of the world's other major powers and the "rogue" nations identified as potential enemies by the Defense Department.

Military Budgets, 2003

(In $ billions)

U.S. $396**; Allies* $198; Russia $60; China $42; "Rogue" states* $15

*Allies include the NATO countries, Australia, Japan and South Korea. Rogue states are Cuba, Iraq, Iran, Libya, North Korea, Sudan and Syria.

**Includes requests for Energy Department nuclear-weapons programs and military construction in addition to the core Defense Department budget request.

Source: Center for Defense Information, *Military Almanac, 2001-2002*, based on data from the International Institute for Strategic Studies and the Department of Defense.

"But that is almost entirely separate from the military establishment," Thompson said. "Defense spending has increased, but for the most part not because of Sept. 11. So it is somewhat misleading to think that the surge in money for homeland security is synonymous with increased defense spending."

But others warn against radical changes in the Pentagon's ongoing effort to transform the military. "There is danger in taking an overly militarized view of the war on terrorism," said Joseph Nye, dean of Harvard University's John F. Kennedy School of Government. "It's important to realize that the military is only a part of what is needed to protect against terrorism, and maybe not even the dominant part."

Nye, who served as assistant Defense secretary for international security affairs under former President Bill Clinton, says the attacks did not significantly change the nature of emerging post-Cold War threats to U.S. security—such as the possibility that Iraq and other so-called rogue states may be developing nuclear weapons. "We have to have an intelligent defense strategy" to deal with such threats, he said.

In fact, Bush's recent war to effect "regime change" in Iraq represents one of the major shifts in the administration's military policy. Bush has often warned that he would consider preemptive strikes against any states or terrorist groups trying to develop nuclear, biological or chemical weapons—so-called weapons of mass destruction—that could be used against the United States.

Bush's Go-It-Alone Nuclear Policy

The Bush administration's call to overthrow Iraqi President Saddam Hussein—suspected of developing nuclear weapons for possible use against the United States or its allies—represents a radical departure in U.S. arms-control policy. That policy, in essence, called for negotiation rather than unilateral action.

During the Cold War, the United States and the Soviet Union developed a series of negotiated agreements to avert a potentially catastrophic nuclear exchange. Those treaties included the 1972 Anti-Ballistic Missile Treaty (ABM) and the SALT I and II treaties, negotiated in the 1970s and 1980s.

When the Soviet Union dissolved in 1991, the SALT treaties became obsolete, and the United States and leaders of the new Russia negotiated new treaties, starting with the 1991 Strategic Arms Reduction Treaty (START I). It limited each side to 6,000 warheads and 1,600 long-range bombers and missiles. The treaty also applied to the Soviet successor states of Russia, Ukraine, Belarus and Kazakhstan, then the repositories for the former Soviet arsenal.[1]

As bilateral relations steadily improved, the United States and Russia agreed to further nuclear-arms reductions. In January 1993, even before START I took effect (December 1994), they signed START II, which called for nearly halving each country's strategic nuclear warheads, to 3,500. The U.S. Senate ratified the treaty in January 1996, the Russian legislature in 2000.

---

[1] Information in this section is based in part on Amy F. Woolf, "Nuclear Arms Control: The U.S.-Russian Agenda," Congressional Research Service, June 13, 2002.

In March 1997, President Bill Clinton and Russian President Boris Yeltsin agreed to begin negotiations on START III, once START II entered into force. The new treaty would have reduced each side's nuclear arsenals to 2,000-2,500 warheads and set limits on shorter-range, or tactical, nuclear weapons.

By 2001, when President Bush took office, START II had yet to enter into force. As a critic of traditional arms-control policy, Bush strongly supported the accelerated construction of a national missile-defense system. But the ABM Treaty prohibited such a nationwide defensive system, on the theory that it would spark the building of more nuclear arms to overcome it.

The ABM Treaty allowed each country to install a single missile-defense site, with no more than 100 interceptors, provided they did not provide nationwide coverage. The treaty was part of a broad agreement limiting both sides' ballistic-missile arsenals. (The 1979 SALT II Treaty contained a second set of limits, but the Senate refused to ratify it after the Soviets invaded Afghanistan in 1980.)

On Dec. 13, 2001, Bush announced his intention to unilaterally withdraw from the ABM Treaty, calling it out of date. Over Russian objections, the United States officially withdrew from the treaty on June 13, 2002.

At the same time, Bush announced—again unilaterally—plans to continue reducing the U.S. nuclear arsenal. Instead of pursuing his predecessor's efforts to conclude START III, Bush bypassed the negotiation process and declared that the United States would cut its nuclear arsenal to below the levels agreed to under START II. Russia,

---

"We must . . . confront the worst threats before they emerge," Bush told the graduating class of West Point on June 1, 2002. "In the world we have entered, the only path to safety is the path of action. And this nation will act."

Preemptive-strike proposals stem from frustration over the U.S. military's inability to prevent the Sept. 11 attacks as well as from fear that in the era of the suicide bomber, America's longstanding strategy of deterrence may not be enough.

"Most countries are deterred from attacking us, even if they have nuclear weapons, by the fact that we also have nuclear weapons and could do considerable damage to them," said Peter W. Galbraith, a professor at the

National War College, which trains senior Pentagon officers. But al Qaeda has "no return address," he pointed out. "If they smuggle [a nuclear weapon] in and blow it up in Washington or New York, we can do nothing to hit back except what we've been trying to do, apparently unsuccessfully, for the last year, which is to get Mr. bin Laden, dead or alive."

Bush enjoyed widespread bipartisan support for his military actions in Afghanistan following the Sept. 11 attacks. But the war to oust President Saddam Hussein of Iraq, absent overt aggression against the United States, raised concerns at home and abroad. Senate Foreign Relations Committee Chairman Joseph R. Biden Jr., D-Del., held a hearing on the issue several months before

however, called for a formal, bilateral agreement binding the two sides to any further nuclear arms reductions.

On May 24, 2002, Bush and Russian President Vladimir Putin signed a new Strategic Offensive Reductions Treaty. Known as the Treaty of Moscow, it calls for cuts in each country's deployed nuclear warheads to between 1,700 and 2,200 by the end of 2012. As the Senate prepares to consider the treaty, Senate Foreign Relations Committee Chairman Joseph Biden Jr., D-Del., and some other lawmakers are pressing for controls on short-range nuclear warheads as well. Russia's stockpile of thousands of tactical weapons is poorly guarded, and lawmakers worry that terrorists could obtain some warheads and make easily concealed "suitcase bombs" that could be detonated in a U.S. city.[2]

Meanwhile, the administration has stated it will not seek ratification of the 1996 Comprehensive Nuclear Test Ban Treaty (CTBT). By prohibiting all nuclear tests, the treaty aims to halt the improvement of existing nuclear arsenals and the development of new nuclear weapons. Signed by

Iraq's Saddam Hussein meets in August with Foreign Minister Sheikh Hamad of Qatar, the first Gulf state to re-establish ties with Iraq after the 1991 gulf war.

President Clinton and 164 other countries, it would enter into force after ratification by the 44 countries that already have nuclear weapons or nuclear reactors. To date, 31 have done so, including Russia, the United Kingdom, and France.

In the United States, critics have argued that some signatories might secretly test weapons or improve their nuclear stockpiles while the treaty-abiding United States would be left with a deteriorating arsenal. On the basis of these objections, the Senate rejected the treaty in 1999.

But a panel of experts convened by the National Academy of Sciences recently found that fear unfounded. "We judge that the United States has the technical capabilities to maintain confidence in the safety and reliability of its existing nuclear weapon stockpile under the CTBT," the panel concluded, "provided that adequate resources are made available."[3]

Although the administration will not seek ratification of the CTBT, it says it intends to observe a nuclear-testing moratorium in place since October 1992.

---

[2] See Miles A. Pomper, "U.S.-Russia Nuclear Arms Treaty Debated," *CQ Weekly*, July 13, 2002, p. 1897.

[3] National Academy of Sciences, "Technical Issues Related to the Comprehensive Nuclear Test Ban Treaty," July 31, 2002.

---

the U.S. invasion began in March. "I want [administration officials] to define their objectives in Iraq," Biden said. "I want to know what scenarios there are for eliminating the chemical and biological weapons that Iraq may use if we attack. I'd like to know how important our allies are in this."[6]

In response to such concerns, Bush announced on Sept. 3 he would not take action before seeking the approval of Congress. Later, he discussed his concerns about Iraq with leaders from Britain, France, Russia, China and other nations. Only Britain agreed to join the United States in the war.

As lawmakers debate the nation's post-9/11 defense policy, these are some of the issues being considered:

Should the United States embrace the preemptive-strike doctrine?

President Bush has described Iraq, Iran and North Korea as part of an "axis of evil" bent on destroying the United States and its allies. Iraqi President Hussein rose to the top of that list, the administration said, because he had biological and chemical weapons, was developing nuclear weapons and allegedly supported anti-U.S. terrorist groups.

The president's father, former President George Bush, ousted Iraq from Kuwait in 1991 but stopped short of invading Baghdad and going after Hussein.[7]

Hussein defied a United Nations resolution mandating inspections of suspected Iraqi nuclear, biological and

Defense Dominates Discretionary Spending

Defense spending is expected to comprise 18 percent of the nation's $2.1 trillion budget this fiscal year. However, military spending comprises almost half of the $792 billion the nation spends annually on discretionary items, such as foreign aid.

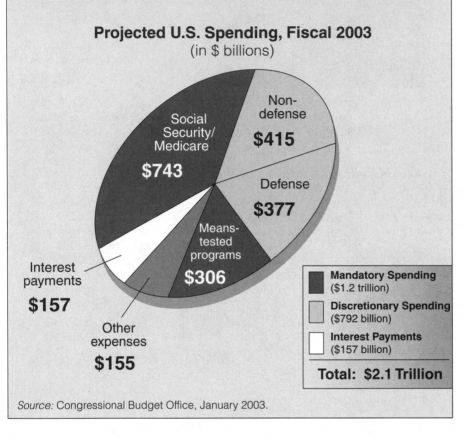

Projected U.S. Spending, Fiscal 2003
(in $ billions)

Non-defense $415

Social Security/Medicare $743

Defense $377

Means-tested programs $306

Interest payments $157

Other expenses $155

Mandatory Spending ($1.2 trillion)

Discretionary Spending ($792 billion)

Interest Payments ($157 billion)

Total: $2.1 Trillion

Source: Congressional Budget Office, January 2003.

chemical weapons production sites—a provision of the peace agreement Iraq signed when it surrendered. The second Bush administration charged that Iraq continued to develop weapons of mass destruction despite U.N. economic sanctions intended to force Hussein to readmit weapons inspectors.

After the 1991 Persian Gulf War, the U.S. sought to prevent further Iraqi aggression. Britain and the United States enforced "no-fly" zones designed to keep Iraqi forces out of northern and southern regions of the country, home to persecuted Kurdish and Shiite Muslim populations.

But after the Sept. 11 attacks, the administration turned up the rhetorical heat against Iraq. "It's the stated policy of this government to have a regime change," Bush said on July 8, 2002. "And we'll use all the tools at our disposal to do so." Earlier that year, the president reportedly signed an order directing the Central Intelligence Agency (CIA) to initiate a covert program to overthrow Hussein.[8]

To justify such an offensive, the administration articulated a new preemptive doctrine allowing the president to initiate military action—without congressional approval—against rogue states with weapons of mass destruction.

"Deterrence—the promise of massive retaliation against nations—means nothing against shadowy terrorist networks with no nation or citizens to defend," the president said at West Point. "If we wait for threats to fully materialize, we will have waited too long. [O]ur security will require all Americans to . . . be ready for preemptive action when necessary to defend our liberty and to defend our lives."

In fact, preemption isn't a new doctrine, said the war college's Galbraith. "It's long been the case that if we thought that someone was about to attack the United States we would take action against them," he said. "This is an evil regime that has practiced genocide against its own people, would do it again if unrestrained and certainly is going to cheat on every agreement it has made with regard to weapons of mass destruction. The Iraqi people will be very supportive of our taking action to liberate them."

Galbraith wonders, however, about the administration's logic of announcing—and then debating—preemptive action. "It doesn't make sense to announce it, particularly if you're dealing with someone like Saddam Hussein," he said. In fact, he added, announcing it in advance removes any reason for Hussein "not to use whatever weapons he has."

Supporters of Bush's emerging preemptive-strike policy argue that terrorist organizations and hostile governments that threaten the United States are unlikely to respond to traditional methods of deterrence.

"There is no give and take between such regimes and our country," said Lurie of the CSIS. The fact that North Korea, Iran and Iraq either have or are developing nuclear weapons and are hostile to the United States fully justifies a preemptive doctrine, he added. "The danger is immense. I would hate to see a situation where people are standing around scratching their heads, if they still have heads, and wondering, 'Why didn't we see it coming?'"

But preemptive action may have unintended consequences, critics say. Because it would permit the United States to launch a military operation unilaterally, the doctrine would alienate longstanding U.S. allies and may undermine the credibility of the United Nations and other international institutions, which the United States helped build. Indeed, widespread opposition from France, Germany and other allies to the U.S.-led war has produced the biggest strains in transatlantic relations since the end of World War II.

"It is not only politically unsustainable but diplomatically harmful," wrote G. John Inkenberry, a political science professor at Georgetown University. "And if history is a guide, it will trigger antagonism and resistance that will leave America in a more hostile and divided world."[9]

Others are more concerned about the administration's suggestion that a preemptive strike against Iraq might involve the use of nuclear weapons. After the gulf war, the Iraqi military moved some of its essential communications—and weapons—into deep underground bunkers. To destroy those installations, the Pentagon called for developing small, "bunker-busting" tactical nuclear warheads.[10]

"Tac-nukes," as they are called, were first developed as a last-resort defense against a massive Soviet invasion of Europe. They have never been used, and critics warn that deploying such nuclear weapons would lower the threshold for the future use of similar or even more lethal weapons. Although none were used in the war against Iraq, Congress has approved funds to develop nuclear bunker busters in the 2004 budget.

"It is politically inconceivable that the United States could ever be the first to use nuclear weapons," Galbraith said, adding that it would also be "militarily disastrous" for the United States. "If you have, as we do, the most powerful conventional forces in the world, the last thing you want is for it to become acceptable for people to ever think about using nuclear weapons against our forces."

Moreover, said Michael E. O'Hanlon, a senior fellow at the Brookings Institution, it is doubtful that conditions favorable to implementing a nuclear first-strike would ever arise. "You'd have to have Saddam deep in some underground bunker out in the middle of nowhere, where prevailing winds would not carry the fallout toward major cities," he says. "He's more likely to be where there are a lot of civilians, because that's his best defense against attack.

Supporters of preemption say the changing security environment warrants an equally radical shift in thinking. "During the Cold War, we had one enemy that mattered, and we relied on deterrence because we couldn't defend ourselves against a large Soviet attack," said the Lexington Institute's Thompson. "Today, we not only have other options, but we've also got lots of other enemies, and we don't understand some of them. So the administration's basic logic is valid: Not only are new enemies less predictable, but they may be less deterrable. So just trying to discourage aggression isn't enough any more."

Should the Pentagon play a bigger role in homeland security?

Traditionally, the Defense Department was charged with defending the United States abroad while a broad array of agencies protected Americans on U.S. soil. Tragically, the Sept. 11 attacks revealed a gaping hole in that division of labor.

The Bush administration responded immediately by creating the White House Office of Homeland Security, headed by former Gov. Tom Ridge of Pennsylvania. On June 6, 2002, Bush proposed transforming the office into a new, Cabinet-level Department of Homeland

Security, merging all or parts of the 22 agencies that protect the United States from terrorist attacks. Congres approved the new department, and Ridge was sworn in as its secretary on Jan. 24, 2003.

The Pentagon has a limited role in the new department, due in large part to the longstanding legal separation of military and police functions. The 1878 Posse Comitatus Act prohibited using military forces for domestic law enforcement. Adopted in response to excesses by federal troops deployed in the South during Reconstruction, the law has been amended to allow for limited military involvement in drug interdiction and a few other exceptions.

Pentagon officials traditionally have opposed exceptions to the law, fearing domestic assignments could weaken the military's readiness overseas. However, the terrorist attacks blurred that distinction. While the attacks took place on U.S. soil, they were conducted by foreign nationals and supported by overseas leadership and funding. As a result, the military was immediately pressed into service after the attacks: Air Force jets patrolled over American cities while National Guard troops guarded airports and assisted at border checkpoints.

The administration, eager to strengthen local defenses against terrorist attack, has asked for a review of the law's ban on domestic military involvement.

The Pentagon's new domestic role is managed through the recently created office of the assistant secretary of Defense for homeland security. But Air Force Gen. Ralph E. Eberhart, who heads the Northern Command, created after Sept. 11 to boost domestic security, is among a handful of military brass who advocate amending the law to enhance the military's contribution to homeland defense. "My view has been that Posse Comitatus will constantly be under review as we mature this command," he said.

The command, which began operations Oct. 1, 2002, at its headquarters in Colorado Springs, is authorized to deploy military personnel to back up domestic agencies such as the FBI and the Federal Emergency Management Agency (FEMA), as needed in emergencies.[11]

Some experts say the ban on military involvement in domestic law enforcement is a waste of vital military know-how and manpower. "Our Department of Defense has more tools, training, technology and talent to help combat the terrorist threat at home than any other federal agency," said Sen. Joseph I. Lieberman, D-Conn., chairman of the Senate Armed Services Airland Subcommittee. He would give the 460,000-member National Guard—essentially a 50-state militia that can be mobilized in state and national emergencies—an especially prominent role in homeland security.

"Our military has proven capable of brilliance beyond our borders," Lieberman said. "Now we must tap its expertise and its resources within our country by better integrating the Defense Department into our homeland security plans."[12]

But some experts agree with Pentagon officials who say the line between the military and law enforcement should remain strong. "The job of the Pentagon is to deter and defeat adversaries," said Thompson of the Lexington Institute. "Dragging them into an already overcrowded homeland defense arena would be a big mistake. We really don't need aircraft carriers defending our coastlines."

Other experts want the National Guard and the reserves to focus primarily on external threats, because that's where the risk is most serious. "If there is a catastrophe here at home, the National Guard is not going to be on hand quickly enough to be the most important player in the first few hours after an attack," said O'Hanlon of the Brookings Institution. "It's going to be local fire, police and rescue personnel. These first responders should get most of the resources, and the Guard should remain focused primarily on overseas combat."

Would a national missile-defense system protect the United States?

In one of the first major arms-control agreements of the Cold War era, the United States and the Soviet Union agreed to refrain from building defenses against the biggest perceived threat of the time—a massive nuclear attack by one superpower against the other. By prohibiting defenses against such a nuclear holocaust, the 1972 Anti-Ballistic Missile (ABM) Treaty assured each Cold War adversary that the other side was essentially defenseless. Moreover, the strategy—known as Mutual Assured Destruction (MAD)—theoretically reduced the incentive to build more nuclear weapons.[13]

Toward the end of the Cold War, however, President Ronald Reagan rejected the ABM Treaty's logic and called for the development of a space-based system capable of intercepting incoming missiles. Although critics ridiculed the plan as technically unfeasible—dubbing it "Star Wars" after the popular movie of the time—the Strategic Defense Initiative received funding that continued even after the Soviet Union's collapse in 1991. President Clinton later endorsed a more limited approach aimed at deflecting attacks from hostile states like Iraq, Iran and North Korea that had or were developing nuclear weapons.

George W. Bush entered the White House promising to remove the main legal obstacle to missile defenses by jettisoning the ABM Treaty altogether, which he did, effective June 14, 2002. The next day, on June 15, construction began on a missile-defense facility at Fort Greely, Alaska, the first component of a larger system that could total $238 billion by 2025.[14]

The attacks of Sept. 11 merely confirmed the views of missile-defense critics who had warned all along that long-range missiles no longer posed the biggest threat to U.S. security and that defending against them entailed huge technical obstacles.

"President Bush will not and cannot deploy any meaningful missile defense anytime this decade," wrote Joseph Cirincione, an analyst at the Carnegie Endowment for International Peace, who argues that the program has greater political than practical value. "Missile defense plays well for the Republicans. It shows that President Bush is keeping the faith with the Reagan revolution, and it remains an applause line for his core, conservative constituency."[15]

Harvard's Nye argues that the missile-defense program would be useless against today's immediate threats. "The idea of being able to defend ourselves against missiles from second-tier states at some point in the future is a worthy objective," he said. "The key questions are how much you spend, how fast you develop the program and how effective it will be."

Nye worries that emphasizing missile defenses may divert resources away from other weapons of mass destruction, such as nuclear "suitcase" bombs that could be smuggled across inadequately policed borders. "The danger is that we spend a lot of money nailing the door shut while leaving the windows open," he said.

Moreover, he said, "Getting rid of the ABM Treaty may make people think that other threats have gone away, and they haven't."

Some missile-defense advocates say that the terrorist attacks strongly suggest the program's design should be altered. O'Hanlon of Brookings supports a "relatively small" system, partly to avoid fueling a nuclear arms race with China, which has a limited nuclear arsenal.

But, he concedes, the threat from China is "not so dire as to constitute [an] urgent reason for investing huge numbers of national security dollars."

In addition, huge technical obstacles to developing an effective missile-defense system remain. "The administration is probably right that countries that don't now have missiles will be more inclined to acquire them if we are defenseless," said Thompson of the Lexington Institute. "But that doesn't address the main question, which is whether the defenses will work, and on that the jury is still out."

Like O'Hanlon, Thompson worries that a major missile-defense system would spur China to expand its nuclear arsenal. "But the missile defense system we are planning to deploy, at least during the Bush years, will be very modest," Thompson said. "It could cope with a North Korean missile attack or a handful of missiles accidentally launched by China or Russia, but not much else."

Meanwhile, Thompson echoed the skeptical views of many defense experts on both sides of the debate. "Although missile defense is still a worthwhile undertaking, Sept. 11 essentially confirmed the critics' complaints that there are many other ways that we could be attacked."

BACKGROUND

Post-Cold War Shift

The ongoing evolution in U.S. military strategy dates from the Soviet Union's collapse in December 1991.[16] Besides ending the Cold War, it abruptly eliminated the rationale for America's military strategy since the end of World War II.

The United States and the communist-led Soviet Union spent the early years of the Cold War in a race to build nuclear arsenals. As it became clear that neither country could defeat the other without destroying itself in the process—the MAD notion—they negotiated a series of bilateral arms-control agreements to slow the arms race. (*See sidebar, p. 28.*)

The Cold War also shaped the superpowers' arsenals of non-nuclear weapons. Assuming that the biggest

CHRONOLOGY

1950s-1970s *Cold War shapes U.S. defense policy; superpowers sign nuclear arms control treaties.*

1972 The U.S.-Soviet Anti-Ballistic Missile (ABM) Treaty is signed, prohibiting the superpowers from erecting a ballistic missile-defense system.

1973 War Powers Resolution calls for Congress and the president to share in decision-making over going to war.

1980s-1990s *As the Cold War winds down, hostile "rogue" states and Islamic terrorists replace the Soviet Union as the United States' main security concern.*

1991 The U.S. leads an international coalition to drive Iraq from Kuwait. The Soviet Union collapses in December, ending the Cold War. U.S. and Russia sign START I treaty limiting nuclear weapons.

1993 The first major study on transforming the military after the Cold War reaffirms the "two-war strategy"— calling for military preparedness to fight two regional wars at once. In January, Russia and the U.S. sign START II, calling for halving each country's nuclear warheads. On Feb. 23 Arab terrorists bomb the World Trade Center, killing six and injuring 1,000.

1994 The National Defense Authorization Act orders a Pentagon review of broad strategic goals every four years. U.S. forces withdraw from Somalia on March 25 after 18 American soldiers are killed during a failed U.N. peacekeeping mission. U.S. troops oust a Haitian military regime that had seized power from the elected president.

June 25, 1996 Terrorists bomb U.S. military barracks in Saudi Arabia, killing 19.

1997 The first Quadrennial Defense Review (QDR) directs the military to prepare for a broad range of conflicts and threats. Critics say retaining the two-war strategy fails to consider new security threats, such as terrorism, requiring more mobile forces.

August 1998 On Aug. 7, terrorists bomb U.S. embassies in Tanzania and Kenya, killing 224; U.S. retaliates on Aug. 20 by attacking al Qaeda camps in Afghanistan.

1999 The United States leads a NATO campaign to halt Serb repression of ethnic Albanians in Kosovo. Critics blame civilian casualties on the U.S. military's reluctance to place troops on the ground.

2000s *Continued terrorist attacks prompt changes in defense policy.*

Oct. 12, 2000 *USS Cole* is bombed in Yemen by militant Muslims, killing 17.

January 2001 President George W. Bush asks for the largest defense budget increase since the 1980s and orders review of the nation's military capability.

Sept. 11, 2001 Al Qaeda terrorists attack World Trade Center and the Pentagon, killing 3,000.

May 8, 2002 Defense Secretary Donald H. Rumsfeld says he wants to cancel the $11 billion Crusader cannon, one of several weapons systems that critics say are ill-suited to current threats.

May 24, 2002 U.S. and Russia sign Treaty of Moscow, calling for more cuts in nuclear arms.

June 1, 2002 Bush announces plans to use preemptive strikes against states or terrorist groups trying to develop weapons of mass destruction.

June 13, 2002 Bush withdraws U.S. from ABM treaty.

July 8, 2002 Bush says his government wants "a regime change" in Iraq.

Sept. 4, 2002 Bush promises to ask Congress and the U.N. Security Council for approval to attack Iraq.

Sept. 12, 2002 Bush is scheduled to address the U.N. General Assembly to present his case for attacking Iraq.

March 20, 2003 The United States and Britain invade Iraq and topple the government of President Saddam Hussein.

May 1, 2003 Bush declares victory in Iraq.

threat was a massive land invasion of Warsaw Pact forces across West Germany's Fulda Gap, the United States arrayed heavy tanks, artillery and ground troops along the so-called Iron Curtain—the border between Soviet-dominated communist Eastern Europe and democratic Western Europe.

As the superpowers refrained from direct hostilities in Europe, the Cold War devolved into a series of U.S.-Soviet proxy wars in Africa, Asia and Latin America— wherever socialist- or communist-leaning rebels were active in a country run by a pro-U.S. government. These far-flung conflicts and face-offs required the deployment of troops and equipment at military bases around the world.

The prevailing military doctrines were containment and deterrence. Containment—a term coined in 1947 by U.S. diplomat George F. Kennan—called for preventing the Soviet Union from expanding beyond a handful of bordering countries, which together became known as the Communist Bloc. Deterrence, reflecting President Theodore Roosevelt's admonition to "speak softly and carry a big stick," called for building a military strong enough to dissuade the enemy from attacking.

But both doctrines became less relevant after democratically elected governments replaced the communist regimes in the former Soviet states and Eastern Europe. U.S. policymakers anticipated a hefty "peace dividend"—more funds for domestic needs—as overseas military commitments, military bases and defense spending were cut. The transformation left Pentagon planners scrambling to define new strategies for dealing with a radically different set of security concerns.

Some of these threats had been emerging even before the Soviet collapse, as Iraq, North Korea and a few other regional powers began building arsenals of advanced conventional weapons and, in some cases, weapons of mass destruction.[17] To cope with the threat of what the State Department called rogue states, Pentagon planners began assembling the forces necessary to prevail against two regional powers simultaneously. They also began shifting procurement priorities from massive tanks and artillery to lighter, more mobile weapons that could be quickly transported from bases in the United States.

Iraq's Hussein put the new plans to the test in 1990, when he invaded Kuwait, launching the Persian Gulf

Weapons of Choice
In an effort to save money, the Pentagon is retaining the less-expensive F-35 Joint Strike Fighter (top), while some older warplanes may be dropped or phased out. Pentagon planners also may shelve plans to replace the Navy's nine *Nimitz*-class aircraft carriers (bottom) with a new generation of nuclear-powered carriers.

War. Equipped with the latest in high-technology hardware, from night-vision equipment to precision-guided "smart" bombs, the 500,000 U.S. and allied forces of Operation Desert Storm drove Iraq out of Kuwait in just seven weeks in 1991.

The United States' first major post-Cold War conflict also revealed some weaknesses in the new U.S. strategy. Lightly armed 82nd Airborne Division soldiers—who were deployed early—were vulnerable to

Despite calling for a sweeping transformation of the U.S. military, the Bush administration has canceled only one major weapon system to date—the Crusader, a heavy cannon designed for old-style battlefield combat. Defense Secretary Donald H. Rumsfeld asked that the $475 million initially requested for the $11 billion Crusader program in 2003 be used instead to speed development of lighter, more mobile artillery.

Iraqi attack for weeks before more heavily armed reinforcements could arrive by ship. In addition, several "smart" bombs missed their targets and killed civilians, and Iraqi Scud missile launchers evaded detection long enough to cause significant damage in Israel and Saudi Arabia.

There was another problem with the smart bombs and other precision weapons that could be employed far from the battlefield. While they kept U.S. combat casualties to a minimum, they also fostered a reluctance to place U.S. troops in harm's way. It was this caution, crit-

ics say, along with fears that Iraq might disintegrate, that led then-President George Bush not to pursue Iraqi troops to Baghdad.

Clinton's Changes

President Clinton (1993-2001) continued the process of "transforming" the military. During his administration, calls mounted for more than just modernization but for a true revolution in military affairs that would incorporate rapidly developing technology into weapons systems and adjust strategy to accommodate them.

Such a technological transformation would be as revolutionary as the introduction of gunpowder or the development of aircraft carriers before World War II. Military planning, advocates said, should acknowledge that future adversaries, unable to match the United States' overwhelming force superiority, would try to use surprise and unconventional uses of the weapons at hand to engage the world's sole superpower in "asymmetrical" warfare.

However, the most visible changes during this period were in so-called force downsizing. The Clinton administration closed 97 major bases—including 24 in California and seven in Texas—and downsized 55 others. Gen. Colin L. Powell, then-chairman of the Joint Chiefs, supported the development of a "base force"—the minimum number of troops and weapons needed to protect U.S. national interests while maintaining enough capacity to win two major regional wars simultaneously.

In 1993, the first major study on transforming the military after the Cold War—the so-called Bottom Up Review—reaffirmed the two-war strategy, despite criticism that it was unrealistic and expensive to fund, and supported a controversial new role for the military as peacekeepers.[18]

Meanwhile, the Clinton administration faced several military challenges that tested the president's goal of broadening the role of U.S. forces to include peacekeeping and other non-traditional missions. These would take U.S. troops to parts of the world where the United States had little or no prior military presence. On March 25, 1994, one such operation ended in disaster, when U.S. forces withdrew from Somalia after 18 American soldiers were killed during a failed U.N. peacekeeping mission in Mogadishu. A more successful operation came on Sept. 19, 1994, when Clinton sent troops to Haiti to oust a military regime that had seized power from the elected president.

A congressionally mandated commission reassessed the international-security environment as part of the 1994 National Defense Authorization Act and recommended retaining the two-war standard. But in view of the rapidly changing global situation—including regional conflict in the Balkans and threats from Iraq and North Korea—the commission suggested that the Pentagon review its broad strategic goals every four years. In 1996, Congress agreed with the panel and required the Defense Department to conduct a comprehensive examination of America's defense needs at four-year intervals.

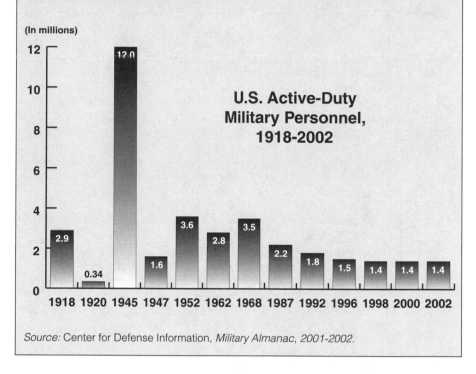

U.S. Military Manpower Has Declined

The number of active-duty military personnel declined and then leveled off in the post-Cold War period. High levels in previous years reflect the world wars and the Korean and Vietnam wars.

(In millions)

U.S. Active-Duty Military Personnel, 1918-2002

Year	Value
1918	2.9
1920	0.34
1945	12.0
1947	1.6
1952	3.6
1962	2.8
1968	3.5
1987	2.2
1992	1.8
1996	1.5
1998	1.4
2000	1.4
2002	1.4

Source: Center for Defense Information, *Military Almanac, 2001-2002.*

The first Quadrennial Defense Review (QDR), issued in 1997, directed the military to prepare for a variety of conflicts and threats, ranging from illegal drug trafficking to terrorism to major wars. But because it kept the two-war standard for determining force strength, critics continued to accuse the Pentagon of exaggerating defense needs to meet budget targets.

Congress had stepped into the debate in 1996 when it passed the Military Force Structure Review Act, which created another panel to assess ongoing defense policy changes. The following year, the National Defense Panel challenged the two-war scenario as a Cold War holdover and faulted the 1997 QDR for failing to adequately plan for the kind of military transformation required to deal with future challenges, such as asymmetric threats.

To pay for new weapons better suited for dealing with the emerging threats, the panel also asked the Pentagon to consider scaling back or eliminating several programs that critics said were either too expensive or antiquated "legacy systems," such as the Army's Crusader artillery vehicle, the Comanche helicopter, the Navy's last *Nimitz*-class aircraft carrier and several tactical, or short-range, aircraft.

By the end of the Clinton administration, some of the Pentagon's efforts to transform the military had begun to bear fruit. In early 1999, Clinton ordered U.S. forces to lead NATO's Operation Allied Force to halt Serb repression of ethnic Albanians in Kosovo. The almost exclusive use of air power and precise munitions enabled the allies to prevail in 11 weeks with few U.S. casualties. However, the deaths of some 500 civilians from stray bombs once again demonstrated the shortcomings of such heavy reliance on long-distance warfare.

Operation Allied Force also demonstrated the limited usefulness of some Cold War systems, such as the Army's

European Allies Oppose Attack on Iraq

Almost from the moment President Bush took office last year, America's European allies have accused him of adopting unilateral defense and foreign policies. One of the sole exceptions to such complaints was the outpouring of sympathy and solidarity after the Sept. 11 terrorist attacks.

Bush has strained transatlantic relations by rejecting several international agreements that enjoy broad support in Europe—including the Kyoto treaty to slow global warming, the U.S.-Soviet Anti-Ballistic Missile (ABM) Treaty and the treaty creating the new International Criminal Court.

Now, his insistence on preemptive U.S. military action to overthrow Iraqi leader Saddam Hussein has injected a new source of tension between the United States and its military allies in the North Atlantic Treaty Organizaton (NATO).

Ever since the president's father—President George Bush senior—led a broad, U.N.-sanctioned coalition to expel an Iraqi invasion of Kuwait in 1991, America's staunchest ally in the quest to contain Iraq has been Britain. Since the Persian Gulf War, British and U.S. air forces have jointly enforced "no-fly" zones over northern and southern Iraq to prevent Iraq from threatening its neighbors and persecuting Kurdish and Shiite Muslim minorities. Since 1998, U.S. and British aircraft have stepped up their attacks on Iraqi ground installations, completing more than 40 so far this year alone.

On Sept. 10, in one of his strongest statements yet, British Prime Minister Tony Blair called Hussein "an international outlaw" and said he believed it was right to deal with the Iraqi leader through the United Nations. "Let it be clear," Blair said, "that he must be disarmed. Let it be clear that there can be no more conditions, no more games, no more prevaricating, no more undermining of the U.N.'s authority. And let it also be clear that should the will of the U.N. be ignored, action will follow."[1]

America's other NATO allies have been adamantly opposed to military action against Iraq from the start. It's not that the Europeans are unconcerned about threats posed by Iraq, but they insist on obtaining a clear mandate from the international community before undertaking any military action. French President Jacques Chirac, who on Aug. 29 criticized "attempts to legitimize the use of unilateral and preemptive use of force" in Iraq, argues that the U.N. Security Council must approve any military operation. German Chancellor Gerhard Schroeder opposes an attack even with U.N. blessings, and indeed has made his opposition to invading Iraq a part of his current campaign for reelection. The goal, he said, should be to pressure

---

[1] Quoted in Terrance Neilan, "Blair Says 'Action Will Follow' if Iraq Spurns U.N. Resolutions," *The New York Times online*, Sept. 10, 2002.

---

big tanks, which were too wide and heavy for Kosovo's narrow roads and rickety bridges.

Bush's Priorities

During the 2000 presidential campaign, candidate George W. Bush criticized then-President Clinton for underfunding U.S. defenses and failing to prepare both military strategy and weaponry for 21st-century contingencies. He repeatedly promised the military, "hope is on the way."

Upon taking office in January 2001, Bush ordered Rumsfeld to conduct a comprehensive review of the nation's military capability. "To meet any dangers, our administration will begin building the military of the future," Bush said after asking for the biggest increase in

military spending since President Ronald Reagan's massive Cold War buildup in the 1980s. "We must and we will make major investments in research and development."[19]

High on Bush's priority list was the national missile-defense system. Although Clinton had supported research into a similar system, he had opposed its actual development because the ABM Treaty banned such systems. Declaring the treaty obsolete, Bush abandoned the agreement and pushed ahead.

When the Pentagon released its second Quadrennial Defense Review on Sept. 30, 2001—barely two weeks after the terrorist attacks—its central objective was to "deter and defeat adversaries who will rely on surprise, deception and asymmetric warfare to achieve their objec-

Hussein to allow weapons inspectors—whom he expelled in 1998—back into Iraq, not to go to war regardless, as Vice President Dick Cheney has suggested. "The problem is that [Cheney] has or seems to have committed himself so strongly that it is hard to imagine how he can climb down. And that is the real problem, that not only I have but that all of us in Europe have."

Non-European voices have been equally forceful. "We are really appalled by any country, whether it is a superpower or a poor country, that goes outside the United Nations and attacks independent countries," said former South African President Nelson Mandela. Russian Foreign Minister Igor Ivanov warned, "Any decision to use force against Iraq would not only complicate an Iraqi settlement but also undermine the situation in the gulf and the Middle East." The Arab League warned that an attack on Iraq would "open the gates of Hell" in the Middle East. Foreign ministers from 20 Arab states called for a "complete rejection of

threats of aggression against some Arab countries, in particular Iraq."[2]

Joseph Nye, dean of Harvard University's John F. Kennedy School of Government, says European allies might support U.S. action if the emphasis were not just on changing the regime but rather on stopping Hussein from obtaining weapons of mass destruction. "That means going through the U.N. inspection system and proving that he's not living up to his multilateral commitments, that he's developing nuclear weapons and that those pose an imminent threat," says Nye, who was former President Bill Clinton's assistant secretary of Defense for international security affairs. "Those are the key steps for gaining international support."

British Prime Minister Tony Blair, left, meets with President Bush at Camp David in early September. Blair supports military action against Iraq only if the U.N. fails to resolve the conflict.

AFP Photo/Paul J. Richards

---

[2] Quoted in Nicholas Blanford, "Syria worries US won't stop at Iraq," *The Christian Science Monitor*, Sept. 9, 2002.

---

tives," said Rumsfeld. "The attack on the United States on Sept. 11, 2001, will require us to move forward more rapidly in these directions, even while we are engaged in the war against terrorism."[20]

But many defense analysts were disappointed that the QDR lacked clear recommendations on how to achieve such a radical shift in focus.

"There is nothing in the QDR that envisions a significant increase in the new war-fighting technologies everyone agrees are critical," wrote Steven J. Nider, director of foreign and security studies at the Progressive Policy Institute, a liberal think tank. Calling the review "maddeningly vague," he charged the Rumsfeld Pentagon with the same inertia that had stymied change since the end of the Cold War.[21]

"More than just a broken campaign promise," he concluded, "it represents a missed opportunity to reshape our military to wage a new kind of war against new threats and enemies."

CURRENT SITUATION

Afghanistan Victory

The most salient lesson learned from Operation Enduring Freedom is that it was an astounding success, said Lurie of the CSIS. "What happened in Afghanistan was definitely an American victory," he said. "Someone may still be shooting a mortar here and there, but the fact of the matter is, we took over Afghanistan in a

U.S. soldiers search for enemy forces in eastern Afghanistan in March, 2002. Despite its success in routing the Taliban, Operation Enduring Freedom fell short of its primary objective, capturing Osama bin Laden and destroying his terrorist organization. Critics say the United States' unwillingness to commit adequate manpower to the Tora Bora campaign allowed Taliban and al Qaeda forces to slip away.

few weeks, something that the Soviets couldn't do in 10 years."

Thanks to the Bush administration's coherent reaction to the Sept. 11 attacks, "Every country now knows what to expect if it allows its own forces or terrorists acting from its territory to attack the United States," Lurie said. "As the old saying goes, 'If you can't kill the lion, don't sting it.'"

Enduring Freedom also introduced several innovations in hardware and tactics. Special-operations forces used laser range-finders and global-positioning systems to help pilots home in on and destroy targets with much greater precision even than during the Gulf War.[22] Unmanned aerial vehicles (UAVs), together with older imaging satellites and the Joint Surveillance Target Attack Radar System, enabled U.S. commanders to obtain vital information about remote battlefield conditions without placing American pilots in danger. And improvements in communication networks relayed the information faster than ever.

Moreover, for the first time unmanned planes, like the CIA's Predator UAVs, were used offensively to fire Hellfire air-to-surface missiles at enemy targets. And precision weapons—such as laser-guided missiles and JDAMS (guided bombs better suited to poor weather)—were first used as the predominant form of ordnance fired on enemy targets.

With the hostilities winding down, Pentagon planners said they had learned several lessons that would guide them in further transforming the military. Brookings' O'Hanlon argues that the mission's success depended not so much on the latest aircraft, ships and ground vehicles, as on improved communications, better-prepared troops and more coordination between special-operations forces on the ground and Air Force and Navy aircraft.

"It's dangerous to infer too much from one conflict, especially in this situation, where the Taliban really didn't have good air defenses," O'Hanlon said. "But I would still argue that Operation Enduring Freedom makes the case for smart munitions being very effective, and sometimes being good enough that you don't need to have the fanciest airplane from which to drop them."

But others warn about the unwillingness to commit adequate manpower to complete the job. "Instead of putting American troops on the ground in the Tora Bora campaign, which would have been costly and might have involved more casualties, we relied on Afghan allies who were hardly tested," said Galbraith of the National War College. "These guys weren't trained, and they operated in the Afghan manner, which is to serve whomever pays the highest price. They simply let the al Qaeda people slip away. There should have been more U.S. forces up there to seal up the escape routes."

Galbraith also questions the growing reliance on high-technology munitions. "There's a belief that high-tech is a magic wand, and that's not true because it depends on intelligence, which is never going to be that good," he said.

Galbraith cites the tragic U.S. bombing of a July 1 wedding party in Oruzgan Province, killing at least 54 civilians. American forces reportedly mistook the traditional firing of rifles into the air by wedding guests for an al Qaeda attack.

"You're just not going to ever get 100 percent intelligence as to whether something is a wedding or a gathering of [Taliban leader] Mullah Omar and his buddies," Galbraith said. "[So,] troops on the ground are probably essential."

Indeed, despite its success in routing the Taliban, the Afghanistan campaign fell short of its primary objective, capturing bin Laden and destroying his organization.

Some critics contend that no matter how well equipped, the U.S. military cannot win this kind of war on

AFP Photo/David Marck Jr.

AT ISSUE

Are the Pentagon's efforts to transform the military on track?

YES   Paul Wolfowitz
Deputy Secretary of Defense

From Testimony Before The Senate Armed Services
Committee, April 9, 2002

Our overall goal is to encourage a series of transformations that, in combination, can produce a revolutionary increase in our military capability and redefine how war is fought. . . .

Long before Sept. 11, the department's senior leaders—civilian and military—began an unprecedented degree of debate and discussion about where America's military should go in the years ahead. Out of those intense debates, we agreed on the urgent need for real changes in our defense strategy. The outline of those changes is reflected in the Quadrennial Defense Review (QDR) and the 2003 budget request. . . .

Setting specific transformation goals has helped to focus our transformation efforts, from investments to experimentation and concept development. The six goals identified in the QDR are:

- To defend the U.S. homeland and other bases of operations, and defeat nuclear, biological and chemical weapons and their means of delivery;
- To deny enemies sanctuary—depriving them of the ability to run or hide—anytime, anywhere;
- To project and sustain forces in distant theaters in the face of access-denial threats;
- To conduct effective operations in space;
- To conduct effective information operations; and,
- To leverage information technology to give our joint forces a common operational picture. . . .

Taken together, these six goals will guide the U.S. military's transformation efforts and improvements in our joint forces. Over time, they will help to shift the balance of U.S. forces and capabilities. U.S. ground forces will be lighter, more lethal and highly mobile. . . . Naval and amphibious forces will be able to assure U.S. access even in area-denial environments, operate close to enemy shores and project power deep inland. Air and space forces will be able to locate and track mobile targets over vast areas and strike them rapidly at long ranges without warning. . . .

Even as we fight this war on terror, potential adversaries scrutinize our methods, they study our capabilities, they seek our weaknesses. . . . So, as we take care of today, we are investing in tomorrow. We are emphasizing multiple transformations that, combined, will fundamentally change warfare in ways that could give us important advantages that can help us secure the peace.

We realize that achieving this goal requires transforming our culture and the way we think. We must do this even as we fight this difficult war on terrorism. We cannot afford to wait.

NO   Andrew F. Krepinevich
Executive Director, Center for Strategic and Budgetary Assessments

From Testimony Before The Senate Armed Services
Committee, April 9, 2002

While the Defense Department's rationale for transformation is persuasive, its process for effecting transformation is more difficult to discern and, hence, to evaluate. A transformation process is needed to validate vision, to identify the best means for addressing critical challenges and to determine if opportunities can be realized. . . .

The process should enable feedback on transformation initiatives (for example, new operational concepts, doctrines, systems, networks, force structures). This will enable senior Defense leaders to gauge whether the transformation path being pursued is, in fact, the correct path, or to make the appropriate adjustments if it is not. Such a process can help inform choices about investments in future capabilities—R&D, procurement, personnel and force structure—so as to reduce uncertainty in a resource-constrained environment.

Unfortunately, the Defense Department's modernization strategy today remains much the same as it was during the Cold War era, with its emphasis on large-scale, serial production of relatively few types of military systems and capabilities. To the extent possible, we should avoid premature large-scale production of new systems . . . until they have clearly proven themselves helpful in meeting critical operational goals. . . .

The United States military must transform itself, and it must begin now. As [Defense] Secretary [Donald] Rumsfeld has said, "Transformation is not a goal for tomorrow, but an endeavor that must be embraced in earnest today. The challenges the nation faces do not loom in the distant future, but are here now."

To its credit, the Bush administration has both clearly defined what transformation is, and provided a persuasive case as to why the world's best military needs to transform. Unfortunately, it has not yet developed either a transformation strategy or a process to ensure that transformation will come about. This is most clearly demonstrated in the absence of plausible service and joint war-fighting concepts for addressing the new, emerging critical operational goals, and finds its ultimate expression in the administration's program and budget priorities, which for the most part sustain the course set by the Clinton administration. . . .

If the Defense Department fails to seize the opportunity to transform our military—we run a very real risk of investing a substantial sum of our national treasure in preparing our military to meet the challenges of today, and yesterday, rather than those of tomorrow. Should that occur, payment could be exacted not only in lost treasure but also in lives lost.

its own. "The military solution was very good in toppling the Taliban, but not at getting rid of al Qaeda, which still has cells in some 50 countries," says Harvard's Nye. "The only way you're going to get rid of them is through very careful intelligence-sharing with many other countries."

But other countries may not be so willing to share intelligence if another potentially sweeping change in Pentagon planning and missions is adopted. Rumsfeld reportedly is considering expanding the role of special-operations forces to capture or kill al Qaeda leaders.

Such clandestine missions—usually limited to the CIA under legally defined conditions—could potentially involve U.S. combat forces in covert actions inside countries with whom the United States is not at war, without the knowledge or consent of the local governments. Pentagon officials reportedly said the expansion of the military's role into covert missions could be justified as "preparation of the battlefield" in the war against terrorists who do not recognize national boundaries.[23]

Defense Budget

The Bush administration has called for speeding plans to transform the military. In 2002, for example, it canceled the $11 billion Crusader cannon. Rumsfeld asked that the $475 million initially requested for the Crusader in 2003 be used instead to speed development of lighter artillery weapons for the Army.[24]

"So little is certain when it comes to the future of warfare, but on one point we must be clear," Rumsfeld wrote in defending his decision to drop the program. "We risk deceiving ourselves and emboldening future adversaries by assuming [the future] will look like the past. Sept. 11 proved one thing above all others: Our enemies are transforming. Will we?"[25]

Besides the Crusader, four other major programs may be sacrificed in the interest of transformation, though the Pentagon has deferred a final decision on their fate. The list includes key weapons currently under development by all four branches of the armed services.

For instance, the F-22 fighter—designed to replace the Air Force's F-15—may be dropped in favor of the cheaper F-35 Joint Strike Fighter, which is already under development. The Marine Corps' V-22 Osprey, which has a tilt rotor that enables it to land and take off like a helicopter and fly like a plane, also is under review. Development of the Osprey has been plagued by accidents that have cost the lives of 23 servicemen. The Army is also scrutinizing its

Comanche helicopter, another troubled program under development for nearly two decades and still at least 10 years from becoming operational. Finally, Pentagon planners are eyeing the Navy's proposed CVNX nuclear-powered aircraft carriers, designed to replace the nine *Nimitz*-class carriers deployed beginning in 1975.

"The administration [believes] the world is changing very rapidly and that something more than evolution [in strategy and weapons design] is required to prepare for future threats," said Thompson of the Lexington Institute. He sees two problems with the administration's approach.

"First, they don't have a clear idea of what the future threat is," he said, "so there's a danger that much of what they do may be inappropriate. Secondly, it's much easier to kill programs . . . than to build a legacy of replacement programs, which takes more time than a single administration has to complete. So the danger is that the Bush administration will be all too effective at eliminating key programs and not effective at all at building a foundation for modernization that is sustained by its successors."

Some experts applaud Rumsfeld's decision to terminate the Crusader as a step in the right direction. "Up to now, every service has been getting their dream piece of equipment, and killing the Crusader dealt a blow at that trend," Harvard's Galbraith said. "It certainly hasn't completely transformed the military, but looking for lighter, more mobile forces is the right idea."

Galbraith is less supportive of the administration's $7.8 billion request for the national missile-defense program, which Congress is expected to approve in full.[26] "The threat isn't a rogue country firing off a missile, because wherever that missile comes from it's going to have a return address," he said. "The real threat is that somebody will acquire or build a nuclear weapon, smuggle it into the country and set if off in Manhattan or Washington, and we won't know where it came from."

In his view, a far better use of those funds would be to develop technologies to detect nuclear weapons and inspect everything that enters the country. "I'm no techno-wizard," he said, "but I sense that money spent that way would be much better than on a missile defense that deals with a very unlikely threat."

Other experts say the Pentagon has not fully applied the lessons of either Desert Storm or Enduring Freedom to the military budget. "I would put more money into munitions, command-and-control networks, information processing and unmanned aerial vehicles and less into the major combat platforms that are carrying those smaller capabilities," O'Hanlon of Brookings said.

Lurie of the CSIS agrees that large weapons systems continue to receive an inordinate share of the defense budget.

"I would like to see a much bigger chunk dedicated to intelligence," he said. "That is probably our most crucial weapon to counter terrorism."

OUTLOOK

Lessons from Iraq

The past year has put the Bush administration's defense priorities under the spotlight. Faced with growing concern in Congress about the potential risks involved in preemptively attacking Iraq, administration officials insisted that Hussein possessed chemical, biological and nuclear weapons and that the risks of inaction were far greater.

Left to deploy nuclear weapons, Vice President Dick Cheney warned, the Iraqi leader would "seek domination of the entire Middle East, take control of a great portion of the world's energy supplies, directly threaten America's friends throughout the region and subject the United States or any other nation to nuclear blackmail."[27]

Bush assured legislators he would seek congressional approval before taking action against Iraq and consulted with the other members of the United Nations Security Council—the leaders of Russia, China, Britain and France—to explain his position.[28] Finally, the president presented his case to the United Nations in New York on Sept. 12—the day after the one-year anniversary of the terrorist attacks.

In effect, Bush was seeking approval from Congress, the country and America's allies for his preemptive-strike policy. "We're in a new era," Bush said. "This is a debate the American people must hear, must understand. And the world must understand, as well, that its credibility is at stake."[29]

As the months wore on, Bush's argument swayed many in the United States, but hardly anyone else. He won overwhelming approval in Congress for a war resolution, and he convinced the Security Council to unanimously adopt Resolution 1441, ordering Iraq to fully and voluntarily disclose the status of its weapons programs. Even after the war began, he kept the unwavering support of the American people, who backed the conflict by a ratio of three-to-one.

But Bush's determination to proceed with the invasion even after weapons inspectors failed to disclose evidence that Iraq possessed weapons of mass destruction alienated many of America's traditional allies. After France and Germany condemned the administration's preemptive war plan, the United States was left with just Britain as a major partner in what Bush called the "coalition of the willing" to invade Iraq. Fellow NATO member Turkey refused to let U.S. forces use its territory across the border from Iraq as a staging area for the impending invasion.

On March 20, Operation Iraqi Freedom began with heavy air strikes, dubbed "shock and awe," against military targets in Iraq, followed by a ground invasion of coalition tanks from Kuwait northward toward Baghdad, the Iraqi capital. From the beginning, critics charged that Rumsfeld had placed too great an emphasis on high-tech weaponry and left ground forces with too few troops. But Iraq's armed forces failed to mount a strong counterattack, and Baghdad fell to coalition forces within weeks. On May 1, Bush formally claimed victory.

In the end, the United States lost just 110 in Operation Iraqi Freedom, fully a quarter of whom died in non-combat accidents. Supporters of Rumsfeld's military transformation attribute the rapid victory and lack of massive casualties to the United States' advanced, satellite-assisted communications equipment, advanced aircraft and smart munitions.

But the military victory left the administration with the much more arduous task of rebuilding Iraq, devastated not only by the war but also by decades of authoritarian rule. Indeed, the post-war mission may prove to be a far greater challenge than the war itself.

Bush has long criticized the use of American troops in peacekeeping operations in the Balkans and elsewhere. But U.S. allies contribute the bulk of peacekeepers now deployed in Afghanistan.

"You would have to assume that we'd be looking at a multiyear stability operation that would make the efforts in the Balkans look relatively modest by comparison," Brookings' O'Hanlon said.

The United States provides about 15 percent of peacekeeping forces in the Balkans. "We'd have to be closer to 25 percent of the total force in Iraq because it would be seen as very much our war," O'Hanlon predicted. "We couldn't do what we've done in Afghanistan and essentially ask our allies to do the whole thing for us."

Indeed, while transatlantic relations have improved somewhat since the war's end, the job of peacekeeping and nation-building in Iraq has fallen squarely on the shoulders of the United States and Britain. Some 150,000 U.S. soldiers—and only 12,000 allied troops—remain in Iraq, helping restore basic services, hunting for weapons of mass destruction and acting as policemen in anticipation of a new civilian government that can take over these missions. That could take months or even years, analysts predict. Meanwhile, persistent attacks on U.S. troops have prompted the military to launch a new mission, dubbed Operation Desert Scorpion, to aggressively hunt down Hussein supporters and beef up humanitarian aid to win over Iraqi public opinion.

Although a majority of Americans still support the military action in Iraq, the administration is coming under scrutiny by critics who charge that Bush misled Americans about the dangers posed by Hussein's regime. Nine weeks after the war's end, the United States had failed to produce clear evidence that Iraq possessed weapons of mass destruction.

NOTES

1. For background, see David Masci and Kenneth Jost, "War on Terrorism," *The CQ Researcher*, Oct. 12, 2001, pp. 817-848.

2. Donald H. Rumsfeld, Foreword, *Quadrennial Defense Review Report*, Department of Defense, Sept. 30, 2001, p. iv.

3. See Carl Hulse, "Senate Easily Passes $355 Billion Bill for Military Spending," *The New York Times*, Aug. 2, 2002.

4. " 'The American People Have Got the Staying Power for This,'" *The New York Times*, Sept. 3, 2002.

5. Adriel Bettelheim, "Congress Changing Tone Of Homeland Security Debate," *CQ Weekly*, Aug. 31, 2002, pp. 2222-2225.

6. See James Dao, "Senate Panel to Ask Bush Aides to Give Details on His Iraq Policy," *The New York Times*, July 10, 2002.

7. Mary H. Cooper, "Energy Security," *The CQ Researcher*, Feb. 1, 2002, pp. 73-96.

8. See Bob Woodward, "President Broadens Anti-Hussein Order," *The Washington Post*, June 16, 2002.

9. John G. Inkenberry, "America's Imperial Ambition," *Foreign Affairs*, September/October 2002, p. 45.

10. See William J. Broad, "Call for New Breed of Nuclear Arms Faces Hurdles," *The New York Times*, March 11, 2002.

11. Quoted by Eric Schmitt, "Wider Military Role in U.S. Is Urged," *The New York Times*, July 21, 2002.

12. Lieberman addressed a June 26, 2002, forum on homeland security sponsored by the Progressive Policy Institute.

13. For background, see Mary H. Cooper, "Missile Defense," *The CQ Researcher*, Sept. 8, 2000, pp. 689-712.

14. See Pat Towell, "Bush Wins on Missile Defense, But With Democratic Stipulation," *CQ Weekly*, June 29, 2002, pp. 1754-1757.

15. John Cirincione, "No ABM Treaty, No Missile Defense," *Carnegie Analysis*, June 17, 2002, www. ceip.org.

16. This section is based in part on Mary H. Cooper, "Bush's Defense Strategy," *The CQ Researcher*, Sept. 7, 2001, pp. 689-712.

17. For background, see Mary H. Cooper, "Weapons of Mass Destruction," *The CQ Researcher*, March 8, 2002, pp. 193-216.

18. Unless otherwise noted, information in this section is based on Jeffrey D. Brake, "Quadrennial Defense Review (QDR): Background, Process, and Issues," *CRS Report for Congress*, Congressional Research Service, June 21, 2001.

19. Speech at the American Legion convention, San Antonio, Texas, Aug. 29, 2001.

20. Rumsfeld, *op. cit.*, p. iv.

21. Steven J. Nider, "New Military Strategy Falls Short," *Blueprint Magazine*, Nov. 15, 2001.

22. Unless otherwise noted, information in this section is based on Michael E. O'Hanlon, *Defense Policy Choices for the Bush Administration*, Second Edition (2002), pp. 99-102.

23. See Thom Shanker and James Risen, "Rumsfeld Weighs New Covert Acts by Military Units," *The New York Times*, Aug. 12, 2002.

24. See Pat Towell, "Crusader May Be Precursor to More Defense Cuts," *CQ Weekly*, July 20, 2002, pp. 1963-1967.

25. Donald Rumsfeld, "A Choice to Transform the Military," *The Washington Post*, May 16, 2002.

26. See Pat Towell, "Missile Defense Money Pivotal for House and Senate Conferees," *CQ Weekly*, Sept. 7, 2002, pp. 2321-2322.

27. Cheney addressed a convention of veterans in Nashville, Tenn., on Aug. 26, 2002. See Elisabeth Bumiller and James Dao, "Cheney: Nuclear Peril Justifies Iraq Attack," *The New York Times*, Aug. 27, 2002.

28. Elisabeth Bumiller, "President to Seek Congress's Assent Over Iraq Action," *The New York Times*, Sept. 5, 2002.

29. Bush's remarks are found at www.whitehouse.gov/news/releases/2002/09/20020904-1.html.

BIBLIOGRAPHY

Books

Butler, Richard, *Fatal Choice: Nuclear Weapons and the Illusion of Missile Defense*, Westview, 2002.
The former head of the U.N. Special Commission on Iraqi weapons programs argues that the Bush administration's plan to build a missile-defense system will only prompt China and other countries to build more nuclear weapons.

Cohen, Eliot A., *Supreme Command: Soldiers, Statesmen, and Leadership in Wartime*, The Free Press, 2002.
A defense analyst argues that the Powell doctrine has severely limited the military's ability to defend U.S. national interests. Attributed to Secretary of State Colin Powell, the doctrine directs the U.S. to abstain from foreign military incursions unless vital national interests are at stake and to use overwhelming force once it decides to act.

O'Hanlon, Michael E., *Defense Policy Choices for the Bush Administration (2nd ed.)*, Brookings Institution, 2002.
A Brookings analyst argues that the Bush administration, despite promises of a radical overhaul, has essen-

tially continued the "transformation" begun by its predecessors.

Articles

Boyer, Peter J., "A Different War," *The New Yorker*, July 1, 2002, pp. 54-67.
The Army, with its legacy of heavy, slow-moving weapons, is the target of much of Defense Secretary Donald Rumsfeld's campaign to revolutionize the military, including increased reliance on long-distance precision strikes using Navy and Air Force aircraft and weapons.

Carr, David, "The Futility of 'Homeland Defense,' " *The Atlantic Monthly*, January 2002, pp. 53-55.
Carr argues the U.S. cannot defend itself completely against attacks involving nuclear, biological or chemical weapons, which could be smuggled in shipping containers, without destroying its free-trade policy.

Homer-Dixon, Thomas, "The Rise of Complex Terrorism," *Foreign Policy*, January/February 2002, pp. 52-62.
The Sept. 11 attacks offer a glimpse of future terrorist actions, a University of Toronto political scientist writes. Wealthy countries, with their widespread energy and industrial facilities, provide myriad targets for far more devastating attacks.

Kagan, Fred, "Needed: A Wartime Defense Budget," *The Wall Street Journal*, April 3, 2002.
A military historian argues that the U.S. armed forces have been so profoundly weakened over the past decade that they will be unable to conduct future operations, including an incursion against Iraq, unless defense spending grows by at least triple the $150 billion increase requested this year by President Bush.

Nather, David, "For Congress, a New World— And Business as Usual," *CQ Weekly*, Sept. 7, 2002, pp. 2274-2288; 2313-2322.
Nather's comprehensive report leads off the magazine's Special Report on congressional and defense issues on the one-year anniversary of the Sept. 11 terrorist attacks. Topics covered include President Bush's efforts to sell lawmakers on preemptive strikes against Iraq, missile defense and Attorney General John Ashcroft and national security.

Perry, William J., "Preparing for the Next Attack," *Foreign Affairs*, November/December 2001, pp. 31-45.
Former President Clinton's Defense secretary says the most immediate threat to the U.S. is a small nuclear or biological weapon unleashed in a major city, and that the best defense is vigorous efforts to halt weapons proliferation.

Wallerstein, Immanuel, "The Eagle Has Crash Landed," *Foreign Policy*, July/August, 2002, pp. 60-68.
A Yale University historian argues that the U.S., like all other great powers before it, is destined to decline in power, and indeed has been losing ground since the 1970s.

Weinberg, Steven, "Can Missile Defense Work?" *The New York Review of Books*, Feb. 14, 2002, pp. 41-47.
A Nobel laureate in physics argues that the national missile-defense system being pursued by the Bush administration will not work against the most dangerous threat—an accidental launch of one of Russia's 3,900 nuclear warheads—and may prompt other countries to develop or expand their own nuclear arsenals.

Reports and Studies

Grimmett, Richard F., "War Powers Resolution: Presidential Compliance," *Issue Brief for Congress*, Congressional Research Service, updated June 12, 2002.
The 1973 War Powers Resolution, meant to ensure that the president and Congress share in war-making decisions, is coming under scrutiny once again as President Bush contemplates action against Iraqi leader Saddam Hussein.

U.S. Department of Defense, "Quadrennial Defense Review," Sept. 30, 2001.
The Bush administration's first QDR provides few major changes from earlier calls for "transforming" the military by developing more flexible, high-tech weapons to deal with new threats to U.S. security.

For More Information

Brookings Institution, 1775 Massachusetts Ave., N.W., Washington, DC 20036; (202) 797-6000; www.brook. edu. An independent research organization devoted to public policy issues.

Center for Defense Information, 1779 Massachusetts Ave., N.W., Washington, DC 20036; (202) 332-0600; www.cdi.org. A nonpartisan, nonprofit educational organization that focuses on security policy and defense budgeting.

Center for Strategic and International Studies, 1800 K St., N.W., Washington, DC 20006; (202) 887-0200; www.csis.org. A bipartisan organization that analyzes challenges to U.S. national and international security.

Council on Foreign Relations, 58 E. 68th St., New York, NY 10021; (212) 434-9400; www.cfr.org. A nonpartisan research organization dedicated to increasing America's understanding of the world and contributing ideas to U.S. foreign policy.

Lexington Institute, 1600 Wilson Blvd., Suite 900, Arlington, VA 22209; (703) 522-5828; www.lexington institute.org. A nonprofit, nonpartisan organization that supports a limited role for government and a strong military.

Nuclear Threat Initiative, 1747 Pennsylvania Ave., N.W., 7th floor, Washington, DC 20006; (202) 296-4810; www.nti.org. Co-chaired by Ted Turner and Sam Nunn, this nonprofit organization works to reduce the global threats from nuclear, biological and chemical weapons.

U.S. Department of Defense, Washington, DC 20301-7100; www.defenselink.mil. The Pentagon's Web site is the most complete source of DOD information.

3

Re-examining 9/11

Kenneth Jost

National security adviser Condoleezza Rice defended the Bush administration's anti-terrorism policies in April 2004 before the commission investigating the Sept. 11, 200l, attacks. Former U.S. counterterrorism coordinator Richard A. Clarke generally praised the Clinton administration's policies in his testimony but sharply criticized Bush's anti-terrorism record.

AFP/Paul Richards (Rice) and Luke Frazza

When President Bush's national security adviser, Condoleezza Rice, agreed after weeks of pressure to testify before the independent commission investigating the Sept. 11, 2001, terrorist attacks, relatives of victims filled the first three rows immediately behind her.

Many listened on April 8 with a mixture of frustration and anger as Rice fended off questions about the administration's anti-terrorism policy in the months before the attacks.

"To listen to her not recall things, to hear those kinds of statements was very frustrating," says Carie Lemack, whose mother was on the first plane that crashed into the World Trade Center. "It was all very surreal."

Rice stoutly defended the administration's anti-terrorism policy, saying that the White House was working overtime to develop a comprehensive strategy to eliminate the al Qaeda terrorist organization. She also discounted the importance of an intelligence briefing that Bush had received on Aug. 6 warning of Osama bin Laden's intention to attack within the United States—possibly an airline hijacking.[1]

The so-called Presidential Daily Brief, or PDB, was "historical information based on old reporting," Rice said. "There was no new threat information."

After more than three hours, Rice stepped down from the witness stand, embracing some 9/11 family members on her way out. But Lemack kept her distance. "Accountability, ma'am, accountability," Lemack shouted at her.

"That's the word that resonates with me: accountability," Lemack explains today. "If my mother was the CEO of a company,

From *The CQ Researcher*, June 4, 2004.

Can Separate, Secret Agencies . . .

The U.S. intelligence community "was not created and does not operate as a single, tightly knit organization," a congressional commission wrote in 1996. "It has evolved over nearly 50 years and now amounts to a confederation of separate agencies and activities with distinctly different histories, missions and lines of command."

As a result, there is no single place where intelligence-gathering can be coordinated and collected information can be analyzed. In the wake of hearings by the independent Sept. 11 commission, some lawmakers say the intelligence network should be restructured.

DOMESTIC INTELLIGENCE AGENCIES

HOMELAND SECURITY DEPARTMENT

Secret Service — Primary duties are protecting the president and stopping counterfeiters.

Customs Service — Inspecting cargo coming into the country by land, sea and air.

Border Patrol — Identifying and stopping illegal aliens before they enter the country.

Coast Guard Intelligence — Processing information on U.S. maritime borders and homeland security.

JUSTICE DEPARTMENT

Federal Bureau of Investigation — Lead agency for domestic intelligence and operations. Has offices overseas.

Drug Enforcement Administration — Collects intelligence in the course of enforcement of federal drug laws.

DEPARTMENT OF ENERGY

Office of Intelligence — Key player in nuclear weapons and non-proliferation, energy security, science and technology.

TREASURY DEPARTMENT

The Office of Intelligence Support — Collects and processes information that may affect fiscal and monetary policy.

STATE AND LOCAL POLICE AGENCIES

Coordinate with the FBI through joint counterterrorism task forces.

Trying to Pull It All Together

Several agencies were created before and after the Sept. 11 terrorist attacks primarily to analyze and integrate intelligence data. Among them:

Terrorist Threat Integration Center — Created by President Bush in 2003, this analysis center located in the CIA is designed to assess all terrorism-related information from U.S. and foreign intelligence sources.

Counterterrorist Center — CIA unit that coordinates counterterrorist efforts of the intelligence community; feeds information to the Terrorist Threat Integration Center.

Information Analysis and Infrastructure Protection Directorate — Part of the Department of Homeland Security created in 2002 to analyze terrorist-related intelligence and assess threats to critical infrastructure.

Terrorist Screening Center — A multi-agency center administered by the FBI to develop a watch-list database of suspected terrorists.

The Intelligence Community

As director of the CIA, George J. Tenet is the titular head of the U.S. intelligence community, a network of 15 departments and agencies. These agencies conduct both domestic and international intelligence-gathering.*

. . . Learn to Share?

INTELLIGENCE AGENCIES OPERATING OVERSEAS

CIVILIAN AGENCIES

Central Intelligence Agency (CIA) — Lead agency for collecting and analyzing foreign intelligence, including information on terrorism. Briefs the president daily.

Department of State Counterterrorism Office — Coordinates efforts to improve counterterrorism cooperation with foreign governments.

Bureau of Intelligence and Research — Analyzes and interprets intelligence on global developments for secretary of State.

MILITARY AGENCIES

National Security Agency (NSA) — Collects and processes foreign signal intelligence from eavesdropping and signal interception. Also charged with protecting critical U.S. information security systems.

Defense Intelligence Agency (DIA) — Provides intelligence to military units, policymakers and force planners. It has operatives in many U.S. embassies.

National Geospatial-Intelligence Agency (NGA) — The intelligence community's mapmakers, able to track movements of people and machines or changes in topography.

National Reconnaissance Office (NRO) — Builds and maintains the nation's spy satellites. Provides information to the Defense Department and other agencies.

Army Intelligence

Navy Intelligence

Marine Corps Intelligence

Air Force Intelligence

TAKING STEPS TO IMPROVE COORDINATION

The weakest link in the intelligence campaign against terrorism has been the analysis and sharing of millions of bits of raw data swept up by government agencies operating in the United States and abroad.

The original plan for correcting this flaw after the Sept. 11 attacks was to centralize analysis in the Department of Homeland Security, which Congress created in 2002. After the law was passed, however, President Bush changed tack. By executive fiat in early 2003 — no written executive order was issued — Bush created the Terrorism Threat Integration Center (TTIC), housed in the Central Intelligence Agency, to coordinate terrorism-related analysis.

Except for a passage in Bush's 2003 State of the Union speech and an address to FBI employees, the administration did not formally outline the roles and responsibilities of agencies participating in the center. A memorandum signed in 2003 by Attorney General John Ashcroft, Director of Central Intelligence George J. Tenet and Homeland Security Secretary Tom Ridge explained the information-sharing responsibilities of the center's participants.

It was not until an April 13, 2004, letter from Tenet, Ridge, FBI Director Robert S. Mueller III and TTIC Director John O. Brennan to several members of Congress that the administration made clear that terrorism-related intelligence would be analyzed by the threat center Bush had created.

The letter was sent in response to a series of inquiries dating to February 2003 from Susan Collins, R-Maine, chairwoman of the Senate Governmental Affairs Committee, and Carl Levin of Michigan, the panel's second-ranking Democrat.

The letter said Brennan's unit controls "terrorism analysis (except for information relating solely to purely domestic terrorism)," which is the province of the FBI. Homeland Security manages information collected by its own components, such as the Coast Guard and Secret Service, and is responsible for analyzing material "supporting decisions to raise or lower the national warning level."

and somebody messed up, at the end of the day it was her fault. She would be accountable."[2]

Lemack helped found one of the major 9/11 survivors' groups, the Family Steering Committee, which vigorously lobbied a reluctant Bush administration in 2002 to create the independent National Commission on Terrorist Attacks upon the United States, the so-called 9/11 commission.[3] Family groups have kept up the pressure since then. Most recently, they forced an equally reluctant House Speaker J. Dennis Hastert, R-Ill., to give the commission more time to complete its report; it is now due on July 26.

Judging by questions from the 10 commission members and from several "staff statements" already released, the panel's final report is likely to fault the anti-terrorism policies of both Bush and his Democratic predecessor, Bill Clinton.[4] For Bush, the report is likely to intensify the political problems generated by legal attacks on the administration's post-9/11 detention policies and the recent, high-profile disclosures—including shocking photographs—of Iraqi prisoners being abused by U.S. servicemembers.[5]

The commission gained most attention with its reconstruction of events immediately leading up to the four hijackings of Sept. 11, which ultimately took some 3,000 lives. The actions of the 19 hijackers also have been dissected to try to understand how they eluded detection by immigration, law enforcement and aviation-security personnel on Sept. 11 and in the days, months and years beforehand.[6]

In its first interim report, released on Jan. 26, 2004, the commission staff documented numerous holes in immigration procedures that allowed some of the hijackers to enter or remain in the United States despite detectable visa violations. Another staff report released the same day reconstructed how the hijackers exploited "publicly available vulnerabilities of the aviation-security system" to pass through checkpoint screening and board their flights.[7] (*See sidebars, pp. 54, 60.*)

"I would not say that 9/11 was preventable, but I would certainly say we had a chance," says Amy Zegart, an assistant professor of public policy at UCLA who specializes in national security issues. "We could have been better organized than we were. Whether that could have made a difference, we'll never know."

The commission is also examining how the Clinton and Bush administrations dealt with al Qaeda since its first attack: the 1993 truck-bomb explosion at the World Trade Center that killed six persons and injured more than 1,000.

In sharply critical statements in April, the commission staff said the Central Intelligence Agency (CIA) failed through the 1990s to develop a "comprehensive estimate" of al Qaeda. In a second report, the staff said the FBI had failed to go beyond its law enforcement role to try to detect and prevent possible terrorist incidents. That report also criticized Bush's attorney general, John Ashcroft, for giving terrorism a low priority in the months before 9/11.[8]

Officials from both the Bush and Clinton administrations testified before the panel to defend their actions, including CIA Director George J. Tenet,* who served in both administrations; FBI Director Robert S. Mueller III and his Clinton administration counterpart, Louis Freeh; and Ashcroft and his predecessor, Janet Reno.

The parade of high-ranking officials came after the commission's most dramatic witness before Rice's appearance: Richard A. Clarke, a career civil servant whom Clinton named in 1998 as the nation's first national counterterrorism coordinator and who continued in that position under Bush for more than two years, though with downgraded status.

Clarke appeared before the panel after publication of his first-person account, *Against All Enemies*, which paints a fairly positive picture of the Clinton administration's counterterrorism policies but sharply criticizes the Bush administration's record. Bush "failed to act prior to Sept. 11 on the threat from al Qaeda despite repeated warnings," Clarke writes. He goes on to blame Bush for having launched "an unnecessary and costly war in Iraq that strengthened the fundamentalist, radical Islamic terrorist organization worldwide."[9]

Zegart, who is writing a book on U.S. intelligence agencies' response to terrorism, faults both the CIA and the FBI for organizational deficiencies and "cultural" blind spots in dealing with the problem.[10] But she also criticizes policymakers in both the Clinton and Bush administrations. "It seems fairly clear that terrorism was not a high enough priority for either administration," she adds.[11]

---

* Tenet abruptly resigned "for personal reasons" on June 10, 2004, just after this report went to press. President Bush said Tenet had done a "superb job for the American people" and that CIA Deputy Director John McLaughlin will become acting director after Tenet's resignation takes effect in mid-July.

Under widespread pressure, Bush himself agreed to submit to questioning by the commission, but only after insisting that Vice President Dick Cheney accompany him and that no recording or transcript be made of the closed-door session. (The commission had earlier heard separately from Clinton and former Vice President Al Gore.) The April 29 meeting with Bush and Cheney lasted more than three hours. Afterward, the commission said Bush and Cheney had been "forthcoming and candid." Bush described the meeting as "very cordial."

As the 9/11 commission continues its hearings and deliberations, here are some of the major questions being considered by the panel and by policymakers, experts and the public:

Did the Clinton administration miss good opportunities to take action against al Qaeda?

The CIA's Counterterrorism Center knew enough about bin Laden's role in financing and directing al Qaeda that it created a special "Issue Station" in January 1996 devoted exclusively to tracking his activities. But the unit's "sense of alarm" about bin Laden was not widely shared, according to the 9/11 commission staff. "Employees in the unit told us they felt their zeal attracted ridicule from their peers," the staff's March 24, 2004, statement said.[12]

The skepticism even among intelligence professionals about targeting bin Laden was one of many difficulties the Clinton administration faced in confronting al Qaeda in the late 1990s. Clinton today gets some credit, even from political conservatives, for recognizing the threat. But he is also criticized for failing to mobilize support in or outside the government for strong action or to make effective those initiatives he was willing to authorize—most significantly, an Aug. 20, 1998, cruise missile attack against an al Qaeda base in Afghanistan aimed at killing bin Laden after he was linked to the Aug. 7, 1998, bombings of embassies in Kenya and Tanzania.

Moreover, many of the intelligence agencies' missteps occurred on Clinton's watch—most notably, the CIA's and FBI's mutual failure in 2000 to track two al Qaeda operatives into the United States and their eventual roles as 9/11 hijackers. Many experts fault Clinton for adopting a law enforcement approach toward al Qaeda—focusing on criminal prosecutions inside the United States—instead of a military approach using armed force.

"They continued to have largely a criminal-justice model for al Qaeda rather than a military model, rather

than a counterinsurgency model," says John Pike, director of GlobalSecurity.org, an Alexandria, Va., think tank.

Mark Riebling, editorial director at the conservative Manhattan Institute and author of a history of the relationship between the CIA and the FBI, says it was "patently absurd" for Clinton to designate the Justice Department as the lead agency in his 1995 Presidential Decision Directive on terrorism. Both men, however, say Clinton's approach matched what Riebling calls the "conventional wisdom" of the time.

Some other experts are less forgiving of what they regard as the Clinton administration's misdirection. "There was a strategic failure to understand the magnitude of the threat—that the 1993 World Trade Center bombing and the other incidents were part of a larger campaign," says Steven Aftergood, a senior research analyst at the liberal-oriented Federation of American Scientists.

But Aftergood also says the administration's attitude coincided with the public's. "There was a kind of post-Cold War relaxation that did not properly assess the rising hostility in parts of the Islamic world," he says. "It seems to have been a blind spot."

On the other hand, Richard Betts, a professor at Columbia University and member of the Hart-Rudman commission on terrorism in the late 1990s, says Clinton could have done more to mobilize public support for stronger action against al Qaeda. "There would have been political support for much more decisive military action" after the embassy bombings in Africa, Betts says.

Pike gives the administration credit for the strike against the al Qaeda camp in Afghanistan. Stronger action—an invasion of Afghanistan—was unrealistic at the time, he says. "I don't think they could have convinced anybody even if they had convinced themselves," he says.

In any case, Betts notes that Clinton faced personal and political problems in trying to overcome the military's reluctance to go after al Qaeda. "Clinton, being Clinton, had no moral authority to challenge the military on anything," Betts says.

"The other problem is that there was that whole impeachment business," Pike adds. "The last two years of the administration, they were politically paralyzed."

Intelligence experts also emphasize that the administration inherited a decades-old lack of CIA and FBI coordination. "The problem was deeply structural," says Greg Treverton, a RAND Corporation senior research

9/11 Commission Bucked White House

The special commission created to investigate the 9/11 terrorist attacks has clashed with the Bush administration ever since its creation.

Congress approved creating the 10-member National Commission on Terrorist Attacks upon the United States on Nov. 15, 2002, a month after the White House had blocked a version passed by both the House and the Senate that summer. President Bush signed the bill into law on Nov. 27 and immediately named former Secretary of State Henry Kissinger to chair the commission.[1]

Congressional Democrats chose former Senate Majority Leader George Mitchell of Maine as the vice-chair of the panel. But both men resigned from the posts barely two weeks later: Mitchell cited the time demands of the job; Kissinger refused ethics requirements to disclose the clients of his international consulting firm.

Bush then picked former New Jersey Gov. Thomas F. Kean to chair the panel on Dec. 16. Kean, currently president of Drew University, is well regarded as a political moderate but lacks any foreign policy experience. In the previous week, congressional Democrats had tapped former Rep. Lee Hamilton of Indiana as vice chair. Hamilton had extensive foreign affairs experience during 34 years in the House and was widely respected.

The law creating the commission required it to complete its work within 18 months—by May 27, 2004. The timetable, insisted on by the White House, was aimed at getting the commission's report published before the 2004 presidential campaign. By late 2003, however, the commission was saying that it needed more time to complete its work. House Speaker J. Dennis Hastert, R-Ill., opposed

Commission Chairman Thomas Kean, left, and Vice Chairman Lee Hamilton.

AFP Photo/Timothy A. Clary

the request, but finally agreed in late February 2004 to a 60-day extension for the commission's report—now due on July 26.

The commission said it needed more time in part because federal agencies—chiefly, the Defense and Justice departments—had responded slowly to requests for information. The commission also tangled with the White House over access to intelligence briefings Bush received on terrorism issues—including the now famous Aug. 6 "Presidential Daily Brief" warning of Osama bin Laden's interest in attacking the United States.

Bush eventually bowed to the commission's demands. He also agreed under pressure in April 2004 to meet and answer questions from all 10 members of the commission. The commission now states on its Web site that it has had access to every document and every witness it has sought, and that Bush has yet to assert executive privilege on any document request.

Kean and Hamilton have maintained the appearance of bipartisan unity in public statements and hearings. However, Attorney General John Ashcroft complained that Jamie Gorelick, deputy attorney general under President Bill Clinton, should have recused herself from discussions of Justice Department guidelines limiting information sharing between intelligence agencies and the FBI. Both Kean and Hamilton defended Gorelick.

Other Democrats on the panel include Richard Ben-Veniste, a former Watergate prosecutor; former Sen. Bob Kerrey of Nebraska; and former Rep. Timothy Roemer of Minnesota. Besides Kean, the Republican panel members are Fred Fielding, White House counsel under President Ronald Reagan; former Sen. Slade Gorton of Washington; former Navy Secretary John F. Lehman; and former Illinois Gov. James R. Thompson.

---

[1] The legislation was part of the Intelligence Authorization Act for Fiscal Year 2003, Public Law 107-306. The text of the law is on the commission's Web site: www.9-11commision.gov.

analyst who has held intelligence-related positions in government. "We built these agencies to fight the Cold War. But they set us up to fail in the war on terror."[13]

The "most stunning" of the agencies' missteps, Zegart and others say, was the lack of effective follow-up after two of the eventual hijackers—Nawaf al Hazmi and Khalid al Mihdhar—were observed at an al Qaeda meeting in Kuala Lumpur, Malaysia, in 2000. After receiving pictures of the two from Malaysia's security service, the CIA tracked both men into the United States. Subsequent events are bitterly disputed by the agency and FBI.[14]

In one version, the CIA never told the FBI about the two men; in the other, the FBI had access to the information but failed to act on it. In any event, the two men were never put on a terrorism "watchlist" and lived openly in San Diego—under their real names—until the hijackings. The 9/11 commission staff says the episode illustrates the failure "to insure seamless handoffs of information" among intelligence agencies—including the ultrasecret National Security Agency.[15]

Was the CIA or the FBI more to blame for the foul-up? "There's plenty of blame to go around," Zegart says bluntly.

Clinton left office with actions against al Qaeda again under discussion after the bombing of the *USS Cole* off Yemen in October 2000. But delays in linking the bombing to al Qaeda and reluctance to engage in a quick tit-for-tat response combined to quash any proposals to retaliate. Instead, Clinton and his national security team told incoming President Bush that he should put al Qaeda at the top of the list of national-security problems.

Did the Bush administration miss telltale clues that might have prevented the 9/11 attacks?

Intelligence agencies picked up a high volume of al Qaeda-related "threat reporting" in summer 2001. More than 30 possible overseas targets were identified in various intercepted communications. Officers at the CIA's Counterterrorism Center felt a sense of urgency, but some felt administration policymakers were too complacent. In fact, two veteran officers "were so worried about an impending disaster that . . . they considered resigning and going public with their concerns."[16]

Their frustration further buttresses the damning picture of the Bush administration's view of al Qaeda drawn by Clarke. He says in his book that his initial briefing on al Qaeda in January 2001 was greeted with sharp skepticism from Paul Wolfowitz, the deputy secretary of Defense. "I just don't understand why we are beginning by talking about this one man bin Laden," Clarke quotes Wolfowitz. Moreover, he describes Wolfowitz as linking the 1993 trade center bombing and other incidents to "Iraqi terrorism"—a theory Clarke says was "totally discredited."[17]

Experts representing a range of political views say Clarke's account rings true. "They took a long time to get off the mark studying this," the Manhattan Institute's Riebling says.

The American Federation of Scientist's Aftergood agrees: "In its first eight months, the Bush administration received warnings [about al Qaeda], but nevertheless moved at a leisurely pace until the crisis was upon us."

RAND's Treverton says the new administration apparently regarded state-sponsored terrorism as a greater threat than al Qaeda, and thus discounted Clinton officials' warnings. "It's pretty plain that terrorism—particularly, the brand represented by al Qaeda—was not quite on their radar scope," he says.

Some experts are less critical, acknowledging the difficulties that a new administration faced in taking office and setting policies on a range of foreign-policy and national-security issues. "Six months into a new administration, they were still getting their sea legs," says Pike of GlobalSecurity.org.

In both interviews and her sworn testimony before the 9/11 commission, national security adviser Rice insisted Bush understood the threat posed by al Qaeda. She told the commission on April 8 the administration was seeking to develop "a new and comprehensive strategy to eliminate" al Qaeda.

"I credit the administration with recognizing that at some point they were going to have to make really hard strategic choices," says James Jay Carafano, senior research fellow for defense and homeland security at the conservative Heritage Foundation. "That's a real testament to the administration."

Still, Carafano and others say the administration would have been hard-pressed to take stronger action against al Qaeda before 9/11. "Can you imagine if Bush had walked in the door and said let's invade Afghanistan?" Carafano asks. Pike says there were "missed opportunities, but they probably were not attainable, not realistic

Improved Aviation Security Still Has Gaps

The American airline industry was virtually brought to its knees on Sept. 11, 2001, by 19 men with box cutters like those available at any hardware store.

The federal government's response to the hijackings—creation of a massive, new security agency with 45,000 passenger screeners—created a more secure atmosphere at U.S. airports. But two years after its creation, the Transportation Security Administration (TSA) finds itself consistently criticized by politicians and the public. Occasional security gaffes—including a North Carolina college student's efforts last October to expose security glitches by hiding box cutters on two Southwest Airlines flights—have not helped the agency's image.

Moreover, lawmakers have complained the TSA is understaffed at some airports and

Weapons confiscated from passengers at Los Angeles International Airport last year include a knife hidden inside a belt.

AFP Photo/Robyn Beck

overstaffed at others. For example, Rep. Harold Rogers, R-Ky., pointed out at a March hearing that the tiny Rutland, Vt., airport had seven screeners to handle just seven passengers a day.[1]

In addition, those lawmakers who in 2001 opposed the idea of taking airport security away from private contractors and making it a federal responsibility remain critical of the agency. Rep. John Mica, R-Fla., chairman of the Aviation Subcommittee of the House Transportation and Infrastructure Committee, believes more and more private companies should be given the opportunity to take screening back from the government in order to prove

---

[1] Martin Kady II, "TSA Shouldn't Expect an Easy Ride From This Appropriations Cardinal," *CQ Today*, March 12, 2004, p. 1.

opportunities that you could have convinced people to implement."

The debate over the administration's response has come to focus on the now-famous PDB warning that bin Laden was "determined" to strike in the United States. The two-page document was first described in press accounts in May 2002, but the White House refused to provide it to the joint inquiry by House and Senate Intelligence committees investigating 9/11 and declassified it on April 10 only under pressure from the 9/11 commission.[18]

The brief describes bin Laden as wanting to retaliate "in Washington" for the 1998 missile strike in Afghanistan. It also quotes a source as saying in 1998 that

a bin Laden cell in New York "was recruiting Muslim-American youths for attacks." Since that time, the brief continues, the FBI had noticed "patterns of suspicious activity" in the U.S. "consistent with preparations for hijackings or other types of attacks." Rice, in her testimony, described the brief as "historical," and Bush later insisted that it contained no "actionable intelligence."

Some experts agree. "That does not seem to me to be a case of something that was egregiously overlooked and that should have prompted a response that could have made a difference," says Columbia University's Betts. "I don't think that was politically realistic before the fact."

that businesses can do as good a job as the government in keeping terrorists off airplanes.

"Private screening companies are required to meet the same rigorous security standards as . . . federal screeners," Mica said. "As long as the highest-level security standards are met or exceeded, how that is accomplished should be determined by those most closely involved."[2]

But a recent investigation of five airports still using private security firms gave private screeners a mixed review. Clark Kent Ervin, inspector general of the Department of Homeland Security (DHS), said private contractors and the TSA performed "equally poorly."[3] But he blamed the problem largely on the slow hiring and screening process, which is still overseen by the TSA, even for the few airports still using private screeners.

As the summer travel season unfolds and the commercial airline industry continues its financial recovery, the TSA is nearing a crossroads.[4] In November, airports will be able to "opt out" of the federalized screening programs and outsource the work to private contractors. Mica predicts up to 25 percent of the nation's airports will opt out, primarily out of frustration with the TSA's bureaucracy.

About the same time, controversial passenger database programs like the Computer Assisted Passenger Pre-screening System (CAPPS II) and the entry-exit immigration tracking system known as US VISIT will be in place at many airports, adding a new layer of scrutiny while raising questions about privacy.

TSA executives insist they have made the skies safer, noting that there have been no terrorist attacks on airlines since 9/11. In addition, the agency has confiscated 1.5 million knives and incendiary devices and 300 guns, just since last October, said TSA Deputy Administrator Stephen J. McHale.[5]

Despite the progress, several security gaps still exist in passenger aviation: There are no shields to protect commercial airliners from attacks with shoulder-fired missiles, and there is no mandatory screening of air cargo. Rep. Jim Turner, D-Texas, the top Democrat on the House Homeland Security Committee, has introduced a bill that would require cargo screening and hardened cockpit doors on foreign airliners flying in U.S. airspace.

"There are still some security gaps. We need to do more, faster on this troubled system. It's not foolproof," Turner says. "But the good news is that it is clearly more difficult for a terrorist to use an airplane as a weapon."

---

[2] Quoted in *CQ Today*, April 23, 2004, p. 3.

[3] Testimony to House Transportation and Infrastructure Committee's Subcommittee on Aviation, April 22, 2004.

[4] Although some older airlines are still struggling, overall revenues for the industry have recovered somewhat since 9/11. See Eric Torbenson, "Airlines Get Lift from Rise in Revenue," *The Dallas Morning News*, May 21, 2004.

[5] Testimony to House Transportation and Infrastructure Committee Subcommittee on Aviation, May 13, 2004.

Aftergood is more critical. "The fact that Bush received the Aug. 6 PDB while on vacation in Texas tells us something," he says. "What it tells us is that more could have been done; greater vigor could have been exercised." As one example, Bush named Cheney on May 8, 2001, to head a task force to look into responding to a domestic attack with biological, chemical or radioactive weapons. The task force was just getting under way in September.

In line with existing procedure, the Aug. 6 PDB was not disseminated outside the White House. So, the Federal Aviation Administration (FAA) was given no special reason to step up airport security. Perhaps more significantly, the Justice Department never received the warning about possible domestic airline hijackings—which might have heightened attention to concerns raised by FBI agents in Phoenix and Minnesota in the months before Sept. 11.

In Minnesota, FBI lawyer Coleen Rowley had raised suspicions about a French-Algerian man, Zacarias Moussaoui, who attended flight school without being able to identify who was paying his tuition. But FBI officials in Washington said Rowley did not have enough information to justify searching his computer. Moussaoui is now charged with conspiracy in the attacks. Meanwhile, an FBI counterterrorism agent in Phoenix had

CHRONOLOGY I: THE CLINTON YEARS

1993-2000 *Al Qaeda grows into worldwide terrorist organization under Osama bin Laden; U.S. attacked at home and abroad; Clinton administration tries but fails to stunt group's growth and kill or capture bin Laden.*

Feb. 26, 1993 Truck bomb at World Trade Center kills six, injures more than 1,000; conspirators are later identified, indicted and some convicted.

June 1995 Presidential Decision Directive 39 labels terrorism a "potential threat to national security," vows to use "all appropriate means" to combat it; FBI designated lead agency.

January 1996 CIA's Counterterrorism Center creates special "Issue Station" devoted exclusively to bin Laden.

May 1996 Bin Laden leaves Sudan for Afghanistan.

June 25, 1996 Attack on Khobar Towers, U.S. Air Force residential complex, in Saudi Arabia kills 19 servicemembers.

April 1998 Taliban declines request to turn bin Laden over to United States.

May 1998 Presidential Decision Directive 62 lays out counterterrorism strategy; Richard A. Clarke named first national director for counterterrorism.

August 1998 U.S. embassies in Kenya and Tanzania bombed on Aug. 7; Clinton orders cruise missile strike ("Operation Infinite Reach") on al Qaeda base in Afghanistan; Aug. 20 strike hits camp, but after bin Laden had left. . . . Plan for follow-up strikes readied ("Operation Infinite Resolve") but not executed; Pentagon opposed.

December 1998 Plans prepared to use Special Operations forces to capture leaders of bin Laden network, but never executed; strikes readied after bin Laden possibly located, but intelligence deemed not sufficiently reliable, and strikes not ordered.

February, May 1999 Bin Laden located in February and again on several nights in May, but no strike ordered due to risk of killing visiting diplomats from United Arab Emirates (February), doubts about intelligence (May).

Summer 1999 High volume of threat reporting tied to Millennium celebrations.

July 1999 Clinton imposes sanctions on Taliban; U.N. sanctions added in October; through end of year, administration debates diplomatic vs. military approach but comes to no conclusion.

January 2000 Al Qaeda unsuccessfully tries to bomb *USS The Sullivans*; plot undisclosed until after attack on *USS Cole.* . . . Two future 9/11 hijackers tracked by CIA from al Qaeda meeting in Malaysia to United States; CIA and FBI trade accusations later over failure to place them on terrorism watch list.

Oct. 12, 2000 Attack on *Cole* kills 17 sailors; after the attack is linked to al Qaeda, strikes readied, but not ordered.

CHRONOLOGY II: THE BUSH YEARS

2001-Present *Bush administration developing anti-terrorism policies on eve of 9/11 attacks; president rallies nation, launches invasion of Afghanistan to eliminate haven for al Qaeda; later, investigations by congressional committees, independent commission focus on missed clues, possible reforms.*

January 2001 President Bush takes office Jan. 20, administration officials briefed on *USS Cole* attack, but no strikes ordered; national security adviser Condoleezza Rice retains Richard A. Clarke in White House post but has him report to lower-level officials and asks him to draft new counterterrorism strategy.

March-July 2001 Various options for Afghanistan discussed at deputies level.

May 8, 2001 Bush names Vice President Dick Cheney to head counterterrorism task force; it was just getting organized in September.

Summer 2001 Increased threat reporting prompts concern by Clarke, CIA Director George J. Tenet.

June 2001 Draft presidential directive circulated by deputy national security adviser Stephen Hadley calls for new contingency military plans against al Qaeda and Taliban.

July 2001 Federal Aviation Administration issues several security directives; agency is aware that terrorist groups are active in United States and interested in targeting aviation, including hijacking. . . . Internal FBI memo urges closer scrutiny of civil aviation schools and use of schools by individuals who may be affiliated with terrorist organizations.

Aug. 6, 2001 Bush receives Presidential Daily Brief (PDB) warning, "Bin Ladin Determined to Strike in U.S."; two-page brief notes interest in hijacking; no immediate follow-up.

Late August 2001 Immigration and Naturalization Service arrests Zacarias Moussaoui in Minnesota after FBI lawyer raises suspicions about his enrollment in flight school; FBI headquarters rejects bid to search his computer.

Sept. 4, 2001 Top officials approve draft directive on terrorism for submission to Bush, calling for covert action, diplomacy, financial sanctions, military strikes.

Sept. 10, 2001 Three-phase strategy on Afghanistan agreed on at interdepartmental meeting of deputies.

Sept. 11, 2001 Hijackers fly airliners into World Trade Center and Pentagon as well as field in Pennsylvania; 3,000 persons killed; nation reacts with shock, anger.

October-December 2001 U.S.-led coalition ousts Taliban regime in Afghanistan.

2002 House, Senate Intelligence committees launch joint investigation of 9/11; under pressure, Bush administration also agrees to separate probe by independent commission.

2003 CIA, FBI, other intelligence agencies sharply criticized in report by joint congressional intelligence committees; panels call for intelligence overhaul, including new director of national intelligence.

2004 9/11 commission's interim staff reports fault CIA, FBI, other agencies for pre-9/11 lapses; Clarke book blasts Bush administration as slow and weak on terrorism; Bush, aides rebut criticisms; commission due to report in late July.

become suspicious of the number of Arab men taking flight lessons, but FBI headquarters also rejected his request for an investigation.

Are intelligence reforms needed to better guard against future terrorist attacks?

After weeks on the defensive following publication of Clarke's book and the 9/11 commission hearings, the Bush administration sought to regain control of the agenda by leaking word in mid-April of possible plans to back major changes in intelligence gathering. The White House was said to be considering a longstanding proposal from the intelligence community to create a new "director of national intelligence" with budgetary and operational control over all of the government's 15 intelligence agencies. In addition, the White House was said to be eyeing the creation of a new FBI domestic-intelligence unit.[19]

The proposed organizational changes draw mixed reactions. Some experts say the changes are long overdue, others that they would be ill-advised. Several say the greater need is for changes in procedures and attitudes better adapted to confronting the threat of terrorism in an age of instant global communication.

"I'm skeptical of large institutional changes," says Aftergood. Instead, he favors "steady, incremental reform and learning directly from experience, including, above all, learning from mistakes."

The proposal for a director of national intelligence, or DNI, at first seems simply a new title for the current director of central intelligence, or DCI. The 1947 National Security Act empowers the DCI to coordinate all the intelligence agencies with overseas operations.

In practice, however, the DCI has had no control over individual agency's budgets or other matters. "Almost every major study of the intelligence agencies has recommended bolstering the authority of the DCI," UCLA's Zegart says.

She would prefer to increase the DCI's power instead of creating a new position. "George Tenet needs more power over the entire community," she says. In particular, Zegart says the preponderant role of the military units—with around 80 percent of the estimated $40 billion intelligence budget—skews priorities in favor of identifying and locating military targets ("tactical intelligence") at the expense of broader research and analysis ("strategic intelligence").

Other experts, however, envision a DNI with a broad analytical role and no operational authority. "A director

of national intelligence is probably a pretty good idea," RAND's Treverton says. "Someone looking across the spectrum and asking how we're spending the money, and what we're getting for it."

"You have to break up the two hats that Tenet wears," says Melvin Goodman, a former CIA officer who teaches at the National War College. "To be director of central intelligence and director of the CIA is an impossible task."

Tenet told the 9/11 commission, however, that he opposed separating the DCI's overall role from operational control of the CIA. The Defense Department has also resisted taking the military intelligence agencies' budgets out of the Pentagon. "Politically, it would be a very bloody fight to bring it about," says Columbia University's Betts, "and [very] expensive."

Proposals to reorganize the FBI reflect the view that the bureau's historic law enforcement role short-changes intelligence collection and analysis. The methodical collection of evidence for use in courtroom prosecutions is "not quick enough" to prevent terrorist incidents, Zegart says. In addition, she says the FBI's "culture" is ill-suited to intelligence work.

Mueller says he is reorienting FBI policies and procedures to deal with the problems. "That kind of cultural change takes a long time," says a dubious Zegart. But Pike is more optimistic. "I found the argument compelling that the FBI has the matter in hand," he says.

In any event, Pike and other experts strongly oppose one widely discussed proposal: To create a freestanding domestic-intelligence unit comparable to Britain's MI-5. "We're citizens; we are not subjects," Pike remarks.

The Heritage Foundation's Carafano calls it "a really bad idea. We don't need another intelligence organization. We probably have too many now."

Zegart acknowledges the criticisms and suggests a "semiautonomous" domestic-intelligence unit within the FBI might be the answer. Other experts, however, say leadership is more important than organizational change. "If you've got a director who has a mission to reorient [the agency's priorities], it's not absolutely clear to me that a reformed FBI might not be able to do the job," Betts says.

Apart from organizational issues, several experts say 9/11 exposed above all the need for better information sharing. Much of the debate has focused on the "wall"— guidelines restricting the CIA's ability to provide intelligence to the FBI or other domestic agencies.

Several other experts, however, say cultural and organizational barriers may be more significant. "We have a CIA that is very much focused on secrets," Treverton says. The problem, he says, is "getting people to talk to people more."

Aftergood agrees. "The age of central intelligence is behind us," he says. "What we need to move toward is distributed intelligence"—making information more readily accessible for use in enhancing security and preventing terrorist incidents.

In any event, he says, organizational changes alone will not solve the problems. "Institutional arrangements are all less important than the ability of the people who are engaged," he says.

BACKGROUND

Dysfunctional Systems?

The 9/11 attacks disclosed huge gaps in the ability of U.S. intelligence, law enforcement and security systems to detect or prevent terrorist incidents at home. In hindsight, government agencies gave too little attention to domestic terrorist attacks, while airlines and the government agency that regulated them were lax in instituting and enforcing security measures. In addition, both the CIA and the FBI were constrained by reforms instituted after surveillance abuses by both agencies against domestic political groups in the 1960s and '70s.

Neither the CIA nor the FBI was created with counterterrorism in mind.[20] The FBI was established within the Justice Department by President Theodore Roosevelt. It first drew critical scrutiny during and after World War I for its aggressive investigations of sedition, espionage and anti-draft cases. A public and congressional backlash prompted Attorney General Harlan Fiske Stone in 1924 to appoint J. Edgar Hoover, then the bureau's assistant director, as director with a charge to professionalize the organization.

Hoover gained national celebrity by leading the FBI's anti-gangster efforts in the 1930s. With the Cold War, however, the bureau again turned its attention to suspected subversives. Hoover also directed FBI investigations of civil rights groups—notably, by eavesdropping on the Rev. Dr. Martin Luther King Jr. Investigations by journalists and congressional committees in the late '60s and early '70s uncovered a wide-ranging counter-intelligence program—known as COINTELPRO—that used illegal or dubious practices to investigate or disrupt domestic political groups.

The Central Intelligence Agency traces its origins to the famed World War II Office of Strategic Services (OSS), which combined research and analysis functions with espionage, counterespionage, sabotage and propaganda. In late 1944, OSS chief Gen. William J. Donovan outlined to President Franklin D. Roosevelt a plan for a centralized peacetime civilian intelligence agency.

After Roosevelt's death, President Harry S Truman in 1946 created a weak coordinating body called the "Central Intelligence Group." A year later, the National Security Act created the CIA in its present form to coordinate and evaluate intelligence affecting national security.

The CIA became notorious for Cold War covert operations against communist or anti-American regimes in the 1950s and '60s. It toppled leftist governments in Iran and Guatemala, supported anti-Castro rebels in Cuba and encouraged U.S. entry into the war in Southeast Asia. The Watergate scandals under President Richard M. Nixon in the early 1970s led to evidence of illegal domestic political spying by the agency.

Despite its prominence, the CIA is actually dwarfed by Department of Defense intelligence agencies. The biggest is the National Security Agency (NSA), which grew from World War II codebreaking into intensely secretive, electronic surveillance worldwide. Another DoD unit, the National Reconnaissance Office, manages satellite-collection systems, and the National Geospatial Intelligence Agency processes images gleaned from the satellites. Each of the military services also has its own intelligence unit.

The Pentagon also has its own analytical office: the Defense Intelligence Agency, which—like the State Department's Bureau of Intelligence and Research—provides assessments and policy advice independent of, and often at variance with, CIA conclusions. Coast Guard Intelligence and the Department of Homeland Security's (DHS) Information Analysis and Infrastructure Protection Directorate have been added to the intelligence community since 9/11.

Aviation safety is the province of the Federal Aviation Administration (FAA). Hijacking and sabotage emerged gradually as a major FAA concern after hijackings of planes to and from Cuba became common in the early 1960s. After the first passenger death in a U.S. hijacking in 1971 and a rash of violent hijackings, the agency began scanning carry-on baggage and passengers for potential weapons in December 1972.[21] Additional security measures were adopted after other deadly incidents in the 1980s: air marshals in 1985 and X-raying of checked baggage following the bombing of Pan Am Flight 103 over Lockerbie, Scotland, in 1988.

During the '90s, there were no hijackings or aircraft bombings within the United States, possibly leading to increased security laxness. Two Department of Transportation reports in 1999 and 2000 faulted airport-security procedures—specifically for failing to control access to secure areas.

Meanwhile, several studies in 2000 and early 2001 found overall counterterrorism policies deficient.[22] The reports drew attention for short periods but then largely disappeared from the national agenda.

Frustrating Initiatives

Terrorism became a major domestic concern for the United States in the 1990s, but al Qaeda became a major focus of that concern only slowly. The deadly 1995 bombing of the federal office building in Oklahoma City turned out to be the work of domestic rather than international extremists. Meanwhile, bin Laden's buildup of his organization into a wide-ranging, paramilitary operation largely escaped attention—even from intelligence agencies—until the middle of the decade. Even after al Qaeda was linked to the 1998 bombings of two U.S. embassies in Africa, bin Laden remained little known to Americans.

Bin Laden began his path to international terrorism as a "freedom fighter" in Afghanistan in the 1980s, seeking to undo the Soviet invasion of the predominantly Islamic country.[23] He founded al Qaeda (Arabic for "the base") in 1987 to mount a global Islamic crusade. The son of a wealthy Saudi family, he turned against the Saudi government—and the United States—after the Saudis allowed U.S. troops on the Arabian peninsula during and after the Persian Gulf War (1991).

Bin Laden was known at the time only as a "terrorist financier" working from Sudan.[24] Clarke, who handled counterterrorism at the National Security Council (NSC) early in President Bill Clinton's first term, pressed the CIA for more information. In 1996, according to Clarke's account, the CIA got its first big break when a top aide to bin Laden defected. Jamal al-Fadl described bin Laden as the mastermind of a widespread terrorist network with affiliate groups or sleeper cells in 50 countries. By this time, bin Laden had moved his base of operations to Afghanistan.

The administration had tried without success while bin Laden was in Sudan to persuade Saudi Arabia to take him into custody for prosecution and trial. Once bin Laden was in Afghanistan, the Counterterrorism Security Group that Clarke headed drew up plans to abduct him—plans never executed because of logistical difficulties.

When al Qaeda was linked to the 1998 embassy bombings, however, Clinton authorized cruise missile strikes at an al Qaeda base in Afghanistan; they missed bin Laden by minutes.*

Tasked by Clinton, Clarke then designed a strategy to eliminate al Qaeda, including diplomatic efforts to eliminate its sanctuary in Afghanistan; covert action to disrupt terrorist cells; financial sanctions beginning with the freezing of funds of bin Laden-related businesses; and military action to attack targets as they developed.

In his book, Clarke voices great frustration with efforts to put the plan into effect—particularly the military's reluctance to get engaged. The 9/11 commission staff says the strategy "was not formally adopted" and that Cabinet-level officials have "little or no recollection of it."

Clarke writes that Clinton also approved assassinating bin Laden. Tenet told the 9/11 commission, however, that the agency considered the instructions unclear, at best. Clarke writes that he viewed the CIA's demurrals as an "excuse" for its inability to carry out the mission. Efforts to enlist the FBI's help in counterterrorism also proved difficult, according to the commission's staff report. Clinton's national security adviser, Samuel R. Berger, told the panel that despite regular meetings with Attorney General Reno and FBI Director Freeh, the FBI "withheld" terrorism information, citing pending investigations.

In Clinton's final year in office, al Qaeda was viewed as an increasing threat in the United States and overseas. Al Qaeda had been linked to plans to disrupt celebrations of the new Millennium: A plot to plant bombs at

---

* Clinton also approved a missile strike against a pharmaceutical plant near Khartoum, Sudan, suspected of manufacturing precursors of chemical weapons. The Sudanese government denied that the factory had any connection to chemical weapons—denials credited today by many U.S. intelligence experts.

Reorganizing Immigration Triggers Growing Pains

Rep. Harold Rogers, R-Ky., was so fed up with the Immigration and Naturalization Service's efforts to stop illegal immigrants from crossing the borders that he introduced a bill to abolish the agency. The 2000 measure went nowhere.

But the Sept. 11, 2001, terrorist attacks accomplished what Rogers could not: They ushered in the demise of the INS. The agency had spectacularly failed to track the comings and goings of the 19 hijackers, some of whom were in the United States on student visas—allowing them to operate without fear that the government would realize they had overstayed their visas.

The Homeland Security Act of 2002 broke up the old INS into separate pieces and assigned its duties to different divisions within the newly created Department of Homeland Security (DHS). Immigration investigations and administration were assigned to the new Bureau of Immigration and Customs Enforcement, while border enforcement became the responsibility of Customs and Border Protection.

However, reorganizing the INS has not come without bureaucratic growing pains. According to a May 11 General Accounting Office report, the department lacks adequate long-term estimates of the cost of its proposed US VISIT program, a multibillion-dollar computer system designed to track the entry and exit of every foreign visitor.[1] Meanwhile,

The Department of Homeland Security's US VISIT program uses digital cameras and computers to track immigrant entries and exits at airports.

AFP Photo/Robyn Beck

the so-called "visa waiver" program, which allows citizens of 27 U.S.-friendly countries to travel in the United States without visas, is underfunded and poorly organized, according to an April report by the DHS's inspector general. That report also noted that DHS has not adequately tracked lost or stolen foreign passports to determine whether they were used to enter the country.

By October 2004, the passports of visitors without visas must include biometric data, such as fingerprint or facial recognition, to make them less susceptible to fraud. All 27 countries—which include England, France and Japan—will likely miss the deadline, according to DHS Secretary Tom Ridge and Secretary of State Colin L. Powell, who both asked Congress to extend the deadline.

"Rushing a solution to meet the current deadline virtually guarantees that we will have systems that are not operable," Powell said in April 21 testimony before the Senate Judiciary Committee's Subcommittee on Immigration. Sen. Saxby Chambliss, R-Ga., has introduced a bill to extend the deadline.

U.S. citizens will not be exempt from such biometric identities. This fall, the State Department will begin a pilot project to equip U.S. passports with biometric identifiers, with nationwide production of biometric passports beginning some time next year.

---

[1] U.S. General Accounting Office, "First Phase of Visitor and Immigration Status Program Operating, but Improvements Needed," GAO-04-586 (May 11, 2004).

Los Angeles International Airport was foiled when an Algerian man later linked to al Qaeda was stopped at the U.S.-Canadian border on Dec. 18, 1999, driving a car filled with bomb-making materials. Clarke reported afterward that al Qaeda "sleeper cells" might have taken root in the United States.[25]

In March, officials approved a four-part agenda that included disruption, law enforcement, immigration enforcement and U.S.-Canadian border controls. The White House also approved Predator aircraft attacks on al Qaeda bases—or on bin Laden himself. But CIA opposition to the flights derailed the plan. And Clinton left office in January 2001 with retaliation for al Qaeda's role in the October 2000 attack on the *Cole* still under consideration.

Postmortems

The Bush administration gave little visible attention to counterterrorism before 9/11. Bush drew wide public approval for rallying the nation immediately after the attacks and then leading a broad international coalition in ousting the pro-al Qaeda Taliban government in Afghanistan. But both the Clinton and Bush administrations have come under critical scrutiny since then—first from a joint inquiry by two congressional committees and now from the 9/11 commission.

Both administrations were blamed for not better coordinating the various agencies involved in counterterrorism. The Bush administration is also faulted for failing to appreciate the gravity of the threat that al Qaeda posed and for missing potential opportunities to disrupt or prevent the 9/11 attacks.

Clarke briefed Rice on al Qaeda during the transition period in January 2001. He writes that Rice seemed ill-informed about al Qaeda and voiced doubts about the need for a 12-person NSC unit devoted to counterterrorism. Rice told the 9/11 commission that Bush's national security team fully appreciated the threat from al Qaeda and wanted to make sure there was "no respite" in the fight against the organization. She says she took "the unusual step" of retaining Clarke and his staff despite the change in administrations. But Clarke says his position was downgraded so that he reported to deputies rather than to Cabinet-level "principals."

Rice directed Clarke to prepare a new counterterrorism strategy. Clarke says the work proceeded slowly, even with the spike in "threat reporting" in summer 2001. But

Rice stressed in her testimony that the final document—approved by Cabinet-level officials on Sept. 4—was the administration's first major national-security policy directive.

The multipart strategy parallels Clarke's unacted-on 1998 plan: diplomacy, financial sanctions, covert actions and military strikes. But Rice stressed to the 9/11 commission one difference: Whereas Clinton had called for bringing terrorists from Afghanistan to the United States for trial, the Bush plan directed the Pentagon to prepare for military action in Afghanistan itself.

When the war in Afghanistan ended, Congress in 2002 decided to examine the events leading up to 9/11. The House and Senate Intelligence committees completed their joint investigation in December 2002, but the 900-page report was not released until July 24, 2003—while the Bush administration reviewed the document for classified material.

When finally released, the report painted a sharply critical portrait of both the CIA and the FBI. Prior to 9/11, intelligence agencies had received "a modest, but relatively steady, stream of intelligence reporting" indicating the possibility of terrorist attacks in the United States, but they "failed to capitalize on both the individual and collective significance" of the information, the panels reported. Intelligence agencies were "neither well organized, nor equipped, and did not adequately adapt" to meet the threats posed by global terrorism.[26]

The intelligence committees laid out ambitious recommendations, beginning with the proposal—periodically recommended by the intelligence community—to create a powerful director of national intelligence (DNI) over the entire intelligence apparatus. The Cabinet-level position would be separate from the CIA director. The panels also called for Congress and the executive branch to "consider promptly" whether the FBI should retain responsibility for domestic intelligence or whether "a new agency" should take over those functions.

The 16-page laundry list included a host of other recommended changes—less visible but equally or even more important, including developing "human sources" to penetrate terrorist organizations; upgrading technology to "better exploit terrorist communications"; maximizing "effective use" of covert actions; and developing programs to deal with financial support for international terrorism.

The panels also called for "joint tours" for intelligence and law enforcement personnel in order to "broaden their experience and help bridge existing organizational and cultural divides" between the different agencies.

In addition, the committees asked that the 9/11 commission study Congress' own record in monitoring the intelligence community, including whether to replace the separate House and Senate oversight panels with a single committee and whether to change committee membership rules. Currently, members are limited to eight-year terms, but many say the restriction prevents them from developing sufficient expertise on intelligence agencies before they are forced to leave the panel.[27]

CURRENT SITUATION

Ground Zero

Police, firefighters and other emergency personnel were universally celebrated for their rescue efforts on Sept. 11 once the World Trade Center towers had been turned into raging infernos. However, in emotional hearings on May 18 and 19—punctuated by angry outbursts from several victims' family members in the audience—the 9/11 commission sharply criticized the Police and Fire departments' overall management of the disaster.

Inadequate planning, poor communications and interdepartmental rivalries significantly hampered rescue efforts, the commission staff suggested in two interim reports.[28] The critique—and barbed comments from some commissioners during the hearing—drew sharp retorts from current and former city officials. Former Mayor Rudolph W. Giuliani conceded "terrible mistakes" were made, but he denied any problems of coordination.[29]

But the staff reports said longstanding rivalry between the Police and Fire departments led each to consider itself "operationally autonomous" at emergency scenes. "The Mayor's Office of Emergency Management had not overcome this problem," the report said. Commissioner John Lehman called the command-and-control system "a scandal" and the city's disaster-response plans "not worthy of the Boy Scouts."

The staff reports also said 911 and Fire Department dispatchers had inadequate information and could not provide basic information to callers inside the buildings about the fires. "The 911 operators were clueless," said Commissioner Slade Gorton. The staff report also suggested that fire officials were slow to recognize the likelihood of the towers collapsing and therefore slow to order the buildings evacuated.

Thomas Von Essen, the fire commissioner at the time, called Lehman's remark "outrageous." For his part, Giuliani said firefighters were "standing their ground" in the building in order to get civilians out. Giuliani, who now runs his own security-consulting firm, called for Lehman to apologize. The former Navy secretary declined.

The staff reports also criticized the World Trade Center's owner, the Port Authority of New York and New Jersey. Despite biannual fire drills, civilians were not directed into stairwells or given information about evacuation routes, the report said. Civilians were "never instructed not to evacuate up" or informed that rooftop evacuations "were not part of the . . . evacuation plan." The report also noted that evacuation drills were not held and participation in fire drills "varied greatly from tenant to tenant."

The emergency response at the Pentagon, on the other hand, was "generally effective," the staff reports said, praising the "strong professional relationships and trust" established among emergency responders and "the pursuit of a regional approach to response" by departments from different jurisdictions.

New York's current mayor, Michael Bloomberg, told the commission on May 19 that the city was taking steps to "improve communications within and between the Police and Fire departments." Earlier, however, the commission's vice chairman, Lee H. Hamilton, had described the city's plan as a "prescription for confusion."

Bloomberg also criticized the allocation of post-9/11 federal emergency-preparedness assistance, saying that New York ranked 49th out of 50 states in per-capita funding received despite its prominence as a terrorist target. Homeland Security Secretary Tom Ridge told the commission the Bush administration had been trying to get Congress to change the allocation formulas, but he also said it was important to help each state.

In his appearance, Giuliani was asked about the significance of federal officials' failure to tell the city about the threat warnings described in Bush's Aug. 6 intelligence briefing. "I can't honestly tell you we would have done anything differently," Giuliani said. "We were doing, at the time, all that we could think of that was consistent with the city being able to move and to protect the city."

High Court Review

As President Bush was taking flak for his actions before Sept. 11, the administration was also awaiting Supreme

Should Congress create the new position of director of national intelligence?

YES
Sen. Dianne Feinstein, D-Calif.
Ranking Minority Member,
Subcommittee on Terrorism,
Technology and Homeland Security

Written for *The CQ Researcher*, May 2004

Intelligence failures on Iraq's weapons of mass destruction and in the months prior to Sept. 11, 2001, have made clear the need for reform within our nation's intelligence community. The place to start with this reform effort is at the top. We should begin by establishing a single director of national intelligence with the statutory and budgetary authority to truly oversee our nation's intelligence-gathering efforts.

The lack of coordination between intelligence agencies is well known. This disunity was described thoroughly in last summer's report by the Senate-House Inquiry into Sept. 11 and was echoed in the recent 9/11 commission hearings. Our intelligence-gathering efforts are plagued by territorial battles and reluctance among agencies to work together—reluctance that has caused the misreading of threats and endangered our nation.

This post-Cold War era of non-state, asymmetric threats demands cooperation among intelligence agencies. In an age when we must be prepared for the dangers of suitcase nukes, dirty bombs and bioterrorism, our entire government must share information to keep us safe.

The current intelligence structure is inadequate to address the threats posed by al Qaeda and other terrorist organizations. With 15 separate agencies, offices and departments charged with collecting or analyzing intelligence—including such little-known bodies as the National Reconnaissance Office and the National Geospatial-Intelligence Agency—our intelligence community is fragmented and inefficient.

The intelligence leadership structure exacerbates these divisions. The director of central intelligence (DCI) is charged with overseeing an agency while also acting as the leader of the entire intelligence community—two widely divergent functions that limit his effectiveness.

The DCI is further hampered by the fact that he oversees a mere one-fifth of the intelligence budget while the secretary of Defense controls most of the remaining 80 percent.

The best way to address this structural defect is to establish a single director of national intelligence with the statutory and budgetary authority to concentrate full time on coordinating intelligence resources, setting priorities and deciding strategies for the intelligence community and advising the president on intelligence matters.

Referring to the way we gather and analyze intelligence, 9/11 commission member and former Navy Secretary John Lehman recently said, "A revolution is coming."

Serious threats to our national security remain. We cannot afford to wait any longer to reform our intelligence community.

NO
Harold Brown
Counselor/Trustee, Center for Strategic and
International Studies, Secretary of Defense
(1977-1981)

Written for *The CQ Researcher*, May 2004

The present structure of the intelligence community is not working well. We need better connections between the various intelligence agencies. But there are reasons to be careful about inserting an additional position called director of national intelligence (DNI).

One suggestion is to have the DNI be a staff person in the White House. But that would merely add another layer to dealing with intelligence issues. If a referee among departments and agencies with intelligence functions is needed, the president's national security adviser or a deputy can do that.

Another suggestion is to have a DNI with line authority, budget authority and personnel authority over all of the intelligence agencies, including both CIA and those in the Department of Defense. But intelligence support is so important to military operations that any functions taken out of the Pentagon's control would likely be duplicated. And further centralizing of intelligence analysis would suppress alternative views and estimates, which recent history shows to be a mistake.

A DNI who is also director of the CIA cannot be an impartial overseer of the other agencies. But if there is a separate, subordinate, CIA head, the DNI will be too remote from the sensitive area of covert operations. Burying those further down the chain would provide more opportunity for uncontrolled activity.

Perhaps the biggest gap revealed by 9/11 is that between the FBI and the CIA. Discussion about the scope of DNI control usually omits the national security section of the FBI. If the Defense Department is recalcitrant about transferring large segments of its intelligence activities, that's nothing compared to the resistance from the Department of Justice and the FBI to taking away their national security functions.

Some suggestions for better organization can be found in the report of the Commission on the Roles and Capabilities of the U.S. Intelligence Community, which I headed in the mid-1990s. We suggested "double-hatting" heads of the separate intelligence agencies, so that they would report both to the secretary of Defense and the director of central intelligence. That's awkward, but it does correspond to the need for the DCI and the secretary of Defense to thrash out differences, which is necessary in any structure of intelligence. That report also proposed giving the DCI additional budgetary authority and training responsibility.

I would move in the direction of assuring better coordination of planning and operations, including across the sensitive boundary between domestic and foreign intelligence operations, but cautiously. Most of the proposals that have been suggested so far would likely make things worse, not better.

Court rulings on the legality of aggressive detention policies adopted in the post-9/11 war on terrorism.

The justices will decide whether the government has crossed constitutional bounds by denying judicial review to some 600 foreign nationals detained at Guantánamo Bay Naval Base in Cuba since being captured in Afghanistan and Pakistan and to two U.S. citizens held as "enemy combatants" in the United States. One was captured in Afghanistan; the other was arrested at the Chicago airport in May 2002 and charged with conspiring to explode a radioactive bomb somewhere in the United States.

Civil-liberties and human-rights organizations say the lack of access to courts is inconsistent with the U.S. Constitution and international law. But the government argues courts have very limited authority to review the president's authority as commander in chief to detain enemy combatants.

The justices seemed divided along their usual conservative-liberal fault line during arguments in the three cases in late April: Justices Sandra Day O'Connor and Anthony M. Kennedy, moderate-conservatives who often hold the balance of power on the court, gave mixed signals.

In the first case to be argued, a former federal appeals court judge told the justices on April 20 that the government had created "a lawless enclave" at Guantánamo by blocking the foreigners from going to court to challenge their detention. "What's at stake in this case is the authority of the federal courts to uphold the rule of law," said John Gibbons, a lawyer in Newark, N.J., and former chief judge of the federal appeals court in Philadelphia.[30]

Most of the 600 detainees being held at Guantánamo were captured during operations against al Qaeda or the Taliban in Afghanistan or Pakistan. The high court case stemmed from *habeas corpus* petitions filed by Kuwaiti, British and Australian nationals, all of whom claimed they had not been fighting the United States. Two lower federal courts dismissed the petitions, saying Guantánamo was outside U.S. jurisdiction.

In his argument, Solicitor General Theodore Olson noted that the United States was still fighting in Afghanistan and warned that judicial review of the detainees' cases would invite legal challenges to combat-zone treatment of captured enemy soldiers. "Judges would have to decide the circumstances of their detention, whether there had been adequate military process,

The mother of a World Trade Center victim reacts angrily to former New York Mayor Rudolph W. Giuliani's testimony before the 9/11 commission in May 2004. While conceding "terrible mistakes" were made, Giuliani denied any problems of coordination between the Police and Fire departments. Commissioner John Lehman had called the city's disaster-response plans "not worthy of the Boy Scouts."

what control existed over the territory in which they were kept," Olson said.

The administration urged a similarly broad view of executive authority in the cases of the two citizens, argued on April 28.[31] Deputy Solicitor General Paul Clement told the justices it was "well established and long established that the government has the authority to hold both unlawful enemy combatants and lawful prisoners of war captured on the battlefield to prevent them from returning to the battle."

Lawyers representing the two detainees, however, insisted the government's position amounted to authorizing "indefinite executive detention." Frank Dunham, a federal public defender, told the justices, "We could have people locked up all over the country tomorrow without any due process, without any opportunity to be heard."

Dunham was representing Yaser Hamdi, an American-born Saudi seized in Afghanistan. The second case involved José Padilla, a Chicagoan arrested at O'Hare Airport on May 8, 2002, after a flight originating in Pakistan. Both men were held at a Navy brig in Charleston, S.C., without charges and without access to lawyers. The federal appeals court in Richmond, Va., upheld Hamdi's detention, while the federal appeals court in New York ordered the government to charge Padilla or release him.

The cases raise legal questions that the high court has not considered since two pro-government rulings in World War II-era cases: One involved German saboteurs captured in the United States and later executed and the other German soldiers captured in China and later tried by military tribunals.[32]

The administration argued that both decisions supported its position in the current cases, while the detainees' attorneys maintained the rulings were factually and legally distinguishable. Decisions in the current cases are due before the justices' summer recess at the end of June.

OUTLOOK

Law of Averages?

Could 9/11 happen again? Federal officials warn that a new terrorist attack could come this summer or during the presidential campaign this fall. And they concede that despite tightened security measures, there is no assurance that an attack could be thwarted.

"Those charged with protecting us from attack have to succeed 100 percent of the time," national security adviser Rice told the 9/11 commission. "To inflict devastation on a massive scale, the terrorists only have to succeed once, and we know they are trying every day."

"I tend to be somewhat fatalistic about surprise attacks," says Columbia University's Betts. "We're dealing with a problem of batting averages. You're never going to bat 1,000."

The terrorist attacks have already brought about significant changes in the federal government and in Americans' daily routines. In Washington, the new Department of Homeland Security in 2002 consolidated existing border and transportation security functions and emergency preparedness and response under one department. And Americans in all walks of life have grown accustomed to tighter security, while aviation experts are warning of long security lines this summer. Meanwhile, many employers have increased their fire and evacuation drills.

Intelligence reorganization has emerged as the most significant issue in the two official investigations of 9/11. Leading Democratic members of the House and Senate Intelligence committees have proposed creating a new "director of national intelligence" with budget authority over all 15 intelligence agencies and who would no longer head the CIA itself.

A bill by Rep. Jane Harman, D-Calif., ranking member of the House panel, would give the proposed DNI substantial budgetary authority over the intelligence community but leave responsibility for "execution" with the Pentagon or other departments that house existing agencies. The DNI would serve at the pleasure of the president, while the bill would give the director of the CIA a 10-year term—the same as the FBI director. Senate Intelligence Committee member Dianne Feinstein, D-Calif., has sponsored similar legislation since 2002. Her current bill is somewhat less detailed than Harman's and does not give the CIA director a fixed term.[33]

Neither Feinstein nor Harman has any Republican cosponsors. Harman says there is "no reason" Republicans should not support the measure. "This is not a partisan bill," she says. GOP staffers on the Intelligence panels say Republican members are taking a wait-and-see approach. For its part, the administration has given no additional specifics since Bush said in mid-April that the intelligence agencies need to be overhauled.

"We will see no major reforms before another major catastrophic attack," says UCLA's Zegart. "Even then, I don't put the odds better than 50/50. The barriers to intelligence reform are exceptionally high."

The National War College's Goodman is more optimistic but sees the 9/11 commission report as the key to any significant changes. "The only hope is that this 9/11 report will be so strong and so shocking that people will suddenly say, 'Stop. Something's got to be done.' "

Commission Chairman Kean has repeatedly said he hopes the panel's final report will be unanimous. But some commission members are saying the panel may be divided on such major issues as intelligence reorganization. "Unanimity is a nice goal, but it isn't going to be a necessary goal," former Sen. Slade Gorton said.[34] A divided report is assumed likely to have less impact than a unanimous one.

Proposals to reorganize the FBI seem unlikely to advance, largely to allow time to evaluate the changes being put into effect by Director Mueller. Meanwhile, Rep. Christopher Cox, R-Calif., chairman of the House Select Homeland Security Committee, plans to give DHS' intelligence unit more authority over terrorism intelligence in the department's authorization bill. Cox says he is concerned that the unit—known as the Information Analysis and Infrastructure Protection Directorate—is not playing the role intended when the DHS was created.

As for local emergency preparedness, Homeland Security Secretary Ridge told the 9/11 commission his department has disbursed $8 billion to states, regions and cities to train and equip first responders. Noting the communications problems in New York City, Ridge also said the department was working to make communications and equipment "interoperable" between different departments and jurisdictions. Democrats have criticized the administration for not spending enough money to strengthen local emergency preparedness.

Republican and Democratic lawmakers are also squaring off already over renewing the USA Patriot Act, which Congress passed after 9/11 to strengthen law enforcement powers in anti-terrorism cases. Bush is urging Congress to extend the legislation this year, but Democrats are criticizing some of its provisions and questioning the need for action now. Some of the provisions expire in 2005.

Many observers fear that no matter how hard the government tries, the threat of terrorism cannot be eliminated. "There are going to be terrorist attacks, and there are going to be successful terrorist attacks," says the Heritage Foundation's Carafano. "We're never going to be immune from terrorism."

NOTES

1. For background, see David Masci and Kenneth Jost, "War on Terrorism," *The CQ Researcher*, Oct. 12, 2001, pp. 817-848.

2. Some eyewitness material taken from David Lightman, "A Frustrating Day for 9/11 Families," Knight Ridder/Tribune News Service, April 8, 2004.

3. The Family Steering Committee's Web site can be found at www.911independentcommission.org. For other victims' organizations, see Families of Sept. 11 (www.familiesofseptember11.org) and World Trade Center United Family Group (www.wtcufg.org).

4. The commission maintains a thorough and well-organized Web site: www.9-11commission.gov.

5. For background, see Kenneth Jost, "Civil Liberties Debates," *The CQ Researcher*, Oct. 24, 2003, pp. 893-916, and David Masci and Patrick Marshall, "Civil Liberties in Wartime," *The CQ Researcher*, Dec. 14, 2001, pp. 1017-1040.

6. For background, see Martin Kady II, "Homeland Security," *The CQ Researcher*, Sept. 12, 2003, pp. 749-772.

7. Staff Statement No. 1 (immigration), Jan. 26, 2004. Staff Statement No. 3 (aviation security), Jan. 27, 2004.

8. Staff Statement No. 11 (intelligence community), April 14, 2004. Staff Statement No. 9 (law enforcement), April 13, 2004.

9. Richard A. Clarke, *Against All Enemies: Inside America's War on Terror* (2004), p. x. See also Masci, *op. cit.*

10. For an overview, see the Intelligence Community's Web site: www.intelligence.gov.

11. Zegart's book is tentatively titled *Stuck in the Moment: Why American National Securities Agencies Adapted Poorly to the Rise of Terrorism After the Cold War* (Princeton University Press, forthcoming 2005). Zegart notes as disclosure that Condoleezza Rice, President Bush's national security adviser, was her dissertation adviser at Stanford University.

12. Staff Statement No. 7 (intelligence policy), March 24, 2004.

13. For background, see Brian Hansen, "Intelligence Reforms," *The CQ Researcher*, Jan. 25, 2002, pp. 49-72.

14. See Michael Isikoff and Daniel Klaidman, "The Hijackers We Let Escape," *Newsweek*, June 10, 2002; and David Johnston and James Risen, "Inquiry Into Attack on the Cole in 2000 Missed Clues to 9/11," *The New York Times*, April 11, 2004, Section 1, p. 1.

15. Staff Statement No. 2 ("Three 9/11 Hijackers: Identification, Watchlisting, and Tracking") Jan. 26, 2004.

16. Staff Statement No. 7, *op. cit.*

17. Clarke, *op. cit.*, pp. 231-232.

18. The document is appended to Staff Statement No. 10.

19. See Douglas Jehl, "Administration Considers a Post for National Intelligence Director," *The New York Times*, April 16, 2004, p. A1.

20. Background drawn from entries in George T. Kurian (ed.), *A Historical Guide to the U.S. Government* (1998).

21. History drawn from undated "Aviation Security" entry on Web site of U.S. Centennial of Flight Commission:

www.centennialofflight.gov/essay/Government_Role/security/POL18.htm.

22. See Scott Kuzner, "U.S. Studied Terrorist Threat for Years," in David Masci and Kenneth Jost, *op. cit.*, p. 840.

23. For a compact biography, see Charles S. Clark, "Bin Laden's War on America," in Masci and Jost, *op. cit.*, pp. 824-825.

24. Remainder of section drawn from 9/11 commission Staff Statement No. 8; Clarke, *op. cit.*, pp. 134-154, 181-204.

25. For background on computer-related Millennium problems, see Kathy Koch, "Y2K Dilemma," *The CQ Researcher*, Feb. 19, 1999, pp. 137-160.

26. House Permanent Select Committee on Intelligence/Senate Select Committee on Intelligence, Report of the Joint Inquiry into Intelligence Community Activities before and after the Terrorist Attacks of Sept. 11, 2001, December 2002 (S. Rept. 107-351, H. Rept. 107-792; www.gpoaccess.gov/serialset/creports/911.html).

27. See Dana Priest, "Congressional Oversight of Intelligence Criticized," *The Washington Post*, April 27, 2004, p. A1.

28. Staff Statements Nos. 13 (emergency preparedness and response), May 18, 2004, and 14 (crisis management), May 19, 2004.

29. Some quotes taken from coverage in *The New York Times*, May 19-20.

30. The case is *Rasul v. Bush*, 03-334. For information, including a transcript of the oral argument, see the Supreme Court's Web site: www.supremecourtus.gov.

31. The cases are *Hamdi v. Rumsfeld*, 03-6696, and *Rumsfeld v. Padilla*, 03-1027.

32. The decisions are Ex parte Qirin, 323 U.S. 283 (1944) (saboteurs), and *Johnson v. Eisentrager*, 339 U.S. 763 (1950) (POWs).

33. Harman's bill is HR 4104, Feinstein's S 190. Feinstein's legislation was also incorporated in a broad intelligence reorganization measure (S1520) introduced July 31, 2003, by Sen. Bob Graham, D-Fla.

34. Quoted in Philip Shenon, "9/11 Panel May Not Reach Unanimity on Final Report," *The New York Times*, May 26, 2004, p. A19.

BIBLIOGRAPHY

Books

Bamford, James, *Body of Secrets: Anatomy of the Ultra-Secret National Security Agency from the Cold War Through the Dawn of a New Century,* **Doubleday, 2001.**
Published before 9/11, this informative general history of the NSA has two index entries for Osama bin Laden. Includes detailed notes.

Benjamin, Daniel, and Steven Simon, *The Age of Sacred Terror,* **Random House, 2002.**
Former National Security Council staffers in the Clinton administration provide a comprehensive account of the rise of al Qaeda. Benjamin is a senior fellow at the Center for Strategic and International Studies in Washington and Simon is an assistant director of the International Institute for Strategic Studies in London. Includes glossary, detailed notes.

Clarke, Richard A., *Against All Enemies: Inside America's War on Terror,* **Free Press, 2004.**
The former national coordinator for security, infrastructure and terrorism under both Clinton and Bush offers his controversial first-person account of the government's anti-terrorism efforts leading up to the 9/11 attacks.

Lowenthal, Mark M., *Intelligence: From Secrets to Policy* **(2d ed.), CQ Press, 2003.**
This updated overview of the structure, role and operations of the various agencies in the nation's intelligence community was written when Lowenthal worked with a security-consulting firm. He is now assistant director of central intelligence for analysis and production. Includes suggested readings, Web sites and other appendix material.

Riebling, Mark, *Wedge: From Pearl Harbor to 9/11. How the Secret War Between the FBI and CIA Has Endangered National Security,* **Touchstone, 2002 (originally published, 1994).**
The director of the Manhattan Institute for Policy Research provides a detailed history of policy differences and bureaucratic rivalry between the CIA (and its precursors) and the FBI. An epilogue and afterword in the paperback edition relate continuing tensions between the agencies through 9/11. A 14-page list of sources is

included; sources for the epilogue and afterword are posted at secretpolicy.com/wedge/epilogue.

Treverton, Greg, *Reshaping National Intelligence for an Age of Information*, Cambridge University Press, 2001.
A RAND Corporation expert argues for a "sweeping" reshaping of national intelligence to make it more open and decentralized in the post-Cold War information age.

Articles

Dlouhy, Jennifer A., and Martin Kady II, "Lawmakers Eager to Weigh In on Overhaul of Intelligence," *CQ Weekly*, April 17, 2004, pp. 902-905.
Overview of lawmakers' views on various proposals to reorganize the U.S. intelligence community.

Gup, Ted, "The Failure of Intelligence," *The Village Voice*, April 13, 2004.
A veteran journalist and author provides a critical overview of terrorism-related intelligence collection and analysis before 9/11. Gup is now a journalism professor at Case Western Reserve University.

Johnston, David, and Eric Schmitt, "Uneven Response Seen to Terror Risk in Summer '01," *The New York Times*, April 4, 2004, Section 1, page 1.
The author reconstructs the Bush administration's limited follow-up to increased threat reporting during summer 2001; includes chart detailing some of the 33 intercepted messages with threat warnings.

Paltrow, Scot J., "Detailed Picture of U.S. Actions on Sept. 11 Remains Elusive," *The Wall Street Journal*, March 22, 2004, p. A1.
The reporter provides a meticulous reconstruction of the government's actions on Sept. 11, with some evidence contradicting previous official accounts.

Reports and Studies

House Permanent Select Committee on Intelligence/ Senate Select Committee on Intelligence, *Report of the Joint Inquiry into Intelligence Community Activities before and after the Terrorist Attacks of September 11, 2001*, December 2002 (S. Rept. 107-351, H. Rept. 107-792; www.gpoaccess.gov/serialset/creports/911.html).
The 900-page report includes a summary of major findings and conclusions and a list of 17 recommendations. The report is dated December 2002 but was released in July 2003 following executive branch review for redaction of classified material.

National Commission on Terrorist Attacks upon the United States (www.9-11commission.gov).
The 9/11 commission's extensive Web site includes testimony and transcripts from all hearings and interim reports by the commission or staff. The commission's final report is scheduled to be released on July 26; the report will be published by W.W. Norton on the day of release and available for $10.

For More Information

Center for Strategic and International Studies, 1800 K St., N.W., Washington, DC 20006; (202) 887-0200; www.csis.org.

Families of September 11, 1560 Broadway, Suite 305, New York, NY 10036-1518; (212) 575-1878; www. familiesofseptember11.org.

Federation of American Scientists, 1717 K St., N.W., Suite 209, Washington, DC 20036; (202) 546-3300; www.fas.org.

National Commission on Terrorist Attacks Upon the United States, 301 7th St., S.W., Room 5125, Washington, DC 20407; (202) 331-4060; www. 9-11commission.gov.

World Trade Center United Family Group, P.O. Box 2307, Wayne, NJ 07474-2307; (973) 216-2623; www.wtcufg.org.

4

Nuclear Proliferation and Terrorism

Mary H. Cooper

AFP Photo/Philippe Lopez

Terrorist leader Osama bin Laden, left, with his deputy, Ayman al-Zawahiri, has said he wants to use a nuclear bomb against the West. The recent sale of black-market nuclear-weapons technology to North Korea and Iran and the terrorist bombing of passenger trains in Madrid, killing more than 190 people, have intensified concerns about nuclear weapons falling into the hands of "rogue" states or terrorists.

From *The CQ Researcher*, April 2, 2004.

Concern about nuclear terrorism rose to new levels when A.Q. Khan, the revered father of Pakistan's nuclear bomb, confessed recently to peddling nuclear weapons technology to Libya and other rogue states.

Khan's dramatic confession punctured any remaining illusions that 60 years of nonproliferation efforts had kept the world's most dangerous weapons out of the hands of countries hostile to the United States and its allies. Moreover, he enhanced fears that terrorist groups bent on destroying the United States—like Osama bin Laden's al Qaeda network—may be closer than anyone had realized to acquiring nuclear weapons.

"A nuclear 9/11 in Washington or New York would change American history in ways that [the original] 9/11 didn't," says Graham Allison, director of Harvard University's Belfer Center for Science and International Affairs. "It would be as big a leap beyond 9/11 as 9/11 itself was beyond the pre-attack illusion that we were invulnerable."

Khan's January confession followed the revelation that he had operated a busy black-market trade in centrifuges, blueprints for nuclear-weapons equipment to enrich uranium into weapons-grade fuel and missiles capable of delivering nuclear warheads. Khan's vast network involved manufacturers in Malaysia, middlemen in the United Arab Emirates and the governments of Libya, North Korea and Iran.[1]

Several countries in Khan's network were known to have violated the 1968 Nuclear Non-Proliferation Treaty (NPT) and hidden their weapons programs from inspectors for the U.N.'s International Atomic Energy Agency (IAEA).[2] NPT signatories promise

Russia Has Most Nuclear Warheads

Russia and the United States have most of the more than 28,000 nuclear warheads stockpiled today. India, Israel and Pakistan — which have not signed the Nuclear Non-Proliferation Treaty (NPT) — have enough nuclear materials to produce more than 300 warheads. North Korea and Iran are both thought to be developing nuclear bombs. It is unknown whether terrorist groups have or are developing nuclear weapons.

Worldwide Nuclear Stockpiles

Country	Nuclear Weapons (estimated)
NPT Signatories	
China	410
France	350
Russia	18,000
United Kingdom	185
United States	9,000
Non-NPT Signatories *	
India	95 (max.)
Israel	200 (max.)
Pakistan	52 (max.)
Maximum total	28,292

* The number of warheads that could be produced with the amount of weapons-grade nuclear material these countries are thought to possess. The total number of assembled weapons is not known.

Source: Carnegie Endowment for International Peace, 2004

Threat Initiative, an advocacy group that calls for stronger measures to stop the spread of nuclear weapons. "While there had been suggestions that the Pakistanis were nefariously engaged in both Iran and North Korea, the extent of the engagement in Libya and indications that there was an attempt to market proliferation technology in Syria exceeded the darkest suspicions of the intelligence community."

Given the grim realities of the post-9/11 world, fear of nuclear terrorism has dominated the international response to Khan's revelations. President Bush has proposed several measures to strengthen international anti-proliferation efforts. "In the hands of terrorists, weapons of mass destruction would be a first resort," Bush said. "[T]hese terrible weapons are becoming easier to acquire, build, hide and transport. . . . Our message to proliferators must be consistent and must be clear: We will find you, and we're not going to rest until you're stopped."[3]

But many experts say the president's proposals will not provide adequate safeguards against these lethal weapons. Wade Boese, research director of the Arms Control Association, a Washington think tank, commends the administration for emphasizing proliferation and pointing out that it is the most serious threat facing the United States today. However, he notes, since 9/11, the Bush administration has only "maintained the status quo" on funding for programs that deal with the threat of nuclear proliferation.

"The Khan network underscores the fact that we're in a race to tighten down security around [nuclear-weapons technology] so the terrorists can't get it," Boese says. "If this is such an urgent priority, which it is, why not fund it like it is and recognize that we're in a race with the terrorists?"

During the Cold War, both the United States and the Soviet Union understood that using nuclear weapons

to forgo nuclear weapons in exchange for help from the world's five official nuclear powers—the United States, Russia, China, France and Britain—in building civilian nuclear power plants.

In fact, North Korea has bragged that it is developing nuclear weapons, Iraq tried for years to produce weapons-grade fuel, and Iran recently barred IAEA inspections from its nuclear facilities amid allegations that it was developing a bomb. Libya's admission in December that it, too, had tried to build the bomb blew the cover on Khan's network. (*See sidebar, p. 82.*)

But the extent of Khan's black-market activities stunned even the most seasoned observers. "I was surprised by the level of commerce in the supporting supply network," says Charles B. Curtis, president of the Nuclear

would amount to mass suicide. The doctrine of mutual assured destruction—MAD—ensured that a nuclear attack by one superpower would unleash a full-scale response by the other, resulting in annihilation on a national, if not global, scale. Consequently, the theory went, rational leaders would avoid using nuclear weapons at all costs.

But al Qaeda and other radical Islamist organizations don't appear to operate under such constraints. Their suicide bombers embrace death as martyrdom in their quest to destroy the "Great Satan."[4] And because they operate in a number of countries and have no permanent, identifiable headquarters, terrorist groups also have no "return address" to target for a counterattack.

As a result, keeping weapons-grade plutonium and highly enriched uranium out of the hands of terrorists is the only sure way to block terrorists from building nuclear bombs, many experts say.

"The essential ingredients of nuclear weapons are very hard to make and don't occur in nature," notes Matthew Bunn, a nuclear-terrorism expert at the Belfer Center. "But once a well-organized terrorist group gets hold of them, it could make at least a crude nuclear explosive."

Instructions for making a nuclear bomb are not secret; they are even on the Internet. "The secret is in making the nuclear material," Bunn points out, "and that, unfortunately, is the secret that A.Q. Khan was peddling."

While the ability of terrorists to stage a full-scale nuclear attack is of paramount concern, experts say the use of a conventional explosive device containing radioactive waste—a so-called dirty bomb—is far more likely. A dirty bomb in an urban area could contaminate dozens of city blocks, fomenting panic and costing tens of billions of dollars in lost revenues and devalued real estate, even if it claimed no human lives.[5]

"A dirty bomb is pretty likely to happen," says Leonard S. Spector, director of the Center for Nonproliferation Studies' Washington office, a part of the Monterey Institute of International Studies. A dirty bomb can be made easily with radioactive materials, such as cesium, used in X-ray machines and other commonplace diagnostic equipment. Moreover, he points out, civilian nuclear-waste facilities are much easier to penetrate than weapons facilities.

"We have to do our best to control as much of the radioactive material as possible," he says, "but it's already the subject of criminal activities. So we're recommending that people get ready for this one."

As policymakers examine the impact of Khan's nuclear black marketeering on U.S. counterproliferation policy, these are some of the questions being considered:

Is the Non-Proliferation Treaty still an effective shield against the spread of nuclear weapons?

The United States launched the atomic age when it detonated the first atomic bomb in 1945. But After Britain, China, France and the Soviet Union developed their own nuclear weapons, the great powers sought to put the nuclear genie back in the bottle. The landmark 1968 Non-Proliferation Treaty embodied a "grand bargain," by which the five countries with nuclear arsenals agreed to help the rest of the world develop nuclear power for peaceful uses in exchange for the non-nuclear states' promise to forgo nuclear weapons. The IAEA was to oversee compliance with the treaty, which enjoyed near universal support.

However, India, Israel and Pakistan—all of which have since developed nuclear weapons—never signed the treaty. And North Korea, which signed but later renounced the treaty, recently boasted that it is on the threshold of developing nuclear weapons.

The absence of universal adherence to the NPT reveals the treaty's basic weakness. "The fact that a very small number of individuals—nobody believes that A.Q. Khan was acting alone—can create a network that provides some of the most worrisome states on the planet with the technology needed to produce nuclear weapons

Protesters in Seoul, South Korea, burn a North Korean flag and an effigy of Kim Jong Il on Dec. 28, 2003, calling on North Korea's leader to end the country's efforts to build a nuclear bomb.

A Chronology of Nuclear Close Calls

The superpowers came close to using nuclear weapons several times during the Cold War, sometimes due to tensions that might have escalated, and sometimes due to simple accidents or mistakes. The end of the Cold War in 1991, however, did not end the threat of nuclear conflict.

First year of Korean War, 1950-51—President Harry S. Truman sends atomic weapons to Guam for possible use against North Korea; Strategic Air Command makes plans to coordinate an atomic strike. Gen. Douglas MacArthur pushes for attacks on China, possibly using atomic weapons.[1]

The Offshore Islands Crises, 1954-55, 1958—Testing America's resolve, China bombs Quemoy and Matsu, two Nationalist-held islands near the mainland. U.S. officials warn they will use atomic weapons to defend the islands.[2]

Mistake in Greenland, October 1960—The American early-warning radar system in Thule, Greenland, mistakenly reports a "massive" Soviet missile launch against the United States. A reflection on the moon 250,000 miles away is thought to be a missile launch 2,500 miles away.[3]

Flashpoint Berlin, 1961—Soviet threats regarding West Berlin prompt President John F. Kennedy to consider a nuclear first-strike against the U.S.S.R. if it attacks the city.[4]

Cuban Missile Crisis, October 1962—President Kennedy considers invading Cuba to remove Soviet nuclear missiles, unaware the Soviets plan to respond with nuclear weapons. The Strategic Air Command goes to Defense Condition 2 (DEFCON 2), the second-highest state of readiness, for the only time in U.S. history. After an American naval quarantine of the island, Soviet Premier Nikita Khrushchev withdraws the missiles.[5]

B-52 Crash in Greenland, January 1968—A B-52 carrying four thermonuclear bombs crashes near the U.S. early-warning base in Greenland. If the bombs' safety features had failed, the detonation could have been viewed as a surprise attack on America's early-warning system, prompting nuclear retaliation.[6]

Sino-Soviet Conflict, 1969—Soviet Defense Minister Andrei Grechko advocates a nuclear strike against China to deal with what is perceived as an inevitable future war. Fearing the U.S. reaction, the Soviets refrain.[7]

---

[1] Burton Kaufman, *The Korean Conflict* (1999).

[2] John W. Garver, *Foreign Relations of the People's Republic of China* (1993), pp. 50-60.

[3] Center for Defense Information (CDI), www.cdi.org/Issues/NukeAccidents/accidents.htm.

[4] Fred Kaplan, "JFK's First Strike Plan," *The Atlantic Monthly*, October 2001, pp. 81-86.

[5] Graham Allison and Philip Zelikow, *Essence of Decision* (1999).

[6] Scott D. Sagan, *The Limits of Safety* (1993), pp. 180-193.

[7] Garver, *op. cit.*, pp. 305-310.

---

is very troubling," Bunn says. "It shows that the NPT regime is only as strong as its weakest links. We can secure 90 percent of the nuclear material to very high levels, but if the other 10 percent is vulnerable to theft, we still won't have solved the problem because we're dealing with intelligent adversaries who will be able to find and exploit the weak points."

In fact, some experts say that weaknesses doom the NPT to failure. "Arms-control regimes are not capable of dealing with the hard cases," says John Pike, a defense policy expert and founding director of GlobalSecurity.org, a nonprofit organization that studies emerging security threats.

"The logic of the NPT just doesn't get you very far in Tehran [Iran] or Pyongyang [North Korea]," Pike says. "It's not going to matter to India or Pakistan, which have

their own fish to fry. And the Israelis are not going to let go of their arsenal until there is a just and lasting peace in the Middle East," Pike says. "I'm afraid we're rapidly approaching a situation in which there are more nuclear-weapons states outside the NPT than inside, and the treaty itself provides no way whatsoever of addressing that problem."

The nonproliferation regime also lacks adequate verification and enforcement provisions, critics say. "The NPT was a confidence-building measure, not a true arms-control treaty," says C. Paul Robinson, director of Sandia National Laboratories, a division of the Energy Department's National Nuclear Security Administration. Robinson also was chief U.S. negotiator of the U.S.-Soviet Threshold Test Ban and Peaceful Nuclear Explosions Treaties, both ratified in 1990. None of the

Yom Kippur War, October 1973—Egypt and Syria attack Israel, and after initial successes face military disaster. The Soviet Union indicates it might intervene to rescue its client states if Israel continues to refuse a cease-fire; Soviet airborne forces are put on alert, and U.S. military forces also go on alert. Israel agrees to a cease-fire and the superpower crisis ends.[8]

War Game Turns 'Real' at NORAD, 1979-80—In November 1979, a technician at the North American Air Defense (NORAD) facility in Cheyenne Mountain, Colo., accidentally places a training tape simulating a nuclear attack on the United States into the base computer system. The mistake is corrected in six minutes—but after the president's airborne command post is launched. Twice in June 1980, false attack warnings caused by faulty computer chips send bomber crews racing for their planes.[9]

Tension in Europe, Early 1980s—After the Soviet Union deploys new nuclear missiles in Europe, the United States follows suit. Soviet leader Yuri Andropov fears NATO is planning a nuclear first-strike and orders Soviet intelligence to find the non-existent evidence. Tension in Europe decreases when Mikhail Gorbachev replaces Andropov.[10]

Soviet Pacific Fleet, August 1984—A rogue officer at the Soviet Pacific Fleet in Vladivostok broadcasts an un-authorized war alert to Soviet naval forces, which, like American vessels, are armed with nuclear weapons. Soviet, U.S. and Japanese forces all prepare for battle. After 30 minutes, the alert is determined to be false.[11]

Norwegian Sea, January 1995—Russian radar detects an inbound missile over the Norwegian Sea, and President Boris N. Yeltsin opens his nuclear command briefcase and confers with his military commanders. The missile turns out to be a Norwegian weather rocket.[12]

Kargil, Kashmir, May-July 1999—A year after nuclear tests by India and Pakistan, Pakistan invades Kargil, in Indian-controlled Kashmir, and battles Indian forces from May until July. The crisis between the two rival nuclear powers is described as "warlike." Pakistan withdraws in July under heavy international pressure.[13]

Attack on the Indian Parliament, December 2001-January 2002—Islamic militants probably connected to Pakistan's intelligence service attack India's Parliament. India demands that Pakistan cease supporting Islamic fighters. Hundreds of thousands of troops face off at the Indo-Pakistani border; both sides discuss a possible nuclear exchange. Tensions ease after Pakistan cracks down on Islamist groups.[14]

---

[8] P. R. Kumaraswamy (ed.), *Revisiting the Yom Kippur War* (2000).

[9] Sagan, *op. cit.*, pp. 228-233.

[10] Christopher Andrew and Vasili Mitrokhin, *The Sword and the Shield* (1999).

[11] CNN, www.cnn.com/SPECIALS/cold.war/episodes/12/spotlight/.

[12] CNN, *op. cit.*

[13] Yossef Bodansky, "The Kargil Crisis in Kashmir Threatens to Move into a New Indo-Pak War, With PRC Involvement," *Defense & Foreign Affairs Strategic Policy*, May/June 1999, p. 20.

[14] Seymour M. Hersh, "The Getaway," *The New Yorker*, Jan. 28, 2002, p. 36.

---

requirements normally found in arms-control treaties to verify compliance were included in the NPT, he says. "So there's nothing in the original NPT designed to catch cheaters."

After the 1991 Persian Gulf War, the nuclear non-proliferation community was surprised to learn that Iraq had been secretly developing nuclear weapons. So an "Additional Protocol" was added to the NPT allowing for more thorough inspections of suspected weapons facilities, but only 38 countries have ratified it. In any case, Robinson dismisses the protocol as little more than a "Band-Aid."

Even IAEA Director Mohamed ElBaradei said the NPT regime does not prevent nuclear proliferation. "You need a complete overhaul of the export-control system," he said. "It is not working right now."[6]

But the Bush administration says if the NPT and the IAEA oversight powers are strengthened, nonproliferation can remain a credible goal. On Feb. 11, Bush outlined seven steps designed to make the regime more effective in dealing with the threat of what the State Department calls "rogue" states and nuclear terrorism, including U.S. Senate approval of the Additional Protocol (*see p. 86*).

Other analysts say world dynamics have changed so dramatically since the NPT took effect that the nonproliferation regime needs a revolutionary overhaul. "The treaty was about controlling states and governments, not rogue individuals or terrorists who get their hands on these weapons," says Boese of the Arms Control Association. "The nonproliferation regime needs to be modified to better address this gap."

"The system has been pretty remarkable and successful, but is now in sufficient need of radical repair that we need a big jump forward," says Allison of the Belfer Center, who as assistant Defense secretary oversaw the Clinton administration's efforts to reduce the former Soviet nuclear arsenal. "We should now build a global alliance against nuclear terrorism, and the core of its strategy should be the doctrine of what I call the three 'Nos:' "[7]

- "No loose nukes"—Allison coined the phrase a decade ago to describe weapons and weapons-grade materials inadequately secured against theft. "These weapons and materials must be protected to a new security standard adequate to prevent nuclear terrorists from attacking us," he says. Under Allison's proposal, all nuclear states would have to be certified by another member of the nuclear club that all their nuclear materials had been adequately secured. The NPT has no such requirement.

- "No new nascent nukes"—New production of highly enriched uranium and plutonium would be barred. "If you don't have either one of them, you don't have a nuclear weapon," Allison says.

- "No new nuclear weapons"—Noting North Korea's nuclear ambitions, Allison acknowledges that this is the most difficult but potentially most important goal. "To accept North Korea as a new member of the nuclear club would be catastrophic," Allison says, "because North Korea historically has been the most promiscuous proliferator on Earth."

North Korea has sold nuclear-capable missiles to Iraq, Pakistan and other would-be nuclear powers. If Pyongyang develops a nuclear arsenal, most experts agree, other countries in the region, including South Korea, Japan and Taiwan, would be tempted to jettison the NPT and develop their own arsenals in defense, setting off a potentially disastrous regional arms race. "A nuclear North Korea," Allison says, "would blow the lid off the previous arms control and nuclear proliferation regime."

Is the United States doing enough to halt nuclear proliferation?

Since the fall of the Soviet Union in 1991, the United States has concentrated its nonproliferation efforts on preventing the theft or sale of nuclear weapons and materials left in Russia, Ukraine and other former Soviet republics. The 1991 Soviet Nuclear Threat Reduction Act — renamed the Cooperative Threat Reduction (CTR) program in 1993—was designed to help former Soviet satellite countries destroy nuclear, chemical and biological weapons and associated infrastructure. Nicknamed Nunn-Lugar after the law's original sponsors (Sens. Sam Nunn, D-Ga., and Richard G. Lugar, R-Ind.), it also established verifiable safeguards against the proliferation of such weapons.

Recent U.S. efforts to control the worldwide supply of nuclear weapons and materials have focused almost solely on the CTR program: More than 50 former Soviet nuclear-storage sites have been secured and new security systems installed. Besides locking up nuclear materials and establishing security perimeters around the storage sites, says Robinson of Sandia Labs, the CTR program installs detection equipment to warn of any movement of the guarded material. "This material is being locked up and safeguarded," Robinson says. Sandia designs and installs the nuclear-security systems and trains foreign technicians on their use.

But critics say the agreement is woefully inadequate. "Very, very little progress has taken place," says Curtis of the Nuclear Threat Initiative, which Nunn co-founded. "There is an inertia that simply must be overcome with presidential leadership in all the participant countries."

The Bush administration recognizes the importance of securing Russia's nuclear stockpiles. In 2002, the United States, along with Britain, France, Canada, Japan, Germany and Italy, agreed to spend $20 billion over 10 years to support CTR programs—with half of it, or $1 billion a year, to come from the United States.

But that amounts to only about a quarter of 1 percent of the current Defense Department budget of about $401 billion, Bunn points out. "Amazingly," he adds, despite the new terrorist threats throughout the world, U.S. funding for the CTR programs "hasn't increased noticeably since Sept. 11."

Bunn is not alone. A task force led by former Sen. Howard H. Baker Jr., R-Tenn., and former White House Counsel Lloyd Cutler in January 2001 called for a tripling in annual CTR spending—to $3 billion a year.[8]

Inadequate funding has slowed the pace of securing Russia's nuclear sites, critics say. "We're not doing all that we know how to do and all that we must to keep these weapons and materials safe," Curtis says. After more than a decade of Nunn-Lugar efforts, only half of Russia's nuclear weapons have been adequately secured, Curtis points out.

Critics of the war against Iraq suggest that the campaign to topple Saddam Hussein expended precious resources that could have gone toward halting the spread of nuclear materials. The first order of business in combating nuclear terrorism, Allison says, is to list potential sources of nuclear weapons, in order of priority. "Saddam clearly had nuclear ambitions, and the CIA said that over the course of a decade he might realize them," Allison says. "So he deserved to be on the list somewhere down there, but he wasn't in the top dozen for me."

The nuclear weapons and materials that remain vulnerable to theft in Russia are at the top of Allison's list, primarily because of the magnitude of the problem. "We've still got 120 metric tons of highly enriched uranium and plutonium in Russia alone that we haven't even begun security upgrades on," Curtis points out.

Second on Allison's list is North Korea. By repudiating the Clinton administration's "Agreed Framework" with North Korea and refusing to engage in negotiations with the regime until it renounces its nuclear program, Allison says the Bush administration has allowed "North Korea to just about declare itself a nuclear-weapons state. For the past three years, they have been given a pass. And what have they been doing while they got a pass? They've been creating more plutonium every day, as they are today." Recent six-party talks in Beijing aimed at halting North Korea's nuclear-weapons program ended without significant progress.[9]

Third on Allison's priority list is Pakistan. Because it is not a party to the NPT, Pakistan's nuclear-weapons inventory is unknown. But according to a recent CIA analysis, Pakistan's Khan Research Laboratories has been providing North Korea with nuclear fuel, centrifuges and warhead designs since the early 1990s.[10] No one knows how many other customers Khan supplied over the past decade.

"A coherent strategy has got to deal with the most urgent potential sources of supply to terrorists first," Allison says. "When all this other stuff has been happening, why was Iraq the focus of attention for two years?"

Although no evidence that Iraq had recently pursued nuclear weapons has been found since the United States invaded the country over a year ago, Bush continues to defend his decision to overthrow Hussein's regime in the name of counterproliferation.

"The former dictator of Iraq possessed and used weapons of mass destruction against his own people," Bush said on Feb. 11. "For 12 years, he defied the will of the international community. He refused to disarm or account for his illegal weapons and programs. He doubted our resolve to enforce our word—and now he sits in a prison cell, while his country moves toward a democratic future."

Although Russia and Pakistan are widely regarded as the biggest potential sources of nuclear proliferation, the United States has a mixed record on safeguarding its own nuclear materials. The United States exported highly enriched uranium to 43 countries for nearly four decades as part of the Atoms for Peace program, sanctioned by the NPT, to help other countries acquire nuclear technology for peaceful purposes. The uranium was supposed to be returned to the United States in its original form or as spent fuel. But according to a recent report by the Energy Department's inspector general, the United States has made little headway in recovering the uranium, which is enough to make about 1,000 nuclear weapons.[11]

"While we should be locking up materials at risk wherever we can and recovering them when needed, the Department of Energy has been leisurely pursuing its program to recover highly enriched uranium at risk in research facilities around the world," Curtis says. "This is a leisure that we can ill afford."

Should nonproliferation policy aim to eliminate all nuclear weapons?

Article VI of the NPT requires countries with nuclear weapons to take "effective measures" to end the arms race and work toward nuclear disarmament. This was an essential component of the "grand bargain" used to lure the rest of the world to forgo nuclear arms.

As the sole remaining superpower, the United States plays a key role in leading the world toward disarmament. "Nonproliferation strategies have always been linked to U.S. efforts to reduce reliance on its nuclear forces, so there's always been an arms control link to the NPT as part of the essential bargain," says Curtis of NTI. "The world community also considers it a prerequisite for the United States to exercise its moral leadership on nonproliferation, that it be seen to be living up to its side of that bargain."

During the Cold War, the United States and the Soviet Union, which had amassed vast nuclear arsenals, signed a series of treaties that first limited, and then began to reduce, the number of nuclear weapons on each side.[12] On May 24, 2002, President Bush and Russian

Defusing North Korea and Iran

The good news: Only two so-called rogue nations are suspected of trying to build nuclear weapons. (Libya recently promised to end its bomb-making efforts, and Iraq never was close to having a bomb, U.N. inspectors say.) The bad news: The two rogue nations are North Korea and Iran.

North Korea is considered the more immediate threat. The shaky truce that ended the bloody Korean War (1950-53) has not removed the threat of hostilities between the reclusive, authoritarian regime and U.S.-supported South Korea, which relies on a large U.S. military presence for much of its defense.

Under the 1994 Agreed Framework brokered by President Bill Clinton, North Korea agreed to freeze production of plutonium—needed in the production of some nuclear weapons—in exchange for U.S. energy assistance and improved diplomatic relations. That agreement fell apart in October 2002, when the Bush administration accused North Korean leader Kim Jong Il of trying to enrich uranium in violation of the Non-Proliferation Treaty (NPT).

In January 2003, North Korea withdrew from the NPT and kicked out U.N. International Atomic Energy Agency (IAEA) inspectors. North Korea has continued to deny it has a uranium-enrichment program but openly acknowledges its plutonium program, which may already have produced one or two nuclear weapons.

North Korean leader Kim Jong Il

The most recent talks aimed at ending North Korea's nuclear-weapons ambitions, held in late February 2004 in Beijing, also involved China, Russia, Japan and South Korea. The talks failed to overcome the impasse between the Bush administration, which insists on the "complete, verifiable and irreversible dismantlement " of North Korea's nuclear programs before the United States will agree to improve bilateral relations, provide economic and energy assistance and offer "security guarantees" that it will not invade North Korea.

Prospects for the success of follow-up talks soured further on March 20, when North Korea warned it would expand its nuclear-weapons program if the yearly U.S.-led military exercises in South Korea proceed as scheduled in late March.[1]

Iran's nuclear ambitions raised concern two years ago with the discovery of a large uranium-enrichment plant south of Tehran, the capital. Iran, a signatory to the NPT, claims its nuclear program is used purely to generate electricity. In mid-March, after the IAEA censured Tehran for not fully disclosing its nuclear program, Iran temporarily barred the agency from the country. Inspections were set to resume on March 27.

Meanwhile, IAEA Director Mohamed ElBaradei has appealed to President Bush to launch talks with Iran aimed at improving bilateral relations, which have remained hostile since Islamic clerics wrested control of Iran from the U.S.-supported regime of Shah Mohammed Reza Pahlavi in 1979.

Ending Iran's and North Korea's nuclear ambitions will require convincing both countries that they don't need nuclear weapons to defend themselves, experts say. "To strengthen the international nonproliferation regime, we're going have to provide security assurances as well as economic aid," says Matthew Bunn, a nuclear-weapons expert at Harvard University's Belfer Center for Science and International Affairs. "There's going to have to be some kind of security assurance that the United States isn't going to invade Iran and overthrow its government. That's the center of the discussion with North Korea as well."

Failure to do so may lead to regional arms races that could quickly get out of control. If North Korea produces a nuclear arsenal, predicts John Pike of GlobalSecurity.org, Japan may feel sufficiently threatened to transform some of its civilian power-plant nuclear materials to build nuclear weapons in self-defense. "Then South Korea is going to need them, and Taiwan's going to need them," he says. "That will make China want to have more, which will prompt India to need more, and then Pakistan will, too."

---

[1] United Press International, "N. Korea Warns U.S. over War Exercises," March 20, 2004.

President Vladimir V. Putin signed the latest of these, the Strategic Offensive Reductions Treaty (SORT). It called on the two countries to reduce their current number of strategic nuclear warheads by nearly two-thirds by Dec. 31, 2012—to 1,700-2,200 warheads.

"President Putin and I have signed a treaty that will substantially reduce our strategic nuclear warhead arsenals to . . . the lowest level in decades," Bush declared at the Moscow signing ceremony. "This treaty liquidates the Cold War legacy of nuclear hostility between our countries."

But critics say the so-called Moscow Treaty will be far less effective in ridding the world of nuclear weapons than the president's comments suggest. "The agreement doesn't require the destruction of a single warhead or a single delivery vehicle," says Boese of the Arms Control Association. Warheads that are removed from deployment could be disassembled or stored rather than destroyed. "Also, the agreement's limit is actually in effect for just one day—Dec. 31, 2012," Boese says. "Because neither side has to destroy anything after that day, presumably they could then rebuild their arsenals."

After the Sept. 11 terrorist attacks, the Bush administration toughened U.S. policy on nuclear weapons and other weapons of mass destruction (WMD). The new national strategy to combat nuclear, biological and chemical weapons, issued in December 2002, called for strengthening "traditional measures—diplomacy, arms control, multilateral agreements, threat-reduction assistance and export controls." But for the first time, the United States openly warned that it would pre-emptively attack adversaries thought to be preparing to use weapons of mass destruction against the United States.

"U.S. military forces . . . must have the capability to defend against WMD-armed adversaries, including, in appropriate cases, through pre-emptive measures," the administration declared. "This requires capabilities to detect and destroy an adversary's WMD assets before these weapons are used."[13]

Meanwhile, the administration's latest Nuclear Posture Review, sent to Congress on Dec. 31, 2001, called for research into new types of nuclear weapons and outlined new uses for them.[14] As part of that policy, the administration has initiated research into the "bunker buster," a missile armed with a low-yield (less than five kilotons) nuclear warhead designed to penetrate and destroy enemy arsenals or other targets buried deep underground. To enable research to proceed, Congress last year overturned a Clinton-era ban on research and development of low-yield nuclear weapons.[15]

"The reason it was important to reduce or get rid of the prohibition on low-yield nuclear weapons was not because we're trying to develop or are developing low-yield nuclear weapons," said National Nuclear Security Administrator Linton Brooks. "That's a misconception. . . . What we said was that the amendment was poorly drawn and it prohibited research that could lead to a low-yield nuclear weapon."[16] In fact, research on high-powered "bunker buster" bombs commenced in 2003, after Congress overturned the ban.[17]

Since taking office, the administration has rejected arms control as an essential tool for reducing the nuclear threat. Shortly after being sworn into office, Bush said he would not resubmit the 1996 Comprehensive Test Ban Treaty to the Senate for ratification. He also abrogated the 1972 U.S.-Soviet Anti-Ballistic Missile Treaty, which barred signatories from building national defense systems to protect against ballistic-missile attack—a move designed to discourage the superpowers from building more nuclear weapons to overcome such defenses.

Bush instead announced he would pursue earlier plans to build a National Missile Defense System while seeking a "new strategic framework" for dealing with Russia that would focus on reductions in nuclear weapons.[18] The first U.S. anti-missile defense facility, scheduled for deployment in Alaska this summer, has faced criticism for its technical flaws and for undermining the United States' credibility as a strong advocate of nuclear disarmament.[19]

"The current U.S. approach to proliferation emphasizes non-treaty methods and military means, including the effort to deploy a national missile defense system," said John Cirincione, director for nonproliferation at the Carnegie Endowment for International Peace. "The system faces formidable technical challenges and is unlikely to be militarily effective anytime in this decade. Every system within the missile-defense program is behind schedule, over budget and underperforming."[20]

While supporters of the administration's nuclear policy say the changes were needed to protect the United States in a new era of uncertainty, critics say they undermine the administration's credibility in its calls to strengthen global anti-proliferation measures.

"If you're trying to build a consensus [on halting proliferation] while at the same time saying we need a few more different nuclear weapons, I would say those are inconsistent arguments," Allison says. "I've negotiated on behalf of the U.S. government many times when I felt I had a weak hand, but I couldn't imagine keeping a straight face in trying to argue these two goals at the same time."

BACKGROUND

Manhattan Project

The nuclear age traces its origins to 1938, when scientists in Nazi Germany split the nucleus of a uranium atom, releasing heat and radiation. The potential of nuclear fission, as the process was called, to produce weapons of unparalleled power prompted a recent refugee from Germany—Albert Einstein—to alert President Franklin D. Roosevelt. "[T]he element uranium may be turned into a new and important source of energy in the immediate future," the already-legendary physicist wrote. ["T]his new phenomenon," he added, could lead "to the construction of bombs . . ., extremely powerful bombs of a new type."[21]

In 1939, even before the United States entered World War II or realized the full implications of Einstein's warning, Roosevelt established the first federal uranium-research program. Fission research led to further advances, including the 1940 discovery of the element plutonium by physicists at the University of California, Berkeley. After the United States entered the war against Japan, Germany and Italy in December, the race to beat Germany in developing an atomic bomb accelerated under a secret Army Corps of Engineers program known as the Manhattan Project.*

By September 1944, after less than two years of work, Manhattan Project researchers had begun producing plutonium for weapons. On July 16, 1945, they detonated an experimental atomic bomb known as "the Gadget" from a tower in the New Mexico desert. Less than three weeks later, on Aug. 6, U.S. airmen dropped an atom bomb nicknamed "Little Boy" on Hiroshima, followed on Aug. 9 by the detonation of "Fat Man" over Nagasaki.

Two days later, Japan surrendered. World War II was over and the "Atomic Age" had begun. Within weeks of the bombings, the death toll had climbed to more than 100,000 people—mainly civilians.

The enormous loss of civilian lives sparked intense debate over the future of atomic weapons. The Manhattan Project cost the U.S. government almost $20 billion (in today's dollars), including the construction of reactors and lab facilities at more than 30 sites, such as Los Alamos, N.M., Oak Ridge, Tenn., and Hanford, Wash. In 1946, the American representative to the newly created United Nations Atomic Energy Commission, Bernard M. Baruch, proposed the elimination of atomic weapons, but the Soviet Union rejected the proposal. In 1947, Congress replaced the Manhattan Project with the civilian Atomic Energy Commission, which assumed control over atomic research and weapons facilities around the country.

The postwar deterioration of relations with the Soviet Union effectively ended the nuclear debate in the United States and prompted the administration of President Harry S Truman to intensify production of nuclear weapons, especially the next generation of more powerful, thermonuclear weapons. The first Soviet atomic bomb test and the rise of communism in China in 1949, followed the next year by the outbreak of the Korean War, fueled U.S. policymakers' support of the weapons program. By the early 1950s, both sides in the rapidly escalating Cold War had developed hydrogen bombs.

With momentum building for still more nuclear research, calls to abandon the new technology ran into resistance from those promoting nuclear power as a cheap, virtually inexhaustible source of energy. Fission releases large amounts of heat, which can be harnessed to power a steam turbine to generate electricity.

On Dec. 8, 1953, President Dwight D. Eisenhower presented his "Atoms for Peace" proposal to the United Nations, calling for creation of an international atomic energy agency "to devise methods whereby this fissionable material would be allocated to serve the peaceful pursuits of mankind."

The Soviet Union beat the United States in the race to introduce nuclear power, starting up the world's first plant in 1954. With federal support and AEC oversight, General Electric, Westinghouse Electric and other U.S. companies invested heavily in the new technology. On May 26, 1958, Eisenhower opened the first U.S. nuclear power plant, at Shippingport, Pa.

---

* Atomic weapons get their energy from the fission, or breaking apart, of the nucleus of an atom of uranium or plutonium. Hydrogen—or thermonuclear—weapons get their energy largely from fusion, the formation of a heavier nucleus from two lighter ones. Both types of weapons are known collectively as nuclear weapons.

C H R O N O L O G Y

1930s-1980s *Atomic Age begins and evolves into the Cold War.*

1938 Scientists in Nazi Germany split the nucleus of a uranium atom. A year later, the U.S. Manhattan Project enters the race to create an atomic bomb.

Aug. 6, 1945 U.S. drops an atomic bomb on Hiroshima, Japan, followed on Aug. 9 by another on Nagasaki, killing a total of more than 250,000 people. Two days later, Japan surrenders, ending World War II.

1949 The Soviet Union tests its first atomic weapon.

Dec. 8, 1953 President Dwight D. Eisenhower's "Atoms for Peace" proposal calls for using fissionable material "to serve the peaceful pursuits of mankind."

1957 International Atomic Energy Agency (IAEA) is created to promote peaceful use of nuclear energy.

May 26, 1958 Eisenhower opens first U.S. nuclear power plant, at Shippingport, Pa.

1964 China joins the United States, Soviet Union, Britain and France in the "nuclear club" of officially recognized nuclear-weapons states.

July 1, 1968 Nuclear Non-Proliferation Treaty (NPT) is signed by 98 countries after a decade of talks.

1969 Treaty of Tlatelolco bars nuclear weapons from Latin America. Brazil and Argentina are the last nations to sign, in the 1990s.

1981 Israel destroys an Iraqi nuclear reactor, claiming it was being used to produce fuel for weapons.

1990s *Cold War ends, posing new proliferation threats.*

1991 Soviet Union collapses. . . . Persian Gulf War against Iraq, an NPT signatory, reveals that Saddam Hussein had been trying to develop nuclear weapons. . . . Soviet Nuclear Threat Reduction Act sponsored by Sens. Sam Nunn, D-Ga., and Richard G. Lugar, R-Ind., authorizes the United States to help former Soviet-bloc countries destroy nuclear, chemical and biological weapons and establishes verifiable safeguards against their proliferation.

1993 Nunn-Lugar program is broadened and renamed the Cooperative Threat Reduction (CTR) program. . . . South Africa becomes first country with nuclear weapons to renounce its nuclear program and join the NPT.

October 1994 North Korea agrees to freeze its plutonium production in exchange for U.S. assistance in producing energy.

1996 President Bill Clinton signs the Comprehensive Test Ban Treaty.

1998 India and Pakistan join Israel on the list of non-NPT signatories with nuclear weapons.

2000s *Massive terrorist attacks raise the specter of nuclear terrorism.*

Sept. 11, 2001 Suicide airline hijackers linked to Osama bin Laden's al Qaeda terrorist group kill nearly 3,000 people in the worst terrorist attacks in U.S. history.

2002 President Bush disavows the U.S. pact with North Korea and calls on Kim Jong Il to renounce his nuclear ambitions as a condition of the resumption of U.S. aid.

March 19, 2003 U.S. troops invade Iraq but find no weapons of mass destruction.

Dec. 19, 2003 Libya agrees to terminate its nuclear-weapons program, revealing evidence of a Pakistan-based black market in nuclear technology.

Feb. 6, 2004 Pakistani President Pervez Musharraf pardons Abdul Qadeer Khan, founder of Pakistan's nuclear-weapons program, for selling nuclear technology to Iran, North Korea, Libya and possibly others.

Feb. 11, 2004 President Bush responds to the revelations about Khan's network with a seven-point plan to strengthen the NPT and IAEA's enforcement powers.

Fall of a Nuclear Black Marketeer

As A. Q. Khan tells it, the horrors of religious intolerance he witnessed as a 10-year-old Muslim in India turned him into the world's leading black-market merchant of nuclear-bomb materials.[1]

"I can remember trains coming into the station full of dead Muslims," Khan recalled recently, describing the sectarian violence that broke out in Bhopal following Indian independence from Britain. "The [Hindu] Indian authorities were treating the Muslims horribly."[2]

Six years later, Khan fled north to the newly independent Islamic nation of Pakistan. But the slaughter he had seen as a youngster left Khan with an enduring enmity toward India and shaped his life's work, spurring him to develop Pakistan's nuclear bomb.

In the 1960s, Khan pursued postgraduate studies in metallurgy in Western Europe and later worked in the Netherlands at a uranium-enrichment plant run by Urenco, a Dutch-British-German consortium. There he learned about uranium enrichment and the design of sophisticated centrifuges needed to produce weapons-grade nuclear fuel.

Khan reportedly smuggled Urenco's centrifuge designs into Pakistan in the mid-1970s after Prime Minister Zulfikar Ali Bhutto invited him to establish the country's nuclear-weapons program. A Dutch court in 1983 convicted him in absentia of attempted espionage for stealing the designs, but the conviction was overturned.

As the director of Pakistan's nuclear program, Khan became adept at procuring equipment and technology—both legally and on the black market—and did little to conceal his activities. He even published a brochure with a photo of himself and a list of nuclear materials available for sale or barter, including intermediate-range ballistic missiles. Investigators say Khan's network stretched from Europe to Turkey, Russia and Malaysia. Khan himself traveled to North Korea at least 13 times to swap his nuclear technology for Korean missile technology, and U.N. inspectors have discovered documents in Iraq suggesting that he offered to help Saddam Hussein build a nuclear weapon in 1990, just before the first Gulf War.[3]

By 1998, when India first tested nuclear devices, Khan was quick to follow suit. Now the bitter adversaries were both in the "nuclear club."

Khan became an instant hero to Pakistanis, whose hatred of India permeates the national culture. Schools, streets and children were named after him. Indeed, most Pakistanis appeared forgiving when Khan confessed in February following revelations he had illegally supplied nuclear technology to North Korea, Libya and Iran.

But Khan's admissions—and the fact that he was not punished for selling nuclear secrets to rogue states—infuriated

[1] Unless otherwise noted, information in this section is based on Peter Grier, Faye Bowers and Owais Tohid, "Pakistan's Nuclear Hero, World's No. 1 Nuclear Suspect," *The Christian Science Monitor*, Feb. 2, 2004.

[2] Khan was interviewed by the Human Development Foundation, an expatriate Pakistani group in Shaumburg, Ill., www.yespakistan.com.

[3] "The Black Marketeer," "Nightline," ABC News, March 8, 2004.

For the next 20 years—until the partial meltdown at Pennsylvania's Three Mile Island nuclear plant in 1979 and the catastrophic accident at the Soviet plant at Chernobyl in 1986—nuclear power accounted for a growing percentage of the world's electricity.

Today nuclear power accounts for 16 percent of global electricity generated at some 440 plants in 30 countries.[22] A handful of countries depend on nuclear power for more than half of their electricity, but only about 20 percent of the power generated in the United States comes from nuclear reactors.

Nonproliferation Efforts

Eisenhower's Atoms for Peace proposal bore fruit in 1957, when the IAEA was established as an independent U.N. body charged with promoting the peaceful use of nuclear energy. The agency was responsible for inspecting nuclear research facilities and power plants to ensure that they were not being used to build nuclear weapons.[23]

It already was becoming clear, however, that stronger measures were needed to prevent nuclear proliferation. Britain, which had participated in the U.S. nuclear development program, tested its first nuclear device in 1952 and quickly built several hundred warheads. France developed its nuclear capability independently and began building a nuclear arsenal in 1960. In 1964, China tested its first nuclear weapon, becoming the fifth and last nuclear-weapon state recognized under the NPT.

Faced with the prospect of dozens more countries acquiring the bomb within a few decades, the United

many Americans and others in the West. "It sends a horrible signal," said David Albright, president of the Institute for Science and International Security, a nonpartisan think tank dedicated to educating the public on scientific issues affecting international security. "It basically says, 'Yeah, your wrists will be slapped, but, boy, you're going to make millions of dollars.' "[4]

Khan professes bewilderment at the outrage his proliferation activities have engendered. "They dislike me and accuse me of all kinds of unsubstantiated and fabricated lies because I disturbed all their strategic plans, the balance of power and blackmailing potential in this part of the world," he said. "I am not a madman or a nut. . . . I consider myself a humble, patriotic Pakistani who gave his best for his country."

Indeed, while Islamic extremism is rising in Pakistan, the moderate Khan is married to a Dutch national, and neither

Pakistani nuclear scientist Abdul Qadeer Khan

AFP Photo

she nor their daughters wear the veil typically worn by conservative Muslims.

Kahn's enduring popularity helps explain why Pakistani President Pervez Musharraf pardoned him— and why the Bush administration accepted Musharraf's claim that he knew nothing of Khan's illicit activities. Others say the United States did not push Musharraf to punish Khan because of a deal in which Pakistan would help U.S. troops find terrorist leader Osama bin Laden, thought to be hiding in Pakistan's northwest territories (*see p. 86*).

(see p. 86)

"They correctly judged that the United States would blow hot and cold on the question of nuclear proliferation, depending on the temper of the times," says defense-policy analyst John Pike, director of Global-Security.org, a nonprofit organization studying emerging security threats. "Blaming the black market all on A.Q. Khan and letting Musharraf say he had no idea what was going on is just a way for everybody to have their cake and eat it, too."

[4] *Ibid*

States and 17 other countries began talks in 1958 aimed at halting the further spread of nuclear weapons. A proposal by Ireland envisioned a commitment by all nuclear-weapons states not to provide the technology to other countries. In theory, non-nuclear countries would benefit from such an arrangement because it would ensure that their neighbors would also remain nuclear-free. But non-nuclear states called for more incentives to accept this permanent state of military inferiority.

In 1968, after a decade of negotiations, 98 countries signed the Nuclear Non-Proliferation Treaty (NPT). The agreement recognized the original five nuclear-weapons states—the United States, the Soviet Union, France, the United Kingdom and China—defined as countries that had "manufactured and exploded a

nuclear weapon or other nuclear explosive device prior to 1 January 1967." The IAEA was charged with monitoring compliance with the treaty. Countries that signed the treaty agreed to refrain from producing, obtaining or stockpiling nuclear weapons.

The treaty expanded on the Irish resolution by offering more incentives to refrain from building nuclear weapons. The nuclear states agreed to help other countries develop civilian nuclear power plants and also, under Article X, to take "effective measures" to end the arms race and work toward nuclear disarmament.

But the treaty set no timetables for disarmament, enabling the nuclear powers to keep their arsenals virtually indefinitely. The NPT's Article X contains another important loophole—it allows signatories to withdraw

AP Photo/Wade Payne

Components from Libya's nuclear weapons program are displayed by Secretary of Energy Spencer Abraham at the Y-12 National Security Complex in Oak Ridge, Tenn., on March 15, 2004. Libyan leader Muammar el-Qaddafi ended the country's isolation by renouncing weapons of mass destruction and joining the world nonproliferation regime.

from the treaty without penalty for unspecified "supreme interests."

With 188 parties, the NPT has the broadest support of any arms control treaty. Only three countries—India, Israel and Pakistan—have not signed the pact and are believed to possess finished nuclear weapons or components that could be rapidly assembled. Israel began developing its nuclear capability in the 1950s with French assistance. The United States has refrained from pressing its chief Middle Eastern ally on its nuclear program, and Israel has never acknowledged its arsenal, thought to number 98-172 warheads. In 1998, India and Pakistan—engaged in a longstanding border dispute—acknowledged their nuclear status. Both India with (50-90 warheads) and Pakistan (30-50 warheads) are believed to store their nuclear weapons in the form of separate components that can be assembled at short notice.[24]

Over the past decade, the international nonproliferation regime has scored some important successes. In the 1990s, Argentina and Brazil agreed to abandon their nuclear-weapons ambitions, signed the NPT and became the last two Latin American countries to sign the 1969 Treaty of Tlatelolco, which barred nuclear weapons from the 33-nation region. After the Soviet Union's collapse, the former Soviet republics of Belarus, Kazakhstan and Ukraine voluntarily relinquished to Russia all the nuclear weapons Moscow had deployed on their territory

during the Cold War. And, in 1993, after the fall of apartheid, South Africa became the first nuclear-armed country to voluntarily dismantle its entire nuclear-weapons program.

Mushrooming Nukes

For all the NPT's success in containing nuclear weapons, it has failed to keep non-signatories, and even some "renegade states" that signed the treaty, from pursuing nuclear capabilities. Almost as soon as it signed the NPT in 1968, Iraq began developing nuclear weapons with help from France and Italy, presumably to counter Israel's arsenal. Israel destroyed an Iraqi reactor in 1981, claiming it was being used to produce fuel for weapons. Nevertheless, Iraq continued its clandestine program, as weapons inspectors discovered upon entering Iraq after its defeat in the 1991 Gulf War.

After the war, U.S.-led condemnation of Iraq's nuclear-weapons program resulted in U.N. sanctions that prohibited trade with Iraq. The sanctions were later eased to allow Iraq to sell a limited amount of oil to buy food and medical supplies, but by the end of the 1990s, Iraq was in the throes of an economic crisis.

Although the Bush administration cited evidence that Iraq had continued its nuclear-weapons program to justify last year's invasion and toppling of Hussein, recent inspections have turned up no signs Hussein was pursuing nuclear weapons. "It turns out we were all wrong," said former weapons inspector David Kay of U.S. suspicions that Iraq possessed weapons of mass destruction. "And that is most disturbing."[25]

Another NPT "renegade," North Korea is considered to pose a far greater risk. A party to the NPT since 1985, North Korea launched a clandestine nuclear program centered on production of plutonium, which could be used to make nuclear weapons. Although North Korea insisted that its program was intended only to generate electricity, in 1993 it barred IAEA inspectors from viewing its facilities, precipitating a crisis in the nonproliferation regime. In October 1994, the Clinton administration brokered an "Agreed Framework," whereby North Korea agreed to freeze plutonium production in exchange for U.S. assistance to compensate for any energy lost due to the reactor shutdown. President Bush disavowed the pact in 2002 as bowing to nuclear blackmail and called on North Korea's Kim Jong Il to renounce his nuclear ambitions as a condition of resuming aid to the impoverished country.

Concerned that nuclear weapons or weapons-grade materials might fall into the hands of renegade states or terrorist groups, the United States, the Soviet Union and 38 other countries with nuclear technology established the Nuclear Suppliers Group in 1985, agreeing to control exports of civilian nuclear material and related technology to non-nuclear-weapon states. And to restrict the proliferation of nuclear-capable missiles, the United States and six other countries in 1987 set up the Missile Technology Control Regime, a voluntary agreement that has since been expanded to more than 30 countries.

The collapse of the Soviet Union signaled the end of both the Cold War and the nuclear standoff dominated by the military doctrine of mutual assured destruction But the post-Cold War peace, welcome as it was, ushered in a new era of uncertainty in which concern over nuclear proliferation took the place of superpower nuclear brinkmanship. The resulting economic and political upheavals left Russia—the Soviet successor state—poorly equipped to maintain security over the vast nuclear arsenal it inherited.

Recognizing the proliferation risk posed by Russia's arsenal, Congress passed the so-called Nunn-Lugar measure. Since it became law in 1991, the United States has helped Russia deactivate some 6,000 nuclear warheads, retrain 22,000 nuclear-weapons scientists and remove all the nuclear weapons deployed in the former Soviet republics of Belarus, Kazakhstan and Ukraine. Nunn-Lugar also has helped destroy hundreds of Soviet missiles, seal nuclear test facilities and dismantle submarine-based nuclear warheads.

CURRENT SITUATION

Black Market Revealed

A.Q. Khan's black market in nuclear weapons and materials began to unravel on Dec. 19, 2003, when Libya told the United States and Britain it would terminate its nuclear-weapons program. Although the North African country had not developed warheads, it was found to have imported numerous key components, including sophisticated centrifuges needed to enrich uranium into fuel for bombs.

The Bush administration claims much of the credit for this unexpected victory in the fight against nuclear proliferation. "The success of our mission in Libya underscores

the success of this administration's broader nonproliferation efforts around the world," said Energy Secretary Spencer Abraham at a special press tour of seized Libyan nuclear materials and equipment on display at the department's Oak Ridge labs on March 15. "What you have witnessed represents a big, big victory in the administration's efforts to combat weapons of mass destruction."

Administration critics dispute this claim, citing reports that Libyan leader Muammar el-Qaddafi had been convinced by his son and presumptive heir, 31-year-old Saif al-Islam Qaddafi, to end the country's isolation by renouncing weapons of mass destruction and joining the world nonproliferation regime.[26] Libya has suffered severe economic privation since coming under U.N.-sponsored economic sanctions for its involvement in the 1988 bombing of a Pan-Am flight over Lockerbie, Scotland, which killed 270 people.

U.N. sanctions, imposed in 1992, were lifted in September 2003, after Libya accepted responsibility for the bombing and agreed to pay $2.7 billion in compensation to families of the Pan Am victims. Although the Bush administration lifted a ban on travel to Libya after it renounced its nuclear program, other U.S. economic sanctions remain in place.[27]

"Muammar's son thought his dad had run the country into a ditch," says Pike of GlobalSecurity.Org. "But

Vehicles entering the United States from Canada pass through radiation detectors at the Blaine, Wash., border crossing. Experts say terrorists are far more likely to deploy a small, easily transported conventional explosive device containing radioactive waste—a so-called dirty bomb—than to explode a nuclear bomb.

when the dynastic handoff of a country from father to son becomes the primary determinant of our disarmament success, then we're running on a pretty thin reed."

When they entered Libyan facilities in January, IAEA inspectors said they discovered crates of nuclear equipment that only could have come from sources with advanced nuclear programs of their own. Subsequent investigations uncovered a complex web of international transactions that led to a factory in Malaysia, transshipment facilities in Dubai, an intercepted cargo ship in Italy, shipments to Iran and ultimately to Khan himself. In January, after acknowledging his role in establishing the nuclear black market, Khan was pardoned by Pakistani President Pervez Musharraf, who claimed he knew nothing of Khan's undercover business.

Nuclear experts dismiss Musharraf's disavowal as ludicrous. Khan's prominent role as the father of Pakistan's nuclear arsenal made him a highly visible national hero who made no attempt to conceal his lavish lifestyle in his impoverished country and who actually had published brochures describing nuclear materials and equipment that were for sale from his lab for more than a decade.

"The pattern of activity was at such a large scale that it's inconceivable that the Pakistani government didn't know about this all along," Pike says. "It's like asking me to believe that [U.S. nuclear pioneer] Ed Teller was secretly selling hydrogen bombs out of the back of a pickup truck."

But the Bush administration did not question Musharraf's disavowal of knowledge about Khan's activities. Since the Pakistani leader emerged as an outspoken ally of the United States in its war on terrorism after Sept. 11, the administration clearly has been loath to undermine his standing in an Islamic country where anti-American feelings and support for al Qaeda run high. Musharraf has narrowly escaped two assassination attempts, attributed to al Qaeda, in recent months.[28]

Moreover, the Bush administration needs Musharraf's cooperation in order to find al Qaeda leader Osama bin Laden—considered by some to be the mastermind of the 9/11 attacks—and his top lieutenants. Some observers suggest that the Bush administration decided to accept Musharraf's denial of knowledge about Khan's network in exchange for permission for U.S. forces to enter the rugged area on the Pakistani side of the border with Afghanistan, believed to be a key stronghold of al Qaeda

militants and possibly bin Laden himself.[29] Up to now, U.S. forces have had to limit their searches to the Afghan side of the border.

Although administration spokesmen deny the existence of such a deal, American military officials have announced plans for a "spring initiative" on the Afghan side of the border.[30] Already, signs are emerging that an offensive is under way. On March 16, on the eve of a visit to Pakistan by Secretary of State Colin L. Powell, Pakistani troops suffered numerous casualties in gun battles in the border region.[31]

Bush's Response

President Bush responded to the revelations about Khan's network with a seven-point plan to strengthen the NPT and IAEA's enforcement powers. On Feb. 11, the president called for the expansion of his Proliferation Security Initiative, a year-old international effort to seize nuclear materials on the high seas while in transit to or from rogue states. In 1999 and 2000, years before Bush's initiative, Indian and British authorities seized two North Korean shipments of missile components and related equipment en route to Libya.[32]

Bush also called on the U.N. Security Council to adopt a resolution requiring all states to criminalize proliferation of components that could be used to make weapons of mass destruction and to strengthen export controls on them. And he proposed expanding U.S. efforts to secure Russia's nuclear weapons and materials under the Nunn-Lugar program.

In addition, Bush called for closing the loophole in the NPT that allows aspirants to the nuclear club to enrich and reprocess fuel used in civilian nuclear reactors and proposed that only signatories of the Additional Protocol be allowed to import equipment for civilian reactors. To strengthen the IAEA, Bush proposed a new measure to beef up the agency's safeguards and verification powers. Finally, he recommended barring countries being investigated for alleged NPT violations from holding positions of influence in the IAEA.

"We've shown that proliferators can be discovered and can be stopped," Bush said. "Terrorists and terror states are in a race for weapons of mass murder, a race they must lose."

Weapons analysts praised Bush's recommendations. "It was a very important speech," says Curtis of the Nuclear Threat Initiative. "It addressed a number of

AT ISSUE

Will U.S. policies keep nuclear weapons away from terrorists?

YES President George W. Bush

From a speech at the National Defense University, Feb. 11, 2004

On Sept. 11, 2001, America and the world witnessed a new kind of war. We saw the great harm that a stateless network could inflict upon our country, killers armed with box cutters, mace and 19 airline tickets. Those attacks also raised the prospect of even worse dangers—of other weapons in the hands of other men. The greatest threat before humanity today is the possibility of secret and sudden attack with chemical or biological or radiological or nuclear weapons. . . .

America, and the entire civilized world, will face this threat for decades to come. We must confront the danger with open eyes, and unbending purpose. I have made clear to all the policy of this nation: America will not permit terrorists and dangerous regimes to threaten us with the world's most deadly weapons. . . .

We're determined to confront those threats at the source. We will stop these weapons from being acquired or built. We'll block them from being transferred. We'll prevent them from ever being used. One source of these weapons is dangerous and secretive regimes that build weapons of mass destruction to intimidate their neighbors and force their influence upon the world. These nations pose different challenges; they require different strategies. . . .

I propose to expand our efforts to keep weapons from the Cold War and other dangerous materials out of the wrong hands. In 1991, Congress passed the Nunn-Lugar legislation. Sen. [Richard] Lugar had a clear vision, along with Sen. [Sam] Nunn, about what to do with the old Soviet Union. Under this program, we're helping former Soviet states find productive employment for former weapons scientists. We're dismantling, destroying and securing weapons and materials left over from the Soviet . . . arsenal. . . .

Over the last two years, a great coalition has come together to defeat terrorism and to oppose the spread of weapons of mass destruction—the inseparable commitments of the war on terror. We've shown that proliferators can be discovered and can be stopped. We've shown that for regimes that choose defiance, there are serious consequences. The way ahead is not easy, but it is clear. We will proceed as if the lives of our citizens depend on our vigilance, because they do.

Terrorists and terror states are in a race for weapons of mass murder, a race they must lose. Terrorists are resourceful; we're more resourceful. They're determined; we must be more determined. We will never lose focus or resolve. We'll be unrelenting in the defense of free nations, and rise to the hard demands of dangerous times.

NO Natural Resources Defense Council

From a statement, Feb. 12, 2004, www.nrdc.org.

Nunn-Lugar funds are not being used to "dismantle and destroy" Russian nuclear weapons (as opposed to missile silos and obsolete strategic bombers and submarines). In fact, the recently signed Moscow Treaty between the United States and Russia allows Russia to keep SS-18 "heavy" strategic ballistic missile systems that would otherwise have been destroyed under the START II and START III treaties.

Despite years of cooperation, the United States still has no firm idea of how many and which types of Russian nuclear warheads and bombs have been dismantled. As former Sen. Sam Nunn has indicated, the Nunn-Lugar program suffers from inadequate funding. President Bush cites the 2002 G-8 Summit agreement to provide $20 billion over 10 years, but even here the participating countries used accounting tricks to avoid increasing previous commitments. Moreover, some of this money is earmarked to build a plutonium fuel-fabrication plant in Russia that many observers believe will increase the potential that plutonium will be diverted and used for illicit purposes.

President Bush so far has refused to commit to destroying more than a few hundred of the more than 10,000 nuclear weapons still in the United States' nuclear weapons stockpile. The Strategic Offensive Reduction Treaty (SORT) negotiated with Russia in 2002—the Moscow Treaty—does not require the elimination of a single nuclear missile silo, submarine, missile warhead, bomber or bomb. . .

President Bush failed to address the longer-term problem, and long-term proliferation pressures, arising from a world permanently and inequitably divided into declared nuclear weapons states under the Non-Proliferation Treaty (NPT), de-facto nuclear weapon states outside the treaty (India, Pakistan and Israel), nonweapon states that have abandoned the treaty (North Korea) and states with varying degrees of nuclear expertise (Iran) that are presently bound by their treaty commitment not to acquire nuclear weapons but could elect to withdraw from the NPT at any time.

Nor did President Bush discuss how and when the United States and other nuclear weapon states would take further steps to fulfill their Non-Proliferation Treaty commitments to eliminate their nuclear arsenals. On the contrary, the Bush administration is spending record amounts revitalizing the U.S. nuclear weapons complex. . . .

There are two distinct kinds of threats facing the United States, one having to do with the proliferation of [weapons of mass destruction] by nation states and the second with threats posed by terrorists. The president's proposals focused on threats posed by the spread of nuclear weapons, materials and technologies to nation states rather than those by terrorists.

areas that require U.S. leadership and international cooperation."

But Curtis also says the United States needs to do more to dispel the perception that it holds itself to a different standard than the rest of the world regarding proliferation. "Missing from the speech was some meaningful initiative on addressing the strategic nuclear weapons that the United States and Russia still maintain in very large numbers and, under the Treaty of Moscow, may retain into the indefinite future," Curtis says.

To others, Bush's speech exemplified the administration's unilateral approach to pursuing U.S. interests. "President Bush's speech was a series of measures that would constrain everybody else," says Bunn of Harvard's Belfer Center. "There was no mention of anything that would constrain the United States."

In Pike's view, the Bush administration's nuclear policies have left the United States with few viable options. "Right now, our declaratory policy is one of attacks to disarm our enemies' weapons infrastructure, followed up by military invasion and regime change," he says. That's the policy that led to the war in Iraq, which did not yet possess nuclear weapons. But the same policy cannot be applied to a state like North Korea, which may harbor nuclear weapons, for fear of igniting a global holocaust. "So we have an extraordinarily alarming declaratory policy that's basically frightened the living daylights out of the rest of humanity, [but which] we're not prepared to implement. That puts us in the worst of all possible worlds."

OUTLOOK

Crumbling Coalition?

The March 11 bombing of commuter trains in Madrid has lent further urgency to the international war on terrorism. Ten separate explosions at the rush hour ripped through the trains, killing more than 190 commuters and wounding some 1,400.[33] After initially blaming Basque separatists for the attacks, the government announced two days later that it had arrested five people with suspected links to al Qaeda.

The next day, March 14, Spaniards went to the polls and removed Prime Minister José Maria Aznar, a staunch U.S. ally in the war against terrorism, from office. Spain's new leader, Socialist José Luis Rodríguez Zapatero, renewed Spain's commitment to fight terror-

ism. But he promised to fulfill a campaign pledge to withdraw Spain's 1,300-man contingent of peacekeepers in Iraq by June 30. He is one of Europe's most outspoken critics of the war.

Calling the occupation of Iraq "a fiasco," Zapatero has outlined an approach to fighting terrorism that relies on international cooperation, which he says differs sharply from the administration's tactic. "Fighting terrorism with Tomahawk missiles isn't the way to defeat terrorism," he said. "I will listen to Mr. Bush, but my position is very clear and very firm. . . . Terrorism is combated by the [rule] of law."[34]

Zapatero may be expressing the views of more than a demoralized Spanish electorate. According to a new international survey, opposition to the war in Iraq and U.S. international policies has intensified in Europe. A growing percentage of Europeans polled said they want to distance their fate from the United States by adopting independent foreign and security policies through the European Union. More than half support a European foreign policy independent from that of the United States. Even in Britain, the administration's strongest war on terrorism ally, support for an independent European foreign policy has risen from 47 percent in April 2002 to 56 percent in the current poll.[35]

The Bush administration has downplayed any notion of a rift between the United States and its European allies. "We don't think countries face a choice—being European or being trans-Atlantic," said an administration official following Secretary of State Powell's March 24 trip to Spain to attend a memorial service for victims of the Madrid bombing. "All of us, especially in the NATO alliance, are almost by definition both. . . . European nations don't have to choose between good relations with Europe and good relations with the United States."

Foiling Nuclear Terror

The Madrid bombing—the worst incident of terrorist violence in Europe since the Pan Am bombing—coming as it did on the heels of the exposure of Khan's nuclear-smuggling network, will likely intensify debate over how to deal with the threat of nuclear terrorism. Bin Laden has made no secret of his desire to use a nuclear bomb as the ultimate weapon against the West, and weapons experts say events are fast outpacing policies deigned to avert such a catastrophe.

"The Bush administration and the president himself have rightly said that the ultimate specter is al Qaeda with a nuclear weapon," says Harvard's Allison. "But this administration has no coherent strategy for preventing nuclear terrorism. That's a pretty serious charge, but I think it's correct."

Administration supporters reject that view. "President Bush has transported the fight the terrorists began back to their land," wrote former Sen. Alfonse M. D'Amato, R-N.Y. "He refuses to allow them to contaminate our soil with their hatred. He has stood firm in the face of the terrorist threat, despite constant harping from critics who would second-guess his leadership."[36]

Still, IAEA Director General ElBaradei paints a grim picture of nuclear proliferation's future and calls for a revolutionary overhaul of international systems and policies to prevent nuclear terrorism. "Eventually, inevitably, terrorists will gain access to such materials and technology, if not actual weapons," he wrote. "If the world does not change course, we risk self destruction."

ElBaradei calls for globalization of worldwide security. "We must abandon the traditional approach of defining security in terms of boundaries—city walls, border patrols, racial and religious groupings," he wrote recently in *The New York Times*. "The global community has become irreversibly interdependent, with the constant movement of people, ideas, goods and resources.

"In such a world, we must combat terrorism with an infectious security culture that crosses borders—an inclusive approach to security based on solidarity and the value of human life. In such a world, weapons of mass destruction will have no place."[37]

NOTES

1. See Ellen Nakashima and Alan Sipress, "Insider Tells of Nuclear Deals, Cash," *The Washington Post*, Feb. 21, 2004, p. A1.

2. For background, see Mary H. Cooper, "Non-Proliferation Treaty at 25," *The CQ Researcher*, Jan. 27, 1995, pp. 73-96.

3. From a speech at the National Defense University in Washington, D.C., Feb. 11, 2004.

4. For background, see Mary H. Cooper, "Hating America," *The CQ Researcher*, Nov. 23, 2001, pp. 969-992, and David Masci and Kenneth Jost, "War on Terrorism," *The CQ Researcher*, Oct. 12, 2001, pp. 817-840.

5. See Michael A. Levi and Henry C. Kelly, "Weapons of Mass Disruption," *Scientific American*, November 2002, pp. 76-81.

6. ElBaradei spoke at IAEA headquarter in Vienna, Feb. 5, 2004. See Peter Slevin, "U.N. Nuclear Chief Warns of Global Black Market," *The Washington Post*, Feb. 6, 2004, p. A18.

7. For a detailed description, see Graham Allison, "How to Stop Nuclear Terrorism," *Foreign Affairs*, January/February 2004, pp. 64-74.

8. Howard Baker and Lloyd Cutler, "A Report Card on the Department Of Energy's Nonproliferation Programs with Russia," Jan. 10, 2001.

9. See Steven R. Weisman, "Lasting Discord Clouds Talks on North Korean Nuclear Arms," *The New York Times*, March 14, 2004. For background, see Mary H. Cooper, "North Korean Crisis," *The CQ Researcher*, April 11, 2003, pp. 321-344.

10. See David E. Sanger, "U.S. Sees More Arms Ties between Pakistan and Korea," *The New York Times*, March 14, 2004, p. A1.

11. See Joel Brinkley and William J. Broad, "U.S. Lags in Recovering Fuel Suitable for Nuclear Arms," *The New York Times*, March 7, 2004, p. A8.

12. For a list of nuclear arms-control treaties and their provisions, see "Treaties and Agreements," U.S. State Department, www.state.gov, and Nuclear Threat Initiative, "WMD411," www.nti.org. For background, see Mary H. Cooper, "Weapons of Mass Destruction," *The CQ Researcher*, March 8, 2002, pp. 193-116.

13. "National Strategy to Combat Weapons of Mass Destruction," The White House, December 2002, p. 3.

14. "Findings of the Nuclear Posture Review," U.S. Department of Defense, released Jan. 9, 2002; www.defenselink.mil.

15. The measure was included in the 1994 Defense Authorization Act.

16. From an interview with *Arms Control Today*, January/February 2004; www.armscontrol.org.

17. See Joseph C. Anselmo, "Opponents See New Arms Race in Push for Nuclear Research," *CQ Weekly*, Feb. 21, 2004, pp. 498-500.

18. For background, see Mary H. Cooper, "Bush's Defense Policy," *The CQ Researcher*, Sept. 7, 2001, pp. 689-712.

19. See Bradley Graham, "Missile Defense Still Uncertain," *The Washington Post*, March 12, 2004.

20. Cirincione testified before a special meeting of the Danish Parliament, April 24, 2003.

21. For the text of Einstein's letter, see Robert C. Williams and Philip L. Cantelon, eds., *The American Atom* (1984), cited in Stephen I. Schwartz, ed., *Atomic Audit* (1998). Unless otherwise noted, information in this section is based on Schwartz.

22. Data from www.iaea.org and the Nuclear Energy Institute, www.nei.org.

23. For background, see David Masci, "The United Nations and Global Security," *The CQ Researcher*, Feb. 27, 2004, pp. 173-196.

24. For background, see David Masci, "Emerging India," *The CQ Researcher*, April 19, 2002, pp. 329-360.

25. Kay testified before the Senate Armed Services Committee, Jan. 28, 2004.

26. See Michael Evans, "Libya Knew Game Was Up Before Iraq War," *The Times* (London), March 23, 2004, p. 8.

27. See "Top U.S. Official Visits Libyan Leader," The Associated Press, March 23, 2004.

28. See Salman Masood, "Link to Qaeda Cited in Effort to Assassinate Pakistan Chief," *The New York Times*, March 17, 2004.

29. See Seymour M. Hersh, "The Deal," *The New Yorker*, March 8, 2004, pp. 32-37.

30. See David Rohde, "U.S. Announces New Offensive Against Taliban and al Qaeda," *The New York Times*, March 14, 2004, p. 4.

31. See Sulfiqar Ali, "Firefight in Pakistan Claims 32 Lives; Troops Hunting for Militants Clash with Tribesmen in a Region Bordering Afghanistan," *Los Angeles Times*, March 17, 2004, p. A13.

32. See J. Peter Scoblic, "Indefensible," *The New Republic*, March 8, 2004, p. 14.

33. See Aparisim Ghosh and James Graff, "Terror on the Tracks," *Time*, March 22, 2004, p. 32.

34. From an interview on radio Onda Cero quoted in "New Spain PM Firm on Troop Withdrawal," The Associated Press, March 17, 2004.

35. Pew Research Center for the People & the Press, "A Year After Iraq War, Mistrust of America in Europe Ever Higher, Muslim Anger Persists," March 16, 2004; people-press.org.

36. Alfonse D'Amato, "Bush Will Win War on Terrorism," *Newsday*, March 22, 2004.

37. Mohamed ElBaradei, "Saving Ourselves from Self-Destruction," *The New York Times*, Feb. 12, 2004, p. A37.

BIBLIOGRAPHY

Books

Allison, Graham, *Nuclear Terrorism: The Ultimate Preventable Catastrophe,* Henry Holt, 2004.
A former Defense Department official outlines his strategy for strengthening the nuclear nonproliferation regime to prevent the spread of nuclear weapons to terrorists.

Blix, Hans, *Disarming Iraq,* Pantheon, 2004.
The head of the U.N. weapons inspection team in Iraq asserts that the inspectors would have proved conclusively that Iraq no longer possessed weapons of mass destruction had the Bush administration given them more time before invading.

Frum, David, and Richard Perle, *An End to Evil: How to Win the War on Terror,* Random House, 2003.
A former Bush speechwriter (Frum) and a former administration Defense official call current policies in the war on terrorism a choice between "victory or holocaust."

Weissman, Steve, and Herbert Krosney, *The Islamic Bomb,* Times Books, 1981.
Two authors describe how Pakistan and Iraq launched programs to develop nuclear weapons more than two decades ago.

Articles

Cirincione, Joseph, and Jon B. Wolfsthal, "North Korea and Iran: Test Cases for an Improved Nonproliferation Regime?" *Arms Control Today,* **December 2003.**
Innovative measures to strengthen anti-proliferation measures may be needed to keep North Korea and Iran from developing nuclear weapons.

Hersh, Seymour, "The Deal," *The New Yorker,* **March 8, 2004, pp. 32-37.**
President Bush may have accepted Pakistani President Pervez Musharraf's pardon of his top nuclear scientist's black marketing activities in exchange for letting U.S. troops pursue al Qaeda inside Pakistan.

Kagan, Robert, and William Kristol, "The Right War for the Right Reasons," *The Weekly Standard,* **Feb. 23, 2004.**
Although weapons of mass destruction have not been uncovered, two conservative commentators say that ridding the world of Saddam Hussein more than justifies the war against Iraq.

Pollack, Kenneth M., "Spies, Lies, and Weapons: What Went Wrong," *The Atlantic Monthly,* **January/ February 2004, pp. 78-92.**
A former CIA analyst examines how U.S. intelligence wrongfully concluded that Saddam Hussein's regime was actively pursuing nuclear, biological and chemical weapons.

Sokolski, Henry, "Taking Proliferation Seriously," *Policy Review,* **October/November 2003.**
A conservative analyst argues the United States should call for strong measures to close loopholes in the Nuclear Non-Proliferation Treaty.

Weisman, Steven R., "Lasting Discord Clouds Talks on North Korea Nuclear Arms," *The New York Times,* **March 14, 2004, p. 10.**
A proposal to overcome an impasse in six-party talks to end North Korea's nuclear-weapons program has failed to gain acceptance, forcing a postponement of future talks.

Reports and Studies

Baker, Howard, and Lloyd Cutler, "A Report Card on the Department of Energy's Nonproliferation Programs with Russia," Russia Task Force, Secretary of Energy Advisory Board, Jan. 10, 2001.
The panel calls for greater efforts to keep nuclear weapons and materials in the former Soviet Union out of the hands of terrorists.

Cochran, Thomas B., and Christopher E. Paine, "The Amount of Plutonium and Highly-Enriched Uranium Needed for Pure Fission Nuclear Weapons," Natural Resources Defense Council, April 15, 1995.
The environmental-protection advocacy organization questions the standards the International Atomic Energy Agency (IAEA) uses to determine the amount of weapons-grade material needed to build a nuclear weapon.

Federation of American Scientists, Natural Resources Defense Council and Union of Concerned Scientists, "Toward True Security: A U.S. Nuclear Posture for the Next Decade," June 2001.
Three organizations that support arms control say drastically reducing the U.S. nuclear arsenal is essential to countering nuclear proliferation.

Ferguson, Charles D., *et al.,* **"Commercial Radioactive Sources: Surveying the Security Risks," Center for Nonproliferation Studies, Monterey Institute of International Studies, January 2003.**
Numerous sources of commercial radioactive material are vulnerable to terrorist theft. The authors call for an education campaign to prepare the public for a "dirty-bomb" attack.

The White House, "National Strategy to Combat Weapons of Mass Destruction," December 2002.
The Bush administration's post-Sept. 11 strategy contemplates preemptively attacking adversaries armed with nuclear, chemical or biological weapons before they can attack the United States.

For More Information

Arms Control Association, 1726 M St., N.W., Washington, DC 20036; (202) 463-8270; www.armscontrol.org. A nonpartisan membership organization dedicated to promoting support for effective arms-control policies.

Belfer Center for Science and International Affairs, John F. Kennedy School of Government, Harvard University, 79 JFK St., Cambridge, MA 02138; (617) 495-1400; http://bcsia.ksg.harvard.edu. Provides information on technical and political aspects of nonproliferation policy.

Bureau of Nonproliferation, U.S. Department of State, 2201 C St., N.W., Washington, DC 20520; (202) 647-4000; www.state.gov/t/np. Administers policies to prevent the spread of weapons of mass destruction.

Center for Nonproliferation Studies, Monterey Institute of International Studies, 460 Pierce St., Monterey, CA 93940; (831) 647-4154; http://cns.miis.edu. A nongovernmental organization devoted to research and training on nonproliferation issues.

GlobalSecurity.org, 300 N. Washington St., Suite B-100, Alexandria, VA 22314; (703) 548-2700; www.globalsecurity.org. A Web site maintained by veteran defense-policy analyst John Pike containing exhaustive information on U.S. defense policies, including nonproliferation strategy.

Nonproliferation Policy Education Center, 1718 M St., N.W., Suite 244, Washington, DC 20036; (202) 466-4406; www.npec-web.org. A project of the Institute for International Studies that promotes understanding of proliferation issues.

Nuclear Cities Initiative, U.S. Department of Energy, NA-24, 1000 Independence Ave., S.W., Washington, DC 20585; (202) 586-1007; www.nnsa.doe.gov/na-20/nci/index.shtml. Helps the Russian Federation downsize its nuclear weapons complex by establishing private business opportunities for nuclear scientists living in three of the former Soviet Union's closed cities.

Nuclear Threat Initiative, 1747 Pennsylvania Ave., N.W., 7th Floor, Washington DC 20006; (202) 296-4810; www.nti.org. Seeks to increase global security by reducing the risk from nuclear, biological and chemical weapons. The Web site contains a wealth of information.

Thai members of a United Nations peacekeeping force in East Timor participate in a ceremony marking the handover of authority to the new country's military in July 2002. U.N. intervention in the former Indonesian province ended with the creation of a stable, new state, a rare success for the organization.

From *The CQ Researcher,*
February 27, 2004.

5

The United Nations and Global Security

David Masci

On Aug. 19, 2003, a gleaming, new cement truck packed with explosives crashed through a chain-link fence and into a corner of the Canal Hotel, the U.N.'s headquarters in Baghdad, Iraq. The resulting explosion was massive, virtually destroying the three-story building.

The bombing killed 22 people and wounded more than 100, prompting the U.N. to withdraw all its non-Iraqi staff. Among the dead was the apparent target of the attack, Brazilian diplomat Sergio Viera de Mello, the U.N.'s special representative in Iraq and a key player in efforts to rebuild the war-torn nation.

But the destruction of U.N. headquarters was more than just the worst attack on the U.N. in its history. To many observers, the strike at the very heart of U.N. efforts in Iraq symbolized the political battering the 59-year-old organization has been taking lately.

"They've been getting it from all sides," says Stephen Zunes, an associate professor of politics at the University of San Francisco. "The right in the United States thinks the U.N. is irrelevant and that the U.S. doesn't need it, while a lot of people on the left don't want it legitimizing what the U.S. has done in Iraq."

The Iraq war severely strained relations between the U.N. and its most important member, the United States. After months of bitter debate between America and other permanent Security Council members—notably France and Russia—the United States and Britain invaded Iraq without U.N. authorization. Moreover, after toppling Saddam Hussein's regime, President Bush made it clear he envisioned only a limited U.N. role in rebuilding Iraq.[1]

The war and its aftermath have prompted many, Bush included, to question whether the United Nations—founded at the end of

Most U.N. Peacekeepers Serve in Africa

The oldest U.N. peacekeeping operation — in the Middle East — was deployed in 1948, soon after the creation of Israel. Today, 70 percent of the U.N.'s 55,000 peacekeepers are deployed in Africa.

Current U.N. Peacekeeping Operations

Location	Date Begun	Total U.N. personnel deployed (military and civilian)
Middle East	1948	367
India/Pakistan	1949	115
Cyprus	1964	1,402
Golan Heights	1974	1,162
Lebanon	1978	2,406
Western Sahara	1991	497
Georgia	1993	408
Kosovo	1999	7,570
Sierra Leone	1999	12,527
Democratic Republic of the Congo	1999	12,068
Ethiopia/Eritrea	2000	4,498
East Timor	2002	3,369
Liberia	2003	8,994

Source: U.N. Department of Peacekeeping Operations.

World War II to promote global security through dialogue and consensus—can still play a significant geopolitical role in the world following the Sept. 11, 2001, terrorist attacks.

"When it comes to the U.N. and issues of security, the world is moving on," says Daniel Goure, vice president of the Lexington Institute, a defense and foreign policy think tank. "The major centers of power either act unilaterally or within the context of regional alliances like NATO—not the U.N."

Even U.N. Secretary-General Kofi Annan has questioned whether his organization can remain relevant in the new world of terrorists and rogue states with weapons of mass destruction—a world in which U.N. members like the U.S. and Britain feel justified in launching preemptive attacks without the organization's blessing.

"We have come to a fork in the road," Annan told the U.N. General Assembly on Sept. 23. "We must decide whether . . . to continue on the basis agreed upon or whether radical changes are needed."

Many U.N. critics say radical changes are indeed needed, starting with the organization's all-important Security Council, which has the power to authorize sanctions or even military action. Critics say the council's permanent members—the United States, Russia, Britain, France and China—reflect bygone geopolitical realities. Only if important countries like India and Japan became permanent members would the council truly reflect today's world, they say.

Other critics trace many of the U.N.'s problems to its charter, specifically Article 51—which allows nations to defend themselves if attacked. They say it is an anachronism in an era when terrorists armed with weapons of mass destruction (WMDs) could leave millions dead in an instant.

"We need to redraft the charter" to give nations more freedom to respond to these new threats, says Nile Gardiner, a senior fellow at the Heritage Foundation, a conservative think tank.

But others counter that countries would merely use an expanded charter to justify military action against one another. "What would keep us from just whacking each other whenever we felt like it?" responds William J. Durch, a senior associate at the Henry L. Stimson Center, a national-security think tank.

U.N. peacekeeping efforts also have come under fire. In particular, critics have questioned the organization's ability to enforce its own treaty outlawing genocide. Genocide has killed more than 20 million people worldwide since the U.N.'s founding in 1945, according to Gregory Stanton, president of Genocide Watch and coordinator of the International Campaign to End Genocide.

"The United Nations has been ineffective in preventing genocide," because its members "wave the flag of national sovereignty whenever anyone challenges their 'domestic jurisdiction,' " he writes.[2] Such criticisms were raised in the 1990s, when U.N. troops failed to stop the slaughter of hundreds of thousands of civilians in Bosnia, Rwanda and Kosovo.

More recently, the organization's ability to stop the proliferation of WMDs, especially nuclear weapons, also has come under scrutiny.

But it was the U.N.'s unwillingness to sanction an invasion of Iraq, many critics say, that most seriously undercut its credibility, especially after the overthrow of Hussein revealed that the regime had tortured and murdered hundreds of thousands of civilians. The U.N. can only regain credibility—both as a political player and protector of human rights—if it returns to Iraq in a significant political and humanitarian capacity, critics say.

Tentative steps in this direction have been taken by both the United States and the U.N. On Jan. 19, the U.S. administrator in Iraq, L. Paul Bremer III, traveled to U.N. headquarters in New York to personally ask Annan to send a team to Iraq to assess the prospects for direct elections before the United States turns over power to local authorities on June 30. On Feb. 7, a U.N. team went to Baghdad and spent almost a week trying to resolve disagreements among Iraqi political leaders over upcoming elections.

But some observers think the world body should play more than an advisory role and that the United States should turn over significant amounts of authority to U.N. officials now. "The U.N. should be put in control of the whole political process immediately, replacing Bremer and the Americans," says Robert Boorstin, senior vice president for national security and international policy at the Center for American Progress, a liberal think tank. "They have the most experience at policing, reconstruction and institution-building."

Others say the U.N. has a mixed record on nation-building and would likely fail in Iraq—a large country plagued by ethnic tensions and a low-level insurgency. "It would be a disaster," Goure says. "The U.N. bureaucracy has a slow and consensual style of decision making, which would make everything much harder to accomplish in a country that needs things to move forward quickly and decisively."

Meanwhile, the decades-old battle over differing perceptions of what the U.N. can and cannot accomplish continues—a Catch-22 situation prophetically recognized by the first secretary-general, Trygve Lie.

"Some have too great expectations and others too little faith in what the United Nations can do," he once said.[3]

Not surprisingly, some foreign policy experts today say the United Nations will become increasingly irrelevant while others predict it will play a much greater role in promoting peace and security.

As U.N.-watchers ponder the organization's future role in the world, here are some of the questions they are asking:

Should the Security Council be expanded to include new members?

The Security Council is the most important arm of the United Nations grappling with vital issues of war and peace. It dispatches peacekeepers to war-torn countries and authorizes economic and other sanctions and even military action against aggressors. And unlike General Assembly resolutions, those passed by the Security Council are binding.

When the U.N. was established shortly before the end of World War II, the principal victors in the conflict—the United States, Britain, France, the Soviet Union and China—became the council's five permanent members, each with veto power over all decisions. Six non-permanent members were to be elected by the General Assembly to two-year terms.

Nearly 60 years later, that system remains largely in place—changed only once, in 1965, when the number of non-permanent members was increased from six to 10. The same five permanent members—called the P5—still preside over the body.

For decades, Security Council critics have said the arrangement is out of date. "The current council in no way reflects the reality of today's world," says Boorstin of the Center for American Progress. "We don't need representation exactly according to [current] population and geography, but we need some new, realistic approximation of the two."

A new Security Council should at least include some economic or regional powers as new permanent members, Boorstin says. India, the world's largest democracy, could easily represent South Asia, and Japan and Germany—the world's second- and third-largest economies—also should be included. In addition, mammoth Brazil could be Latin America's representative while important Muslim and African countries could represent those peoples, he suggests.

Adding new permanent members also would renew the U.N.'s standing in the world, supporters of expansion

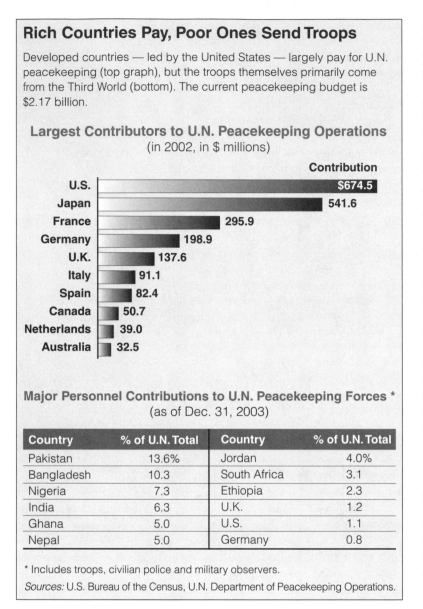

Rich Countries Pay, Poor Ones Send Troops

Developed countries — led by the United States — largely pay for U.N. peacekeeping (top graph), but the troops themselves primarily come from the Third World (bottom). The current peacekeeping budget is $2.17 billion.

Largest Contributors to U.N. Peacekeeping Operations
(in 2002, in $ millions)

Contribution

Country	Contribution
U.S.	$674.5
Japan	541.6
France	295.9
Germany	198.9
U.K.	137.6
Italy	91.1
Spain	82.4
Canada	50.7
Netherlands	39.0
Australia	32.5

Major Personnel Contributions to U.N. Peacekeeping Forces *
(as of Dec. 31, 2003)

Country	% of U.N. Total	Country	% of U.N. Total
Pakistan	13.6%	Jordan	4.0%
Bangladesh	10.3	South Africa	3.1
Nigeria	7.3	Ethiopia	2.3
India	6.3	U.K.	1.2
Ghana	5.0	U.S.	1.1
Nepal	5.0	Germany	0.8

* Includes troops, civilian police and military observers.
Sources: U.S. Bureau of the Census, U.N. Department of Peacekeeping Operations.

the U.N. Foundation. "These countries could use their energies more productively. They wouldn't be spoilers like they often are now."

But Tom Weiss, a professor of political science at Columbia University, thinks new permanent members would "cripple the council with infighting," because existing permanent members won't want to give up power.

Indeed, deciding who would get the new permanent slots would "[tick] off a lot of countries that didn't make it," agrees the Stimson Center's Durch. "You're going to end up with a lot of resentment, and nobody's going to win."

Others say it is in America's interest to maintain the status quo. "Bringing in the countries they always point to—like India, Brazil and Indonesia—means there will simply be more members who are likely to oppose the United States and Britain," says the Heritage Foundation's Gardiner.

Finally, even if agreement could be reached on new members, the larger council would be too big to be effective, expansion opponents say. "This would make it much harder to get anything done," Weiss says. "Adding new members translates into adding new agendas and interests, and this would become even more unwieldy than it is now."

argue. "For the council to be credible in the world today, it has to include the real powers of the world," the Lexington Institute's Goure says.

Bringing on new members would also facilitate more cooperation in solving international crises, say others.

"Things are so difficult today partly because those who feel excluded are less cooperative than they otherwise might be," says Johanna Mendelson-Forman, senior program officer for peace, security and human rights at

Should the U.N. change its charter to broaden a nation's right to self-defense?

During Security Council debates before the Iraq war, the United States and its allies sought authorization to depose Hussein for his violations of more than a dozen U.N. resolutions passed since the end of the first Persian Gulf War in 1991. Chief among them was Resolution 1441—which called on Iraq to dismantle its alleged weapons of mass destruction.

But, in making its case for war to the American people and the world community, the Bush administration also argued that Iraq posed a threat to the region and, ultimately, to the United States. Indeed, since the Sept. 11 terrorist attacks, the administration has repeatedly argued that it has the right to take pre-emptive action, alone if necessary, against any potential threat to the country's safety.

"America will never seek a permission slip to defend the security of our country," President Bush said in his State of the Union address on Jan. 20, 2004.

However, the U.N. charter requires member states to "refrain from the threat or use of force" and to settle international disputes by peaceful means.[4] Military force is allowed—under Article 51—only when a nation is threatened or attacked and is acting in self-defense.

Secretary-General Annan argues that by ignoring the letter and spirit of Article 51, the United States and its allies have made the world more dangerous, because now other nations will justify pre-emptive strikes against other countries by claiming they posed potential threats.

"If nations discount the legitimacy provided by the U.N. and feel they can and must use force unilaterally and pre-emptively, the world will become even more dangerous," Annan told the General Assembly on Sept. 23, 2003.[5]

But critics of Article 51 say the U.N. does not offer countries the right to deal with threats *before* they become imminent—an approach the critics say is more appropriate in the dangerous environment that has emerged since the attacks on the World Trade Center and the Pentagon. "If we wait for threats to materialize," Bush said, "we will have waited too long."[6]

The Heritage Foundation's Gardiner agrees. "We are now living in an age of international terrorism and rogue states, but that's not reflected in Article 51," he says. The article should be updated to allow nations "to attack countries that harbor terrorists," Gardiner says. "This has to be explicit."

"This debate is not about terrorists or even weapons of mass destruction," adds the Lexington Institute's Goure. "It's about failed states that allow terrorists to thrive. Terrorists cannot be effective without access to state assets—like banks, training bases and laboratories to develop weapons."

According to Goure, countries should be allowed to take "anticipatory self-defense" actions against entities

The United Nations' distinctive headquarters was built in New York City in 1953. The U.N. was founded in 1945 in the wake of both World War II and the failed League of Nations.

that might threaten them. "This needs to be written simply and directly" into the U.N. charter, he says.

But Columbia University's Weiss counters that Article 51 already has evolved to encompass new global realities. "The U.N. charter—like the U.S. Constitution—is a living document that changes with the times," Weiss says. "No one, not even international lawyers, dispute the fact that Article 51 now gives you a right to pre-emptively defend yourself if you're threatened. But that has always meant that a verifiable threat is pointed in your direction."

Christopher Preble, director of foreign policy studies at the libertarian Cato Institute, notes, "The United Nations wouldn't have opposed our intervention in Iraq if the majority of member states believed that Iraq was a threat to the U.S. That was the problem: They didn't believe that we were genuinely threatened."

Indeed, the Stimson Center's Durch points out, the Security Council had no qualms about authorizing American action against Afghanistan. "It came under the purview of Article 51 and was fine, because, in this case, the United States had legitimately been threatened."[7]

Should the U.N. have a greater role in running Iraq?

Even before the fall of Baghdad, debate had begun over the U.N.'s role in postwar Iraq. President Bush said he favored a "vital" role for the international body, but the administration ultimately decided its primary responsibility should be to deliver humanitarian assistance. Britain—America's primary ally in the war—wanted the U.N. to help build political and other institutions while the French, Russians and others—who had opposed the war—argued for direct U.N. administration of the country.

Last May, it was agreed that a U.N. special representative would be sent to Baghdad to assist in reconstruction efforts. Although his job description was not entirely spelled out, de Mello quickly found ways to meaningfully aid reconstruction efforts.[8] Most notably, he helped create the Iraqi governing council, convincing American administrator Bremer to grant the 25-person body greater authority.

Then came the Aug. 19 attack on U.N. headquarters, leading Annan to withdraw all non-Iraqi staff. After the U.N. elections team visited Baghdad in February, there was talk of U.N. staff returning to Iraq, but nothing has been decided.

Some U.N. supporters say the only way for Iraq to evolve into a stable, democratic state is for the United States to hand over day-to-day authority to the United Nations. "It seems more and more necessary all the time," says the University of San Francisco's Zunes. "Things are getting worse, with even the Shiite community—which has been quiescent until now—getting more restless. It's time to bring in someone else to do the job."

The Center for American Progress' Boorstin agrees. "The U.N. should be given control of the whole political process," he says. "If we had done this earlier, many fewer Americans would be dead, and the American taxpayer wouldn't be footing the bill for reconstruction."

Indeed, Boorstin says, the United Nations is better suited to nation-building than the U.S.-led coalition running the country, partly because Iraqis perceive it as more even-handed and trustworthy. "No institution is completely trusted by Iraqis, but the United Nations is trusted more than any other," he says.

"The U.N. still has a lot of legitimacy in Iraq," agrees Durch. "After all, they kept about half the country's population alive for more than a decade with their oil-for-food program." Established after the 1991 Persian Gulf War, the program embargoed oil exports except to finance food and medicine imports.

Moreover, he adds, if the United Nations had a greater role in rebuilding Iraq, it would unleash a flood of additional outside help now being withheld because the U.N. isn't involved.

"The U.N. isn't just the U.N., it's the whole U.N. system," Durch says. "So when they come in, they bring in the NGOs [non-governmental organizations], and they do a lot of the work on the ground. They also bring the World Bank with them, and that means there will be a lot of money to spend."

But getting the United Nations more involved would significantly slow down the hand-over of power to the Iraqis, opponents of the idea say. "The United Nations, by its nature, is a very slow and cumbersome organization because it is a government of governments," says Cato's Preble. "Decisions will be made by committee, and you're going find yourself with too many cooks spoiling the broth, so it will inevitably be less effective than the U.S."

Others contend that—based on its experience with nation-building elsewhere—the United Nations simply can't deal with the kinds of potentially explosive issues that could erupt. "You have a lot of immediate, right and wrong issues that pop up, but the U.N. doesn't have the political inclination to handle them because they are trying to treat all sides equally," Goure says. "In Bosnia, you had the U.N. trying to balance three ethnic groups—Serb, Croat and Muslim—to the point of not moving effectively to stop the Serbs [from committing genocide]." As a result, he adds "you had things like the massacre at Srebrenica," where an estimated 10,000 Muslim men and boys were executed.

The same scenario could unfold in Iraq, Goure says, where three major ethnic and religious groups—the Kurds, Sunni Arabs and Shiite Arabs—are jockeying for power. "If the U.N. replaced Bremer, they would have much less strength and inclination to keep these groups apart, and the chances for ethnic conflict would be much greater."

Finally, some observers disagree that Iraqis would view the United Nations as evenhanded or trustworthy.

"The U.N. really isn't liked or seen as part of the solution by most people in Iraq," largely because of its role in imposing and administering the post-Gulf War sanctions, says Edward Luck, director of the Center on International Organizations at Columbia University.

Indeed, the U.N.'s comprehensive economic sanctions (which were partially softened by the oil-for-food program) took a heavy toll on the country's civilian population.

"For the Iraqis, foreigners are foreigners, whether they are wearing the blue helmets of U.N. peacekeepers or the patch of the 82nd Airborne," Preble adds. "They'll be seen as occupiers, just like the U.S. is today."

BACKGROUND

Outgrowth of War

The United Nations arose from the ashes of the failed League of Nations and the devastation of World War II.

The league, established in 1919 by the Treaty of Versailles following World War I, was the world's first attempt to prevent war by creating an international forum to air grievances. But the U.S. Senate refused to ratify America's membership, and without U.S. support the league soon became ineffective.

In 1931, Japan left the league after invading Manchuria in northern China. Germany withdrew in 1933, the year Adolf Hitler came to power. And in 1937, Italy left after the organization condemned its unprovoked invasion of Ethiopia.

Germany, Japan and Italy, of course, were the primary "Axis powers" responsible for the Second World War. Although the league continued to function after the war began in 1939, it had little impact.

The notion of replacing the league with something more effective emerged two years before the war ended, in 1943, when the major allies—the United States, the

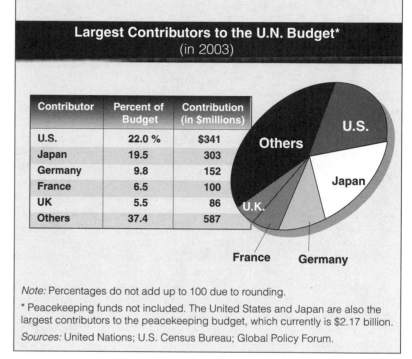

U.S. and Japan Contribute the Most

Five countries contribute 63 percent of the U.N.'s $1.6 billion annual budget, with the United States and Japan paying almost 43 percent of the total.

Largest Contributors to the U.N. Budget*
(in 2003)

Contributor	Percent of Budget	Contribution (in $millions)
U.S.	22.0 %	$341
Japan	19.5	303
Germany	9.8	152
France	6.5	100
UK	5.5	86
Others	37.4	587

Note: Percentages do not add up to 100 due to rounding.

* Peacekeeping funds not included. The United States and Japan are also the largest contributors to the peacekeeping budget, which currently is $2.17 billion.

Sources: United Nations; U.S. Census Bureau; Global Policy Forum.

Soviet Union, Britain and China—began discussing proposals for a new international body.

Problems that arose during the talks foreshadowed many of the issues that would arise later: The Soviets were wary of a body that might block its own geopolitical ambitions, and Britain worried such an institution might try to control its many colonies.

But President Franklin D. Roosevelt pushed the negotiations forward. Although he died in April 1945—less than two weeks before the allies were to meet in San Francisco to hammer out a final agreement—the new president, Harry S Truman, strongly supported the project, and a final accord emerged.

All 51 nations attending the San Francisco negotiations ratified the new U.N. charter on Oct. 24. Its primary goal was "saving succeeding generations from the scourge of war," promoting fundamental human rights, establishing "justice and respect" for international law and treaties and working for "social progress."[9]

Kofi Annan's U.N. Balancing Act

When Kofi Annan became the U.N.'s seventh secretary-general in early 1997, he quickly found himself in the midst of a crisis.

The organization was on the brink of bankruptcy, in part because the United States and other key members were refusing to pay their back dues. The United States alone had withheld $1.6 billion in funds, largely in an effort to pressure the institution—which many Americans saw as wasteful and corrupt—to reform itself.

Annan responded by immediately traveling to Washington to lobby Congress, promising to trim staff and spending. Annan's reform plan, combined with his personal charm, won the support of even the U.N.'s toughest critics on Capitol Hill, including Sen. Jesse Helms, R-N.C., and prompted the United States to pay the bulk of its dues.

But those first few months were merely a warm-up for the challenges he was to face in the years ahead, from "ethnic cleansing" in Kosovo to the bitter debate over the invasion of Iraq.

"You're always dealing with crisis, and some country or countries are always upset with you, and then you always have to placate the U.S. and other big powers," says Stephen C. Schlesinger, director of the World Policy Institute at New School University in New York City and author of *Acts of Creation: The Founding of the United Nations*. "No doubt: It's a tough job."

"It's a Catch-22 kind of job," says Johanna Mendelson-Forman, a senior program officer at the U.N. Foundation.

"You're the most powerful man in the world with limited resources, which can be very frustrating."

Despite the challenges, the 66-year-old Ghanaian generally gets high marks from U.N.-watchers.

"He's the best secretary-general since Dag Hammarskjold" of Sweden, Schlesinger says. "He's been able to restore the U.N.'s moral authority by bringing people together and stressing the original ideals of the U.N."

"He's an extremely patient and calm man, which is needed in that job," Mendelson-Forman says. "Also, he's a creature of the system, which means that he knows all about the U.N.'s internal problems and understands its great potential."

Annan was a popular and respected senior U.N. officer when he was elected to the post in 1996 as a compromise candidate after a bitter battle between the United States and France over whether the controversial Egyptian diplomat Boutros Boutros-Gali, should serve a second term.

During his tenure, Annan has worked hard to heal the rift that developed in the last few decades between the U.N. and its most important member: the United States. Most recently, he went against the advice of his own staff and, in response to a request from President Bush, sent a high-level representative, Algerian diplomat Lakhdar Brahimi, to Iraq to assess the country's political future.

"He understands that he basically doesn't have any choice but to try to keep the United States happy, since the U.N. is so dependent on the U.S. for money and other things," says

---

The General Assembly—comprised of all U.N. members, each with one vote—was given responsibility for overseeing operations and considering non-binding resolutions on international issues. The Security Council was charged with maintaining international peace, authorizing economic and military sanctions and approving the use of force to restore peace.

The five major World War II victors—the United States, the Soviet Union, Britain, France and China—were designated as veto-wielding permanent members of the council, to ensure that every council decision was supported by the globe's strongest nations. The General Assembly elected the council's six non-permanent members—increased to 10 in 1965—to two-year terms.

The assembly met for the first time on Jan. 10, 1946, in London. "It is in your hands to make or mar the happiness of millions yet unborn," King George VI told the delegates. "It is for you to lay the foundations of a new world where such a conflict as that which lately brought our world to the verge of annihilation must never be repeated."[10]

Early Tests

The new organization's first test, in 1947, involved the fate of British-ruled Palestine, which was claimed by both Arabs and Jews. A fierce debate ensued over whether to create an Arab-Jewish federation, favored by Arab states, or to partition the country into ethnic enclaves, which the United States favored.

Frederick D. Barton, a senior adviser at the Center for International and Strategic Studies' International Security Program.

On occasion, however, Annan has opposed the United States and other big powers. "In 1999, for instance, he said the need for humanitarian intervention in places like Bosnia and Rwanda overrode national sovereignty—something the United States was not comfortable with," Schlesinger says.

More recently, in a speech to the General Assembly last November, Annan chided the United States for unilaterally attacking Iraq. At the same time, he criticized opponents of the war—and the U.N. itself—for not adequately taking America's legitimate security concerns into account. "He's good, very good, at balancing interests," Barton says. "That's one of his great strengths."

After Annan joined the U.N. in 1962 as a budget analyst for the World Health Organization, he quickly moved up the U.N. ladder—taking a break in 1972 to obtain a mas-

U.N. Secretary-General Kofi Annan.

ter's degree in management from the Massachusetts Institute of Technology. He became under-secretary for peacekeeping in 1993.

His three-year tenure as head of peacekeeping coincided with one of the most active periods in U.N. peacekeeping history, with blue helmets deployed in Bosnia, Cambodia, Somalia and Rwanda, among others. At one point in 1995, the under-secretary was overseeing 70,000 military and civilian personnel from 77 countries.[1]

Annan's term ends in 2006, and he says he will not seek a third term. Still, Schlesinger says, "it's not impossible to imagine the big powers asking him to stay on one more term, since he's so well respected. Given the divisions at the U.N. right now, they may just be looking for someone they can all agree upon."

---

[1] Figure cited in the secretary-general's official biography at www.un.org/News/ossg/sg/pages/sg_biography.html.

The U.N's decision in 1948 to partition prompted the first of several regional wars between Jews and Arabs.[11] After Israel repelled the attacking Arabs and established a new state, U.N. "military observers" went to the Middle East to monitor the cease-fire between Israel and its neighbors. Their mission continues to this day in the Golan Heights, Egypt and along the border of Israel and Lebanon.[12]

The U.N.'s next big test occurred in Korea, where U.S.-Soviet Cold War rivalry had split the country into the communist north and pro-Western south. Although the superpowers eventually agreed to withdraw from the Korean peninsula, the Soviets left behind a well-armed, North Korean army that invaded the south in 1950.[13]

The United States and its allies condemned the invasion, and the U.N. authorized an international force to defend the south. The resulting Korean War dragged on for three years, with U.N. forces trading huge swaths of territory several times with the north and its Chinese communist allies. The war ended in 1953 with Korea still divided.[14]

Secretary-General Lie declared the Korean War a triumph for collective security, but others said it proved the U.N.'s ineffectiveness. Indeed, many Americans argued an international organization could not deal with communism—the major threat of the day—and that the United States should develop regional alliances to meet the challenge.

CHRONOLOGY

1940s *United Nations is founded in the closing days of World War II.*

June 26, 1945 Delegates from 51 countries sign the U.N. charter; it is formally approved on Oct. 24.

1948 U.N. observers monitor a shaky cease-fire between newly independent Israel and its Arab neighbors.

1950s-1980s *Cold War rivalry hampers but does not entirely quash U.N. efforts to promote peace and security.*

June 25, 1950 U.N. authorizes a U.S.-led international force to help defend South Korea after communist North Korea invades.

November 1956 The first U.N. peacekeepers are sent to the Suez Canal to monitor a cease-fire between Israel and Egypt.

1957 International Atomic Energy Agency is founded with U.N. support to promote the peaceful use of nuclear power.

July 14, 1960 The first large-scale U.N. peacekeeping force is sent to Congo, where independence from Belgium has led to civil unrest.

1965 U.N. peacekeepers begin patrolling the India-Pakistan border following warfare over the disputed Kashmir region.

Nov. 29, 1982 U.N. General Assembly condemns Soviet Union's 1979 invasion of Afghanistan.

Oct. 25, 1983 United States invades Grenada without seeking Security Council authorization.

1990s-Present *Cold War ends, leading to increased U.N. peacekeeping operations.*

1990 Iraq's Aug. 2 invasion of Kuwait prompts Security Council on Nov. 29 to authorize intervention by an American-led coalition.

1991 Coalition forces liberate Kuwait. . . . U.N. arms inspectors search Iraq for weapons of mass destruction

(WMDs) as part of a postwar peace agreement; none are found.

1993 U.N. sends 28,000 peacekeepers to Somalia to alleviate famine and restore order during a civil war. U.S. and other casualties lead to a U.N. withdrawal in 1995.

1994 Almost 1 million civilians die in ethnic fighting in Rwanda between the Hutus and Tutsis. A small U.N. force in the country takes no action.

1995 U.N. efforts to establish "safe havens" in Bosnia to prevent genocide fail as Serbs overrun Srebrenica and kill thousands of civilians.

1996 Kofi Annan, a U.N. official from Ghana, is elected secretary-general.

1998 Iraqi leader Saddam Hussein expels U.N. weapons inspectors.

1999 NATO intervenes in the Yugoslav province of Kosovo without seeking U.N. Security Council authorization.

Sept. 12, 2002 President Bush addresses the General Assembly on WMDs and Iraq and challenges the U.N. to be "relevant."

March 22, 2003 United States and Great Britain lead an invasion of Iraq without seeking Security Council authorization, toppling Hussein's regime in a month.

Aug. 1, 2003 Security Council passes a resolution authorizing the dispatch of U.N. peacekeepers to Liberia.

Aug. 19, 2003 Suicide bomber destroys U.N. headquarters in Baghdad killing U.N. Representative Sergio Viera de Mello and 21 other people.

Nov. 23, 2003 President Bush returns to the U.N. to ask the international community to assist in rebuilding Iraq.

Feb. 7, 2004 Secretary-General Annan sends a U.N. team to Baghdad to assess the prospects for direct elections.

June 30, 2004 United States is scheduled to turn over sovereignty in Iraq to Iraqi authorities.

Dec. 31, 2006 Secretary-General Annan's second term ends.

In 1956, the United Nations enjoyed its first real triumph as a peacemaker. Egypt had nationalized the Suez Canal, taking control from Britain. The British, along with France and Israel, attacked and retook the canal, but the United States condemned the action.

The legendary Secretary-General Dag Hammarskjold—who coined the term "peacekeeping"—stepped into the stalemate and proposed that U.N. troops supervise a truce. The allies withdrew, and 6,000 lightly armed U.N. soldiers from 10 countries took up positions between Israeli and Egyptian troops along their borders. The force remained until May 1967.

In the following decades, U.N. peacekeepers were involved in several other conflicts. In 1962, 20,000 so-called blue helmets were dispatched to newly independent Congo to restore order and supervise the withdrawal of Belgian troops. Three years later, peacekeepers took up positions along the India-Pakistan border, after the two countries fought a war over the Indian province of Kashmir. Later missions included Cyprus, Namibia and Sri Lanka.

But Cold War rivalries severely hampered the U.N.'s peacekeeping success. Although the United States largely dominated the organization, the Soviets repeatedly vetoed Security Council resolutions authorizing interventions, resulting in U.N. missions that were too narrowly defined to be effective.

During the 1960s, '70s and '80s, the United Nations did little to halt civil wars in Vietnam, Angola, Mozambique and El Salvador, which were often seen as surrogate struggles in the Cold War, because the two superpowers supported the opposing sides.

New World Order

In the late 1980s, the geopolitical situation started to change as communist governments in the Soviet Union and its client states began collapsing. By the early 1990s, the Cold War rivalry that long had dominated international relations was gone, and the United States emerged as the world's sole superpower.

President George Bush, the current president's father, declared a "new world order" based on respect for the rule of law and human rights. His rhetoric was soon put to the test when Iraq invaded and occupied Kuwait in August 1990. Bush quickly sought an international coalition at the United Nations that drove the Iraqis out of Kuwait in early 1991.

The U.N. Security Council, which can impose economic sanctions and authorize military action, has five permanent members—the United States, Russia, Britain, France and China. Reformers say other great powers, like India and Japan, should be added to the exclusive club to reflect contemporary global realities.

Many saw the Persian Gulf War as the beginning of a new, bold era for the United Nations. As historian William Jay Jacobs notes in his book *Search for Peace:* "Although leadership [in the Gulf War] undoubtedly came from Washington, it was the United Nations that had broadened the wartime alliance, even isolating Iraq from most of the Arab world. In a major way, the United Nations had served as a unifying force, bringing together nations of widely different backgrounds—including former communist governments—for the task of armed peacekeeping."[15]

Around this time, the U.N. began taking on greater peacekeeping and nation-building challenges. From 1988 to 1993, it established 14 new peacekeeping efforts—more than in its first four decades. In 1992 alone, the number of blue helmets in the field quadrupled, along with peacekeeping expenses, which grew from $700 million to $2.8 billion.[16]

The role of peacekeepers also began to change. Past U.N. forces had been deployed to keep opposing armies apart following ceasefires. Now, U.N. forces were entering ongoing conflicts in war-torn countries like Cambodia, Somalia and Bosnia.

But the peacekeepers were unable to establish stability in any of the conflicts. In Somalia, for instance, 28,000 U.N. forces (including Americans) could not stop the

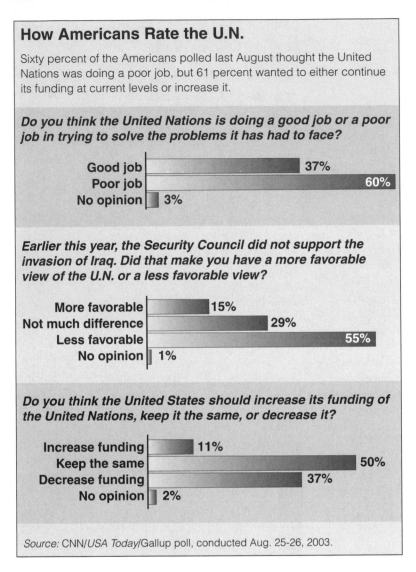

How Americans Rate the U.N.

Sixty percent of the Americans polled last August thought the United Nations was doing a poor job, but 61 percent wanted to either continue its funding at current levels or increase it.

Do you think the United Nations is doing a good job or a poor job in trying to solve the problems it has had to face?

Good job — 37%
Poor job — 60%
No opinion — 3%

Earlier this year, the Security Council did not support the invasion of Iraq. Did that make you have a more favorable view of the U.N. or a less favorable view?

More favorable — 15%
Not much difference — 29%
Less favorable — 55%
No opinion — 1%

Do you think the United States should increase its funding of the United Nations, keep it the same, or decrease it?

Increase funding — 11%
Keep the same — 50%
Decrease funding — 37%
No opinion — 2%

Source: CNN/USA Today/Gallup poll, conducted Aug. 25-26, 2003.

Muslims. A tenuous cease-fire took hold in 1995, only after American-led NATO military forces intervened in the wake of an international outcry.

"In places like Bosnia and Somalia, you had active civil wars going on and the U.N. just wasn't equipped to deal with all of that," says the Stimson Center's Durch. "There was a shortage of troops and money, and an overage of optimism that led to the problems on these missions."

Optimism eventually turned to fatigue, both at the United Nations and in the international community. When another ethic conflict erupted in the central African nation of Rwanda in 1994, the U.N. and its members reacted without energy or commitment.

A small group of U.N. peacekeepers had been sent to Rwanda at the end of 1993 to quell rising ethnic tensions, but they could not prevent the wholesale slaughter the following year. Indeed, U.N. troops stood aside as an estimated 800,000 mostly Tutsi Rwandans were massacred by the Hutu majority.

Four years later, on his first visit to Rwanda since the genocide, Secretary-General Annan—after touring gravesites and buildings filled with victims' skulls—apologized for his organization's inaction. "Now we know that what we did was not nearly enough," he said, "not enough to save Rwanda from itself, not enough to honor the ideals for which the United Nations exists."[18]

President Bill Clinton later echoed Annan's apology: "We did not act quickly enough after the killing began. We did not immediately call these crimes by their right name: genocide."[19]

The Security Council later established international tribunals to prosecute war crimes, genocide and crimes against humanity in Bosnia and Rwanda. But the U.N.'s

violence between rival clans that had brought chaos and famine to the East African nation. While the U.N. efforts did alleviate the devastating famine, attempts in 1993 to end the civil war resulted in some 18 U.S. fatalities and prompted the withdrawal of the entire peacekeeping mission by 1995.[17]

Genocide and the U.N.

A genocidal civil war that began in Bosnia in 1992 also proved intractable for the United Nations. A European-led U.N. force proved unwilling to stand up to Serbian troops, who murdered tens of thousands of ethnic

earlier inaction raised serious questions as to whether it is able or willing to act before mass murders happen. The U.N. Convention on the Prevention and Punishment of the Crime of Genocide—established after Nazi Germany's atrocities during World War II—requires its 129 signatory countries to intervene to halt genocide if they determine that it is occurring.

Criticism about the U.N.'s slowness in responding to atrocities erupted again in 1999, when evidence emerged of "ethnic cleansing" by the Serbians against Albanians in Kosovo. "It is right to stop the ethnic cleansing, war crimes, crimes against humanity and other indicators of genocide that we see," Secretary of State Madeleine K. Albright said in April 1999.[20]

Although the Security Council passed several resolutions demanding the hostilities in Kosovo cease, it did not step in to stop the slaughter, which continued. Once again, NATO bypassed the Security Council and launched an American-led bombing campaign in March, which brought the Serbians to the peace table three months later. The NATO countries did not seek U.N. authorization for the bombings because they knew permanent Security Council members China and Russia—which have been accused of ethnic atrocities in Tibet and Chechnya—would veto the plan.

"If military intervention is used against a country for a human rights issue, that will create a very bad precedent for the world," Chinese Premier Zhu Rongji said. "With that, people will wonder whether foreign powers should take military actions" against China over ethnic issues in Tibet.[21]

Frustrated with the U.N.'s marginalization in the Kosovo affair, Annan criticized both the Security Council's "inaction in the face of genocide" and NATO's unauthorized action. "Unless the Security Council is restored to its pre-eminent position as the sole source of legitimacy on the use of force," Annan said, "we are on a dangerous path to anarchy."[22]

After the peace accord, NATO and Russian peacekeepers helped maintain the ceasefire in Kosovo, and U.N. administrators came in to help restore civil government.

Since Kosovo, U.N. peacekeepers have had some successes, primarily in smaller conflicts. In 1999, for instance, the organization helped shepherd the former Indonesian province of East Timor toward democracy and independence, after decades of bloody conflict between separatists and the Indonesian government.

Confronting Iraq

The terrorist attacks on Sept. 11, 2001, like the end of the Cold War a decade before, imbued the U.N. with a new, if brief, sense of unity and focus. With smoke still rising from the World Trade Center just three miles south of U.N. headquarters, the Security Council authorized several anti-terrorism operations, including military action against Afghanistan, where Osama bin Laden and his al Qaeda terrorist group were operating.

But within a year of the 9/11 attacks, the U.N.'s newfound unity began to crack. With Afghanistan under American control and al Qaeda on the run, the U.S. turned its attention to Iraq's Hussein, who continued to defy U.N. mandates to publicly account for his alleged WMDs.

International Atomic Energy Agency (IAEA) chief Mohamed ElBaradei (left), shown with Iranian President Mohammad Khatami in Tehran last year, has been criticized for not demanding more accountability from Iran and other nations suspected of trying to produce nuclear weapons. The U.N.-supported IAEA is charged with ensuring that civilian nuclear programs are not used to create nuclear weapons.

U.S.-U.N. Relationship Has Ups, Downs

The recent dispute over America's decision to go to war with Iraq was not the first time the United States and the United Nations have been at loggerheads. In recent decades, the two have sparred on issues ranging from the Kyoto treaty on global warming to U.N. family-planning programs.

Some observers find the tension surprising, even ironic, since the United Nations is largely an American creation, established despite Soviet and British ambivalence about creating a successor to the failed League of Nations.

But Stephen C. Schlesinger, author of *Act of Creation: The Founding of the United Nations*, sees no contradiction between U.S. attitudes then and now. The United Nations "was bound to clash with our need to get our own way," he says. "We're the biggest guy on the block, and naturally we don't want to be restricted or limited by anyone else—including the U.N."

Johanna Mendelson-Forman, senior program officer for peace, security and human rights at the U.N. Foundation, agrees. "The U.S. doesn't want to be constrained by the U.N., and it doesn't want to live up to some of the international obligations we made in the past," she says.

Yet others blame the nature of the institution. "The United Nations is wedded to the Cold War model of preserving the balance of power between the U.S. and Soviets," says Thomas Donnelly, a resident fellow at the American Enterprise Institute who studies defense and foreign policy issues. "But times have changed. Although we don't live in a multipolar world anymore, the U.N. is still acting like we do."

According to Donnelly, the world body should help America, not block it. "The United States is the most effective agent for peace and order in the world today," he says. "The U.N. should be trying to support U.S. goals, not just in Iraq and the Middle East, but elsewhere too, as we work to open markets and bring democracy."

Others say that as decolonization in the 1950s and '60s brought more and more new members from the developing world into the United Nations family, the institution became less amenable to America's interests. In addition, right-wing and white-supremacist militia groups in America have long seen the United Nations as bent on dismantling the United States in favor of a world government. And anti-abortionists have attacked the institution's family-planning efforts.[1]

---

[1] For background, see Mary H. Cooper, "United Nations at 50," *The CQ Researcher*, April 18, 1995, pp. 729-752.

In his first post 9/11 State of the Union address, on Jan. 29, 2002, President Bush put Iraq and the world on notice that continued defiance of the United Nations would prompt American military action: "The Iraqi regime has plotted to develop anthrax, and nerve gas, and nuclear weapons for over a decade. . . . America will do what is necessary to ensure our nation's safety."

In fall 2002, the United States and Britain began lobbying other Security Council members for a resolution that would give Iraq a time limit to reveal and destroy its WMDs or face invasion. Permanent members France and Russia were strongly opposed, as was Germany, which held one of the rotating council seats. Along with other countries, they argued that any effort to disarm Iraq should work within the U.N. system and that no U.N. resolution demanding Iraqi cooperation should be used to justify a war.

Finally, in November, a compromise emerged. Security Council Resolution 1441, which passed 15-0, authorized the return of U.N. arms inspectors to Iraq, required Baghdad to account for all WMDs within 90 days and promised "serious consequences" for non-cooperation. The U.N. quickly dispatched International Atomic Energy Agency (IAEA) inspectors to look at Iraq's nuclear program and the Monitoring, Verification and Inspection Commission to search for chemical and biological weapons.

The passage of 1441 initially was hailed as a triumph for international cooperation and for the United Nations system. But the resolution, with its vague threat of "consequences," had merely delayed the inevitable big clash over whether war would ever be justified.

By the end of January, head U.N. arms inspector Hans Blix had reported back to the Security Council

In recent years, several issues have produced new U.N.-U.S. friction. In the 1990s, the two sparred over U.N. efforts—or lack of them, critics said—to reform its large bureaucracy. In fact, Congress refused to pay its back dues until the U.N. adopted reforms, a tactic it has used more than once to force policy changes.[2] Eventually, the United States paid the bulk of its back dues, after the U.N. cut its staff and improved efficiency.

In 2002, the United States withheld $34 million in funds earmarked for the U.N. Population Fund, which promotes family planning in the developing world. Anti-abortionists in America argued that the fund supports China's one-child population program, which critics say forces women to have abortions. In defending the move, State Department spokesman Richard Boucher said, "After careful consideration, we came to the conclusion that U.N. Population Fund moneys go to Chinese agencies that support coercive abortions."[3]

But Secretary-General Kofi Annan denied there was coercion. "We have made it clear [the fund] does not go around encouraging abortions," he said.[4]

The U.S. government also rejected the 1997 Kyoto Protocol, a U.N.-sponsored treaty designed to reduce global emissions of "greenhouse" gases believed to cause global warming. The protocol required the United States to reduce its emissions by 7 percent by 2008 compared with 1990 levels.[5]

While American officials helped negotiate the treaty, President Bill Clinton did little to promote it before a hostile U.S. Senate, which feared it would severely slow economic growth. President Bush, similarly concerned about its economic impact, rejected the document soon after taking office in 2001.

"Bush, by dismissing Kyoto and the whole Kyoto process, is really dismissing the United Nations and the international community," says Kert Davies, research director of Greenpeace U.S.A., an environmental advocacy group. "He's done incalculable damage to the [U.N.] and the environment."

Still, some experts say that for all their differences, the U.N. and United States have a more cooperative and productive relationship than appearances would indicate. After all, the United States still provides the largest share—22 percent—of the U.N.'s annual budget.

"The U.S. supports the U.N. a lot more than people think," Mendelson-Forman says. "In areas like refugee assistance, food aid and health care, the U.S. and U.N. work very closely and very well together."

[2] *Ibid.*

[3] Quoted in "U.S. to Withhold Family Planning Funds, CNN.com, www.cnn.com/2002/US/07/22/un.funds/. For background, see Mary H. Cooper, "Population and the Environment," *The CQ Researcher*, July 17, 1998, pp. 601-624.

[4] Quoted in CNN, *op. cit.*

[5] For background, see Mary H. Cooper, "Global Warming," *The CQ Researcher*, Jan. 26, 2001, pp. 41-64.

that Iraq "appears not to have come to a genuine acceptance . . . of the disarmament that was demanded of it," leaving the great powers once again deadlocked over what to do next.[23] France and its allies favored expanded arms inspections while the United States and Britain wanted authorization for the use of force unless Iraq immediately disarmed.

Negotiations dragged on for weeks with each side growing increasingly critical of the other. German Chancellor Gerhard Schröeder dismissed U.S. plans to invade Iraq as "an adventure," an anti-American position that had helped him secure re-election the year before. For his part, Secretary of Defense Donald Rumsfeld ruffled feathers when he labeled France and Germany as part of "old Europe," compared to the ex-communist Central and Eastern European states that supported the U.S. position.

In February, the opposition, led by France, threatened to veto any American or British resolution authorizing military action. French President Jacques Chirac argued that he would never opt for war when there was still a chance that Iraq could be disarmed peacefully. Some observers say France was trying to create a new bloc of powerful countries to serve as a counterweight to the United States, which the French had labeled a "hyperpower."

But the U.S said it would invade Iraq with or without the U.N.'s blessing. The old cooperative spirit evident during the first Persian Gulf War and Afghanistan was gone.

The split in the Security Council endured right up to the war on March 17 and despite last-minute efforts to reach a compromise. Miscalculations apparently played a part. The French held out hope that America and Britain would not really attack on their own, while the Americans continued to believe the French ultimately would not oppose ousting Hussein.

But the biggest loser in the struggle may have been the U.N. itself. "This was a terrible blow to the U.N. system," the U.N. Foundation's Mendelson-Forman says. "By excluding the U.N. from the process, by taking a unilateral as opposed to a multilateral approach to this problem, we ended up saying that the U.N. didn't matter. We made a laughing stock of the U.N."

CURRENT SITUATION

Peacekeeping Lessons

Although its charter requires the U.N. to help ensure the "collective security of nations," it does not actually authorize peacekeeping missions. Secretary-General Hammarskjold half-jokingly said peacekeeping—the term he coined—was authorized by "Chapter Six and a Half" of the charter because it fell between resolving disputes peacefully (Chapter 6) and using embargos and other more forceful means (Chapter 7).

In the past, critics have called the U.N.'s peacekeeping efforts ineffective and even negligent. But U.N.-watchers of varying political stripes say the international community sends insufficient numbers of peacekeepers to deal with intractable problems. "People try to throw in U.N. forces as a substitute either for a lack of will by the parties involved to settle their differences or lack of willingness by the great powers to deal with the issue," says Columbia University's Luck. "So, of course, peacekeeping missions turn out badly. What do people expect?"

The so-called safe havens created in Bosnia were just the kind of situation where the U.N. was expected to perform miracles, Luck says.* "The fighting was still raging in Bosnia, and no one really wanted to put outside forces on the ground," he says. "So they put inadequate peacekeepers on the ground and substituted words like 'safe haven' in lieu of real protection."

Nancy Soderberg, vice president of the International Crisis Group, a conflict-resolution think tank in New York, agrees. "The Serbs wanted to keep fighting, so

everything quickly got out of control," she says. "The situation didn't improve until the U.S. bombed, and a NATO force was put in place, which should have happened in the first place."

Indeed, Bosnia taught the U.N. some valuable lessons about peacekeeping. Soderberg says. "They've learned they can't fight the war or enforce the peace," she says. "Those things have to be taken care of before they come in."

Soderberg says Kosovo and—more recently Sierra Leone and Ivory Coast—are examples of the U.N.'s more practical approach to peacekeeping. "They're not rushing into these places," she says. Peacekeepers went into Liberia and the Congo only after military forces from the region, the United States or France had established peace. "The U.N. can come in when there's truly a peace to keep."

Peacekeeping is now among the U.N.'s most important and visible activities, along with humanitarian efforts, such as assisting refugees and providing food aid.[24] The mission to Congo is the largest of the 13 active operations, with 10,500 U.N. troops helping maintain a fragile ceasefire following a brutal civil war that left 3 million dead.

Some experts have suggested the U.N. should establish a permanent peacekeeping force. Currently, the U.N. must ask members to contribute troops or money whenever peacekeepers are needed—a time-consuming process that prevents rapid response.

"Better early-warning systems must be developed, and the international community must become willing to

> ## "The international community must become willing to react in the early stages of a conflict."
>
> — **Sir Brian Urquhart**
> Former U.N. Undersecretary for Peacekeeping

react in the early stages of a conflict," Sir Brian Urquhart, former U.N. under-secretary for peacekeeping operation and perhaps the most well-regarded proponent of a permanent peacekeeping force, said. "Some sort of highly trained standing force seems needed."[25]

---

* The havens were areas set aside to protect Muslim refugees, but Serb troops entered the areas with no resistance from U.N. guards and murdered thousands of Muslims.

AT ISSUE

Should the U.S. transfer administrative power in Iraq to the U.N.?

YES
Stephen Zunes
*Associate professor of politics,
University of San Francisco;
author, Tinderbox: U.S. Middle East Policy
and the Roots of Terrorism*

Written for *The CQ Researcher*, February 2004

With the original justifications for the U.S. invasion of Iraq in doubt and discontent growing over U.S. occupation policies, increasing numbers of Iraqis are challenging the U.S. role in their country—even those who opposed Saddam Hussein's brutal regime.

Although extremist elements would not be satisfied if administrative responsibilities were transferred from U.S. occupation forces to the United Nations, such a move would dramatically decrease the extremists' support and facilitate restoring basic services, maintaining stability and establishing peaceful and democratic self-governance.

U.S. forces could remain in Iraq under U.N. command. However, even if the Bush administration chose to withdraw, there would still be sufficient forces available from other U.N. member states for peacekeeping and administrative responsibilities. Several Western European and South Asian governments, which refused to contribute troops under what they see as an illegal U.S. occupation, would do so under the U.N. flag.

It is unlikely that any Iraqi regime that emerges from the U.S. occupation—particularly under the proposed system of caucuses chosen by U.S. appointees—would be accepted as legitimate. Both popular resistance and terrorism would therefore continue, requiring an ongoing presence of U.S. forces.

By contrast, an Iraqi government that would emerge under an international mandate through the United Nations would be far more credible, both inside and outside Iraq, and could thereby take responsibility for its own security needs a lot sooner.

The financial burdens of administrative and security functions in Iraq have thus far fallen upon the American taxpayer. Under U.N. leadership, the United States would be responsible for no more than 20 percent of the costs.

The challenges facing any interim administration in Iraq are daunting, and the United Nations, like other intergovernmental bodies, is an imperfect organization. The U.N. has had a lot more experience in nation-building, however, than the U.S. armed forces, whose primary function should be defending America.

East Timor was a U.N. trusteeship for two years after the withdrawal of Indonesian forces in 1999; the new East Timorese government is a stable democracy and a strong U.S. ally. The U.N. also successfully administered postwar Kosovo, even as NATO remained in charge of security. Turning administration of Iraq over to the U.N. makes sense for Iraq, for America and for the world.

NO
Thomas Donnelly
*Resident Fellow,
American Enterprise Institute*

Written for *The CQ Researcher*, February 2004

The recent visit by U.N. envoy Lakhdar Brahimi to Iraq invites a question as to what role the U.N. can play in American-occupied Iraq, and whether the United States should shape its policies to attract greater international support.

Brahimi's trip was a whopping success, to judge by the headlines. He got in to see the leading Shi'a cleric, Grand Ayatollah Ali Sistani, something Ambassador Paul Bremer III hasn't accomplished. And Brahimi seemed to broker a deal that split the difference between the American plan for a quick transfer of Iraqi sovereignty through regional caucuses and Sistani's demand for direct elections.

Moreover, the U.N. saved Iraq from civil war and conferred a long-sought legitimacy on post-Saddam Iraq, according to the press.

But whether the U.N. can serve as a real powerbroker in Iraq remains very doubtful. First of all, the U.N. has little in the way of real power to bring to the table, and that's what Iraqis and the American-led coalition are jockeying over at the moment. Just because some negotiations may be held in the U.N.'s tent does not mean the U.N. is actually participating in the talks. And, to Iraqi factions trying to summon a minimum of political trust, there is little doubt that the United States is the most trustworthy and most attractive partner.

Two indisputable facts underscore this truth. First is the matter of political legitimacy. As the American Founders wrote repeatedly, the source of a government's legitimacy lies in its ability and commitment to secure the natural political rights of its citizens. This is as true in Iraq today as it was in the English colonies two centuries ago. But the U.N. was founded on state sovereignty and political stability—the principles that helped preserve Saddam Hussein in power for decades, a fact not forgotten by the Iraqi people. Iraqi factions know what the various warring factions in the Balkans knew: America and its real allies are most likely to be their honest broker.

Secondly, in a less-than-utopian world, legitimacy without power is meaningless—indeed, worse than meaningless. The U.N. already has been a target for Iraqi rejectionists, as U.N. forces in the Balkans were. This suggests something less than a respect for the legitimacy of the U.N.

While the Bush administration rightly welcomes the positive contributions of the U.N. to the immense task of reconstruction in Iraq, it cannot delude itself that the world body can be any substitute for the exercise of U.S. power.

However, many U.N.-watchers doubt that a permanent force would help. "They could never afford to have the kind of force that could operate without the assistance of the great powers," Luck says. "And if the great powers are on board, you don't need some sort of U.N. group, because they can raise a sufficient force to deal with the problem."

To make peacekeeping more effective, the Security Council should pass "sober and realistic resolutions and stop overreaching in its goals," says Luck at the Center on International Organizations.

The operational quality of U.N. peacekeepers also needs improvement, Soderberg says. "Most of the troops come from developing countries, and they are often not well-equipped or trained," she says. "The U.S. should help train and equip U.N. forces."

Thomas Donnelly, a resident fellow at the American Enterprise Institute, agrees, arguing that troops from many of the peacekeeping nations can't "do much more than man roadblocks."

Nuclear Watchdog

When the United Nations was created in 1945, only the United States had nuclear weapons. Today, eight countries are nuclear powers and several others—North Korea and Iran among them—either possess nuclear weapons or are close to developing them.[26]

Moreover, there is widespread fear that terrorist groups like al Qaeda will attack civilian targets using a nuclear device or conventional explosives packed with nuclear material—so-called "dirty bombs."

The U.N-affiliated IAEA promotes the peaceful use of nuclear power. It inspects nuclear-power and research facilities to ensure that they are not being used to produce weapons. Under the 1970 Nuclear Non-Proliferation Treaty—signed by 187 nations—countries with nuclear facilities must follow certain safeguards and allow IAEA inspections.[27]

Recently, the IAEA has played a constructive role in several anti-proliferation efforts. For instance, after the first Persian Gulf War in 1991, Iraq was found to have a much more advanced nuclear weapons program than anyone had suspected. Under the peace agreement following the war, the IAEA supervised the dismantling of the program while inspectors from the ad hoc U.N. Special Commission (UNSCOM) searched for chemical and biological weapons.

In the months leading up to the invasion of Iraq last March, IAEA inspectors returned to determine whether Hussein was continuing to develop nuclear weapons. They found little evidence that the program had been resuscitated.

But critics complain that several countries have "gone nuclear," unbeknown to the IAEA, including India, Israel and Pakistan. In fact, North Korea claims to have built one or more bombs while a small IAEA team was in the country monitoring a plutonium reactor. More recently, Libya admitted to the existence of four nuclear sites that were part of its secret WMD program.[28]

The agency has also drawn fire because Iran allegedly has been developing nuclear weapons, despite the past presence of IAEA inspectors. Iran finally agreed to new IAEA oversight only after Britain, France and Germany brought pressure on Iranian officials.

Critics of the agency say it has been too trusting of some states. "They told countries that if they would forgo nuclear weapons, they could get access to nuclear technology for civilian use," the Lexington Institute's Goure says. "Well guess what? Iran and North Korea ended up using the technology to develop a nuclear weapons program."*

Goure says the agency tries to be evenhanded, even with states that are less responsible about the use of their civilian nuclear programs. "The IAEA sees this as an equality issue, but the fact of the matter is that some of these countries, like Iran, just shouldn't be getting this technology, period."

Others say the agency's current director general, Egyptian scientist Mohamed ElBaradei, sympathizes more with nations seeking nuclear weapons than with those trying to halt their spread. ElBaradei "has routinely acted in a way better calculated to thwart U.S. counter-proliferation efforts than to prevent the spread of nuclear weaponry," according to Frank Gaffney, president of the Center for Security Policy, a defense think tank.[29]

"ElBaradei has gone to great lengths to prevent the Bush administration from bringing Iran's illegal nuclear-weapons program before the U.N. Security Council," Gaffney writes, a step mandated by the Nuclear Non-Proliferation Treaty. ElBaradei also has slanted IAEA reports on Iran "to make sure the conclusions do not

---

* Iran continues to deny accusations from many in the international community that it has a nuclear weapons program.

support a Security Council referral, often by inserting unjustified findings that obscure or downplay the actual evidence," Gaffney charges.[30]

IAEA supporters acknowledge past mistakes by the agency but say it has made the best of what has often been a bad situation. The "bleeding between civilian and military nuclear programs" is inevitable because of the "Siamese-twin relationship" that exists between the two, points out Rose Gottemoeller, a senior associate at the Carnegie Endowment for International Peace and former head of Department of Energy non-proliferation policy. "This leaves the IAEA with a very tough job." But the agency has taken the lead on important issues and "generally done good work," she adds. "I think you can call them a success."

In addition, Goure says, "ElBaradei is getting much tougher," in part because the United States and the Europeans are pressing him not to be too soft.

But Gottemoeller says his tougher attitude is driven more by recent developments than outside pressure. "I talked to him after he returned from Iran, and he's deadly serious about getting a handle on this," she says. "The problem cases, like Iran and North Korea, have really made him want to deal with these issues."

OUTLOOK

Regaining Relevance?

In a speech before the U.N. on Sept. 12, 2002, President Bush asked: "Will the United Nations serve the purpose of its founding, or will it be irrelevant?"[31]

Although Bush was referring to the U.N.'s lack of action in Iraq, the question resonated beyond the Middle East. Some U.N.-watchers contend the organization has proven incapable of meeting the president's challenge.

The Lexington Institute's Goure says the major powers already acknowledge in their actions, if not always their words, the U.N.'s lack of importance in global security issues. "The U.S. has shown that it's willing to act alone if it needs to," he says, "and you have other players like the Europeans forming an E.U. [European Union] rapid-reaction force. Recently, even the ASEAN [Association of Southeast Asian Nations] nations created a security structure to deal with these kinds of issues. All of this points away from the U.N. and toward alternatives."

Indeed, Goure argues, "Since the early 1950s, [the U.N.] hasn't lived up to its mandate 'To prevent wars and chase down aggressors.' Recent events just showed how much this is the case."

Other skeptics contend that the U.N. could still carve out an important role if it took a tougher line on the world's biggest security threat: the development of WMDs by rogue states. "A lot hinges on how the U.N. handles the biggest security concerns we're facing right now: namely Iran and North Korea," says the Heritage Foundation's Gardiner. "And I'm not optimistic.

"If the U.N. were to disarm these countries, then they would be a serious player," he continues. "But if there is more inaction and appeasement, then the organization will be written off. And, given the bipolar power structure at the Security Council—with the U.S. and Britain on one side and France and Russia on the other—I really don't see any strong response from the U.N. on this issue any time soon."

But the University of San Francisco's Zunes says the United Nations plays too important a role in the world to sink into irrelevance. "Eventually, we'll realize how much we need the United Nations to help keep the peace and make the world a better place," he says. "Unfortunately, given the attitude of the current administration, we'll probably hobble the U.N. more than help it in the short run, but I'm optimistic over the longer term."

Columbia University's Luck also sees signs of the U.N.'s future relevance. "Even when you look at Iraq, which was supposed to be the U.N.'s darkest hour, you see evidence that it is terribly relevant," he says. "Why has the United States gone back to the United Nations over and over again with regard to Iraq? Because the U.N. is a vital part of the furniture of international relations, and the U.S. knows that."

Indeed, Luck says, most states see the continued existence of the U.N. as very much in their interest. "On one hand, smaller countries want to have a voice—especially on the big issues of war and peace—and where else can they go except the U.N.?" he asks. "On the other hand, big powers, even the U.S., need partners and help, and the U.N. is still the best place for that."

Others share the view that the U.N. will always be seen as necessary for global stability. "No matter how often we criticize the U.N., it's necessary to have a forum like it," says Boorstin of the Center for American Progress. "If the U.N. didn't exist, we'd have to build it."

NOTES

1. See David Masci, "Confronting Iraq," *The CQ Researcher*, Oct. 4, 2002, pp. 793-816, and David Masci, "Rebuilding Iraq," *The CQ Researcher*, July 25, 2003, pp. 625-648.

2. Gregory Stanton, "Create a United Nations Genocide Prevention Focal Point and Genocide Prevention Center," *Genocide Watch*; www.genocidewatch.org/UnitedNationsGenocidePreventionFocalPoint.htm.

3. Quoted in Bill Spindle, "U.N. Strives to Define Its Role in a Single-Superpower World," *The Wall Street Journal*, Aug. 21, 2003, p. A1.

4. See www.un.org/aboutun/charter/

5. Quoted in "Binding the Colossus," *The Economist*, Nov. 20, 2003.

6. *Ibid.*

7. See David Masci and Kenneth Jost, "War on Terrorism," *The CQ Researcher*, Oct. 12, 2001, pp. 817-848, and Kenneth Jost, "Rebuilding Afghanistan," *The CQ Researcher*, Dec. 21, 2001, pp. 1041-1064.

8. Spindle, *op. cit.*

9. For background, see Mary H. Cooper, "United Nations at 50," *The CQ Researcher*, Aug. 18, 1995, pp. 729-752.

10. Quoted in Max Harrelson, *Fires All Around the Horizon: The U.N.'s Uphill Battle to Preserve the Peace* (1989), p. 5.

11. For background, see David Masci, "Prospects for Mideast Peace," *The CQ Researcher*, Aug. 30, 2002, pp. 673-696.

12. *Ibid.*, pp. 31-39.

13. For background, see Kenneth Jost, "Future of Korea," *The CQ Researcher*, May 19, 2000, pp. 425-448.

14. William Jay Jacobs, *Search For Peace: The Story of the United Nations* (1994), p. 44.

15. Quoted in *ibid.*, pp. 90-91.

16. Figures cited in *ibid.*, p. 85.

17. For background, see David Masci, "Aiding Africa," *The CQ Researcher*, Aug. 29, 2003, pp. 697-720.

18. Quoted in James C. McKinley Jr., "Annan Given Cold Shoulder by Officials in Rwanda," *The New York Times*, May 8, 1998, p. A9.

19. Quoted in Brad Knickerbocker, "Grappling with the century's most heinous crimes," *The Christian Science Monitor*, April 12, 1999, p. 1.

20. *Ibid.*

21. Quoted in Peter Ford, "World weighs in on NATO's war," *The Christian Science Monitor*, April 14, 1999, p. 1.

22. Judith Miller, "Annan Takes Critical Stance on U.S. Actions in Kosovo," *The New York Times*, May 19, 1999, p. A11.

23. Quoted in "When Squabbling Turns Too Dangerous," *The Economist*, Feb. 15, 2003.

24. For background, see Mary H. Cooper, "Global Refugee Crisis," *The CQ Researcher*, July 9, 1999, pp. 569-592, and Brian Hansen, "Children in Crisis," *The CQ Researcher*, Aug. 31, 2001, pp. 657-688.

25. Urquhart's 1995 speech is at www.colorado.edu/conflict/peace/example/urqu5486.htm.

26. See Mary H. Cooper, "North Korean Crisis," *The CQ Researcher*, April 11, 2003, pp. 321-344.

27. Treaty at www.un.org/Depts/dda/WMD/treaty/; for more information on the IAEA see www.iaea.org. For background, see Mary H. Cooper, "Non-Proliferation Treaty at 25," *The CQ Researcher*, Jan. 27, 1995, pp. 73-96.

28. Patrick Tyler, "Libya's Atom Bid in Early Phases," *The New York Times*, Dec. 30, 2003, p. A1.

29. Frank Gaffney, "A Fateful Choice," *The Washington Times*, Feb. 10, 2004, p. A17.

30. *Ibid.*

31. Full speech at www.whitehouse.gov/news/releases/2002/09/20020912-1.html.

BIBLIOGRAPHY

Books

Harrelson, Max, *Fires All Around the Horizon: The U.N.'s Uphill Battle to Preserve the Peace*, Praeger, 1989.

An Associated Press foreign correspondent and editor details the U.N.'s various efforts to promote peace and security, from its founding to the late 1980s.

Schlesinger, Stephen C., *Acts of Creation: The Founding of the United Nations,* Westview Press, 2003.
The director of the World Policy Institute chronicles the negotiations and intrigues that accompanied creation of the United Nations, including the crucial, persistent efforts of President Harry S Truman and Secretary of State Edward Stettinius.

Articles

Barringer, Felicity, "U.N. Senses It Must Change, Fast, or Fade Away," *The New York Times,* Sept. 19, 2003, p. A3.
Barringer looks at the debate over the United Nations' relevance after the Iraq war.

"Binding the Colossus," *The Economist,* Nov. 20, 2003.
The article examines the tension between the world's sole superpower, the United States, and its premier international institution, the United Nations.

Block, Robert, and Alix Freedman, "U.N. Peacekeeping is a Troubled Art," *The Wall Street Journal,* Oct. 1, 2003, p. A1.
The article examines the difficulties of organizing and executing a peacekeeping operation, especially in a place embroiled in civil war, like Congo.

Cooper, Mary H., "United Nations at 50," *The CQ Researcher,* Aug. 18, 1995, pp. 729-752.
Cooper's overview is still on target almost a decade after it was written.

ElBaradei, Mohamed, "Toward a Safer World," *The Economist,* Oct. 18, 2003.
The head of the International Atomic Energy Agency lays out his vision for improving nuclear non-proliferation.

Freedman, Alix, and Bill Spindle, "Now at the Top of the U.N.'s Agenda: How to Save Itself," *The Wall Street Journal,* Dec. 19, 2003, p. A1.
Part of a six-part series on the U.N. examines how the organization is determining its role in a post-Iraq war environment.

Fuerth, Leon, "America Need Not be a Law Unto Itself," *The Financial Times,* May 12, 2003, p. 17.
Vice President Al Gore's former national security adviser argues the United States can operate effectively as a world power within the parameters set by Article 51 of the U.N. charter, which grants a nation the right of self-defense.

Jordan, Michael J., "Who's In, Who's Out: U.N. Security Council Mulls Reform," *The Christian Science Monitor,* Oct. 16, 2002, p. 7.
The author reviews the various arguments for reforming the Security Council.

Khanna, Parag, "One More Seat at the Table," *The New York Times,* Dec. 6, 2003, p. A15.
A research analyst at the Brookings Institution proposes reforms to make the Security Council more effective, including eliminating the five permanent members' veto.

Lander, Mark, "U.N. Atom Agency Gives Iran Both a Slap and a Pass," *The New York Times,* Nov. 27, 2003, p. A22.
The author details recent efforts to contain Iran's alleged nuclear weapons development program.

Urquhart, Brian, "A Force Behind the U.N." *The New York Times,* Aug. 7, 2003, p. A23.
Urquhart, who served as U.N. under secretary-general for political affairs from 1974 to 1986, proposes development of a permanent U.N. peacekeeping force.

Weiss, Thomas G., "The Illusion of U.N. Security Council Reform," *The Washington Quarterly,* Autumn 2003, p. 147.
A political science professor at Columbia University argues that the Security Council, in its current configuration, is more than capable of effectively working toward the promotion of international peace and security.

Reports

"Enhancing U.S. Leadership at the United Nations," Council on Foreign Relations and Freedom House, 2002.
Analysts urge the United States to work more closely with other democratic nations at the United Nations to promote democracy and increase counterterrorism efforts.

Gardiner, Nile, and Baker Spring, "Reform the United Nations," *The Heritage Foundation,* Oct. 27, 2003.
Conservative analysts call for significant changes at the United Nations, including the broadening of a nation's right to self-defense and the removal from the U.N. Human Rights Commission of regimes that abuse human rights.

For More Information

American Enterprise Institute, 1150 17th St., N.W., Washington, DC 20036; (202) 862-5800; www.aei.org. A major Washington think tank.

Center for American Progress, 805 15th St., N.W., Suite 400, Washington, DC 20005; (202) 682-1611; www.americanprogress.org. A nonpartisan research and educational institute.

International Crisis Group, 1629 K St., N.W., Suite 450, Washington, DC 20006; (202) 785-1601; www.crisisweb.org. A nonprofit, non-governmental organization devoted to resolving conflicts around the globe.

United Nations Association, 801 2nd Ave., 2nd Fl., New York, N.Y. 10017; (212) 907-1300; ww.unausa.org. A nonprofit group that supports the U.N.

United Nations Foundation, 1225 Connecticut Ave., N.W., Suite 400, Washington, DC 20036; (202) 887-9040; www.unfoundation.org. Supports U.N. activities through grants and public-private partnerships.

World Policy Institute, New School University, 66 5th Ave., Suite 900, New York, NY 10011; (212) 229-5808; www.worldpolicy.org. An international-relations think tank.

6

Exporting Jobs

Mary H. Cooper

Workers at a call center in Bangalore, India, service customers from around the world 24 hours a day. U.S. and other firms are increasingly outsourcing their service operations to India, the Philippines, Russia and other sources of skilled, cheap labor. Proponents of so-called "offshoring" say it ultimately helps the U.S. economy, but critics say sending high-paying jobs overseas forces laid-off Americans into less desirable jobs.

From *The CQ Researcher*, February 20, 2004.

Computer programmer Robin Tauch rode the technology boom to a salary of nearly $100,000 a year at Dallas-based Computer Sciences Corp. But the ride ended last August, when she joined legions of fellow computer professionals on the unemployment rolls.

"I've got tons of friends who are looking for work," she says. "We're all people who have been employed for 20-some years. For the first time in our lives, we've just been dumped on the street."

But losing her job was doubly painful to Tauch because she had to train the two technology workers brought in from India to replace her.

Similar scenarios are playing out across the United States. Eager to reduce labor costs, a U.S. firm imports qualified foreign information technology (IT) workers by obtaining temporary visas for the new employees. Once they learn the host company's specific needs, the foreign workers often return home to establish an IT department for the firm. Or they replace the workers who trained them.

India is one of several countries with relatively low-wage, highly educated, English-speaking populations—Ireland and the Philippines among them—benefiting from U.S. cost-cutting efforts.

Workers in such countries provide a broad range of business services, such as answering customer-service calls, accounting, reviewing insurance claims and processing bills.

The export of American jobs has touched so many sectors of the economy, in fact, that it has generated a new term to describe the trend—"offshoring," short for offshore outsourcing.

"A lot of these offshored positions replace very high-wage jobs," says Lester Thurow, dean of the Sloan School of Business at

Nearly 3 Million Factory Jobs Were Lost

More than 2.8 million U.S. factory jobs have been lost since 2000, mainly in the computer/electronics and textile industries. Offshoring accounted for about 10 percent of the losses, according to one estimate. In the next 15 years, other studies predict the loss of up to 14 million service jobs, such as answering customer calls, accounting, insurance claim review and bill processing.

Lost U.S. Manufacturing Jobs
Selected Industries, 2000-2003

Industry	Jobs Lost
Computers and electronics	455,000
Textiles and apparel	395,000
Machinery	301,000
Transportation equipment	297,000
Fabricated materials	288,000
Primary metals	154,000
Electrical equipment/appliances	135,000
Plastics	131,000
Printing	132,000
Furniture	107,000

Source: Labor Department, Bureau of Labor Statistics, Feb. 4, 2004; www.bls.gov

is emerging as a key issue in the coming presidential campaign.

U.S. job outsourcing began in the manufacturing sector in the 1980s, when disappearing worldwide trade barriers forced U.S. companies to compete with foreign manufacturers using cheap labor. To survive, U.S. manufacturers exported factory jobs from the higher-wage, heavily unionized Northeast and Midwest to Asia and Latin America, as well as to the largely non-unionized and lower-wage Southern United States.

In addition, many factory jobs fall victim to computerization and robotization.

As a result, many blue-collar workers and middle managers were "downsized," forcing many former assembly-line workers to seek lower-paid jobs in the rapidly expanding retail and business-service industries. Nearly 5 million U.S. factory jobs have been lost in the United States since 1979, more than half of them—2.8 million—since 2000 alone.[2]

Massachusetts Institute of Technology (MIT). "Here in Boston, for example, Massachusetts General Hospital is even outsourcing radiologists. Instead of having a $450,000 radiologist read an X-ray or an MRI here, they send it to India and have it read by a $50,000 radiologist."

Meanwhile, General Electric, Microsoft and other big firms are expanding their operations in India to include everything from basic customer service to high-end research and development.[1]

Business advocates say offshoring is nothing more than the latest cost-saving technique and that it will benefit Americans in the long run by allowing companies to be more efficient and to invest the savings in more valuable, cutting-edge U.S. jobs of the future.

Labor advocates counter that offshoring threatens U.S. living standards by forcing Americans whose jobs have gone overseas to take lower-wage positions. The debate over whether offshoring helps or hurts the economy also

Lately, however, American businesses have been offshoring more of their highly paid professional staffs, who until now had been insulated from job insecurity by their specialized skills, usually acquired after years of costly college and graduate education.

"The Web makes it much easier for a skilled job to move to India, where you have plenty of people trained not just at MIT but at various high-tech Indian academic institutions," says Susan Aaronson, director of globalization studies at the University of North Carolina's Kenan Institute of Private Enterprise, in Washington, D.C. "The only thing that's new about this is that middle-class jobs are now being affected."

Estimates of the number of American jobs lost to the trend vary widely, largely because U.S. companies are not required to report their offshoring practices. One report blames offshoring for 300,000 of the 2.4 million total jobs lost since 2001. Various studies project that from

3 to 14 million service jobs could go overseas in the next 15 years.[3]

Economists say offshoring helps explain why the nation is undergoing its so-called jobless recovery. Since the last recession ended in 2001, the U.S. economy has rebounded—except for employment.

Last year, America's output of goods and services, or gross domestic product (GDP), rose by 3.1 percent, up from 2.2 percent in 2002 and just 0.5 percent in 2001.[4] Business investment and consumer spending also has picked up.[5] But employment, which typically improves during recoveries, has lagged: Only 112,000 new jobs were added to private payrolls in January, about 38,000 fewer than economists had expected.[6]

President Bush declared on Feb. 9, 2004, that "America's economy is strong and getting stronger" and predicted the creation of 2.6 million jobs this year, increasing non-farm payroll employment to 132.7 million. Last February, the White House predicted that 1.7 million jobs would be created in 2003. In fact, non-farm payrolls showed a small decline. Since Bush took office, the country has lost 2.2 million payroll jobs, as non-farm employment dipped to 130.2 million.

One explanation for the disappointing employment numbers lies in the economy's blistering productivity rate—9.4 percent in the third quarter of last year.

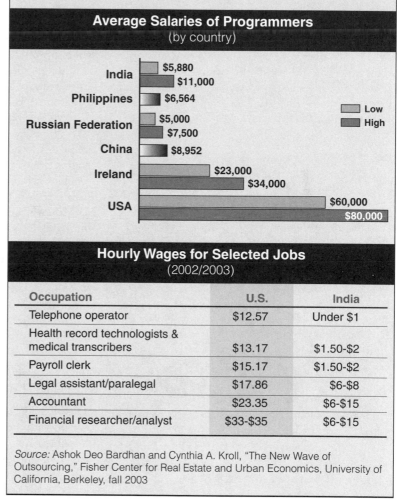

Outsourced Jobs Abroad Pay Lower Wages

Computer programmers in countries where U.S. companies are outsourcing their technology jobs earn far less than American programmers (top). Similarly, low wages are paid in other countries, like India, where U.S. firms also are outsourcing non-technology jobs (bottom).

Average Salaries of Programmers
(by country)

Country	Low	High
India	$5,880	$11,000
Philippines	$6,564	
Russian Federation	$5,000	$7,500
China	$8,952	
Ireland	$23,000	$34,000
USA	$60,000	$80,000

Hourly Wages for Selected Jobs
(2002/2003)

Occupation	U.S.	India
Telephone operator	$12.57	Under $1
Health record technologists & medical transcribers	$13.17	$1.50-$2
Payroll clerk	$15.17	$1.50-$2
Legal assistant/paralegal	$17.86	$6-$8
Accountant	$23.35	$6-$15
Financial researcher/analyst	$33-$35	$6-$15

Source: Ashok Deo Bardhan and Cynthia A. Kroll, "The New Wave of Outsourcing," Fisher Center for Real Estate and Urban Economics, University of California, Berkeley, fall 2003

"Moving all the low-productivity stuff from the American economy to China or India raises the productivity level of what's left," Thurow says. "Outsourcing is the big reason why—even though we've got an economic recovery in terms of rate of growth—we don't have an economic recovery in terms of jobs."

Proponents of offshoring say it simply reflects the way the U.S. economy is evolving and that bumps in the road must be expected. "This trend of moving jobs to other locations, both onshore and offshore, started when we moved from an agrarian-based society to where we are today, and it's been a continuous evolution," says Robert Daigle, co-founder of Evalueserve, an offshoring company in Chappaqua, N.Y. Evalueserve's far-flung staff includes 270 people in India who conduct market research and write patent applications for corporate clients worldwide.

"Companies are outsourcing and offshoring to remain competitive."

Business representatives say that attempts to block the hiring of foreign workers would only hurt the economy, and eventually American workers. In addition to cutting labor costs, they say, globalizing work forces lets companies offer round-the-clock customer service, with workers in the Philippines and other overseas call centers answering customers when American employees are sleeping.

But critics say offshoring reflects the corporate quest for profits no matter the human cost. "Every time we hear a story like the one about the young lady [Tauch] in Texas, it just drives us crazy," says Mike Gildea, executive director of the AFL-CIO's Department for Professional Employees.

Getty Images/Tim Boyle

A job-seeker looks for tips at a state employment center in Arlington, Ill., last October. Although the economy is improving, economists call it a "jobless" recovery because of sluggish job growth. In December, manufacturers shed 26,000 jobs, bringing to 516,000 the number of U.S. factory jobs that disappeared last year. Moreover, a half-million tech jobs have been lost since 2001.

In addition, he says, offshoring could send a negative signal to the next generation of workers about the value of a college education. "These are American workers who have tried to do the right thing to get the American dream," Gildea says. "They've gone through years of schooling. Collectively, we're talking about billions of dollars invested in education going to waste. It makes no economic sense."

Nevertheless, offshoring is a $35-billion-a-year business and reportedly is growing 30-40 percent annually, gobbling up 1 percent of the world's service sector, according to the *Financial Times*.[7] As Nandan Nilekani, chief executive of Infosys Technologies, said at the World Economic Forum in Davos, Switzerland, recently: "Everything you can send down a wire is up for grabs."[8]

Still, offshoring advocates insist the threat to U.S. jobs has been overblown. According to the British information firm Datamonitor, only 2 percent of the world's 4 million call-center agents work outside the parent company's territory.[9]

Meanwhile, with the presidential campaign intensifying, candidates for the Democratic Party's nomination are beginning to blame offshoring for the loss of good jobs. And labor groups complain that a new immigration amnesty plan recently proposed by President Bush could flood the country with even more low-wage workers from Mexico, depressing U.S. wages for low-end jobs.

Here are some of the issues likely to fuel the coming debate:

Does offshoring threaten Americans' standard of living?

Traditionally during recessions, American workers were laid off with the implicit promise they would be rehired when demand for goods and services picked up again. Unemployment benefits generally lasted long enough to tide workers over until they returned to work, and pre-recession living standards were typically restored.

But the downsizing and offshoring trend of the past several decades marks a structural, or permanent, shift in the U.S. labor market, many economists say.[10] Domestic and offshore outsourcing often causes job losses. Unemployment benefits are no longer used to wait out recessions but to help workers retrain and find entirely different jobs—a process that frequently outlasts the benefits themselves.

Terminated workers frequently are forced to take jobs at much lower wages, forcing families to accept reduced living standards or compensate for the loss by sending a second family member to work. In the past, a single worker with a factory job could support a family, but today two-thirds of all working households are supported by two or more workers.[11] Even so, the shifting labor market is shutting many American workers out of the middle class: The Census Bureau reports that 67 percent of full-time workers earn less than $45,000 a year; half of all American workers make less than $33,636, hardly enough for a family to purchase the trappings of the American dream.[12]

But most economists cite the result of the 1980s downsizings—the economic boom of the 1990s—as evidence that offshoring will improve living standards for Americans and other workers over the long term.

"Globalization and the movement of jobs offshore are creating new markets for goods and services for U.S. companies," Daigle says. "In India, an emerging middle class lives the same lifestyle we Americans are familiar with; it didn't exist a decade or two ago. Not only are we bringing jobs to a place that sorely needs them, but there's a benefit to U.S. companies as well."

But critics of work force globalization say the benefits to developing countries and American companies are not trickling down to U.S. workers in all sectors of the economy. "We dispute the notion that workers have come out well in the end," Gildea says. "Any number of studies have shown that the lost manufacturing jobs have been replaced by jobs principally in the service sector, which are much, much lower-paying and have few, if any, benefits."

Workers' advocates say the same thing is happening to higher-paid technology specialists whose jobs are going overseas. "We are becoming a Wal-Martized country, where the only place you can afford to shop is at Wal-Mart, and the only thing you can get there is stuff made in China," says John A. Bauman, president of The Organization for the Rights of American Workers (T.O.R.A.W.), an advocacy group formed in 2002 to raise public awareness of IT offshoring. Bauman's job as a computer programmer was terminated in 2002, ending his 25-year career. Unable to find work, he says he delivered FedEx packages over the holidays.

Both sides agree on one thing: Globalization produces winners and losers. "Outsourcing doesn't threaten everybody's standard of living," says Josh Bivens, an economist at the Economic Policy Institute. "What it really does is redistribute a lot of income." Outsourcing boosts corporate profits, he explains, benefiting stockholders but not workers whose only income comes from wages.

Income redistribution already has widened the gap between rich and poor Americans. The share of aggregate income going to the wealthiest 5 percent of U.S. households has risen from 16 percent to 22 percent since 1980, while that received by the poorest 20 percent of all households has fallen by more than 80 percent, to just 3.5 percent of total U.S. income.[13]

Bivens says the trend is only likely to worsen as the offshoring of U.S. jobs escalates. "The winners are going to be people who own stock in large corporations," he says, "while people who get most of their money from a paycheck are going to see their standard of living hurt—the blue-collar workers who have had it rough for the past couple of decades."

Former U.S. Trade Representative Carla Hills likens the current anxiety about offshoring to the 1980s, when Americans feared the exodus of high-tech jobs to Japan. "They were going to make the computer chips, we were going to be left with the potato chips," she recalled. "But that didn't happen. Computer prices came down . . . and all of us, every business could afford a computer. We created jobs not only in computers, but across the spectrum."[14]

The new jobs may take longer than usual to materialize after the recent recession, she said, because the economy has undergone a major "structural change," and recovering from such changes "takes longer to get over the hump than when it's just cyclical."[15]

But Sen. Charles E. Schumer, D-N.Y., says the structural changes represent a fundamental, triple-threat, "paradigm shift" in the world economy, which may prevent classic economic theories from bearing fruit. First, capital flows more freely across borders, allowing American companies to invest in facilities abroad. Second, broadband allows information and jobs to be sent "around the world at no cost in the blink of an eye," he said.[16]

"Thirdly, and most importantly, we have 50 to 100 million well-educated, highly motivated Chinese and Indians coming on the market that can compete" with American workers, Schumer says. "If high-end jobs, middle-end jobs and low-end jobs can all be done better overseas, . . . what's left here?

"Yes, our companies will do better, but if 80 percent, 90 percent of their employees are overseas and if American wages are forced to go down in the new jobs [that are created], what do we do?" he asked.[17]

Craig R. Barrett, CEO of Intel, the world's leading computer chip maker, would seem to agree. "The structure of the world has changed," he said. "The U.S. no longer has a lock on high-tech, white-collar jobs."[18]

The solution, says Hills, is tax incentives to encourage "investment in human capital" so Americans could do the higher-end jobs that will be created in the coming decade.[19]

Manufacturers defend outsourcing as the only way they can stay in business and protect their remaining U.S. jobs. "Manufacturing, more than any other economic activity, is on the world stage," says Hank Cox, spokesman for the National Association of Manufacturers. "The service or retail companies compete with the business in the next block, but our guys compete with China, Korea and the rest of the world, so they face a relentless downward pressure on prices."

Cox says that while prices for manufactured goods have dropped by about 1 percent a year over the past seven years, production costs—including wages and especially health benefits—continue to rise. "A lot of our members have gone under, and we've lost a lot of jobs because of that. A lot of them have been faced with a choice between outsourcing and closing their doors."

Indeed, proponents of offshoring say Americans should embrace the practice, not deplore it. A study by the McKinsey Global Institute shows the U.S. economy gets up to $1.14 in profits for every dollar outsourced.[20]

Furthermore, the proponents say, given America's huge budget deficit, rather than restricting the offshoring of government jobs, the country should be shipping even more government jobs overseas—in order to save taxpayers money.[21]

Would better education and job training protect American jobs?

During the 1980s downsizing, factory workers were encouraged to retrain for the computer-related jobs the fledgling high-tech revolution was creating. While some did get retrained, others took service positions, though generally at lesser wages and benefits than their old jobs.

Now, as offshoring begins taking the jobs of higher-wage workers, many experts are once again urging unemployed Americans to retrain for the new, highly skilled positions expected to become available.

President Bush echoed the call. "Many of the fastest-growing occupations require strong math and science

preparation, and training beyond the high school level," Bush said in his State of the Union address in January. "I propose increasing our support for America's fine community colleges, so they can train workers for the industries that are creating the most new jobs." The president announced a Jobs for the 21st Century proposal that would provide $100 million for education and training, including retraining of displaced workers, in fiscal 2005.[22]

But Bush's initiative ignores the plight of specialists with advanced degrees who are already unemployed or underemployed. The unemployment rate among science and engineering Ph.D.s stands at around 10 percent.[23] Gene Nelson, a biophysicist in Dallas, Texas, says he cannot find a job in his field that pays a living wage. "As a condition of being a postdoctoral worker, you must have a science or engineering doctorate, which is a very substantial investment of time and money," he says. "Postdocs today, by and large, are paid less than the high school graduate who manages the fast-food restaurant down the road. So there you are. You've earned your Ph.D., and there are no jobs; people are being trained for nonexistent positions at the Ph.D. level."

Nelson attributes the lack of demand for postdoctoral workers in part to an influx of foreign advanced-degree holders that followed dire warnings in the late 1990s that the United States was not graduating enough engineers and scientists.[24] Unless Congress increased the number of non-immigrant, H-1B, visas for skilled foreign workers, American firms argued, they could not maintain their competitive edge in the high-tech revolution. "Basically, we had a situation designed by employers and lobbied for by government agencies that was totally fraudulent," Nelson says, "because they alleged that we faced a looming shortage of scientists and engineers. Nothing could be further from the truth."

Thurow says the warnings were justified for IT specialists, but only temporarily. "In the late 1990s, there was a huge shortfall of IT professionals in the United States," he says. Even though many out-of-work, older programmers questioned whether there truly was a shortage, Congress expanded the temporary visa program for high-tech workers and those with advanced degrees. Between 1995 and 2000, millions of workers entered the country under the program.

But then the bubble burst. "When the dot-coms collapsed, they disgorged hundreds of thousands of experienced IT professionals," Thurow says. Today, about

800,000 American IT professionals are unemployed.[25]

Workers who lost IT jobs to off-shoring doubt education and training will ease their plight. After she lost her job at CSC, Tauch went to a community college to update her bachelor's degree in computer science. "But once you get the training and look for a job, they won't give it to you unless you have experience," she says. "President Bush keeps telling us to go to community college, but it's a joke."

Nevertheless, U.S. manufacturers agree with Bush on the need for a better-educated work force, particularly among high school graduates. "Our members say education is one of their biggest concerns," says the NAM's Cox. "They say the kids coming out of school today can't pass a writing test, can't pass a reading test, can't pass a math test and can't pass a drug test."

Cox supports Bush's community-college initiative and thinks it will help high school graduates transition to an increasingly demanding workplace. "The modern manufacturing workplace is like Star Trek," Cox says. "It's high-tech, and a dummy can't just go in there and handle it. These are advanced jobs that pay well, and we have to start directing some of our brightest young people into manufacturing."

Yet veterans of the labor-market turbulence of recent decades dispute the value of education and training, even for young people entering the job market. For instance, among computer programmers—the sector that has taken one of the biggest hits from outsourcing—unemployment has risen from just 1.6 percent two years ago to 7.1 percent today, significantly higher than the overall U.S. unemployment rate of 5.7 percent.[26]

"They tell you that if you take computer courses you're going to get a job in the computer field," says IT specialist Bauman. "You can go and get an education, but for what jobs? Those of us who are already under-employed are working as FedEx drivers, selling cars and selling insurance. I've got two kids who have all their certifications, and they can't find jobs. It's all because they listened to Dad, and this is one time I wish they hadn't."

Do current work-visa rules hurt American workers?

Bringing foreign workers into the United States on a temporary basis is an indirect form of exporting American jobs, critics of U.S. work-visa programs say. Although the work contributes to the U.S. economy,

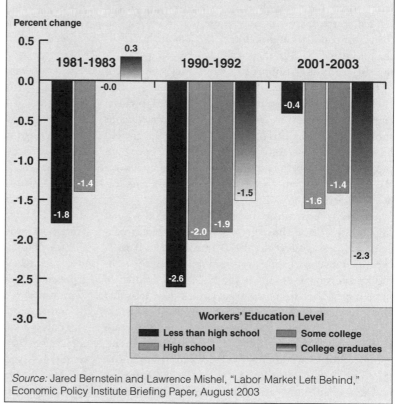

College Graduates Were Hit Hardest

Highly educated American workers suffered a greater drop in employment rates in the current economic recovery than less well-educated workers. In the previous two recoveries, by contrast, employment rates dropped farther for less-educated workers.

Changes in Employment Rates by Education Level

Percent change

1981-1983: 0.3, -0.0, -1.4, -1.8

1990-1992: -2.6, -2.0, -1.9, -1.5

2001-2003: -0.4, -1.6, -1.4, -2.3

Workers' Education Level
- Less than high school
- High school
- Some college
- College graduates

Source: Jared Bernstein and Lawrence Mishel, "Labor Market Left Behind," Economic Policy Institute Briefing Paper, August 2003

many of the workers will likely return to their native lands when their visas expire. Although some end up getting green cards and working in the United States permanently, many are hired with the understanding that they will open satellite U.S. offices back home after their training in the United States.

"Importing visa workers facilitates the offshoring of American jobs," Bauman says. "The foreign workers learn about the technology from people here in the United States, figure out how to use that technology in their own countries and then take the jobs offshore." In the meantime, he says, the foreign workers are performing the computer support for which they were hired. "The Americans are already gone."

Temporary work-visa programs were created to satisfy employers' demands for workers during perceived labor shortages.[27] In the early 20th century, Mexican field hands entered the country under the "Bracero" program supported by Western farm interests, followed by Basque sheepherders, Caribbean sugar cane harvesters and academic researchers from Europe and Asia.

In 1990, responding to what industry said was an impending critical shortage of skilled high-tech workers, Congress passed the 1990 Immigration Act. It expanded several existing non-immigrant visas for technical professionals—notably the H-1B visa, granted to foreign professionals for up to six years to take jobs that employers said they could not find qualified U.S. workers to fill. The visa also has been used to import physical therapists and, more recently, elementary and kindergarten teachers. In addition, the L-1 visa program, introduced in 1970, permits foreign executives and managers of U.S.-based multinationals to work in the United States for up to seven years; workers with special knowledge of an employer's products can stay up to five years.

Last year, more than 217,000 work visas were approved for foreign nationals under the H-1B program.[28] Since 1985, more than 17 million H-1B foreign workers have been admitted to the United States, according to ZaZona.com, an online monitoring service run by a critic of the programs. It estimates that almost 900,000 H-1B workers were in the United States at the end of 2001.[29]

Industry supporters say the visas help ensure American competitiveness in the global marketplace. "Access to the best-educated engineering talent around the world is critical to [our] company's future success," said Patrick J. Duffy, human resources attorney for Intel Corp. The U.S. semiconductor giant, with some $27 billion in revenues, employs almost 80,000 workers worldwide, and H-1B workers account for around 5 percent of its U.S. work force. "We expect . . . to sponsor H-1B employees in the future for the simple reason that we cannot find enough U.S. workers with the advanced education, skills and expertise we need."[30]

Moreover, supporters say, the visa programs help protect American jobs by keeping U.S. companies competitive. "When companies are competing in an international market, the inability to effectively manage their work force can mean the difference between gaining the edge and being put out of business," wrote Randel K. Johnson, a vice president of the U.S. Chamber of Commerce. "The result can mean even greater job losses in the long run."[31]

But critics say the visa programs simply have been used to replace American professionals with lower-wage foreigners. Although the visa law specifically says imported workers must receive prevailing wages, critics say enforcement is nearly nonexistent and that H-1B workers make between 15 and 33 percent less than their American counterparts.[32]

Dallas biophysicist Nelson says American universities took an early lead in promoting the visa programs, depressing wages for American scientists across the board. "This was all about bringing in cheap labor," he says.

Furthermore, Nelson says, because H-1B visa holders may only work for the employer who submitted their visa application, they are unlikely to object to adverse working conditions—such as lower pay scales or longer hours.

"This visa was designed to give the employer incredible leverage," Nelson says. "It is conditioned on the foreign national maintaining continuous employment. So if the employer gets unhappy and terminates that worker, the worker is immediately subject to deportation. In practice, it's been rarely done, but this is a very, very powerful tool."

That leverage extends beyond the foreign workers themselves, critics say. "By robbing the foreign workers of bargaining power, the visa program robs everyone else in the industry of that bargaining power as well," says the Economic Policy Institute's Bivens. If employers have access to cheaper labor, he explains, they can ignore American workers' demands for higher wages.

"There's nothing intrinsically wrong with guest workers, or even immigrants who wish to become citizens, having these jobs," Bivens adds. "What's wrong is the way the program is structured, which is quite bad for wages overall in these industries."

Many critics want work-visa programs eliminated altogether. "The H-1B program amounts to a government subsidy, because it provides economic benefits to a narrow class of entities, while the rest of us either have no benefit or—in the case of people like me—a negative benefit," Nelson says. "Our investment in our education, training and experience has been reduced to an economic value approaching zero."

In fact, he adds, because he's considered overqualified for most of the jobs now open—such as retail clerks and administrative assistants—"I've actually had to keep it a secret that I have a Ph.D."

BACKGROUND

Postwar Boom

As Western Europe, Japan and the Soviet bloc struggled to rebuild after World War II, U.S. manufacturing enjoyed a golden age. Expanding production and exports brought new jobs by the millions, feeding a rapidly growing American middle class.

Bolstered by union protections, a blue-collar wage earner in the leading manufacturing sectors—steel, appliances and automobiles—took home "family wages" sufficient to support an entire family, plus employer-provided health insurance and pensions. Even low-wage textile jobs offered opportunities for betterment to impoverished Southern farm workers.

For most of the 1950s and '60s, the United States was largely self-sufficient. As Europe and East Asia rebuilt their economies, they provided a vast market for U.S. goods while slowly emerging as significant trade competitors. Japan expanded its manufacturing sector by applying U.S. production techniques and became a leading exporter of plastic toys and other inexpensive products, and eventually high-end electronics and automobiles. Europe focused on exporting cars and other high-value manufactured goods to American consumers.

U.S. manufacturers began building factories in the South and overseas, where wages were much lower. The practice accelerated in the 1970s, when a series of energy crises signaled the beginning of the end of U.S. self-reliance in oil production—the basic fuel driving the

U.S. economy. Rising energy prices caused a series of recessions, and steel- and automakers and other manufacturers laid off thousands of workers.

For their part, American consumers sought cheaper imported products, including the increasingly popular Japanese cars. Labor unions responded with "Buy-American" campaigns intended to shore up the beleaguered Midwest, which became known as the Rust Belt for its numerous shuttered factories.

But by the mid-1980s, rising production costs and growing foreign competition had prompted more and more industries to restructure. Many permanently downsized their work forces, often using automation. Others outsourced at least part of the production, either to lower-cost—non-union—domestic producers or overseas, where labor was cheaper still. The textile and apparel industries, usually in Southern mill towns, were among the first to export large numbers of American jobs, especially to emerging economies in Asia.

In the early 1980s, U.S. makers of auto and electronic equipment pioneered the overseas production of basic components for U.S. assembly—providing the technological foundation for other countries to develop their own industries.[33]

With Japan emerging as a major industrial power, Hong Kong, Taiwan, Malaysia, South Korea and Singapore assumed Japan's earlier role of low-cost producer of components shipped to the United States for assembly into finished products.

Meanwhile, to reduce the cost of transporting their own finished products to the U.S. market, foreign companies began opening factories in the United States, partly offsetting the loss of American jobs offshore. European and Japanese automakers, in particular, created thousands of new jobs for Americans in the late 1980s. But they mostly built their facilities outside the industrial heartland, hiring non-union workers for less pay than their unionized peers in the upper Midwest.

Wages also suffered as the manufacturing sector declined. Laid-off factory workers often took low-paying, non-union jobs in the burgeoning service sector as retail clerks and cashiers.

NAFTA and More

The export of U.S. manufacturing jobs accelerated in the 1990s, especially after Congress in 1993 approved the North American Free Trade Agreement (NAFTA),

CHRONOLOGY

1970s–1980s *Growing international competition prompts U.S. companies to reduce labor costs by moving factories to lower-wage countries.*

1970 Congress establishes the L-1 visa program to permit foreign executives and managers of U.S.-based multinationals to work in the United States.

1976 The Immigration and Nationality Act Amendments increase the number of visas allocated to foreign workers and their families.

1990s *Americans flock to information-technology (IT) jobs after government and industry vow that manufacturing jobs shifted overseas would be replaced by domestic computer jobs and warn of a coming high-tech labor shortage.*

1990 The Immigration Act expands the H-1B non-immigrant visa program. It permits up to 65,000 foreign technical professionals a year to work in the U.S. for up to six years at jobs employers claim cannot be filled by U.S. workers.

1993 Congress approves the North American Free Trade Agreement (NAFTA) removing trade barriers among the United States, Canada and Mexico. U.S. manufacturers set up plants just south of the border hiring low-wage Mexican workers.

1998 Congress expands the number of H-1B visas issued each year after U.S. businesses plead for more foreign computer specialists to help prevent widespread computer failures at the turn of the millennium.

2000s *High-tech unemployment increases after the "Y2K" crisis never materializes, the technology boom collapses and U.S. companies begin shifting high-tech and other white-collar jobs offshore.*

October 2000 Congress again raises the annual H-1B visa cap, to 195,000.

November 2001 The current "jobless" recovery begins, featuring rising stock prices, economic output and productivity, loss of manufacturing jobs and few new jobs.

2002 Recently fired technology professionals establish the Organization for the Rights of American Workers (T.O.R.A.W.) to raise public awareness of IT off-shoring. . . . Forrester Research predicts that 3.3 million service-sectors jobs will move offshore by 2015.

July 10, 2003 Rep. Rosa DeLauro, D-Conn., and Sen. Saxby Chambliss, R-Ga., introduce the L-1 Non-Immigrant Reform Act to address reported abuses of the L-1 visa program.

July 24, 2003 Sen. Christopher J. Dodd, D-Conn., and Rep. Nancy L. Johnson, R-Conn., introduce the USA Jobs Protection Act, which would beef up enforcement of the H-1B and L-1 visa programs to prevent companies from illegally replacing qualified American workers and underpaying foreign workers.

Sept. 30, 2003 Rising unemployment in the high-tech industry prompts Congress to slash the annual cap on H-1B visas from 195,000 to 65,000 in response to concern over the impact of guest workers on U.S. jobs.

December 2003 On the 10th anniversary of NAFTA, studies show that more U.S. jobs have been created than lost since the law was passed.

Jan. 7, 2004 President Bush proposes a plan to offer temporary legal status to illegal immigrants working in the United States.

Jan. 20, 2004 In his State of the Union address, Bush calls for a new education and job-retraining program to be based in the nation's community colleges.

Jan. 23, 2004 Bush signs into law a measure prohibiting American companies from subcontracting some government jobs to companies outside the United States.

Feb. 6, 2004 Labor Department reports that American employers added only 112,000 new jobs in January, about 38,000 fewer than economists had expected.

Poor Nations Thrive on Job Exporting

For all the controversy surrounding the offshore outsourcing of American white-collar jobs, one of its consequences is undisputed—higher living standards in developing countries that have just joined the global economy.

In the late 1980s, when U.S. corporations first began exporting "back-office" work like bill processing, they turned to developed countries with large English-speaking populations but lower prevailing wages, such as Ireland and Israel. Many were allies, reducing the political risks associated with outsourcing.

But by the 1990s, the end of the Cold War had opened up new labor markets in the former Soviet bloc, while the embrace of free markets and the gradual lowering of trade barriers by many formerly closed economies—such as India and China—made still more countries attractive targets for offshoring.[1]

Today, U.S. and European companies are shifting a growing array of white-collar jobs—500,000 in the past five years—to poorer countries all over the world, from the Philippines to Russia and its former allies in Hungary, Romania and the Czech Republic—virtually any country with broadband Internet access and a technically literate work force.[2]

But no country has benefited more from recent white-collar job outsourcing by American industry than India, where such work now accounts for 2.5 per cent of gross domestic product.[3] After gaining independence in 1947, India missed out on the industrial revolution that had enriched its imperial overlord, Britain, remaining mired in poverty along with the rest of the Third World.

Successive Indian governments adopted protectionist policies to promote self-sufficiency as the engine of India's economy, but they also invested heavily in education, notably a large university system focusing on engineering and science. In addition, the colonial experience left most of India's 1 billion inhabitants with an enduring asset: proficiency in English.

In short, India offers highly educated, English-speaking workers for about a tenth of Americans' salaries. White-collar outsourcing has helped fuel a 33-percent increase in India's share of global economic output since 1991.[4]

Some of the newfound wealth is ending up in the pockets of Indian high-tech workers, whose wages are climbing.[5] Young college graduates are flocking to offshore centers such as Bangalore and Mumbai (formerly Bombay) and gaining the independence that comes with a generous paycheck. In addition, India's strict class and caste divisions are loosening, and a newly emerging middle class of young professionals is adopting the consumption habits of their American peers and casting aside such time-honored traditions as arranged marriages

India may soon face stiff competition from such budding offshore locations as Bangladesh, Brazil, Singapore, Thailand, Venezuela and Vietnam, the United Nations reports.[6] As wages rise in India, it is likely to see competition from China, whose fast-growing industrial base and even bigger labor pool are making it a tempting alternative for cost-cutting American firms. China is likely to overcome its big shortcoming—a dearth of English speakers—as a new generation of workers graduates from China's schools, where English instruction is now mandatory.

Outsourcing of manufacturing jobs from the United States and other industrial countries has already benefited workers in special economic zones located along China's coastline that were opened to trade in the 1980s. "There are 300 million people in those eastern coastal provinces who have seen an extraordinary pickup in their standard of living," said Edmund Harriss, portfolio manager of the Guinness Atkinson China and Hong Kong Fund.[7]

In 2001, China was granted normal trade status by the United States after joining the World Trade Organization, two moves that forced it to significantly liberalize its trade policies. "You're seeing an economy that is just about to take wing because you now have consumers who were never able to participate in the economy before," Harriss said.

China's opening to foreign investment, including job offshoring, is being felt beyond the U.S. As a result of the 1993 North American Free Trade Agreement, Mexico enjoyed a decade of rapid job growth as U.S. firms seeking low-wage workers set up factories south of the border. But today Mexico is losing many of those jobs to even lower-wage countries, including China.

"Five years ago, Mexico was the logical place for manufacturers to go," said Jonathan Heath, an economist with LatinSource, a consulting firm in Mexico City. "Now China is logical."[8]

[1] See Andy Meisler, "Where in the World Is Offshoring Going?" *Workforce Management*, January 2004, p. 45.

[2] Christopher Caldwell, "A chill wind from offshore," *Financial Times*, Feb. 7, 2004.

[3] *Ibid.*

[4] International Monetary Fund, "IMF Survey," Feb. 2, 2004.

[5] See David E. Gumpert, "U.S. Programmers at Overseas Salaries," *Business Week Online*, Dec. 2, 2003.

[6] U.N. Conference on Trade and Development, "E-Commerce and Development Report 2003," Nov. 20, 2003.

[7] Quoted by Erika Kinetz, "Who Wins and Who Loses as Jobs Move Overseas?" *The New York Times*, Dec. 7, 2003, p. A5.

[8] Quoted by Chris Kraal, "NAFTA 10 Years Later," *Los Angeles Times*, Jan. 2, 2004, p. A1

which removed trade barriers among the United States, Canada and Mexico. U.S. companies seeking cheap labor close to the American market built hundreds of factories, called *maquiladoras*, just south of the border, employing tens of thousands of Mexicans. By 2000, American textile workers—already hit by outsourcing to Asia—had lost more than 80,000 additional jobs to Mexico as a result of NAFTA.[34]

But according to Mack McLarty, former chief of staff and special envoy for the Americas under President Bill Clinton, NAFTA created more U.S. jobs than it eliminated. While about 500,000 American factory jobs went to Mexico because of NAFTA, U.S. private-sector employment grew by 15 million jobs—with hourly wages up 10 percent—in the decade since the law went into effect, McLarty wrote recently.[35]

Even as traditional manufacturing jobs continued to disappear during the 1990s, increasing productivity transformed several U.S. manufacturing sectors. A newly organized American steel industry emerged, even after such industry leaders as Bethlehem Steel and LTV went under, crushed by lower-cost imports from Japan and other countries. Incorporating the latest technologies, International Steel Group and other new companies over the past two decades increased U.S. steel production from 75 million tons to 102 million tons. But they did so by increasing productivity, not jobs: Today there are

just 74,000 U.S. steelworkers, down from 289,000 in the early 1980s. And while wages remain high, at $18 to $21 an hour, the generous pension and health benefits their predecessors enjoyed are gone.[36]

Still, the enormous shift from traditional manufacturing to telecommunications, retail trade, finance and other industries continued apace. Between 1980—when manufacturers began downsizing—and 2002, General Motors eliminated 53 percent of its work force, Kodak 46 percent and Goodyear 36 percent. Over the same period, United Parcel Service boosted its payroll by 224 percent, McDonald's by 253 percent and Wal-Mart by a whopping 4,715 percent.[37] A quarter of the factory workers who found new jobs took pay cuts of at least 25 percent, according to the Institute for International Economics.[38]

During the 1990s, makers of electronic equipment and computers began emulating older manufacturers by sending production overseas. Despite rapid productivity improvements—accompanied by high profits and rising stock prices—high-tech companies were eager to improve their competitive edge in a rapidly globalizing industry.

The service sector also sought cheaper labor overseas.[39] Software companies led the way, quickly establishing Bangalore, India, as a major U.S. outpost. Other countries benefited from U.S. offshoring as well. Ireland, which largely had missed Europe's postwar boom, blossomed in the 1990s as American corporations outsourced their billing and other "back-office" operations. The Philippines and Malaysia emerged as leading call-center locations, China became an important back-office service center, and Russia and Israel began providing customized software and computer systems.

Several unrelated developments further energized offshoring during the 1990s. Access to the Internet through high-speed broadband connection spread from the industrial countries to the developing world, enabling managers in the U.S. to communicate quickly and cheaply with satellite offices. The use of English as the *lingua franca* of businesses around the world enabled workers in India, the Philippines and other English-speaking countries to take part in the outsourcing boom. And locating offices in different time zones allowed call centers to service customers around the clock.

Y2K Impact

Before U.S. employers began exporting large numbers of IT and other white-collar jobs, they clamored for relax-

President Bush called for "stronger math and science preparation" in his State of the Union address in January. "I propose increasing our support for America's fine community colleges, so they can train workers for the industries that are creating the most new jobs," he said.

ation of the laws limiting non-immigrant visas. Fueling these efforts were dire predictions by the National Science Foundation and the conservative Hudson Institute that American universities were not turning out enough skilled technical professionals.[40]

Congress cited the studies in 1990, when it substantially increased the number of skilled workers allowed into the country. The Immigration Act of 1990 nearly tripled the number of permanent, work-based admissions allowed each year and created tens of thousands of slots for various types of temporary skilled workers, including 65,000 under the controversial H-1B program. The 1990 law also created new visas for other skilled temporary workers, including nurses, scientists, teachers and entertainers, and expanded the L-1 program enabling multinational corporations to bring key executives to the United States for up to seven years.

As the 20th century came to an end, there was widespread fear that computer systems would crash worldwide on Jan. 1, 2000, because their internal clocks were not set to change from 1999 to 2000.[41] As U.S. companies scrambled to hire extra workers to circumvent the so-called Y2K bug, programmers became scarce. Employers renewed their claims of a dire shortage of skilled American workers and brought in thousands of foreign programmers under the H-1B program.

Either the fears had been overblown—or enough computers had been fixed to avert the problem. In any event, the new century arrived without incident. But companies that had hired costly specialists to rewrite their codes were left with a new incentive to cut costs.

"When 2000 came, employers started laying off more employees," says T.O.R.A.W. President Bauman. "But the foreign visa workers, who were supposedly getting a fair wage, were costing them less." Seasoned professionals like Bauman received higher compensation than H-1B workers, who often were just out of college. "Employers were saving on salaries with foreign workers, and they decided to keep them on."

As the new millennium began, the elimination of U.S. high-tech jobs only accelerated when the nation went into recession after the telecom "bubble" burst. The economy took a further nosedive after the Sept. 11, 2001, terrorist attacks. U.S. employers decided to more fully tap India's vast, cheap, labor pool, setting up operations in Bangalore and other cities. The offshoring boom had begun.

Vietnamese computer programmers attend a job fair in Hanoi in April 2002. Vietnam has emerged as a major outsourcing base for U.S., European and Japanese high-tech firms.

CURRENT SITUATION

'Jobless' Recovery

The U.S. economy continues on its uneven path to recovery. The Dow Jones Industrial Average rose an encouraging 25 percent last year after two disappointing previous years. GDP growth—8.2 percent in the third quarter and 4 percent in the fourth—suggests that the recovery, which officially began in November 2001, is finally picking up. Business investments in equipment and software are up, and inflation remains low, prompting the Federal Reserve to keep interest rates at their lowest levels in decades.[42]

"Exports are growing," Bush declared during his State of the Union address. "Productivity is high, and jobs are on the rise."

But Labor Department data show why economists call the recovery "jobless." A net total of just 1,000 jobs were added to industry payrolls in December. Temp agencies and other service companies hired 45,000 workers; construction workers and health-services workers also posted gains. But the new-job gains were offset by the continuing hemorrhaging of manufacturing jobs, which tend to pay middle-class wages and benefits. In December, manufacturers shed 26,000 jobs, bringing to 516,000 the number of U.S. factory jobs that disappeared last year. Moreover, in addition to the 2.8 million manufacturing jobs lost since July 2000, a half-million tech jobs have been lost since 2001.[43]

Although no figures are kept on how much of the job loss can be attributed to outsourcing or offshoring, economists are sure that outsourcing is a factor.

"It certainly plays a role in manufacturing," M.I.T.'s Thurow says. "A lot of the automobile components that used to be made in the United States are now made in various Third World countries. And that basically leads some blue-collar workers and their managers to lose their jobs. This outsourcing started back in the '90s, but the economy was growing so fast in the high-tech sector, we didn't notice it."

Former Labor Secretary Robert B. Reich contends most manufacturing jobs are not disappearing due to offshoring but because of the higher productivity that comes with enhanced efficiency and new technology. "I recently toured a U.S. factory containing two employees and 400 computerized robots," Reich wrote in *The Wall Street Journal*.[44]

Moreover, he noted, although more than 22 million factory jobs worldwide vanished between 1995 and 2002, the United States lost fewer than many other countries, both rich and poor. The United States lost 11 percent of its manufacturing jobs during the period, he noted, while Japan lost 16 percent, China 15 percent and Brazil 20 percent.[45]

Several business-research firms have estimated the extent of offshoring today and its likely growth in the future. The Information Technology Association of America found that 12 percent of its member companies had opened offshore operations, usually for programmers and software engineers.[46] Forrester Research predicts that 3.3 million U.S. service jobs—mostly IT-related positions like software developers and help-desk operators—will move offshore over the next 15 years.[47] Goldman Sachs estimates that 200,000 service jobs have been lost to offshoring so far—with 6 million more to follow over the next decade.[48] A University of California, Berkeley, study put the number at close to 14 million over the next 15 years.[49]

Lower costs for software and other services will allow "huge segments" of the economy to improve productivity, said former U.S. Trade Representative Hills, creating 20 million new American jobs in the coming decade. "That's faster than last decade," she said, noting that even the booming 1990s only created 15 million jobs. "Every metric study shows that . . . job growth [will rise]

faster than it did in the last decade. This is an amazing prospect."[50]

Some economists say the estimates ignore the economy's ability to absorb job losses. "The number of high-tech jobs outsourced abroad still accounts for a tiny proportion of America's 10-million strong IT work force," Reich also has noted. "When the U.S. economy fully bounces back from recession (as it almost certainly will within the next 18 months), a large portion of high-tech jobs that were lost after 2000 will come back in some form."[51]

But MIT's Thurow says white-collar outsourcing is still in its infancy—totaling only about $8 billion in a $400 billion, U.S.-dominated global software market. "White-collar outsourcing is rising very rapidly," Thurow says. "The issue is a little bit like rape. Not that many women have been raped, but you don't need a very large fraction of women who've been raped before everybody's worried about it."

Those fears seem likely to intensify as more American technology companies announce they are moving key jobs offshore. America Online reportedly is planning to hire additional Indian software engineers for its facility in Bangalore to help build its Internet software. Yahoo and Google may soon follow AOL's lead.[52] IBM plans to move as many as 4,730 white-collar jobs from the United States.[53] They would be joining the ranks of such American icons as AT&T, Dell, Microsoft, Proctor & Gamble and Verizon.

Legislative Action

Offshoring is turning into a hot political issue in this presidential election year, as the economic recovery fails to generate all the new jobs anticipated by the administration. The shortfall is prompting Congress and the states to consider proposals aimed at stemming the loss of American jobs.

A bipartisan measure pending in Congress would close what critics see as major loopholes in the H-1B and L-1 visa programs. The USA Jobs Protection Act, cosponsored by Democratic Sen. Christopher J. Dodd and GOP Rep. Nancy L. Johnson—both from Connecticut—would beef up federal enforcement of the programs to prevent companies from illegally replacing qualified American workers and underpaying the temporary workers.

Another proposal, sponsored in the House by Rep. Rosa DeLauro, D-Conn., and in the Senate by Sen. Saxby Chambliss, R-Ga., addresses reported abuses of the L-1 program. Since Sept. 30, 2003, when Congress slashed the annual cap on H-1B visas from 195,000 to 65,000, critics charge that companies have abused the L-1 program, which has no annual cap, to import non-managerial tech workers.

"The availability of the L-visa category to those applying under 'specialized knowledge'—a vague term at best open to multiple and elastic interpretations—has done clear harm to the American work force and contributed directly to the job loss since the most recent recession began," House International Relations Committee Chairman Henry J. Hyde, R-Ill., told a Feb. 4, 2004, committee hearing on visa reform. "Lax procedures, for L visas or any other category of non-immigrant visa, are clearly a prescription for chaos in both visa policy and border security. It is time for reform."

Business representatives counter that any attempt to restrict corporate America's ability to hire workers anywhere in the world would only hurt the U.S. economy, and eventually American workers. "The use of certain categories of visas, such as the H-1B or the L-1, by multinational companies has been an effective means of maintaining our competitive edge," the Chamber of Commerce's Johnson wrote. "In the long run, expansion of international trade and investment in the United States is in the best interests of all."[54]

"Unless U.S. and foreign companies are able to bring key personnel to their American operations, U.S. companies will be put at a competitive disadvantage and foreign companies will be unlikely to establish or expand their presence in our country," Harris N. Miller, president of the Information Technology Association of America, told the committee. Foreign investment "means more U.S. factories, offices and jobs, and the L-1 program facilitates these investments."

Another measure, introduced by Sens. John Kerry, D-Mass., the current front-runner for the Democratic presidential nomination, and Minority Leader Tom Daschle, D-S.D., seeks to help Americans understand how widespread the offshoring phenomenon really is by requiring employees at overseas call centers of U.S.-based companies to disclose the center's physical location.

On Jan. 23, President Bush signed into law a measure preventing American companies from subcontracting some government jobs to companies outside the United States. The ban, originally sponsored by Sens. George V. Voinovich, R-Ohio, and Craig Thomas, R-Wyo., was included in the fiscal 2004 omnibus appropriations bill. It remains uncertain how many of the 1.8 million civilians who work for the federal government will be affected. The Bush administration has accelerated the pace of outsourcing of federal jobs, and 102,000 jobs are currently slated to come up for competitive bidding.[55]

Some states that have been especially hard-hit by IT outsourcing are considering prohibiting government work from being contracted to non-Americans or barring employers from requiring workers slated for layoff to train their foreign replacements. Anti-outsourcing bills are now pending in a dozen legislatures, and up to 20 could consider such measures before the legislative season ends, according to Justin Marks, an analyst at the National Conference of State Legislatures (NCSL). Marks said eight states debated such bills last year, but none passed—largely due to Republican opposition.[56]

Even California—home to Silicon Valley companies that have been heavy users of offshoring and H-1B visas—is considering anti-offshoring legislation. A bill introduced by Assemblywoman Carol Liu, D-Pasadena, would prevent the use of overseas call centers for state services like welfare and food stamps. "There's a great irony here that we're telling people on welfare to find jobs, and the kind of jobs they could do are not here anymore," said Richard Johnson, Liu's legislative aide.[57]

> **Anti-outsourcing bills are now pending in a dozen legislatures, and up to 20 could consider such measures before the legislative season ends.**
>
> **— Justin Marks,**
> Analyst, National Conference of
> State Legislatures

Should the government slow the outsourcing of high-tech jobs?

YES — Ron Hira
Chairman, R&D Policy Committee, Institute of Electrical and Electronics Engineers

From testimony before the House Small Business Committee, Oct. 20, 2003

According to the most recent data from the Bureau of Labor Statistics, electrical, electronics and computer hardware engineers continue to face a higher unemployment rate than the general population, and over double the rate for other managers and professionals. The news for engineering managers is even worse, with an unemployment rate of 8 percent. . . .

To put this in historical context, in the 30-plus years that the Department of Labor has been collecting statistics, the past two years are the first in which unemployment rates for electrical, electronics and computer engineers are higher than the unemployment rate for all workers. . . . And throughout the 1980s, at a time when unemployment rates for all workers got as high as 9.5 percent, electrical and electronics engineering unemployment rates never rose above 2 percent. . . .

It is entirely misleading to describe offshore outsourcing as a "win-win" proposition for America and other countries, as free-trade advocates so often do. Those advocates [should be required] to demonstrate how workers who have been adversely affected will be compensated and helped to become productive citizens once again.

These advocates assume, as part of their argument, that displaced American workers will be redeployed. Instead of assuming, we should ensure that such workers are redeployed in equally high-skill and highly paid positions. . . .

The federal government must begin regularly tracking the volume and nature of the jobs that are moving offshore. Companies should be required to give adequate notice of their intentions to move work offshore, so displaced employees can make appropriate plans to minimize the financial hardship, and government support agencies can prepare to provide the necessary transition assistance. Congress should rethink how U.S. work force assistance programs can be designed to help displaced high-tech workers become productive again.

We are in a new era of work and lifelong learning, and new and more flexible methods are needed to provide meaningful assistance. Congress should strengthen H-1B and L-1 work force protections and their enforcement to ensure that the programs serve their respective purposes without adversely affecting employment opportunities for U.S. high-tech workers.

The United States needs a coordinated national strategy designed to sustain its technological leadership and promote job creation in response to the concerted strategies being used by other countries to attract U.S. industries and jobs.

NO — Harris N. Miller
President, Information Technology Association of America

From testimony before the House Small Business Committee, Oct. 20, 2003

In statistical terms, the trend towards offshore outsourcing is a cloud on the horizon, not a hurricane sweeping everything in its midst. We should keep our eye on how the weather pattern is changing, but we should not start boarding up our windows and stashing the patio furniture. The U.S. IT industry is facing new challenges, but it is not disappearing.

Over 10 million Americans earn their living in the IT work force . . . nine out of 10 of [them] employed by businesses outside of the IT industry: banks, law firms, factories, stores and the like. Eight out of 10 of these jobs are found in small businesses—the firms arguably least likely to [send their jobs offshore]. Even the most doom-and-gloom analysts predict that fewer than 500,000 computer-specific jobs will move offshore in the next 10 years. . . .

If we have seen any storm at all, it has been the three-year "perfect storm" of trends converging to depress the short-term demand for U.S. IT workers: the dot-com bust, the telecom collapse, the recession and jobless recovery and slow customer spending—domestically and globally—for new IT products and services. . . .

I do not mean to downplay the very real impacts of offshore competition to American IT workers or their families. Thousands of IT professionals have played by the rules: studied hard in school, worked long hours, made a sweat equity investment in the future of their companies, only to find themselves now unemployed or underemployed. A more vibrant economy and greater capital spending by the private sector will greatly help these individuals. Not all of the current concerns, however, can be attributed to the economy, and we need to better understand this new competitive reality, using logic—not emotion—as our filter. . . .

While it may be emotionally satisfying to try to protect jobs by throwing up barriers, free trade and global markets spark investment, trade and job creation. For Americans caught in the riptide of a transitioning job market, economic abstractions like positive trade balances and expanding free markets may be the source of cold comfort. I reject, however, the notion that offshore development is a zero sum game or that every job shipped offshore is a job permanently lost to an American worker. On the contrary, evidence abounds that the working capital that U.S. companies save by moving jobs and operations offshore results in new investment, innovation and job creation in this country.

At least one of the bills to be introduced in California is expected to apply to private employers that handle customers' confidential information. Controversies have erupted around the country in recent months when patients learned that insurance companies increasingly are having confidential medical records transcribed by companies overseas, where U.S. medical-privacy laws do not apply. During an employment dispute in October, a Pakistani contract worker handling confidential medical records from California threatened to disclose the information.[58]

Marks says political pressure to pass anti-outsourcing measures this year is growing in some states. "In any event, I think we'll see a ripple effect in policymaking," he said, "with greater efforts at local job creation in places most affected by outsourcing."[59]

Marks says offshoring public-sector jobs may not end up saving taxpayers money in the long run, because hidden long-term costs could outweigh short-term taxpayers' savings. "If you compare the savings to the loss in taxable income [from local workers laid off due to the offshoring] with the state's cost of paying unemployment benefits [to those laid off], it's possible states are not saving that much money," Marks said.[60]

Northeastern University labor economist Paul E. Harrington warns of another hidden, long-term cost: the erosion of a state's middle-class base. States that value "full employment, upward mobility and a solid middle class as an important and essential feature" of their economies should warn their companies to "think about this outsourcing issue," Harrington advised.[61]

Business spokesmen say anti-outsourcing measures amount to protectionism and will only hurt American workers. "The focus should be making sure that America stays a nimble, highly educated, forward-thinking, innovative economic presence, not one that's trying to hold onto things while the world around them is changing," says Daigle of Evalueserve. "That strategy is a going-out-of-business strategy."

But Bauman says displaced IT workers are counting on the offshoring bills. "If we don't see any action on this problem soon," he says, "we can kiss our careers good-bye forever."

Bush's Amnesty Plan

On Jan. 7, President Bush announced an initiative to permit the estimated 8 million illegal immigrants to remain in the United States for six years as long they are employed. The undocumented workers would receive identification cards enabling them to travel between the United States and their home countries. Employers also could bring in additional "guest workers" under the same conditions if they cannot find qualified American workers.

"We must make our immigration laws more rational and more humane," Bush said. "I believe we can do so without jeopardizing the livelihoods of American citizens."[62]

Critics say the proposal would worsen working conditions for American employees just as existing visa programs do—by tying a worker's legal status to steady employment with a single employer. "One of the ways you get ahead in the U.S. labor market is by making employers bid for you, and it doesn't sound like these guest workers are going to have that ability at all," says Bivens of the Economic Policy Institute. If employers can rely on low-wage immigrants to fill their job openings, he says, they will have no incentive to hire American workers who demand higher wages. "It doesn't really provide a big improvement over the status quo for the undocumented," Bivens says, "and it is one more way to subvert the bargaining power of other workers here."

Business groups welcome the proposal, saying immigrants would take jobs Americans don't want, not manufacturing or white-collar positions. "Manufacturing workers tend to be more sophisticated, higher-level workers," says Cox of the NAM. "Guys don't come here from Guatemala or Mexico and go to work in manufacturing. You have to know too much high-tech stuff."

But critics say similar efforts in other industrial countries offer little grounds for encouragement. "Guest-worker systems haven't worked anywhere in the world because eventually people just don't go home," MIT's Thurow says.

But Switzerland's program works, Thurow says, because every worker must return home for a certain period each year and is barred from bringing family members into the country. "The only way you can deport temporary workers is the way Switzerland does it," he says, "and they are just ferocious."

Few observers expect Congress to take up Bush's immigration plan this year. Many Republicans oppose any immigration initiative that rewards illegal immigrants for breaking the law, while many Democrats say the plan does not do enough to help them gain U.S. citizenship.

A bipartisan alternative presented on Jan. 21 by Sens. Daschle and Chuck Hagel, R-Neb., calls for eventual citizenship for illegal immigrants who meet a series of requirements and would admit no more than 350,000 new temporary workers each year.[63]

OUTLOOK

Election Debate

As presidential campaign rhetoric intensifies, many observers expect the globalization of American jobs to become an increasingly important issue, especially if offshoring continues to threaten white-collar jobs.

"If I were President Bush, professional white-collar outsourcing would give me nightmares," Thurow says. "When a factory moves to China or India, that's blue-collar jobs. They're Democratic voters anyway. But white-collar outsourcing? That's Republican voters."

The administration recently got a taste of how politically sensitive the offshoring issue is. N. Gregory Mankiw, chairman of the White House Council of Economic Advisers, stunned Democrats and Republicans alike when he recently described offshoring as "just a new way to do international trade. Outsourcing is a growing phenomenon, but it's something that we should realize is probably a plus for the economy in the long run."[64]

House Speaker J. Dennis Hastert, R-Ill., issued a stern rebuttal to his fellow Republican. "I understand that Mr. Mankiw is a brilliant economic theorist, but his theory fails a basic test of real economics," Hastert said. "An economy suffers when jobs disappear. Outsourcing can be a problem for American workers, and for the American economy. We can't have a healthy economy unless we have more jobs here in America."[65]

Mankiw subsequently hedged his statement. "It is regrettable whenever anyone loses a job," he wrote. "At the same time, we have to acknowledge that any economic change, whether arising from trade or technology, can cause painful dislocations for some workers and their families. The goal of policy should be to help workers prepare for the global economy of the future."

But the basic thrust of Bush's policy on outsourcing stands, as reflected in this year's "Economic Report of the President": "When a good or service is produced more cheaply abroad, it makes more sense to import it than to make or provide it domestically."[66]

President Bush asserts that his income tax cuts, which the administration says will total $1.3 trillion over 10 years, are the key to speeding the recovery and stimulating job growth. "Americans took those dollars and put them to work, driving this economy forward," Bush said during his State of the Union address.

The president went on to ask Congress to fund new programs to improve science and math education at the middle- and high-school levels and help community colleges "train workers for the industries that are creating the most new jobs."

The job-export issue is creeping into the tax debate. Democratic candidates have lambasted a tax loophole that enables corporations to avoid paying U.S. taxes on offshore revenues that already have been taxed by foreign governments.

"George Bush continues to fight for incentives to encourage Benedict Arnold companies to ship jobs overseas at the same time he cuts job training for our workers and cuts help for small businesses that create jobs here at home," Kerry charged.[67]

But the campaign oratory does not impress T.O.R.A.W. President Bauman and other Americans who have lost their jobs to foreign workers.

"Neither side is addressing this problem adequately," Bauman says. "Some of the candidates have outwardly said they would do something, but nobody has come out and said exactly what they would do to stop offshoring. I don't want to wait until November. I want to see action now."

"The issue is going to be exaggerated and manipulated by both sides in the political debate," predicted Dean Davison, an analyst at the Meta Group, a technology research and advisory firm in Stamford, Conn.[68]

Former Trade Representative Hills warns, "We really must be very wary about making the wrong economic move, even when it's politically attractive to be sloganistic."[69]

NOTES

1. Saritha Rai, "Indians Fearing Repercussions Of U.S. Technology Outsourcing," *The New York Times*, Feb. 9, 2004, p. C4.

2. See Nelson D. Schwartz, "Will 'Made in USA' Fade Away?" *Fortune*, Nov. 24, 2003, p. 98, and

"Employees on Nonfarm Payrolls by Major Industry Sector, 1954 to Date," Bureau of Labor Statistics.

3. See Karl Schoenberger, "Kerry, Dean Compete to Stress Hot Issue," *San Jose Mercury News*, Jan. 30, 2004.

4. The Commerce Department released its most recent GDP data on Jan. 30, 2004.

5. See Nell Henderson, "Growth Again, but Slower," *The Washington Post*, Jan. 31, 2004.

6. See "Unemployment Rate Falls; Few Jobs Added," The Associated Press, Jan. 9, 2004.

7. Christopher Caldwell, "A chill wind from offshore," *Financial Times*, Feb. 7, 2004.

8. *Ibid.*

9. "Global Offshore Call Center Outsourcing: Who Will Be the Next India?" *Datamonitor*, Jan. 8, 2004.

10. See Erica L. Groshen and Simon Potter, "Has Structural Change Contributed to a Jobless Recovery?" *Current Issues in Economics and Finance*, Federal Reserve Bank of New York, August 2003.

11. Census Bureau, 2002. See Andrew Hacker, "The Underworld of Work," *The New York Review of Books*, Feb. 12, 2004, pp. 38-40.

12. *Ibid.*

13. U.S. Census Bureau, "Historical Income Tables—Income Equality," Table IE-3, www.census.gov. For background, see Mary H. Cooper, "Income Inequality," *The CQ Researcher*, April 17, 1998, pp. 337-360.

14. Quoted on ABC's "This Week," Feb. 15, 2004. Hills was citing a study by Catherine L. Mann, "Globalization of IT Services and White Collar Jobs: The Next Wave of Productivity Growth," International Economics Policy Briefs, Institute for International Economics, December 2003.

15. *Ibid.*

16. *Ibid.*

17. *Ibid.*

18. Quoted in Steve Lohr, "Many New Causes for Old problem of Jobs Lost Abroad," *The New York Times*, Feb. 15, 2004, p. A17.

19. ABC, *op. cit.*

20. www.mckinsey.com/knowledge/mgi/offshore/.

21. Caldwell, *op. cit.*

22. From Bush's State of the Union address, Jan. 20, 2004.

23. See Peter D. Syverson, "Coping with Conflicting Data: The Employment Status of Recent Science and Engineering Ph.D.s," Council of Graduate Schools, 1997.

24. See, for example, Committee for Economic Development, "Reforming Immigration: Helping Meet America's Need for a Skilled Workforce," 2001.

25. *Ibid.*

26. See Eric Chabrow, "The Programmer's Future," *InformationWeek*, Nov. 17, 2003, pp. 40-52.

27. For background, see Kathy Koch, "High-Tech Labor Shortage," *The CQ Researcher*, April 24, 1998, pp. 361-384.

28. U.S. Citizenship and Immigration Services Fact Sheet, "H-1B Petitions Received and Approved in FY 2003," Oct. 22, 2003. Citizenship and Immigration Services, part of the Department of Homeland Security, has administered work-visa programs since the department absorbed the Immigration and Naturalization Service in 2003.

29. Ron Sanchez administers ZaZona.com as a source of information on the H-1B program.

30. Duffy testified Sept. 16, 2003, before the Senate Judiciary Committee.

31. From a June 18, 2003, letter to House Small Business Committee Chairman Donald A. Manzullo, R-Ill.

32. Norman Matloff, "Needed Reform for the H-1B and L-1 Work Visas: Major Points," Feb. 5, 2003, http://heather.cs.ucdavis.edu/itaa.html.

33. See "The Impact of Global Sourcing on the U.S. Economy, 2003-2010," *Evalueserve*, 2003.

34. See Jane Tanner, "Future Job Market," *The CQ Researcher*, Jan. 11, 2002, p. 14.

35. See Mack McLarty, "Trade Paves Path to U.S. Prosperity," *Los Angeles Times*, Feb. 1, 2004, p. M2.

36. Schwartz, *op. cit.*

37. Hacker, *op. cit.*

38. See Steve Lohr, "Questioning the Age of Wal-Mart," *The New York Times*, Dec. 28, 2003.

39. Information in the following paragraphs is based on Ashok Deo Bardhan and Cynthia A. Kroll, "The New Wave of Outsourcing," Research Report, Fisher Center for Real Estate and Urban Economics, University of California, Berkeley, fall 2003.

40. Koch, *op. cit.*

41. For background, see Kathy Koch, "Y2K Dilemma," *The CQ Researcher*, Feb. 19, 1999, pp. 137-160.

42. See Bureau of Economic Analysis, Commerce Department, "Growth Moderates in Fourth Quarter but Is Up for the Year," Jan. 30, 2004.

43. Bureau of Labor Statistics, Department of Labor, "Employment Situation Summary," Jan. 9, 2004. Also see Jonathan Krim, "Grove Says U.S. Is Losing Edge in Tech Sector," Forbes.com, Oct. 10, 2003.

44. See Robert B. Reich, "Nice Work If You Can Get It," *The Wall Street Journal*, Dec. 26, 2003, p. A10.

45. *Ibid.*

46. Information Technology Association of America, "2003 IT Workforce Survey," May 5, 2003.

47. John C. McCarthy *et al.*, "3.3 Million U.S. Services Jobs to Go Offshore," *Forrester Tech Strategy Brief*, Nov. 11, 2002.

48. Andrew Tilton, "Offshoring: Where Have All the Jobs Gone?" Goldman, Sachs & Co., *U.S. Economics Analyst*, Sept. 19, 2003.

49. Bardhan, *op. cit.*

50. ABC, *op. cit.*

51. Robert Reich, "High-Tech Jobs Are Going Abroad! But That's OK," *The Washington Post*, Nov. 2, 2003, p. B3.

52. See Jim Hu and Evan Hansen, "AOL Takes Passage to India," CNET News.com, Dec. 22, 2003.

53. See William M. Bulkeley, "IBM to Export Highly Paid Jobs to India, China," *The Wall Street Journal*, Dec. 15, 2003, p. B1.

54. Johnson, *op. cit.*

55. Andrew Mollison, "GOP Ban on 'Offshoring' Federal Jobs Angers Business Groups," Cox News Service, Jan. 29, 2004.

56. Karl Schoenberger, "Legislator wants to keep jobs in state, limits sought on overseas contracts," *San Jose* [California] *Mercury News*, Feb. 5, 2004.

57. *Ibid.*

58. *Ibid.*

59. *Ibid.*

60. Quoted on "Marketplace," National Public Radio, Feb. 16, 2004.

61. *Ibid.*

62. Quoted in Mike Allen, "Bush Proposes Legal Status for Immigrant Labor," *The Washington Post*, Jan. 8, 2004, p. A1. For background, see David Masci, "Debate Over Immigration," *The CQ Researcher*, July 14, 2000, pp. 569-592.

63. See Helen Dewar, "2 Senators Counter Bush on Immigrants," *The Washington Post*, Jan. 22, 2004, p. A4.

64. Mankiw spoke as he released the "Economic Report of the President 2004" on Feb. 9, 2004.

65. Statement, "Hastert Disagrees With President's Economic Advisor On Outsourcing," Feb. 11, 2004, http://speaker.house.gov. See Mike Allen, "Hastert Rebukes Bush Adviser," *The Washington Post*, Feb. 12, 2004, p. A17.

66. "Economic Report of the President 2004," Chapter 12, International Trade and Cooperation.

67. From a Feb. 3, 2004, statement posted at Kerry's campaign Web site, johnkerry.com.

68. Quoted in Karl Schoenberger, "Offshore Job Losses on Voters' Agendas," *San Jose Mercury News*, Jan. 30, 2004.

69. ABC News, *op. cit.*

BIBLIOGRAPHY

Books

Bardhan, Ashok Deo, *et al.*, *Globalization and a High-Tech Economy*, Kluwer Academic Publishers, 2003.
High-tech U.S. firms are outsourcing white-collar jobs offshore to cut labor costs, according to a University of California, Berkeley, economist and his colleagues.

Thurow, Lester C., *Fortune Favors the Bold: What We Must Do to Build a New and Lasting Global Prosperity*, HarperBusiness, 2003.
The dean of MIT's business school calls on policymakers to take steps to reduce the threat of problems that could result from rapid globalization.

Articles

Cullen, Lisa Takeuchi, "Now Hiring!" *Time*, **Nov. 24, 2003, p. 48.**

The stagnant U.S. labor market is slowly improving, but the average job search today takes four to six months, while senior-level positions take more than a year.

Fox, Justin, "Where Your Job Is Going," *Fortune*, **Nov. 10, 2003, p. 84.**

Bangalore, India, has become a major center for call centers and computer services for U.S. businesses.

Hacker, Andrew, "The Underworld of Work," *The New York Review of Books*, **Feb. 12, 2004, pp. 38-40.**

Three recent books on U.S. employment trends describe the shift from high-wage manufacturing jobs to low-wage service jobs over the past 20 years.

Irwin, Douglas A., "'Outsourcing' Is Good for America," *The Wall Street Journal*, **Jan. 28, 2004, p. A16.**

Outsourcing gives consumers lower prices and employers higher profits that they can use to create high-skilled U.S. jobs.

Krugman, Paul, "For Richer," *The New York Times Magazine*, **Oct. 20, 2003, pp. 62-142.**

Tax policies favoring the wealthiest Americans are widening the income gap and worsening living standards for American workers.

Lind, Michael, "Are We Still a Middle-Class Nation?" *The Atlantic Monthly*, **January/February 2004, pp. 120-128.**

As the number of well-paid jobs shrinks, low-wage service jobs are growing, but the cost of living for middle-class workers is rising.

Overby, Stephanie, "U.S. Stays on Top," *CIO Magazine*, **Dec. 15, 2003.**

As companies continue to outsource computer jobs overseas, information-technology professionals will find high-level jobs in strategy, implementation and design.

Reich, Robert, "High-Tech Jobs Are Going Abroad! But That's OK," *The Washington Post*, **Nov. 2, 2003, p. B3.**

The former secretary of Labor explains why he believes the flow of high-tech jobs abroad is not a problem.

Risen, Clay, "Missed Target: Is Outsourcing Really So Bad?" *The New Republic*, **Feb. 2, 2004, p. 10.**

Instead of banning outsourcing, Congress should create a new program to retrain displaced manufacturing workers and help white-collar workers find alternative jobs.

Reports and Studies

Bernstein, Jared, and Lawrence Mishel, "Labor Market Left Behind," Briefing Paper, Economic Policy Institute, August 2003.

The current recovery has produced fewer jobs than any other during the post-World War II era.

Evalueserve, "The Impact of Global Sourcing on the U.S. Economy, 2003-2010," Oct. 9, 2003.

Some 1.3 million U.S. jobs will be shifted offshore from 2003-2010, compensating for the shrinking of the work force as the Baby Boomers retire.

Information Technology Association of America, "2003 IT Workforce Survey," May 5, 2003.

Twelve percent of U.S. information-technology companies outsourced jobs overseas, primarily programming jobs.

Matloff, Norman, "On the Need for Reform of the H-1B Non-Immigrant Work Visa in Computer-Related Occupations," *University of Michigan Journal of Law Reform*, **Dec. 12, 2003.**

In a special issue on immigration, a University of California expert on the H-1B visa program contends that employers abuse the program to import low-wage programmers and other professionals.

U.S. Department of Commerce, Economics and Statistics Administration, "Digital Economy 2003," December 2003.

The information-technology sector promises to continue on a modest, steady growth path, thanks in part to offshoring.

For More Information

Bureau of Labor Statistics, U.S. Labor Department, 2 Massachusetts Ave., N.E., Suite 4040, Washington, DC 20212-0001; (202) 691-5200; www.bls.gov.

Department for Professional Employees, AFL-CIO, 1025 Vermont Ave., N.W., Suite 1030, Washington, DC 20005; (202) 638-0320; www.dpeaflcio.org. This labor group representing more than 4 million white-collar workers calls for policy changes to stem the export of U.S. jobs.

Economic Policy Institute, 1660 L St., N.W., Suite 1200, Washington, DC 20036; (202) 775-8810; www.epinet.org. This nonprofit research group contends Americans lose jobs because of free-trade agreements.

National Association of Manufacturers, 1331 Pennsylvania Ave., N.W., Washington, DC 20004-1790; (202) 637-3000; www.nam.org. The 14,000-member organization defends outsourcing as essential to U.S. competitiveness.

Organization for the Rights of American Workers (T.O.R.A.W.), PO Box 2354, Meriden, CT 06450-1454; www.toraw.org. A worker-advocacy group demanding that U.S. jobs be preserved for American citizens and calling for legislation to limit offshoring and worker-visa programs.

U.S. Chamber of Commerce, 1615 H St., N.W., Washington, DC 20062-2000; (202) 659-6000; www.uschamber.com. The largest U.S. business lobby opposes legislative obstacles to offshore outsourcing.

7

Oil Diplomacy

Mary H. Cooper

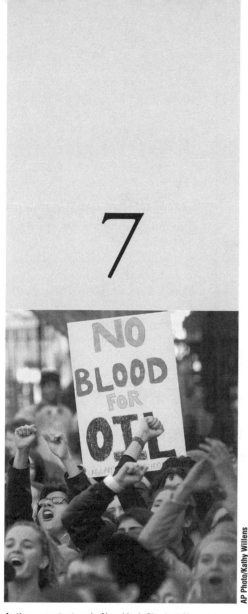

Anti-war protesters in New York City last November oppose President Bush's plan to overthrow oil-rich Iraq. Critics say America's need for oil lies behind the possible invasion as well as the friendly relations it maintains with nations that have been questionable allies in the war on terrorism or are accused of human-rights abuses. The administration says its concern in Iraq is eliminating Saddam Hussein's weapons of mass destruction.

From *The CQ Researcher*, January 24, 2003.

Following in the footsteps of world leaders like Russia's Vladimir Putin and China's Jiang Zemin, Crown Prince Abdullah of Saudi Arabia journeyed to Crawford, Texas, last April to meet with President Bush at his 1,600-acre ranch.

"I was honored to welcome Crown Prince Abdullah to my ranch . . . a place where I welcome very special guests to our country," Bush said later that day. "We spent a lot of time alone, discussing our respective visions, talking about our families. I'm convinced that the stronger our personal bond is, the more likely it is relations between our countries will be strong."[1]

The president's warm embrace of the Saudi leader struck many observers as inappropriate in the wake of the Sept. 11, 2001, terrorist attacks. Fifteen of the 19 Islamic extremists who crashed hijacked airliners into the World Trade Center and the Pentagon were Saudis, a fact the Riyadh government was slow to acknowledge. And when the Bush administration froze the assets of organizations and individuals believed to have ties to Osama bin Laden and his al Qaeda terrorist organization, the Saudi government initially failed to cooperate. Moreover, while expressing outrage at the attacks, Saudi leaders continued to tolerate anti-American teachings in *madrassas*, schools funded by Saudi charitable contributions, at home and overseas.

Few would disagree with the notion that U.S. diplomatic priorities around the world center on America's need to maintain the oil lifeline. The United States is by far the world's largest consumer of oil, a fact that shows no sign of changing. The wildly popular sport-utility vehicle (SUV) and other gas-guzzlers now account for more than half of new-car sales. Domestic oil reserves are dwindling fast,

OPEC Produces 40 Percent of World's Oil

The Organization of Petroleum Exporting Countries (OPEC) — including Venezuela, Nigeria and the Persian Gulf nations — produces about 40 percent of the world's oil. Russia, the United States and other non-OPEC nations produce the rest. OPEC's disproportionate influence on prices and supplies has prompted the U.S. and other industrial countries to seek new oil sources outside OPEC.

World Oil Production
(In thousands of barrels per day)

OPEC	**26,044**
Major OPEC producers	
Persian Gulf nations	17,437
Venezuela	2,701
Nigeria	2,102
Libya	1,308
Indonesia	1,274
Non-OPEC producers	**40,355**
Major non-OPEC producers	
Russia	7,298
United States	5,827
China	3,360
Mexico	3,168
United Kingdom	2,244
World Total	**66,399**

Source: Energy Information Administration, *Monthly Energy Review*, December 2002; online at www.eia.doe.gov/emeu/mer/inter.html

senior fellow at the Cato Institute, a conservative think tank in Washington, D.C. "It's the world's major holder of oil resources. There's no doubt that the friendliness of the U.S. relationship with Riyadh flows out of the desire to maintain access to oil."

Today, the United States imports more than half of the oil it consumes, a percentage expected to rise to 64 percent by 2020. And, despite efforts to develop oil sources away from the politically volatile Middle East, the United States still relies on oil from the region for a fifth of its imports.[2]

As the Bush administration prepares for possible war against Iraq, concern is mounting that the United States may be in for a new energy crisis, reminiscent of two oil "shocks" in the 1970s that saw oil prices increase nearly sevenfold. Not that Iraq wields much of an oil weapon, despite sitting astride the world's second-largest oil reserves after Saudi Arabia. Its oil exports have been limited to a bare minimum in the wake of the 1991 Persian Gulf War and Iraq's subsequent refusal to allow thorough U.N. inspections for weapons of mass destruction.

Thus, even a complete shutdown of Iraq's current production of 2.5 million barrels a day may have little impact on world oil markets. "Iraqi oil is important, but it's more important for Iraq than for the rest of the world," says John Lichtblau, a leading oil analyst and chairman of the nonprofit Petroleum Industry Research Foundation in New York City. "The rest of the world can live without Iraqi oil."

But Iraqi output is not the only uncertainty in the outlook for world oil supplies. A labor strike in Venezuela has halted exports from America's fourth-largest foreign oil supplier since early December. Strike leaders, who want to end the presidency of populist Hugo Chávez, have declared

so the United States grows more dependent on foreign oil each year.

But critics say the United States' growing need for oil is behind the administration's willingness to maintain friendly relations with Saudi Arabia and other allies with either poor human-rights records or questionable efforts to aid the U.S. war on terrorism. Moreover, the critics say Iraq's massive oil reserves, not concern about Iraq's weapons of mass destruction (WMD), are driving U.S. plans to invade Iraq.

"The United States is friendly with the Saudis for one reason and for one reason only," says Doug Bandow, a

that no resumption of oil exports can be expected before Feb. 2. Bush administration officials have suggested that any military operations against Iraq may begin in February as well, meaning that oil exports from both Iraq and Venezuela could be suspended at the same time.

Thus, at a time of unusual uncertainty, U.S. diplomacy is clearly targeted at ensuring access to oil. But critics insist the Bush administration may be going too far in accommodating unsavory regimes just to keep the oil flowing. Perhaps the biggest example, they say, is the House of Saud, America's second-largest oil supplier, which maintains an iron grip over the country, bans political opposition and rigidly suppresses women's rights. "You don't have to have the prince out to the ranch and have cuddly sessions with him talking about how wonderful everybody is," Bandow says. "We certainly should be willing to push for human rights."

Critics like Bandow say America's relentless quest for oil is compromising its reputation as the world's leading champion of democracy and human rights. Diplomacy fueled by oil interests only aggravates anti-American sentiment abroad, they say, by resurrecting the Cold War specter of a United States espousing democracy and human rights abroad while bankrolling unsavory dictators just because they were anti-communist.

Critics also worry about the U.S. government's recent efforts to establish more friendly relations with corrupt leaders in poor West African nations and the Caspian Sea area—potential new sources of sizable oil reserves—to fill the potential gap caused by a prolonged disruption of Persian Gulf oil. (*See sidebar, p. 140.*)

For example, President Nursultan Nazarbayev of Kazakhstan, a key oil producer in the Caspian Sea region, is widely regarded as a despot whose nation is infamous for human-rights abuses. He is currently under

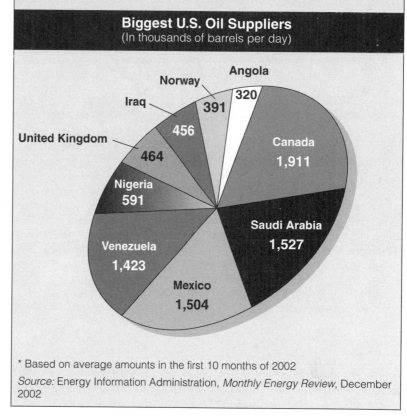

Canada Is Top U.S. Supplier

The United States imports more oil from Canada than from any other nation, including Saudi Arabia. Only two Middle Eastern nations rank among the nine biggest U.S. suppliers.

Biggest U.S. Oil Suppliers
(In thousands of barrels per day)

- Angola 320
- Norway 391
- Iraq 456
- United Kingdom 464
- Nigeria 591
- Venezuela 1,423
- Mexico 1,504
- Saudi Arabia 1,527
- Canada 1,911

* Based on average amounts in the first 10 months of 2002

Source: Energy Information Administration, *Monthly Energy Review*, December 2002

investigation by federal prosecutors who charge that he accepted bribes in exchange for U.S. oil-company concessions during the 1990s and lobbied the Bush White House to halt the inquiry.[3]

"History shows that oil producers don't fare as well in terms of democracy or economic well-being as non-oil producers," says Arvind Ganeshan, director of the business and human-rights program at Human Rights Watch, an international advocacy group. "The bulk of them, including the major oil producers, don't have a very good record on human rights, particularly in terms of democratic accountability."

In West Africa, for instance, the countries that stand to profit the most from developing and selling oil to consumers like the United States—including Nigeria,

Search for Non-OPEC Oil Pays Off

The rise of Islamic extremism among some of the leading members of the Organization of Petroleum Exporting Countries (OPEC) has intensified concern about U.S. dependence on Middle Eastern oil, especially since the terrorist attacks of Sept. 11, 2001.

Of OPEC's 11 members, all but two—Nigeria and Venezuela—are predominantly Muslim. Violence by re–ligious extremists has broken out in several member countries, including Indonesia and Nigeria, and threatens to destabilize Saudi Arabia and other key Persian Gulf producers.

Since the 1973 Arab oil embargo against the United States, a frantic search for non-OPEC oil supplies has paid off. Major new oil deposits were found in Alaska's North Slope, Mexico and the North and Caspian seas. As a result, the share of U.S. oil imports that come from OPEC producers has fallen from 70 percent to 40 percent since 1977.

Diversification has been made possible by technological advances in oil-detection and drilling equipment. Seismic devices allow geologists to find deposits that once lay undetected beneath thick layers of non-porous rock, and horizontal-drilling technology enables oil companies to reduce costs and speed production by tapping a number of deposits from a single bore. Most important, floating platforms and equipment that can probe ever-increasing depths for underwater deposits have made the largest discoveries accessible for extraction.

The most recent major oil find is in the Atlantic Basin, a vast region of underwater oil deposits stretching from Latin America to West Africa. The only OPEC member that stands to benefit from oil drilling in the basin is Nigeria. Non-OPEC West African nations that may profit from the expected bonanza include Angola, which has the most promising reserves, Ivory Coast, Sierra Leone, Equatorial Guinea, Congo, Namibia and Gabon.

On the other side of the ocean, Brazil and, to a lesser extent, Argentina have most of the Latin American portion of the reserves.[1] Experts are uncertain just how much oil these countries may produce. Brazil stands to quadruple its output by 2020, to 4.1 million barrels a day. But that probably won't be available for export because it will be needed to meet Brazil's domestic oil needs.

---

[1] Information on the Atlantic Basin is found in Energy Information Administration, *International Energy Outlook 2002*, pp. 35-36.

Angola and Equatorial Guinea—are among the world's poorest countries, and some have been embroiled in civil unrest, widespread corruption and blatant human-rights violations.

In Nigeria, a member of the influential Organization of Petroleum Exporting Countries (OPEC), lawmakers have threatened to impeach President Olusegun Obasanjo more than once for allegedly violating the constitution, abetting corruption and allowing ethnic massacres by the military. Angola's 4.1 million displaced people, uprooted by a long-running civil war that ended last year, are routinely subjected to physical harassment and abuse by security forces. And in Equatorial Guinea, where the State Department closed the U.S. Embassy for eight years in part to protest the government's rampant abuses, "human-rights abuse went unabated in 2002," Human Rights Watch reports.[4]

Critics like Ganeshan say both the U.S. government and American oil companies with production-sharing or joint-venture arrangements in foreign countries can help improve economic and social conditions in countries that supply oil to the U.S. market. "Companies have an obligation to ensure that their operations respect human rights," Ganeshan says. "The U.S. government can press for transparency and accountability in how governments receive and spend oil money."

For now, though, most criticism centers on U.S. relations with Saudi Arabia. "Unfortunately, our dependence on relatively inexpensive Saudi oil has caused successive U.S. administrations to adopt what might be called a 'see-no-evil' attitude toward the kingdom's efforts to manage and suppress potentially threatening internal opposition by encouraging virulent hostility towards America and her allies, most especially Israel," said Frank J. Gaffney Jr., president of the conservative Center for Security Policy and a former Reagan administration Pentagon official. "Clearly, we can no longer afford to indulge in such a dangerous stance."[5]

West Africa is a different matter, however. Angola may more than quadruple its output by 2020, judging from the positive findings of exploratory probes. The impoverished country's economy, devastated by civil war, is unlikely to be able to absorb much of the oil it produces for the foreseeable future.

West Africa's oil is an attractive target for U.S. oil companies because it is a light, high-quality variety. Also, the region lies just on the other side of the Atlantic Ocean, only days away from East Coast ports, with no perilous choke points like the Middle East's Straits of Hormuz standing in the way of tanker traffic.

It's uncertain how the Atlantic Basin reserves will affect U.S. oil diplomacy. While they appear likely to reduce U.S. energy dependence on OPEC and the Middle East, there are other concerns surrounding relations with the region's governments. Human-rights advocates are calling on the U.S. government to break with the priorities of a century of oil diplomacy to address the extreme poverty and widespread human-rights abuses that have afflicted most emerging oil producers of West Africa.

Compounding the region's social and economic ills is pervasive corruption among government leaders, a situation that is unlikely to abate with an influx of oil money.

"In countries where power is concentrated in the hands of just one or a few individuals, adding the economic power that flows from control over oil revenues is a tremendous disincentive to accountability," says Arvind Ganeshan, director of the business and human-rights program at Human Rights Watch, an advocacy group. "If the government is the biggest political actor and the biggest company in town, which dictator wants to give that up?"

But Ganeshan says there are steps the United States could take to improve so-called transparency and accountability in the way host governments use the investments they receive from foreign oil companies and the revenues they receive from selling oil. "That can be done through bilateral diplomacy," he says. "Washington also can encourage the World Bank and the International Monetary Fund [IMF] to insist on that."

The IMF is in a particularly strong position to enforce accountability, he says, because it has the authority to call for audits into government finances and has a code of good practices for fiscal transparency.

Finally, Ganeshan says, as a key element of its oil diplomacy the U.S. government should enlist the help of American oil companies in these countries. "Washington should press very strongly for human-rights improvements and accountability," he says. "But it also should press American companies to maintain the highest human-rights standards possible in their operations."

But others say the criticism of Saudi Arabia is overblown. Saudi leaders are helping ensure America's energy security by trying to maintain calm in world oil markets, they point out. On Jan. 12, Saudi-led OPEC announced it would increase production to compensate for the potential loss of Iraqi and Venezuelan exports.

"Saudi Arabia holds more than a quarter of the world's proven oil reserves, and as such has more capacity than anyone else to affect the oil supply," says Shibley Telhami, a Middle East expert at the University of Maryland. "If the Saudis chose to play the game irresponsibly, they could flood the market, throw a lot of people out of the oil business and then dominate the market themselves. But they have chosen to play largely a moderating role in the oil arena."

The administration also cites the Saudi's cooperation in allowing U.S. troops to be stationed on Saudi soil—a move that has triggered strong condemnation from Osama bin Laden. As confrontation with Iraq draws more imminent, these are some of the questions being asked about U.S. oil diplomacy:

Is American concern about weapons of mass destruction in Iraq a smokescreen for a grab for Iraq's oil?

The Bush administration's march toward war with Iraq began in earnest on Jan. 29, 2002, with the president's State of the Union address. In it, he branded Iraq, Iran and North Korea as an "axis of evil" bent on developing weapons of mass destruction to use against America and its allies or to supply to terrorists.

"States like these, and their terrorist allies, constitute an axis of evil, arming to threaten the peace of the world," Bush said. "By seeking weapons of mass destruction, these regimes pose a grave and growing danger. I will not wait on events, while dangers gather. I will not stand by, as peril draws closer and closer. The United States of America will not permit the world's most dangerous regimes to threaten us with the world's most destructive weapons."

Last October, Bush singled out Iraq as the most immediate threat to U.S. interests and defiantly dismissed U.N. efforts to halt weapons development in Iraq. Instead he called for a "regime change" in Baghdad. "The stated policy of the United States is regime change," Bush explained, "because, for 11 years, Saddam Hussein has ignored the United Nations and the free world, [and] we don't believe he is going to change."[6]

Although in the past Hussein has had programs to develop nuclear, biological and chemical weapons—and indeed used gas in 1988 to massacre separatist Kurds in northern Iraq—the administration has yet to present to the public clear evidence that Iraq has or is pursuing such a capability today.

The lack of proof prompts some critics to charge that Bush's concern about weapons masks another agenda—gaining control of Iraq's vast oil reserves, the world's second-largest after Saudi Arabia. "Weapons of mass destruction don't have much to do with this at all," says Mark Weisbrot, co-director of the Center for Economic and Policy Research, a liberal think tank. "There have been 230 weapons inspections now, and they haven't found anything. On the other hand, controlling the world's oil resources always has been a major strategic goal of the U.S. government."

Meanwhile, uncertainty over the stability of Saudi Arabia, the world's leading oil producer, has mounted since the Sept. 11 terrorist attacks and repeated threats from terrorist leader bin Laden against the regime for allowing the United States to base troops on Saudi soil. That makes it all the more important for the United States to gain access to Iraq's crude, Weisbrot says. "The administration doesn't know how long the Saudi regime is going to last, so they need another stable place where they can be based and control oil reserves. What's important here is the strategic power that comes from controlling oil resources."

Pulitzer Prize-winning *New York Times* columnist Thomas L. Friedman agrees that oil would be high on the list of U.S. objectives in any war on Iraq. "Any war we launch in Iraq will certainly be—in part—about oil," he wrote recently. "To deny that is laughable."

Moreover, Friedman said war would be justifiable, so long as it spawned a democratic government in Iraq and meaningful efforts to conserve energy in the United States.

"I have no problem with a war for oil—provided that it is to fuel the first progressive Arab regime and not just our SUVs, and provided we behave in a way that makes clear to the world we are protecting everyone's access to oil at reasonable prices—not simply our right to binge on it."[7]

But protesters in European capitals recently brandished anti-war placards demanding "No blood for oil."[8] A recent Pew Research Center poll found that more than half the people in Russia, France and Germany thought "the U.S. wants to control Iraqi oil."[9]

Even in Britain, where Prime Minister Tony Blair has been Bush's strongest ally against Hussein, public opinion is divided over the true reasons why Bush and Vice President Dick Cheney—both former oil-company executives—are bent on targeting Iraq. "American oil companies stand to gain billions of dollars in the event of a U.S. invasion," wrote British columnist Robert Fisk. "Once out of power, Bush and his friend could become multibillionaires on the spoils of this war."[10]

These suspicions are even more pronounced in the Middle East, where anti-U.S. sentiment runs even higher because of the Bush administration's support of Israel's relentless suppression of the Palestinian uprising. "Clearly, oil is seen as a key factor in the region," says Telhami of the University of Maryland. "But, even worse, the common wisdom in the Middle East is that all of this is an effort to serve Israeli interests," since Israel has been attacked by Iraq in the past. "This is even more serious to people in the region than just the assumption that U.S. policy is based simply on oil."

But Secretary of State Colin L. Powell flatly rejects that notion. "The oil fields are the property of the Iraqi people," he said recently on NBC's "Meet the Press. "If a coalition of forces goes into those oil fields, we would want to protect those fields and make sure that they are used to benefit the people of Iraq and are not destroyed or damaged by a failing regime on the way out the door."[11]

Even if the United States takes control of Iraq's oil fields, it could require years and up to $40 billion to rehabilitate the country's aging oil infrastructure, bring it back into full production and develop new fields.[12] Such a monumental investment to control oil—that wouldn't even be available for years—would not justify conducting a military campaign, some experts say.

"No U.S. administration would launch so momentous a campaign just to facilitate a handful of oil-development contracts and a moderate increase in supply—half a decade from now," wrote Daniel Yergin, chairman of Cambridge Energy Research Associates.[13]

Oil-industry representatives agree that the benefits to Western oil companies would be far outweighed by the risks of war. "If we really wanted the oil, we could do a deal with Hussein right now, but that's not in our national interest," says John Felmy, chief economist at the American Petroleum Institute. He emphasizes that Iraq wants to sell more oil but is constrained by U.N. sanctions. "Oil is not even relevant to policy toward Iraq," he says. "Statements to the contrary are just ludicrous."

Should Saudi Arabia be held more accountable for its role in the spread of Islamic fundamentalism?

Since the Sept. 11 terrorist attacks, intelligence officials and Middle East experts alike have scrutinized U.S.-Saudi relations in an effort to understand why so many of the hijackers—as well as bin Laden—were Saudis. Of particular interest has been Islam's Wahhabi sect, a uniquely Saudi Arabian fundamentalist branch of the faith and a key institutional ally of the ruling House of Saud. Wahhabi clerics teach anti-American attitudes in Saudi-funded Islamic schools—known as *madrassas*—around the world.

"It is violent, it is intolerant and it is fanatical beyond measure," wrote Stephen Schwartz, author of a recently published book on Wahhabism and a convert to Islam. "Not all Muslims are suicide bombers, but all Muslim suicide bombers are Wahhabis."[14]

William Kristol, editor of *The Weekly Standard* and chairman of the Project for the New American Century—a conservative nonprofit organization dedicated to American global leadership—told a congressional subcommittee last May: "The Saudis have been deeply implicated in the wave of suicide bombers that have attacked Israeli citizens—and American citizens in Israel—in recent years. [Yet,] initial Saudi official reaction has been to deny the link."[15]

Scrutiny turned to hostility in some camps as the Saudi government dragged its feet in acknowledging the hijackers' origins and stemming the flow of Saudi donations to Muslim charities thought to be supporting al Qaeda and other terrorist organizations.

"Saudi Arabia is a corrupt, totalitarian regime at sharp variance with America's most cherished values, including religious liberty," Bandow, of the Cato Institute, testified

Nigerian villagers celebrate last December after Chevron-Texaco agreed to spend $100 million building a modern town in the oil-rich Niger Delta. The local Itsekiri people had blocked production facilities to protest the U.S. oil giant's failure to share its profits from the region's oil.

AFP Photo/David Clark

on Capitol Hill last June. "By any normal assessment, Americans should care little if the House of Saud fell, as have other illegitimate monarchies, such as Iran's peacock throne. Except for one thing: Saudi Arabia has oil. For this reason, Washington has long been hesitant to treat Saudi Arabia the way Washington treats most other nations."[16]

But it's not just conservative supporters of Israel who condemn Saudi Arabia's post-Sept. 11 conduct. "One way [Saudi rulers] have held power is to allow and even encourage some of the extremists," says Weisbrot, one of the Bush administration's most vocal liberal critics. "Look at how long it took them—and how much pressure it took—for them to even freeze the assets of these people. So it's understandable that somebody should make a stink over that. The criticism is just a logical outcome of the Saudi government's gross hypocrisy."

Anti-Saudi criticism mounted still further in November, when it was reported that Princess Haifa, wife of the Saudi ambassador to Washington, Prince Bandar bin Sultan, had donated money to Saudis connected with the Sept. 11 hijackers. Although there was no suggestion that the princess had knowingly funded anti-American terrorists, the scandal prompted the Saudi government to launch a public-relations campaign on U.S. television aimed at quelling anti-Saudi sentiment.

However, some Middle East experts say the criticism of the House of Saud is overblown. They note that in the 1980s the Reagan administration asked the Saudis to help get Islamic fundamentalists to join U.S.-supported "freedom fighters" trying to expel the Soviet Union from Afghanistan. Bin Laden and many of his followers received U.S. training, weapons and support, as did future members of Afghanistan's oppressive Taliban regime, which sheltered al Qaeda before being driven from power by a U.S.-led coalition after Sept. 11.

"We found that utilizing Islamic motivation to rid a Muslim country of the infidel Soviets was very convenient," says Walter L. Cutler, president of the Meridian International Center think tank and U.S. ambassador to Saudi Arabia in the late 1980s. "We worked very closely with not only the Saudis but also a lot of other Arab governments in trying to get the Soviets out of Afghanistan. It was still the Cold War, and when that was crowned with success in 1989 we tended to relax a bit and focus more on walls falling down in Berlin than we did on what was going on elsewhere."

Cutler says American critics of Saudi behavior fail to recognize that charitable giving is central to the Islamic faith. "We have a right to expect the Saudis to be more accountable," he says. "But one has to realize that when Muslims give to charity it is not within their religious or cultural tradition to check up on where every rial is going. That is almost counter to the spirit of giving."

The Saudis themselves are baffled by the degree of U.S. hostility, says the University of Maryland's Telhami. "From the Saudi point of view, they've been extremely cooperative in the war on terrorism," he says. "They don't know what the United States wants them to do, other than crack down on charities. We have to recognize that these charities are an important part of life in Saudi Arabia, and that most of them pose no danger and are truly peaceful."

Some critics even advocate pressuring the regime to adopt domestic reforms, liberalizing the education system, affording greater civil rights to women and granting freedom of religion to non-Muslims in the country, including American military personnel based there. "We're a tolerant country that allows Muslims to worship freely," says Bandow of the Cato Institute. "It's outrageous that U.S. soldiers aren't allowed to publicly worship according to their own faith when they're over there to defend the Saudis. On issues like that we have to be much more pushy with the [Saudi] government."

But defenders of strong U.S.-Saudi ties point out that during the Cold War the United States maintained close diplomatic relations with plenty of regimes with even weaker democratic credentials than the Saudis—as long as those regimes were anti-communist. The totalitarian regimes of Augusto Pinochet's Chile during the 1970s and Shah Mohammad Reza Pahlavi in Iran are but two examples. Even Hussein's Iraq enjoyed cordial relations with the United States for most of the 1980s, when he was fighting Iran, then considered one of America's principal enemies.

In any event, some experts warn, critics of Saudi Arabia's rulers should consider the likely alternative to the current regime. "Even though we would like to see greater economic, social and political reform in Saudi Arabia, we should bear in mind that there could be something much worse in power in Saudi Arabia," Cutler says. "I'm talking about a real Taliban regime, one that might not mind cutting off exports of oil for awhile if it thought that could bring down Western civilization and do huge harm to our economy.

"So we should think twice before we open fire with both barrels at the Saudis," he continues. "They have been very cooperative out of self-interest and out of valuing the relationship with the United States. We need their oil, and they need our security."

Can the United States greatly reduce its dependence on Persian Gulf oil?

Ever since the painful 1973 Arab oil embargo, politicians and conservationists have declared reducing U.S. dependence on Middle East oil a vital national priority. At the height of the oil crisis of 1978-79, President Jimmy Carter introduced an array of proposals aimed at improving auto fuel economy, developing alternative-energy sources and stocking a strategic reserve of crude oil to soften the blow of future oil cutoffs.

But relatively low oil prices since the early 1980s have dampened Americans' enthusiasm for saving energy, especially gasoline. Gone are the days when U.S. consumers opted for fuel-efficient Japanese cars, nearly driving the Big Three Detroit automakers out of business after gasoline prices skyrocketed in the 1970s. Today the cars of choice are SUVs and other large gas-guzzlers. And because U.S. oil production has been declining since reaching its peak in 1970, a growing portion of America's thirst for oil is being met by imports. Since the 1973 oil embargo, in fact, U.S. oil imports have increased from 36 percent of consumption to more than 50 percent today.

Alternative sources of oil from Nigeria to the North Sea have come on line to diminish reliance on the Persian Gulf region, while new technology is tapping the potential oil wealth of the Caspian Sea and other sources. "The development of deep-water technology has enabled us to drill under thousands of feet of water, which has led to some dramatic discoveries in the Gulf of Mexico and particularly West Africa," says the API's Felmy. "Also, the development of seismic technology has improved our ability to find the oil. The combination of those two technologies has been very important to our efforts to diversify oil sources."

Nevertheless, the world's largest known crude reserves still lie under the deserts of Saudi Arabia, Iraq and other states in the region. And many oil experts say energy independence is neither possible nor urgent, because the United States—by far the world's largest single consumer of crude—is just one player in a huge, interdependent oil market. "Independence from foreign oil is impossible because more than half of our oil supplies are imported today," says Lichtblau of the Petroleum Industry Research Foundation. "So there's no way we could become independent; neither is it necessary or even desirable to try."

"Most industrial countries are net importers of substantial amounts of oil," Lichtblau explains. "Japan, South Korea and the European countries—with the exception of the United Kingdom—are all net importers of much more of their oil supplies than we are. That's been the nature of the world oil market for many decades, and it's not going to change because there's plenty of oil around."

Lichtblau downplays the potential threat to U.S. energy supplies of political instability in the Middle East. "These countries that sell us the oil must sell it," he says. "It's their principal or only source of foreign exchange. So we are interdependent with Saudi Arabia, and to a lesser degree with Iraq, Kuwait and the United Arab Emirates."

In addition, three Western Hemisphere producers—Canada, Mexico and Venezuela—rank among the top-four suppliers, along with Saudi Arabia, of oil imports into the United States. "Venezuela right now has trouble, but normally it must sell oil in order to survive, as must Mexico."

Still, many experts say the United States should do more to wean itself from its dependence on foreign oil. "I'm very much in favor of our developing a serious, long-term strategic plan for reducing our dependence on imported oil from wherever," says Cutler of the Meridian International Center. "We tend to worry about the Middle East, with possible boycotts and instability in that region, but look at some of the other major suppliers." Besides the industrywide strike in Venezuela, unrest in Nigeria, Colombia, Indonesia and other oil-supplying countries puts those sources at risk as well, he points out.

But energy security is not simply a question of foreign supplies, Cutler emphasizes. There is much the U.S. government and consumers could do to reduce demand for oil, he says. "We should have started back in 1973, when we had the first oil crisis, to reduce our consumption of oil, no matter what the source," he says.[17]

But consumer demand for uneconomical vehicles appears stronger than ever. The recent North American International Auto Show in Detroit featured such behemoths as a 16-cylinder, 1,050-horsepower Cadillac.[18]

"Here we are worried about being vulnerable to energy shortages," Cutler says, "but so far we have failed to take energy security seriously."

BACKGROUND

Strategic Commodity

Blessed with abundant energy supplies, the United States enjoyed a distinct advantage over other emerging industrial powers from the Industrial Revolution well into the 20th century.[19] Coal powered the factories and railroads during the 1800s, and the discovery of vast oil deposits in Texas in the early 1900s paved the way for a new revolution that would be based on the gasoline-powered automobile.

Henry Ford's innovative manufacturing system of mass production brought the cost of personal autos within reach of many Americans. That led to a boom in auto sales that prompted massive highway building and shaped patterns of suburban development that ensured the dominant place of oil in the country's energy mix.

While the United States developed its industrial economy with few initial concerns about energy, other industrial nations were forced to look outside their boundaries to meet their growing demand for oil. The 1908 discovery

CHRONOLOGY

1900s-1940s *The United States and Europe discover and extract oil in the Middle East.*

1927 British-dominated Iraq Petroleum Co. becomes one of Persian Gulf region's first significant oil exporters after the discovery of a major Iraqi oil field at Kirkuk.

1933 Standard Oil Co. of California (Socal) obtains a 60-year concession for exclusive rights to oil in eastern Saudi Arabia, breaking Britain's control over the region's oil resources and securing a major source of cheap oil for U.S. consumers.

1948 The creation of Israel after World War II fosters enduring conflict with neighboring Arabs.

1950s-1970s *Middle Eastern nations take possession of their oil fields, enabling Organization of Petroleum Exporting Countries (OPEC) to assert control over the global oil market.*

1970 U.S. oil production peaks at 11.3 million barrels a day, but growing subsequent demand sparks increasing need for imports.

1973 Saudi Arabia and other Arab OPEC members impose an oil embargo against the United States in retaliation for its support of Israel in the October 1973 Arab-Israeli War.

1974 The United States and other industrial countries establish the International Energy Agency (IEA), which requires member countries to stockpile oil to minimize the impact of future supply disruptions.

1975 The Energy Policy and Conservation Act establishes Corporate Average Fuel Economy (CAFE) standards mandating an increase in auto fuel economy to an average of 27.5 miles per gallon by 1985 and authorizes the creation of the Strategic Petroleum Reserve.

1978-1979 Islamic revolutionaries topple the shah in Iran, a major oil producer and U.S. ally, and install an anti-American Islamic government.

1980s-1990s *The United States, with help from Saudi Arabia and other Arab countries, recruits religious Muslims to help expel Soviet forces from Afghanistan.*

September 1980 War between Iran and Iraq breaks out. The eight-year war sparks oil shortages and price increases that contribute to recession in the United States.

1991 A U.S.-led military coalition forces Iraq to retreat from its occupation of neighboring Kuwait. The Soviet Union collapses, eliminating the United States' chief adversary during the previous half-century and eroding OPEC's hold on world oil markets by making some of the world's most promising oil reserves—under and around the Caspian Sea—available to world markets.

2000s *Terrorism prompts changes in U.S. oil diplomacy.*

April 2001 Bush administration's energy plan calls for more oil production in the United States, including Alaska's Arctic National Wildlife Refuge (ANWR).

May 2001 President Olusegun Obasanjo of Nigeria, the fifth-largest U.S. oil supplier, meets with President Bush in the first White House visit by an African leader since Bush took office.

Sept. 11, 2001 Nineteen hijackers—15 of Saudi origin—crash commercial aircraft into the World Trade Center and the Pentagon in the worst act of terrorism ever on U.S. soil.

April 2002 President Bush welcomes Saudi Crown Prince Abdullah to his Crawford, Texas, ranch, prompting critism that the administration is not pressing the Saudis to cooperate more aggressively with the U.S. "war on terrorism" out of a desire to ensure continued access to Saudi oil.

Jan. 18, 2003 Chanting "No blood for oil," tens of thousands of protesters in Washington, D.C., and other U.S. cities demand that Bush call off plans to oust Iraqi President Saddam Hussein.

of a vast oil deposit in Iran focused European attention on the region surrounding the Persian Gulf as a promising source of crude. European demand for oil took off on the eve of World War I, when Winston Churchill, then First Lord of the Admiralty, converted Royal Navy ships from domestic coal to oil.

The quest for oil became a primary focus of energy-poor Europe's policies toward the oil-rich Middle East in the early 20th century, particularly in the Persian Gulf region. But Britain quickly consolidated a near-monopoly over Middle Eastern oil fields, edging out Germany and other European competitors by negotiating exclusive production concessions with the region's kings and sheikhs. After the discovery of a major oil field at Kirkuk in 1927, the British-dominated Iraq Petroleum Co. became one of the region's first significant oil exporters.

America's presence in the region began in earnest in the early 1930s. Even though the United States still had plenty of oil to satisfy domestic

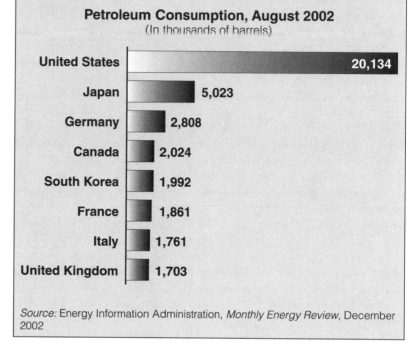

U.S. Oil Use Dwarfs Other Nations'

The United States used more than 20 million barrels of oil in August 2002, or more than all the petroleum used by seven other industrialized nations in the Organization for Economic Cooperation and Development (OECD).

Petroleum Consumption, August 2002
(In thousands of barrels)

United States	20,134
Japan	5,023
Germany	2,808
Canada	2,024
South Korea	1,992
France	1,861
Italy	1,761
United Kingdom	1,703

Source: Energy Information Administration, *Monthly Energy Review*, December 2002

demand, the strategic importance of controlling access to the world's major oil sources was becoming increasingly apparent as European powers jockeyed for influence in the Middle East. After the discovery of another large field, in the Persian Gulf island nation of Bahrain in 1932, geologists from Standard Oil Co. of California (now ChevronTexaco) began searching for deposits in neighboring Saudi Arabia. In 1933, Standard Oil obtained from King Abdul Aziz (known as Ibn Saud) a 60-year concession for exclusive rights to oil in eastern Saudi Arabia, breaking Britain's control over the region's oil resources and securing a major source of cheap oil for American consumers.

As the immensity of Saudi Arabia's oil reserves became apparent, Standard Oil negotiated a six-year extension to its original concession and extended its rights over almost 80,000 square miles of Saudi territory. The American concession underwent several ownership changes and in 1944

was renamed the Arabian American Oil Co.—Aramco. By then, all the major U.S. oil companies—including the predecessors of ExxonMobil and ChevronTexaco—had interests in the Saudi concession.

Americans' reliance on the family car for commuting and other daily needs was well established by the time demand for gasoline and other petroleum products began to outstrip domestic supplies. In 1970, American oil production reached its all-time peak of 11.3 million barrels a day and began its inexorable decline as domestic deposits began to run out of easily recoverable oil. As population growth, economic prosperity and suburban development continued to fuel U.S. consumers' demand for gasoline-driven automobiles, oil imports slowly rose as a portion of the country's total energy supply, from 2.2 million barrels a day in 1967 to 6 million barrels a day in 1973. Over the same period, imports as a share of total U.S. oil consumption rose from

19 percent to 36 percent, the vast majority from the Middle East.[20]

'73 Oil Embargo

But the era of cheap Middle Eastern oil soon came to an abrupt halt. Resentment over the Western powers' exploitation of their precious resource and opposition to the creation of Israel in 1948 fueled a broad movement of Arab nationalism that spread from Egypt to the major oil producers. Over the next two decades, Saudi Arabia, Iraq, Iran and smaller states surrounding the Persian Gulf expelled Western oil companies, nationalized their oil fields and created state-run companies to take over oil production.

In 1973 the Saudi government assumed a 25 percent stake in Aramco and expanded its ownership to 100 percent in 1976. In 1989, the last vestige of American control over Aramco ended when American John J. Kelberer ceded the presidency of the company to a Saudi, Ali Naimi. The Saudi government describes this event as a key moment in national self-determination: "Thus the oil of the kingdom, which had lain for so long beneath Saudi Arabia's deserts and which then for decades had been exploited by foreign interests, became at last a national resource controlled and managed by those under whose soil it lay."[21]

In addition to resenting Western control of the region's oil supply, Saudi Arabia and other Arab countries were outraged by U.S. support of Israel during the 1973 Arab-Israeli War. In retaliation, Saudi Arabia led several other Arab countries in a five-month oil embargo that caused nationwide gasoline shortages in the United States. As the leading producer in OPEC, Saudi Arabia convinced the other members to reduce their exports, causing a quadrupling of world crude oil prices to about $12 dollars a barrel and demonstrating OPEC's control of the world oil market.

The United States and other industrial countries quickly responded to the embargo in 1974 by establishing the International Energy Agency (IEA), which helped coordinate supplies among nations and required member countries to stockpile enough oil to last for three months.

For its part, the U.S. government responded with a flurry of programs to conserve energy, including a largely unsuccessful program to develop alternative fuels for automobiles and equally unsuccessful oil-price and allocation controls. The 1975 Energy Policy and Conservation Act established "Corporate Average Fuel Economy" (CAFE) standards mandating an increase in auto fuel economy to an average of 27.5 miles per gallon by 1985. The act also authorized creation of the Strategic Petroleum Reserve, an underground repository aimed at cushioning the impact of future oil shortages. In 1977 the Energy Department was created to consolidate energy-related functions into a single, Cabinet-level agency.

More Instability

The U.S. conservation efforts did not insulate the economy from a second "oil shock" in 1979, caused by increasing turmoil in Iran and OPEC's announcement that it would raise prices.

World crude spot prices skyrocketed in early 1979, as buyers snapped up product before OPEC's price hikes went into effect. Spiraling gasoline prices produced long lines at service stations, which shortened their hours and limited purchase quantities. Some localities restricted gasoline purchases according to whether the buyer's license plate ended in odd or even numbers.

In Iran, oil production plummeted by 4 million barrels a day in early 1979 after the shah's government was overthrown by religious extremists. And on Nov. 4, militant students overran the U.S. Embassy, taking more than five dozen Americans hostage for more than a year—a crisis that lasted for the rest of Carter's presidency and further accentuated how vulnerable America was due to its dependence on Middle Eastern oil.

The outbreak of the eight-year Iran-Iraq War in September 1980 further reduced Persian Gulf oil output. By 1981, total OPEC production had fallen to 22 million barrels a day, 7 million less than in 1978. At the same time, prices shot up from around $14 a barrel in early 1979 to more than $35 in early 1981. It was not until 1983 that oil prices stabilized at around $28 a barrel.[22]

By the early 1980s, many oil deposits in the United States were running low, and producers had capped off thousands of wells as the cost of extracting the hard-to-reach dregs of these "marginal" well exceeded the revenue they could generate. But with world oil prices soaring and foreign supplies tight, American producers reopened many marginal wells, especially after President Ronald Reagan abolished Nixon-era domestic price controls within days of taking office in 1981.

High oil prices also prompted the United States and other industrial countries to seek new foreign oil sources outside OPEC and develop new technologies to detect and extract oil from previously inaccessible deposits.

Deep-sea oil rigs began tapping huge underwater deposits in the North Sea and the Gulf of Mexico, and Alaska's frigid North Slope became a major source of oil. As these sources came on line, the share of world oil production controlled by OPEC shrank from 50 percent in 1978 to 30 percent by 1985. By increasing imports from Canada, Mexico, Britain and other non-OPEC countries, the United States was able to cut its dependence on OPEC sources by an even greater margin, from 82 percent to 41 percent over the same period.

As still more alternative sources of crude came on line, OPEC gradually lost its power to control world oil output and prices. OPEC's leading producer, Saudi Arabia, acted as the group's "swing producer," and tried to prop up oil prices by cutting its own output, from 10 million barrels a day in early 1981 to just 2.3 million barrels a day by mid-1985. But even this drastic action failed to significantly buoy oil prices, and Saudi Arabia resumed normal production to win back market share. Other OPEC members followed suit, and oil flooded the world market, depressing oil prices to less than $10 a barrel by the end of 1985.

Low oil prices had a mixed impact on U.S. producers and consumers. Once again, producers could no longer afford to extract oil from marginal wells, which they shut down. Consumers lost the price incentive to conserve energy, as cheap gasoline encouraged sales of increasingly large, gas-guzzling vehicles. The sport-utility vehicle, with its appeal as a youthful, off-road vehicle, became an instant hit among American consumers. Classified as "light trucks," SUVs were not covered by even the lax CAFE standards for passenger cars, which remained at their 1985 levels. The popularity of SUVs has slowed improvement in the fuel efficiency of the American auto fleet.

Persian Gulf Crisis

A third spike in oil prices occurred after Iraq invaded neighboring Kuwait on Aug. 2, 1990. The United Nations approved an embargo on oil exports from both countries—removing more than 4 million barrels a day from world markets. By September, the price of crude had risen from about $16 a barrel before the invasion to around $36 a barrel.

But unlike earlier supply shortfalls, this one was short-lived, thanks to the new non-OPEC sources of oil that had come on line in Central America, Western Europe and Africa. Plus, the United States and other International Energy Agency members now had emergency

supplies to cushion sudden cutoffs. As a result, the U.S.-led Persian Gulf War to expel Iraq from Kuwait in early 1991 had little impact on oil markets, despite the near-destruction of Kuwait's oil fields by retreating Iraqi forces, who set them afire as they left.

The 1980s also had seen a shift in U.S. diplomatic relations in the Persian Gulf that helped dampen the impact of the oil embargo. Saudi Arabia and Iran, enemies of the United States and its allies at different times during the 1960s and '70s, shared America's opposition to Hussein and boosted oil production during the Gulf War. Iran had suffered enormous casualties during its eight-year war with Iraq in the 1980s; Saudi Arabia feared Hussein's destabilizing influence in the region, especially inside its own kingdom, where dissidents were fomenting unrest. The Saudi government even allowed the United States to station troops on Saudi territory during the war—a decision bin Laden would later cite as his main grievance against the House of Saud.

The Soviet Union's 1991 collapse dramatically impacted oil diplomacy. Besides eliminating the United States' chief Cold War adversary, it further eroded OPEC's influence by making some of the world's most promising oil reserves, located under and around the Caspian Sea, available to world markets. Chevron, Amoco and other U.S. producers quickly formed joint-production projects with the former Soviet countries of Kazakhstan and Azerbaijan.

As American oil companies developed production facilities in the region, the U.S. government pursued diplomatic ties with the Caspian Sea nations in hopes of ensuring access to this promising new source of oil. The U.S. government also spearheaded a plan to build an oil pipeline from the Caspian oil fields through Turkey, a NATO ally, to the Turkish port of Ceyhan on the Mediterranean Sea.

Meanwhile, Russia's need for foreign exchange prompted it to maximize oil exports from its own vast oil fields.

In the 1990s, the relative stability of oil supplies and prices was a boon to the global and U.S. economy, which was experiencing astounding prosperity and growth. But as the booming '90s progressed, the United States was quietly but inexorably losing the quest for energy independence. Falling domestic oil production and rising demand fueled by low oil prices pushed U.S. imports to 9.1 million barrels a day in 2000—triple the imports in 1985.

New Attack on Greenhouse Gases

In 1992, the first President George Bush and other world leaders met in Rio de Janeiro, Brazil, to sign the historic Framework Convention on Climate Change—the first international agreement that recognized the environmental threat posed by petroleum and coal use.

But concern over the cost of complying with the treaty soon mounted in the United States, by far the world's largest oil consumer and emitter of so-called greenhouse gases. In 1997, the Senate went on record opposing the 1997 treaty that implemented the Rio agreement—the Kyoto Protocol—by calling for mandatory reductions in greenhouse gases. Scientists widely agree that the gases released by burning oil and other carbon-based fuels trap the sun's heat inside Earth's atmosphere like a greenhouse, causing a gradual but potentially disastrous warming.

In January 2001, within days of taking office, the current President Bush reversed his campaign pledge to support controls on global warming and renounced the Kyoto Protocol. Arguing that mandates would harm the U.S. economy, he called instead for further research into global warming and economic incentives to encourage individuals and industries to voluntarily reduce carbon emissions.

This January, Canada became the 100th nation to ratify the Kyoto treaty, leaving the United States as the only major industrial power refusing to accept the protocol's mandate to reduce greenhouse emissions. Meanwhile, the Bush administration has launched its promised research into the causes of climate change—causes that most of the world has agreed lie with fossil-fuel use.

Frustrated by the president's refusal to begin reducing carbon emissions, Sens. John McCain, R-Ariz., and Joseph I. Lieberman, D-Conn., introduced a bill on Jan. 8, 2003, calling for mandatory greenhouse-gas reductions. The emission caps, which would apply to all sectors except agricultural and residential energy use, are less stringent than those laid out in Kyoto. By 2010, carbon emissions would have to decline to the level reported in 2000; by 2016, they would have to fall to the 1990 level—about 12 percent below the current U.S. emission level. By comparison, the Kyoto Protocol requires industrialized countries to cut their carbon emissions an average 5 percent below 1990 levels by 2012.

"Today we take the first step up a long mountain road—a road that will culminate with this country taking credible action to address the global problems of our warming planet," Lieberman testified at a Jan. 8 hearing before the Senate Commerce, Science and Transportation Committee. "The rest of the world is now taking on the

CURRENT SITUATION

Sept. 11 Aftermath

The terrorist attacks on the World Trade Center and the Pentagon added a new and lethal twist to U.S. relations with the Muslim world. "I was surprised by the nature of the attack," says Cutler of the Meridian International Center, who as ambassador to Saudi Arabia became aware of rising Islamic extremism long before the attacks. "There was a pretty clear trail left by al Qaeda, but nobody was anticipating a dramatic strike in the heart of America."

Despite endless U.S. efforts to negotiate peace between Israel and Palestinian leaders during the 1990s, antipathy toward the United States had grown throughout the region because of U.S. support of Israel, Cutler says. "Underneath it all there was a kind of love-hate relationship toward the United States," he says. "Together with admiration of our technology and universities, there were feelings of inadequacy and vulnerability to the West going back generations, and this all came together after Afghanistan."

Because the United States was instrumental in driving the Soviet army out of Afghanistan, many Saudis and other Middle Easterners resented the United States, blaming them for the rise of al Qaeda. Al Qaeda grew out of the resistance movement in Afghanistan, notes Telhami of the University of Maryland. "We solicited the help of Saudi Arabia, Egypt and other allies, asking them specifically to recruit fanatical believers of Islam to fight the infidel communists. Of course, it was inadvertent, and people didn't understand the consequences of mobilizing a force of that sort, but the Saudis and the Egyptians have some reason to be frustrated with America's forgetting that part of history."

Aggravating this sense of frustration, Telhami says, is what Arabs see as the Bush administration's abandoning the challenge this problem presents. The United States, as the world's largest emitter of the gases and the home of the world's strongest economy, must not have its head in the clouds."

Transportation, which is fueled almost exclusively by oil products—gasoline and diesel—accounts for about a third of U.S. greenhouse emissions. The bill would apply to oil producers and refiners, as well as to automakers, who would be allowed to buy and sell credits earned under the Corporate Average Fuel Economy (CAFE) program, which requires carmakers to achieve an average 27.5 miles per gallon across their fleets. Manufacturers that fail to meet the standard would be allowed to buy credits from automakers that produce more fuel-efficient cars.

The bipartisan nature of the McCain-Lieberman bill has prompted cautious optimism about its prospects for passage by the new, Republican-controlled Congress. "The admin-

Sens. John McCain, R-Ariz., and Joseph I. Lieberman, D-Conn., introduced legislation early this month calling for mandatory greenhouse-gas reductions.

istration suggests that little or nothing can be done to reduce emissions," said Senate Minority Leader Thomas A. Daschle, D-S.D. "The Senate will lead the United States to address the problem of global warming since the president is unwilling to."[1]

But the impact of such efforts on the United States' enduring dependence on oil imports may be limited, says oil analyst John Lichtblau, chairman of the Petroleum Industry Research Foundation in New York City. "More efficient automobiles would reduce gasoline consumption and have a positive impact on the environment," he says. "It also probably would reduce somewhat our oil import dependence, but not by very much."

---

[1] See Eric Pianin, "Reductions Sought in Greenhouse Gases," *The Washington Post*, Jan. 9, 2003, p. A4.

---

lead role previous administrations had played in advancing the Arab-Israeli peace process. President Bush has instead appeared to come down heavily on the side of Israeli Prime Minister Ariel Sharon in the ongoing exchange of violence between Israel and the Palestinian Authority led by Yasser Arafat. Bush has undermined Arafat's authority in the decades-old dispute by calling for new Palestinian elections as a necessary pre-condition for peace.

Bush's decision to step back from an active role in mediating Arab-Israeli tensions has fed anti-American opinion throughout the Middle East. Telhami says surveys consistently place the Arab-Israeli conflict at the top of the list of Arab concerns. "They look at the United States through the prism of the Arab-Israeli issue," he says. "So while the United States is angry at Arab Muslims over issues that the Arabs think they are not centrally to blame for, they are very frustrated that the United States is not responding to their most immediate and pressing concern."

U.S.-Saudi Relations

Opinion polls and commentators suggest that Americans continue to blame Saudi Arabia for contributing, at least indirectly, to the rise in Islamic extremism and for not cooperating fully with the Bush administration's war on terrorism. According to an online survey in early December, 69 percent of respondents answered "no" to the query, "Is Saudi Arabia a true friend of the United States?"[23]

"The House of Saud must end the Faustian bargain it originally made with the country's extremist Wahhabist sect," columnist Jim Hoagland wrote in *The Washington Post*.[24]

"The Bush administration and the Saudis have done a masterful job of turning attention away from . . . the trail that leads to the possibility that a foreign government provided support to some of the Sept. 11 hijackers," said Sen. Bob Graham, D-Fla., then-chairman of the Senate Intelligence Committee.[25]

Israeli Prime Minister Ariel Sharon meets with President Bush at the White House last Oct. 16. Arabs widely see the Bush administration as heavily favoring Israel in the ongoing exchanges of violence between Israel and the Palestinian Authority, led by Yasser Arafat.

The Saudi government, meanwhile, is trying to smooth over its damaged relations with the United States. Adel al-Jubeir, foreign policy adviser to Crown Prince Abdullah, came to Washington in December to defend the kingdom's record on fighting terrorism and denounced anti-Saudi sentiment as part of a campaign that "borders on hate."

"We believe that our country has been unfairly maligned," al-Jubeir said. "We believe that we have been subjected to criticism that we do not deserve. We believe that people have been misinformed about Saudi Arabia and what Saudi Arabia has done, or, frankly, that people have lied about what we have done and what we allegedly have not done."[26]

On Jan. 11, the Saudis convinced OPEC to increase the group's daily oil production by 1.5 million barrels in an effort to thwart a significant increase in oil prices in the event of war in Iraq. The move was welcome news in Washington, where the U.S. economy is in a year-long slump, and a prolonged rise in oil prices, which already exceed $30 a barrel, could tip the economy into a recession.

Saudi Arabia also has taken the politically risky step of agreeing to allow the Pentagon to use its airspace and air bases in the event of war with Iraq, including a command center that would provide vital coordination for air attacks.[27] Since the Gulf War, the Saudi government had barred U.S. forces from conducting bombing strikes in retaliation for Iraqi attacks against U.S. and British planes that patrol no-fly zones in northern and southern Iraq. But after the U.N. Security Council resolution of Nov. 8, 2002—which demanded that Iraq fully account for its weapons of mass destruction and cooperate with U.N. inspectors—the Bush administration, after weeks of diplomatic negotiations, persuaded the Saudis to rescind that restriction in case of war with Iraq.[28]

The Bush administration has stood by Saudi Arabia throughout the criticism. During the crown prince's visit to Bush's ranch last April, the president spoke of "the strong relationship" between the two countries. "Our partnership is important to both our nations," Bush said. "And it is important to the cause of peace and stability in the Middle East and the world."

On Dec. 13, Secretary of State Powell announced a program to encourage economic, political and educational changes in Saudi Arabia and other Arab countries. The U.S.-Middle East Partnership Initiative, with an initial funding of $29 million, would focus on improvements in the status of women. "Until the countries of the Middle East unleash the abilities and potential of their women, they will not build a future of hope," he said.[29]

Some experts say the Saudi government has made progress in reforming its institutions and warn against weakening Washington's close diplomatic relations with the House of Saud, because the alternative could be a Taliban-like regime.

"The country is changing, but it's important to the Saudis, and it should be important to us, that this change be evolutionary and not revolutionary," says Cutler of the Meridian International Center. "Because, if sometimes we're critical of the Saudis, let's not help move them into a situation where we would say, 'My God, what have we done?'"

Should the U.S. demand more support from Saudi Arabia?

YES   William Kristol
Chairman, Project for the New American Century;
Editor, The Weekly Standard

From Testimony before the House International Relations Subcommittee on the Middle East and South Asia, May 22, 2002

It is time for the United States to rethink its relationship with Riyadh. For we are now at war . . . with terror and its sponsor, radical Islam. And in this war, the Saudi regime is more part of the problem than part of the solution.

The case for re-evaluating our strategic partnership with the current Saudi regime is a strong one. Begin with the simple fact that 15 of the 19 participants in the Sept. 11 attacks were Saudi nationals. That's something the Saudis themselves could not initially admit. A large proportion—perhaps as high as 80 percent, according to some reports—of the "detainees" taken from Afghanistan to Guantanamo Bay are Saudis. And although Osama bin Laden has made much of his antipathy to the Saudi regime, his true relationship with the royal family is certainly more complex and questionable. . . .

The Saudis also have been deeply implicated in the wave of suicide bombers that have attacked Israeli citizens—and American citizens in Israel—in recent years. Again, initial Saudi official reaction has been to deny the link. . . .

But even more important [is] the Saudi regime's general and aggressive export of Wahhabi fundamentalists. . . . Wahhabi teachings, religious schools and Saudi oil money have encouraged young Muslims in countries around the world to a jihad-like incitement against non-Muslims. The combination of Wahhabi ideology and Saudi money has contributed more to the radicalization and anti-Americanization of large parts of the Islamic world than any other single factor. . . .

Clearly, the long tradition of quiet diplomacy with the Saudi monarchy no longer serves American purposes. The royal family has taken silence as consent in its strategy of directing Arab and Islamic discontent away from the House of Saud and toward the United States, Israel and the West. This is a strategy inimical to American security and a dangerously crippling problem in President Bush's war on terrorism. . . .

Only by applying pressure can we encourage whatever modernizing movement there may be within the royal family and the armed forces while isolating the radical Wahhabi clerics and their supporters. Prince Abdullah is sometimes seen as a reformer. We should give him every incentive to reform the current Saudi regime, and the main such incentive would be to tell him, privately and publicly, that the status quo is unacceptable.

NO   F. Gregory Gause III
Associate Professor of Political Science,
University of Vermont

From testimony before the House International Relations Subcommittee on the Middle East and South Asia, May 22, 2002

We expected our friends to stand with us after Sept. 11, without question and without hesitation. Since the Gulf War, we have counted Saudi Arabia in the camp of our friends. . . .

[T]he Saudis are strategic partners who share a number of common interests with us. We can work with them when those interests coincide, as they frequently do. The Saudis' first reaction to any policy choice is not, "How can we help the Americans on this?" but, "How can we help, or at least not hurt, ourselves?" In this, Saudi Arabia is like almost every other country in the world. Those who thought otherwise, who put the Saudis in the "friends" category, have swung to the other extreme and now come close to labeling them as "enemies." This is equally mistaken. . . .

We have pressed the Saudis for more open intelligence sharing, with some positive results, and we should continue to press them on that score. In short, we have gotten what we need, even if we have not gotten all that we want from the Saudis during the first phase of the war against terrorism. . . .

Those who call for American pressure on the al-Saud to open up their political process should be careful what they wish for. Saudi cooperation on Iraqi and Arab-Israeli issues will be more, not less, difficult to achieve if the Saudi public has a greater say in the country's foreign policy. If you are worried about the level of anti-Israeli rhetoric in the Saudi press, permitting more press freedom will not solve your problem. . . .

Moreover, any elections in Saudi Arabia now would be won by people closer to bin Laden's point of view than to that of liberal democrats. . . .

There is an active debate in Saudi Arabia, predating Sept. 11, about the need to reassess the educational system in light of the changing world economy. Pressure from the United States on this issue will only work against those in Saudi Arabia who seek reform.

Americans can offer advice if asked. In general, however, Washington ought to resist suggesting that it knows better than the Saudis themselves how to manage their society.

What would come after al-Saud rule, if reformist openings lead to revolutionary fervor, would not be an improvement from the point of view of either American interests or American values.

OUTLOOK

Oil Diversification

While maintaining close relations with Saudi Arabia, the Bush administration has expressed concern over the reliability of Middle Eastern oil supplies. Shortly after taking office in January 2001, Bush and Vice President Cheney introduced an energy plan they said would reduce U.S. vulnerability to future oil shortages.[30]

To the dismay of environmentalists, who prefer reducing the high demand for petroleum products through higher energy taxes and incentives to develop alternative power sources, the Bush plan focuses on increasing oil supplies. Among other things, it calls for opening public land, most controversially in the 23-million-acre Alaskan Arctic National Wildlife Refuge (ANWR) to oil exploration and production. But critics say even if the Republican-dominated Congress approves the plan this year, ANWR oil would do little to reduce U.S. dependence on foreign oil, because production would not begin until 2011 and would only add an estimated 800,000 barrels a day to U.S. crude output—enough to reduce from 62 percent to 60 percent the share of foreign oil used by American consumers in 2020.[31]

The Bush plan also calls for continuing the diversification of foreign oil sources under way since the 1973 Arab oil embargo. A prime target for this effort is West Africa, which already supplies about 12 percent of U.S. oil imports and could double that share over the next decade or so.[32] Nigeria currently accounts for the bulk of U.S. oil imports from West Africa, making it the fifth-largest supplier of crude, behind Canada, Saudi Arabia, Mexico and Venezuela.[33]

But some analysts fear that by simply increasing reliance on West African oil without promoting economic development and government reform in that beleaguered part of the world, the Bush administration risks repeating the same mistakes previous administrations have made in the Middle East. Nigeria and the other regional producers—Angola, Equatorial Guinea, Chad, Cameroon and the Republic of Congo—are beset with government corruption, internal strife and extreme poverty. As corrupt leaders siphon off Western oil-company payments with no public oversight, the region's population sinks ever deeper into poverty, setting the stage for the kind of unrest that has afflicted other countries that rely heavily on oil exports.

"Anybody can see that if we're going to rely on Africa as an alternative source of supply, then we mustn't fall into the same trap that we're trying to extricate ourselves from in Saudi Arabia," said international financier George Soros, who is calling for changes in securities law to force oil companies to make public their investments in foreign countries.[34]

Russia and the Caspian Sea region also are promising sources of non-Middle Eastern crude. Their current combined production of 9 million barrels a day is expected to increase by half eventually. Russia is eager to maximize oil exports to improve its ailing economy, while U.S., European and Russian oil companies are developing production facilities and pipelines to carry Caspian oil to ports on the Mediterranean and Black seas.

The promise of Russian oil and Russia's tolerance of the growing U.S. oil-industry presence in the Caspian—a region of Russian strategic interest even after the Soviet Union's fall—have been a key focus in the Bush administration's rapprochement with Russian President Putin.

The U.S. interest in Russian oil even trumps the widespread U.S. misgivings about Putin's brutal supression of dissent in the breakaway province of Chechnya.

"The growth of oil supplies from Russia and the Caspian can be one of the most important new contributions to stability in world oil markets—especially in the face of non-OPEC declines elsewhere," said Yergin of Cambridge Energy Research Associates. "By working with the Russian government to facilitate energy development, the U.S. government can make one of its most important contributions to energy security."[35]

Latin America, a third major area of potential new oil development, is closer than other foreign suppliers. It takes just five days to ship oil from Venezuela to the United States, compared to about 45 days from the Persian Gulf. But, as in West Africa and the Middle East, oil production in several Latin American countries has come at a price. Pipeline construction and oil spills have polluted pristine jungle habitat in Ecuador, threatening indigenous communities. An ongoing civil war and rampant drug trade jeopardize Colombia's oil production, while the oil industry faces an uncertain future in Brazil, where the country's newly elected populist president, socialist Luiz Inacio Lula da Silva, has vowed to review his country's social and economic policies.

In Venezuela—Latin America's leading oil producer and the world's fifth-largest oil exporter—the striking oil workers claim leftist President Chávez is mismanaging the oil industry by resisting calls to increase oil production to slow rising world oil prices.

"The management of [the state-run oil company] wants to produce 6 million barrels a day, which is what the United States wants them to do," says Weisbrot of the Center for Economic and Policy Research. "Chávez has taken a different strategy, which is probably better for Venezuela, which is to obey the OPEC quotas as much as he can and produce a lower amount. Venezuela is actually better off with lower levels of production at a higher price, a fact that no one in the United States is considering because we just want more oil and cheaper oil."

Iraqi Wild Card

Despite the upheavals in Venezuela, the greatest source of uncertainty in world oil markets, however, is Iraq. U.N. weapons inspectors are scheduled to report their findings from the ongoing search for weapons of mass destruction in Iraqi on Jan. 27. Even if they report no evidence of violations, the Bush administration, which is massing troops, ships and weapons in the region, may dismiss their conclusions and proceed with an invasion.

The impact of a war against Iraq would depend on its duration, outcome and effect on the region's other oil producers. "If the war lasts three days—we've blown everything up, we've found all the weapons of mass destruction, the U.N. is coming in and everybody's happy—the oil-price impact could be pretty modest," says Amy Myers Jaffe, a senior energy adviser at the Baker Institute.

"But suppose the campaign turns out to be a little bit more drawn out," Jaffe continues, "and the U.S. military does what it's done in the past—knocks out electrical power stations. That's going to slow down the resumption of Iraq's exports, which would make for a less optimistic scenario."

Some analysts say their biggest concern is the chance that Iraq's oil production will be interrupted by war before Venezuela resumes production. "It will be a much tighter and much more expensive market if both of these countries are out at the same time," says Lichtblau of the Petroleum Industry Research Foundation. "This is entirely possible, because we don't know when the Venezuelan situation will actually improve to the point where they can again become normal oil exporters. Even if the strike ended in a week or two, it would take them

maybe another four or five weeks, or longer, to get back to where they were before Dec. 2."

Meanwhile, critics charge that the Bush administration's desire for Venezuela's oil makes it more than a passive bystander in the crisis. When opposition leaders staged a coup against the democratically elected Chávez last April 12, Washington refrained from condemning the action. The coup failed two days later, but the administration continues to support the strikers' demand for early elections to replace the leftist Chávez.

With so much attention focused on the Middle East and the potential for war with Iraq, Washington's diplomatic initiatives in Venezuela have attracted little attention. But that may soon change. Nineteen liberal members of Congress recently sent a letter of support to Chávez, decrying "unconstitutional" plans to hold early elections in the South American nation.

"The purpose of the letter is to express to the democratically elected president of Venezuela that that there are members of Congress who believe in the principles of our own country," said Rep. Maurice D. Hinchey, D-N.Y., the letter's author. "Our country is supposed to respect democratic policies and principles, but this administration doesn't seem to understand that."[36]

NOTES

1. From remarks after the meeting in Crawford on April 25, 2002.

2. Energy Information Administration, *Monthly Energy Review*, December 2002, pp. 49, 55.

3. See Jeff Gerth, "Bribery Inquiry Involves Kazaks Chief, and He's Unhappy," *The New York Times*, Dec. 11, 2002, p. A16.

4. Human Rights Watch, "World Report 2003." See also Warren Vieth, "U.S. Quest for Oil in Africa Worries Analysts," *Los Angeles Times*, Jan. 13, 2003, p. A1.

5. Gaffney testified June 20, 2002, before the House International Relations Committee.

6. Bush's comment was in answer to a reporter's question on Oct. 21, 2002.

7. Thomas L. Friedman, "A War for Oil?" *The New York Times*, Jan. 5, 2003, p. A11.

8. See, for example, "Protesters Denounce U.S. Navy Presence," *Chicago Tribune*, Dec. 27, 2002.

9. Pew Research Center for the People & the Press, "How Global Publics View Their Lives, Their Countries, the World, America," released Dec. 4, 2002.

10. Robert Fisk, "What the U.S. President Wants Us to Forget," *The Independent* (London), Sept. 10, 2002, p. A17.

11. Speaking with host Tim Russert on NBC's "Meet the Press," Dec. 29, 2002.

12. "Guiding Principles for U.S. Post-Conflict Policy in Iraq," James A. Baker III Institute for Public Policy and Council on Foreign Relations, December 2002.

13. Daniel Yergin, "A Crude View of the Crisis in Iraq," *The Washington Post*, Dec. 8, 2002, p. B1.

14. Schwartz's book, *The Two Faces of Islam*, is described by Ira Rifkin, "Author Sees Terrorist Roots in Saudi Religious Code," *The Washington Post*, Jan. 11, 2003, p. B9.

15. From testimony before the House International Relations Subcommittee on the Middle East and South Asia, May 22, 2002.

16. Bandow testified on June 12, 2002, before the House Government Reform Committee.

17. For background, see Mary H. Cooper, "Energy Security," *The CQ Researcher*, Feb. 1, 2002, pp. 73-96.

18. See Brock Yates, "Car Talk," *The Wall Street Journal*, Jan. 9, 2003, p. A10.

19. For a comprehensive history of oil diplomacy, see Daniel Yergin, *The Prize* (1991).

20. *Ibid.*, p. 567.

21. From a Saudi government information Web site, www.saudinf.com.

22. U.S. Department of Energy, Energy Information Agency, "Petroleum Chronology of Events 1970-2000," www.eia.doe.gov.

23. From a Dec. 6, 2002, survey at www.doubtcome.com.

24. Jim Hoagland, "Saudi Arabia's Choice," *The Washington Post*, Dec. 1, 2002, p. B7.

25. Quoted in "U.S. Sen. Graham Critical of Bush Administration, Saudi Arabia," *Dow Jones International News*, Dec. 3, 2002.

26. Speaking at a press conference at the Saudi Embassy in Washington, Dec. 3, 2002.

27. See Thomas E. Ricks, "American Way of War in Saudi Desert," *The Washington Post*, Jan. 7, 2003, p. A1.

28. See Michael R. Gordon, "Iraq's Neighbors Seem to Be Ready to Support a War," *The New York Times*, Dec. 2, 2002, p. A1.

29. See Edward Walsh, "Powell Unveils U.S.-Arab Initiative," *The Washington Post*, Dec. 13, 2002, p. A22. For background on women's rights, see David Masci, "Emerging India," *The CQ Researcher*, April 19, 2002, pp. 329-360; Kenneth Jost, "Rebuilding Afghanistan," *The CQ Researcher*, Dec. 21, 2001, pp. 1041-1064; and Mary H. Cooper, "Women and Human Rights," *The CQ Researcher*, April 30, 1999, pp. 353-376.

30. For background, see Mary H. Cooper, "Energy Policy," *The CQ Researcher*, May 25, 2001, pp. 441-464.

31. Energy Information Administration, "The Effects of the Alaska Oil and Natural Gas Provisions of H.R. 4 and S. 1766 on U.S. Energy Markets," February 2002.

32. See Warren Vieth, "U.S. Quest for Oil in Africa Worries Analysts," *Los Angeles Times*, Jan. 13, 2003, p. A1.

33. Energy Information Administration, "Nigeria," January 2002.

34. Quoted in Vieth, *op. cit.*

35. Yergin testified June 20, 2002, before the House International Relations Committee.

36. See Jonathan Riehl, "House Liberals Defend Leftist Venezuelan President Chávez," *Congressional Quarterly Daily Monitor*, Jan. 14, 2003.

BIBLIOGRAPHY

Books

Schwartz, Stephen, *The Two Faces of Islam: The House of Saud from Tradition to Terror*, Doubleday, 2002.
The author, a convert to Islam, blames Wahhabism—Saudi Arabia's strict interpretation of the faith—for instilling hatred of Western values in young Arab men.

Telhami, Shibley, *The Stakes: America and the Middle East*, Westview Press, 2002.
A University of Maryland political scientist writes that so long as the United States is viewed in the Middle East as arrogant, pro-Israel and supportive of authoritarian regimes such as Saudi Arabia, it will not win the war on terrorism.

Yergin, Daniel, *The Prize: The Epic Quest for Oil, Money, and Power,* **Simon & Schuster, 1991.**
This Pulitzer Prize-winning history of the oil industry provides a comprehensive review of how oil shaped U.S. foreign policy toward the Middle East. Yergin is president of Cambridge Energy Associates and former chairman of the Energy Department's Task Force on Strategic Energy Research and Development.

Articles

"Don't Mention the O-Word," *The Economist,* **Sept. 14, 2002.**
Fears that a U.S.-led invasion of Iraq would disrupt global oil supplies are exaggerated, according to this overview of Middle Eastern oil supplies, because Iraqi oil exports are already low.

Morse, Edward L., and James Richard, "The Battle for Energy Dominance," *Foreign Affairs,* **March/April 2002, pp. 16-31.**
Efforts to buy oil from suppliers outside the Middle East have intensified since the Sept. 11, 2001, terrorist attacks, putting Russia in a position to surpass Saudi Arabia in coming years as the world's leading exporter.

Ottaway, Marina, "Reluctant Missionaries," *Foreign Policy,* **July-August 2001.**
Oil companies are drawing criticism for polluting the environment and tolerating human-rights abuses in countries where they operate. But oil companies are not in a position to effect human-rights reforms, the author writes.

Ratnesar, Romesh, "The Unending War," *Time,* **Dec. 9, 2002.**
Critics question the Bush administration's cordial relations with Saudi Arabia after revelations that the wife of its U.S. ambassador contributed to charities that may have ties to al Qaeda.

Vieth, Warren, "U.S. Quest for Oil in Africa Worries Analysts, Activists," *Los Angeles Times,* **Jan. 13, 2003, p. 1.**
The Bush administration's search for more secure sources of oil is leading it to the doorsteps of some of the world's most repressive regimes: the petroleum-rich countries of West Africa.

Reports and Studies

Congressional Budget Office, "Reducing Gasoline Consumption: Three Policy Options," November 2002.
Tightening fuel-efficiency standards for cars, raising the federal tax on gasoline and setting carbon-emission limits on companies that produce cars and other gasoline-powered products would reduce U.S. energy dependence and emissions of gases linked to global warming.

Friends of the Earth, Taxpayers for Common Sense and the U.S. Public Interest Research Group Education Fund, "Running on Empty: How Environmentally Harmful Energy Subsidies Siphon Billions from Taxpayers," 2002.
Three advocacy groups argue the U.S. government is impeding the development of alternative-energy sources by spending more on fossil fuel research than it devotes to developing renewable-energy sources and encouraging energy efficiency.

James A. Baker III Institute for Public Policy and Council on Foreign Relations, "Strategic Energy Policy Challenges for the 21st Century," 2001.
Before the next crisis erupts, the U.S. government should urgently overhaul its international energy policy with a view toward achieving energy independence, according to this report.

National Intelligence Council, "Global Trends 2015: A Dialogue about the Future with Nongovernment Experts," December 2000.
The CIA's research branch predicts that Asia will replace North America as the world's leading energy-consumption region and account for more than half the world's total increase in demand for oil by 2015.

Natural Resources Defense Council and Union of Concerned Scientists, "Dangerous Addiction: Ending America's Oil Dependence," January 2002.
The report calls on the government to reduce U.S. dependence on Middle Eastern oil by tightening fuel economy, providing tax credits to buyers of hybrid vehicles and providing incentives to speed the development of hydrogen-powered fuel-cell cars.

For More Information

American Petroleum Institute, 1220 L St., N.W., Washington, DC 20005; (202) 682-8000; www.api.org. A membership organization representing U.S. oil and natural-gas companies that provides information about the industry and oil-supply forecasts.

Energy Information Administration, U.S. Department of Energy, 1000 Independence Ave., S.W., #7B058, Washington, DC 20585; (202) 586-8800; www.eia.doe.gov. Provides data, forecasts and analyses on all U.S. energy sectors.

Human Rights Watch, 350 Fifth Ave., 34th floor, New York, NY 10118; (212) 290-4700; www.hrw.org. A nonprofit advocacy group that issues detailed reports on human rights around the world.

International Energy Agency, 2001 L St., N.W., #650, Washington, DC 20036; (202) 785-6323; www.oecdwash.org. This branch of the Organization for Economic Cooperation and Development provides information on industrial countries' emergency stockpiles of oil.

Middle East Institute, 1761 N St., N.W., Washington, DC 20036; (202) 785-1141; www.mideasti.org. This nonprofit educational organization provides information on the Middle East in an effort to increase Americans' knowledge and understanding of the region.

8

Japan in Crisis

David Masci

A homeless man finds shelter in one of the many parks and gardens in Tokyo. Japan's unemployment rate has doubled in the past decade, triggering a jump in homelessness. Last year alone, homelessness spiked 25 percent.

From *The CQ Researcher,*
July 26, 2002.

On the surface of Japan's orderly society, all appears to be well. Most streets are clean, the crime rate is relatively low and people are generally polite and cooperative. Throngs visit fashionable shopping districts, and many live comfortably in tidy, elegant suburbs.

But under the patina of harmony and affluence, all is not as it seems. "There's a lot more pain in Japan than people are willing to admit or talk about," says Eugene Mathews, an expert on Japan at the Council on Foreign Relations in New York City. "There is a sense of paralysis and great despair."

Indeed, many experts say Japan is in a crisis. A near-continuous recession for more than a decade has cost hundreds of thousands of jobs—devastating in a country where lifetime employment with a single company traditionally has been central to the social compact. One result of the rise in unemployment: Homelessness is up, rising 25 percent in the last year alone, according to the Health, Labor and Welfare Ministry.[1]

The nation's historically low crime rate also has been rising rapidly—12 percent last year—although it is still nowhere near American or European levels.[2]

Even Japan's much-vaunted educational system, once the envy of the world, is now seen as an anachronism that fosters rote learning instead of the creativity and independent thinking needed in today's competitive global economy. "Our whole school system now seems antiquated because it's good at producing bureaucrats and middle managers, but not the entrepreneurs that Japan needs right now," says Mariko Ikehara, director of the Washington office of CNET, a Japanese public service cable-TV station.

Land of the Rising Sun

The ancient Japanese, unaware of any lands east of their own, called their realm Nippon — "Land of the Rising Sun." The California-sized island nation is home to about 127 million people — nearly half the population of the United States.

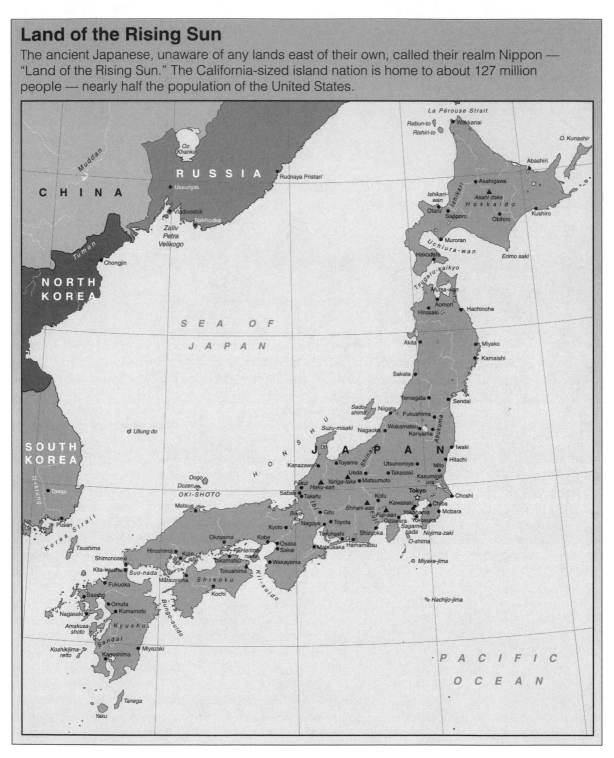

Japan at a Glance

Population: 126,771,662 (July 2001 estimate)

Ethnicity: Japanese, 99.4 percent; Koreans, 0.6 percent

Life Expectancy: 80.8 years

Fertility Rate: 1.4 children are born to each woman. (2.06 in the United States)

Religion: Buddhism and Shinto, 84 percent; secular and smaller sects, 16 percent.

Total Area: 152,200 square miles. (About the same as California and Germany)

Gross Domestic Product: $3.15 trillion. (2000 estimate)

Monetary Unit: The yen. One dollar equals about 116 yen.

Major Industries: Among the world's largest manufacturers of autos, electronic products, steel, ships and chemicals.

Government: Japan is a parliamentary democracy with a bicameral legislature. The 252 members of the upper house (Shang-in) are elected for six years, while the 480 members of the lower house (Shugi-in) serve for four years. The prime minister, who is elected by the lower house, leads the government. The chief of state is the emperor, a largely ceremonial office currently held by Emperor Akihito.

Sources: CIA World Factbook; The World Almanac (2002).

pass the United States as an economic and geopolitical superpower.

Today, however, bookstores in both countries carry volumes explaining what went wrong in Japan, and newspaper editorials exhort the Japanese to adopt American-style economic reforms and business practices. "We used to say that Japan had third-rate politicians but a first-rate economy," Ikehara says. "Now, everything is third-rate."

Despite the pessimism, Japan's still boasts the world's second-largest economy behind the United States. And it is still home to some of the world's most successful and innovative companies, like Toyota, Sony and Honda. But the island nation is drowning in debt and seemingly incapable of sustained growth.

Much of the trouble can be traced to Japan's banking system, which lent trillions of dollars to land developers and other businessmen during the high-flying 1980s—when unparalleled economic growth sparked gravity-defying spikes in stock and real estate prices. When the "bubble" burst in the early 1990s, massive loan defaults saddled the banks with almost unimaginable losses. (*See story, p. 166.*)

Economist Adam Posen of the International Institute for Economics in Washington, D.C., is among the analysts who believe Japan's banking system could collapse by year's end, creating economic chaos. Others think the banks could continue to limp along for another two or three years. But all agree that unless the government of Prime Minister Junichiro Koizumi bails out the banks—and soon—they will crumble under the weight of their non-performing loans.

The banks' troubles have left them with little cash, making them less likely to extend new loans—even to creditworthy borrowers—thus sending the economy into more of a tailspin.[3] The cash shortage has also triggered deflation, or falling prices, further hurting Japan's already battered economy. Lower prices mean that businesses earn less for selling goods and services. Moreover, since a scarcity of money makes it more valuable, borrowers have a harder time paying back loans.

And debt problems aren't limited to the private sector. The government's 8 percent annual budget deficit shows no sign of decreasing. Total public debt is now nearly 160 percent of the annual gross domestic product (GDP)—more than three times the U.S. government's debt rate and by far the highest level in the developed world.

Yet only a decade ago, scholars and journalists on both sides of the Pacific saw Japan as the world's new great power and a model society. In books such as *Japan as Number One* and *The Rise and Fall of the Great Powers*, they predicted that Japan would soon rival or even sur-

When he was elected 18 months ago, Koizumi promised to fix the banking system, bring the budget under control and make the political process more open and responsive. But so far, he has been unable to make meaningful changes.

Many Japan-watchers blame Koizumi's inability to effect change on the country's political system. The prime minister's own Liberal Democratic Party (LDP)—which has been in power almost continuously since 1955—stifles any attempt at radical change and owes its long rule to support from Japan's many entrenched special interests. But others note that Koizumi came into power with an 80 percent approval rating and a mandate for change, both of which they say he squandered in his first year and a half.

However, the prime minister has been able to make a few changes, most notably to Japan's military posture. The country's constitution—imposed by occupying American forces after World War II—prohibits the armed forces from engaging in combat outside Japan. But following the Sept. 11 attacks on the United States, Koizumi convinced the Diet, or parliament, to ease some of the strict limits on the military by allowing naval vessels to provide non-combat support for U.S. forces in the Middle East.

Many Japanese citizens, as well as U.S. Japan-watchers, want the country to scrap the constitutional ban on sending troops into combat. As the largest pro-Western democracy in Asia and a key American ally, Japan should contribute to multilateral military actions, they argue, such as the current efforts to fight terrorism in Afghanistan.

But others say the so-called Peace Constitution has served Japan well and should not be changed. "We can do other things, non-military things, to help, like give humanitarian assistance," says Mariko Tamanoi, a Japanese national teaching at the University of California at Los Angeles (UCLA).

Debate over the country's proper military role, of course, stems from Japan's aggression before and during World War II, when the Japanese attacked China, the United States and many other countries throughout Asia and the Pacific. Some observers say Japan—in stark contrast to Germany, its former wartime ally—has yet to fully atone for its wartime actions, including the Bataan death march and other unspeakable atrocities.

But Japan's greatest challenge lies not in coming to grips with its past but in charting a path into an uncertain future. In the coming decades, the Japanese will have to grapple with the economic and social costs of an aging population, as well as increasing competition from neighboring Asian countries. As Japan deals with its past, present and future, here are some of the questions being asked:

Is substantial economic reform possible under Japan's current political system?

When Koizumi swept to victory last April 26, he had assets any politician would envy—striking good looks, charisma and extensive political experience. But perhaps his greatest strength was that he came to office having convinced the public that he could change the country and end its persistent recession.

Talk of bold reforms marked Koizumi's first months. He promised to overhaul the tax system, deal with the banking crisis and control Japan's massive budget deficits. He also pledged to show no favoritism to Japan's sacred political cows—most notably farmers, the construction industry and small-business owners—and the old leaders of his own party. The tantalizing promises netted Koizumi astounding 80 percent approval ratings—a level of popularity unparalleled in the nation's modern political history.

But today, more than a year after the election, few of Koizumi's proposals have been enacted. Moreover, his approval rating has dropped since the beginning of the year by half—to 40 percent—as hopes fade that he could revive the economy and effect systemic change.

Some analysts say Koizumi's dreams of reforming Japan never really stood a chance against the country's entrenched ruling party, special interests and powerful bureaucracy. But others remain hopeful. "The Japanese political system is capable of reform and change," says Steven Vogel, an associate professor of political science at the University of California at Berkeley. "It may not be easy, but it's possible."

Koizumi's popularity gave him a golden opportunity to make meaningful changes, Vogel and others contend. "He had real room to maneuver and space to make real reforms because he was so overwhelmingly popular," he says. "But he squandered it."

Indeed, the prime minister's critics say, Koizumi could have tackled what many consider Japan's most pressing problem: the banking crisis. "With his immense popularity in the beginning, Koizumi could have tried to reform the banking sector, but essentially he has done nothing about this," says Edward J. Lincoln, an expert on the Japanese economy at the Brookings Institution.

Instead, the prime minister ignored the facts and declared the banking situation much less serious than it is, according to Lincoln and others. "He basically said it wasn't that big of a problem by grossly underestimating the amount of bad loans the banks had and then said they could deal with it themselves by writing these loans off over the next three years," Lincoln says.

Koizumi's critics also say he lacks both a clear agenda and a genuine commitment to reform. "I don't think he really understands what the problems are and so doesn't know what to do to solve them," Vogel says.

"He put himself forward as 'Mister Reform' because that's what the people wanted," Lincoln says. "Beyond the rhetoric, I don't think he has concrete ideas on how to tackle the real problems facing Japan."

But others say the prime minister faces structural obstacles that would hamstring even the most dedicated or persuasive reformer. "Given the way things work in Japan, it's hard to blame Koizumi," says Marie Anchordoguy, a professor of political science at the University of Washington at Seattle. "Koizumi had a mandate from the people, without the power to carry out that mandate."

Japan's problems "have nothing to do with economics but everything to do with the political system," says Frank Gibney, a professor of political science at Pomona College in Claremont, Calif. Indeed, Koizumi's biggest obstacle is his own party, which has dominated Japan since the mid-1950s, he adds.

"Members of the LDP are so tied to special interests they won't do anything to go against them, even if it's clearly in the interests of the society as a whole," agrees Tsuneo Watanabe, a Japan specialist at the Center for Strategic and International Studies (CSIS).

The special interests contribute huge amounts to keep certain Diet members in office. "Basically, each special interest has at least 20 or 30 members of the Diet, usually in the ruling party, that are in their pocket," Gibney says. "These members can be counted on to jam up any effort that threatens whatever interest is supporting them."

The construction industry ranks among the biggest offenders, Gibney says. To keep their firms busy and prof-

Prime Minister Junichiro Koizumi follows a Shinto priest during his controversial visit last April to Tokyo's Yasukuni Shrine—resting place for 2.5 million Japanese war dead, including former Prime Minister Hideki Tojo and other convicted war criminals from World War II.

itable, the industry presses the government to spend billions on unnecessary infrastructure projects every year, he says. "They pass these huge economic-stimulus bills that fund the building of roads in remote areas or bridges that are not needed," Gibney says. "But, of course, this spending ultimately does nothing to end the recession."

Moreover, because its opposition parties are usually weak, Japan essentially is a one-party state, critics point out.

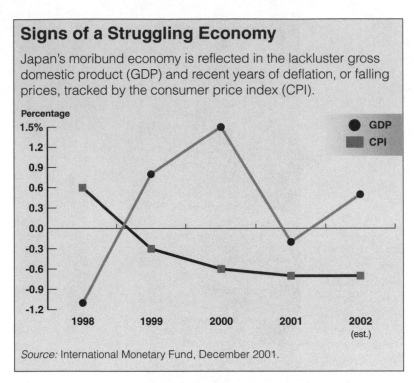

Signs of a Struggling Economy

Japan's moribund economy is reflected in the lackluster gross domestic product (GDP) and recent years of deflation, or falling prices, tracked by the consumer price index (CPI).

Percentage

● GDP

■ CPI

Source: International Monetary Fund, December 2001.

allies overseas—but only in a non-combat capacity. By November, three Japanese ships were in the Indian Ocean, providing logistical and supply help to the U.S. Navy.

The limits on Japan's armed forces stem from its 1947 constitution—a pacifist document drafted largely by the United States—whose Article 9 decried war and initially prohibited Japan from even maintaining a military. But the prohibition—written when memories of World War II carnage were still fresh—soon fell victim to the realities of the Cold War. Prodded by the United States, Japan in 1954 set about creating a "self-defense force" that could help the Americans stave off Soviet aggression. Japan has since built a small, but state-of-the-art, military.

The Japanese have been chipping away at Article 9 for years. The changes often come when a world crisis like Sept. 11 creates pressure for Japanese military assistance. And yet Japanese forces are still prohibited from direct combat, to some extent because of public opposition. According to a recent poll, only 42 percent of the Japanese favor allowing their forces to join others in military actions that include combat.[4]

Many experts dismiss Article 9 as an anachronism with no real purpose except to handicap Japan's efforts to be a responsible world power. "No one wants the constitution changed to allow for military aggression," says CSIS's Watanabe, "but the overseas ban on combat missions must be lifted so Japan can take her place along with the United States and other nations in peacekeeping operations and other multilateral missions."

"Japan has a moral obligation, as a prosperous nation, to help others, and that includes peacekeeping," says T. J. Pempel, director of the Institute of East Asian Studies at the University of California at Berkeley. "So in a place like East Timor in 1999, Japan should have been there with combat troops, helping to protect the East Timorese," he adds, referring to an Australia-led peace-

"There are other political parties, but there's really no practical alternative to the LDP," Anchordoguy says. "And, even so, these parties are often filled with old LDP guys."

Thus, the ruling party has little incentive to respond to the will of the people, she says. "The LDP can afford to ignore the voice of the Japanese people because they know there is nowhere else to turn."

Should the Japanese military be allowed to engage in combat missions overseas?

After Sept. 11, Japan joined other close U.S. allies in pledging support in the war against terrorism. But unlike the others—including Japan's former World War II ally, Germany—Japan was constitutionally blocked from providing combat forces.*

Koizumi immediately pushed a bill through the Diet that allowed the nation's armed forces to assist

---

* Because the United States needed Germany to be a partner in the North Atlantic Treaty Organization, Germany was allowed to build a military after World War II, but it, too, was prohibited from deploying troops overseas. That prohibition was lifted in the mid-1990s, when Germany participated in peacekeeping operations in Bosnia. Today, Germany's chancellor can send troops into overseas combat, but only after obtaining parliament's approval.

keeping mission to the island, which was then part of Indonesia.*

Allowing Japan to send soldiers into harm's way will pay handsome geopolitical dividends, say critics of the current system. "Japan would increase its influence around the world," says William Breer, an expert on Japan at the CSIS. "It would give them a seat at the table that they don't have right now because they can't commit troops."

For instance, the Japanese tried to play an important role during the Persian Gulf War by contributing $13 billion to the allied effort, Breer points out. But even with such a large sum of money, "Japan was not taken seriously," he says.

Finally, opponents of Article 9 say that abolishing the ban on combat will help Japan exorcise the ghosts of its militaristic past. "If Japan could show both itself and the world that it is a responsible military power, then it would finally be able to move on from its history," says Pempel.

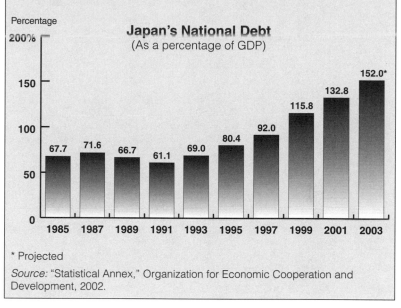

National Debt Has Doubled

Japan's national debt has more than doubled since its lowest point in 1991. It is projected to reach more than 150 percent of the country's annual gross domestic product (GDP) in 2003 — about triple the relative size of the U.S. government's debt and by far the highest in the developed world.

Japan's National Debt
(As a percentage of GDP)

Year	Percentage
1985	67.7
1987	71.6
1989	66.7
1991	61.1
1993	69.0
1995	80.4
1997	92.0
1999	115.8
2001	132.8
2003	152.0*

* Projected

Source: "Statistical Annex," Organization for Economic Cooperation and Development, 2002.

But proponents of the prohibition say one of the enduring lessons of World War II is that Japan should eschew the use of the military to solve problems. "The pacifist movement and the pacifist impulse is still very popular in Japan for a reason," says UCLA's Tamanoi. "Japan suffered so much during wartime, especially with the allied bombing of Tokyo and other cities. But we also remember that we bear responsibility for these tragedies because we started the conflict."

Instead, the Japanese should focus on continuing to contribute to peacekeeping and other missions in non-military ways, Tamanoi and others say. "Japan can do many things to pull its weight in ways that don't involve the military," she says. "For example, in Afghanistan, we have sent many people to provide humanitarian assistance, such as digging wells."

Such endeavors would be much more useful than military assistance, says Miles Fletcher, a professor of history at the University of North Carolina at Chapel Hill. "They just don't really have a big military that they can project far from home, so I don't see them making much of a difference, beyond symbolism," he says.

Thus, opponents of lifting the ban insist Japan would probably gain little influence from taking on military missions. "Given what they could contribute, I really doubt they would all of a sudden acquire all of this new influence if they allowed their armed forces to engage in combat," Fletcher says. "They'd have to have a huge military buildup in order to make a difference."

Moreover, say supporters of Article 9, removing the ban on combat could bolster nationalist forces in Japan— a vocal minority that wants to move the country toward a more aggressive foreign and military policy. "If the nation began thinking more in military terms, you could end up encouraging the wrong people," Fletcher says. "The pacifist constitution is a check on these tendencies."

---

* Japan did send 600 non-combat soldiers to East Timor, which since has achieved independence.

Banking System Faces Collapse

During the 1980s, Japanese banks were among the world's largest and most profitable. But today, the industry is headed for a total meltdown.

"The banking system is on the verge of collapsing, and many of Japan's biggest banks are already technically bankrupt," says Edward J. Lincoln, an expert on the Japanese economy at the Brookings Institution.

Although estimates vary, most private analysts say the nation's banks have between $1 trillion and $2 trillion in bad loans on their books, an amount equal to between 20 percent and 40 percent of Japan's gross domestic product (GDP). By contrast, the value of bad loans during America's savings and loan crisis in the late 1980s and early '90s represented 5 percent of the U.S. GDP.

"I think [Japan's] system will begin to collapse in the next six months," predicts Adam Posen an economist at the International Institute for Economics.

But others say predictions of imminent collapse may be premature. "There are a lot of non-performing loans, and, of course, that's bad," says Miles Fletcher, a professor of history at the University of North Carolina at Chapel Hill. "But people have been talking about the dire condition of Japan's banks for almost a decade and they haven't collapsed yet."

The roots of Japan's banking crisis lie at the heart of the system that vaulted the country from a post-World War II basket case into an economic superpower. After the war, the economy was micromanaged by an army of government bureaucrats, who directed and oversaw every industrial sector.

Banks were often directed to lend money to certain parts of the economy—like steel or petrochemicals—deemed by government officials as crucial to the country's economic health. The usual factors that lending institutions consider, such as whether the loan would be put to good use or paid back, often were set aside in favor of political considerations.

"The system is comparable to the command economy in the old Soviet Union in the sense that market forces aren't really the major consideration," says Tsuneo Watanabe, a fellow at the Center for Strategic and International Studies.

The system worked remarkably well through the 1980s. Indeed, the Japanese model of directing the economy was often touted as the wave of the future. But government officials during the 1980s nudged banks to lend massive amounts of money to the construction and real estate sectors, which were growing almost exponentially. The almost complete collapse of real estate prices in the early 1990s left banks holding hundreds of billions in bad loans. Moreover, many other businesses that had nothing to do with construction had borrowed money to invest in real estate, widening the circle of heavily indebted businesses.

Since then, according to Lincoln, the government has largely ignored the problem. "They say that there are $300 billion in bad loans and the industry can solve its own problems," Lincoln says. But Japan's banks are beyond self-help, he contends. "Prime Minister Koizumi needs to go on TV, declare a national emergency and tell the Japanese people that everything that they've heard about the banks, including from his own government, is untrue."

Watanabe agrees, arguing that the banks should be nationalized. "They need to take over all of the banks and close the ones with too many bad loans on their books and clean up the ones that can be revived," he says. The government should finance part of the cleanup by selling the banks' assets, he says, with the rest coming from the taxpayers. In a few years, the banks would be fiscally healthy and could be resold to private investors.

The cleanup costs would surpass the hundreds of billions in taxpayer funds needed to resuscitate the banks. "Thousands of companies would be forced into bankruptcy because their loans would be called in," Lincoln says. "The construction and real estate industries would suffer the most, but retailing and manufacturing would also have some bankruptcies."

Such a radical overhaul would lead to a near doubling in unemployment, Lincoln predicts, from the current 5.5 percent rate to about 9 percent.

"It would be very painful, but in the years following [the bankruptcies] the people laid off would be reabsorbed back into more productive parts of the economy, and the rate of unemployment would drop."

Should Japan do more to atone for its wartime past?

World leaders routinely visit memorials dedicated to their war dead, but for Japan—a nation whose only major recent war ended in defeat and ignominy—honoring the fallen can be very complicated.

Japan's major war memorial, the Yasukuni Shrine, holds the remains of more than 1 million soldiers, sailors and airman who died in service to the emperor during World War II. Honoring their sacrifice is not controversial. But the shrine also contains the remains of 12 people executed by the United States in the late 1940s as war criminals.

As a result, Yasukuni has become a litmus test for Japanese politicians. Visiting the shrine pleases the country's nationalists, who say that it is correct and natural for their leader to honor those who served the nation in war.

Prime Minister Koizumi has visited the shrine twice since taking office, once last August and then again this past April. But while the pilgrimage mollified nationalists, many Japanese criticized it as a repudiation of Japan's post-World War II pacifist policies.

The visit has also drawn fire from countries attacked by Japan before and during the war, particularly China and Korea, where millions perished. Honoring war criminals is grossly insensitive to the memories of the victims of Japan's wartime aggression, the two nations claim.

The controversy is just the tip of a larger ongoing debate in Japan and throughout much of Asia over how Japan handles its wartime past. Although Japan no longer threatens its neighbors, critics claim events like the Yasukuni visit show that the Japanese, unlike the Germans, have not fully accepted their culpability for the horrors they perpetrated before and during World War II. "I just don't think that they've come to grips with what they did, as a nation," says the University of Washington's Anchordoguy. "It's hard to look at what they've done since then and argue that they've been accurate and responsive on this."

Anchordoguy and others point to the fact that Japanese textbooks downplay or try to mitigate the country's aggressive and brutal behavior during the period. For example, last year, the South Korean government complained that many Japanese textbooks do not even mention that tens of thousands of Asian women, many from Korea, were forced into sexual slavery by the Japanese military during World War II.[5]

"German textbooks portray the war and Germany's role in it in an accurate light," Pempel says. "But in Japan the Ministry of Education has pushed textbook publishers to 'balance' the view of the Japanese as aggressors by reminding students of such things as the fact that there was white colonialism in Asia."

Critics also dismiss apologies for the country's past aggression offered by Japan's prime ministers. "Sure, they've made these half apologies saying that they regret this or that," says the University of Washington's Anchordoguy. "They haven't really made heartfelt apologies to these countries. If they made a good faith effort at contrition, they would mollify many of these countries, like China."

But others say the critics, both Japanese and foreign, are hypersensitive. "Japan totally subjugated itself to the victorious allies, paid reparations to the countries we conquered and has been the most peaceable nation on Earth since World War II," says Yoshishisa Komori, editor-at-large at *Sankei Shimbun*, one of Tokyo's largest daily newspapers. "What else do people want?"

"I think the Japanese are getting a bit of a bum rap on this whole thing," agrees the University of North Carolina's Fletcher. "Sure, there is still a lot of ignorance and apathy among the Japanese about the war, but there's a lot of the same in the United States and elsewhere too, so we can't really use that as proof that they haven't done enough."

Japan has gone to great lengths to face its past, apologizing to every nation it invaded and paying some of those countries reparations, according to Komori, Fletcher and others. In some cases, such as China, Japanese prime ministers have apologized on more than one occasion. "They've issued all kinds of apologies to most of these countries, but it never seems to be enough," says Breer of CSIS.

According to Breer, the apologies usually fall on deaf ears because countries like China and Korea use Japan's wartime guilt to put the country's leaders on the defensive. "Other nations, especially China, are reluctant to put it to rest because it gives them political leverage over the Japanese," he says. "It gives them a wonderful political and diplomatic button to push anytime they want anything from the Japanese. So, of course, they don't want to give it up."

The country's defenders insist the Japanese are not afraid to face the grim reality of what they did. For instance, Fletcher says, Japanese historians have examined various atrocities committed by Japan during the years right before and during World War II, including the infamous "Rape of Nanjing," which led to an estimated 200,000 Chinese deaths and countless rapes and other human rights abuses.[6]

Finally, supporters say, the proof is in the pudding. Japan has turned from an aggressive, imperialist power into a tolerant democracy and model world citizen. "Japan has made such great strides, politically, economically and otherwise and they should feel proud of the kind of country they've created," Mathews of the Council on Foreign Relations says.

BACKGROUND

The Rising Sun

The Japanese have always perceived foreigners with a mixture of fascination and fear. But throughout much of Japan's history, fear—often justified—has trumped curiosity. Even today, 150 years after the country was "reopened" to the world, many Japanese still view foreigners, or *gaijin*, with trepidation.

Europeans first came to Japan in the middle of the 16th century, when competing warlords (or shoguns) ruled the country. Portuguese traders and missionaries arrived first, quickly followed by the Spanish and Dutch. By the 1580s, the newcomers were engaging in a brisk trade in silks, silver and gold, and about 150,000 Japanese—2 percent of the population—had converted to Christianity.[7]

But in the following decades, Japan was unified under one warlord, and encroaching European influence was deemed a threat to the new state. Both Christianity and foreign commerce were suppressed. By the 1640s, Christianity was heavily proscribed and foreigners largely expelled from the country. For the next 200 years, Japan existed in virtual isolation.

By the 1840s, Western encroachments in the rest of Asia, especially China, were increasingly threatening to Japan. Its isolation ended in July 1853, when American Commodore Matthew C. Perry sailed into Tokyo Bay with four warships. The overwhelming power of the then-modern naval vessels forced the Japanese to accede to some American terms—namely the opening of diplomatic and trade relations with the United States. Soon,

other European countries had wrested similar treaties from the Japanese.[8]

Partly as a result of Western incursions, an already weak Japanese shogunate began to totter and eventually collapsed. In 1868, he was replaced by an emperor, a hereditary office that had been largely symbolic until then.

The 16-year-old Emperor Meiji transformed Japan. He largely abolished the old feudal social order in favor of a more egalitarian model, legalized private ownership of land and replaced a crushing taxation system—which had kept many average Japanese in penury—with a more progressive tax structure.

Japan also instituted a crash modernization program, aimed at bringing the nation up to American and European standards. Shipyards, telegraphs, railroads and factories were built at a rapid pace.[9] The emperor also created a Western-style financial system—with a convertible currency, stock exchange and central bank—and overhauled the military using modern Western methods and weapons.

Meanwhile, the Japanese harkened back to the past to glorify the emperor. Meiji became the head of the state Shinto religion—a Japanese offshoot of Buddhism—and was declared a living god.

But peasants, vestiges of the old aristocracy and others opposed at least some of the modernization. In the 1870s several armed rebellions broke out, which were put down by the new government.

Yet the unrest led to a partial democratization of the political system and establishment of an independent judiciary. In 1889, a new constitution was enacted, creating an assembly with limited legislative powers, elected by wealthy male Japanese men.[10] Despite these reforms, most political power in Japan still rested with the emperor and a clique of elder statesmen around him.

Imperial Overreach

By the end of the 19th century, Japan had become a modern power with typical modern-power ambitions: It wanted to expand its influence and acquire territory.

Throughout the 1880s, Japan and China each maneuvered to become the dominant power in nearby Korea, wrangling that in 1894 pushed the two countries into war.

The Sino-Japanese conflict, which lasted only nine months, resulted in China's complete defeat. In subsequent peace talks, Japan gained control of the island of Taiwan and the southern part of the northern Chinese

CHRONOLOGY

Before 1850 *European efforts to influence Japan lead to 200 years of isolation.*

1543 Portuguese traders arrive in Japan, followed by the Spanish and Dutch.

1580s Trade with Europe expands. Some Japanese convert to Christianity.

1603 A military dictatorship, or shogunate, unifies the country.

1622 The shogunate drives Christianity and European commerce from Japan. For the next two centuries, Japan bars foreigners.

1850-1945 *Japan opens up to the West and quickly modernizes. Expansionism ultimately leads to war with the Allies and defeat.*

1853 Commodore Matthew C. Perry forces the Japanese to open diplomatic and trade relations with the United States. European states establish similar treaties soon after.

1868 The shogunate collapses and Emperor Meiji becomes ruler of Japan.

1894 Japan and China go to war over Korea. Japanese forces destroy the Chinese military, and Korea comes under Japanese sway.

1905 Japan defeats Russia in a war over Manchuria.

1937 Japan conquers eastern China, slaughtering thousands of civilians in Nanjing.

Dec. 7, 1941 In a surprise attack on Pearl Harbor, the Japanese destroy much of the U.S. Pacific fleet. The United States joins the war against Japan and the Axis.

1942 Japan is defeated at Midway. The Allies begin pushing Japanese forces back toward Japan.

1945 Japan surrenders after atomic bombs devastate Hiroshima and Nagasaki. U.S. troops occupy the country until 1952.

1946-1990 *Japan becomes Asia's pre-eminent economic power.*

1947 Under American guidance, the country adopts a new constitution establishing democratic institutions, guaranteeing individual rights and forswearing war.

1951 Japan signs Mutual Security Assistance Pact with the United States.

1955 The Liberal Democratic Party (LDP) is formed.

1965 The Japanese economy begins growing 11 percent a year.

1968 Japan surpasses West Germany to becomes the world's second-largest economy, behind the U.S.

1973 The Arab oil embargo hurts Japan's economy but gives Japanese automakers a toehold in the U.S. market.

1989 Japan's Nikkei index has tripled in value since 1986.

1991-Present *A decade of recession stalls Japan's economic miracle.*

1991 Nikkei stock index has lost nearly two-thirds of its value since 1989.

1993 The ruling LDP loses power for the first time since 1955. It returns to power in 1995.

April 26, 2001 Junichiro Koizumi becomes prime minister, promising reforms.

Aug. 13, 2001 Koizumi sets off controversy by visiting Yasukuni Shrine, where Japanese war dead are interred, including World War II war criminals.

Oct. 29, 2001 In response to Sept. 11 attacks on the U.S., the Diet authorizes the deployment of Japanese forces overseas in a non-combat capacity.

May 31, 2002 For the fourth time since 1996, Japan's credit rating is downgraded.

Women and Immigrants to the Rescue?

Of the many social and economic problems that Japan faces, the rapidly aging population is perhaps its most daunting challenge.

Coupled with a shrinking pool of young people, the burgeoning elderly population is "already a huge problem, and it's just going to get worse, much worse, as time goes on," says Yoshihisa Komori, editor-at-large at *Sankei Shimbum*, a daily newspaper in Tokyo.

Already, 17.2 percent of the population is over 60, one of the highest rates in the industrialized world.[1] By 2050, a whopping 42.3 percent of the population will be 60 or older.[2] By contrast, only 26.9 percent of the U.S. population will be in that age category by mid-century.

At the same time, the Japanese are having fewer children because birth rates in the Land of the Rising Sun have been dropping since the 1960s. In the 1970s, Japan's fertility rate fell below 2.1 births per woman, the number needed to maintain the population at its current size. Today, the fertility rate is a mere 1.41.[3]

Several factors explain the alarming statistics. First, the Japanese citizen lives an average of 81.5 years—longer than the residents of most other developed countries—thanks to Japan's traditionally healthy diet and excellent health-care system.[4]

Low birth rates are caused in part by a drop in the rate at which the Japanese marry. Many young Japanese women prefer to live at home with their parents and work, rather than to tie themselves to a husband and children in a country where women are still expected to be homemakers after marriage. In addition, women traditionally are expected to care for their husband's parents, as well as their own, making marriage even less attractive. The average age for marriage among Japanese women has increased from 22 in 1950 to 26 today. At the same time, the divorce rate rose 50 percent from 1990 to 1998.[5]

The impact of having fewer children and more seniors will wreak social havoc. The cost of providing the current, generous level of health care and pensions will rise dramatically, even as the number of working people shrinks. Indeed, by 2050, the ratio of working-age people to dependents—both children and the aged—is expected to approach one-to-one.[6]

If current trends continue, say experts, pension benefits will have to be cut and the retirement age increased. "Everyone understands that the current pension system will not survive," says Shinji Fukukawa, chief executive officer of the Dentsu Institute for Human Studies, a Tokyo think tank.[7] Indeed, the Japanese government is already running huge annual budget deficits, making any social-service spending increases in coming years unlikely.

Some experts say there are several ways to mitigate the coming demographic crisis. Japanese women comprise an

[1] The worldwide average is 6.9 percent and 14.3 present in the industrialized countries. *World Population Prospects: The 2000 Revision and World Urbanization Prospects:* The 2001 Revision, Population Division of the Department of Economic and Social Affairs of the United Nations Secretariat, http://esa.un.org/unpp/index.asp?panel=2.

[2] *Ibid.*

[3] *CIA World Factbook*, www.cia.goc/cia/publications/factbook/

[4] *Ibid.*

[5] Figures cited in Sonni Efron, "Japan's Demographic Shock," *Los Angeles Times*, June 25, 2002.

[6] *Ibid.*

[7] Figures cited in "Consensus and Contraction," *The Economist*, April 18, 2002.

province of Manchuria and became the primary foreign influence in Korea.[11]

However, Japan soon found itself facing another Asian power. In the years after the victory over China, Russia tried to clip Japan's wings by forcing the Japanese to return to China the portion of Manchuria it had occupied and trying to mitigate Japan's influence in Korea. Tensions between the two countries boiled over in 1904 when war broke out. Unlike China—whose days as a great power were long past—Russia was a key

player in world affairs. Most statesmen and diplomats predicted the Russians would crush the Japanese.

But to the shock of many, Japan beat the Russians, sinking the czar's Pacific fleet in a surprise attack in 1904. The following year, Japan also destroyed the enemy's huge Baltic fleet—which had been moved to the Pacific—leaving Russia without a sizable navy.[12] A peace treaty negotiated by the United States confirmed Japan's primacy in Korea and its influence in southern Manchuria.

underutilized segment of the work force. Only 60 percent of single women have a job, and only half of all married women work outside of the home. "Women are still subjected to a lot of discrimination in Japanese society," says Mariko Tamanoi, an associate professor of anthropology at the University of California at Los Angeles. "To a great extent, they are still banned from business and government."

"Women are really an untapped resource in Japan," agrees Marie Anchordoguy, a professor of political science at the University of Washington. Japan needs to open up opportunities for women so they can be more productive members of society, she adds.

Yet some would say that Japan's working women are already carrying more than their share of the workload: Many married women only work part time because they are solely responsible for keeping house and caring for both the children and the elderly.[8]

The country needs to encourage employers to be more flexible with its male employees, Anchordoguy says. "We need to allow men to be able to come home and participate in family life so women are not the only caregivers," she says. "This would free up a lot of women to go out, find work and lead their own lives."

AFP Photo/Chiaki Tsukumo

Residents of a Japanese nursing home are entertained by a visiting musician. Today, 17 percent of the Japanese population is over 60—one of the highest rates in the world. By 2050 the level is expected to reach 42.3 percent, producing what some have called a "demographic crisis of epic proportions."

Experts also argue that Japan cannot tackle its demographic trouble without overhauling its very restrictive immigration policy. Currently, less than 1 percent of Japan's population is foreign-born (compared to more than 10 percent in the United States), and many are ethnic Japanese from Latin America, where many emigrated in the early 20th century.

Accepting newcomers who are not ethnic cousins is difficult for the Japanese. "They've never really accepted foreigners because, unlike us, they consider themselves an ethnic group as well as a state," says Edward J. Lincoln, a senior fellow for foreign policy studies at the Brookings Institution. "As a result, you've got fourth-generation Koreans in Japan who don't yet have citizenship and are discriminated against."

According to Lincoln, to sustain the economy and support the growing numbers of retirees Japan must open its borders to new immigrants. "They need 500,000 immigrants a year if they really want to have enough workers," Lincoln says. "Will they do it? I'm not sure the Japanese are flexible enough to accept new people coming and staying."

But the Japanese don't really have a choice, says Miles Fletcher, a professor of Asian studies at the University of North Carolina at Chapel Hill. "They need these new people, so they're going to have to change their values," he says. "They're going to have to become a multiethnic society."

---

[8] Figures cited in *ibid.*

The Russo-Japanese War put Japan on the geopolitical map. The Great Powers, which had dismissed the island nation as an Asian upstart, now began to treat it as an equal.

In 1914, shortly after World War I broke out, Japan declared war against Germany and occupied its interests in China and on some South Pacific islands. After the war, Japan was one of the "big five" powers at the Versailles peace conference and was given a permanent seat in the newly formed League of Nations, the precursor to the United Nations.

As Japan was integrating into the world community, ultranationalists at home were gaining strength and influence. They sought to check the growing trend toward democracy, elevate the emperor and the Shinto religion to an even higher level in society and accelerate Japan's dominance of Asia. By the early 1930s, parts of the military were openly hostile to civilian rule.

In 1932, the elected Japanese prime minister was assassinated and a new government composed of military men and nationalists took power. That same year, Japan

U.S. Gen. Douglas MacArthur, who helped put Japan on the road to economic and political recovery after its defeat in World War II, allowed Emperor Hirohito to remain on the throne.

expanded its holdings in Manchuria, using the province to set up a puppet state, Manchukuo, with the last Chinese emperor as its titular head.[13]

In the next five years, Japan built up its military might and edged closer to Nazi Germany and away from its former World War I allies—the United States, Britain and France. In 1937, Japan entered into a full-scale war with China, invading south from its Manchurian territories. The Japanese army eventually conquered much of eastern China.

World War II

In 1940, Japan officially entered World War II on the side of the Axis allies, Germany and Italy. That year, the Japanese conquered the northern half of French Indochina, greatly expanding Japan's territories in East Asia, and called for the creation of a "Greater East Asia Co-Prosperity Sphere" uniting China, Korea and other parts of the region under Japanese control. The announcement was tantamount to a public declaration of the country's territorial ambitions.[14]

But while Japan sought an Asian empire, the United States had a presence throughout much of Asia and was also a major Pacific power. As the 1930s wore on, the two countries' interests were increasingly at cross-purposes.

The U.S. government wanted to prevent Japan from becoming the dominant power in resource-rich Asia. The U.S. economy depended on raw materials from Europe's Southeast Asian colonies—like Holland's Indonesia, Britain's Malaysia and Burma and France's Vietnam and Cambodia.

Moreover, news accounts of Japanese atrocities, especially in the Chinese city of Nanjing, helped turn American public opinion against Japan. But Japan resented U.S. efforts to take the moral high ground, especially since the United States still held the Philippines and other colonies in the Pacific. Indeed, many Japanese thought their country was liberating Asia from white imperialism. Resource-poor Japan also viewed its new Asian colonies as its only avenue to economic self-sufficiency.

By 1941, relations between Japan and the United States had seriously deteriorated and talk of war was in the air. America had imposed severe economic sanctions against Japan after its invasion of China and other aggressive actions. For the Japanese, the sanctions only confirmed Japan's need for extensive colonies to ensure economic self-reliance. As the year came to a close, the Japanese decided that a bold gamble on their part was needed to resolve the standoff.

On Dec. 7, 1941, the Japanese navy destroyed much of the U.S. Pacific fleet in a surprise dawn raid at its Hawaiian headquarters at Pearl Harbor. On the same day, Japanese forces invaded the Philippines as well as British and European colonies in Asia.

The Japanese did not think the attacks would lead to the total defeat of the United States. Instead, they hoped to cripple American naval power and confidence, leading to a quick armistice and peace talks on Japan's terms.

But the attack on Pearl Harbor, though a stunning surprise, accomplished none of its objectives. America's most valuable naval vessels, its aircraft carriers, survived because they were not in port when the attack occurred. Moreover, the American government and people, far from being cowed into peace talks, demanded total war against Japan.

America's economic and technological superiority made it unlikely that Japan would prevail in an all-out war. Indeed, within a year of the attack—before the full force of American industry could be felt—the U.S. military had already turned the tide. At an engagement near Midway Island in early June 1942, American naval forces destroyed much of Japan's aircraft-carrier fleet.

By 1943, the Americans were pushing Japan back toward its home islands. The following year, U.S. forces began massive bombing raids against Japan itself. The war ended on Sept. 2, 1945, less than a month after the Americans dropped atomic bombs on the Japanese cities of Hiroshima and Nagasaki, killing an estimated 190,000-210,000 people.

Some historians said that the devastation caused by these new weapons of mass destruction convinced the Japanese that any hopes of fighting to even a stalemate were unrealistic. But others said the Japanese were on the verge of surrendering and that the bombings were inhumane and purely retribution for Pearl Harbor.

Post-War Recovery

After the surrender, the United States set out to completely reorder Japanese society to prevent future military aggression. The Japanese armed forces were dissolved and all munitions factories converted to civilian use. More than 4,000 Japanese officers were found guilty of war crimes and 700 were executed. Tens of thousands of nationalist officials were purged from the government.[15]

In the interest of social stability, Emperor Hirohito was retained as the country's symbolic leader, but he was no longer to be considered divine. In addition, Shintoism was disestablished as the state religion.

U.S. forces under the command of Gen. Douglas MacArthur occupied Japan from the time of its surrender until 1952. Initially, they focused on helping the Japanese house, clothe and feed themselves. The war, and especially allied bombing, had destroyed much of the country, leaving millions homeless and hungry.

By 1947, MacArthur had imposed a new constitution on Japan, establishing a British parliamentary political system under the symbolic leadership of the emperor. The document contained many of the guarantees contained in the U.S. Constitution, such as freedom of worship and speech. In addition, it committed Japan to pacifism, renouncing war as an instrument of international relations and prohibiting the maintenance of a military.[16]

Japan signed a formal peace treaty with the United States and its allies in 1951. In it, Japan gave up all claims to China, Korea and other territories it conquered before or during the war. The treaty also acknowledged Japan's right to defend itself against foreign aggression, the first crack in the pacifist constitution ratified only four years before.[17] Just hours after accepting the peace treaty, the Japanese signed the Japan-United States Mutual Security Assistance Pact, which linked Japan's military policy to America's aims in Asia. Three years later, Japan's armed forces were resuscitated as "self-defense forces."

Meanwhile, Japan was beginning to experience some normalcy on other fronts. Elections first took place in 1947, with many parties jockeying for power. Although party squabbling and collapsing coalitions characterized the first seven years of Japanese politics, one man, Yoshida Shigeru, held office as prime minister during most of the period from 1948 until 1954.

The economy also was beginning to pick up, helped by more than $2 billion in U.S. assistance. Under the leadership of its Ministry of International Trade and Industry (MITI), Japan began rebuilding its shattered economy. Export industries—notably electronics, automobile manufacturing and steel—began to expand rapidly after receiving low-interest loans and other special treatment. This led to higher exports and greater economic growth. The Korean War (1950-1953) also helped the economy in these early years, as the United States bought large quantities of Japanese goods to help supply its armed forces stationed in nearby Korea.

By 1954, the average Japanese income had returned to its mid-1930s level. Four years later, living standards had risen another 27 percent.[18] In the 1960s, the country's GDP increased at an almost unparalleled rate. Indeed, in the second half of the decade, GDP was galloping an average of 11 percent each year.[19]

With economic growth came a new political stability. In 1955, Japan's two largest conservative parties merged to form the LDP. Several socialist parties also merged in 1955 to become the largest opposition group in the Diet. Another major party, Komeito, or Clean Government, was formed in 1964.

The LDP dominated politics during the post-war decades, largely because of Japan's ever-burgeoning economy. So long as the standard of living continued to rise, voters saw no reason to punish the ruling party.

But the LDP's popularity was based on more than just a consistently growing economy. It built rock-solid support among various sectors of Japanese society—notably farmers and small-business men—by assiduously catering to their political desires. Farmers, for instance, were protected from cheaper food imports. Small businesses likewise benefited from rules that contained the growth of large retailers.

In short, the LDP tried to be all things to as many Japanese as it could—a particularly effective formula in a consensus-driven country like Japan. Plus, the party's policies were producing a harmonious and prosperous society. Indeed, by the 1980s, Japan was enjoying a level of prosperity fast becoming the envy of the world. Even the United States began to worry about being outpaced by its protégé.

Economic Dynamo

On almost every economic front, the Japanese were beating their American and European competitors. Its electronic companies, including Sony and Matsushita (owner of the Panasonic brand) put most competitors out of business and produced the bulk of the world's consumer electronics goods, such as televisions, stereos and VCRs. Rising oil prices in the 1970s gave Japanese automakers like Toyota and Honda—which specialized in small, fuel-efficient cars—a foothold in the U.S. market, which Japan exploited by marketing reliable and increasingly upscale cars. Japanese steel, ships and memory chips also dominated world markets.

In addition, Japanese manufacturing practices became the world's quality standard, making their products much sought-after, even as the country's home market was protected from outside competition. Companies like Sony and Toyota reaped huge profits.

Export success overseas and protected markets at home drove the stock and real estate markets through the roof. In the four years from 1986 to 1989, the Nikkei index of leading stocks tripled in value, rising from 13,000 to 39,000.[20] Meanwhile, property values rose so high that the imperial palace and grounds in downtown Tokyo were worth more than all the real estate in California.

But by the end of 1989, the Japanese miracle began to grind to a halt. Western nations, led by the United States, were in a recession. New, low-cost competitors from South Korea and other Asian countries were taking market share and profits away from Japanese companies. The result was a spiral into recession.

With profits down, the Nikkei plunged, losing 65 percent of its value in a year and a half.[21] Since the stock market boom had fueled the real estate boom, land prices began to plummet. Soon, many developers and speculators were bankrupt, leaving the country's banking system with more than $1 trillion in bad loans. As a result, banks stopped lending, further adding to the economy's woes.

The LDP tried to bring the country out of recession by enacting massive new public-spending programs aimed at jump-starting the economy. But the efforts only led to brief spurts of economic growth.

By 1993, the Japanese were frustrated with the LDP's inability to end the recession. The party's standing dropped further when LDP bigwigs were implicated in several damning bribery scandals. Voters turned to opposition groups, including new parties formed by LDP defectors. By August, a seven-party coalition was running the country—the first non-LDP government since its formation in 1955.

But the newcomers also proved ineffective. During the next two and a half years, the coalition devoted most of its energies to political infighting and did not address the nation's problems. In 1996, the LDP retook power under the leadership of the charismatic Hashimoto Ryutaro.

Hashimoto promised to clean up the banking system and restore Japan's economic health. But his policies—which included more spending and a tax cut to stimulate the economy—also proved ineffective.[22]

While 1998 election losses did not oust the LDP, disappointment within the party led to Hashimoto's resignation and the elevation of several caretaker prime ministers. During the tenure of the second leader, Mori Yoshiro, the LDP's popularity dropped to new lows.

In March 2001, Mori resigned, and the party searched for a new leader. For a time, it looked as though Hashimoto might make a political comeback, but Koizumi, who had the support of the party's rank and file, beat him, promising "a total reversal of the past."[23]

CURRENT SITUATION

An Important Friendship

When the last U.S. troops left Japan in 1952, the two countries had already signed a mutual-security treaty charging America with protecting Japan in case of attack.

Should Japan revise its constitution to allow Japanese forces to engage in combat missions?

YES
Ted Galen Carpenter
Vice president, defense and foreign policy studies, Cato Institute

Written for *The CQ Researcher*, July 2002

Article 9, the "pacifist clause" in Japan's constitution, has outlived whatever usefulness it may have had when it was adopted at the insistence of the United States after World War II.

Japan is now the only major power that does not play a security role commensurate with its political and economic status. Even Germany, the other principal defeated power in World War II, has sent peacekeeping troops to the Balkans and Afghanistan. Tokyo cannot forever limit its security role to cheerleading for U.S. military exertions.

A more vigorous Japanese role in East Asia is essential. North Korea poses a significant security problem, and there are concerns about China's rising power and ambitions. A militarily capable, assertive Japan is indispensable for stability and an effective balance of power. Otherwise, the United States ends up shouldering all of the region's security burdens by default.

In recent years, Japan has moved away from a rigid interpretation of Article 9. The 1997 revisions to the defense guidelines of the U.S.-Japanese alliance allowed Japan's Self-Defense Forces (SDF) to help U.S. forces repel a security threat in the western Pacific. Four years later, the Diet adopted anti-terrorism legislation allowing the SDF to play a similar role outside the western Pacific theater.

But one must not overstate the significance of those mildly encouraging changes. In both cases, the SDF is only empowered to provide non-lethal, logistical support to U.S. forces—not engage in combat operations—unless Japan itself is under attack. That restriction needs to end.

Many argue that if Japan played a more active military role it would upset its East Asian neighbors, who still remember the outrages committed by imperial Japan in the 1930s and '40s. But that argument oversimplifies reality.

Several of Japan's neighbors -including Australia, Singapore, Taiwan and the Philippines—have signaled unmistakably in recent years that they would accept, perhaps even welcome, a more assertive Japan to balance China's growing power.

It is time for Japan to fully rejoin the ranks of the great powers, and the United States must help with that transition. Washington should make it clear to Japan and to its neighbors that it would welcome the repeal of Article 9.

NO
David Krieger
President, Nuclear Age Peace Foundation

Written for *The CQ Researcher*, July 2002

Article 9 of the Japanese constitution is a statement of intent and limitation, highly unusual in the constitution of any state and particularly in that of a powerful nation such as Japan. In it, Japan renounces war as a "sovereign right" and further renounces "the threat or use of force as a means of settling disputes."

This article was accepted by Japanese leaders after World War II under pressure from the occupying U.S. forces. But for more than 50 years Japan has retained and supported this constitutional provision against internal nationalist forces and, ironically, against pressure from the United States, which wants Japan to accept more military responsibility in its alliance with the United States.

The intent of Article 9 was to transform Japan from a warlike, aggressor nation into a peaceful nation. In this sense, the article has been very successful. For more than half a century—despite international pressure—Japan has forsworn participation in war.

However, it has developed extremely powerful self-defense forces and sent Self-Defense Force ships to the Indian Ocean to provide refueling and other logistical support to British and U.S. forces in the war in Afghanistan.

Article 9 conforms to international law as set forth in the United Nations Charter. If all states relied only on self-defense forces and adopted their own version of Article 9, war would be effectively abolished as a sovereign right. This would clearly be a step forward in a world of increasingly powerful and destructive weapons.

As the first nation to experience the effects of nuclear weapons, Japan has a special responsibility to be a messenger to the world of the need to end the Nuclear Age. Article 9 is, in part, a way of fulfilling this responsibility.

Article 9 is helping to establish a new international norm necessary to assure the continuation of civilization. Should Japan amend Article 9 to allow it to participate in multilateral military missions, including combat duty, it would signal to the world that the renunciation of war and force is not practical and has failed.

The Japanese people need to hold to the high ideals of their constitution and help lead the world out of the Nuclear Age and into a new age, in which conflicts are settled without force. Japan's, or any nation's, status as a great nation need not rest on military prowess.

Unemployment Doubles

Japan's unemployment rate has doubled during the nation's long recession, a devastating development in a country where lifetime employment with a single firm is central to the social compact.

Percentage

Unemployment Rate
(As percentage of the civilian work force)

Year	Rate
1983	2.7
1985	2.6
1987	2.8
1989	2.3
1991	2.1
1993	2.5
1995	3.1
1997	3.4
1999	4.7
2001	5.0

Source: Organization for Economic Cooperation and Development, 2002.

More recently, the U.S. war on terrorism has prompted the Japanese government to expand its security cooperation with the United States. Besides allowing Japanese forces to support U.S. forces in the Indian Ocean near Afghanistan, the Diet also allowed the country's military to protect U.S. forces in Japan. "There's no question that the events of Sept. 11 have propelled Japan toward a more active security role with the United States," says Vogel, of the University of California. "And of course that has pleased the Americans."

On economic matters, relations between the two countries have been on a less secure footing. During the 1980s, American politicians and others worried that an increasingly successful Japan would eventually dominate the U.S. economy. The Japanese purchase of American icons like Columbia Studios and New York's Rockefeller Center fed fears that "Japan Inc."—as the country was often called—would supplant America as the world's preeminent economic power. Moreover, as Japanese companies were aggressively exporting products and investing overseas, the Japanese prevented foreign competition in their home market. U.S. producers of goods ranging from rice and apples to automobiles were prevented from making significant inroads into the Japanese market.

Today, economic tensions between the two nations remain, but for very different reasons. No longer the economic juggernaut it was in the 1980s, Japan has seen its economic prospects sink so low that the United States is now chiding the government for not making its economy more competitive.

Other issues also cause tension. For instance, the Bush administration's abrogation of both the Kyoto Protocol on Global Warming and the Anti-Ballistic Missile (ABM) Treaty have been unpopular in Japan.[24]

Even the vaunted security alliance may be buffeted in the coming decade, as the war against terrorism inevitably leads the United States to ask Japan to carry a greater share of the responsibility for regional defense. "I think things will be fine in the short term, because of

In exchange, the Japanese promised to allow U.S. military bases in the country.

In the ensuing decades, Japan's security policy remained tied to the American military. The new Japanese Self-Defense Force essentially supplemented the U.S. defense of the country.

Although the military relationship between the two countries has been generally good, tensions exist. The United States routinely prods Japan to beef up its armed forces, especially when U.S. military power is stretched thin, such as during the 1991 Persian Gulf War. And the Japanese have been troubled by the occasional misconduct of American servicemen, as occurred in 1995 when three U.S. Marines were convicted of gang-raping a teenager on the island of Okinawa, where most U.S. forces are based.

Still, most experts agree that security relations between the two remain on a sound footing. "Military relations between the two countries are very strong," the University of California's Pempel says. "I see no real threat to that in the near future."

Indeed, in 1996, when the relationship was last subjected to a thorough mutual review, both countries declared it in robust health. "The U.S. and Japan essentially said they were on the same page militarily and that they were happy with the way things were going," Pempel says.

the momentum in Japan created by Sept. 11," Vogel says. But, he adds, trouble may come when America looks to Japan to significantly enhance its military capability to better supplement American power in the region.

"Because of politics and the peace constitution, I'm not sure the Japanese will want to upgrade their forces and expand their military's mission," he says. "This could cause a real increase in tension."

Economic Trouble

On May 31, Japan's creditworthiness was downgraded two levels by Moody's, an influential U.S. credit-rating firm. The rating measures a country's ability to pay its debts.

While the new A2 rating implies that Japan is still likely to pay back the money its government has borrowed, it puts the creditworthiness of the world's second-largest economy far below most other advanced economies and on par with Botswana and Estonia.[25]

The downgrade was the fourth endured by Japan since 1998 and reflects the size of the government's debt, now nearly triple that of the United States. But the lower rating is also a sign of the economy's fundamental weakness.

The Japanese now refer to the 1990s as the "lost decade," when the country's once-mighty economy was mostly contracting, with only short bursts of growth. The decade before had been the nation's best, with high corporate profits and ever-rising stock and real estate markets.

But in the early 1990s, the bubble burst. The Nikkei index has lost three-quarters of its value since its 1988 high.[26] The real estate market has fallen even further: Commercial real estate prices in Japan's six biggest cities have dropped 84 percent since 1991.[27]

The current decade also may be lost, some economists say. Last year, the country's economy shrank by 1.9 percent. In the first quarter of 2002, GDP decreased by a whopping 4.8 percent.[28] Even though the economy is expected to grow about 1.3 percent in 2003, few see an end to the overall trend toward recession.

The economic gloom can be puzzling to Americans, who see Japanese corporations like Sony, Toyota and Honda as world leaders in manufacturing. However, the successful multinationals produce less than 10 percent of Japan's economic output.

"The other 90 percent has some bright spots—like the convenience-store sector, which is very competitive—but, overall, most of the country's business sectors are not competitive at all," says the Brookings Institution's Lincoln. "Many industries in Japan—like the construction, real estate, agricultural and hotel sectors—have been made inefficient by government protection and coddling."

That "protection and coddling" include trade barriers and what Lincoln calls government-subsidized "informal cartels" that allow companies to edge out even domestic competitors.

Deflation, another major problem facing Japan, has caused prices for goods and services to drop from 1 to 2 percent a year over the last three years, a situation that creates difficulties for everyone. Deflation, caused by a shortage of currency in circulation, causes prices to fall and reduces the average person's assets. Workers suffer because employers ultimately cut wages, even as the cost of servicing a mortgage or other consumer debt rises because money is worth more.[29]

Businesses suffer, too. "Companies get less for the goods and services they provide," says Posen of the International Institute for Economics. "At the same time, they may have debt payments to make or wage agreements with unions that prevent them from cutting wages." To stay afloat, some businesses are forced to cut back and some "just go under," he says.

According to Posen, deflation has been caused in part by the Bank of Japan's refusal to print more currency and create inflation. The central bank's unwillingness to act is based on the belief that sparking even mild inflation will ease pressure on the government to tackle the country's greatest short-term problem: the huge number of bad loans at the nation's banks.

"The cost of servicing debt would decrease, providing some breathing room for the banks," Posen says. "The [central] bank is playing a game of chicken with the government, saying it won't deal with the deflation problem until the government begins to take on the bad-loan crisis at the banks."

But Posen thinks the central bank's policy is misguided. "Ignoring one problem isn't a way to solve another," he says.

Still, there is some good news amid the gloom. Thanks to the weaker yen, Japanese exports are more attractive overseas, particularly in America, which may be coming out of its own recession. Thus, profits for

Japanese manufacturers are expected to grow by an astonishing 43 percent this year.[30]

OUTLOOK

Epic Crisis Ahead?

History teaches that Japan is capable of instituting rapid change, from its breakneck industrialization in the middle of the 19th century to the miraculous recovery from devastation in the middle of the 20th. But experts are divided over whether Japan can emerge from its current economic and social slump anytime soon.

Some, like the University of California's Pempel are "increasingly pessimistic. They have these huge economic problems," he says, "but, they show absolutely no sign of even starting to deal with them anytime soon."

"It will be at least a decade before they've sorted out the structural problems with their economy," says Brookings' Lincoln. "And even if they manage to eventually deal with their economy in the next 10 years, they face a demographic crisis of epic proportions."

Many say the projected graying of Japan's population is the next big challenge casting a long shadow over the future. "Their population is going to be falling and aging at the same time," says Lincoln. "This just doesn't bode well for Japan remaining a vibrant economic force in the world."

Moreover, the pessimists say, the country lacks a tradition of encouraging entrepreneurial risk-taking that produces new industries that could help create new wealth. "Japan is behind and it's falling further behind in information technology and biotechnology," Pempel says, "because they don't push this entrepreneurial spirit like we do in the United States.

Moreover, says UCLA's Tamanoi, Japanese society is not well positioned to embrace globalization. "It's a very closed society, with a difficult language and complicated social rules and mores," she says. "It just doesn't seem like it will fit easily into the global economy."

But others see Japan's long-term future as quite bright. "Japan is going to come back and come back strong," the University of California's Vogel says. "The next few years are going to be very tough as they sort out their economic troubles—especially the banks. But afterwards, they will be strong again."

Vogel and others are optimistic because, for all its recent troubles, Japan is still, at its heart, a strong and competitive country. "All of the fundamentals are still there," says Mathews of the Council on Foreign Relations. "They have a hard-working, highly educated populace and some of the world's most competitive companies. There's no reason why they shouldn't bounce back."

According to Mathews, Japan is transitioning from its past reliance on manufacturing to new, service-oriented industries, as the United States did in the 1970s and '80s. "The future for Japan lies in industries like financial services," he says. "No other country in Asia has anything like the capital that Japan does. It will rely on these kinds of industries to stoke its prosperity."

NOTES

1. "Out of Site, Out of Mind," *Yomiuri Shimbun*, May 28, 2002.

2. Figure cited in "Crime Rate in Japan on the Rise," *The Globe and Mail*, Dec. 22, 2001.

3. For background, see Christopher Conte, "Deflation Fears," *The CQ Researcher*, Feb. 13, 1998, pp. 121-144.

4. Figure cited in "Poll Shows 57 Percent Favor Revision of Constitution," *The Yomiuri Shimbun*, April 5, 2002.

5. "Japan's Sins of Omission," *The Economist*, April 14, 2001.

6. James L. McClain, *Japan: A Modern History* (2002), p. 449.

7. Robert Dolan and Robert Worden (eds.), *Japan: A Country Study* (1992), p. 24.

8. Richard Tames, *A Traveller's History of Japan* (1993), pp. 115-117.

9. Marius B. Jansen, *The Making of Modern Japan* (2000), p. 374.

10. *Ibid.*, pp. 389-395.

11. Louis G. Perez, *The History of Japan* (1998), p. 120.

12. Jansen, *op. cit.*, p. 440.

13. *Ibid.*, p. 586.

14. *Ibid.*, p. 633.

15. Dolan and Worden, *op. cit.*, p. 60.

16. *Ibid.*, pp. 306-318.

17. McClain, *op. cit.*, pp. 557-558.

18. Figures cited in Tames, *op. cit.*, pp. 180-181.

19. Figures cited in *ibid.*, p. 184.

20. Figures cited in McClain, *op. cit.*, p. 601.

21. *Ibid.*

22. *Ibid.*, pp. 604-605.

23. Quoted in "A New Face for Japan," *The Economist*, April 26, 2001.

24. For background, see Mary H. Cooper, "Transatlantic Tensions," *The CQ Researcher*, July 13, 2001, pp. 553-576.

25. Jason Singer, "Moody's Downgrades Japan's Credit Rating by Two Levels to A2," *The Wall Street Journal*, June 3, 2002.

26. John Grimon, "What Ails Japan?" *The Economist*, April 18, 2002.

27. *Ibid.*

28. Conte, *op. cit.*

29. Figures cited in "Economic and Financial Indicators," *The Economist*, June 1, 2002.

30. "The Bottom Line," *The Economist*, April 27, 2002.

BIBLIOGRAPHY

Books

Jansen, Marius B., *The Making of Modern Japan*, Harvard University Press, 2000.
An emeritus professor of Japanese history at Princeton University presents a detailed chronicle of Japanese history from 1600 to the present, emphasizing the various forces working for and against modernizing the country through four centuries.

McClain, James, *A Modern History of Japan*, W.W. Norton, 2002.
A professor of history at Brown University describes the panorama of Japanese history from the beginning of the 17th century to the present. His chronicle of the country's political and social transformation after World War II is particularly clear and insightful.

Tames, Richard, *A Traveller's History of Japan*, Interlink Books, 1993.
A prolific author of books on Japan has written an engaging, concise history of the Japanese.

Articles

Brooke, James, "Japan Braces for a 'Designed in China World,'" *The New York Times*, April 21, 2002, p. A1.
No longer just a venue for cheap manufactures, China is now a haven in Asia for high-technology research and development, eroding Japan's last real competitive advantage in the region.

Efron, Sonni, "Japan's Demographic Shock," *Los Angeles Times*, June 25, 2002, p. A12.
The article examines the implications for Japan of its rising elderly population and looks at options, like increasing immigration, which could help mitigate the cost of caring for increasing numbers of seniors.

Gibney, Frank, "Koizumi Spirals Down," *Los Angeles Times*, Feb. 11, 2002, p. B11.
A professor of political science at Pomona College criticizes Prime Minister Junichiro Koizumi for being indecisive and not pursuing reform vigorously enough.

Grimond, John, "What Ails Japan?" *The Economist*, April 18, 2002.
The British magazine's most recent survey on Japan explores how the country's political and economic systems are failing the Japanese. The author concludes that Japan may have to endure a catastrophe even greater than the banking crisis before both the people and the political elites take the kinds of steps needed to overhaul the country.

Kruger, David, "Despite Failures, Japan's Koizumi Revives Office," *The Wall Street Journal*, April 30, 2002, p. A15.
Kruger argues that although Prime Minister Junichiro Koizumi has failed to push through his promised reforms, he has made some important changes, including strengthening the office of prime minister and expanding the role of Japan's military since the Sept. 11 terrorist attacks on the United States.

Landers, Peter, Jason Singer and Phred Dvorak, "Silver Lining? Amid Japan's Gloom, Corporate Overhauls Offer Hints of Revival," *The Wall Street Journal*, Feb. 21, 2002, p. A1.
As politicians dither on economic reform, some Japanese companies are trying to deal with the near-continuous

recession by laying off workers and redirecting other employees to more productive operations.

"The Politics of Nationalism," *The Economist,* **April 25, 2002.**
The article describes Prime Minister Junichiro Koizumi's April visit to the Yasukuni Shrine, where Japanese war criminals are interred along with other World War II servicemen.

Struck, Doug, and Kathryn Tolbert, "In Japan, a Growing Gap Between Haves and Have-Nots," *The Washington Post,* **Jan. 4, 2002, p. A22.**
According to Struck and Tolbert, "Japan's unrelenting decade-long recession is increasingly . . . exposing a host of social strains and removing the mythical cloak of equality."

Williams, Michael, and Phred Dvorak, "Japan Seethes Over Comparisons to Botswana," *The Wall Street Journal,* **May 13, 2002, p. C1.**
The recent downgrading of Japan's creditworthiness to the level of Botswana has touched off a firestorm of anger and protest in the country.

Reports

Hwang, Balbina, and Brett Shaefer, "Assessing the Looming Financial Crisis in Japan" *The Heritage Foundation,* **March 26, 2002.**
Two Heritage Foundation analysts urge the United States to push Japan to reform its banking sector. Failure to take action, they say, could lead to a financial meltdown that ultimately drags the world economy into recession.

For More Information

Center for Strategic and International Studies, 1800 K St., N.W., Suite 400, Washington, DC 20006; (202) 887-0200; www.csis.org. Provides information on global issues, including Japan's role in the world economy and its security relationship with the United States.

Council on Foreign Relations, 58 East 68th St., New York, NY 10021; (212) 434-9400; www.cfr.org. Generates ideas and educates the public about foreign policy.

Institute of East Asian Studies, University of California at Berkeley, 2223 Fulton St., Suite 2318, Berkeley, CA 94720-2318; (510) 642-2809; ieas.berkeley.edu. Offers a broad range of courses and programs on East Asia and hosts the Center for Japanese Studies.

Institute of International Economics, 1750 Massachusetts Ave., N.W., Washington, DC 20036-1903; (202) 328-9000; www.iie.com. A private, nonprofit, nonpartisan research institution devoted to the study of international economic policy, including that of Japan and East Asia.

9

Democracy in the Arab World

Kenneth Jost and Benton Ives-Halperin

AFP Photo/Ahmad Al-Rubaye

Thousands of Shiite Muslims march through Baghdad on Jan. 19, demanding that Iraq's new government be selected through direct elections rather than caucuses, as the United States has proposed. Some monarchies in the Arab world have taken tentative steps toward electoral governance, but others continue to struggle under the grip of authoritarian regimes. President Bush recently called on all Arab states to join "the global democratic revolution."

From *The CQ Researcher,*
January 30, 2004.

Egyptian sociologist Saad Eddin Ibrahim was lecturing in the United States last November when President Bush called for democratization in the Middle East. "I could not have written a better speech," Ibrahim, a longtime critic of Egyptian strongman Hosni Mubarak, wrote in *The Washington Post*.[1]

Back in Egypt, Ibrahim's op-ed remarks caused an uproar. Pro-government newspapers insinuated that he had actually written Bush's Nov. 6 speech—and that his entire trip was designed to embarrass Egypt and secure U.S. funding for Ibrahim's pro-democracy center in Cairo. Declared a headline in the pro-government weekly *Al-Osbou:* "Saad in Washington to incite the U.S. against Egypt and the Arab world."[2]

Political dissidents in many countries can shrug off newspaper innuendoes. But government critics in Egypt must take care. Ibrahim himself served more than a year in prison and was twice convicted of receiving foreign funds for his Ibn Khaldun Center without permission—a $225,000 grant from the European Union for voter-awareness projects—and spreading defamatory information about Egypt. The convictions sparked international protests that died down only after Ibrahim won a reversal and subsequent acquittal in March 2003. The center, which the government had ordered closed, reopened in November.

Hafez Abu Saada, head of the Egyptian Organization for Human Rights, was arrested five years ago and charged with similar offenses. He was never tried, but he says the government can revive the case any time in the next 15 years. Meanwhile, he has been waiting for more than six months to find out whether the Egyptian Ministry of Social Affairs will allow his group to accept a grant from the U.S.-government-funded National Endowment for Democracy to help pay for its human rights monitoring work.

Egypt's law regulating non-governmental organizations is just one of the many statutes tightly controlling civic life in a country that is a critical American partner in the Middle East and—with about 75 million people—the most populous nation in the Arab world. According to the U.S.-based human rights group Freedom House, a government committee must license all political parties, and the Ministry of the Interior must approve public demonstrations in advance. In addition, the government owns all the broadcast media, along with three major daily newspapers, whose editors are appointed by the president. Direct criticism of the president, his family or the military can result in imprisonment of journalists or closure of publications.

Egypt has an elected president and a bicameral legislature with an elected lower house and a mostly elective upper chamber. But Mubarak—who has ruled by decree since taking office after the assassination of President Anwar el-Sadat in 1981—is nominated by parliament and then voted on in a single-candidate referendum for a five-year term. Further, the political licensing laws combine with what Freedom House calls "systematic irregularities" in election procedures to assure the ruling National Democratic Party (NDP) a lock on governmental power. "Egyptians cannot change their government democratically," the group concludes.[3]

As in Egypt, so in the rest of the Arab world—which stretches across North Africa, south through the Arabian peninsula and east to Iraq. (*See map, p. 183.*) With around 300 million people, the 22 members of the League of Arab States include only one rated by Freedom House as "free"—tiny Djibouti on the Horn of Africa. None of the other members allows a free election to choose the national leader, and only one—Kuwait—has a parliament with effective power to control the executive branch of government.

"There is no substantial and significant movement toward full democracy in any of the majority-Arab countries," says Adrian Karatnycky, a senior counselor and former president of Freedom House.

Other human rights advocates and experts agree. "Legitimate democracy is non-existent in the Arab world," says James Phillips, a Mideast expert at the conservative Heritage Foundation.

Thomas Carothers, vice president of the more liberal Carnegie Endowment for International Peace, says, "There is very little democratic trend in the region."

Arab leaders, however, profess support for democracy and claim to see progress toward the goal in many countries in the region. "More than a few people are committed to the democratization process, committed to widening and consolidating political participation," says Nassif Hitti, a diplomat in the Paris mission of the League of Arab States. "It's a process. It's moving on, perhaps not as fast as one would like to see it. It's moving on at different speeds depending on different cases."

A leading American spokesman for Arab-Americans also sees advancing democratization in the region. "It's proceeding apace," says James Zogby, president of the Arab American Institute. "While there are problems, to be sure, changes have been occurring that should not be ignored but all too frequently are ignored."

A major 2002 human rights report by a leading Arab development group, however, takes a more critical view. "The wave of democracy . . . has barely reached the Arab States," the Arab Fund for Economic and Social Development said in a 2002 report co-published by the United Nations Development Program. Representative democracy "is not always genuine and sometimes absent," the group said, while freedoms of expression and association are "frequently curtailed."[4]

Bush raised the profile of the issue in his Nov. 6 speech marking the 20th anniversary of the National Endowment for Democracy, calling on the Middle East and North Africa to join what he called "the global democratic revolution." Bush cataloged signs of democratization in many Arab lands—from the first-ever parliamentary elections in the island emirate of Bahrain and planned elections in Saudi Arabia to a new constitution in Qatar and a call by Morocco's king to extend rights to women.

In a widely noted passage, Bush also directly criticized the United States and other Western nations for supporting autocratic governments in the past. "Sixty years of Western nations excusing and accommodating the lack of freedom in the Middle East did nothing to make us safe," Bush said, "because in the long run, stability cannot be purchased at the expense of liberty."[5]

Bush also vowed to press on with building a democracy in Iraq following last year's U.S.-led invasion and ouster of the country's former dictator, Saddam Hussein.[6]

Political Freedom Rare in the Arab World

Only one member of the 22-member League of Arab States — tiny Djibouti on the Horn of Africa — is rated "free" by the human-rights group Freedom House. No other Arab country allows free elections of national leaders, and only Kuwait has a parliament that can effectively control the executive branch. Yemen is the only Arab country whose freedom status improved over the past year.

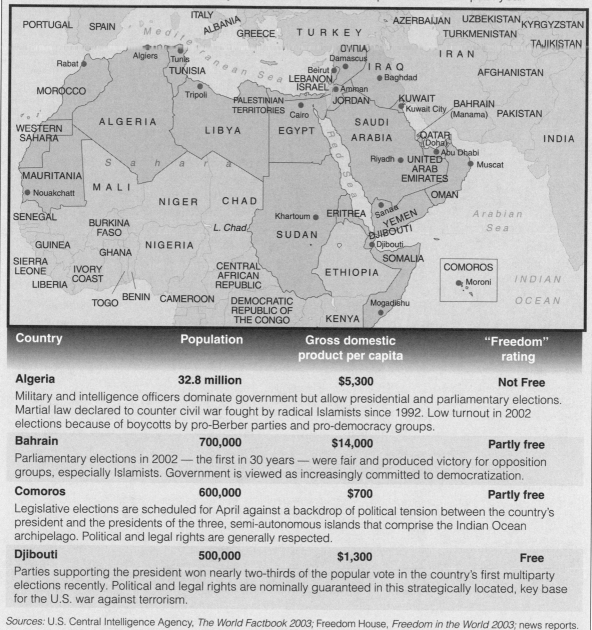

Country	Population	Gross domestic product per capita	"Freedom" rating
Algeria	**32.8 million**	**$5,300**	**Not Free**
Military and intelligence officers dominate government but allow presidential and parliamentary elections. Martial law declared to counter civil war fought by radical Islamists since 1992. Low turnout in 2002 elections because of boycotts by pro-Berber parties and pro-democracy groups.			
Bahrain	**700,000**	**$14,000**	**Partly free**
Parliamentary elections in 2002 — the first in 30 years — were fair and produced victory for opposition groups, especially Islamists. Government is viewed as increasingly committed to democratization.			
Comoros	**600,000**	**$700**	**Partly free**
Legislative elections are scheduled for April against a backdrop of political tension between the country's president and the presidents of the three, semi-autonomous islands that comprise the Indian Ocean archipelago. Political and legal rights are generally respected.			
Djibouti	**500,000**	**$1,300**	**Free**
Parties supporting the president won nearly two-thirds of the popular vote in the country's first multiparty elections recently. Political and legal rights are nominally guaranteed in this strategically located, key base for the U.S. war against terrorism.			

Sources: U.S. Central Intelligence Agency, *The World Factbook 2003;* Freedom House, *Freedom in the World 2003;* news reports.

Country	Population	Gross domestic product per capita	"Freedom" rating
Egypt	**74.7 million**	**$3,900**	**Not free**

President Hosni Mubarak has ruled under a continuous state of emergency since assuming office in 1981 after the assassination of Anwar el-Sadat but said he supports limited reforms drafted by a party committee headed by his son Gamal. Some easing of previous crackdowns on internal dissent has occurred; Islamic militancy is seen as fueled by socioeconomic problems.

Iraq	**24.7 million**	**$2,400**	**Not free**

The United States is pressing transition to democratic self-rule after a U.S.-led coalition ousted Saddam Hussein last spring. Captured in December 2003, Hussein faces trial by an Iraqi tribunal. L. Paul Bremer III — administrator of the American-led occupation — is working to transfer power to Iraqi entities; elections possible in 2004.

Jordan	**5.5 million**	**$4,300**	**Not free**

King Abdullah II promises to continue pushing democratic reforms following victory for allies in previously postponed parliamentary elections in June 2003. He dissolved parliament in 2001 to counter Islamist opposition to pro-Western foreign policy he continued after 1999 death of his father, King Hussein.

Kuwait	**2.2 million**	**$15,000**	**Partly free**

Fundamentalist Muslims and supporters of the royal-backed cabinet improved their standing in parliamentary elections last June; the aging emir appointed his 74-year-old brother as prime minister in July in an apparent effort to boost economic and political reforms, but succession issues still cloud prospects.

Lebanon	**3.7 million**	**$5,400**	**Not free**

Opposition to Syrian military occupation increasing, although Syria downsized its military presence in 2001. The elected, pro-Syrian government continues to hold power since winning control after the end of Christian-Muslim civil war in 1990.

Libya	**5.5 million**	**$7,600**	**Not free**

Muammar el-Qaddafi has ruled by decree since seizing power in 1969. Independent political parties and non-authorized Islamic groups are banned. Qaddafi recently has been seeking U.S. goodwill by cooperating in the war against terrorism, while domestic support wanes.

Mauritania	**2.9 million**	**$1,700**	**Partly free**

Longtime President Maaouiya Ould Taya was re-elected in November after his main opponent was charged with plotting a coup d'etat. Elections in October 2001 were seen as generally fair and open, but Ould Taya's political control was left undisturbed.

Morocco	**31.7 million**	**$3,900**	**Partly free**

King Mohammed VI instituted political and economic liberalization after assuming the throne in 1999. Free and fair elections for parliament were held in 2002, but turnout was low. Palace still holds decision-making power.

Oman	**2.8 million**	**$8,300**	**Not free**

An 83-member advisory council was elected by universal-suffrage election in October; parliamentary elections planned in 2004. Political liberalization and economic modernization have been pushed since 1990s by Sultan Qaboos, who overthrew his father in 1970.

Palestinian Territories	**3.2 million**	**$930**	**Not free**

Progress toward limited self-rule by the Palestinian Authority in the Israeli-occupied West Bank and Gaza Strip has stalled following the outbreak of the Palestinian intifada (uprising) in September 2000, a continuing dispute over Israeli settlements and a stalemate in peace talks. The first popular election in 1996 was seen as legitimate; municipal elections have been postponed since 1998.

Country	Population	Gross domestic product per capita	"Freedom" rating
Qatar	800,000	$21,500	**Not free**

Parliamentary elections have been promised for 2004. Liberalization has been directed by the ruling emir, who overthrew his father in 1995. The government's Al-Jazeera all-news satellite TV station and close military ties with the United States have raised the country's profile.

Saudi Arabia	24.3 million	$10,500	**Not free**

Crown Prince Abdullah favors political and economic liberalization but faces family opposition. Popular discontent among religious and liberal dissidents fueled by declining living standards has been put down by harsh measures. Under U.S. pressure, the government is moving against al-Qaeda terrorist activities.

Somalia	8 million	$600	**Not free**

Delegates to a peace conference agreed in July 2003 to create a new federal government after more than a decade of civil war and virtual anarchy, but the plan has yet to be implemented. The breakaway Republic of Somaliland in the north has not won diplomatic recognition.

Sudan	38.1 million	$1,420	**Not free**

The Arab Muslim government reached a cease-fire agreement in September with black African rebels in the south in 20-year-old civil war that has claimed 2 million lives. Accord envisions a six-year transition to autonomy for the southern region and Islamic law in north.

Syria	17.6 million	$3,500	**Not free**

President Bashar Assad has mixed record on reform since the death of his autocratic father, Hafez al-Assad, in 2000. Bashar allowed reform movement to form during "Damascus Spring" but began clamping down in February 2001. Calls for reform were renewed last September, but broad political change is seen as unlikely.

Tunisia	10 million	$6,500	**Not free**

President Zine el-Abidine Ben Ali gained power in a 1987 coup and won 99 percent approval in a 2002 referendum to seek election for a fourth five-year term. Elections for parliament are heavily orchestrated. The country has a strong, diversified market economy, but political and civil liberties are restricted.

United Arab Emirates	2.5 million	$22,000	**Not free**

Council of seven dynastic families have ruled the federation since its formation in 1971. No elections have been held and political parties are banned. The diversified modern economy supports high per capita income. The federation has a moderate foreign policy stance and new anti-money laundering laws to stem terrorism financing.

Western Sahara	300,000	N/A	**Not free**

Morocco virtually annexed the country in late 1970s, but the territory is still contested by the so-called Polisario guerrillas; guerrilla activities continued sporadically until a U.N.-monitored cease-fire on Sept. 6, 1991.

Yemen	19.3 million	$840	**Partly free**

President Ali Abdullah Saleh, in office since unification of North and South Yemen in 1990, won approval in a 2001 referendum to extend presidential and parliamentary terms. Elections for parliament were deemed free and fair, but it exercises little power. Under U.S. pressure, government is cracking down on al-Qaeda cells and radical Islamist schools.

"This work is not easy," he said. But, he added, "We will meet this test."

Egypt merited a mention in the speech, with the president hailing a "great and proud nation" but calling on it to "show the way toward democracy in the Middle East." President Mubarak answered the next month by insisting that Egypt is already a democracy. "We do not need any pressure from anyone to adopt democratic principles," he told a news conference in December.[7]

Indeed, many Arabists say the United States should not try to impose democracy on the Arab world. "It might be considered by many as an interference, for right

President Bush has urged Egyptian President Hosni Mubarak, left, and other Arab leaders to allow more democracy in the Middle East. "For too long, many people in that region have been victims and subjects—they deserve to be active citizens," Bush said in a Nov. 6 speech.

or wrong reasons, and this might frustrate at some times the progress of this process," Hitti says.

Mubarak's son Gamal, in fact, heads an NDP committee that has called for revising the political licensing laws and invited legal opposition parties and non-governmental organizations to join a "national dialogue." Most Egyptian democracy advocates are unimpressed. "I find all policies unchanged," Abu Saad says. As for Mubarak's assessment, Abu Saad flatly disagrees: "You can't say we have democracy at all."

As the debate on democratic reforms continues in Egypt and elsewhere in the Arab world and in Washington, here are some of the questions being considered:

Is democracy taking root in the Arab world?

The U.S.-led liberation of Kuwait in the first Gulf War in 1991 raised hopes for democratic changes in the oil-rich emirate. Pressure from Washington helped persuade the ruling al-Sabah family to restore the previously suspended national assembly.

Today, Kuwait's parliament is regarded as the only legislative body in an Arab country with the power to check decisions by the executive branch. The parliament's most notable use of that power came in 1999 when it nullified a decree by the ruling emir to allow women the right to vote. And the prospect for further reforms is clouded by fractiousness within the ruling family and the strong showing by Islamist, or Muslim

fundamentalist, forces in the most recent parliamentary elections in 2003.

Kuwait's al-Sabah regime serves as one example of the many obstacles to democratization in the Arab world. While historic, cultural and religious factors are all cited as important, the Carnegie Foundation's Carothers says the most important obstacle is political: the power and survival skills of existing, undemocratic governments.

"These are well-entrenched, non-democratic regimes that have learned to survive over the years and are able to mobilize resources—either oil or foreign aid—to co-opt opposition movements, to repress and to tell their peoples that they are forces of order that are necessary to keep societies together," Carothers says.

Arab League diplomat Hitti acknowledges that established regimes are part of the problem. "The official elements are in many instances part of the constraining factors," he says. But he declines to comment on specific countries or leaders.

Contemporary political conditions, however, have developed from a history largely without democratic institutions or procedures. The Heritage Foundation's Phillips says Arab culture itself is ill disposed toward democracy. For example, the Arab word for politics translates most closely as "control," he points out, while the English word derives from a Greek root meaning cooperation.

"Arabs in general don't handle equality very well because in their system you're either giving orders or taking orders," Phillips says.

"The Muslim and Arab countries do not have a culture or heritage or traditions of democratic practices or liberties as such," says Laith Kubba, an Iraqi-born U.S. citizen who is senior program officer for the Middle East and North Africa at the National Endowment for Democracy. "They have more traditional tribal cultures, where consensus is valued and dissent is not appreciated or welcome."

The 2002 Arab human rights report itself acknowledges that "traditional Arab culture and values" are often "at odds with those of the globalizing world."[8] The report calls for Arab countries to adopt an attitude of "openness and constructive engagement" toward other cultures, but Carothers says outside influences are generally unwelcome. "There is a sense in the Arab world that there is a particular Arab way to do things, and they should resist change from the outside," he says.

Arabs and Arab-Americans say cultural factors are less important in inhibiting democracy than historical factors—specifically, the legacy of colonial rule, first by the Ottoman Empire and then by European powers beginning in the 19th century. "During the colonial era, whatever existed before was wiped out," says Radwan Masmoudi, a Tunisian-born U.S. citizen who heads the Center for the Study of Islam and Democracy in Washington.

After independence in the early 20th century, Masmoudi continues, "the new states were created in an ad hoc fashion. They weren't established to represent the will of the people or even to serve the people."

Zogby agrees. "You've got a region that for the last 150 years has not controlled its own destiny," he says. "This region was not free to advance and develop at its own rate, and that's never a positive factor in promoting democracy."

The region's largely Muslim population and character are often cited as another barrier to democratization, but the relationship between Islam and democracy is complex and susceptible to what the Arab League's Hitti calls "contradictory interpretations." Many experts see support for democracy in Islam's central tenets, while others view Islam's fusion of religion and the state as antithetical to democracy.

For his part, President Bush insisted in his Nov. 6 speech that Islam and democracy are not in conflict. And Arab and U.S. experts alike stress the multiplicity of views among Muslims themselves. "There are versions of Islam that are pretty anti-democratic, but they're just versions," Carothers says.

But Abdelwahab El-Affendi, a senior research fellow at the Centre for the Study of Democracy at the University of Westminster, in London, says the strong differences among Muslims themselves are part of the problem. "The many visions are often incompatible," says El-Affendi, a Sudanese. "The holders of each vision are not ready to negotiate."

The Arab human rights report cataloged a host of factors underlying what it called the "freedom deficit" in the region. It listed high rates of illiteracy and low rates of economic development as important factors, along with such political conditions as the unchecked power of executive branches of government, little popular participation and limited freedom of expression or association. "Remedying this state of affairs," the report concluded, "must be a priority of national leaderships."[9]

Will democracy help promote economic development in the Arab world?

Saudi Arabia may be oil-rich, but the kingdom is beset with economic problems, according to Freedom House's most recent annual country profile. The report blames "declining oil prices," "rampant corruption within the royal family" and "gross economic mismanagement" for a steep decline in living standards—represented by a 50 percent drop in per capita income since the 1980s. Meanwhile, unemployment is estimated at 35 percent and expected to rise in coming years.[10]

Saudi Arabia provides just one example—though the most dramatic—of the paradoxical economic conditions in the Arab world. Arab nations control about half of the world's oil reserves, but the region has higher unemployment and poverty than much of the developing world. Unemployment averages 15 percent, according to the Arab human rights report, and more than one out of five people live on less than $2 per day. Combined, the Arab states' gross national product is less than that of Spain—which has less than one-seventh of the Arab world's population.[11]

The region's economic problems are widely seen as an obstacle to democratization, which in turn is viewed as one of the keys to improved economic performance. "Opening up markets is tied directly to opening up the political process," says diplomat Hitti. "There is a direct relationship between the issues."

Many advocates and experts say the region's dependence on oil as its primary source of wealth has had a negative effect on democratization. "Energy-rich societies have been able to use oil and wealth to buy quiescence and consent from portions of their population, and they've used repression to deal with the balance," says Freedom House's Karatnycky.

"Oil is an incredibly corrupting influence," says Stephen Krasner, director of the Center on Democracy, Development and the Rule of Law at Stanford University's Institute of International Studies, in Palo Alto, Calif.

In states with oil wealth, Krasner explains, "People want to get control of the state [because] the state gives you resources that you can use to repress your enemies. You don't have to compromise. You don't have to think about responsive fiscal systems. It's a huge problem."

Michael Ross, a political scientist at the University of California, Los Angeles, says oil dependence also hampers democratization because it fails to produce the kind of social modernization usually associated with

Are Islam and Democracy Incompatible?

Politics and religion are a volatile mix in many countries, but nowhere more so than in the Arab world. Islam has a special status in Arab states—not only because it is the nearly universal faith but also because many Muslims view Islam as an essential source of government law.

Even in non-Arab Islamic countries, fundamentalists, or Islamists, often claim a religious basis for repressive policies against political opponents, women and other religions—notably, in Iran after the Islamic revolution of 1979 and in Afghanistan under the now-deposed Taliban. In addition, Islamist groups bring a sometimes deadly religious zeal to their battles against secular Arab regimes, not to mention Israel and the United States.

As a result, many Westerners regard Islam and democracy as inherently incompatible. Muslims in and outside the Arab world resent that view, and human rights advocates take pains to try to refute it.

"Islam, per se, is not an obstacle to democracy," says Thomas Carothers, director of the Project on Democracy and the Rule of Law at the Carnegie Endowment for International Peace. But, Carothers adds, "there are certain patterns of Islam that are inhospitable to democracy."

"There is a long tradition of people who want to combine liberalism with Islam," says Abdelwahab El-Affendi, coordinator of the Project on Democracy in the Muslim World at the University of Westminster in London and a native Sudanese. But he concedes that groups with "illiberal" Islamic views have more adherents in the Arab world today. "They say if liberalism and Islam conflict, then the Islamic way should be supreme," he explains.

In its most recent annual survey, the human rights group Freedom House says there is "no inexorable link between Islam and political repression."[1] Nearly half of the world's 1.5 billion Muslims live in countries with elective democracies, according to the survey. The list includes such majority-Muslim countries as Bangladesh, Nigeria and

Turkey as well as more religiously diverse nations like India, Indonesia and the United States.

Nevertheless, the survey reports, "The largest freedom gap exists in countries with a majority-Muslim population, especially in the Arab world." Out of 44 majority-Muslim countries, only eight are electoral democracies—none of them Arab states. And only two are classified as "free": Mali and Senegal in West Africa. The other 42 countries—home to more than 1 billion Muslims—are rated either as "partly free" or "not free."

Human rights advocates blame the limited advance of democracy in the Islamic world more on history and politics than on religion. Radwan Masmoudi, the founding president of the Center for the Study of Islam and Democracy in Washington, says that European colonial rulers of the early 20th century were succeeded by ideologues of various stripes—Arab nationalists, communists and Baathists—who adopted authoritarian policies to hold power.

Properly understood, Islam has been fully consistent with democracy, according to Masmoudi, a Tunisian-born U.S. citizen who founded the center partly with U.S.-government funding in 1999. "From a historical perspective, Islam has been a fairly tolerant religion," Masmoudi says, ever since its birth with the teachings of Muhammad in the seventh century A.D. "The sayings of the Prophet are clearly for freedom, democracy and tolerance," he explains.

Other experts also see support for democratic government in such Islamic principles as consultation (*shurah*), consensus (*ijma*) and independent judgment (*itjihad*). But John Esposito, director of the Center for Christian-Muslim Understanding at Georgetown University in Washington, notes that Islamic thinkers adapt these concepts in ways that reflect criticisms of what they see as the secularism and materialism of Western-style democracy.[2]

Other U.S. scholars, however, say that fundamentalists interpret Islam in ways that are antithetical to democracy. "For [fundamentalists], the truth is knowable, and so there

---

[1] "Global Freedom Gains Amid Terror, Uncertainty," Freedom House, Dec. 18, 2003 (www.freedomhouse.org).

[2] See John L. Esposito and John O. Voll, *Islam and Democracy* (1996), pp. 27-32.

is no need to discuss it in an open forum," says Daniel Pipes, director of the Middle East Forum, a think tank in Philadelphia. "That strikes me as undemocratic."[3]

Islamic fundamentalists "regard liberal democracy as a corrupt and corrupting form of government," writes Bernard Lewis, a leading historian of the Middle East. "They are willing to see it, at best, as an avenue to power, but an avenue that runs one way only."[4]

Masmoudi and others say that U.S. policymakers must accept that secularism and separation of church and state will not be accepted by most Muslims. "People tend to think that democracy is equal to secularism, that religion will play no role in society whatsoever," he explains. If people view Islam and democracy in conflict, Masmoudi says, "Eighty percent of them will say, 'We want to be good Muslims. We don't care about good democracy—if it is against Islam, we don't want it.' "

"The Islamists in the Middle East are there to stay," says Mohamed Ben-Ruwin, an assistant professor of political science at Texas A&M International University in Laredo. "You have to engage them in some kind of dialogue."[5]

"We should have a dialogue of civilizations, not 'a clash of civilizations,' " Ben-Ruwin adds, referring to the widely discussed book by Harvard political scientist Samuel Huntington forecasting an increasing threat of violence

AFP Photo/Getty Image/Hani al-Obeidi

Shiite Muslim Iraqis have become increasingly vocal in supporting their spiritual leader Grand Ayatollah Ali al-Sistani's unrelenting call for direct elections. The majority Shiites were repressed by the ruling Sunnis during the regime of deposed President Saddam Hussein.

from countries and cultures with religiously based policies and traditions.[6]

Democracy advocates point to the success of a moderate Islamic party in Turkey as a promising example for majority-Muslim countries. Since taking office after an overwhelming election victory in November 2002, the Justice and Development Party has moved to expand political rights in a nation founded in 1923 as a secular republic.

"Turkey shows us that Islamists in a democratic environment modify their policies over time," says Adrian Karatnycky, counselor and former president of Freedom House. "Just because this is a religiously informed movement doesn't mean it is going to be anti-democratic."

In Iran, the reform-minded Mohammad Kha-tami won election as president in 1997 and re-election in 2001 after reformers had also won the overwhelming majority of parliamentary seats in 2000. But hard-line conservatives still dominate the judiciary and security services—producing a stalemate between pro- and anti-liberalization forces.[7]

Many Arab leaders resist free elections by pointing to the danger of a victory for extremist Islamist groups—a fear shared though not always voiced among U.S. policymakers. Masmoudi says the danger is exaggerated.

"I trust the people," he says. "The Islamist parties that will win are not against democracy. I believe it will be the moderate Islamists, not the radical Islamists who are opposed to democracy."

---

[3] Quoted in David Masci, "Islamic Fundamentalism," *The CQ Researcher*, March 24, 2000, pp. 241-264.

[4] Bernard Lewis, "A Historical Overview," in Larry Diamond, Marc F. Plattner and Daniel Brumberg (eds.), *Islam and Democracy in the Middle East* (2003), p. 210.

[5] See Mohamed Berween, "Leadership Crisis in the Arab Countries and the Challenge of the Islamists," *Middle East Affairs Journal*, Vol. 7, No. 1-2 (winter/spring 2001), pp. 121-132.

[6] Samuel P. Huntington, *The Clash of Civilizations and the Remaking of World Order* (2000).

[7] For background, see David Masci, "Reform in Iran," *The CQ Researcher*, Dec. 18, 1998, pp. 1097-1120.

Anti-U.S. Views Dominate Arab World

Unfavorable attitudes about the United States were twice as prevalent, on average, as favorable attitudes, according to a poll in five Arab nations.

Country	Favorable	Unfavorable
Lebanon	41%	40%
Kuwait	28	41
Jordan	22	62
Morocco	22	41
Saudi Arabia	16	64
Total	26%	50%

Note: Percentages are not included for respondents with neither favorable nor unfavorable attitudes.

Source: Gallup Organization, poll of nearly 10,000 residents, February 2002.

democratic change, such as urbanization, education and occupational specialization. Without those changes, Ross writes in a detailed examination of the issue, the public is "demobilized"—ill equipped to organize and communicate and unaccustomed to thinking for itself.[12]

The 2002 Arab human rights report viewed government policies as unhelpful to economic development. "[T]he state's role in promoting, complementing and regulating markets for goods, services and factors of production has been both constrained and constraining," the 2002 report stated. As a result, "the private sector's contribution to development has often been hesitant and certainly below expectations."[13]

Today, however, Hitti claims that Arab governments are adopting free-market policies. "Almost all of our countries are moving along market economic lines," he says.

Some experts say they expect democratic changes will encourage more economic development. "You may liberate a lot of economic free-wheeling activity," says the Heritage Foundation's Phillips. "The Arabs are great traders and merchants, but the problem is that the merchant class has been kept down except in Kuwait, where the merchants run the place."

Other experts, however, caution against expecting democratic change alone to solve the region's economic problems. "No statistical relationship can be shown be-

tween democracy and economic growth," Krasner says. He puts greater emphasis on instilling "decent levels of governance," including reducing corruption, adopting a "reasonable level of rule of law" and delivering government services more effectively.

For Saudi Arabia itself, broad democratic changes would have "a huge positive effect" on economic development, says Jean-Francois Seznec, an adjunct professor at Georgetown University's Center for Contemporary Arab Studies, in Washington. "If you have democratization, the private sector will be much more able to invest."

Seznec notes that Saudi Arabia has been developing an industrial base—notably, in petrochemical manufacturing. The Saudi Ministry of Labor is calling for investing $200 billion a year in further industrialization. But investment is hampered by the government's tight control of the economy and the lack of an independent judiciary.

"Right now, the civil service controls the economy, and the royal family is above the law," Seznec explains. An independent judiciary, he says, "would allow people to invest more freely, and there's plenty of money to invest."

Without democratization, Seznec concludes, economic changes "will occur, but very, very slowly."

Should the United States do more to promote democracy in Arab countries?

As Secretary of State Colin L. Powell prepared to visit Morocco, Algeria and Tunisia last December, human rights groups urged him to lobby their leaders for democratic reforms. "Secretary Powell should make bold and specific statements calling for the countries in the region to take serious steps to enhance the rule of law, strengthen independent media and expand democratic freedoms," Freedom House Executive Director Jennifer Windsor urged.

Powell did raise the issue in each country. He praised Morocco's holding of parliamentary elections in 2002, called on Algeria to ensure "free and fair" elections for the national assembly in April 2004 and pressed Tunisia's longtime president, Zine el-Abidine Ben Ali, to move faster on political reforms. But Powell was careful to soften any implied criticism. In Tunis, for example, Powell said that Tunisia "has accomplished so much that people are expecting more to happen."

Human rights groups had mixed reactions. Human rights "was not a major theme of his public statements," Freedom House's Karatnycky commented afterwards. But Tom Malinowski, Washington advocacy director for Human Rights Watch, was more impressed. "Human rights were raised in a manner in which they haven't been raised in the past by the United States in these countries," he remarked.

Powell's careful diplomacy illustrates the recurrent tension between human rights advocacy and present-day strategic considerations. "We still need and value our close cooperation with some of the non-democratic governments in the region—like Egypt and Saudi Arabia—on security matters as well as on economic matters like oil," says the Carnegie Endowment's Carothers. "It's hard for us to take a genuinely tough line toward governments that know we need them."

But human rights advocates and experts also stress that the United States is hampered in pushing for democratic change in the region because of its past record of supporting autocratic Arab governments. "The United States has been, over time, interested in stability and generally indifferent to democracy," Karatnycky says.

"We have very little credibility as a pro-democratic actor," Carothers says. "We will have to earn that credibility by word and deed over a sustained period of time."

Arab-American advocates make the same point, even more critically. "We've never been a supporter of democracy in this region," Zogby says. "We lack both the moral authority and credibility at this point to be an agent for that kind of change."

For their part, Arab governments and Arab-American advocates also say that U.S. support for Israel undermines the United States' position in pushing for democratic changes. "The American position—particularly as it pertains to the Arab-Israeli conflict—has been damaging," Hitti says. He complains today of U.S. "immobilism" in peacemaking efforts in the Mideast.[14]

Bush's Nov. 6 speech drew mixed reactions from U.S. experts and advocates. The Heritage Foundation's Phillips calls it a "great speech," but Joe Stork, acting director for the Middle East and North Africa at Human Rights Watch, is more restrained. "It was a positive signal, but now we have to see if he can walk the walk," Stork says.

"The rhetoric is very dramatic," Karatnycky says, "but as yet the programmatic resources are relatively modest, and the pressure [from the U.S.] is still very, very mild."

The administration's vehicle for pro-democracy programs in the region is the Middle East Partnership Initiative, a State Department program that was headed by Elizabeth Cheney, daughter of the vice president, until her resignation in December 2003 to join President Bush's re-election campaign. Funding for the initiative was $129 million for 2002 and 2003 and up to $120 million for 2004.[15]

For his part, the Arab League's Hitti says Bush's speech failed to resolve concerns about U.S. hypocrisy in pushing for democratization. "There is a great feeling in the region that there is a double standard in America," he says. "You use democracy in certain aspects and not in other aspects."

Apart from any questions about the administration's sincerity, some experts also say that the push for democratization may be too narrowly focused on elections rather than on the full range of political reforms needed to sustain democratic government. Daniel Brumberg, an associate professor of government at Georgetown and a senior associate at the Carnegie Endowment, complains that Bush's speech lacked "any discussion of fundamental constitutional reforms." He points in particular to the need for Arab governments to create what none of them now has: legislative bodies "with the authority and power to speak for elected majorities."[16]

"We are deeply hamstrung by thinking that we must only focus on having free elections," Stanford's Krasner says. "What we should be talking about is good governance and accountability, of which democracy is a part, but only one part."

Despite those criticisms, Kubba at the National Endowment for Democracy believes the United States is on the way to becoming a positive force for democratization—not only for moral reasons but also for national self-interest, particularly after the Sept. 11, 2001, attacks on New York's World Trade Center and the Pentagon by Arab terrorists.

"There has been a genuine shift after Sept. 11 toward supporting democracy in the Middle East," Kubba says, "because [the administration] now believes that democracy-building enhances not only the security and stability in the region but also America's interest and security."

CHRONOLOGY

Before 1900 *Arab empire extends from Spain to India; Ottoman Turks conquer the Arabs in 15th century; European powers gain foothold in 1800s.*

1900-1945 *Britain, France establish "mandates" after defeating Ottomans in World War I; House of Saud establishes kingdom on Arabian peninsula.*

1946-1970 *Arab nationalism grows with independence after World War II and creation of Israel; U.S. bolsters sitting leaders to protect oil supplies, aid Cold War struggle.*

1948-1949 Israel established as Jewish homeland, defeats Arab states in nine-month war; 960,000 Palestinians displaced.

1952 Gamal Abdel Nasser becomes Egypt's president after military coup, promotes pan-Arab unity but loses prestige after Arab defeat in Six-Day War with Israel in 1967.

1967 Israel occupies Gaza Strip, West Bank after victory in Six-Day War.

1968 Sadaam Hussein assumes power in Iraq as leader of Baath Party.

1970s-1980s *Oil, terrorism raise U.S. stakes in Arab lands.*

1973 Saudi Arabia leads oil embargo against U.S. by Organization of Petroleum Exporting Countries (OPEC).

1981 Egyptian President Anwar el-Sadat assassinated; new president, Hosni Mubarak, institutes rule by decree that continues to present day.

1990s *U.S. role in Iraq grows after Iraq's defeat in Gulf War; radical Islamist movements advance.*

1990-1991 Iraq's Hussein invades Kuwait; U.S. leads United Nations coalition in Gulf War to force

withdrawal, but President George Bush, the current president's father, decides not to seek Hussein's ouster.

1992 Algerian military cancels legislative elections to forestall victory by radical Islamic Salvation Front, touching off protracted civil war.

1996 With King Fahd ailing, Crown Prince Abdullah gains authority in Saudi Arabia; he later pushes for reforms but faces opposition from other members of royal family.

1999 Jordan's King Hussein, key U.S. ally, dies; his son, Abdullah, succeeds him, continues pro-U.S. policies while promoting limited political reform.

2000-Present *Democracy makes limited gains in region; U.S. promotes democracy after ousting Iraq's Hussein.*

2000 Syrian President Hafez al-Assad dies, succeeded by his son, Bashar, who adopts, then backs off from, limited reforms.

2001 Terrorist attacks against U.S. by Osama bin Laden's al-Qaeda leave nearly 3,000 dead; President Bush promises war against global terror.

2002 Bahrain holds first parliamentary elections in 30 years . . . Parliamentary elections in Morocco . . . Arab report criticizes "freedom deficit" in Arab world.

2003 U.S.-led invasion ousts Hussein in Iraq . . . Bush vows transition to democracy, promotes democracy for all Middle East on Nov. 6 . . . Gamal Mubarak, president's son, pushes limited reforms in Egypt.

2004 Democratic elections planned in many Arab states; Saudi Arabia eyes balloting for municipal councils . . . U.S. plans for handoff to Iraqi authorities by June 30 roiled by dispute over timing of elections. . . . Thousands of Shiites march through Baghdad and other major cities on Jan. 19, demanding direct elections to choose a new government. . . . U.N. Secretary-General Kofi Annan announces on Jan. 27 he will send a fact-finding mission to determine whether early elections are feasible.

BACKGROUND

A Vast Empire

The earliest known Arab governments were established during a period of imperial expansion in the seventh century—shortly after the Islamic religion was established.[17] Led initially by the prophet Muhammad, nomadic peoples of the Arabian Peninsula conquered a vast empire stretching from Spain and North Africa to the Middle East and present-day Pakistan, spreading their religion, language and culture throughout the region. Islam reached Central Asia and the South Caucasus Mountains in the eighth century and spread to India and Indonesia in the 12th and 13th centuries, largely via Muslim traders and explorers.

Arab leaders exercised a tolerant but absolutist rule over their empire. Democratic governance was largely non-existent. Although the empire collapsed in the 15th century, Arabs have remained the principal power in the Middle East well into the modern era.

Pre-imperial Arab society had been organized around tribal allegiances, with little central authority or government and no common legal system. Most Arabs were nomadic shepherds, tending herds of goats, sheep or camels. All males were expected to be warriors, and competition over scarce resources often led to conflict between various tribal groups. Despite their differences, most Mideast tribes shared Arabic as a common language, and overland trade routes required inter-tribal cooperation and interaction.

The emergence of Islam ("surrender" in Arabic), a new monotheistic religion, on the Arabian Peninsula in 622 A.D. heralded the beginning of the transformation of the Arabs from desert nomads to a world power. Established by an Arab merchant known only as Muhammad, Islam provided a framework for running early Arabian society. The *Koran*—Islam's holy book and a record of God's revelations to Muhammad—provided rules for business contracts, marriages, inheritance and other societal institutions.

Under Muhammad's spiritual and military leadership, early Arab-Islamic society rose to prominence in Arabia, gaining control of religious and trade centers like Mecca and Medina. Muhammad exercised supreme authority over his nascent empire.

Following Muhammad's death in 632 A.D., two factions struggled for control of Arab-Islamic society, producing a schism in Islam. Sunni Arabs believed that a politically selected successor, or caliph, should become ruler. Shiites, on the other hand, claimed that the direct descendents of Muhammad, called imams, were the legitimate rulers of Islam. Sunnis won the power struggle, and the secular caliphs dominated the Arab empire until the 16th century, with Shiite imams wielding only negligible power.

By the middle of the eighth century, the caliphs ruled from Spain to the Indian subcontinent. In theory, a central Arab ruler governed outlying territories with absolute secular and Islamic authority. In practice, the size and breadth of the sprawling empire made direct governance difficult, so Arab rulers often left local administrative and governmental structures intact. Nonetheless, occasional uprisings produced breakaway caliphates in places like North Africa and Egypt.

During the heyday of the Arab-Islamic empire—generally from the eighth to the 10th centuries—poetry, agriculture, trade and intellectual pursuits flourished. Arab scholars made valuable contributions to trigonometry, algebra and philosophy. Religious scholars developed the five pillars of Islam, a framework of prayers and rituals that formed a common and universal religious experience for Arabs.

By the standards of its day, the Islamic empire showed remarkable religious tolerance. Other monotheistic faiths like Christianity or Judaism were protected under the *Koran*. While early caliphs discriminated against non-Arab Muslim converts, later rulers universalized Islam and granted all Muslims equal rights.

Eventually, the increasingly diverse Arab empire proved difficult to govern with only the *Koran* for guidance. Arab leaders and intellectuals developed Sharia, a "legal system that would recognize the requirements of imperial administration and the value of local customs while remaining true to the concept of a community guided by divine [Islamic] revelation," writes William Cleveland, in his book, *A History of the Modern Middle East*. Sharia allowed Islamic officials to interpret Islamic principles to mediate situations not explicitly covered by the *Koran*.

By the 11th century, the central power of the Arab caliphate in Baghdad began to wane. Turkish nomads from Asia—who had converted to Islam—carved out large dynasties of their own within the Arab empire, previewing the coming Ottoman Empire. European crusaders invaded Arab lands and maintained a tenuous occupation

Women Benefit From Top-Down Reforms

Women's groups are working in many Arab countries to change what an Arab development group describes as a "glaring deficit in women's empowerment" in the region. But recent advances in voting rights and family law in some countries amount to "top-down" reforms pushed by progressive-minded leaders rather than victories for grass-roots women's movements, experts say.

Qatar and Bahrain recently extended the right to vote for women, thanks to changes pushed by the ruling emirs in the tiny Persian Gulf states. Jordan and Morocco have recently given women limited rights to divorce at the behest of their ruling monarchs: King Abdullah II in Jordan and Mohamed VI in Morocco.

Egypt similarly enacted a "personal status" law in 2000 giving women the right to divorce if they relinquish financial rights. Women's associations "indirectly contributed" to passage of the law, according to a 2002 human rights report by the Arab Fund for Economic and Social Development, but the reform ultimately "was decided by the political powers."[1]

"Most of the progress in women's rights has come from progressive-minded rulers or rulers who want to be considered progressive and have tried to impose top-down reforms on society," says Amy Hawthorne, an expert on Mideast politics at the Carnegie Endowment for International Peace in Washington.

Arab countries rank below every other world region except sub-Saharan Africa on a "gender-empowerment measure," according to the Arab human rights report. The statistical measure—created by the United Nations Development Program—combines women's per capita income and the percentages of professional and technical positions and parliamentary seats held by women.[2]

"Women have a lower social and political status" in Arab countries compared to the rest of the world, Hawthorne says. But she also notes that women's status "varies considerably" through the region. She notes that women have had the right to vote in most Arab countries for some time—even if elections in many of those countries are blatantly undemocratic.

Diane Singerman, a professor of political studies at American University in Washington, also says that women are not subjected to second-class status throughout the Arab world. Women's illiteracy is high because education is not encouraged for women, she says, and unemployment is high—especially among educated women.

On the other hand, "there are a lot of very high-powered, very serious professional women," Singerman says. "In many cases, when women do well, they're not discriminated against in ways that are common" in the United States.

Islamic groups inhibit advances for women's rights. Moroccan women's groups mounted a demonstration with

---

[1] United Nations Development Program/Arab Fund for Economic and Social Development Report, "Arab Human Development Report 2002," p. 117.

[2] *Ibid.*, p. 28.

---

of some Arab territory for 200 years. Ultimately, though, the crusades had minimal impact on the Middle East.[18]

Later foreign invasions spelled the end of the Arab empire. In the 13th century, Mongol conquerors from Asia sacked Baghdad and killed the caliph, ending 500 years of Arab imperial rule. And, at the beginning of the 15th century, the armies of Timur Lang (Tamerlane) swept over the empire, splintering it into several, smaller and weakened dynasties.

Ottoman Empire

Beginning in the 15th century, Ottoman Turks established a new empire that encompassed almost all of the

Arabic-speaking lands in the Middle East.* But Ottoman imperial rule failed under external pressure from the rising European powers, and after World War I the Middle East fell under European control. Following World War II, the region struggled to shed the yoke of European dominance and adopt independent governments, even as new concepts of Arab identity emerged.

By the late 17th century, the sultans—supreme monarchs of the Ottoman Empire—ruled lands that stretched

---

* The Ottomans were Turks who organized under Osman I, a tribal chieftain who lived from 1290-1326.

some 800,000 marchers in the capital city of Rabat in March 2000 in support of the proposed divorce law. But on the same day, some 2 million people took to the streets of Casablanca, warning that the proposal was a threat to Islam. Religious conservatives relented only after the king's intervention.[3]

Islamist-minded legislators led the successful opposition to granting women the right to vote in Kuwait in 1999. The strict school of Islam known as Wahhabism serves as the basis for a host of restrictions on women in Saudi Arabia—such as a ban on driving.

Egypt passed its new divorce law, however, after women's groups claimed the *Koran* itself approved dissolving a marriage if a woman gave up financial rights created by the marital contract. "What's happening throughout the area is that women and other people in the re-

A veiled Jordanian woman casts her ballot. Women have limited voting rights in the Arab world. Bahrain became the first of the Persian Gulf states to allow women to vote in 2002. Kuwait's parliament nullified a decree by the ruling emir in 1999 that would have allowed women to vote.

gion are saying that Islam may say something else," Singerman says. "It's a revisionist history of the record instead of a patriarchal interpretation."

Improving the status of women is "a critical aspect of human freedom," according to the Arab human rights report.[4] But Hawthorne cautions against assuming that granting women political rights will necessarily lead to political change. Some of the countries with broadest rights for women—for example, Syria—are also among the most autocratic of Arab states, she says.

"In the long run, any country that is going through a genuine process of democratization needs to include the empowerment of women," Hawthorne says. "But the addition of women won't necessarily result [right away] in increased democratization."

---

[3] See Kent Davis-Packard, "Morocco Pushes Ahead," *The Christian Science Monitor*, Nov. 12, 2003, p. 15.

[4] "Arab Human Development Report," *loc. cit.*

---

from Hungary in Europe to Algiers in North Africa to Baghdad in the Middle East. The empire was an agrarian, absolutist monarchy, with a strong bureaucracy of educated ruling elites. The sultans implemented Sharia throughout the empire and conferred with a counsel of advisers on policy issues.[19]

The Ottomans employed a flexible system of imperial governance—similar to earlier Arab empires—that allowed local authorities to retain traditional customs, so long as they supplied adequate tax revenue to the Ottoman rulers. The Ottomans also continued Arab traditions of religious tolerance, granting non-Muslims significant civil rights and powers of self-governance.

In the 18th and 19th centuries, faced with the rise of European economic and military might, the Ottoman Empire entered a period of governmental reform and Europeanization. Ottoman officials who knew European languages and supported reforms were promoted, while old-style Ottoman institutions, like the *ulama* (religious scholars), increasingly were bypassed.

The first Ottoman constitution was adopted in 1876, providing for the election of government deputies and an appointed senate. But constitutional reforms proved short-lived, and the sultan reclaimed absolute authority in 1878.

But with central Ottoman authority weakened, several Islamic reformist movements emerged on the rural outskirts of the empire. In Arabia, the puritanical Wahhabi movement rose to power, advocating a return to strict interpretation of the *Koran* and adherence to Sharia.

European 'Mandates'

Elsewhere, intellectuals and scholars called for an Arab cultural renaissance, which reinvigorated the Arabic language and Arab identity, producing a kind of proto-Arab nationalism. And in 1916, an Arab insurrection—supported by the British—founded a short-lived Arab kingdom centered in Damascus.

Although the Ottomans reinstated a constitution in 1908, World War I doomed the empire. The victorious Allies partitioned the empire—which had been allied with Germany—into European-controlled "mandates." Britain maintained control of Egypt—which it had held since 1914—and gained control over Iraq, Palestine and Transjordan (later called Jordan). France assumed control of Syria.

Under international agreement, Britain and France were expected to guide the Arab mandates toward self-governance. In actuality, the mandates allowed the British and French to protect their interests in the Middle East through the end of World War II.[20]

Not surprisingly, the Arabs chafed under the mandates, and many grew to distrust European-imposed political reforms. In Egypt, the Wafd—a political group opposed to British rule—established a secularist parliamentary constitution in 1924. But continued British influence over Wafd governments spawned popular opposition groups, most notably the fundamentalist Muslim Brotherhood, which advocated a return to an Islamic Egyptian state.

Nominally, Iraq achieved early independence in 1932, with a constitutional monarchy and bicameral legislature, as Britain had little interest in governing Iraq's volatile population of Sunnis, Shiites and ethnic Kurds. But Iraqi nationalists battled British-backed governments until 1958, when they succeeded in evicting the monarch.

Transjordan achieved independence in 1946, although the constitutional monarchy owed much of its authority to British support. In Syria, the French retained almost total control over the government until 1946, despite attempts by the Syrians to form a popular government.

Meanwhile, in Arabia—an area outside of European interest—a strong Islamic government took root in the wake of the Ottoman Empire. The Arabian tribal chief Abd al-Aziz ibn Saud, in an alliance with the Wahhabis, founded the kingdom of Saudi Arabia. Saud gained con-

trol of key Islamic religious sites, like Mecca and Medina and instituted strict Sharia law.

Some historians say the period of British and French control in the Middle East marked a high point for Arab democracy. "The Anglo-French domination also gave the Middle East an interlude of liberal economy and political freedom. The freedom was always limited and sometimes suspended but . . . it was on the whole more extensive than anything experienced before or after," writes noted historian Bernard Lewis, in his book, *The Middle East.*[21]

But other historians say Anglo-French domination merely installed a new class of ruling elites. "The same elite that had enjoyed power and prestige before 1914—the European-educated landed and professional classes in Egypt and the traditional notables in Syria, Lebanon and Palestine—continued to exercise their privileges during the 1920s and 1930s," Cleveland writes.[22]

With the twin failures of Ottoman imperialism and European-backed governments in the Middle East, Arabs increasingly looked to nationalism and Islamism as political organizing principles.

Arab Nationalism

After World War II, the creation of Israel threw much of the Middle East into turmoil. Arab efforts to dislodge the Jewish state failed, and military coups replaced many of the defeated Arab governments. Although Arab military leaders espoused reform and pan-Arabism in the 1960s and '70s, they steadily moved toward authoritarianism. Meanwhile, the Cold War extended U.S. influence throughout the Middle East, and the Arabian oil boom cemented U.S. interests in the region. By the new millennium, Arab governments had stymied democratic reform, and radical Islamic groups increasingly targeted the United States for supporting the autocratic regimes.

After the Nazi Holocaust killed millions of Jews in World War II, international support for a Jewish state rose dramatically, culminating with Israel declaring its independence in 1948. Members of the Arab League—a federation of Arab states including Syria, Egypt and Jordan—promptly declared war on the new state.

Following a nine-month war, Arab forces were defeated, and hundreds of thousands of Arabs fled or were forced out of Palestine. By 1950, more than 960,000 Palestinians were refugees.[23] The Arab League later sponsored the Palestine Liberation Organization (PLO), a resistance group that battled Israel and became a Palestinian government in exile.

After the 1948 war, many post-imperial Arab governments were swept away by military regimes promising democratic and social reforms. But the new governments reverted to authoritarianism, which some historians attribute to a legacy of authoritarian rule under the European mandates.[24]

In Egypt, a military coup in 1952 led by Col. Gamal Abdel Nasser ousted the old Wafd government and brought some constitutional reforms, including an elected legislature. But Nasser quickly consolidated power and undermined democratic measures by adopting broad presidential powers.

Nasser also championed the cause of pan-Arab unity, hoping to unite all the Arab countries under a single Egyptian-Arab authority. Nasser achieved some success: Egypt and Syria united as a single nation for a short while, and strong Arab alliances formed in opposition to Israel. But the crushing defeat of Egypt (along with Syria and Jordan) by Israel in 1967—during the so-called Six-Day War—damaged Nasser's reputation and derailed his hopes for pan-Arabism.

Nasser's successor, Sadat, renewed efforts to liberalize Egyptian politics. But Sadat's Western-style reforms failed to satisfy calls for democratic reform. Resistance groups, including the Muslim Brotherhood, called for a return to the successful theocratic governments of the past, and Muslim dissidents assassinated Sadat in 1981. Hosni Mubarak's autocratic government, which assumed power after Sadat's death, continued to control the electoral process and brutally suppress rising Islamic dissent.

In other Arab nations, radical nationalist movements—more focused on ejecting Western-influenced leaders and social reform than in democratization—installed similarly autocratic regimes. A series of military coups in Syria eventually empowered the radical Baath Party, which advocated social reform, pan-Arab unity and nationalism. But Baathist rule brought little reform, prompting militant Islamic groups to battle with the government for power throughout the 1980s and '90s.

Baathist radicals—under Hussein's leadership—assumed power in Iraq in 1968. Hussein's regime produced some social reforms, like increased literacy, but opposition and dissent were violently snuffed out.

Muslims and Freedom

The vast majority of people in Muslim-majority nations are only "partly free" or "not free," according to Freedom House.

Freedom Status in Muslim-Majority Nations

Free Population	Partly Free Population	Not Free Population
20.4 million	577.1 million	532.4 million

Source: CIA Factbook, www.islamicpopulations.com; Freedom House.

Democratic reforms also remained elusive in Arab countries that avoided military insurrection. Jordan's King Hussein assumed power in 1953 and ruled over a monarchy until his death in 1999—a longevity often attributed to Western support. In Lebanon—a state carved out of Syria by the French—democratic governance was pushed aside by Syrian occupation in 1976. And in Algeria's 1991 free elections, voters overwhelmingly chose an Islamic government that vowed a return to Sharia. Military leaders quickly halted the elections, sparking a civil war between radical fundamentalists and the government.

Many of the Arab autocracies received aid from the superpowers during the Cold War. The U.S. provided billions of dollars in military and economic assistance to Israel, Jordan and Iran, while the Soviets armed Syria, Egypt and Iraq. But continued U.S. support for Israel after the Cold War further inflamed anti-American Arab sentiment, even though since 1979 Egypt has been the second-largest recipient of U.S. foreign aid, after President Jimmy Carter brokered the Egypt-Israeli "Camp David" peace accord the year before.[25]

On the Arabian peninsula, the discovery in the early 20th century of vast oil reserves transformed the desert monarchies into world powers. By 1973, Saudi Arabia was producing 13 percent of the world's crude oil, and surging oil wealth strengthened Arabian monarchs' grip on power, enabling them to sidestep democratic reforms.

The monarchies turned to petroleum-hungry Western powers for military protection, particularly the United States. When Hussein invaded the Kuwaiti monarchy in 1990 and threatened Saudi oil fields, a U.S.-led coalition destroyed Iraq's army.[26]

After the Persian Gulf War, popular resistance to the monarchies grew. Radical Islamic groups objected to

AFP Photo/Nicolas Asfouri

A demonstrator outside No. 10 Downing Street in London, the official residence of British Prime Minister Tony Blair, protests Egypt's arrests, torture and detentions of Islamic activists, scholars and civilians. Egypt's ruling National Democratic Party recently has proposed some democratic reforms, but not competitive presidential elections.

Western military and social influence in Saudi Arabia—home of Islam's holiest cities and shrines—and secular interests pushed for more democracy. In Egypt, radicals battled to overthrow the government, while moderates called for democratic reforms.

In the 1990s, America's ties to autocratic regimes and its continued support for Israel led militant Islamic radicals to launch terrorist attacks against American targets. In 1993, Islamic terrorists bombed New York's World Trade Center, killing six and injuring 1,000. And in 1998, hundreds were killed—including 12 Americans—when U.S. embassies in Kenya and Tanzania were bombed by terrorists linked to the al-Qaeda Islamic terrorist organization run by Saudi dissident Osama bin Laden.

Calls for Reform

In response to the murders of nearly 3,000 people in the Sept. 11 terrorist attacks, many Arab governments helped the United States hunt down the bin Laden followers who had helped put the plan to hijack four airliners into action.[27] Under mounting internal and external pressure, some Arab governments also unveiled new democratization efforts, but widespread reform faltered. Israeli-American ties continued to undermine Arab support for U.S. policies in the Middle East, even though the United States and Britain overthrew the murderously repressive Hussein and tried to establish democracy in Iraq.

The Arab world's initial reaction to the Sept. 11 attacks was mixed. Some news reports showed Arabs celebrating in the Palestinian territories. But heads of Arab governments unanimously condemned the carnage.[28]

American officials pressured Arab governments to crack down on Islamic extremists, and Arab states formerly antagonistic to the U.S.—including Syria, Libya and Sudan—provided intelligence and assistance to the Americans. In Yemen, U.S. forces assassinated a suspected al-Qaeda leader with the government's tacit approval.[29] Security forces in Saudi Arabia—the homeland of 15 of the 19 hijackers—began restricting the activities of Islamic militants.[30]

Some Arab liberals renewed calls for electoral reform, suggesting that political oppression might have been partly responsible for inspiring the hijackers.[31] Even some members of the Arab ruling elite said democratic reforms could curtail extremism. "If people speak more freely and get more involved in the political process, you can really contain them and make them part of the process," said Saudi Prince Walid bin Talal.[32]

A combination of internal dissent and U.S. pressure inspired some Arab democratization efforts after Sept. 11. Reformers gained some ground in Egypt when Mubarak tentatively backed a democratization package put forward by his son, Gamal. Under pressure from the United States, Egypt also freed and later acquitted Egyptian-American democracy advocate Ibrahim, who had been imprisoned by Mubarak's government, some say in an effort to intimidate critics.

On the Arabian Peninsula, some of the monarchies took tentative steps toward electoral governance. Saudi Arabian officials promised municipal elections but did not set a firm date. In Bahrain, parliamentary elections in 2002 established strong support for opposition candidates, particularly Islamists. Qatar approved a constitution in 2003, opening the way for parliamentary elections later this year.

But other Arab states continue to struggle under the grip of authoritarian regimes. Bashar Assad has maintained strict control over Syria since the death of his father in 2000. Pro-democracy groups boycotted the 2002 elections convened by the military in Algeria.

Recent remarks by Jordan's King Abdullah II seem to represent a growing Arab interest in governmental reform. "We are at the beginning of a new stage in terms of democracy and freedom," said Abdullah at a September

Should the United States increase pressure on Arab countries to democratize?

YES
Adrian Karatnycky
Counselor, Senior Scholar, Freedom House

Written for *The CQ Researcher*, January 2004

Over the last 30 years, nearly 50 countries have established democratic governments rooted in the rule of law. Today, countries that provide basic freedoms represent nearly half the world's 192 states. Democracies can be found on all continents, among all races and creeds. They include prosperous and expanding economies as well as poor countries. Yet not one is part of the Arab world.

There are compelling reasons to try to end this Arab exceptionalism and for the United States to press Arab regimes to change by supporting non-violent democratic civic power.

First, it is in the U.S.'s national security interests to do so. It is no coincidence that much global terrorism originates in the least democratic part of the world. The absence of open discourse means ill-informed and misinformed populations fall under the sway of the disinformation of anti-liberal ideas. As a result, extremists prosper. In short, the war on terrorism cannot be won without waging a war of ideas against the extremist ideologies that fuel terror.

Second, Arabs are the main victims of tyrannical regimes and extremist movements, which wreak mayhem on ordinary people and suppress their basic rights. This is why recent polling data show that Arabs strongly favor government elected by and accountable to the people.

Opponents of a U.S. role in promoting democracy in the Arab world suggest that we are hated in that region and our pressure would be counterproductive. Yet, anti-Americanism is rampant because official media in Arab autocracies preach anti-U.S. messages. We are also disliked because over the years, the United States has been indifferent to the massive violations of the basic rights of Arabs.

Others argue that pressing for democracy would only destabilize the Arab world and empower Islamist extremists. Yet the opening of formerly closed societies to genuine freedom of the press, civic activism and electoral competition has served to moderate Islamist political movements—as last year's elections in Turkey showed.

No one says the promotion of democracy in the Arab world will be easy. It will require working with the region's democratic voices to develop a strong latticework of free and diverse media, political parties, civic organizations and think tanks.

But if we fail to exert constructive pressure, we will only help perpetuate the very political environments that produce the fanatics who threaten our well-being today.

NO
James Zogby
President, Arab American Institute

Written for *The CQ Researcher*, January 2004

Sadly, given our current foreign policy in the Middle East, I do not believe the United States can, at this time, make a meaningful and positive contribution to democratic transformation in the Arab world.

Positive changes are occurring in many Arab countries, largely in response to the evolving circumstances in those countries and independent of U.S. involvement. In some instances, the United States has served as an impediment to this process: As public opinion has turned against the United States, some Arab governments have become more defensive and resistive to democratic change.

The United States lacks credibility and legitimacy when it claims to support democracy and human rights. While Arabs view U.S. values—democracy, freedom and education—positively, they view U.S. Middle East policy so negatively that overall attitudes toward the United States drop into the single digits.

In other words, Arabs like our values, but do not believe that we have their best interests at heart, especially in Palestine—the central, defining issue of Arab attitudes. We are viewed as biased toward Israel and insensitive to Palestinians' needs and rights. This harms not only our overall standing in the region but also our friends' standings and our ability to function as a partner in the Arab world.

For too long, we have not appreciated Arab history. The current state of affairs for the Arab people is the culmination of more than 100 years of a loss of control. During the past century, some Arab areas were colonized by the West. Others were victims of imperial powers that occupied the region, created states out of whole cloth and implanted regimes.

The neo-conservative "idealism" that sees us establishing democracy in this region is, at best, counterproductive, and, at worst, damaging. Our unilateral occupation of Iraq and our behavior vis-à-vis the Palestinians has us viewed today as a continuation of the Western machinations of the last century. If we fail to understand this, we put ourselves at great risk.

If the United States were to do an about-face on Palestine—for example, by directly and dramatically challenging Israeli expansion on the West Bank—our relationship with the region would improve dramatically. It would significantly contribute to our peacemaking ability, as well as our ability to play a more constructive role as an agent for change in the region.

breakfast with human rights and democracy activists in Washington. "If we are successful, if we can get our act together, we can be an agent other Arabs can use."[33]

Some experts say Arab autocrats use Mideast resentment about U.S. support for Israel as a way to divert anger toward the slow rate of reform in their own countries. "The continuing conflict between Israel and Palestine gives [autocratic] regimes an excuse to deflect people's attention away from their own shortcomings," the Carnegie Endowment's Carothers says.

Others say Arab feelings of frustration over the Palestinian issue are more than an excuse. "People see the issue of Palestine as symbolic of their lives," says Zogby, of the Arab American Institute. "It's ever-present, it's very real and it's deeply felt. It's not a game that's being played on them."

The 2003 U.S.-led military campaign to depose Hussein thrust the issue of Arab democracy into the spotlight. While arguing the case for war at the United Nations in September 2002, President Bush said, "Liberty for the Iraqi people is a great moral cause and a great strategic goal." And after a quick and decisive military victory, the U.S. occupying authority established a 25-member Iraqi governing council and organized municipal elections in many Iraqi cities and towns.

But conflict between Iraq's majority-Shiite population and the minority Sunnis has marred efforts to form a popular government. A continued insurgency, thought to be the work of Baathist loyalists, has killed hundreds of American soldiers and further hindered U.S. efforts to democratize Iraq.

Nonetheless, President Bush in his November speech called for more democracy in the Middle East, noting that past U.S. efforts to turn a blind eye to the lack of freedom in the Middle East has made neither America nor the Middle East safer.[34]

But many Arab commentators frostily rejected Bush's calls for reform. "The fundamental problem remains that of Palestine and the scandalous U.S. bias in favor of Israel and against the Arabs, their interests and their aspirations," wrote Lebanese columnist Sahar Baasiri.[35]

CURRENT SITUATION

Casting Ballots

Sometime this year, Saudi Arabia will give its people their first opportunity to elect government officials in four decades. But the balloting will be for only half the nation's municipal councils—which have only limited power anyway.

"It's very symbolic," says Georgetown's Seznec. "It doesn't mean anything, especially in terms of democratization per se."

Still, the planned elections—not yet scheduled but likely to be held in the fall—represent a concession by the ruling House of Saud to the need for some form of public participation in a country beset by economic ills and shaken by violent protests, including a deadly terrorist bombing in Riyadh that left 17 people dead in November.

"There is a strong logic to expanding participation for these ruling families," says Michael Herb, an assistant professor of political science at Georgia State University. "It allows them to hear what their people actually have to say, to show a more liberal face to the outside world and to let off steam—all without the risk of actually losing power."

The Saudi elections—the first since similar balloting in the 1950s and '60s—come as more Arab states are allowing their citizens to vote for government officials. As in Saudi Arabia, however, the elections fall far short of full democracy. Women are barred from voting in most countries, political parties often are restricted or prohibited and the media are either government-controlled or tightly regulated.

As President Bush noted in his November speech, some of the strongest stirrings of democracy are in the smallest Arab states: the Persian Gulf emirates of Kuwait, Bahrain, Oman and Qatar. But Bush did not mention the limitations. In Kuwait, for example, voting for the national assembly is limited to less than one-sixth of the population, and political parties are banned. Western-style liberals fared badly in the most recent parliamentary elections in June 2003, winning only three of 50 seats.

Elsewhere, Bahrain became the first of the Gulf states to allow women to vote, but some opposition groups boycotted the 2002 parliamentary elections because of limits on the national assembly's power. As in Kuwait, Islamists led the balloting. Oman is now preparing for universal suffrage parliamentary elections in 2004 following balloting for an advisory council in October 2003. But Herb says that a ban on campaigning makes it impossible to evaluate the results. Qatar is also preparing for legislative elections sometime in 2004, but the constitution approved by voters in 2003 gives the parliament little power, he says.

Outside the Gulf, democracy is less advanced even when voting is allowed. Morocco and Jordan—two countries praised by Bush—held relatively free parliamentary elections in 2002 and 2003, respectively. But King Mohammed VI in Morocco and Jordan's Abdullah both have supreme power, including the right to dissolve parliament and appoint the prime minister and cabinet. Yemen has held free, universal-suffrage elections, but the elected House of Representatives has never exercised its power to initiate legislation.

In Tunisia, balloting for the presidency is highly orchestrated: President Zine el-Abidine Ben Ali claimed 99.4 percent of the vote in 1999 and won approval of a constitutional change in May 2003 to allow him to seek fourth and fifth five-year terms in 2004 and 2009. Syrian President Assad won 97 percent of the vote in a 2000 referendum after succeeding his father. In Algeria, the electoral process is viewed as highly flawed: All of the rivals to President Abdelaziz Bouteflika withdrew from the 1999 campaign, claiming fraud.

In other countries, elections are simply lacking. Libya's Muammar el-Qaddafi rules by decree, with no signs to date of following his recent moves out of international disgrace with an easing of his domestic powers. The seven ruling families of the United Arab Emirates choose a president and vice president every five years, with no popular elections or political parties. Lebanon holds elections, but Syria effectively controls the government after more than a decade of military occupation.

Democracy also lags in the handful of Arab-minority African countries—all preponderantly Muslim—that belong to the Arab League. Sudan is ravaged by a civil war between the Arab minority in the north and the insurgent black minority in the south, while a secession movement by northern clans racks Somalia. Djibouti—the only Arab League country rated as "free" by Freedom House—held successful multiparty elections in January. A four-party opposition alliance won slightly more than one-third of the vote.

In Egypt, meanwhile, talk of reform is increasing, but the outcome remains uncertain. In a signed editorial, Ibrahim Nafie, editor in chief of the semi-official *Al-Ahram*, praises the ruling National Democratic Party for having taken "big steps" toward reform, but he cautions against moving too fast. Rights advocate Abu Saada notes that the reform package does not call for competitive presidential elections.

In Saudi Arabia as well, experts caution against expecting too much in terms of reform. Former *Washington Post* Mideast correspondent Thomas Lippman, author of

Egyptian-American human rights activist Saad Eddin Ibrahim, a sociology professor at Cairo's American University, enters Egypt's highest court on Feb. 4, 2003, with his wife. After spending more than a year in jail, he was acquitted of tarnishing Egypt's image with his writings on democracy and human rights.

a new book on Saudi Arabia, notes that the country's "basic law"—adopted in 1993—locks in rule by the House of Saud.

"You can talk about the trappings of democracy, various democratic forms, ways in which certain forms of communication with the rulers might be structured to allow more public participation," Lippman says, "but you're not talking about democracy."[36]

Building Democracy?

The United States has what seems an unparalleled opportunity to advance democracy in the Arab world in Iraq, where an American administrator heads a U.S.-led military occupation in consultation with an Iraqi advisory council handpicked by the United States. But forging a stable government—much less a working democracy—is treacherous in a country with longstanding ethnic and religious factionalism and present-day anti-American insurgency.

Bush sees success as important, not only for domestic political reasons but also for the worldwide advance of democracy. "The establishment of a free Iraq at the heart of the Middle East," he said in his November speech, "will be a watershed event in the global democratic revolution."

As 2004 began, however, the administration found itself pressured by the leading cleric of Iraq's majority Shiite Muslims to allow direct elections sooner than envisioned under the U.S. timetable. The United States, citing the difficulties of holding elections, planned instead to hold caucuses around the country to select an interim legislature and executive that would assume responsibility for governing Iraq by June 30. But Grand Ayatollah Ali al-Sistani rejected the plan on Jan. 11, repeating demands he has made since November for direct elections before a U.S. transfer of power.

"The planned transitional assembly cannot represent the Iraqis in an ideal manner," Sistani said after meeting with a delegation of the U.S.-appointed governing council. Sistani described elections as "the ideal mechanism" and insisted balloting could be held in the near future "with an acceptable degree of credibility and transparency."[37]

"It's interesting to see Islamic clerics giving the United States lessons in how to conduct democracy,"

says the Carnegie Endowment's Carothers. "It's funny to see them pushing for early elections and the United States resisting."

Carothers acknowledges that national elections in Iraq would present "huge logistical obstacles," given the lack of security and destruction of Iraqi infrastructure in the invasion. But the dispute is more than procedural. Iraq's 15 million Shiites comprise about 60 percent of the population, but they were politically disadvantaged under Hussein, a Sunni Muslim. The Shiites hope to make political gains with early elections, while the Sunnis and the ethnic Kurds in northern Iraq fear early voting will weaken the influence they currently have with the American-led occupation.

The timing of elections is one of several contentious questions that U.S. Administrator L. Paul Bremer III is grappling with while trying to meet the accelerated timetable for transferring power. One issue—what to do with former members of the ruling Baath Party—appeared in January to be moving toward resolution. The 18-member Governing Council adopted new guidelines that give lower-level party members a better chance to appeal their dismissals or to apply for pensions than under the U.S. "de-Baathification" procedures. American officials were quoted as approving the shift.[38]

The United States appears less content with developments so far on the issue of the Kurds' status in a new Iraq. The Kurds—a non-Arab ethnic group comprising about 17 percent of Iraq's population—were essentially autonomous in Hussein's final 12 years in office following Iraq's defeat in the first Gulf War. They want to maintain their autonomy—or, more ambitiously, gain independence. While the United States supports some form of self-rule, it fears a fragmented Iraq or a weak central government.[39]

Other difficult issues loom in the drafting of the constitution, notably the role of religion. Shiites are widely seen as religiously conservative, the Sunnis and Kurds more liberal. But fears of a religious theocracy appear to have been eased with a formula drawn up by the Governing Council that declares Iraq to be a majority-Muslim community that protects minority rights and in which Islamic law is one—but not the only—source of legislation.[40]

The elections dispute, meanwhile, forced Bremer to return to Washington on Jan. 16 for conferences on how to salvage the administration's timetable. With thousands of Iraqis rallying in the streets demanding prompt

During voting in Qatar last April 29, Qataris approved the gas-rich monarchy's first written constitution, paving the way for parliamentary elections later this year.

elections—the largest protest since the U.S. occupation of Iraq last March—Bremer told reporters that the United States was willing to consider changing the planned method for selecting the interim government.

The administration and the Governing Council also asked the United Nations on Jan. 19 to help broker an agreement with Sistani on transition plans. U.N. Secretary-General Kofi Annan said on Jan. 27 he would send a team to Baghdad to determine whether early elections are feasible.

OUTLOOK

Slow Process

Talk of democracy is spreading in the Arab world, but Arab leaders are resisting outside pressure and insisting on definitions and timetables of their own choosing. The result seems all but certain to be slower and less thoroughgoing change than sought by pro-democracy advocates in and outside the Arab world.

Arab ambivalence can be seen in the proceedings of a recent pro-democracy conference, hosted by Yemen and cosponsored by the European Union (EU) and the U.N. Development Program.[41] The January conference in the Yemeni capital of Sanaa drew 600 delegates from 40 countries, including government representatives and democracy activists from most Arab states.

The conference ended with adoption of a declaration embracing the major tenets of so-called Western-style democracy—from elective legislatures and independent judiciaries to fair-trial guarantees and protection of women's rights.

"Democracy is the choice of the modern age for all people of the world and the rescue ship for political regimes," Yemeni President Ali Abdulla Saleh said as he opened the conference.

But Amr Moussa, secretary-general of the Arab League, said democracy should be viewed "as a process, not a decision imposed by others," a point echoed by U.N. Secretary-General Annan. Democracy, Annan told the conference, "cannot be imposed from the outside."

Human rights advocates both in and outside the Arab world discern mounting political pressures for change from the social and economic gaps between Arab countries and the rest of the world. On a variety of socioeconomic measures, Arab states lag behind developing countries in other parts of the world, as well as the United States and other industrialized nations.

Demographics add to the pressure. Population growth rates in all but one of the Arab League states exceed the worldwide average of 1.4 percent per year. Population increases can be "an engine of material development," notes the 2002 Arab human rights report, if other factors are conducive to economic growth—but a "force for immiserization" if not.[42]

Arab leaders say political changes are necessary to respond to the discontent bred by what others more bluntly describe as deteriorating socioeconomic conditions. "There is a great sense in the Arab world about the necessity of having a new social pact," the Arab League's Hitti says. "Democracy is part and parcel of this process."

Still, human rights advocates are generally cautious, at best, in predicting the pace of democratization. "I would be very surprised to see much genuine movement toward democracy in the next five years," says the Carnegie Endowment's Carothers. "The question is whether we can help foster a trend in the next five years. That would be a realistic goal."

Similarly, the Heritage Foundation's Phillips expects little change over the next few years.

Others are somewhat more optimistic. "You've got a little bit of a trend developing," Freedom House's Karatnycky says. He sees prospects for more liberalization in the gulf countries and some larger states, such as Jordan and Morocco. "There's more of a chance for a liberal trend than a retrenchment or some new dark age of anti-liberal ideologies or more repressive regimes," he concludes.

The University of Westminster's El-Affendi also sounds optimistic. "The undemocratic forces are a spent force," he says. "The desire for democracy is very widespread, and the disillusionment with undemocratic governments is at a very high level, and increasing at all times."

El-Affendi says support for democratization from the United States and the European Union is helpful. Others disagree. U.S. pressure, Hitti says, "might fire back." Zogby of the Arab American Institute says American influence has fallen because of increasingly unfavorable public opinion about America due to the invasion of Iraq, the stalemate in the Arab-Israeli peace process and the mistreatment of people of Muslim or Arab backgrounds in the U.S. war on terror.[43]

Apart from government policies, however, El-Affendi says broader global changes—including the Arab peoples' increased exposure to the world beyond—impel democratic advances in the long run.

"The trend is moving in this direction," he says. "It's now very difficult for any ruler in the Muslim world to just hope that he's going to stay in power forever without being responsive to the people. It's just not going to work."

NOTES

1. See Saad Eddin Ibrahim, "A Dissident Asks: Can Bush Turn Words Into Action?" *The Washington Post*, Nov. 23, 2003, p. A23. The article and other background can be found on the Web site of the Ibn Khaldun Center: www.democracy-egypt.org.

2. See "Flimsy on Facts," *Al Ahram Weekly*, Nov. 27, 2003 (http://weekly.ahram.org.eg). *Al Ahram Weekly* is an English-language version of the Arabic-language daily *Al Ahram*.

3. Freedom House, "Freedom in the World 2004" (www.freedomhouse.org).

4. United Nations Development Programme/Arab Fund for Economic and Social Development, "Arab Human Development Report 2002," p. 2.

5. For coverage, see David E. Sanger, "Bush Asks Lands in Mideast to Try Democratic Ways," *The New York Times*, Nov. 7, 2003, p. A1; Dana Milbank and Mike Allen, "Bush Urges Commitment to Transform Mideast," *The Washington Post*, Nov. 7, 2003, p. A1.

6. For background, see David Masci, "Rebuilding Iraq," *The CQ Researcher*, July 25, 2003, pp. 625-648 and David Masci, "Confronting Iraq," *The CQ Researcher*, Oct. 4, 2002, pp. 793-816.

7. Quoted in Glenn Frankel, "Egypt Muzzles Calls for Democracy," *The Washington Post*, Jan. 6, 2004, p. A1.

8. United Nations Development Programme, *op. cit.*, p. 8.

9. *Ibid.*, p. 9.

10. Country profile in "Freedom in the World 2003," www.freedomhouse.org.

11. United Nations Development Programme, *op. cit.*, pp. 4-6.

12. Michael Ross, "Does Oil Hinder Democracy?" *World Politics*, Vol. 53 (April 2001), pp. 336-337.

13. United Nations Development Programme, *op. cit.*, p. 4.

14. For background, see David Masci, "Prospects for Middle East Peace," *The CQ Researcher*, Aug. 30, 2002, pp. 673-696, and David Masci, "Israel at 50," *The CQ Researcher*, March 6, 1998, pp. 193-215.

15. See Glenn Kessler and Robin Wright, "Realities Overtake Arab Democracy Drive," *The Washington Post*, Dec. 3, 2003, p. A22.

16. See Daniel Brumberg, "Bush Policy or Bush Philosophy," *The Washington Post*, Nov. 16, 2003, p. B3.

17. Background drawn from William Cleveland, *A History of the Modern Middle East* (2000) and Albert Hourani, *A History of the Arab Peoples* (1992).

18. Cleveland, *op. cit.*, p. 36.

19. Bernard Lewis, *The Middle East* (1995), p. 147.

20. Hourani, *op. cit.*, pp. 315-323.

21. Lewis, *op. cit.*, p. 355.

22. Cleveland, *op. cit.*, p. 170.

23. Cleveland, *op. cit.*, p. 261.

24. Shibley Telhami, *The Stakes* (2004), p. 161.

25. For background, see Mary H. Cooper, "Foreign Aid After Sept. 11," *The CQ Researcher*, April 26, 2002, pp. 361-392, and Masci, "Prospects for Mideast Peace," *op. cit.*

26. For background, see Mary H. Cooper, "Oil Diplomacy," *The CQ Researcher*, Jan. 24, 2003, pp. 49-62.

27. For background, see David Masci and Kenneth Jost, "War on Terrorism," *The CQ Researcher*, Oct. 12, 2001, pp. 817-848.

28. See Mary H. Cooper, "Hating America," *The CQ Researcher*, Nov. 23 2001, pp. 969-992.

29. David Johnston and David Sanger, "Fatal Strike in Yemen Was Based on Rules Set Out by Bush," *The New York Times*, Nov. 6, 2002, p. A16.

30. Douglas Jehl, "Holy War Lured Saudis As Rulers Looked Away," *The New York Times*, Dec. 27, 2001, p. A1.

31. *Ibid.*

32. Douglas Jehl, "A Saudi Prince With an Unconventional Idea: Elections," *The New York Times*, Nov. 28, 2001, p. A3.

33. Jackson Diehl, "Jordan's Democracy Option," *The Washington Post*, Sept. 21, 2003, p. B7.

34. Sanger, *op. cit.*

35. Neil MacFarquhar, "Mideast View: Bush Spoke More to U.S. Than to Us," *The New York Times*, Nov. 8, 2003, p. A9.

36. See Thomas W. Lippman, *Inside the Mirage: America's Fragile Partnership with Saudi Arabia* (2004).

37. Quoted in Daniel Williams, "Top Shiite Cleric Hardens Call for Early Iraqi Vote," *The Washington Post*, Jan. 12, 2004, p. A12. See also Edward Wong, "Direct Election of Iraq Assembly Pushed by Cleric," *The New York Times*, Jan. 12, 2004, p. A1; Steven R. Weisman, "Bush Team Revising Planning for Iraqi Self-Rule," *The New York Times*, Jan. 13, 2004, p. A1.

38. See Pamela Constable, "Iraqis Revise Policy on Ex-Baath Members," *The Washington Post*, Jan. 12, 2004, p. A12.

39. Robin Wright, "Kurds' Wariness Frustrates U.S. Efforts," *The Washington Post*, Jan. 9, 2004, p. A13.

40. *Ibid.*

41. Account drawn from John R. Bradley, "Arab Leaders See Democracy Ascendant," *The Washington Times*, Jan. 13, 2004, p. A13. A summary of the conference declaration can be found on the Ibn Khaldun Center's Web site: www.democracy-egypt.org.eg.

42. United Nations Development Programme, *op. cit.*, pp. 37-38.

43. For background, see Kenneth Jost, "Civil Liberties Debates," *The CQ Researcher*, Oct. 24, 2003, pp. 893-916.

BIBLIOGRAPHY

Books

Brynen, Rex, Baghat Kornay and Paul Noble, *Political Liberalization and Democratization in the Arab World: Theoretical Perspectives* (Vol. 1), Lynne Rienner, 1996; Brynen, Rex, Baghat Kornay and Paul Noble, *Political Liberalization and Democratization in the Arab World: Comparative Experiences* (Vol. 2), Lynne Rienner, 1998.

Various experts provide an overview of democratization in the region (vol. 1) and the status of democratization in 10 specific countries (vol. 2). Brynen and Noble are McGill University professors; Kornay is now at the American University in Cairo.

Cleveland, William L., *A History of the Modern Middle East* (2d ed.), Westview Press, 2000 (1st edition, 1994).
A professor of Arab political history at Simon Fraser University in Vancouver traces the history of the Middle East, from the rise of Islam through the radical Islamist movements.

Diamond, Larry, Marc F. Plattner and Daniel Brumberg (eds.), *Islam and Democracy in the Middle East*, Johns Hopkins University Press, 2003.
An anthology of *Journal of Democracy* articles by U.S. and Middle Eastern experts examines the status of democratization in the Mideast and the relationship between Islam and democracy.

Esposito, John L., and John O. Voll, *Islam and Democracy*, Oxford University Press, 1996.
The director (Esposito) and assistant director (Voll) of Georgetown University's Center for Muslim-Christian Understanding examine the "heritage and global context" of Islam and democracy, along with the status of democratization in major Islamic countries.

Humphreys, R. Stephen, *Between Memory and Desire: The Middle East in a Troubled Age*, University of California Press, 1999.
A professor of Islamic and Middle Eastern history at the University of California, Santa Barbara, focuses on four basic conditions in the Middle East: economic stagnation, weakness in the international arena, political instability and ideological confusion.

Lewis, Bernard, *What Went Wrong? Western Impact and Middle Eastern Response*, Oxford University Press, 2002 (reissued by Perennial, 2003, with subtitle *The Clash Between Islam and Modernity in the Middle East*).
A distinguished U.S. historian provides a trenchant critique of the Islamic world's failure to modernize. For a comprehensive history of the region, see *The Middle East: A Brief History of the Last 2,000 Years* (Touchstone, 1995).

Magnarella, Paul J. (ed.), *Middle East and North Africa: Governance, Democratization, Human Rights*, Ashgate, 1999.
Experts examine the status of democratization in major Arab countries, Turkey, Israel and the West Bank and Gaza Strip. Magnarella is a professor of anthropology at the University of Florida.

Telhami, Shelby, *The Stakes: America and the Middle East—The Consequences of Power and the Choice for Peace*, Westview Press, 2002.
A professor of government at the University of Maryland and a senior fellow at the Brookings Institution examines public opinion in the Middle East toward the United States and U.S. policy in the Middle East.

Articles

Anderson, Lisa, "Arab Democracy: Dismal Prospects," *World Policy Journal*, Vol. 18, No. 3 (fall 2001), p. 53.
The dean of Columbia University's School of International and Public Affairs critically examines prospects for Arab democracy. For a more favorable assessment by the Arab League's representative to the U.S., see Hussein A. Hassouna, "Arab Democracy: The Hope," *ibid.*, p. 47.

Reports and Studies

Ottaway, Marina, *et al.*, "Democratic Mirage in the Middle East," Carnegie Endowment for International Peace, October 2002.
A policy brief forecasts a "long, hard, and slow" path to democratization in the Middle East.

United Nations Development Programme, Arab Fund for Economic and Social Development, "Arab Human Development Report 2002: Creating Opportunities for Future Generations," 2002.
Human development in Arab countries is hampered by "deficits in popular freedoms and in the quality of Arab governance institutions," say the authors. A second report, "Arab Human Development Report 2003: Building a Knowledge Society," focuses on education, communication and technology. Available at www.un.org/publications or www.miftah.org.

For More Information

Arab American Institute, 1600 K St. N.W., Suite 601, Washington, DC 20006; (202) 429-9210; www.aaiusa.org.

Arab Information Center/Arab League, 1100 17th St., N.W., Washington, DC 20036; (202) 265-3210; www.arableagueonline.org.

Carnegie Endowment for International Peace, 1779 Massachusetts Ave. N.W., Washington DC 20036-2103; (202) 483-7600; www.ceip.org.

Center for the Study of Islam and Democracy, 1050 Connecticut Ave., N.W., Suite 1000, Washington, DC 20036; (202) 772-2022; www.islam-democracy.org.

Freedom House, 120 Wall St., 26th floor, New York, NY 10005; (212) 514-8040; www.freedomhouse.org.

Heritage Foundation, 214 Massachusetts Ave., N.E., Washington, DC 20002-4999; (202) 546-4400; www.heritage.org.

Human Rights Watch, 350 Fifth Ave. 34th floor, New York, NY 10118-3299; (212) 290-4700; www.hrw.org; Washington office: 1630 Connecticut Ave., N.W., Suite 500, Washington, DC 20009; (202) 612-4321.

National Endowment for Democracy, 1101 15th St., N.W., Suite 700, Washington, DC 20005; (202) 293-9072; www.ned.org.

10

Trouble in
South America

David Masci

A funeral procession for 17 peasants reportedly killed by the Revolutionary Armed Forces of Colombia (FARC) wends through San Carlos on Jan. 19, 2003. The Bush administration is seeking $537 million from Congress for Colombia this year, partly to help protect an oil pipeline from attacks by the guerrillas. Political turmoil in much of South America has some experts worried about the survival of democratic gains made in the 1980s and '90s.

From *The CQ Researcher*,
March 14, 2003.

L a Paz means "peace" in Spanish, but Bolivia's capital was anything but peaceful on Feb. 12, when thousands of angry citizens marched to the center of the city. At one point during the ensuing melee, striking police officers and army troops sent to keep order fired at each other.

By the next day, 29 people were dead, seven government ministries had been ransacked, scores of businesses looted and large downtown sections of the city set ablaze. Protesters even rushed the presidential palace, forcing President Gonzalo Sánchez de Lozada to make his escape by hiding in an ambulance.

The protests were sparked by Sanchez's decision, later rescinded, to raise taxes and cut government spending in order to secure International Monetary Fund (IMF) loans. Aid is desperately needed in the poor Andean nation, where nearly three-quarters of the 8 million people live at or below the poverty line.

Economic and political turmoil has wracked much of South America in recent years, sending protesters into the streets in Argentina, Peru and Venezuela, often with violent results.

"There's a sour mood throughout much of the continent right now," says Michael Shifter, a professor of Latin American studies at Georgetown University and vice president of Inter-American Dialogue, a Washington think tank. "There's a sense that the economic and political models they'd been relying on for years are not working."

Venezuela is perhaps the best example of such failure. President Hugo Chavez—whose 1999 election reflected voter dissatisfaction with the existing government—has responded to massive strikes with dictatorial tactics, such as arresting opponents. (*See sidebar, p. 218.*)

207

Democratic Nations, Elected Leaders

South America's remaining dictatorships evolved into democracies in the last two decades, including those in Brazil, Argentina, Paraguay and Chile. Today, every leader on the continent has either been elected by direct popular vote or by a parliament or other elected body. Brazil, the continent's largest and most populous nation, recently elected the popular Luiz Inácio Lula da Silva — widely known as Lula.

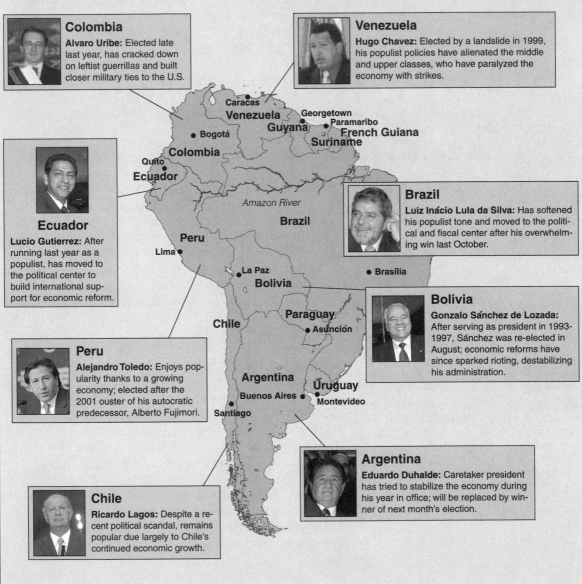

Colombia
Alvaro Uribe: Elected late last year, has cracked down on leftist guerrillas and built closer military ties to the U.S.

Venezuela
Hugo Chavez: Elected by a landslide in 1999, his populist policies have alienated the middle and upper classes, who have paralyzed the economy with strikes.

Ecuador
Lucio Gutierrez: After running last year as a populist, has moved to the political center to build international support for economic reform.

Brazil
Luiz Inácio Lula da Silva: Has softened his populist tone and moved to the political and fiscal center after his overwhelming win last October.

Peru
Alejandro Toledo: Enjoys popularity thanks to a growing economy; elected after the 2001 ouster of his autocratic predecessor, Alberto Fujimori.

Bolivia
Gonzalo Sánchez de Lozada: After serving as president in 1993-1997, Sánchez was re-elected in August; economic reforms have since sparked rioting, destabilizing his administration.

Chile
Ricardo Lagos: Despite a recent political scandal, remains popular due largely to Chile's continued economic growth.

Argentina
Eduardo Duhalde: Caretaker president has tried to stabilize the economy during his year in office; will be replaced by winner of next month's election.

Map labels: Caracas, Venezuela, Georgetown, Paramaribo, French Guiana, Guyana, Suriname, Bogotá, Colombia, Quito, Ecuador, Amazon River, Brazil, Peru, Lima, La Paz, Bolivia, Brasília, Paraguay, Asunción, Chile, Argentina, Uruguay, Buenos Aires, Montevideo, Santiago

Source: Freedom House, 2000, "Freedom in the World, 1999-2000"

Brazil and Argentina Dominate South America's Economy

South America encompasses 13 countries totaling more than 350 million people. Portuguese is spoken in the largest country, Brazil. Most of the rest speak Spanish. About 80 percent of South Americans are Roman Catholic, but in recent years evangelical Protestants have converted millions.

Economic Data, 2002

Country	Population	Gross Domestic Product (GDP)*	Per capita GDP*	Inflation	Main industries
Argentina	37.8 million	$382 billion	$10,202	41.0%	Food processing, motor vehicles, textiles, petrochemicals
Bolivia	8.4 million	$21.4 billion	$2,600	2.5	Mining, tobacco, handicrafts
Brazil	176.0 million	$1.3 trillion	$7,500	12.5	Aircraft, motor vehicles, steel, cement
Colombia	41.0 million	$255 billion	$6,300	7.0	Textiles, food processing, chemicals
Chile	15.5 million	$153 billion	$10,000	2.5	Mining, steel, cement
Ecuador	13.4 million	$48.6 billion	$3,997	12.5	Timber, petroleum, plastics
French Guiana	182,333	$1 billion	$6,000	2.5	Construction, shrimp processing, timber
Guyana	698,209	$2.5 billion	$3,600	6.0	Sugar, textiles, mining
Paraguay	5.9 million	$26.2 billion	$4,600	7.2	Sugar, cement, timber
Peru	27.9 million	$132 billion	$4,800	1.5	Mining, oil, steel, food processing
Suriname	436,491	$1.5 billion	$3,500	5.9	Mining, timber, food processing
Uruguay	3.4 million	$31 billion	$9,200	3.6	Food processing, heavy equipment, chemicals
Venezuela	24.3 million	$146.2 billion	$6,100	31.2	Petroleum, mining, motor vehicles

* All GDP and per capita GDP numbers are calculated in purchasing power parity, or the amount of goods and services purchasable in local currency.

Sources: CIA World Book, 2002; news reports (for inflation)

In Argentina, Bolivia and other countries, economic troubles have discredited political elites and traditional political parties to the point that some South America-watchers fear for the survival of democracy on the continent. Although few believe South America will return to the military dictatorships of the 1970s, some feel that new populist leaders like Chavez may subvert the democratic gains of the 1980s and '90s just to stay in power.[1]

Much of the trouble stems from the troubled world economy, which has been in a slump since the turn of the millennium. The region's gross domestic product (GDP) shrank by more than 1 percent last year, and a similar drop is expected this year, according to Shifter and others.

But some analysts also blame the big multilateral lending institutions, in particular the IMF, for many of the continent's woes. The IMF and the World Bank lend tens of billions each year to South American nations, giving the banks tremendous influence over economic policy.

Brazil's Rags-to-Riches President

His life story sounds like a rags-to-riches Hollywood movie: Born into abject poverty, Brazil's Luiz Inácio Lula da Silva—known simply as Lula—has risen from shining shoes to the nation's highest office.

The miracle of Lula's incredible success is not lost on his fellow citizens, who love him with a passion usually reserved for religious leaders or rock stars. Even before he was officially declared the winner of the country's presidential election on Oct. 27, the streets of Brazil's largest city, São Paulo, were crowded with pro-Lula revelers.

Lula did not disappoint his supporters, winning more than 60 percent of the vote against his government-supported opponent. Indeed, the landslide marked another chapter in his remarkable life: The triumph came after four previous unsuccessful runs for the presidency.

"This is a historic victory because, finally, it represents the will of the people," said Gabriel Brasileiro, a São Paulo social worker. "People want wealth distributed more fairly, and I'm sure Lula will adopt a more social stance right from the start."[1]

But restoring the country's sagging economy while eliminating its crushing poverty will be no easy task for the 56-year-old former factory worker.

Born the son of impoverished farm workers, he dropped out of school after the fifth grade to help support his family. For the next decade, Lula did factory work, often as a lathe operator.

[1] Quoted in Tony Smith, "Music and Victory in the Streets of Brazil," *The New York Times*, Oct. 27, 2002, p. A6.

At 22, Lula joined a union and quickly became a labor activist. He was elected president of a metalworkers' union when he was 30, and by 1980 he had come to national attention after leading several successful strikes. The following year, he formed the Workers Party, bringing together several leftist groups under one banner.

In 1985, Brazil's military dictatorship ended, and Lula ran for president. He lost the first election, as well as the next three, but on each try his share of the vote rose. Still, few believed he would ever get more than 35 or 40 percent of the vote because of his leftist ideology.

Indeed, in his first four campaigns, Lula unabashedly espoused large increases in social spending while criticizing big business, free trade, the International Monetary Fund (IMF) and the United States. He even dressed like the workingman that he was, in casual clothes instead of the business suits most political leaders wear.

For the 2002 election campaign though, Lula changed his stripes—literally. In addition to donning pinstripe suits, candidate Lula moderated his positions, sounding less like the fiery populist of yore and more like the kind of calm, left-of-center democrat one might find in Europe. During the campaign, he reversed his earlier opposition to the proposed Free Trade Area of the Americas and even supported the strict conditions for a new $30 billion IMF loan negotiated by then-President Fernando Henrique Cardoso.

The move won him new support from the country's political center, which had feared the former union leader would lead Brazil to economic ruin. Still, bankers and business leaders were less convinced, leading to a 35 percent drop in the value of the country's currency, the real, and a drop in

Critics of the big lenders say they impose "a one-size-fits-all" economic regimen—including tight monetary policies, privatization and trade liberalization—that does much more harm than good in countries with fragile economies. They point to Argentina, where they say IMF policies helped cause and exacerbate a fiscal crisis of immense proportions.

But IMF officials say the fund tailors its advice to fit each country's situation. "One-size-fits-all is a big myth," says Tom Dawson, chief spokesman for the IMF. "We're always accused of not caring what

[other countries] think, but we look closely at every individual country and try to help them fashion policies to suit their needs." Other experts blame the region's problems on government corruption and inefficiency.

The United States, meanwhile, is hoping to jump-start the region's economies with the proposed Free Trade Area of the Americas (FTAA) treaty—which would encompass all of North and South America plus most of the Caribbean. The U.S. proposal for the FTAA, unveiled in February by U.S. Trade Representative

Brazil's stock market as it became clear Lula would win.

But Lula has surprised the doubters so far. He has stayed within budgetary constraints imposed by the IMF deal and journeyed to Washington even before he was inaugurated to discuss free trade with President Bush. He also picked an economic team known for its commitment to fiscal responsibility. Consequently, the stock market has fully recovered and the *real* has regained about half its lost ground.

At the same time, the new president has not forgotten his leftist supporters, announcing a new campaign, Zero Hunger, to help Brazil's poorest. The food-assistance proposal would spend nearly $1.5 billion over the next four years to help 46 million of the country's 176 million citizens.

"He's really trying to take the middle road of economic and fiscal stability on one side and poverty reduction on the other," says Michael Shifter, vice president for policy at Inter-American Dialogue, a Washington think tank.

So far, the balancing act seems to be working, Shifter and others say. Certainly everywhere the new president goes, crowds cheer him.

Luiz Inácio Lula da Silva, Brazil's populist president in pinstripes, moderated his leftist positions—and his attire—after his victory.

But huge challenges remain. Brazil faces a crippling public debt of more than a half-trillion dollars—about 42 percent of the country's $1.2 trillion gross domestic product (GDP). At 12 percent, inflation is also creeping up too high, economists say. In addition, the public pension system is running huge deficits, and the tax system is not taking in enough revenue.

Lula has pledged to reform pensions and taxes, but that may be difficult given that his Workers Party has only 18 percent of the seats in parliament. He also wants Brazil's economy to grow at 5 percent this year, (more than twice last year's increase)—a tall order considering the sputtering global economy.

Still, Brazil's new president has been underestimated his whole life. And supporters and foes alike acknowledge his unique ability to work with different groups.

"All his political life, he's been a good negotiator," says John Welch, chief Latin American economist at the New York branch of WestLB, a German bank. "Maybe he can pull this one off, too."

Robert Zoellick, would phase out all tariffs for treaty signatories between 2005 and 2015.

Zoellick and other free-trade advocates contend that eliminating trade barriers will promote long-term growth in South America, as countries gain greater access to the giant U.S. market. But some in the region worry that large American multinational corporations will use free trade to overwhelm smaller South American businesses and despoil the continent's environment—especially the vast Amazon basin, whose rain forests are being threatened by loggers and agricultural interests.

America's other major regional policy initiative is "Plan Colombia"—a multiyear program to provide military assistance to the Colombian government. Colombia is in the grip of a brutal, decades-long, civil war fueled by drug money, involving both left-wing guerrillas and right-wing paramilitary soldiers. In recent years, U.S. aid has shifted its focus from just the narcotics trade to countering the guerrillas as well.

Human rights activists and others criticize the new aid, slated to be more than $500 million this year, because the Colombian army is closely linked to the paramilitaries, who—like the guerrillas—have been charged with committing atrocities against civilians. "The concern is that the Colombian military has links to paramilitaries who have committed atrocities, and that those involved at the highest level have not been brought to justice," said Sen. Patrick J. Leahy, D-Vt. "Neither the Colombian military leadership nor the [Colombian] attorney general has shown the will to end the impunity."[2]

Supporters counter that to bring peace to Colombia the army must be strong enough to rein in both sides and restore order.

Some experts are cautiously optimistic that Colombia, along with the continent's other nations, will overcome its problems in the coming decades. Indeed, some optimists say that with its rich resources and new democratic traditions, South America will become a stable and prosperous region over the next 20 years.

"There's no doubt that South America has great untapped potential," says John Williamson, a senior fellow at the Institute for International Economics, a think tank in Washington.

Even in the here and now, the news is not all bad. Brazil's popular, new president is grappling valiantly with the nation's crippling public debt and the social problems that have created its large underclass. And in Chile, democracy and the economy have flourished since military dictator Gen. Augusto Pinochet stepped down nearly 15 years ago.

As South America-watchers look to the future, here are some of the questions they are asking about the continent today:

Are IMF policies partly responsible for South America's current economic woes?

According to a recent World Bank report, South America's GDP will shrink by 1.1 percent this year—its worst performance in 20 years.[3] The decline is driven not only by the limping world economy but also by Argentina's fiscal collapse and economic problems in Brazil, Venezuela and other nations on the continent (*see p. 224*).

But some economists say the IMF bears some of the responsibility for these problems, much more than other international lenders like the poverty-fighting World Bank and much smaller Inter-American Development Bank. "When you look at South America as a whole, the [fund] really has mishandled things," says Sarah Anderson,

director of the Global Economy Project at the Institute for Policy Studies, a Washington think tank. "Especially in a place like Argentina, where they forced an austerity program on them as their economy was collapsing, you see that they've often been a negative force in many places."

During the 1990s, the IMF and other international financial institutions pushed most of South America to adopt the so-called Washington Consensus—a set of policies aimed at liberalizing economies by removing trade barriers, privatizing state-owned industries and opening financial markets to foreign capital.

Left-leaning critics of the IMF like Anderson say the measures exposed South America's fragile economies to often-destructive forces that have usually fallen hardest on the poor and middle class. "Basically, there has been this experiment where they've forced these countries to implement tight fiscal policies and open trade and monetary policies regardless of what was happening on the ground, and it has failed," says Mark Weisbrot, co-director of the Center for Economic Policy Research, a Washington think tank.

"During the 20 years between 1960 and 1980, South America's economy grew 75 percent," he says. "In the next 20 years, between 1980 and 2000, when they were supposedly doing the right thing according to the IMF, their economies grew a total of 6 or 7 percent."

Weisbrot says the IMF pushed a one-size-fits-all policy that didn't take into account individual countries or their economic situations at the time. "So you had countries cutting [government] spending even though they were in a recession," he says. "That's usually disastrous, which is why we in the United States don't do it. But that's what's happening right now in Argentina."

Such criticism is "nonsense," says IMF spokesman Dawson. "The Washington Consensus calls for flexible currency-exchange rates, and yet when Argentina told the fund that they were going to have a fixed rate, we accepted it as the right policy," he says. "So much for one-size-fits-all. Our policies are based on a nuanced, case-by-case analysis."

And, despite economic turmoil in many South American countries, Washington Consensus policies have generally had positive results, Dawson claims. For instance, he says, the IMF, through loans and advice, has helped set Chile on a stable course. "And they've paid off their IMF loans ahead of schedule."

A different example of an IMF success is its push for South American countries to privatize industries. "Of course, there have been setbacks, but in general, the privatized companies lowered prices and offered better service to consumers, and that's good," says Williamson, whose ideas inspired the Washington Consensus.

Defenders of the multilateral lending institutions say South America's troubles are largely homegrown. "They're not doing the things good governments should do to make their economies grow," says Julia E. Sweig, a senior fellow at the Council on Foreign Relations, a New York City think tank. "For instance, they don't have adequate tax systems and often use VAT [value-added taxes] taxes—which are very regressive—to raise revenue." In addition, South American governments tend to spend beyond their means and waste much of their revenue on inefficiency and corruption, she says.

Indeed, IMF Research Director Kenneth Rogoff argues, countries that have been spending beyond their means often criticize the fund when it forces them to confront the obvious: that government budgets must be more in line with revenues. "Blaming the fund for the reality that every country must confront its budget constraints is like blaming the fund for gravity."[4]

But some conservative critics of the international funding institutions blame the continent's problems on the lenders' unwillingness to use their leverage to force South America's countries to make needed systemic changes.

"The IMF has turned into a savings and loan for these countries by perpetually providing money for them no matter what they do," says Stephen Johnson, a senior fellow at the Heritage Foundation. As a result, he says, "the people who run these countries think they can live off the IMF's largess forever, without ever having to really work out their problems. Until the [IMF] is willing to really hold their feet to the fire and cut them off, you won't see South America undertaking the real reforms that they need."

Ian Vasquez, director of the Project for Global Economic Liberty at the libertarian Cato Institute, agrees. The IMF "basically made a bad situation worse by encouraging borrowing and undisciplined spending," he says, pointing to its recent loan to tottering Argentina.

"They stopped lending to Argentina for a year, and I thought maybe they'd turned a corner," he says. "But they blew it when they gave [Argentina] another loan just a year later in spite of the fact that the Argentines hadn't really done anything to warrant more money."

Is South America in danger of retreating from the democratic gains made since the early 1980s?

South America's successful shift to democratic rule over the past two decades has been widely celebrated. Beginning in the early 1980s, several of the continent's largest and most important countries—among them Argentina, Brazil and Chile—replaced military rulers with democratically elected leaders and legislatures.

But in the last two years, severe political turmoil in several Latin democracies has thrown those democratic gains into question. In Argentina, five presidents came and went in a tumultuous two-week period at the end of 2001. The leaders of Peru and Ecuador have been forced from office, and in Venezuela, President Chavez's heavy-handed tactics have prompted his political opponents to respond in kind.

Meanwhile, public support for democracy in South America is faltering. In Brazil, Colombia, Paraguay and Chile, fewer than half the respondents to a 2002 poll favored democracy over other forms of government.[5]

Some observers say South American democracies have been hurt by their new, largely leftist leaders, who they say used the ballot box to seize power and then showed little respect for democratic institutions once in office. "There is no doubt South American democracy is in crisis," says Angel Rabasa, a senior policy analyst at the Rand Corporation, a think tank in Palo Alto, Calif. "You have a trend away from real democratic institutions and toward leftist, authoritarian leaders."

Chavez is widely seen as this group's chief offender. Shortly after his election, he convened a constituent assembly that replaced the elected Congress and reshuffled the Supreme Court. Indeed, says Constantine Menges, a senior fellow at the conservative Hudson Institute, "Chavez has gone further than that, creating paramilitary groups to intimidate and even shoot his opponents." Recently, Chavez arrested political opponents who organized a crippling, nationwide strike late last year.

But Chavez' critics have used undemocratic means to push their agenda as well. Last April, business leaders and some military units briefly deposed Chavez in a coup, only to see him returned to power days later by other elements in the armed forces.

Elsewhere, the situation is little better, according to Menges and Rabasa. They point to Argentina, where a revolving-door presidency has damaged the office to the point that the winner of the May presidential election probably will be severely weakened, possibly creating a power vacuum. In Ecuador, they note, the president is a populist former army officer who was elected after a coup he helped engineer. The governments of Bolivia and Peru also are shaky, with the presidents of both countries in danger of being deposed.

Pundits link the instability to recent economic troubles. "The failure of market-oriented reforms in places like Ecuador and Argentina has led to the [negative] reaction against the governing institutions that are responsible," Rabasa says. "They turn to populists like Chavez."

But others point out that most South American countries, even those in economic trouble, still enjoy robust democratic systems. "In most places they're not getting the guns out, the military is staying in its barracks and they're resolving their differences peacefully with elections," says the Council on Foreign Relations' Sweig.

"With the exception of Chavez in Venezuela, I don't think they're backtracking," agrees Peter Hakim, president of Inter-American Dialogue. "Although many people have lost confidence in their institutions and their leaders, democracy is still the rule."

Hakim disagrees with the notion that the continent is turning toward leftist, populist, authoritarian leaders like Chavez. In Brazil, he points out, newly elected President Luiz Inácio Lula da Silva, widely known as Lula, has forsaken his populist roots to become a pragmatic centrist. (*See sidebar, p. 210.*) "The real story in Brazil isn't of a leftwing firebrand, but of a person who has become much more moderate in power," Hakim says. "Since he was elected, he hasn't tried to tear down his predecessor's more conservative policies, but has accepted them and even built on them."

For instance, Lula has adopted the previous administration's policy of creating government surpluses each year to pay down Brazil's large foreign debt, Hakim points out. "This is very hard for him because it constrains his ability to spend money and to enact new programs," he says. "But he's done it, and he's even proposed running higher surpluses in order to pay down more debt."

In Ecuador, another recently elected populist, Lucio Gutierrez, also has moved toward the political and economic center, winning plaudits from the IMF and the

Bush administration for his fiscal belt-tightening and other reforms.

Moreover, optimists say, most South Americans want to have nothing to do with the kind of populism that has wracked Venezuela. "Chavez scares a lot of people, and they want to avoid becoming anything like what Venezuela has become," says Johnson of the Heritage Foundation. "For example, what's happened in Venezuela has had an effect on Peru, where President Alejandro Toledo may not be popular, but he's muddling through in part because people value stability and don't want to sink into chaos."

Should the United States continue aiding Colombia's fight against leftist guerrillas?

Colombia is South America's most violent country— under siege by leftist guerrillas, rightist paramilitary groups and narco-traffickers. In the last decade, 30,000 Colombians—mostly civilians—were killed. Last year alone, 3,000 people were kidnapped.[6]

Newly elected President Alvaro Uribe Velez is trying to contain the violence with a get-tough policy, targeted especially against the country's 18,000-member left-wing guerrilla group, the Revolutionary Armed Forces of Colombia (FARC).[7] Established in 1964 as the military wing of the Colombian Communist Party, FARC has since largely shed its political agenda to focus more on organized criminal activities like kidnapping and drug-trafficking.

Uribe virtually reversed the policies of his predecessor, Andres Pastrana, who devoted most of his tenure to unsuccessfully trying to negotiate a peace agreement with FARC, even ceding control to the guerrillas of a "safe haven" the size of Switzerland in southeastern Colombia.

Uribe's about-face won strong support from the Bush administration, which casts the country's troubles as a part of the broader war on terrorism. "After Sept. 11, the Bush administration changed its whole focus worldwide to fighting terrorism, so it makes sense that they would see the [Colombian] government's battle against the FARC as a struggle against terrorism," says Rand's Rabasa.

But the United States was helping Colombia even before 9/11. Since 1997, the United States has given Colombia $2 billion—including $411 million last year— to beef up its anti-narcotics and law-enforcement capabilities.[8] But the Sept. 11 terrorist attacks on New York and the Pentagon prompted the U.S. to up the ante.

When Secretary of State Colin L. Powell visited Bogotá on Dec. 4, he announced the administration would seek $537 billion from Congress for Colombia this year, including $98 million for counterinsurgency training. The administration also has sent 60 Special Forces soldiers and intelligence operatives to help train the country's army.[9]

The aid is largely to help the Colombian army protect an oil pipeline from the frequent disruptions by guerrilla attacks. Still, the new emphasis on helping Colombia fight guerrillas is a break from the past, when military aid solely targeted anti-drug efforts.

Some experts applaud the administration's help fighting FARC and other groups, saying that without U.S. aid, Colombia could implode, becoming a state without a real governing authority. Then they warn, the chaos could spread to less stable neighbors, like Venezuela, throwing the region into further turmoil.

"Colombia might very well collapse unless we strengthen the army enough to fight the leftist guerrillas and the right-wing paramilitaries," says the Council on Foreign Relations' Sweig. "Already they don't control half the country, so something needs to be done to restore government control."

"The problem is getting worse and will continue to get worse if something isn't done," agrees Heritage's Johnson. "Any army's job in [such] a situation is to guarantee public safety and the rule of law. The only way they're going to do that in Colombia is to push the FARC back."

And repelling the FARC is the only real option, aid supporters say. "Pastrana's efforts to talk to the FARC ended in failure, because the FARC really weren't interested in making peace," Rabasa says. "The government has exhausted all possibilities and now they have to fight them."

Colombia has only about 40,000 combat soldiers, compared with more than 20,000 leftist, mostly FARC guerrillas and about half that many paramilitaries. The military largely controls the urban areas and some well-populated parts of the countryside. But large swaths are without either a military or civil presence.

Rabasa and others say the U.S. should be doing more, given the army's small size and the task ahead. "Basically we are training and equipping a battalion to guard the oil pipeline," he says. "While that helps, the army is going to need more resources and training from the Americans if it is going to retake control of the country."

But others say beefing up the Colombian military is counterproductive, because they see the war as unwinnable. "Everyone knows that you're not going to end this thing militarily," says Sanho Tree, a fellow at the Institute for Policy Studies.

Effective counterinsurgency usually requires 10 times as many troops as the rebels, he says. "Colombia is the size of Texas and California combined and has about 40,000 soldiers to deal with almost as many insurgents," he says. "The New York City police have almost as many people to deal with in an area a fraction of that size."

Opponents of aid also argue that America's Colombia policy eerily parallels the early years of U.S. involvement in Vietnam. "This has quagmire written all over it," Tree says. "And just as they were saying about Vietnam in the early 1960s, some American hard-liners say we need to help the Colombian military achieve a few big victories to strengthen its position at the bargaining table. That's how we got deeper into Vietnam, and look what happened."

More important, say critics of U.S. aid, the Colombian army has a record of human rights abuses and deep ties to right-wing paramilitary vigilante groups formed in the early 1980s to fight FARC and other guerrillas. "The Colombian military created the paramilitaries and has maintained strong ties to them, even after the government declared them illegal in 1989," says Robin Kirk, a senior researcher with Human Rights Watch and author of the best-selling 2003 book *More Terrible Than Death: Massacres, Drugs, and America's War in Colombia.*

The military "subcontracted out its dirty war against the leftists to the paramilitaries," says Kirk. Indeed, paramilitary groups devote most of their energy and resources to killing civilians suspected of sympathizing with the FARC, she says, rather than the guerrillas themselves.

"The paramilitaries are believed responsible for 70 percent of the human rights abuses in the country," Tree adds. "These are not good guys."

But supporters of aid say U.S. assistance will help the army disassociate itself from the paramilitaries and improve human rights in Colombia. "The army has supported and worked with the paramilitaries [because] they haven't had the resources to combat the guerrillas on their own," Johnson says. "By strengthening the army, you will make them less dependent on the paramilitaries."

In addition, aid proponents say, the U.S. can use military aid to assure that the Colombian military cleans up its human rights record. "When we've pulled aid—as in

Guatemala in the 1970s—things went haywire, and the military committed horrendous abuses," Sweig says. "But when we've used aid to slowly change an army—as we did in El Salvador in the 1980s—things got better."

But Kirk disagrees. "Aid and training never solved a human rights problem," she says. "In El Salvador, soldiers who received full training by the United States went on to commit massacres and atrocities."

BACKGROUND

Discovery and Conquest

Christopher Columbus discovered what is now Venezuela during his third voyage to the New World in 1498. He was soon followed by fellow Italian, Amerigo Vespucci (after whom the Americas were named) and Pedro Alvares Cabral, a Portuguese sailor who discovered Brazil in 1500.

The Europeans who followed these first explorers into South America found an array of cultures and societies. The largest and most technically sophisticated of these indigenous groups were the rapacious Inca, who had used their formidable military and organizational skills to forge a vast empire of 12 million people encompassing much of the Andes Mountains and the Pacific coast.

By contrast, there were the peaceful Guarani, who raised crops in the jungles of central South America. Other areas supported groups ranging from stone-age hunter-gatherers to large-scale agricultural and fishing communities.

The conquest of South America began in earnest in 1530, when Spaniard Francisco Pizarro led a small band of well-armed troops against the Inca. Cunning, skill and vastly superior weaponry helped Pizarro and later conquistadors bring down the huge empire.[10] Old World diseases, like smallpox, also played a role, wiping out millions of potential Inca adversaries. The future Peru, Ecuador, Bolivia and Venezuela soon lay in Spanish hands.

Meanwhile, the Portuguese were consolidating their hold over Brazil. Incursions into the colony by French, English and Spanish adventurers prompted the king of Portugal to grant huge tracts of the territory to rich patrons who promised to colonize and protect the area for Portugal in exchange for the right to exploit the land and its people.

Spanish rule was more centralized. A Council of the Indies—located in Spain and comprised of the king, aristocrats and lawyers—made general policy, which was then carried out by an appointed viceroy, who ruled over the continent from Lima, Peru, through a hierarchy of colonial administrators.[11]

By 1600, the economy of colonial South America flourished on gold and silver mining and large plantations that produced cotton, tobacco and sugar for export. But while Spanish and Portuguese rule made fortunes for many Europeans, it brought misery to the continent's native peoples. Millions succumbed to diseases that had been common in Europe for centuries but were unknown in the Americas, and hence devastating.[12] Millions more were ultimately drafted for forced labor in mines, plantations and other ventures.

Viewing the Indians as potential converts, the Catholic Church urged the Spanish crown to prohibit the mistreatment of indigenous people. Its missionaries fought for their basic human rights, but European settlers resisted the reform efforts.

But the forced-labor system eventually collapsed as more and more Indians died from disease, overwork and the abuses meted out by their Spanish and Portuguese overlords. Many of the Indians who survived became sharecroppers on large European-owned plantations known as haciendas. In turn, millions of African slaves were brought in to do work originally performed by the Indians.

During the 18th century, Spanish kings tried several times to reform the administration of their New World colonies. In an effort to decentralize authority, South America was broken into three territories—the Vice-royalties of New Granada (now Venezuela) in the north, Peru along the Pacific coast and Rio de la Plata (Argentina) in the south. Many trade barriers also were lifted, which helped stimulate the continent's economy.

Push for Independence

In the late 18th century, increased prosperity expanded South America's middle and upper classes—the descendants of the early European settlers and mixed-race mestizos. But prosperity did not trickle down to the continent's Indian or black populations, intensifying the region's social stratification. As the wealth of the new elites grew, so did their wish to run their own affairs. Desire for greater autonomy was further strengthened by revolutions in the 1770s and '80s in the United States and France and by the revolutionary theories of the Age

CHRONOLOGY

16th-18th Centuries *European explorers conquer South America.*

1498 Italian explorer Christopher Columbus, sailing under a Spanish flag, lands in Venezuela, becoming the first known European to see South America.

1500 Portuguese explorer Pedro Alvares Cabral discovers Brazil.

1510 The first African slaves arrive.

1530 Spaniard Francisco Pizarro begins the conquest of the Inca.

1776 The American Revolution inspires South Americans to consider their own independence.

19th Century *South American states become independent.*

1811 Venezuela declares independence, but Spain reasserts its authority in 1815.

1816 Simón Bolívar helps Venezuela resist Spain. . . . Argentina declares independence.

1819 Bolívar liberates Colombia.

1821 Bolívar frees Venezuela and Ecuador.

1822 Brazil becomes a separate state with a Portuguese king.

1823 The U.S. adopts the Monroe Doctrine to keep Europe out of hemispheric affairs.

1888 Brazil abolishes slavery.

1900-1980 *Dictators rule over economic growth and urbanization.*

1914 World War I halts immigration into South America.

1946 Juan and Eva Perón assume power in Argentina.

1948 The U.S. helps establish the Organization of American States (OAS).

1964 A Brazilian coup ousts the elected president.

1973 Gen. Augusto Pinochet overthrows Salvador Allende, Chile's elected president.

1980-Present *Democracy and free markets proliferate.*

1985 Brazil returns to civilian rule.

1989 Pinochet loses a referendum and civilian rule in Chile is restored. . . . Carlos Menem wins Argentina's presidency and institutes free-market reforms.

1994 Fernando Cardoso becomes Brazil's president and institutes free-market reforms.

1998 Populist Hugo Chavez is elected president of Venezuela.

2001 Eduardo Duhalde becomes president of Argentina after the country's slide into recession. . . . Businessmen mount a coup against Chavez on April 12. He returns to power in two days.

May 2002 Alvaro Uribe becomes president of Colombia, promising to crack down on guerrillas.

October 2002 Luiz Inácio Lula da Silva becomes president of Brazil on his fifth try.

December 2002 Businesses and the national oil company begin a two-month strike in Venezuela demanding Chavez's resignation.

January 2003 Venezuela's strike ends; Chavez arrests some strike leaders and forces the state oil company to resume operations.

February 2003 Protests in La Paz, Bolivia, over tax hikes and spending cuts almost bring down the government.

April 2003 Presidential elections are scheduled in Argentina to replace Duhalde.

Venezuela's Leader Hangs onto Power

Venezuela's feisty President Hugo Chavez prefers to stand and fight—even in situations where others might have retreated or resigned.

Within the last year and a half, he has weathered a coup attempt that forced him from office for two days and outlasted a two-month nationwide strike that shut down the entire country. "Chavez actually thrives in situations like this," says Stephen Levitsky, a professor of government at Harvard University. "He's at his best when he's fighting an enemy."

If that is true, President Chavez has had many opportunities lately to be "at his best." Roughly two-thirds of Venezuelans—from almost all sectors of society, including organized labor, business and parts of the military—oppose his leadership. But while his political obituary has been written more than once, Chavez has always managed to confound conventional wisdom and bounce back.

The recent strike, for instance, was initially seen as a huge victory for his opponents. Businesses everywhere were shuttered—at an estimated economic cost of $50 million a day.[1] Many workers at the state-owned oil company—which provides half the government's revenues, 80 percent of the country's exports and is America's fourth-largest foreign supplier of oil—went on strike, completely shutting down the entire industry.[2]

The strikers, led by a coalition of business and labor leaders, demanded that Chavez step down or at least submit his four-year-old rule to a free and fair referendum. The president didn't budge. Instead, he waited until the strikers were so financially strapped they had to reopen their businesses. As for the all-important state oil company, Petroleos Venezuela, Chavez fired 16,000 striking workers—about 40 percent of its workforce—and set the rest to work restarting production.

Chavez may have won his latest political battles, but the victories may turn out to be pyrrhic. Inflation has reached more than 30 percent, and unemployment is expected to reach the same level by June. The economy shrank by 9 percent last year and is expected to decline 20 percent this year. Latin America has never seen such a dramatic economic contraction, said Organization of American States

(OAS) Secretary-General Cesar Gavira—"not even during a civil war."[3]

Moreover, Petroleos is unlikely to return to its pre-strike production level of 3.1 million barrels of oil a day, because the loss of hundreds of experienced workers has hobbled the firm, analysts say. "It will not be the company it once was," said Mazhar al-Shereidah, an oil economist in Caracas, Venezuela's capital.[4]

Petroleos is not the only company in danger of foundering. More than 5,000 private firms have gone bankrupt since Chavez was elected four years ago, and hundreds of others are about to follow suit. "The feeling we have," one business leader told *Newsweek*, "is that this man wants to do away with the private sector altogether."[5]

But Guillermo Garcia Ponce, the Stalinist coordinator of the Political Command of the Revolution—an advisory committee chaired by Chavez—says that rather than wanting to shut down private business, Chavez wants to improve capitalism, so it's "not subject to globalization or U.S. interests."[6]

Venezuela's democracy also has suffered a series of blows since Chavez came to office in 1999. Most notably, in 2000, he pushed through the election of a new Assembly that dismissed and replaced the existing Congress and reshuffled the Supreme Court. The president also expanded the powers of his own office, granting himself the right to rule by decree in matters affecting the economy and crime.

More recently, Chavez arrested some of the strike leaders and promised to put them on trial. Many fear that he will also curb press freedoms.

Venezuela was not always in such a chaotic state. In the 1970s, as one of Latin America's oldest democracies and richest economies, Venezuela was hailed as a model for the rest of the continent. With plentiful supplies of oil, a solid middle class and a strong multiparty democracy, many believed Venezuela would be the first to join the ranks of the developed world.

But plummeting oil prices in the 1980s and '90s sent the petroleum-dependent economy into a tailspin. Falling standards of living eventually led to riots and, in 1992, two

---

[1] Ginger Thompson, "Strike's Efforts Tear at Social Fabric," *The New York Times*, Jan. 16, 2003.

[2] Juan Forero, "Venezuela's Lifeblood Ebbs Even as it Flows," *The New York Times*, Feb. 26, 2003, p. C1.

[3] Quoted in Phil Gunson, "Out for Revenge?" *Newsweek*, Feb. 24, 2003.

[4] Forero, *op. cit.*

[5] Gunson, *op. cit.*

[6] *Ibid.*

coups, one led by then-Col. Chavez.

In 1999, Chavez swept into power as a fiery populist promising a revolution on behalf of the lower and working classes and against the country's wealthy elite. But the new president's heavy-handed tactics failed to jump-start the economy, and by 2001 the former paratrooper was deeply unpopular, except among the very poor.

But if Chavez made mistakes, so did his opponents. In April of 2002, members of the business community joined elements in the military to depose the president. Within 48 hours, Chavez had rallied much of the army to his side and was back in power.

President Hugo Chavez, a former paratrooper, survived a two-day coup and outlasted a recent strike that brought Venezuela to a standstill.

The United States, which traditionally condemns military takeovers of democratically elected governments, appeared to acquiesce to Chavez's overthrow, earning widespread international criticism. In fact, Chavez later alleged that the United States was behind the coup, a charge vehemently denied by U.S. officials.[7]

Meanwhile, the administration continues to support the strikers' demand for early elections, and, with Chavez returned to power, relations between the two countries have been strained.

The two sides have never seen eye-to-eye. Chavez's consistently anti-American rhetoric—such as calling the U.S. assault on Afghanistan as great a crime as the Sept. 11 terrorist attacks in New York and the Pentagon—has irked the United States. Chavez also raised American ire by pushing for the Organization of Petroleum Exporting Countries to limit production and raise world oil prices.

Critics of Chavez say that he will only get more authoritarian as Venezuela's economy continues to decline and he becomes even more unpopular. They point out that he is a close friend and admirer of communist Cuban dictator Fidel Castro (who has advised the Venezuelan president) and allegedly supports leftist guerrillas in neighboring Colombia.

"The defeat of the opposition in the strike is allowing him to consolidate a leftist dictatorship and that will continue," says Angel Rabasa, a senior policy analyst at the Rand Corporation, a Palo Alto, Calif., think tank.

But others argue that the opposition is trying, by hook or by crook, to oust a democratically elected president because he is fighting for the poor and not tending to the interests of the country's elites. "His radical rhetoric favoring the poor over the privileged has alienated the middle class," wrote Steve Ellner, co-editor of the 2003 book *Venezuelan Politics in the Chavez Era: Class, Polarization and Conflict.*[8]

The OAS—along with regional heavyweights like the U.S., Mexico and Brazil—is trying to fashion a negotiated settlement to the country's crisis, possibly an agreement to hold a referendum on the president's rule at the midpoint of his term (August of this year) as is allowed under the country's constitution.

Chavez has largely dismissed the efforts of the OAS as the "meddling" of outsiders.[9] Moreover, while he has said he would submit to a vote in August, many Venezuelans don't believe him.

"They are convinced that in August, when the constitution contemplates a referendum on the president, the government will resort to delaying tactics and dirty tricks," said Moses Naim, former Venezuelan minister for trade and industry and editor of *Foreign Policy* magazine.[10]

Levitsky, at Harvard, agrees that Chavez is unlikely to submit himself to a vote for the simple reason that he would almost certainly lose. "He's deeply unpopular right now, so I just can't see him winning a vote that was fair," he says. "Instead, I think he's going to keep trying to tough it out."

---

[7] Scott Wilson, "Chavez Raises Idea of U.S. Role in Coup; Interview Suggests Rocky Road Ahead," *The Washington Post*, May 5, 2002, p. A20.

[8] Steve Ellner, "Venezuela on the Brink," *The Nation*, Jan. 13, 2003, p. 5.

[9] Quoted in David Buchbinder, "Slowly, Chavez Isolates Himself from the World," *The Christian Science Monitor*, March 5, 2003, p. 7.

[10] Quoted in Moises Naim, "Hugo Chavez and the Limits of Democracy," *The New York Times*, March 5, 2003, p. A23.

of Enlightenment, which held the sovereignty of the individual as a primary tenet.

But the independence movement simmered for decades before being brought to a boil in the early 1800s, during the Napoleonic wars that engulfed Europe. In 1796, Spain joined France in a war against England. The alliance cut the Spanish off from their New World colonies because the English navy was powerful enough to virtually halt Spanish shipping to and from the Americas.

In 1806, the British invaded Argentina and captured Buenos Aires. The Argentines soon organized an armed resistance and drove the foreigners from the city.

But what had seemed a victory for Spain was short-lived. By taking matters into their own hands, the Argentines gained new confidence that they could run their own affairs. Meanwhile, Spain was slowly being absorbed into Napoleon's empire. In 1807, the French leader replaced the Spanish king with his brother and invaded Portugal. The move provoked an uprising by the Spanish, leading to five years of brutal war.

With Spain in turmoil, Venezuelan elites—led by revolutionary leader Francisco de Miranda—took the opportunity to declare independence, creating a constitutional republic in 1811.[13] But bickering within the revolutionary camp (which included a young army officer named Simón Bolívar) and Spanish attempts to reassert authority after Napoleon's defeat in 1812, led to the downfall of the new Venezuelan republic by 1815.

While many revolutionary leaders (including Miranda) were captured, Bolívar escaped to Jamaica, where he began organizing resistance to Spain. In 1816, he returned to a remote part of Venezuela, where revolutionary support was still strong, and organized an army.

In the following years, Bolívar (with British assistance) handed the Spaniards a series of stunning defeats, conquering Colombia in 1819, Venezuela and Ecuador in 1821.[14]

Other parts of the continent were cutting their European bonds at the same time. In Argentina, those who had resisted the British in 1806 slowly pulled away from Spain, first appointing a Congress to rule in the king's name in 1810 and finally declaring independence in 1816. An Argentine army under the leadership of José de San Martin marched north and west, liberating Chile and Uruguay. San Martin also tried to liberate Peru, but it was Bolívar and his lieutenant, José Antonio de Sucre, who ultimately freed the area from Spanish rule in 1823.

Brazil was liberated with much less fighting, in part because the revolution was led by the heir to Portugal's throne, Dom Pedro, who had originally come to South America to escape Napoleon's invasion of his country. In 1822, Dom Pedro resisted calls from Portugal for his return and declared Brazil independent and himself king.[15]

New Troubles

Political chaos and continuing social imbalances characterized the post-independence period. Contrary to the high expectations that followed independence, there was little change in the ills of colonial South America—such as slavery and poverty among Indians and the working class—after Spanish and Portuguese rule had ended. The powerful landowners and urban elites who ran the newly independent states used their new power to advance their own positions, ignoring the great majority of the citizenry.

The cornerstones of good government—such as the rule of law and orderly transfer of political power—were absent in most of the new states. Warlords (called *caudillos*) and violent bands were common in many areas. Established landowners—able to acquire more property through government connections—grew richer while the peasants were forced to pay ever-higher taxes.

By the middle of the 19th century, South American political thinkers were desperate to reverse the continent's downward trajectory. Looking to the United States and Great Britain for inspiration, they noticed the relationship between both countries' political and economic systems and began to see economic advancement as the way to greater political stability and freedom.

The new focus on economic development in the 1850s and '60s came at a propitious time: Foreign investors from Europe and the United States had begun to enter the South American market, attracted by the continent's abundant natural resources and agricultural potential. Over the next 60 years, huge tracts of land were cleared for grains, sugar and later coffee, and cattle ranching became a huge industry, especially in Argentina. Foreign investors also helped develop the continent's mineral wealth.

In some countries, strong new leaders emerged. In Brazil and Argentina, governments established stability and order. Roads, bridges and railroads were built—often by foreigners—further facilitating commerce.

The economic boom also attracted immigrants mostly from Europe. By the end of the century, hundreds of thousands were arriving each year, many from Italy and

Spain as well as northern Europe. Argentina, for instance, received 1.2 million Italian and 1 million Spanish immigrants before 1914. After World War I, immigrants began arriving from Asia. More than 200,000 Japanese came to Brazil between 1920 and 1940.

New wealth and the new immigrants brought a push to modernize society. Slavery was finally eliminated—Brazil was the last nation to act, freeing its slaves in 1888.[16] New universities sprang up, and more and more children entered primary school. Brazil, Chile, Argentina and other countries cast off dictators and kings to become republics.

By the early 20th century, South America had become a major exporter of raw materials and agricultural commodities—minerals from Chile and Bolivia, grain and beef from Argentina and coffee from Brazil. About the same time, heavy industry was developing, particularly in the southern half of the continent, triggering a population shift to urban areas. Brazil's São Paolo, for instance, grew from a large town of 65,000 in 1890 to a metropolis of 350,000 by 1910.

Urbanization brought a newfound sense of entitlement on several levels. Workers unionized and began demanding not only better pay but also pensions and other benefits from the government. By the 1930s, many countries had created large social-welfare schemes and nationalized major sectors of their economies to protect industrial workers.

Relations with U.S.

On a broader level, countries began to seek more independence from the United States, whose enormous economic and military power had made it influential throughout the continent. The Monroe Doctrine of 1823 initially had helped establish U.S. supremacy in the Western Hemisphere, discouraging further incursions by European powers. Moreover, American intervention in Mexico, Central America and the Caribbean in the opening decades of the 20th century made South Americans even more distrustful of U.S. intentions.[17]

Relations improved during the 1930s, with President Franklin D. Roosevelt's Good Neighbor Policy, which pledged the U.S. would not interfere in the continent's affairs. World War II helped cement better ties, as the United States turned to South America to help supply its war effort, bringing new prosperity to the region. In 1948, the United States helped found the Organization of American States (OAS) to promote development and democracy throughout Latin America and the Caribbean.

Despite widespread progress, some countries could not make the transition to stable democratic rule. Strongman Getulio Vargas led Brazil in the 1930s and '40s. In 1946, Juan Perón and his charismatic wife Evita came to power in neighboring Argentina, promising to solve the nation's social ills by nationalizing industry and spending lavishly on social programs.

Vargas and Perón eventually were deposed and both countries returned to more democratic systems. But by the 1960s and early '70s, Brazil, Argentina, Chile, Uruguay and Peru had succumbed to authoritarian and often brutal military dictatorships. Despite its stated preference for democracy, the United States often supported dictators as bulwarks against the spread of communism on the continent.

In addition to being repressive, most of the strongmen—with the exception of Chile's Augusto Pinochet—proved to be poor stewards of the economy. Economic mismanagement and corruption led to runaway inflation, particularly in Brazil and Argentina, and a high level of foreign debt.

By the early 1980s, many of the military regimes had become highly unpopular. Argentina's junta—which "disappeared" thousands of leftist opponents—gave up power in 1983. The military had been discredited over its mishandling of the economy and its humiliating loss in the Falkland Islands war, in which Argentina invaded a British possession off its coast, only to be expelled by the Royal Navy and Marines. Brazil's military handed back power to civilians in 1985. Chileans, tired of Pinochet's dictatorial rule, voted the general from power in 1989.

During the 1990s, democracy and free markets thrived in South America. In Argentina, popular President Carlos Menem tamed hyperinflation and brought the country almost a decade of sustained economic growth. Fernando Cardoso worked similar economic magic in Brazil, first as finance minister and then as president. In Peru, President Alberto Fujimori destroyed a crippling Maoist rebellion by the Shining Path guerrillas and set the economy on a more stable footing.

However, the decade ended on a sour note. Menem left office accused of corruption, while Argentina's economy slid into a deep recession. A corruption scandal also drove out the increasingly authoritarian Fujimori.

CURRENT SITUATION

Free-Trade Proposal

Since the Sept. 11 terrorist attacks in the United States and the ongoing confrontation with Iraq, South American diplomats and political leaders have complained about U.S. neglect of the region. But the United States hasn't been entirely distracted.

In addition to sending U.S. aid to Colombia, the United States has been leading the negotiations to create a free-trade zone linking North and South America and the Caribbean—34 countries stretching from the Antarctic to Canada. The Free Trade Area of the Americas (FTAA) was first proposed in 1994, but the idea has received little attention until recently.

On Feb. 11, the United States presented its opening negotiating stance, offering to eliminate tariffs on 65 percent of imports from other FTAA countries as soon as the treaty took effect in 2005. American textile tariffs, long regarded as unfair by South American competitors, would be phased out over the next five years. By 2015, all treaty signatories would eliminate all tariffs.[18]

"The U.S. has created a detailed road map for free trade in the Western Hemisphere," said U.S. Trade Representative Zoellick. "We've put all our tariffs on the table, and we now hope our trading partners will do the same."[19]

Many trade analysts applaud Zoellick for moving the process forward, but they caution that negotiations could take a long time. "I think it's overly optimistic to set a 2005 deadline for completing the treaty," says the Cato Institute's Vasquez. "There are a lot of sensitive issues and things that will be hard for each country to give up."

Indeed, many signs do not auger well for the treaty's early completion. The U.S. has tarnished its free-trade credentials in the past year, reinstating farm subsides and imposing steel tariffs on many countries, including big steel makers in Brazil, in an effort to protect its own ailing industry.

For its part, South America has a mixed-to-poor record on free trade, with many countries employing high tariffs to protect uncompetitive industries. The major free-trade zone on the continent—Mercusor, encompassing Brazil, Argentina, Uruguay and Paraguay—has fallen on hard times.

The problems began in 1999, when Brazil decided to allow its currency to decline in value, making its exports much cheaper. The move devastated trade with the other big Mercusor member, Argentina, because its currency was pegged to the dollar, keeping it artificially high, and hence its exports very expensive. The zone was also rocked by last year's economic crisis in Argentina, which shuttered much of the country's industry and left its consumers with little money to spend on imports.

On the other hand, the news for free-traders is not all bad. In December, the United States sealed a free-trade deal with Chile, probably South America's most market-oriented economy. South Americans can also look to their Latin cousin to the north, Mexico, where relatively open trade with the U.S. and Canada—spurred by the North American Free Trade Agreement (NAFTA)—has generally been judged a success, leading to increased foreign investment and sustained economic growth for that country.[20]

Finally, Brazil's Lula, formerly a vocal opponent of the FTAA, has shifted his position since taking office late last year. "In order to grow, Brazil needs to increase the amount of its foreign trade," he told an audience at the National Press Club in Washington on Dec. 10. "And the FTAA, in our view, can represent a genuine opening up of the U.S. and Canadian markets."

Lula's newfound willingness to negotiate a free-trade agreement is a big step forward for supporters of FTAA, given that Brazil is South America's largest economy.

Few dispute that better access to the North American market would offer South Americans tremendous opportunities. But opponents of the trade zone worry that it also could devastate already fragile South American economies.

Local farmers and businesses could be hurt—and possibly bankrupted—by a flood of cheaper imports from the more competitive north. Millions of people could lose their jobs, their businesses or their farms, if U.S. multinationals move in with cheaper, better products. "We cannot compete with them," said Ermel Chavez, an activist in Ecuador. "We'll become nothing more than consumers."[21]

The Institute for Policy Studies' Anderson agrees: "Many people down there see free trade as a way for the big American companies to expand their access to and investment in their market in order to make greater profits without improving the standard of living of local people."

Indigenous groups and environmentalists also oppose the pact because they fear it could spur the kind of development (such as mining and logging) that would damage

Should the United States continue aiding Colombia's counterinsurgency efforts?

YES
Stephen Johnson
Senior Policy Analyst for Latin America,
The Heritage Foundation

Written for *The CQ Researcher,* March 10, 2003

Just as Colombia is making progress in its fight against violence, terror and drug trafficking, it would be a mistake to withdraw assistance for its counterterrorism efforts.

Despite having one of South America's longest-running continuous democracies, Colombia has had weak governments and a minimal state presence outside urban areas. Civil conflicts triggered a rural communist insurgency in the 1960s. Meanwhile, marijuana, heroin and cocaine production flourished in the uncontrolled countryside. By the mid-1990s, U.S. counternarcotics aid had helped Colombia defeat its major drug cartels. But when allegations surfaced that President Ernesto Samper had received campaign contributions from one of the kingpins, the United States halted assistance. In the ensuing disarray, Colombian rebels joined with remaining drug producers and took over where the cartels left off.

With the election of President Andrés Pastrana, aid was restored under a bilateral agenda called Plan Colombia. But Pastrana spent most of his term trying to achieve a cease-fire by allowing the largest rebel group, the Revolutionary Armed Forces of Colombia (FARC), to occupy a huge safe-haven in the middle of Colombia. FARC grew from 10,000 to 18,000 troops and began collecting between $50 million and $100 million a month from drug trafficking, extortion and kidnapping. Today, guerrillas—and the paramilitary forces that have risen up to fight them—cause up to 3,500 brutal deaths a year and hundreds of millions of dollars in infrastructure damage, not to mention the public costs of pursuing them.

Last year, newly elected President Alvaro Uribe embarked on an ambitious program to retake the countryside, curb drug trafficking, strengthen public institutions and provide public security. With a decline in coca cultivation, he is already achieving some success. Because America's drug demand fuels much of the problem, the United States should help meet these goals. Counterterrorism aid must be part of the mix. Failure to leverage Colombia's homegrown efforts could easily destabilize the wobbly northern Andean region and lead to terrorist violence in neighboring countries.

Bipartisan consensus exists for continuing military aid, but critics point out that Colombia's security forces still commit human rights abuses, albeit fewer than in the past. Yet, leaving Colombia to the mercy of narco-terrorists is no option. The only alternative is to help the government disarm these criminals and protect innocent citizens—especially when it is beginning to make progress.

NO
Jason Hagen
Associate for Colombia, Washington Office on
Latin America

Written for *The CQ Researcher,* March 10, 2003

U.S. taxpayers should ask what their $2 billion has achieved in Colombia. I have yet to see many positive results: The drug supply has not been curtailed, the country has become more violent and the ranks of the poor are swelling.

Meanwhile, anti-terrorist rhetoric from both governments is drowning out the complexity of the conflict. Instead of providing much-needed creativity, the United States is digging its heels into very hostile terrain alongside a new administration in Colombia that seems committed to repeating historical errors.

Most analysts, including me, see negotiations as the only way to resolve the conflict. But those who believe the country can be pacified through military means should at least be honest with the math. Classic counterinsurgency doctrine requires 10 soldiers for every insurgent in order to win on the battlefield. Right now, the Colombian military has up to 60,000 soldiers ready to be deployed, and the government does not have the money to pay for additional regular soldiers. There are approximately 35,000 illegal, armed guerrillas.

Will the United States provide the missing 290,000 troops for jungle warfare?

Colombian social spending has dried up because the government is devoting its slim resources to the war. Even in areas the government has designated as security priorities, promised social assistance has not arrived. This is a tremendous oversight, considering that more than 60 percent of Colombians make less than $2 a day, roughly 6 percent of the population has been forcibly displaced from their homes and unemployment is nearly 20 percent.

Having soldiers on every corner means little to a family that cannot afford bread. If even a tiny fraction of these desperate people join the insurgency for a paycheck or for political reasons, the guerrilla threat will continue to grow. Colombia and the United States should be investing heavily in social and economic programs to prevent this from happening.

Elements of the Colombian military continue to maintain ties with an illegal paramilitary force that the United States regards as a terrorist organization. Turning a blind eye to terror in order to fight terror is neither morally acceptable nor a smart strategy to bring peace to Colombia.

Rather than waste years dabbling in an intractable conflict—at the cost of thousands of lives and billions of dollars—the United States should put its considerable diplomatic weight behind a peace process.

the continent's environment. Concern is especially great over the Amazon basin.

"I was just in Ecuador, where there is a strong, indigenous movement and a strong sense these wild places need to be protected as a resource for these indigenous people who make their living off the land," Anderson says. "The people I talked to think [the FTAA] will simply be an opening for big foreign companies to exploit the forest, and that average people will not benefit."

Free-trade supporters counter that while these concerns are legitimate, they should not stand in the way of open trade. "At the end of the day, when you argue against free trade, you are arguing against modernization," Vasquez says.

Vasquez admits that dislocations will occur as industries large and small struggle to compete in the new, more open environment. But, he argues, many of those who lose jobs and businesses will find new opportunities as other, more competitive sectors of the economy expand.

Most important, Vasquez says, free trade will benefit all South Americans, especially the poor, by driving down the prices of many goods and services. "When you protect industries from competition, prices stay higher than they should, which is a big deal in South America where so many people are poor."

Shaky Economies

Argentina's economic collapse at the end of 2001 has raised fears of a continentwide meltdown. And indeed, some other countries, including Uruguay, Venezuela and even Brazil, look to be in danger of sliding into a full depression.

The continent's gross domestic product (GDP) shrank by roughly 1 percent last year and is expected to do so again this year as Argentina and Venezuela undergo painful economic contractions, along with other nations. According to the Economic Commission for Latin America, a United Nations-sponsored think tank in Santiago, Chile, poverty in the region is also high, with 44 percent of Latin Americans now poor, nearly half of them living in extreme poverty.[22]

And inflation, once the bane of Brazil and many other South American countries, is creeping back up after years in check. Atop the watch list are Argentina and Venezuela, currently tackling annual inflation rates of nearly 41 percent and 31 percent, respectively. At 12.5 percent, consumer price increases in Brazil are also considered too high.[23]

Argentina is still in deep trouble, with its economy contracting 11 percent last year—its fourth annual consecutive decline in GDP. The country is continuing to struggle through an economic crisis that saw a quarter of its population out of work, private bank accounts frozen and government defaulting on its loan obligations.

In January, the IMF rode to the rescue, giving Argentina a $6.8 billion loan that would enable it to service its debt to the IMF and other lenders through August. But the agreement (which has yet to be ratified by the country's Congress) would impose strict fiscal discipline on Argentina. For instance, under the plan, subsidies on energy and other staples would be cut, which would hurt the poor and could lead to renewed riots and other forms of social instability.

"I don't think anyone really doubts that in the short term, it's going to be pretty rocky for Argentina," says Inter-American Dialogue's Shifter. "I think it will be at least a few years before they're able to turn a corner and get back on their feet."

The other big economy of the region, Brazil, is in better shape, but there is the real risk of an Argentine-style collapse. The economy grew only 1.5 percent last year, and the currency, the *real*, lost 35 percent of its value.[24]

But there are signs of improvement. At 3.4 percent, fourth-quarter GDP growth was higher than the other three quarters, and agricultural exports have surged due to the weaker currency.[25]

Like most other South American countries, Brazil has a high public debt—running at about 56 percent of GDP. In exchange for an IMF loan last year, Brazil agreed to cut government spending in order to pay some of it off. The problem now facing Lula, the country's charismatic president, is that many of the cuts must come from social programs, hard for a leader who campaigned on a platform of helping the poor.[26]

In the continent's Andean region in the north and west, the situation is not much better, possibly worse. "I think this is the most troubled part of the continent," Shifter says. "It's sort of an axis of upheaval."

Deep political turmoil has wracked the economy of oil-rich Venezuela, which shrank about 9 percent last year.[27] And as President Chavez tightens his grip on the country, more stores and factories are expected to close as members of the business community (which vehemently opposes the president) leave the country.

Economists agree that Colombia, with abundant natural resources and a well-educated populace, has great economic potential. But the civil war has prevented foreign and domestic investment while prompting Colombia's best and brightest to emigrate. As a result, the economy grew at only 1.6 percent last year.[28]

Ecuador and Bolivia also are facing civil strife, caused in part by slow economic growth. Among the poorest countries in South America, each grew at about 2.5 percent last year, not fast enough for a developing country to greatly improve the standard of living for most citizens.[29]

Economic troubles throughout the continent are leading to a re-examination of the free-market policies that South Americans embraced, in some places, as early as the 1980s. "After 10 or 15 years of operating with free-market policies, paradise hasn't come," says Julio Carrion, an economist at the University of Delaware. "People are starting to wonder whether the gospel is as good as advertised."

"People are really tired of the current formula because it hasn't paid the dividends they'd hoped for," Georgetown University's Shifter says. "At the same time, they don't want to go back to the discredited socialist policies of the 1970s either."

South Americans are beginning to look for something that combines the best of both policies, Shifter says. "They are groping right now, looking for a mix of the state and the market to solve their problems."

Shifter believes that Brazil's new president is making the first attempt to move in a new direction. "Lula represents the best hope for this middle ground," he says. "He's moderated his attitude toward free trade and the IMF, but he's also committed to dealing with Brazil's poverty."

But others say the problem is not free-market policies but the unwillingness or inability of South American leaders to implement them. "Beginning in the 1980s and picking up steam in the '90s, all of these leaders tried free-market reforms because they'd literally tried everything else, and nothing had worked," says Cato's Vasquez.

"It worked just like it was supposed to, with inflation down and growth up, but none of these guys, like [Argentina's] Menem and [Peru's] Fujimori were really free-marketers. So they abandoned the reforms once the economies picked up and the pressure was off."

Fighting Poverty

The search for a new economic path also reflects the continent's stubbornly high poverty rates. In Brazil, 50 million people—almost a third of the population—live at or below the poverty line, and 19 percent of all households still lack running water.[30] In Argentina, the economic crisis has driven the number of people in poverty from roughly one-third of the population to nearly one-half in the last 18 months. And in the desperately poor Andes region, countries like Ecuador have poverty rates as high as 80 percent.

The World Bank, the world's largest anti-poverty institution, made $4.4 billion in social-development loans to Latin America in 2002. The loans ranged from $200 million to improve access to higher education in Colombia to $600 million to help poor Argentine families make ends meet.

"We lend money for so many things—to improve health care by building clinics in rural areas or education by building schools or training teachers," says Christopher Neal, a World Bank spokesman. Other activities include environmental protection, land distribution and improving the way governments deliver services.

In exchange, Neal says, "we ask countries to make government reforms by, say, improving transparency," or public accountability. For instance, he says, the bank might help the government publish information about government procurement on the Internet so citizens can understand and monitor how and where public money is being spent.

The Inter-American Development Bank (IDB) also makes poverty-alleviation and economic-development loans to South American countries. The IDB lent Latin American countries about $8 billion last year—40 percent of which went directly for anti-poverty programs like building low-income housing or hospitals in poor areas.

Aid organizations are often criticized for being ineffective, given that South America's poverty rates are still shockingly high. But the World Bank's Neal points out that the situation in South America has been steadily improving, especially on certain key social-development indicators. "Life expectancy for the region in 1990 was 68; 10 years later it was 70," he says. Infant mortality and illiteracy rates have also dropped during the same period, he says, from 41 deaths per thousand births to 29, and from 16 percent illiteracy to 12 percent.

Neal argues that poverty is sometimes driven up by outside factors, such as the slumping world economy or the historic and intransigent lack of widespread land ownership in rural areas throughout the continent. Efforts at land reform in the 1970s and '80s failed in most Latin countries, and today institutions like the development banks focus on funding programs that buy land from large property holders and sell it to poor farmers.

Moreover, lenders like the World Bank and IDB can only be effective in those countries with adequate governing institutions, Neal says. "If a government is not functioning well, it's hard to have an impact, because you need to work with effective local institutions to be able to make a difference."

OUTLOOK

New Leaders

Since the late 19th century, South America has been seen as a continent long on potential, both economically and politically, but short on actual results. Argentina actually achieved first-world living standards in the early 1900s, only to fall far behind the United States and Europe by the middle of the century.

Some experts believe the continent will continue failing to live up to its potential in the coming decades, largely because South Americans do not yet have the political maturity needed to create prosperous societies.

"They're going to muddle along for the time being because they don't really have a vision for the future aside from each person's desire to increase their individual wealth," says Johnson of the Heritage Foundation. "Many people in South America don't understand that their personal prosperity is tied to that of their neighbors and of society as a whole, so they don't push hard enough for the kind of change they need, like strong legislatures and judiciaries and a government that actually listens to people."

But others say South Americans will begin to make the changes needed to make their societies work. "It is more likely than not that they will do the things they need to do, like continuing to liberalize their markets, reform labor laws and battle corruption," says Williamson of the Institute for International Economics. "South America will end up looking like North America. If you look at countries like Singapore, they went from being poorer than South America is now to developed-country living standards in less than 30 years. So it is possible."

Inter-American Dialogue's Sifter agrees that the future is bright, in part because the next generation of leaders will be very different from the current crop.

"I've met with a lot of the people who are in their 30s and 40s and are going to be running things soon, and I can tell you that these people are very impressive," he says. "They understand that governments have to be honest and effective and responsive, and that's what they're working for."

NOTES

1. For background, see Kenneth Jost, "Democracy in Latin America," *The CQ Researcher*, Nov. 3, 2000, pp. 881-904.

2. Quoted in Thomas Ginsberg, "Latin Battleground," *The Philadelphia Inquirer*, Dec. 12, 2002, p. A1.

3. Figure cited in "Praying for a Happier New Year," *The Economist*, Dec. 19, 2002.

4. Kenneth Rogoff, "The IMF Strikes Back," *Foreign Policy*, January/February 2003, p. 38.

5. Poll cited in "Democracy Clings On in a Cold Climate," *The Economist*, Aug. 15, 2002.

6. Figures cited in "More Order and Less Law," *The Economist*, Nov. 7, 2002.

7. *Ibid.*

8. Juan Forero, "Colombia Will Tie Aid Request to Terror," *The New York Times*, Feb. 10, 2003, p. A6.

9. Steven R. Weisman, "Powell Says U.S. Will Increase Military Aid for Colombia," *The New York Times*, Dec. 5, 2002, p. A14.

10. Jared Diamond, *Guns, Germs, and Steel: The Fates of Human Societies* (1997), pp. 67-81.

11. Edwin Williamson, *The Penguin History of Latin America* (1992), pp. 91-92.

12. Diamond, *op. cit.*, pp. 210-211.

13. Williamson, *op. cit.*, p. 217.

14. *Ibid.*, p. 223.

15. Rex Hudson (ed.), *Brazil: A Country Study* (1998), p. 37.

16. *Ibid.*, p. 53.

17. Williamson, *op. cit.*, pp. 322-327.

18. Neil Irwin, "U.S. Seeks to End Many Tariffs," *The Washington Post*, Feb. 12, 2003, p. E1.

19. Quoted in *ibid.*

20. For background, see Mary H. Cooper, "Rethinking NAFTA," *The CQ Researcher*, June 7, 1996, pp. 481-504, and David Masci, "Mexico's Future," Sept. 19, 1997, pp. 817-840.

21. Quoted in Edmund Andrews, "Outside the Halls of Power, Many Fear Free Trade," *The New York Times*, Nov. 3, 2002, p. C4.

22. Figures cited at www.eclac.cl.

23. *CIA World Book*, 2002.

24. Tony Smith, "Brazil: Growth Despite Turmoil," *The New York Times*, Feb. 28, 2003, p. W1.

25. *Ibid.*

26. "Gruel Before Jam," *The Economist*, Feb. 13, 2003.

27. Figure cited in Marc Lifsher, "The Andean Arc of Instability," *The Wall Street Journal*, Feb. 24, 2003, p. A13.

28. Figure cited in *ibid.*

29. Figure cited in *ibid.*

30. "Three Square Meals a Day," *The Economist*, Feb. 20, 2003.

BIBLIOGRAPHY

Books

Easterly, William, *The Elusive Quest for Growth: Economists' Adventures and Misadventures in the Tropics*, **MIT Press, 2002.**
A former World Bank economist concludes that aid programs for the developing world fail because people and institutions respond to incentives, not penalties.

Kirk, Robin, *More Terrible Than Death: Massacres, Drugs, and America's War in Colombia*, **Public Affairs, 2003.**
A Human Rights Watch researcher chronicles the human toll of Colombia's drug war.

Skidmore, Thomas E., and Peter H. Smith, *Modern Latin America*, **Oxford University Press, 2000.**
The authors, who teach history at Brown University and political science at the University of California at San Diego, respectively, explore social and political trends in South America.

Williamson, Edwin, *The Penguin History of Latin America*, **Penguin U.S.A., 1993.**
A professor of Hispanic studies at the University of Edinburgh focuses on 19th-century independence movements.

Articles

Andrews, Edmund L., "Outside the Halls of Power, Many Fear Free Trade," *The New York Times,* **Nov. 3, 2002, p. C4.**
Andrews examines the debate over the proposed Free Trade Area of the Americas, focusing on the critics' concerns.

Bluestein, Paul, "IMF's 'Consensus' Policies Fraying," *The Washington Post*, **Sept. 26, 2002, p. E1.**
The article details the small but growing number of economists who oppose the "Washington Consensus" due to South America's anemic growth rates.

Bussey, Jane, "U.S. Trade Chief Offers Zero Tariffs," *The Miami Herald*, **Feb. 12, 2003, p. 1.**
U.S. Trade Representative Robert Zoellick's offer to eliminate tariffs in the Western Hemisphere by 2015 is detailed.

Forero, Juan, "How Venezuelan Outlasted His Foes," *The New York Times*, **Feb. 6, 2003, p. A6.**
The article explores the character traits that help President Hugo Chavez survive political turmoil.

Jost, Kenneth, "Democracy in Latin America," *The CQ Researcher*, **Nov. 3, 2000, pp. 881-904.**
Jost details the strengths and weakness of the democracies that have arisen in South America in the last two decades.

Kristof, Nicholas D., "The Next Africa," *The New York Times*, **Dec. 10, 2002, p. A35.**
Kristof concludes from South America's many troubles that it is "quietly falling apart."

Lifsher, Marc, "The Andean Arc of Instability," *The Wall Street Journal*, **Feb. 24, 2003, p. A13.**
Lifsher explores the extreme poverty and political turmoil in the Andean region.

"Lula's Burden of Hope," *The Economist*, **Jan. 2, 2003.**
Brazil's new president is committed to helping the poor but constrained by IMF spending requirements.

"More Law, Less Order," *The Economist*, Nov. 7, 2002.

The article asks whether Colombian President Alvaro Uribe's get-tough policies will undermine civil liberties.

Naim, Moises, "The Washington Consensus: A Damaged Brand," *The Financial Times*, Oct. 28, 2002.

The editor of *Foreign Policy* magazine argues the free-market prescriptions of the Washington Consensus are worth considering, despite all the criticism.

Stiglitz, Joseph E., "Argentina, Shortchanged; Why the Nation That Followed the Rules Fell to Pieces," *The Washington Post*, May 12, 2002, p. B1.

A former chief economist at the World Bank argues that the orthodox economic prescriptions imposed on Argentina by the Washington Consensus helped derail its economy.

Tobar, Hector, "The Good Life is No More in Argentina," *Los Angeles Times*, Feb. 18, 2003, p. 1.

The piece details Argentina's slide into economic chaos and the impact the country's depression is having on its once well-to-do populace.

Reports

Human Rights Watch, "A Wrong Turn: The Record of the Colombian Attorney General's Office," November 2002.

The advocacy group alleges the attorney general failed to adequately prosecute members of the military for human rights abuses.

World Bank, *Global Economic Prospects and the Developing Countries 2003: Investing to Unlock Global Opportunities*, December 2002.

The report looks at Latin America's economy in 2002 and the prospects for growth in the coming years, focusing on the impact of Argentina's financial collapse.

For More Information

Center for Economic and Policy Research, 1621 Connecticut Ave., N.W., Suite 500, Washington, DC 20009; (202) 293-5380; www.cepr.net.

Council on Foreign Relations, The Harold Pratt House, 58 East 68th St., New York, NY 10021; (212) 434-9400; www.cfr.org.

Council on Hemispheric Affairs, 1250 Connecticut Ave., N.W., Suite 1C, Washington, DC 20036; (202) 223-4975; www.coha.org.

Institute for International Economics, 1750 Massachusetts Ave., N.W., Washington, DC 20036; (202) 328-9000; www.iie.com.

Inter-American Development Bank, 1300 New York Ave., N.W., Washington, DC 20577; (202) 623-1000; www.iadb.org.

Inter-American Dialogue, 1211 Connecticut Ave., N.W., Suite 510, Washington, DC 20036; (202) 822-9002; www.iadialog.org.

International Bank for Reconstruction and Development (World Bank), 1818 H St., N.W., Washington, DC 20433; (202) 473-1000; www.worldbank.org.

Organization of American States, 17th St. and Constitution Ave., N.W., Washington, DC 20006; (202) 458-3000; www.oas.org.

Washington Office on Latin America, 1630 Connecticut Ave., N.W., Suite 200, Washington, DC 20009; (202) 797-2171; www.wola.org.

11

Aiding Africa

David Masci

Protected by a Nigerian peacekeeper, Liberians unload U.N. food aid in the port city of Monrovia. Civil wars have devastated Liberia and other African countries in recent years, as have AIDS and famine. Corruption and economic stagnation also have taken a toll. Now the United States and other industrial nations are calling for new infusions of international humanitarian and development aid.

From *The CQ Researcher*, August 29, 2003.

Sitting on his velvet throne in a crisp, white suit, Liberian President Charles Taylor looked every bit the African strongman. But Taylor's position on a recent August morning was anything but secure. After six violent and chaotic years, he announced he was stepping down and going into exile in Nigeria.

"I have accepted this role as the sacrificial lamb," he said, comparing himself to Jesus Christ and vowing one day to return.[1]

Taylor had been pressured for months, by the United States and most of the rest of the international community, to leave his utterly devastated country, which has seen tens of thousands of civilians die during more than a decade of civil war.

"He was in every way bad for his country, and his departure is long overdue," says Ali A. Mazrui, chancellor of Jomo Kenyatta University of Agriculture and Technology in Thika, Kenya, and a respected Africa scholar. "This is especially good news because Africa has had so many leaders like Taylor, but few of them have ever resigned."

But while Taylor's resignation is unusual, the hallmarks of his rule—authoritarianism, violence and brutality—are all too common in sub-Saharan Africa. Since the late 1950s and early '60s, when most African colonies achieved independence from Europe, scores of repressive dictators have come and gone, from the late Idi Amin of Uganda to Zaire's Mobutu Sese Seko.

Their legacy of underdevelopment, corruption, desperate poverty and violence continues to hobble Africa. The nearly 700 million inhabitants of sub-Saharan Africa are the poorest in the world, with a per-capita gross-domestic product (GDP) of $460—just over a dollar a day. African life expectancy also is the world's

Successes Amid the Crises

Many of sub-Saharan Africa's 48 nations are struggling with life-and-death challenges, such as political instability, war, desperate poverty, famine and the spread of HIV/AIDS. But there are success stories as well: Angola emerged last year from a 25-year civil war, and Kenya and Nigeria both held elections after years of authoritarian rule.

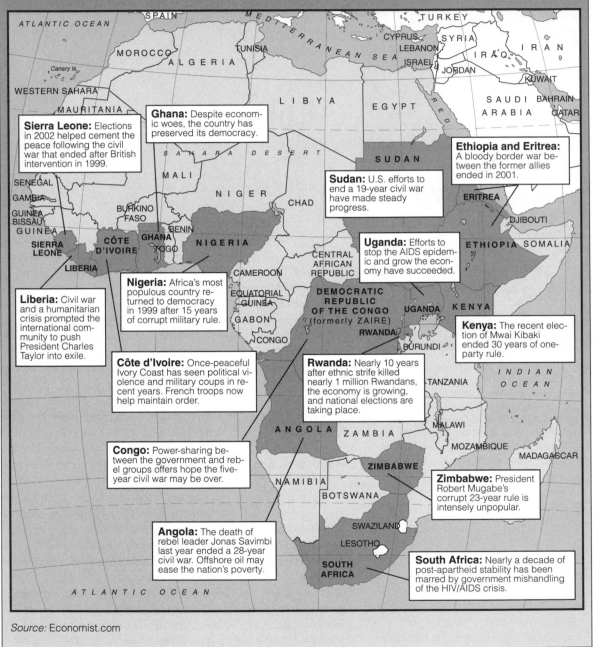

Sierra Leone: Elections in 2002 helped cement the peace following the civil war that ended after British intervention in 1999.

Ghana: Despite economic woes, the country has preserved its democracy.

Ethiopia and Eritrea: A bloody border war between the former allies ended in 2001.

Sudan: U.S. efforts to end a 19-year civil war have made steady progress.

Uganda: Efforts to stop the AIDS epidemic and grow the economy have succeeded.

Liberia: Civil war and a humanitarian crisis prompted the international community to push President Charles Taylor into exile.

Nigeria: Africa's most populous country returned to democracy in 1999 after 15 years of corrupt military rule.

Kenya: The recent election of Mwai Kibaki ended 30 years of one-party rule.

Côte d'Ivoire: Once-peaceful Ivory Coast has seen political violence and military coups in recent years. French troops now help maintain order.

Rwanda: Nearly 10 years after ethnic strife killed nearly 1 million Rwandans, the economy is growing, and national elections are taking place.

Congo: Power-sharing between the government and rebel groups offers hope the five-year civil war may be over.

Zimbabwe: President Robert Mugabe's corrupt 23-year rule is intensely unpopular.

Angola: The death of rebel leader Jonas Savimbi last year ended a 28-year civil war. Offshore oil may ease the nation's poverty.

South Africa: Nearly a decade of post-apartheid stability has been marred by government mishandling of the HIV/AIDS crisis.

Source: Economist.com

Quality of Life Lowest in Sub-Saharan Africa

Sub-Saharan Africa ranks lowest among other regions in several categories used to measure quality of life, including life expectancy, child mortality and access to clean water.

Selected Regions	Population (in millions) 2001	Life expectancy at birth (in years) 2001	GNP per capita (in $US) 2001	Under-5 mortality rate (per 1,000) 2001	Percent with access to clean water 2000
Sub-Saharan Africa	674	46	$460	171	58%
East Asia & Pacific	1,823	69	900	44	76
Europe & Central Asia	475	69	1,970	38	91
Latin America & Caribbean	524	71	3,580	34	86
Middle East & North Africa	301	68	2,220	54	88
South Asia	1,378	63	450	99	84

Source: 2003 World Development Indicators database, World Bank, April 13, 2003

lowest—and falling even lower, dropping from 50 years in 1990 to 46 in 2001.

The decline in lifespan is largely due to HIV/AIDS, which has killed millions in southern and eastern Africa and is still being largely ignored by governments in several affected nations. Now the disease is rapidly spreading into West Africa.

Meanwhile, rulers with little or no democratic legitimacy govern more than half of all African states, even though Zambia, Malawi and several other African countries made the transition to democracy during the 1990s. While some experts point to recent elections in Kenya as evidence that the trend toward elections and freedom continues, others contend that the push for democratic change has largely stalled.

Either way, democratic reform is often hindered by instability, which has plagued many parts of the continent since independence. Civil war, revolution and even genocide have been all too common since African countries began governing themselves roughly 40 years ago.

In the last 10 years alone, wars have been fought in, among other countries, Sierra Leone, Liberia, Congo, Angola, Sudan and Rwanda. Even Côte d'Ivoire (Ivory Coast), once a bastion of stability in West Africa, has recently descended into a bloody civil war.

Since the end of the Cold War, Africa's internecine fighting has occurred largely unhindered by the West, even when the blood-letting reached horrific proportions. In Congo alone, an estimated 3 million people have died from fighting and starvation in a civil war that has embroiled eight other countries. An earlier tragedy in Rwanda, where a 1994 genocide led to an estimated 1 million deaths, also provoked little action from the developed nations.

Lately though, the world community has been paying more attention to African conflicts. Earlier this year, about 8,000 peacekeepers (mostly from France) arrived to try to stop the fighting in Congo. In addition, British forces entered Sierra Leone in 1999 to stop a civil war.

Similarly, the world community had been calling in recent months for the United States to intervene militarily to stop the civil war in Liberia and ensure the flow of humanitarian aid. After more than a month of indecision, President Bush on Aug. 14 finally sent 200 Marines and dozens of helicopters to Monrovia, Liberia's capital, to back up a much larger contingent of Nigerian peacekeepers already there.

The president's hesitation over sending troops to Africa on a humanitarian mission stemmed in part from the deadly 1992 U.S. experience in Somalia, where a military intervention to help feed famine victims thrust American troops into the middle of a civil war. Eventually, 44 Americans died, and the rest of the force was hastily pulled from the country.

Critics of humanitarian intervention say U.S. blood should not be spilled in places like Somalia and Liberia, where American strategic interests are not clear-cut. "We need to focus our military on those areas where we have big interests and allow regional powers to deal with these smaller peacekeeping operations," says Jack Spencer, a senior defense-policy analyst at the Heritage Foundation.

But advocates of intervention contend that saving innocents from violence and starvation—and preventing war and political chaos from spreading to other countries—is in America's strategic interest. "We should understand by now that letting problems fester can lead to horrible consequences," says Joseph Siegle, a senior fellow and Africa expert at the Council on Foreign Relations, noting that al Qaeda terrorists have taken advantage of instability in countries like Somalia, Sudan and, most notably, Afghanistan to recruit and train converts.

Many experts see the deployment of U.S. troops in Liberia as the latest in a series of recent Bush administration actions reflecting almost a sea change in U.S. attitudes about Africa's political, economic and strategic importance. Since the Sept. 11 attacks almost two years ago, the White House has proposed a number of ambitious aid programs, ranging from promoting democratic change and open markets to easing the continent's AIDS crisis.

Indeed, many experts see Bush's recent five-nation trip to sub-Saharan Africa—only the second by an American president—as a sign of America's new interest in the long-neglected continent. In Botswana and Uganda, the president visited AIDS clinics to underscore his recent $15 billion commitment to fighting the disease that has already claimed 20 million Africans and infected 30 million more. And during a speech in Nigeria, Bush stressed the need for both African and Western countries to reverse the continent's history of poverty, instability and underdevelopment.

"Working together," the president said, "we can help make this a decade of rising prosperity and expanding peace across Africa."

The president's emphasis on cooperation is reflected in a proposed U.S. development-assistance program pending before Congress that would reward countries that make political and economic strides. In 2002, he announced a $5 billion aid package for countries that

create more democratic, open and accountable societies. Called the Millennium Challenge Account, the new program has been bolstered by promises of more aid from European and other prosperous nations.

But some Africa-watchers contend that foreign assistance often does more harm than good in Africa, feeding corruption and warping the very market forces that could help lift Africans out of poverty. Like opponents of domestic welfare, critics of foreign aid charge that it creates a damaging dependency, robbing recipients of the incentive to solve their own problems.

The opposing sides in the aid debate do agree on one thing: Much work needs to be done before Africa can begin living up to its enormous potential. And all agree that the West, and the United States in particular, have an important role to play.

As policymakers debate Africa's future, here are some of the questions they are asking:

Should the U.S. intervene militarily in Africa to stop wars and humanitarian crises?

The recent civil war in Liberia has renewed the debate over whether American troops should intervene in African countries that are not considered strategically important.

The dilemma has confronted the United States only in the last decade or so—particularly since the end of the Cold War.

Traditionally, Africa has drawn more attention from European powers, most notably Britain and France, which colonized much of the continent in the late 19th and early 20th centuries. Even the rise of the United States as a superpower after World War II and the breakup of Europe's colonial empires did not lead to direct American military involvement in sub-Saharan Africa. Instead, the United States, then embroiled in the Cold War with the Soviet Union, limited its role to providing money and arms to African countries—often run by corrupt dictators—or rebel forces fighting communist or socialist governments.

But the fall of the Soviet Union in 1991 left the United States as the only nation on Earth able to deploy large numbers of troops in distant theaters. In addition, cable television and later the Internet brought far-off humanitarian crises into Americans' living rooms 24 hours a day, often sparking widespread demands for action.

Such factors drew the United States in 1992 to its first and so far, only major, humanitarian intervention in

Africa. That year a bloody civil war in Somalia had led to widespread famine and American troops were called on, as the lead nation in a United Nations-sponsored coalition, to help feed millions of people and stabilize the country.

At first, the mission succeeded. But efforts to stabilize the country put American soldiers in the middle of a chaotic civil war. After 44 Americans died, and a U.S. soldier's body was dragged through Mogadishu, President Bill Clinton withdrew all the U.S. troops.

Two years later, Clinton faced a similar choice in tiny Rwanda, where tribal tensions between the Hutus and Tutsis were threatening to erupt. But still smarting from the Somalia debacle, the United States and other allies didn't aid Rwanda, and an estimated 1 million people eventually were killed in the worst ethnic genocide in recent history.

Rwanda is often cited by supporters of humanitarian military intervention as an example of what can happen when a chaotic situation is allowed to continue. "I was in an airport hangar waiting to go into Rwanda when the mission was scrapped, and I've never felt good about that," says Army Special Forces Maj. Roger Carstens, a member of the Council on Emerging National Security Affairs, a private think tank. "If sending 2,500 troops in can make a situation like that better and save the lives of millions of people, it seems like a pretty good trade-off, if you ask me."

Carstens and others argue that intervening in trouble spots like Rwanda can prevent them from destabilizing neighboring countries, something that commonly occurs. Indeed, Rwanda's troubles spilled into Burundi and Congo, stoking the flames of Congo's long-running civil war.

"These sorts of humanitarian conflicts are the main source of instability in the world because they move across borders through refugee flows, through slower economic growth and through warfare itself," says the Council on Foreign Relations' Siegle. "Avoiding that has to be in our strategic interest."

As a result, Carstens says, it is folly to say that humanitarian crises like the current troubles in Liberia are not in America's strategic interest. "After 9/11, everything is a strategic interest more or less, especially if it is in a state of chaos," he says. "Look at Afghanistan: When ignored and left to its own devices, it became a haven for drug smugglers and terrorists."

In Carstens' view, African trouble spots could, like Afghanistan, turn into direct threats to American security.

Young workers carry dirt out of a gold mine in the Democratic Republic of Congo. Economists say most African economies are much too dependent on exporting price-sensitive commodities like gold.

"When you look at failing states like Congo and Liberia, you have to remember that we now live in a world where terrorism and weapons of mass destruction have taken on a global dimension," he says. Some experts even say Liberia's Taylor may have laundered money for al Qaeda.[2]

But others counter that while crises like those in Rwanda and Liberia are tragic and even important to the United States, they do not represent the sort of strategic interests that American soldiers should risk their lives protecting.

"The United States has a unique role to play in the world, and that is keeping the big peace, doing the sort of things that other countries can't do," says the Heritage Foundation's Spencer. "Our job is to deter aggression and promote stability in strategically important regions like Europe, the Middle East and Asia, not respond to every flareup everywhere."

As for sending American troops to Liberia, syndicated columnist Charles Krauthammer said recently on Fox News, "In principle, it's a bad idea because foreign policy is not social work. There are a lot of bad guys in the world, but we don't spend our blood and treasure going after all the bad guys. We go after bad guys who are our enemies. . . . The military is to defend the United States, it's not to do relief."[3]

Moreover, Spencer adds, the American military is not trained to do the kind of work necessary to stabilize a Rwanda or Liberia. "U.S. ground forces are trained to fight and win wars, not to do peacekeeping duties," he says.

Opponents of humanitarian missions also contend that they deter other nations capable of doing peacekeeping missions from undertaking them. "We need to stop communicating to the rest of the world that the U.S. has a responsibility to do this because we've created an expectation that we will intervene," says Christopher Preble, director of foreign-policy studies at the Cato Institute. "In most of these situations, there are local and regional powers that have a role to play, and we should let them play it."

For instance, Preble says, Nigerian troops delayed their entry into Liberia by more than a month due to expectations that the United States might intervene. "I got the sense that they were ready to go into Liberia [in June,] but then they decided to wait because they thought we might go in."

But Princeton Lyman, former U.S. ambassador to Nigeria and South Africa, says expectations of U.S. intervention don't delay other countries from carrying out their responsibilities. "No one expected us to go into Congo or Sierra Leone, and we didn't," he says. "Instead, the French and British went in, as they should have."

Even in Liberia, Lyman points out, the Nigerians only delayed their deployment because the United States was very publicly considering intervention. "Bush went all over Africa saying we might go in, so of course the Africans waited until a decision was made."

Will Africa's recent democratic gains be sustained and expanded?

In the 1990s, many African countries made substantial steps toward democratic reform. In Zambia, for instance, longtime dictator Kenneth Kaunda stepped down after losing multiparty elections in 1991. Similar events occurred in Malawi, South Africa and Nigeria.[4]

But Africa's march toward democracy has by no means been smooth, and much of the continent remains mired in dictatorships or quasi-democratic systems that do not give citizens much voice in state affairs. For instance, nations such as Eritrea, Congo and Sudan have repressive, authoritarian governments. And in some places—notably Zimbabwe—governments that once had at least some trappings of democracy have largely lost them.

According to the democracy-advocacy group Freedom House, only 18 of the 48 countries in sub-Saharan Africa are electoral democracies. And of those, only 11 received the organization's highest rating of "free," meaning they respect citizens' full political and civil rights.[5]

Some experts argue that Africa's 1990s trend toward democracy has lost momentum and that the continent is unlikely to make substantial progress on democratic reform in the foreseeable future.

"There is no question that the democratization process that was moving forward in the mid-1990s has stalled today," says George Ayittey, a professor of economics at American University and president of the Free Africa Foundation, which promotes democratic change on the continent.

Robert Rotberg, director of the Program on Intrastate Conflict at the Kennedy School of Government at Harvard University, agrees that Africa's momentum toward democratization has slowed. "I don't think we can say that there is some democratic blossoming in Africa right now," he says. "Until some of the states that are large and influential, like Congo and Sudan, begin going democratic, it will be hard to say that the trends are running in the right direction."

Part of the problem, Ayittey says, is that many African governments are making cosmetic changes just to please aid donors, but are not committed to real democracy. "Many have twisted the rules of the game and then stood for elections, knowing full well that they would win," he says, citing countries like Togo, where the electoral process has been "rigged" to ensure the continuation of the current ruling clique. "That's not democracy."

Moreover, Rotberg says, the ruling elite is perfectly willing to ignore the popular will in order to preserve its privileges. "There is a growing middle class in Africa, and it wants the same things that middle classes in other parts of the world want, including a say in how their country is run," he says. "But you have a determined group of elites ready and willing to stand in the way to protect what they have."

Over the longer term, says Ayittey, a native of Ghana, Africa will continue to be "democracy poor" until local media are truly free. "If Africans really want to re-invigorate democracy, they need to reinvigorate the media," he says. "This is the best way to expose government wrongdoing and cronyism and hold them accountable."

By Ayittey's count, however, only eight countries have a truly free media. "So, you see, they have a long way to go."

But Charles Cobb, senior diplomatic correspondent for AllAfrica.com, a news-gathering organization, says the dire assessment by Ayittey, Rotberg and others is unwarranted. Although Africa is still far from its democratic potential, the trend remains positive, he contends. "On balance, I'd say they are going in the right direction," Cobb says.

Ambassador Lyman agrees, arguing that difficulties in a few countries like Liberia, Zimbabwe and Congo have blinded many people to the progress being made on the continent.

In Kenya, for instance, a new, freely elected president, Mwai Kibaki, has just taken power after 39 years of one-party rule under former president and strongman Daniel Arap Moi. Even in war-torn Congo, Lyman says, a government of national unity has been formed between the sitting government and rebel groups, and an election is to be held in the next two years. "There's real reason to hope there."

Cobb and Lyman also see positive signs that bode well for long-term democratic prospects on the continent. For instance, military coups are becoming much less common, both say, in large part because most African countries now ostracize governments that have taken power by force.

"Coups are just no longer acceptable in institutional Africa," Cobb says. "They recently had coups in Chad and Sao Tome, and African institutions like the African

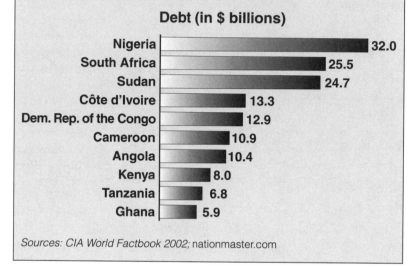

Five Nations Owe More Than $100 Billion

The five sub-Saharan nations with the most national debt owe more than $100 billion, mostly to donor nations and multilateral lenders like the World Bank. Most Africa-watchers contend that the prospects for poverty reduction in these and other African countries will remain bleak until much or all of their debt is forgiven. But some advocates of debt forgiveness argue it should only be granted to countries that successfully move to democracy and open markets.

Debt (in $ billions)

Country	Debt
Nigeria	32.0
South Africa	25.5
Sudan	24.7
Côte d'Ivoire	13.3
Dem. Rep. of the Congo	12.9
Cameroon	10.9
Angola	10.4
Kenya	8.0
Tanzania	6.8
Ghana	5.9

Sources: CIA World Factbook 2002; nationmaster.com

Union pressured these guys to back down and restore civilian rule, and they did. That's progress."

Meanwhile, on a more local level, optimists note, Africans are taking charge of their own future and not leaving it in the hands of corrupt leaders. "There's a great increase in civil-society groups," Cobb says, referring to churches, anti-corruption groups, environmental organizations, labor unions and the like. "These groups are increasingly making a difference all over Africa."

Michelle Carter, deputy regional director for East and Central Africa for the aid group CARE, says the impact of the groups was especially apparent in last year's election in Kenya. "In Kenya, you had a situation where the people were holding their leaders accountable, and it made a real difference," she says. "The rise of these civil-society groups is relatively new, but it is spreading throughout Africa."

Is the foreign aid that goes to Africa generally effective?

Nearly half of all Africans live in dire poverty. And only 15 percent live in an environment conducive to economic

AFP Photo/Issouf Sanogo

Nigerian President Olusegun Obasanjo votes in the presidential election last April. Nigeria is among several African countries that made the transition to democracy in the 1990s, including Zambia and South Africa.

growth and development.[6] Such bleak statistics have helped Africa gain more aid from the developed world in recent years.

The United Nations got the ball rolling in 2001 with its Millennium Development Goals, a series of objectives aimed at cutting world poverty in half by 2015.[7]

Then in March 2002 President Bush weighed in with his own development initiative, the Millennium Challenge Account (MCA), targeted at rewarding Third World countries that meet certain political and economic standards. Only countries with democratically elected governments that protect human rights and foster open markets are eligible for the aid, expected to total

$5 billion over the next three years. Much of the MCA funding will likely go to Africa.[8]

The case for increased foreign assistance gathered more momentum at the G-8 summit near Calgary, Canada, in June 2002, when Russia and the world's seven biggest economies—Japan, Germany, France, Britain, Italy, Canada and the United States—pledged an additional $6 billion in aid for Africa beginning in 2003. The G-8 leaders also pledged to phase out domestic subsidies to their own farmers, which make it hard for Africa's agricultural sector to compete on the international market.

A year later, at the next G-8 summit in Evian, France, several African leaders, including South Africa's President Thabo Mbeki and Nigeria's Olusegun Obasanjo, were invited to speak to the United States and its great-power allies as part of a Third World delegation.[9] The move was meant to underscore the importance of listening to and helping Africa and other underdeveloped regions.

A little more than a week before that meeting, on May 21, Bush pledged $15 billion over five years to combat the AIDS epidemic killing hundreds of thousands throughout sub-Saharan Africa each year.[10] Congress later authorized the money but has yet to appropriate the funds.*

African leaders, aid workers and others applaud these recent steps, arguing that reducing poverty and creating prosperity will require massive new infusions of aid. Moreover, they say, much more money will be needed to meet the U.N.'s ambitious goals. Indeed, U.N. Secretary-General Kofi Annan has called on the world's rich countries to double their development assistance. The total is currently about $50 billion per year—down more than 20 percent from its 1990 peak of $65.5 billion.[11]

But others point out that Africa has received hundreds of billions of dollars in aid over the last four decades, only to slip further into poverty. "The goal of aid, that being sustainable economic development, has not been met," says Paolo Pasicolan, a trade analyst at the Heritage Foundation. "Most African countries are poorer now than when we began giving them assistance after they became independent 30 or 40 years ago."

As William Easterly, a professor of economics at New York University and a senior fellow at the Center for Global Development, noted recently in *Forbes* magazine,

---

* The House has appropriated $2 billion of the $3 billion Bush requested for the first year of the five-year plan. The Senate has yet to act.

"Africa is the most intensive recipient of foreign aid of any continent on the globe. . . . Yet Africa's growth in output per person has declined from 1.5 percent per year in the 1960s and 1970s to zero in the 1980s and 1990s. Meanwhile, foreign aid to Africa increased from 7 percent of its income in the 1960s and 1970s to 16 percent in the 1980s and 1990s."[12]

The reason for the failure, critics say, is that aid doesn't help poor countries, it actually hurts them. "As a general rule, foreign aid is not an effective way to promote prosperity," says Cato's Preble. "Indeed, it makes things worse because it strengthens the very institutions that thwart prosperity."

Preble believes that giving money to African governments or even non-governmental organizations (NGOs) damages the only mechanism that will allow Africans to economically better themselves: the free market. "Everything governments do becomes politicized, and how and what they do with the money is based on political considerations."

For instance, he says, "When we give money to a government to establish a bank to lend money to small-business men, its lending practices will inevitably be based on political considerations." Private banks, by contrast, lend to those businesses they believe will succeed, he adds.

At the same time, Preble contends, establishing a government bank with cheap foreign aid discourages the development of private banks. "If the government is lending money at low rates, private banks won't be able to compete. It would be stupid for them to try."

Others argue that aid creates a damaging dependency for African countries. "Developing countries, especially in Africa, have become much too dependent on aid," Pasicolan says. "It's very much like welfare."

Indeed, Pasicolan and others point out that in many African countries, aid often makes up a huge share of the government budget. In Malawi, for instance, 40 percent of government spending comes from foreign aid. In Zambia and Uganda, the figure is even higher.[13]

The best thing the United States and other developed countries can do for Africa is not to give them more aid but open their domestic markets to the continent's products. "The trade barriers we put up are doing great harm to African countries," Preble says. "We need to eliminate agricultural subsidies and tariffs if we really want to help them."

Aid opponents cite a recent *New York Times* column in which Amadou Toumani Toure and Blaise Compaore, the presidents of Mali and Burkina Faso, call on the U.S. and the European Union to end their domestic subsidies for cotton producers, arguing the subsidies have effectively shut African farmers out of the world cotton market and are helping to impoverish people in rural areas.[14]

But others counter that foreign aid, for all its problems, has helped Africa tremendously. "Things in Africa are not good right now," says Ambassador Lyman. "But if we didn't have aid, I guarantee there would be much more human suffering than there has been."

CARE's Carter agrees. "For all that's wrong, many indicators in Africa in areas like education and health are higher today than they were 50 years ago, and that's due to aid. No question about it."

Carter and others point to U.N. statistics showing that in several areas from infant mortality to literacy, African countries have been making progress. For example, infant mortality has dropped in Uganda from 110 per 1,000 births in 1970 to 79 in 2001. Meanwhile, the percentage of young Ugandans who can read and write has risen from 70.1 percent in 1990 to 79.4 in 2001.[15]

But, according to some supporters, foreign aid is only as good as the policies of the countries that receive it. A recent study by World Bank economists David Dollar and Craig Burnside found that "aid has a positive effect on growth in a good policy environment."[16] In other words, countries with sound monetary policy, the rule of law, open trade and other hallmarks of developed economies will be able to put foreign aid to good use.

Jerry Wolgin, the World Bank's principal economist for Africa, says that although the Dollar and Burnside study sounds obvious, it has helped make aid more effective. "Donors are getting better at putting their money in countries with good environments," he says, adding that there are between 12 and 15 states in Africa, such as Botswana and Ghana, that currently make the grade and would qualify for aid under MCA standards.

On the flip side, Wolgin says, countries without a good aid environment will get help to develop one. "So, for example, in Sierra Leone, where they currently have weak institutions, we're sending experts to help train government officials," he says. "We're helping them bring themselves up to a point where they can put development aid to good use."

Also on the good-news front: Some donors are beginning to reverse the longstanding practice of tying most of their foreign aid to purchases of domestic goods and services, leaving little actual money in the hands of recipients. For instance, foreign aid from Britain no longer must be spent on British products and contractors.

BACKGROUND

Out of Imperialism

During the 19th and early 20th centuries, the British and French—the world's two greatest colonial powers—conquered huge chunks of sub-Saharan Africa. Germany and Italy also grabbed pieces here and there, and even small states, like Belgium and Portugal, seized territories that were many times larger than their own.

European colonizers brought much that was both good and bad to Africa. The English and French, for instance, built roads, railroads and other infrastructure and created a native civil service to assist them in running their territories.

But all the colonizers exploited the land and its people. Some, like the Belgians, literally killed and maimed millions as they stripped their huge colony, Congo, of its natural resources.

But Europe's role as Africa's overseer was short-lived, largely due to the Second World War, which dramatically weakened most of the colonial powers. Many of Africa's masters—notably France and Belgium—had been occupied by Germany. Even Britain, one of the victors, emerged from the conflict considerably diminished. In short, Europe could no longer afford the cost of maintaining vast colonies far from home.

Meanwhile, even before the war ended, the world's new great power, the United States, had been pressuring the Europeans to divest their colonies in Africa and elsewhere.

As a result, independence came to many parts of Africa without the violence that often precedes a colony's separation from its mother country. In more cases than not, power was transferred smoothly and even amicably.

By the late 1940s, the British Colonial Office had begun transferring some governing authority to local elected councils in Africa. It was the first step toward self-government and eventually led to the formation of political parties in each of Britain's colonies.[17]

The establishment of a genuine political process in British Africa led to an independence "domino effect" that began in 1957 in Ghana. Three years later Nigeria—the most populous African country—gained its freedom, and tiny Sierra Leone followed suit in 1961. Over the next five years, Uganda, Tanzania, Kenya and Gambia would all become independent via the peaceful transfer of power.*

The 14 French colonies in West and Central Africa also began to gain more and more autonomy in the late 1940s and '50s, electing local officials and even sending representatives to the French parliament.[18] By 1956, Francophone Africa was largely self-governing, although Paris still controlled the colonies' finance, defense and foreign policies.[19] France hoped to make this arrangement permanent when in 1958 it offered its African possessions two choices: total independence or autonomy within a new "French Community." Colonies that chose autonomy would receive French aid and protection in exchange for continued French oversight of external and finance policy.[20]

Initially, almost all the territories chose continued close association with France. But within months, the new quasi-states began opting out of the community and declaring total independence.

By 1960, all but one of the Francophone countries in sub-Saharan Africa—French Somaliland—had rejected community in favor of independence. The same year, Congo formally declared itself a sovereign state, severing its formal association with Belgium.

Still, the great wave of decolonization did not leave Africa entirely free of white rule. Portugal employed increasingly repressive tactics to retain control of Portuguese Guinea, Angola and Mozambique. Soon, however, the three territories were in open revolt, and by 1970 Lisbon had to maintain 150,000 troops in Africa to hold onto its possessions.[21]

A different but no less explosive situation prevailed in southern Africa. In South Africa, the descendents of 18th-century Dutch and German settlers, known as Afrikaners, held power over the territory's black majority. Upon achieving independence from Britain in 1948, the Afrikaners established a harsh, new system of formal racial

---

* Beginning in 1952, Kenyans rose up against the British in the bloody Mau Mau uprising. But it had been quelled by the time the country won its freedom in 1963.

CHRONOLOGY

1950s-1960s *Europe's colonies in Africa gain independence, often peacefully.*

1957 Ghana becomes the first British colony to gain independence.

1958 France offers its 14 colonies in sub-Saharan Africa independence or semi-autonomy within a new "French Community." Within two years, all but one former colony opt for independence.

1960 Africa's most populous state, Nigeria, gains independence. Kenya, Uganda and other British territories become free over the next five years.

1965 Efforts by Britain to negotiate a power-sharing agreement between blacks and whites in Rhodesia fail, and the white minority declares independence, sparking an uprising by the black majority.

1970s-1980s *Cold War rivalry and economic mismanagement hurt most African states.*

1975 Mozambique and Angola gain independence from Portugal and almost immediately plunge into civil wars.

1980 Minority-white rule ends in Rhodesia, which is renamed Zimbabwe. But white Afrikaners continue to oppress South Africa's black majority under the apartheid system of legal discrimination and segregation.

1990-Present *Much of the continent embraces democracy while it grapples with challenges like economic stagnation, ethnic violence and HIV/AIDS.*

1990 South African opposition leader Nelson Mandela is freed from prison by President F.W. de Klerk after 27 years. Negotiations over the transition to black majority rule begin.

1991 Zambia's president for 30 years, Kenneth Kaunda, is defeated in free elections. . . . Two Marxist dictators in Africa's so-called Horn, Mohammed Siad Barre of

Somalia and Mengistu Haile Mariam of Ethiopia, are overthrown by homegrown rebellions.

1992 American aid efforts in Somalia end in failure, and U.S. troops are pulled from the country.

1994 Ethnic tensions in Rwanda erupt into genocide, killing an estimated 1 million people. South Africa, Mozambique and Malawi hold free elections.

1997 Congo's Mobutu Sese Seko is ousted.

1999 Congress passes the Africa Growth and Opportunity Act, aimed at spurring exports from Africa to the United States. . . . Nigeria holds its first successful multi-party elections after 15 years of army rule. . . . The number of people living with HIV/AIDS in sub-Saharan Africa reaches 25 million.

2001 Ethiopia and Eritrea fight a bloody border war.

March 2002 President Bush proposes the Millennium Challenge Account, a new U.S. aid program aimed at rewarding poor countries that promote democracy and enact sound economic policies. . . . Angola's rebel leader, Jonas Savimbi, is killed, ending his country's 28-year civil war.

June 2002 A G-8 summit in Canada focuses on alleviating Africa's poverty.

December 2002 Kenya's ruling party loses its 30-year grip on power in the wake of the country's first free election in decades.

May 21, 2003 President Bush pledges $15 billion over five years to combat the AIDS epidemic in Africa. Congress later authorizes the money but has yet to appropriate the funds.

July 2003 President Bush visits five nations in sub-Saharan Africa. His trip is only the second by an American president.

August 2003 Liberian President Charles Taylor goes into exile under pressure from the United States and other nations, and a small American force joins Nigerian peacekeepers in an effort to bring stability to the war-torn country.

Leaders Target Bribery and Corruption

When Kenya's minister of local government, Karisa Maitha, found a briefcase with $62,500 outside of his Nairobi office recently, he did something that is unusual in Africa: He found the man who left it, a local developer, and threw him and his money out of the building.[1]

It is so rare for an official in Africa to turn down a bribe, especially such a large one, that Maitha's gesture made headlines in Kenya and beyond. From the lowliest bureaucrat or police officer to cabinet ministers and presidents, bribery and corruption are woven into the fabric of life. Indeed, African civil servants' salaries are the lowest in the world, partly in expectation that paychecks will be supplemented by bribes.

Citizens who need a phone installed, a form processed or a traffic violation overlooked simply slip the appropriate official a little baksheesh. The same holds true for multinational corporations and rich businessmen, who often see kickbacks as part of the price of doing business.

But the custom may be changing, at least in some parts of Africa. In Kenya, recently elected President Mwai Kibaki has launched a "zero corruption" initiative that already has caused Kenya's chief justice, central bank chief and top tax collector to step down.

"Corruption has undermined our economy, our politics and our national psyche," Kibaki said.[2]

Other countries, including Ghana, Mozambique, Zambia and South Africa, also have launched anti-corruption drives. Zambia, which has been developing new standards of conduct for civil servants, recently put former President Frederick Chaluba on trial for allegedly plundering the state treasury during his two terms.

In South Africa, new laws now protect whistleblowers and require public disclosure of public spending. Moreover, a special anti-corruption unit—dubbed the Scorpions—has won fame by netting hundreds of allegedly corrupt officials, including top members of the ruling African National Congress (ANC) party. Indeed, at the end of July, the group was investigating charges that Deputy President Jacob Zuma took a $68,000 bribe from a French defense firm.[3]

But for all of this progress, Africa still ranks among the most corrupt places on Earth. A recent survey of 102 countries conducted by Transparency International, an anti-corruption group, found that many of the world's most corrupt nations were in Africa, including Nigeria, Madagascar, Kenya, Angola and Uganda. Of the 25 least-corrupt countries, only one, Botswana, was African.[4]

In Nigeria, for instance, bribery is rampant at all levels of society. "Nigerians say it is just a normal part of their lives, like anything else," says Chantal Uwimana, a Burundian, who is a program officer for Transparency

---

[1] "Minister Maitha Rejects Bag with a $62,000 Bribe," *The Nation* [of Kenya], April 5, 2003.

[2] Quoted in Marc Lacey, "A Sign of the New Kenya: A Briefcase Filled with Cash is Spurned," *The New York Times*, March 29, 2003, p. A6.

[3] "Just How Bad Is It, Really?" *The Economist*, Aug. 2, 2003.

[4] From Transparency International's "Corruption Perceptions Index 2002" at http://www.transparency.org/cpi/2002/cpi2002.en.html

---

segregation, known as apartheid ("apart"), in an effort to solidify their rule. Under apartheid, blacks were paid less than whites for the same jobs, restricted in where they could travel or live, prohibited from voting and generally not allowed to receive higher education or hold positions of authority in either government or business.

Meanwhile, just north of South Africa another white minority in another British colony was trying to retain its power and privileges. In the early 1960s, as it prepared to grant independence to what was then called Rhodesia, Britain tried to broker a power-sharing deal between whites and blacks. But the effort failed, and whites, though greatly outnumbered by the blacks, declared

independence from the U.K. in 1965 and set about governing on their own.

Britain and most of the world community did not recognize Rhodesia's white-minority government, and soon the United Nations had imposed economic sanctions on the new country. Meanwhile, blacks began actively fighting for independence from white rule, throwing the country into a civil war that lasted almost 15 years.

The Cold War

By 1970, sub-Saharan Africa was largely free of direct European rule. In less than 15 years, 42 new African

International in Berlin. "They don't even wait until someone asks them for a bribe, but just pay it as if it was a normal fee."

Even in Kenya, with all of its recent efforts, bribery still costs the average citizen 20 percent of his salary, according to Uwimana. "They have to pay extra for everything—health care, education, police and judges."

But corruption hurts Africans in other ways as well. "Because of corruption, a significant amount of [foreign] aid doesn't reach its intended target," says George Ayittey, a professor of economics at American University and president of the Free Africa Foundation, which promotes democracy on the continent. "So much of [aid] is embezzled—an estimated 40 percent of World Bank loans in Ghana, for example—so the suffering continues."

In addition to foreign aid, oil and natural gas revenues are also frequently the targets of corruption. Nigeria sits on an estimated 25 billion barrels of petroleum and is Africa's largest oil exporter. Yet past governments and their allies have been accused of stealing about $30 billion in oil revenue and wasting much of the rest.[5] Meanwhile, Nigerian motorists often have to wait in line for gas.

"Oil has been a curse for Africa because it has completely undermined good governance," says Jerry Wolgin, the World Bank's principal economist for Africa. "There are just too many ways to get wealthy, too many temptations and so government officials focus on getting rich instead of doing their jobs."

But here too, some steps are being taken to ensure that oil wealth is used to good purpose. Chad, for example, recently agreed to allow the World Bank to oversee the spending of a new financial windfall from recent oil development.[6]

And in June, British Prime Minister Tony Blair threw his political weight behind efforts to get energy companies to disclose how much they are paying developing nations for oil and gas leases. So far, a number of companies, including British Petroleum and Royal Dutch Shell, have responded positively to the controversial initiative, though none have committed to full disclosure.

"It this succeeds, it will give people a sense of how much money their governments are getting, and that will make these governments more accountable for how they spend it," says Uwimana.

According to experts like Uwimana, Africans are growing more and more weary of corruption. But eliminating bribery and other dirty practices takes a determined effort starting at the top, says Stephen Hayes, president of the Corporate Council on Africa, a group promoting U.S.-Africa trade. "Tackling corruption of all kinds requires a genuine commitment from the leader of the government," he says.

Uwimana goes even further, arguing that anti-corruption efforts must be broad-based. "The commitment has to come from all parts of political society—executive, parliamentary and judicial as well as civil-society groups," she says. "Without that, you won't make real progress."

---

[5] Warren Vieth, "U.S. Quest for Oil in Africa Worries Analysts, Activists," *Los Angeles Times*, Jan. 13, 2003, p. A1.

[6] Daniel Fisher, "Dangerous Liaisons," *Forbes*, Aug. 28, 2003, p. 84.

countries had become members of the United Nations. Only the three Portuguese colonies, South Africa and Rhodesia were not ruled by black Africans.

But the speed and relative ease with which most African countries obtained independence belied the huge challenges they faced. Many of the new states had been left to govern themselves without enough skilled managers and technicians, both in government and business.

As Oxford University historian John Morris Roberts observes: "In practical terms, the speed of decolonization in Africa had often meant that there was little chance of finding native Africans in sufficient numbers to provide administrators and technicians for the new regimes, some of

which continued for a time to rely upon white personnel. Similarly, the supporting structures of higher education, communications and armed forces were often nothing like so evolved as those in say, India; this, too, made new African nations even more dependent on foreign help."[22]

And foreign "help" was always available. As the Cold War raged worldwide, it often had repercussions on the continent. The United States, Soviet Union, China and former colonial powers like Britain and France all jockeyed to gain influence in newly independent Africa. Often this led to economic and military backing for corrupt and even cruel leaders or support for a rebel group that was destabilizing the country.

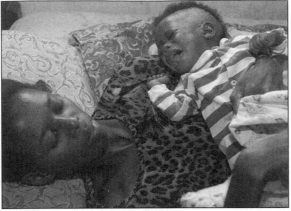

A South African woman with AIDS consoles her HIV-positive child. AIDS has killed some 20 million Africans and infected 30 million more in the last two decades. President Bush has pledged $15 billion over five years to combat AIDS in Africa, but Congress has yet to appropriate the funds.

In Congo, for instance, the Soviet Union and the United States each backed different sides in an internal conflict that began brewing literally as the country gained independence. The Soviets backed the newly elected prime minister, Patrice Lumumba, a fiery nationalist and socialist. The United States opposed Lumumba and eventually supported Army Chief of Staff Joseph Mobutu, who allegedly had Lumumba killed and eventually took control of the government.[23]

But Africa's problems were not entirely imported. Intertribal violence flared up in many new states, which often had been created without regard to traditional tribal boundaries. In eastern Nigeria, for instance, the Ojukwu tribe seceded in 1967, declaring the independent state of Biafra. Three years of bloody war ensued, leading to an estimated 1 million deaths—many from starvation—before the rebels surrendered.[24]

Tribalism often led states to abandon democratic principles in favor of authoritarian, usually military, rule. So-called dictators for life, or strongmen, rose to power in many countries, including Zambia, Kenya, Ethiopia and Uganda, using the specter of intertribal violence as a justification for their heavy-handed rule. These regimes quickly became corrupt and often harshly repressive.

By the 1970s, the repression and corruption, often accompanied by socialist policies, eventually led to economic stagnation and decline. Ten years earlier, during the years immediately following independence, many African countries had experienced moderate economic growth. Rising prices for cocoa, cotton, gold and other commodities had boosted most African economies, which relied heavily on such exports. In addition, many states were bolstered by outside aid, usually spent on large infrastructure or prestige projects, like dams and universities.

But corrupt and inept governance eventually undermined the gains. In the early 1970s, a recession in the West sent world commodity prices plummeting. Africa was hit hard, and throughout the rest of the 1970s and '80s, the gross domestic product (GDP) of most African countries shrank. Between 1980 and '87, for instance, the continentwide GDP dropped an average of 2.6 percent per year. By contrast, Asian countries such as South Korea and Taiwan, which had been poorer than most parts of Africa just two decades before—were growing at a breakneck pace.

By 1989, 30 heavily indebted sub-Saharan African countries were being forced by the World Bank and International Monetary Fund (IMF) to submit to "structural adjustment" programs, or spending restrictions, in an effort to balance budgets and make their economies more market-oriented. But the spending limits also kept many economies in deep recession and hurt Africa's poor.[25]

The economic suffering was compounded by restrictions on political freedom. Only one state, Botswana, was judged in 1989 to be fully democratic.[26]

New Hope

The end of the Cold War in the early 1990s brought dramatic changes to Africa, especially in the political arena. Dictators who had been almost blindly propped up by the United States and Soviet Union began to lose their patronage.

Moreover, as Cambridge University historian David Reynolds writes, the spending limits imposed by the multinational lenders had a political impact as well: "Cutting government projects and slashing state jobs hit the patronage networks created by African rulers."[27] One of the dictators' traditional levers of power was disappearing.

In a few cases, longtime dictators were violently overthrown. In 1991, for example, two brutal Marxists in Africa's so-called Horn, Mohammed Siad Barre of Somalia and Mengistu Haile Mariam of Ethiopia, were toppled by homegrown rebellions. And in 1997 Congo's Mobutu, long backed by the United States, was ousted by a rebel army led by longtime revolutionary Laurent Kabila.

Unfortunately, the abrupt changes left several countries no better off. Somalia descended almost immediately into civil war and famine. Likewise in Congo, Kabila's rule brought about a new and bloodier civil war.

But in much of the rest of Africa, the old order was swept away by more peaceful means. And often, the changes led to real improvements in people's lives. Between 1990 and 1995, 14 leaders were removed from power via the electoral process. Longtime strongmen like Zambia's Kaunda and Malawi's Hastings Banda were forced to step aside and make way for younger leaders who had built grass-roots political movements and enjoyed enormous popularity.

Perhaps the most significant and exciting of the new democratic transitions occurred in South Africa, where apartheid had continued despite the crippling effects of international economic sanctions and the end of white-minority rule in neighboring Rhodesia (renamed Zimbabwe) in 1980.

But South Africa's repressive white government could not withstand international pressure forever. By early 1990, when the nation's last white president, F. W. de Klerk, took office, the economy was reeling from the collapse of investment, international trade sanctions and high military expenditures needed to keep the increasingly rebellious black majority in line.

De Klerk immediately began preparing for the transition to majority rule. Within six months, he legalized the main opposition group, the African National Congress (ANC), and freed its iconic leader, Nelson Mandela, after 27 years in prison.

De Klerk and Mandela worked to shape a new, post-apartheid South Africa. The negotiations were marred by violence and threatened by both white and black extremists, but by late 1993 all sides had reached an agreement to hold elections in April 1994.[28]

The successful election marked the first time South Africans of all races voted. They elected Mandela as president and handed nearly two-thirds of the seats in the new parliament to the ANC. The white-dominated National Party became the chief opposition, and de Klerk was picked as deputy president.[29]

Despite the good news in South Africa and elsewhere, misery and death still burdened many parts of the continent. The same year South Africa held its first multiracial elections, tiny Rwanda exploded in horrific ethnic violence after a power-sharing agreement between the minority Tutsi tribe and majority Hutus broke down. The violence that followed left an estimated 1 million Rwandans, mostly Tutsis, dead—many hacked to death with machetes. A Tutsi rebel army, backed by Uganda, finally entered the country and restored order.

Today, the good news-bad news cycle that has characterized much of the post-independence period continues apace. Economic stagnation still grips the region, and civil wars continue to rage in Congo and Sudan. Even Zimbabwe and Côte d'Ivoire—once touted as examples of stability and economic success for the rest of Africa—recently have been plagued by civil unrest. Zimbabwe's economy has collapsed under the repressive rule of its longtime president Robert Mugabe. Meanwhile, ethnic violence has rocked Côte d'Ivoire, where only the presence of French and West African peacekeepers has allowed a fragile peace to take hold.

But some parts of the continent continue to make progress. In South Africa and in nearby Zambia, Botswana and Namibia strong democratic institutions have taken root and continue to grow.

Yet even there, the good news is tempered by other troubles. The new southern democracies recently have experienced both famine and an HIV/AIDS crisis that is affecting one in every five young adults in some areas and creating millions of orphans.[30]

CURRENT SITUATION

Slow Growth

The peaceful transfer of power throughout sub-Saharan Africa, coupled with rising prices for many African commodities, prompted many economists to predict the continent would outgrow Asia, Latin America and other parts of the developing world. Ghana, for instance, began the 1960s with a per-capita GDP nearly three times that of India.

But by the early 1970s, Africa's economic picture was bleak and getting bleaker. Widespread government mismanagement had created a business environment that discouraged foreign investors, who were needed to help Africa create an industrial base. Thus the continent was dangerously dependent on exports of coffee, cocoa, cotton, gold and other commodities that wildly fluctuated in price,

Progress for Women, But Many Woes

Although African society is largely patriarchal, it is women who often form the social and economic backbone of their communities, doing a substantial portion of the daily work—as high as 80 percent by some estimates.[1]

"Women hold the family together," said Alicen Chelaite, Kenya's deputy assistant minister for gender, sports, culture and social services. "They are the managers—they manage the farm, the house, the children, the water, the firewood."[2]

At the same time, sub-Saharan Africa is a bastion of male chauvinism. Women in many parts of the continent routinely put up with sexual harassment, rampant discrimination in employment, polygamy, genital mutilation and domestic violence.

And yet, little is being done in many places to improve the lot of girls and women. For instance, throughout much of Africa there is a visible gender gap in education. Currently, girls make up 60 percent of all children on the continent who are not in school.[3]

"It's not that most African families don't want to educate their daughters," says Sofia Gruskin, an associate professor of international health and human rights at Harvard University's School of Public Health. "It's more a question of priorities. In most African countries, school fees are very high, and when a family can't afford to send all of their children, sons usually go first. The attitude is: Girls are going to be married away anyway."

Violence, especially rape, is another problem. In South Africa—called the "rape capital of the world"—health officials estimate a woman or girl is raped every 26 seconds, on average. And the numbers are rising. In 1994, the year of South Africa's first multiracial elections, 18,801 rapes were reported. In 2001, 24,892 cases were reported, considered a fraction of the actual number.[4]

And in countries like South Africa or Zambia, where 20 percent of the population between ages 18 and 35 is HIV positive, rape can do more than just physical and emotional damage to the victim: It can kill her. In fact, 58 percent of all HIV/AIDS victims in Africa are women. Since African men are more likely than women to have multiple partners, they also are more likely to infect more than one woman.[5]

Women in sub-Saharan Africa have many other health problems. For instance, according to the United Nations Development Program, they are 100 times more likely to die in childbirth than are women in Western countries.[6]

But there are signs of progress in a number of areas, especially on the political front. "You're seeing more women in real positions of authority, especially in Anglophone [English-speaking] Africa," Gruskin says.

Although there has been only one female president in Africa (Liberia's Ruth Perry, from 1996-1997), women now hold 30 percent of the parliamentary seats in Mozambique and South Africa, 26 percent in Rwanda and 24 percent in Uganda.[7]

More and more countries are also placing women in high cabinet positions, including Mozambique—where Luisa Diogo is minister of finance—and Nigeria, Senegal, South Africa, Botswana and Ethiopia.

Women are also fighting more forcefully and openly for their rights at the grass-roots level. In February, for instance, women from all over the continent met in Ethiopia to publicly denounce female genital mutilation, sometimes called female circumcision, a common practice in sub-Saharan Africa.[8]

And hundreds of civil-society groups have sprung up across Africa to address women's issues. One such group in Senegal surrounds the houses of men who have been accused of domestic violence against their wives or girlfriends and blows whistles to humiliate them and to call attention to the problem.

"This started in Senegal but is spreading all over Africa," Gruskin says. "It's really amazing what women are doing to improve their lives."

[1] Emily Wax, "Africa's Women Beginning to See Progress in Politics," *The Washington Post,* June 6, 2003, p. A14.

[2] Quoted in *Ibid.*

[3] Figure cited in "Human Development Report 2003," United Nations Development Program, 2003, p. 6.

[4] Vincent R. Okungu, "Culture of Sexual Violence Pervades Continent," allAfrica.com, Aug. 18, 2003.

[5] Kofi Annan, "In Africa, AIDS Has a Woman's Face," *The New York Times,* Dec. 29, 2003, p. D9.

[6] United Nations, *op. cit.*, p. 8.

[7] Figures cited in Wax, *op. cit.*

[8] For background, see Mary H. Cooper, "Women and Human Rights," *The CQ Researcher,* April 30, 1999, pp. 353-376.

Should Western donors impose strict conditions for African debt relief?

YES
George B.N. Ayittey, Ph.D.
Associate Professor of Economics, American University, President, Free Africa Foundation

Written for *The CQ Researcher*, August 2003

Africa owes more than $350 billion in foreign debt. Servicing that debt absorbs some 30 percent of export revenue, leaving scant resources to import critical materials for schools, hospitals and national development. About 80 percent of Africa's debt is owed to multilateral financial institutions, such as the World Bank, or to Western foreign-aid programs. But many of these aid programs failed in Africa because of mistakes made by both donors and the recipients.

Donors allocated aid to support Cold War allies and to woo various Marxist leaders from the Soviet bloc. They also tied aid—usually requiring the use of services offered by donor-country companies—reducing its effectiveness. As a result of those tie-ins, about 80 percent of U.S. foreign aid is spent in the United States. Foreign-aid allocations—cocooned in bureaucratic red tape and shrouded in secrecy—lacked transparency, and the people being helped were seldom consulted.

Meanwhile, African governments used loans to finance unproductive, grandiose projects of little economic value or simply squandered or embezzled the money. In many cases, the loans cannot be paid back because there is little to show for them.

But outright, unconditional debt relief would do Africa more harm than good: It would reward past, reckless borrowing behavior and make a mockery of any attempt to enforce accountability. If a person has accumulated a huge consumer credit-card debt, you don't just wipe off their debt and grant him access to the same credit cards without counseling.

Therefore, Africans would like to see the following conditions for debt relief:

- Full public accounting of external loans: The loans were contracted on behalf of the people, and they must know who took what loans and for what purpose.
- Repatriation of the loot stashed abroad by corrupt African leaders: The United Nations has estimated that in 1991 alone, more than $200 billion was siphoned out of Africa by the ruling elites.
- Debt relief should be restricted to the 16 African countries (out of 54) that are democratic; or,
- Debt relief should be given only to those countries with free media: Benin, Botswana, Cape Verde Islands, Ghana, Mali, Mauritius, Sao Tome & Principe and South Africa, according to Freedom House's 2003 Survey.

Without democratic accountability and a free intellectual environment to debate issues, debt relief to Africa would be meaningless.

NO
Michelle Denise Carter
Deputy Regional Director for East and Central Africa, CARE

Written for *The CQ Researcher*, August 2003

Poor countries pay rich countries nine times more in debt repayments than they receive in aid. In Ethiopia, where more than 100,000 children die each year from preventable illnesses like diarrhea, debt repayments amount to four times the amount of public spending on health services As a continent, Africa alone spends four times more to repay its debts than it spends on health care.

Obviously, debt burden continues to be a critical obstacle in Africa's development. Debt burden is a tangible symbol of both the vicious circle of poverty and the widening gap between the world's "haves" and "have-nots."

Strict conditions for debt relief do NOT help Africans, but simply stated, are another form of colonialism. In its poverty-reduction plans, Tanzania was given 157 policies as conditions for debt relief; Benin had 111. The donors decide what these conditions will be, and the donors decide satisfaction of compliance. Strict conditions make any and all reforms part of the donor agenda—with very little, if any, ownership by the recipient country. The Kenyan government, for example, promised many times to enact reforms in exchange for donors' resources, but those promises were broken. Who suffers? Poor people.

"Strings-attached" lending programs have failed to achieve substantial economic growth. Strict conditions are not only coercive but also highly ineffective. In fact, there is little or no evidence that attaching conditions reduces poverty. Too many times, the conditions imposed by donors punish poor performance on specific macroeconomic targets without consideration of appropriateness or capacity.

If donors are serious about reducing poverty in Africa, they cannot impose strict conditions for debt forgiveness. Better recommendations for debt forgiveness would include the promotion of good performance in broader poverty-reduction and development goals. In addition, donors should consider write-offs with no conditions for old unpayable debts and serious dialogue between poor countries and debtor governments, multilateral financial institutions and civil society on how to move forward on macroeconomic policies to further development and poverty reduction.

Donors should provide a platform for African success in reducing poverty that includes debt forgiveness, appropriate foreign aid and fairer trade practices. This will result in an Africa that can be more self-reliant and less dependent on the "generosity" of assistance from rich countries. This will also result in an Africa with a brighter future for generations to come.

even as other developing regions, particularly East Asia, were becoming low-cost exporters of manufactured goods.

"Most African countries were plagued by poor economic policies that discriminated against exporters," said Guy P. Pfeffermann, chief economist at the International Finance Corporation, an arm of the World Bank that promotes private foreign investment in the developing world. "The prevalence of often-inefficient state enterprises, horrendous red tape and uncertain macroeconomic policies generated investor uncertainty."[31]

Even in the booming 1990s, when most of the world was experiencing strong economic growth, most of Africa's economies failed to catch fire. There were some exceptions: Ghana, for example, grew at 6 percent for a few years.

Overall, however, per-capita income in sub-Saharan Africa actually declined by 0.2 percent from 1990 to 2001. Today, Africa remains the world's poorest region, with a per-capita GDP of only $460 per person, compared with $7,640 for Brazil and $36,410 in the United States.[32] In addition, life expectancy—at 46 years—is the world's lowest.[33] In industrialized nations, people routinely live into their late 70s.

Meanwhile, sub-Saharan Africa's share of global trade has dropped to a mere 1.6 percent, less than half the amount it had two decades ago. Similarly, its share of world investment plummeted from 4 percent in 1980 to 1.8 percent.[34]

Most economists blame Africa's economic troubles on a host of causes, but a woeful lack of good governance traditionally tops the list. "There's really no reason that any of these countries can't do well," says the World Bank's Wolgin. "All it takes is good government that is committed to the sorts of policies that promote growth."

For developing economies, promoting growth still means exports: matching foreign investment with cheap African labor. "They still don't have the same vision that Asian governments did when they began to grow" in the 1960s, Wolgin says. "For developing economies to really take off, they need to focus on exporting to the rest of the world."

Gearing up to export requires creating the right conditions for foreign investment, such as a stable currency, the rule of law and respect for property and contract rights, Wolgin says. "There also needs to be political stability," he adds.

Infrastructure is crucial as well. "It's not easy to transport things in Africa," Wolgin says, citing poor road and rail links. "And then once you reach the ports, you find that many of them don't work well either."

In addition, Africans themselves often lack the skills needed for success in a sophisticated, global economy. "Managerial expertise and organizational ability are lacking in many places," says Mazrui of Kenya's Jomo Kenyatta University. "They generally aren't being stressed by schools. The Europeans wanted Africans to do their chores, so they turned them into clerks. Unfortunately, this legacy of imperialism is still with us."

New Optimism

Some African countries—including Uganda, Mozambique and Ghana—are making great strides in opening up their economies to investment and growth. "A new generation of leaders in Africa is much more open to outside investment," says diplomatic correspondent Cobb. "The idea of African socialism, which kept many businesses away because they worried about having their factories nationalized, or whether they'd be able to repatriate their profits, is fading."

African leaders also are more willing to take responsibility for the continent's economic development. "They've turned a corner on this," Wolgin says. "Africans

AFP Photo/Marco Longari

A woman works in a new textile factory in Kampala, Uganda, one of several textile plants built recently in Africa to take advantage of a 2000 U.S. law allowing African countries to export to the United States without paying the usual tariffs.

are beginning to recognize that their problems are theirs and not some outsider's responsibility."

Led by South Africa's Mbeki, African leaders have inaugurated the New Partnership for African Development (NEPAD), a framework for social and economic development. NEPAD's goals—such as government transparency, respect for human rights and greater openness to foreign investment—are not new. But there's a crucial difference: The plan is the handiwork of Africans, not imposed by donor countries, as in the past.

"We are taking responsibility for the success of the program," Mbeki said. "We can't say it's somebody else's plan. It's our plan."[35]

Meanwhile, the West has focused on boosting opportunities for African exporters. In 1999, the U.S. Congress enacted the Africa Growth and Opportunity Act, which allows most African goods to enjoy duty-free status. The law seems to be having the desired effect. Factories, particularly textile plants, have sprung up in Kenya, Uganda, Ghana and Ethiopia, creating jobs and earning foreign exchange for cash-strapped governments.[36] In Kenya, exports to the United States doubled in the first five months of 2003, from $38.5 million during the same period last year to $76.4 million. 37 Foreign investment also has quadrupled, from $14.9 million in 2000 to $60.6 million in 2002.[38]

Meanwhile, after years of stagnation, sub-Saharan Africa has been growing again—by 4.3 percent in 2001 and 3.2 percent last year, according to the United Nations Economic Commission for Africa (ECA)—a huge improvement over the 0.4 percent growth rate of the early 1990s.[39]

In 2003, Africa's GDP is expected to increase by 4.2 percent, the ECA predicts, even though the continent's largest and most sophisticated economy, South Africa, is only growing at a sluggish 1.5 percent.[40]

OUTLOOK

Bleak Future?

On July 8, the U.N. Development Program released its annual "Human Development Report," which measures living standards around the world.

Predictably, Africa fared poorly compared with the rest of the world. But the report also painted a bleak picture of the continent's long-term prospects, predicting

that if current trends continue, sub-Saharan Africa will need roughly 150 years to meet the basic needs of most of its people.[41]

Such predictions are not surprising to American University's Ayittey. "The biggest reason Africa is in so much trouble is its leaders," he says. "They mismanage the economy and steal everything in the treasury and are not held accountable until someone comes along and kills them."

Unfortunately, there is little evidence that Africa's leadership deficit will be eliminated or even reduced in the coming decades, he says. "I'm not optimistic," he says. "For Africa, I see much of the same. It may even grow worse because these [leaders] are compounding already grave problems."

Trade analyst Pasicolan agrees. "There are still too many dictatorships and marginal democracies in Africa, and I don't see that changing any time soon," he says.

Moreover, some African leaders—including those who have been elected or are well-intentioned—are hamstrung by the past, Pasicolan points out. "They still blame Europe and the United States for their problems and think that they are responsible for solving Africa's problems," he says. "But look at Asian governments: They had a colonial period as well, but developed their own successful models in the post-colonial era that brought up people's living standards."

Others, though, wonder whether the problems Africa's leaders face are simply too enormous to handle. "You have this great wave of democratic reform and a real hope that they can make things right," says Hayes of the Corporate Council on Africa. "But it's going to be so hard because they have these crushing problems, like the disparity between rich and poor."

Diplomatic correspondent Cobb agrees. "The leadership in Africa is more open and more committed than ever," he says. "But look at the huge problems they face: high unemployment, massive slums, AIDS, a huge deficit in education. I just hope that they can act on their good intentions before they get overwhelmed."

Some scholars echo these views but argue that the prevalence of HIV/AIDS throughout much of the continent—more than any other factor—is likely to destroy Africa's chances for sustained development in the coming decades, particularly since the disease disproportionately impacts young adults, the most productive members of society. "There is every likelihood that AIDS will be a scourge for at least the next 15 or 20 years, and I can't imagine that will do anything but make matters worse," says the Kennedy School's Rotberg.

In parts of southern and eastern Africa, Rotberg points out, one in five adults has HIV or AIDS. To make matters worse, he notes, the disease is now spreading quickly in Nigeria and other parts of West Africa, where up to this point it hadn't been as bad.

Yet some experts are still optimistic about Africa's future. "Africans will be better off 10 or 20 years from now because they're learning how to better help themselves, and we're learning how to better help them," says the World Bank's Wolgin. "They've turned a corner on a lot of things, like not relying on military coups and learning that you can have a peaceful transfer of power."

Even AIDS, Wolgin says, is not an impossible obstacle. "The lesson of Uganda is that AIDS can be turned around," he says. The East African nation cut new HIV infections by more than half in the last 10 years through an aggressive education and condom-distribution program.[42]

Cato's Preble also thinks Africans themselves hold the key to their own success. "The people are getting a better sense of what they want and how to get it," he says. "On balance, this will inevitably push African governments toward a more democratic and prosperous future."

NOTES

1. Quoted in Somini Sengupta, "Leader of Liberia Surrenders Power and Enters Exile," *The New York Times*, Aug. 12, 2003, p. A1.

2. Frank P. Ardaiolo, "Liberia: U.S. Must Intervene," *The* [Rock Hill, S.C.] *Herald*, July 13, 2003, p. E1.

3. Quoted on "Fox News Sunday," July 6, 2003.

4. For background, see Kenneth Jost, "Democracy in Africa," *The CQ Researcher*, March 24, 1995, pp. 241-272.

5. Figures cited in "Freedom in the World: 2003," Freedom House; available at http://www.freedomhouse.org/research/index.htm.

6. Figures cited in "The Heart of the Matter," *The Economist*, May 13, 2000.

7. For a complete list of the U.N.'s development goals, see: http://www.un.org/esa/africa/africamillennium.htm

8. For background on the MCA program, see Steven Radelet, "Bush and Foreign Aid," *Foreign Affairs*, September/October 2003.

9. David Sanger, "G-8 Adopts Africa Aid Package, With Strict Conditions," *The New York Times*, June 28, 2003, p. A8.

10. Carolyn Skorneck, "AIDS Program Supporters Hope Senate Will Come Through with Full Funding for Program," *CQ Weekly*, July 26, 2003, p. 1876.

11. John Leicester, "Poor Nations Push the Rich for More Aid," The Associated Press, June 1, 2003. For background, see Mary H. Cooper, "Foreign Aid After Sept. 11," *The CQ Researcher*, April 26, 2002, pp. 361-392.

12. William Easterly, "Playing the Aid Game," *Forbes*, Aug. 11, 2003, p. 35.

13. Baffour Ankomah and Khalid Bazid, "Who Says Africa is Independent?" *New African*, July 1, 2003.

14. Amadou Toumani Toure and Blaise Compaore, "Your Farm Subsidies Are Strangling Us," *The New York Times*, July 11, 2003, p. A17.

15. "Human Development Report 2003," *United Nations Human Development Program*, 2003, pp. 264 and 272.

16. David Dollar and Craig Burnside, "Aid, Policies and Growth," *American Policy Review*, May 2000.

17. J.M. Roberts, *The Twentieth Century* (1999), p. 528.

18. *Ibid.*, pp. 528-529.

19. David Reynolds, *One World Divisible: A Global History Since 1945* (2000), p. 90.

20. John Reader, *Africa: A Biography of the Continent* (1998), pp. 645-646.

21. Figure cited in Roberts, *op. cit.*, p. 530.

22. *Ibid.*, p. 534.

23. Reader, *op. cit.*, pp. 656-662.

24. *Ibid.*, p. 670.

25. For background on Africa's structural-adjustment programs, see Kathy Koch, "Africa: Strategies for Economic Turnabout," *Editorial Research Reports*, Nov. 7, 1986, pp. 814-832.

26. Reynolds, *op. cit.*, p. 671.

27. *Ibid.*, p. 519.

28. Roberts, *op. cit.*, pp. 735-736.

29. *Ibid.*, p. 737.

30. For background, see David Masci, "Famine in Africa," *The CQ Researcher*, Nov. 8, 2002, pp. 921-944.

31. Guy P. Pfeffermann, "Africa's Investment Climate," International Finance Corporation, 1998. See http://www.ifc.org/economics/speeches/nov98.htm.

32. Economist.com

33. *Ibid.*

34. John Tagliabue, "Chirac to Call for a Shift from Battling Terrorism to Helping Poor Nations," *The New York Times*, June 1, 2003, p. A15.

35. Quoted in Sebastian Mallaby, "Africans to the Aid of Africa," *The Washington Post*, Sept. 23, 2002, p. A19.

36. Wilson F. Hunt Jr., "Trade With Africa," *The Chicago Tribune*, July 19, 2003, p. A24.

37. Figures cited in "Kenya Doubles U.S. Exports," *The Nation* [Kenya], Aug. 13, 2003.

38. "AGOA Exports Earn SH10 Billion," *The East African Standard*, Aug. 13, 2003.

39. See http://www.uneca.org/.

40. *Ibid.*

41. United Nations Human Development Program, *op. cit.*

42. Edwin Chen, "A Firsthand Look at Battle Against AIDS," *Los Angeles Times*, July 12, 2003, p. A3.

BIBLIOGRAPHY

Books

Freeman, Sharon, T., *Conversations with Powerful African Woman Leaders: Inspiration, Motivation, and Strategy*, American Small Business Exporters Association, 2002.
A business consultant who has worked in Africa profiles 11 African women who hold high-ranking government positions in their native countries.

Reader, John, *Africa: Biography of the Continent*, Knopf, 1998.
A research fellow at University College in London has written a thorough history of the African continent, from its geological formation to the post-independence period.

Articles

Beinart, Peter, "No Answer," *The New Republic*, July 21, 2003, p. 6.
The article examines the political impulses that drive American policy in Africa.

Cannon, Carl M., "Into Africa," *National Journal*, July 5, 2003.
An excellent overview of the continent's problems, written on the eve of President Bush's trip.

Cooper, Mary H., "Foreign Aid Since Sept. 11," *The CQ Researcher*, April 26, 2002, pp. 361-392.
Cooper explores the debate in the United States over foreign assistance.

Dickerson, John F., and Jeff Chu, "The African Bush," *Time*, July 2, 2003, p. 34.
The article chronicles President Bush's recent trip to Africa and details the hopes and expectations his visit created.

Gourevitch, Philip, "Africa Calling," *The New Yorker*, July 14, 2003, p. 29.
Gourevitch details the Bush administration's increasing involvement in Africa and the consequences for American foreign policy.

"A Region in Flames," *The Economist*, July 3, 2003.
An excellent overview of the recent civil wars that have been raging in Liberia, Sierra Leone and other West African countries.

Sachs, Jeffrey D., "A Rich Nation, A Poor Continent," *The New York Times*, July 9, 2003, p. A21.
The noted economist and director of the Earth Institute at Columbia University makes a plea for the rich world, especially the United States, to spend billions more helping impoverished Africa.

Stevenson, Richard W., "New Threats and Opportunities Redefine U.S. Interests in Africa," *The New York Times*, July 7, 2003, p. A1.
The article outlines the risks and potential benefits of increased American involvement in Africa.

Toure, Amadou Toumani, and Blaise Compaore, "Your Farm Subsidies Are Strangling Us," *The New York Times*, July 11, 2003, p. A17.
The presidents, respectively, of Mali and Burkina Faso, ask rich nations to end subsidies on cotton and other crops grown in Africa. Such subsidies, they say, are destroying Africa's agricultural sector and helping to keep the continent poor.

Walsh, Declan, "Liberia's War a Tangled Web," *The Boston Globe*, July 31, 2003, p. A10.
Walsh gives a good overview of the political forces at work pulling the small nation of Liberia apart.

Wax, Emily, "Africa's Women Beginning to See Progress in Politics," *The Washington Post*, June 6, 2003, p. A14.
Wax examines the routine hardships women in sub-Saharan Africa must endure, such as overwork and discrimination, and also charts their progress in the political realm.

Zakaria, Fareed, "Take the Lead in Africa," *Newsweek*, Aug. 18, 2003, p. 35.
A respected journalist and foreign-policy thinker argues in favor of sending American troops into Liberia.

Reports and Studies

Corruption Perceptions Index 2002, **Transparency International, 2002.**
The index ranks 102 countries in the world, from least to most corrupt. Most African states have high corruption indices.

Freedom in the World 2003: An Annual Survey of Political Rights and Civil Liberties, **Freedom House, 2003.**
An annual report on democracy and human rights in 192 countries, including sub-Saharan Africa.

Human Development Report 2003: Millennium Development Goals: A Compact Among Nations to End Poverty, **United Nations Development Program, 2003.**
A massive compendium detailing efforts to meet the United Nations Millennium Development Goals, which aim to halve poverty in Africa and elsewhere in the developing world by 2015.

For More Information

AllAfrica.com, 920 M. St., S.E., Washington, DC 20003; (202) 546-0777; www. allafrica.com. Provides African news from African news outlets.

CARE, 151 Ellis St., Atlanta, GA 30303; (404) 681-2552; www.careusa.org. One of the world's largest private humanitarian organizations.

Council for Emerging National Security Affairs, 1212 New York Ave., N.W., Suite 850, Washington DC 20005; (202) 289-7524; www.censa.net. A nonpartisan think tank founded in 1999.

Freedom House, 1319 18th St., N.W., Washington, DC 20036; (202) 296-5101; www.freedomhouse.org. Co-founded by Eleanor Roosevelt nearly 60 years ago, the non-partisan organization "is a clear voice for democracy and freedom around the world."

Heritage Foundation, 214 Massachusetts Ave., N.E., Washington, DC 20002; (202) 546-4400; www. heritage.org. The conservative think thank opposed U.S. military intervention in Liberia.

TransAfrica Forum, 1426 21st St., N.W., Suite 200, Washington, DC 20036; (202) 223-1960; www. transafricaforum.org. Lobbies on African issues and conducts educational training for minority students.

Transparency International, Otto-Suhr-Allee 97-99, 10585 Berlin, Germany; 49-30-343 8200; www. transparency.org. Monitors corruption around the world.

12

Human Trafficking and Slavery

David Masci

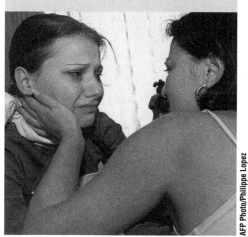

AFP Photo/Philippe Lopez

Tearful Eastern European women comfort each other after being freed in 2000 from an American-owned hotel in Phnom Penh, Cambodia, where they were forced to have sex with businessmen and government officials. Traffickers in Eastern Europe often lure young women into bondage by advertising phony jobs abroad for nannies, models or actresses.

From *The CQ Researcher*,
March 26, 2004.

One morning in May, 7-year-old Francis Bok walked to the market in Nymlal, Sudan, to sell some eggs and peanuts. The farmer's son had made the same trip many times before.

"I was living a very good life with my family," he recalls today. "I was a happy child."

But his happy life ended that day in 1986. Arab raiders from northern Sudan swept into the village, sowing death and destruction. "They came on horses and camels and running on foot, firing machine guns and killing people everywhere," he says. His entire family—mother, father and two sisters—died in the attack.

The raiders grabbed Francis and several other children, lashed them to donkeys and carried them north for two days. Then the children were parceled out to their captors. Francis went to a man named Giema Abdullah.

For the next 10 years, the boy tended his "owner's" goats and cattle. He slept with the animals, never had a day off and was rarely fed properly.

"He treated me like an animal, he even called me an animal, and he beat me," Francis says. "There was no joy. Even when I remembered my happy life before, it only made me sad."

In 1996, Francis escaped to Sudan's capital, Khartoum; then he made his way to Cairo, Egypt, and eventually in 2000 to the United States, which admitted him as a refugee.

As all American students learn, the Civil War ended slavery in the United States in 1865. Internationally, the practice was banned by several agreements and treaties, beginning in 1926 with the Slavery Convention of the League of Nations. But for tens of millions of people around the world, including millions of children like

Where Human Trafficking Occurs

Human trafficking and slavery take place in virtually every country in the world, but the U.N. and other reliable sources say the most extensive trafficking occurs in the countries below (listed at right).

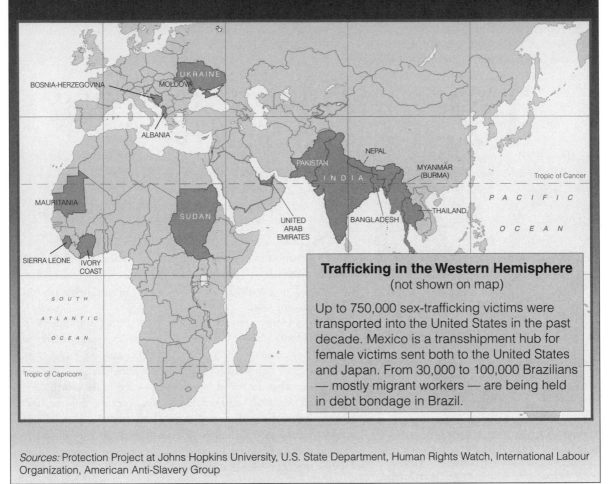

BOSNIA-HERZEGOVINA
UKRAINE
MOLDOVA
ALBANIA
MAURITANIA
SUDAN
SIERRA LEONE
IVORY COAST
PAKISTAN
INDIA
NEPAL
MYANMAR (BURMA)
THAILAND
BANGLADESH
UNITED ARAB EMIRATES
Tropic of Cancer
PACIFIC OCEAN
SOUTH ATLANTIC OCEAN
Tropic of Capricorn

Trafficking in the Western Hemisphere
(not shown on map)

Up to 750,000 sex-trafficking victims were transported into the United States in the past decade. Mexico is a transshipment hub for female victims sent both to the United States and Japan. From 30,000 to 100,000 Brazilians — mostly migrant workers — are being held in debt bondage in Brazil.

Sources: Protection Project at Johns Hopkins University, U.S. State Department, Human Rights Watch, International Labour Organization, American Anti-Slavery Group

Francis, slavery never ended. An estimated 27 million people currently are held in some form of bondage, according to anti-slavery groups like Free the Slaves.[1] From the villages of Sudan and Mauritania in Africa to the factories, sweatshops and brothels of South Asia, slavery in its rawest, cruelest form is very much alive in the 21st century.

Many of those in bondage were kidnapped, like Francis. Others go voluntarily to different countries, thinking they are heading for a better life, only to be forced into a nightmare of prostitution or hard labor. Many more work as bonded laborers, tied to lifetime servitude because their father or grandfather borrowed money they couldn't repay.

Trafficking people across international borders has become a $12-billion-a-year global industry that touches virtually every country. The U.S. government estimates that between 800,000 and 900,000 people are trafficked internationally every year, many of them women and children, transported as sex workers.[2] The total includes

Europe	
Albania	Up to 90 percent of the girls in rural areas don't go to school for fear of being abducted and sold into sexual servitude.
Bosnia and Herzegovina	A quarter of the women working in nightclubs claim they were forced into prostitution. The U.N. police task force is suspected of covering up its involvement in the sex trade.
Moldova	Up to 80 percent of the women trafficked as prostitutes in Western Europe may be Moldovans.
Ukraine	Up to 400,000 Ukrainian women have been trafficked for sexual exploitation in the past decade, Ukraine says. Ukrainian sex slaves can fetch up to $25,000 in Israel.
Africa	
Ivory Coast	A girl can allegedly be bought as a slave in Abidjan for about $7; a shipment of 10 children from Mali for work on the cocoa plantations costs about $420.
Mauritania	Light-skinned Arab Berbers today are thought to exploit hundreds of thousands of black African slaves. Slave raids in the 13th century began systemic slavery in Mauritania.
Sudan	Muslim tribesmen from northern Sudan still stage slave raids on non-Muslim Dinka peoples in the south, taking thousands of women and children.
Asia	
Bangladesh	An estimated 25,000 women and children are trafficked annually from Bangladesh.
India	Parents have sold an estimated 15 million children into bonded labor in return for meager loans from moneylenders.
Myanmar	The ruling military junta coerces minorities into forced labor in factories that benefit the regime and foreign corporations.
Nepal	A major source of women trafficked into Indian brothels; in addition, an estimated 75,000 people are trapped as bonded laborers in Nepal.
Pakistan	Millions of Pakistanis, often members of religious minorities, are forced to work as brick makers or in the fields of feudal landowners.
Thailand	Children sold by their parents make up a significant percentage of prostitutes in Thailand, which is a prime destination for pedophile sex tourists.
United Arab Emirates	Many women trafficked from the former Soviet Union end up in the UAE.

up to 20,000 people forcibly trafficked into the United States annually, according to the Central Intelligence Agency.[3] (*See sidebar, p. 262.*)

Lyudmilla's story is typical. Like many desperately poor young women, the single mother of three from the former Soviet republic of Moldova responded to an advertisement promising work in Italy. Instead she was taken to a brothel in Macedonia, where she spent two horrific years in sexual slavery before escaping in 2002.[4]

Venecija, a Bulgarian, also ended up in a Macedonian brothel. "We were so tired we couldn't get out of bed," she recalled. "But [we had to] put on makeup and meet customers," she said after escaping. Those who refused were beaten until they "changed their minds."[5]

Traffickers control their victims through a variety of coercive means. In addition to rape and beatings, they keep their passports, leaving them with few options if they do manage to escape.

And the violence can follow those who do get away. Mercy, a young West African woman trafficked to Italy, escaped her tormentors only to see her sister killed in retribution after Mercy told human rights groups about her experience.[6]

The vast majority of slaves and victims of human trafficking come from the poorest parts of Africa, Asia, Latin America and Eastern Europe, where, smooth-talking traffickers often easily deceive desperate victims or their parents into believing that they are being offered a "better life."

"Being poor doesn't make you a slave, but it does make you vulnerable to being a slave," says Peggy Callahan, a spokeswoman for Free the Slaves, based in Washington, D.C.

Some Christian groups and non-governmental organizations (NGOs) have tried to buy slaves out of bondage, particularly in Sudan, where two decades of civil war have stoked the slave trade. But many humanitarian groups argue that so-called slave redemption merely increases the demand for slaves.

International efforts to fight slavery and trafficking have increased dramatically over the last 10 years, with the United States playing a leading role. President Bush dramatized America's commitment in an address to the U.N. General Assembly on Sept. 23, 2003. The president had been expected to focus on security issues in the Middle East, but he devoted a substantial portion of his remarks to urging the international community to do more to fight trafficking.

"There is a special evil in the abuse and exploitation of the most innocent and vulnerable," Bush said. "Nearly two centuries after the abolition of the transatlantic slave trade, and more than a century after slavery was officially ended in its last strongholds, the trade in human beings for any purpose must not be allowed to thrive."[7]

The cornerstone of recent American anti-trafficking efforts is the 2000 Trafficking Victims Protection Act, which mandates the cutoff of most non-humanitarian U.S. aid for any nation deemed not trying hard enough to address the problem.

"The act breaks new ground because it actually tries to bring about changes in other countries," says Wendy Young, director of external relations for the Women's Commission for Refugee Women and Children in New York City.

"It's making a difference in countries all over the world," agrees Rep. Christopher H. Smith, R-N.J., one of the law's authors.

But critics contend the act is too weak to force real behavior changes. "It's very easy for countries to avoid sanctions just by taking a few largely meaningless actions," says Katherine Chon, co-director of the Polaris Project, an anti-trafficking advocacy group in Washington. She also accuses the administration of giving a pass to important allies, like Saudi Arabia, regardless of what they do to ameliorate their forced-labor practices.

All sides agree that many countries where trafficking occurs have a long way to go before they attain the level of economic, legal and political maturity needed to entirely eliminate the practice. "I don't think people realize just how desperately poor and chaotic many countries are today," says Linda Beher, a spokeswoman for the New York City-based United Methodist Committee On Relief, which assists trafficking victims.

A tragic consequence of this poverty is child labor, which many experts see as a cousin to slavery. In the developing world today, nearly 200 million children ages 5-14 are put to work to help support their families, according to the International Labour Organization (ILO). Almost half are under age 12, and more than 20 million are engaged in

John Eibner of Christian Solidarity International pays an Arab trader to free 132 slaves in Madhol, northern Sudan, in 1997. Critics of slave-redemption say it only encourages more slave-taking, but supporters say that not trying to free slaves would be unconscionable.

AP Photo/Jean-Marc Bouju

highly hazardous work, such as tanning leather or weaving rugs, exposing them to unhealthy chemicals or airborne pollutants.[8]

Some humanitarian aid workers describe much child labor as inherently coercive, because young children often have no choice.

The ILO argues that eliminating child labor and sending children to school would ultimately benefit nations with child laborers by raising income levels. (*See graph, p. 257.*) But some economists counter that putting even a fraction of the working children in school would be prohibitively expensive.

As experts debate resolving what has been called one of the greatest humanitarian problems of the 21st century, here are some of the questions they are asking:

Does buying slaves in order to free them solve the problem?

In recent years, would-be Samaritans—from Christian missionaries to famous rock musicians—have worked to free slaves in Africa. Although slave trading occurs in many countries, the rescue efforts largely have focused on war-torn Sudan, where Muslim raiders from the north have enslaved hundreds of thousands of Christian and animist tribesmen in the south.

The Sudanese government has done virtually nothing to stop the practice and has even encouraged it as a means of prosecuting the war against the rebellious south, according to the U.S. State Department's 2003 "Trafficking in Persons Report."

Since 1995, Christian Solidarity International (CSI) and other slave-redemption groups operating in Sudan say they have purchased the freedom of more than 60,000 people by providing money for local Sudanese to buy slaves and then free them.[9]

"Women and children are freed from the terrible abuse, the rape, the beatings, the forcible conversions [to Islam]—all of the horrors that are an inherent part of slavery in Sudan," said John Eibner, director of CSI's redemption program.[10]

Halfway around the world, *New York Times* columnist Nicholas D. Kristof had his own brush with slave redemption when he traveled to Cambodia and freed two female sex slaves. "I woke up her brothel's owner at dawn," he wrote of his efforts to purchase one of the prostitutes, "handed over $150, brushed off demands for

interest on the debt and got a receipt for $150 for buying a girl's freedom. Then Srey Neth and I fled before the brothel's owner was even out of bed."[11]

While experts concede that slave redeemers are well-intentioned, many contend the practice actually does more harm than good. "When you have people running around buying up slaves, you help create market demand for more slaves," says Jim Jacobson, president of Christian Freedom International, a relief group in Front Royal, Va., that stopped its slave-repatriation efforts five years ago. "It's really just simple economics."

Kevin Bales, author of *Disposable People: New Slavery in the Global Economy* and president of Free the Slaves, agrees. "This is like paying a burglar to redeem the television set he just stole," says Bales, a noted expert on contemporary slavery. "It's better to find other ways to free people, like going to the police or taking them out of bondage by force."

Indeed, Jacobson says, redemption only puts more money in the pockets of unscrupulous and often violent slave traders. "These people end up taking the money and buying more guns and hiring more thugs to go out and take more slaves," he says.

In addition, the critics say, many "slaves" pretend to be in bondage to defraud Westerners. "If you talk to aid workers in these places, you'll find that [bogus slave traders] are literally picking up [already free] people from across town and 'selling' them an hour later," Free the Slaves' Callahan says.

"So much of it is a huge scam operation," agrees Jacobson. "A lot of these people aren't really slaves."

But supporters of redemption say it would be unconscionable not to attempt to free slaves, even if slavers will go out searching for new victims. "Slaves are treated so badly, especially the women and children, who have been beaten and raped," says William Saunders, human rights counsel for the Family Research Council, a conservative social-policy group, and co-founder of the Bishop Gassis Sudan Relief Fund, both in Washington. "How can you not try to free these people?"

Saunders and others also contend that slave buyers take steps to avoid creating a bigger market for slaves. "In the Sudan, they use the local currency, because a dollar or a [British] pound is the sort of powerful magnet that might give people incentives to take more slaves or present non-slaves," he says.

Fighting the Traffickers

The 2000 Trafficking Victims Protection Act requires the State Department to report each year on global efforts to end human trafficking. Last year, 15 countries were placed in Tier 3, for those deemed to be doing little or nothing against trafficking. Countries in Tier 3 for three years in a row can lose all U.S. non-humanitarian aid. Tier 1 countries are considered to be actively fighting trafficking. Seventy-five countries are in Tier 2, indicating they are making some efforts against trafficking.

State Department Anti-Trafficking Ratings

Tier 1 — Actively Fighting Trafficking

Austria	Hong Kong	Poland
Belgium	Italy	Portugal
Benin	South Korea	Spain
Colombia	Lithuania	Sweden
Czech Republic	Macedonia	Switzerland
Denmark	Mauritius	Taiwan
France	Morocco	United Arab Emirates
Germany	The Netherlands	United Kingdom
Ghana		

Tier 3 — Doing Little or Nothing

Belize	Georgia	North Korea
Bosnia and Herzegovina	Greece	Sudan
Myanmar	Haiti	Suriname
Cuba	Kazakhstan	Turkey
Dominican Republic	Liberia	Uzbekistan

Source: "2003 Trafficking in Persons Report," Office to Monitor and Combat Trafficking in Persons, Department of State, June 2003

ensure that they are true slaves. "They try to repatriate these people directly to their villages," Saunders says. "They don't just buy their freedom and let them go."

But the critics remain dubious. "It's so hard to get anywhere in Sudan that there is no way that they could actually follow all of these people back to their home villages," Jacobson says. "It would take weeks or months."

Moreover, he says, "they don't have any idea whether the people they've freed have been coached or whether the village they're going to is really their village. It's simply impossible to know."

Is the Trafficking Victims Protection Act tough enough?

The $12 billion human-trafficking industry is now the world's third-largest illegal business, surpassing every other criminal enterprise except the drug and arms trades, according to the United Nations.[12]

In October 2000, the U.S. government zeroed in on the problem, enacting the Trafficking Victims Protection Act (TVPA), which targets the illegal trade both at home and abroad.[13] The law established the State Department's Office to Monitor and Combat Trafficking in Persons, which issues an annual report on what countries are doing to end trafficking.

The report uses a three-tiered system to rank countries—from states that actively fight trafficking (Tier 1) to those doing little (Tier 3). Countries classified as Tier 3 for three years in a row are subject to a cut-off of non-humanitarian U.S. aid. (*See sidebar, p. 256.*)

On the domestic side, the law allows U.S. authorities to charge alleged traffickers in the United States under the tough federal anti-racketeering law (RICO). According to the State Department, 111 persons have been charged with trafficking in the first three years since the law was

In addition, redemption supporters say, they usually cap what they will pay per person—typically $50. "There's a real effort to ensure that we don't inflate the value of slaves," says Tommy Ray Calvert, chief of external operations for the Boston-based American Anti-Slavery Group (AASG).

Calvert contends that the redemptions have helped decrease slave raids in Sudan. The redemptions "brought world attention to the issue and forced our government and others to start pressuring the Sudanese to stop this evil practice," he says.

Moreover, Saunders refutes the charge that redeemers simply set people free without trying to enacted, a threefold increase over the three-year period before the TVPA went into effect.[14]

The law also makes it easier for trafficked victims to acquire refugee status in the United States and allows them to sue their victimizers for damages in civil court.

President Bill Clinton signed the bill into law on Oct. 28, 2000, saying it would provide "important new tools and resources to combat the worldwide scourge of trafficking."

Today, however, critics argue that while the act is "a step in the right direction," it is ultimately not tough enough to shake up the industry, especially internationally. "Of course, it's good that we have it, but frankly we have an awfully long way to go," says the Polaris Project's Chon.

She especially criticizes provisions requiring countries to fight trafficking or face American penalties. "It's just not strong enough because it allows countries to avoid sanctions with just superficial acts," she says.

For example, she says, Japan responded to U.S. pressure to curtail sex trafficking by "giving Cambodia a few million dollars in anti-trafficking aid and holding a symposium on trafficking." But the Japanese did "not really do anything to substantially crack down on their own widespread problem."

Yet, she adds, the United States has said Japan has been tackling trafficking enough to avoid a Tier 3 classification and the prospect of sanctions. "Japan is an important ally," she says. "Need I say more?"

Other critics allege that certain countries are treated with "kid gloves" for political reasons. "States like Saudi Arabia and countries from the former Soviet Union, which are important American allies, have been pushed up to Tier 2 because stopping slavery isn't the priority [in U.S. foreign relations] it should be," says Calvert of the AASG.

Calvert is especially incensed that the government failed to classify Mauritania, on Africa's northwestern

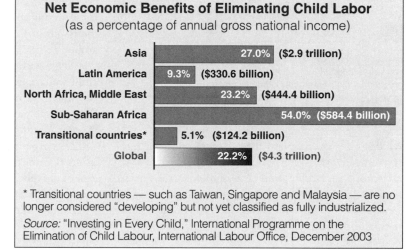

Economic Benefits Cited for Ending Child Labor

Banning child labor and educating all children would raise the world's total income by 22 percent, or $4.3 trillion, over 20 years, according to the International Labour Organization (ILO). The principal benefit would be the economic boost that most countries would experience if all children were educated through lower secondary school, plus substantial but less dramatic health benefits. The ILO analysis assumes countries that banned child labor would pay poor parents for their children's lost wages, something critics say is unrealistically expensive.

Net Economic Benefits of Eliminating Child Labor
(as a percentage of annual gross national income)

Asia	27.0% ($2.9 trillion)
Latin America	9.3% ($330.6 billion)
North Africa, Middle East	23.2% ($444.4 billion)
Sub-Saharan Africa	54.0% ($584.4 billion)
Transitional countries*	5.1% ($124.2 billion)
Global	22.2% ($4.3 trillion)

* Transitional countries — such as Taiwan, Singapore and Malaysia — are no longer considered "developing" but not yet classified as fully industrialized.

Source: "Investing in Every Child," International Programme on the Elimination of Child Labour, International Labour Office, December 2003

coast, in Tier 3, calling it instead a "special case" because of insufficient information to make an accurate determination. "This is a country with literally hundreds of thousands of people in chattel slavery and everyone knows it, and yet it gets a pass," he says. "That is just unbelievable to me."

But supporters contend that the TVPA, while not perfect, helps move problem countries in the right direction. "It's important to have a tool we can use to push foreign governments to act against this terrible abuse of human dignity, and this law does that," says Beher, of the United Methodist Committee On Relief.

In Japan, for instance, the law has helped make the fight against trafficking more effective, raising public awareness of the problem dramatically as a result of the debate over its ranking in the TVPA, supporters add.

"When Japan was dropped from Tier 1 to Tier 2, it was very embarrassing for them, and all of a sudden you saw this real public debate about the trafficking issue—

AFP Photo

Rescuers return 14 children to their native Bangladesh after they were abducted to India. Children in poor countries sometimes are sold by their parents or kidnapped by traffickers and forced to work without pay, frequently in hazardous conditions.

which is a huge problem there," says Diana Pinata, a spokeswoman for Vital Voices, a global woman's advocacy group in Washington. "If nothing else, the [annual State Department trafficking] report and the threat of sanctions keeps the issue in the spotlight in these countries, and that's very positive."

Besides Japan, several other countries, including Russia, Saudi Arabia and Indonesia, have dramatically improved their anti-trafficking efforts as a result of pressure brought to bear by the TVPA, says John Miller, director of the Office to Combat Trafficking. "We've seen real efforts all over the world," he says. "Some have been more substantial than others, but there already has been a lot of progress."

Moreover, Miller rejects the charge of political favoritism. "Look at the Tier 3 list, and you'll see that there are U.S. allies like Greece and Turkey there," he says. "These decisions aren't being made on the basis of politics."

Pinata agrees. "When we speak to NGO workers and others in the field working on this issue, we get the sense that the trafficking report's assessment of these countries is essentially correct," she says.

Should most forms of child labor be eliminated?

Zara Cigay, 12, and her two younger brothers don't go to school. Instead, they help their parents and extended family, migrant farm workers who pick cotton and other crops in southern Turkey.

"Wherever there is a job, we do it," said Huseyin Cigay, Zara's great-uncle. "The children work with us everywhere."[15]

More than 250 million children around the world between the ages of 5 and 17 are working, according to the ILO. Most are in developing countries in Africa and Asia, and nearly half work full time like Zara and her brothers.[16]

Many do strenuous farm labor. In cities, they do everything from retailing and domestic service to manufacturing and construction. In nations beset by civil wars, thousands of children have been forced to fight in rebel armies.[17]

A large portion of child labor is coerced, according to child-welfare experts. Children are often sold by their parents or kidnapped and forced to work virtually as slaves for no pay. In India, children are literally tied to weaving looms so that they cannot run away.

Labor experts uniformly condemn forced and bonded labor. But on the question of child labor in general, the experts are split over whether the practice should be condoned under certain circumstances.

Human rights advocates and others point to the ILO's 1999 Worst Forms of Child Labor Convention, which prohibits all full-time work and any work by children under 12 but sanctions part-time, non-hazardous labor for teenagers that does not interfere with their social development.[18]

"Under international law, children have a right to a basic education," says Karin Landgren, chief of child protection at the United Nations Children's Fund (UNICEF). "Work should never interfere with this."

In addition, Landgren says, "They need to have time to play and participate freely in their country's cultural and social life. This is vitally important if they are to develop into healthy adults."

A recent ILO report says that child labor negatively impacts all levels of society. "Child labor perpetuates poverty, because when children don't have an education and a real chance to develop to their fullest potential, they are mortgaging their future," says Frans Roselaers, director of the organization's international program on the elimination of child labor and author of the report.

Child labor also costs societies economically by producing uneducated adult workers, Roselaers says. "Countries with a lot of child workers are stunting their economic growth," he says, "because they will only end up producing an army of weak and tired workers with no skills."

But some economists counter that child labor, even full-time work, is often a necessity in developing countries. "In an ideal world, children would spend all of their time at school and at play, but poor people in poor countries don't have the kind of options that we in rich countries do," says Ian Vasquez, director of the Project on Global Economic Liberty at the Cato Institute, a libertarian think tank. "When you begin to restrict children's options for work, you can end up hurting children and their families."

Indeed, child labor often is the only thing that stands between survival and starvation, some experts say. "No parents want their child to work, but child labor helps families get by," says Deepak Lal, a professor of international-development studies at the University of California, Los Angeles. "When a country's per capita income rises to about $3,000 or $4,000, child labor usually fades away."

In addition, Lal says, working children often end up with a better education than those who don't work. "The public education system is a failure in many parts of the developing world and really doesn't offer much to the children who attend school," he says. "But if a child works and his family earns enough to send him or his siblings to private school, that can really pay off."

Finally, Vasquez argues that outlawing child labor would only drive the problem underground, where there is no government oversight, and abuses would increase. "In Bangladesh, girls were prevented from continuing to work in textile plants, so many ended up as prostitutes," he says. "People need to make money, and if you deny them one route, they'll take another."

But Roselaers counters that child workers would not be driven to more dangerous and demeaning jobs if the international community eased the transition from work to school. In the case of Bangladesh, he says, the threat of a consumer boycott by Western countries prompted textile factory owners to fire their child employees.

"The factory owners panicked and fired the kids, and so, yes, there were problems," he says. "But when groups like the ILO and UNICEF came in, we started offering the parents stipends to make up for the lost income and easing the children's transition from work to school."

Some 1 million children are now being helped to make the transition from work to school, according to a recent ILO report.[19] In India, for instance, the ILO and the U.S.

Department of Labor are spending $40 million this year to target 80,000 children working in hazardous jobs.[20]

Nonetheless, Lal says, such a program could only make a small dent in the problem. "You can't give a stipend to each of the many millions of families that send their children to work," he says. "There isn't enough money to do this, so it's not a realistic solution, just a palliative that make Westerners feel good about themselves."

BACKGROUND

Ancient Practice

Slavery is as old as human civilization. All of the world's great founding cultures, including those in Mesopotamia, China, Egypt and India, accepted slavery as a fact of life.[21] The practice also was common in sub-Saharan Africa and the Americas.

Neither the Bible nor the great thinkers of Greece and Rome took firm positions against slavery. Some, like the Greek philosopher Aristotle, vigorously defended it.

It was not until Enlightenment philosophers like John Locke and Voltaire established new definitions of human freedom and dignity in the 17th and 18th centuries, that large numbers of people started questioning the morality of keeping another person in bondage.

Ancient societies typically acquired slaves from outside their borders, usually through war or territorial conquest. Captives and conquered people often served as agricultural workers or domestic servants.

Slavery probably reached its zenith in ancient Greece and then Rome, where human trafficking became a huge and profitable industry. In many Greek cities, including powerful Athens and Sparta, as many as half the residents were slaves. In Rome, slavery was so widespread that even common people could afford to have one or two.[22]

Slaves in the ancient world often did more than just menial tasks. Some, especially in the Roman Empire, became physicians and poets. Others achieved great influence, managing estates or assisting powerful generals or politicians.

Great Roman thinkers like Pliny the Younger and Cicero urged masters to treat their slaves with kindness and even to let them "share your conversations, your deliberations and your company," Cicero wrote.[23] Perhaps as a result, manumission, or the freeing of slaves by their masters, was commonplace, usually after many years of service.

CHRONOLOGY

19th Century *After thousands of years, slavery is abolished in much of the world.*

1821 Congress enacts the Missouri Compromise, specifying which new U.S. states will allow slavery.

1833 England outlaws slavery throughout its empire.

1839 The world's first international abolitionist group, Anti-slavery International, is founded in England.

1848 Slavery abolished in French colonies.

1863 President Abraham Lincoln issues Emancipation Proclamation.

December 1865 The 13th Amendment abolishes slavery.

1873 Spain ends slavery in Puerto Rico.

1888 Brazil outlaws slavery.

1900-1990 *International treaties to halt slavery are adopted.*

1919 International Labour Organization (ILO) is founded.

1926 League of Nations outlaws slavery.

1945 United Nations is founded.

1946 U.N. Children's Fund is established.

1948 U.N.'s Universal Declaration of Human Rights prohibits slavery.

1951 International Organization for Migration is founded to help migrants.

1956 Supplementary Convention on the Abolition of Slavery, the Slave Trade, and Institutions and Practices Similar to Slavery outlaws debt bondage, serfdom and other forced-labor practices.

1978 Human Rights Watch is founded.

1983 Sudan's civil war begins, pitting the Muslim north against the Christian and animist south, leading to slave raids in the south.

1990s *The end of the Cold War and other geopolitical changes allow trafficking and slavery to expand.*

1991 Collapse of the Soviet Union leads to a dramatic rise in trafficking in Eastern Europe.

1994 American Anti-Slavery Group is founded.

1995 Christian and non-governmental organizations begin redeeming slaves in Sudan.

June 1, 1999 ILO adopts the Worst Forms of Child Labor Convention.

2000-Present *United States and other countries renew efforts to fight slavery and trafficking.*

March 2000 Free the Slaves is founded.

Oct. 28, 2000 President Bill Clinton signs the Trafficking Victims Protection Act.

Nov. 15, 2000 United Nations approves the Protocol to Prevent, Suppress and Punish the Trafficking in Persons.

Feb. 14, 2002 Polaris Project is founded to fight trafficking.

June 10, 2002 State Department's Office to Monitor and Combat Trafficking releases its first "Trafficking in Persons Report."

March 11, 2003 Brazilian President Luiz Inacio Lula da Silva unveils anti-slavery initiative.

Sept. 19, 2003 President Bush signs Trafficking Victims Protection Act Reauthorization.

Sept. 23, 2003 President Bush delivers a major anti-trafficking address at the U.N. General Assembly.

January 2004 U.N. launches year-long commemoration of anti-slavery movement.

Summer 2004 State Department's Fourth Annual "Trafficking in Persons Report" to be released.

Ultimately, however, Roman slavery was maintained by cruelty and violence, including the use of severe flogging and even crucifixion. Slave revolts, common in the first and second centuries B.C., were brutally suppressed.

The collapse of the western half of the Roman Empire in the 5th-century A.D. led to a new, more fragmented, power structure in Western Europe often centered around local warlords (knights) and the Catholic Church. The new order did not eliminate slavery, but in many areas slaves became serfs, or peasants tied to the local lord's land and could not leave without his permission.[24]

In the East, meanwhile, a new force—Islam—was on the rise. For the Arabs who swept into the Mediterranean basin and the Near East beginning in the 7th century, traditional slavery was a way of life, just as it had been for the Romans. In the ensuing centuries, the Arabs brought millions of sub-Saharan Africans, Asians and Europeans to the slave markets for sale throughout the Middle East.

Meanwhile, slavery remained commonplace elsewhere. In North America, Indians along the Eastern seaboard and in the Pacific Northwest often enslaved members of other tribes taken in war. The more advanced indigenous civilizations to the south, like the Aztec and Mayans in what is now Mexico, and the Inca of Peru, also relied upon slaves. And on the Indian subcontinent, the strict Hindu caste system held tens of millions in virtual bondage.

Slavery Goes Global

In the 15th century, European explorers and adventurers sailing to new territories in Asia, Africa and the Americas began a new chapter in the history of slavery.

By 1650, the Dutch, Spanish, Portuguese, French and English had established colonies throughout the world. The new territories, especially in the Americas, produced new crops such as sugar and tobacco, as well as gold and other minerals. Initially, enslaved indigenous peoples did the harvesting and mining in South America. But ill treatment and disease quickly decimated native populations, prompting the importation of slaves from Africa.

From the mid-1500s to the mid-1800s, almost 9 million Africans were shipped mostly to Latin America—particularly to today's Brazil, Haiti and Cuba—under the most inhumane conditions. About 5 percent—about 400,000—of all the African slaves ended up in the United States.[25]

On the sugar plantations of the West Indies and South America, crushing work and brutal punishment were the norm. Although Spain and Portugal had relatively liberal laws concerning the treatment of slaves—they could marry, sue a cruel owner and even buy their freedom—they were rarely enforced.

In the British colonies and later in the United States, slaves enjoyed somewhat better working conditions and medical care. Nonetheless, life was harsh and in some ways more difficult. Since slaves in Latin America and the Caribbean usually outnumbered Europeans, they were able to retain more of their African customs. In British America, where by 1750 whites outnumbered slaves by more than four to one, Africans quickly lost many of their cultural underpinnings.

Most American slavery was tied to the great Southern plantations that grew tobacco, rice and other cash crops. Although slavery also was practiced in Northern states, it was never as widespread and had been largely abolished by 1800.

By the late 18th century, Southern slavery also appeared headed for extinction, as industrialization and other trends took hold, rendering the plantation system increasingly economically unfeasible. But Eli Whitney's invention of the cotton gin in 1793 gave American slavery a new lease on life. The gin made the labor-intensive process of separating the seeds from the cotton easy, enabling slaves to dramatically increase their output.[26]

Meanwhile, the rise of textile mills in England and elsewhere was creating a new demand for the fluffy, white fiber. By the early 19th century, many Southern plantations that had been unprofitably growing other crops were now making plenty of money using slaves to pick and process cotton.

Around the same time, however, a movement to abolish slavery began to gather steam in the Northern states. For decades, Americans had debated the morality of slavery. During deliberations over independence in 1776, many delegates to the Second Continental Congress—including John Adams, Benjamin Franklin and Virginia slaveholder Thomas Jefferson—had pushed to make the elimination of slavery part of the movement for America's independence. But resistance from the South and the need for colonial unity against the British doomed the proposal.

The debate over slavery, however, did not go away. The issue complicated the new country's efforts to form

Fighting Trafficking in the United States

Seven men were sent to prison on Jan. 29, 2004, for holding several Latin American women against their will in South Texas, forcing them to work without pay and raping them repeatedly.

The case was the latest in a series of sex-trafficking cases prosecuted under the Trafficking Victims Protection Act (TVPA) of 2000, which established stiff penalties for human trafficking and provided mandatory restitution to victims.[1] In the last three years, the Justice Department has prosecuted 132 traffickers—three times the number charged in the three years before the law was enacted.[2]

Last year, Congress updated the law to make trafficking a racketeering offense and allow victims to sue their captors in U.S. courts.

"While we have made much progress in combating human trafficking . . . we have not yet eradicated modern-day slavery," reauthorization sponsor Rep. Christopher H. Smith, R-N.J., said during consideration of the bill by the House International Relations Committee on July 23, 2003.

The Central Intelligence Agency estimates that between 18,000 and 20,000 people are trafficked into the United States each year.[3] Many are women—kidnapped or lured here with promises of marriage or work as nannies, models, waitresses, factory workers and exotic dancers. Once they arrive, they are stripped of their passports and forced to work as sex slaves, laborers or domestic servants until their smuggling or travel "debts" are repaid. The average victim is 20 years old.[4]

"They tell them they'll make a lot of money, they'll be free, they'll have a beautiful life," says Marisa B. Ugarte, executive director of the Bilateral Safety Corridor Coalition, a San Diego organization that assists trafficking victims in Mexico and the United States. "But once they are here, everything changes."

Prior to passage of the TVPA, many of the victims were treated as criminals and subject to deportation. Today, they can apply to the Bureau of Citizen and Immigration Services for one of 5,000 "T" nonimmigrant visas available each year. The visas allow them to remain in the United States if they are assisting in the investigation or prosecution of traffickers. They may then apply for permanent residency if their removal would cause severe hardship.[5]

The Department of Homeland Security had received 721 T-status applications as of June 30, 2003: 301 were granted, 30 were denied and 390 are pending.[6]

Mohamed Mattar, co-director of the Protection Project, a human-rights research institute at Johns Hopkins University, said the visa program has been stymied by victims' reluctance to go to law enforcement authorities for help.

This fear is fed by the fact that many police officers remain unaware of the TVPA and are more likely to arrest the victims than the perpetrators, says Donna M. Hughes, an authority on sex trafficking at the University of Rhode Island.

"We need to start treating [Johns] like the perpetrators they are, and not like lonely guys," Hughes adds. "We need a renewal of ideas at the state and local level."

---

[1] Department of Justice press release, Jan. 29, 2004.

[2] Department of Justice press release, March 2, 2004.

[3] Department of Justice, "Assessment of U.S. Activities to Combat Trafficking in Persons," August 2003, p. 3.

[4] Amy O'Neill Richard, "International Trafficking in Women to the United States: A Contemporary Manifestation of Slavery and Organized Crime," DCI Exceptional Intelligence Analyst Program, pp. 3-5.

[5] John R. Miller, "The United States' Effort to Combat Trafficking in Persons," *International Information Program Electronic Journal*, U.S. State Department, June 2003.

[6] Department of Justice, *op. cit.*, August 2003, p. 9.

---

its governing institutions and to expand westward, forcing increasingly abolitionist Northerners and slaveholding Southerners to craft tortured compromises to keep the nation together.

In 1789, delegates to the Constitutional Convention hammered out the infamous Three-fifths Compromise, permitting each slave to be counted as three-fifths of a person for purposes of apportioning the number of representatives each state had in the new Congress.[27] And in 1821, Congress passed the Missouri Compromise, drawing a line westward along the 36.30 parallel. The new Western states above the line would be admitted to the Union as "free" states, while those below the boundary would be so-called slave states.

Outlawing Slavery

Much of the rest of the world, however, was abolishing slavery. In the early 1800s, many of the newly independent nations of Spanish America won their independence and immediately outlawed human bondage. Simón Bolívar,

Under the TVPA, alien trafficking victims who do come forward can receive federal benefits normally available to refugees.

Historically, most trafficked victims have come from Latin America and Southeast Asia, smuggled across the porous Mexican border by "coyotes" or escorted by "jockeys" pretending to be a boyfriend or cousin.[7] Since the early 1990s, however, there has been an influx of women from the former Soviet Union and Central and Eastern Europe, where trafficking rings recruit women with newspaper ads and billboards beckoning them to prosperous futures in the United States.

Undocumented migrant workers are also vulnerable to traffickers. On March 2, 2004, a federal district judge sentenced Florida labor contractor Ramiro Ramos to 15 years in prison for holding migrant workers in servitude and forcing them to work in citrus groves until they had paid off their transportation debts.[8]

In some instances, diplomats and international civil servants bring domestic workers—often illiterate women from Africa, Asia and Latin America—into the United States legally, but then force them to work long hours for almost no pay. In one case, an Ethiopian maid for an International Monetary Fund staffer says she worked eight years for seven days a week, 15 hours a day for less than 3 cents an hour.[9]

Although the employer claimed the maid was his guest, he disappeared before a lawsuit filed by the maid, Yeshehareg Teferra, could be prosecuted. "I was not their guest," Teferra told a reporter. "I was their slave "[10]

Foreign diplomats bring 3,800 domestic servants into the United States each year under special temporary work visas, which allow them only to work for the employer who sponsored them. The employer promises to abide by U.S. labor laws, but there is almost no oversight of the program, so the abuse of servants remains under law enforcement's radar screen, human rights advocates say.[11]

But foreign nationals are not the only victims of domestic trafficking. Homeless and runaway American children also are preyed upon by pimps, who troll malls and clubs in search of teenagers they can "turn." Typically, the pimps befriend the girls, ply them with drugs and then use their addiction to turn them into prostitutes.[12]

There are between 100,000 and 300,000 such citizen victims in the United States, though they're more often overlooked by police, says Derek Ellerman, co-founder of the Polaris Project, a grass-roots anti-trafficking organization. "There is a glaring bias in enforcement" of the Mann Act, which bans the transport of children and adults across state lines for prostitution, Ellerman says. "U.S. kids who are being targeted [by traffickers] just are not being protected."

For the traffickers—many of them members of gangs or loosely linked criminal networks—trafficking is much more lucrative than smuggling contraband items, because human slaves can provide a source of long-term income through prostitution and forced labor. "There's a market for cheap labor, and there's a market for cheap sex, and traffickers know they can make money in it," Michele Clark, co-director of the Protection Project, says.

---

[7] Peter Landesman, "The Girls Next Door," *The New York Times Magazine*, Jan. 25, 2004.

[8] Justice Department, *op. cit.*, March 2, 2004.

[9] William Branigin, "A Life of Exhaustion, Beatings, and Isolation," *The Washington Post*, Jan. 5, 1999, p. A6.

[10] Quoted in *ibid.*

[11] Richard, *op. cit.*, p. 28,

[12] Janice G. Raymond and Donna M. Hughes, "Sex Trafficking of Women in the United States, International and Domestic Trends," Coalition Against Trafficking in Women, March 2001, p. 52.

---

who liberated much of Latin America, was a staunch abolitionist, calling slavery "the daughter of darkness."[28]

In Europe, the tide also was turning. Largely due to the efforts of abolitionist William Wilberforce, the British Empire outlawed the practice in 1833, although de facto slavery continued in India and some other colonies. In 1848, France also freed the slaves in its colonies.

However, in the United States, peaceful efforts at compromise over slavery failed, and the issue finally helped trigger the Civil War in 1861. In 1863, during the

height of the conflict, President Abraham Lincoln issued the "Emancipation Proclamation," freeing all slaves in the Southern, or Confederate, states. Soon after the war ended with Union victory in 1865, the 13th Amendment to the Constitution abolished slavery altogether.[29]

After the Civil War, the worldwide abolition of slavery continued. Spain outlawed the practice in Puerto Rico in 1873 and in Cuba in 1886. More important, Brazil began dismantling its huge slave infrastructure in 1888.

Nearly 200 Million Young Kids Must Work

Nearly a fifth of the world's young children have to work, including 110 million in Asia and fully a quarter of all the children in sub-Saharan Africa.

Working Children, Ages 5 to 14, By Region
(in millions)

Region	Total Working	Percentage of children in region
Asia	110.4	18.7%
Latin America	16.5	17.0
North Africa, Middle East	9.0	10.2
Sub-Saharan Africa	37.9	25.3
Transitional countries*	8.3	14.6
Total	**182.1**	**18.5%**

* Transitional countries — such as Taiwan, Singapore and Malaysia — are no longer considered "developing" but not yet classified as fully industrialized.

Source: "Investing in Every Child," International Programme on the Elimination of Child Labour, International Labour Office, December 2003

AFP Photo

Six-year-old Ratan Das breaks rocks at a construction site in Agartala, India, where he earns about 40 cents a day to supplement his widowed mother's 60-cents-per-day income. India has more child laborers than any other country—about 120 million— followed by Pakistan, Bangladesh, Indonesia and Brazil.

Today, slavery is illegal in every country in the world and is outlawed by several treaties. "In international law, the outlawing of slavery has become what is called *jus cogens*, which means that it's completely accepted and doesn't need to be written into new treaties and conventions," says Bales of Free the Slaves.

The foundation of this complete acceptance rests on several groundbreaking international agreements, beginning with the 1926 Slavery Convention of the League of Nations, which required signatory countries to work to abolish every aspect of the practice.[30]

Slavery also is banned by the 1948 Universal Declaration of Human Rights, which holds that "no one shall be held in slavery or servitude; slavery and the slave trade shall be prohibited in all their forms."[31]

Other conventions prohibiting the practice include the 1930 ILO Convention on Forced Labor and a 1956 Supplementary Convention on the Abolition of Slavery, the Slave Trade, and Institutions and Practices Similar to Slavery.

More recently, the United Nations in 2001 approved a Protocol to Prevent, Suppress and Punish the Trafficking in Persons as part of a major convention on fighting organized crime. The protocol requires signatories to take action to fight trafficking and protect its victims. It has been signed by 117 countries and ratified by 45.[32] While the United States has not yet ratified the document, it has the support of the White House and is expected to win Senate approval in the near future.

CURRENT SITUATION

Human Trafficking

The poorest and most chaotic parts of the developing world supply most trafficking victims—often women and children destined for the sex trade.

In South Asia, young women and children routinely are abducted or lured from Nepal, Pakistan, India, Bangladesh, Cambodia and Myanmar (Burma) to work in brothels in India's large cities, notably Bombay, and the Persian Gulf states. Thousands also end up in Bangkok, Thailand's capital and an infamous sex-tourism mecca.

In Asia, the victims' own families often sell them to traffickers. "In Nepal, entire villages have been emptied of girls," says Pinata of Vital Voices. "Obviously, this could not have happened without the complicity between traffickers and the victims' families."

Parents sell their children for a variety of reasons—virtually all linked to poverty, Pinata says. "Some think the child will have a better life or that their daughter will be able to send money home," she says. "For some, it's just one less mouth to feed."

"Even when they have a sense of what their children will be doing, many parents feel they don't have a choice," adds UNICEF's Landgren. "They feel that literally anything is better than what they have now."

In Eastern Europe, traffickers often lure women into bondage by advertising in local newspapers for nanny positions in the United States or Western Europe. For instance, Tetiana, a Ukrainian woman, was offered 10 times her salary to be an au pair in Italy. Instead she was forced into prostitution in Istanbul, Turkey.[33]

Others are promised work as models or actresses. In some cases, the victims even put up their own money for their travel expenses, only to find themselves prisoners in a European brothel or in Mexico, awaiting transport across the border to the United States.[34]

Even those who understand at the outset that they are going to be prostitutes are not prepared for the brutality they face. "They're unaware of how much abuse, rape, psychological manipulation and coercion is involved," says the Polaris Project's Chon.

Eastern Europe is particularly fertile ground for sex traffickers, she says. The collapse of communism more than a decade ago has left many parts of the region, especially Ukraine, Moldova and Belarus, economically and politically stunted. "These countries are just full of desperate people who will do anything for a chance at a better life," she says.

To make matters worse, brothel owners prize the region's many light-skinned, blonde women. "Lighter women are very popular in places like the United States,

Europe and Asia," Chon says. "So these women are in demand."

In Africa, more people are trafficked for forced labor than as sex slaves. "In Africa, you have a lot of people being taken and sent to pick cotton and cocoa and other forms of agricultural labor," says Vital Voices' Pinata.

Regardless of their origin, once victims are lured into a trafficking ring, they quickly lose control over their destiny. "If they have a passport, it's usually taken from them and they're abused, physically and psychologically, in order to make them easier to control," says the United Methodist Committee On Relief's Beher.

When victims of trafficking reach their final destination, they rarely have freedom of any kind. "A 16-year-old girl who had been trafficked into Kosovo to be a prostitute told me that when she wasn't working in the bar, she was literally locked into her room and not allowed out," Beher says. "That's the sort of thing we see all the time."

Organized crime plays a key role in most human trafficking. "Most of what you are dealing with here is criminal networks," says Miller of the Office to Combat Trafficking. "You can't take someone out of the Czech Republic and drive her to the Netherlands and hand her over to another trafficker and then to a brothel without real cooperation."

A 16-year-old Cambodian girl rescued from a brothel peers from her hiding place in Phnom Penh. An estimated 300,000 women are trapped in slave-like conditions in the Southeast Asian sex trade. Cambodia recently agreed to join the first U.N. program aimed at halting the trafficking of women in the region.

Is the Trafficking Victims Protection Act tough enough?

YES
Rep. Christopher H. Smith, R-N.J.
Chairman, U.S. Helsinki Commission

Written for *The CQ Researcher*, March 15, 2004

Each year, nearly a million people worldwide are bought and sold into the commercial sex industry, sweatshops, domestic servitude and other dehumanizing situations.

In October 2000, President Clinton signed into law the Trafficking Victims Protection Act (TVPA), which I authored. It provided a multifaceted approach to halting human trafficking through law enforcement, prevention and aid to victims. It also represented two major policy changes: up to life in prison for those who traffic in humans and treatment of the people trafficked—largely women, children, and teenagers—as victims rather than as criminals. In 2003, the law was expanded and strengthened.

As President Bush noted in his historic speech at the United Nations in September 2003, the global community must do more to eradicate human slavery. But significant progress has been made in just a few years, thanks largely to the law's three-tier system and annual "Trafficking in Persons Report" mandated by the law.

When the first report came out, the State Department listed 23 nations in Tier 3 as the worst offenders. It pulled no punches and did not hesitate to name offending nations, including our allies, if they were not making "serious and sustained" efforts to fight trafficking. Naming names was a measure I fought hard to include in the law, even though it was initially opposed by the previous administration.

Thanks to the report and the threat of sanctions, most nations have improved their record on trafficking. Only 15 countries were in Tier 3 during the most recent 2003 report, and most of them made enough progress in the ensuing months to avoid economic sanctions. The State Department is continually improving the scope of the report so it will present the most accurate and thorough picture of the worldwide trafficking problem.

The message from the United States is loud and clear: If you are committed to the fight against human slavery, we welcome you as an ally. But if you continue to look askance when it comes to this horrible crime and pretend you don't have a trafficking problem, we're going to aggressively push you to make reforms, and we'll use economic sanctions as a means to that end.

NO
Tommy Calvert, Jr.
Chief of External Operations, American Anti-Slavery Group

Written for *The CQ Researcher*, March 15, 2004

Most anti-slavery experts would agree the TVPA is a good law, but that slavery can be defeated in our lifetime only if we give the law priority in attention and funding—and apply it equally to friends and foes alike.

The "Trafficking in Person's Report" (TIPS) required by the law does not reveal the full story on global slavery, but only a snapshot. The criteria used to determine progress in the fight against slavery—by focusing on government action rather than on total slavery within a nation's borders—skew our view of realities on the ground.

South Korea, for example, has a serious problem with trafficking—an estimated 15,000 people trafficked per year—but it is ranked in Tier 1, the best ranking a government can receive. Nations can create many seemingly tough laws and programs to fight slavery. However, organized crime may still run thriving trafficking operations in the face of such policies, which may in reality be weak or ineffectual.

Last year marked the first time that countries designated by the "Trafficking In Persons Report" as the worst offenders—Tier 3—would automatically be subject to U.S. sanctions, which can only be waived by the president.

The State Department gave wide latitude to the standards for Tier 2, perhaps to keep strategic allies from being hit with sanctions. Both Brazil and Saudi Arabia, for instance, received Tier 2 designations. But Brazil's president has launched one of the world's most ambitious plans to end slavery, while Saudi Arabia has no laws outlawing human trafficking and has prosecuted no offenders. Thus, the report's rankings equate a major national initiative to end slavery with royal lip service.

Some Middle Eastern and North African countries may have advanced in the rankings because they are being courted by the administration to support the war on terror and our plans for change in the region. But there is evidence these countries have not really progressed in the fight against human bondage.

The long-term effect of such discrepancies is to reduce the credibility of the report and lengthen the time it takes to eradicate slavery.

Indeed, smuggling rings often team up with criminal groups in other countries or maintain "branch offices" there. And most traffickers are involved in other criminal activities, such as drugs and weapons smuggling. "Many drug gangs in Southeast Asia are spinning off into trafficking because it's very low risk and very lucrative," says the Women's Commission's Young, who adds that unlike a shipment of drugs, human cargo can earn traffickers money for years.

These crime networks, especially in Eastern Europe and Asia, operate freely, in large part because they have corrupted many local officials. "So many people are being moved across borders that it's impossible to believe that government officials aren't cooperating," Young says. "Like drugs and other illegal activities, this is very corrupting, especially in poor countries where the police are poorly paid."

In addition to stepping up law enforcement, countries can do many things to fight trafficking, UNICEF's Landgren says. "For example, the United Kingdom has a new system that keeps tabs on children entering the country," she says. "By keeping track of children that come in from abroad, we can better protect them."

And in Brazil, where landowners often lure peasants to their farms with promises of work only to put them in debt bondage, President Luiz Ignacio Lula da Silva has stepped up efforts to free forced laborers. Lula, as the president is called, also has called for a change in the constitution to allow the confiscation of land for those convicted of enslaving workers.

Even countries that have long allowed trafficking are beginning to address the issue. Moldova, for instance, has begun prosecuting traffickers and has created a database of employment agencies that help people find legitimate work abroad.[35]

NGOs have also taken steps to help. For instance, some groups run safe houses where trafficking victims who escape can find shelter and security. "We provide them with medical and psychological care," says Beher, whose group operates a house in Kosovo's capital, Pristina. "We allow them to stay until they recover and then help them to get home, which is usually somewhere else in Eastern Europe, like Romania or Moldova."

The Polaris Project maintains three 24-hour hotlines (in English, Thai and Korean) in the United States to allow both victims and third parties to report trafficking activity. Polaris also has a trafficking database to help law enforcement and other officials gather information about potential cases.

But international organizations and NGOs can only do so much, says Beher, because impoverished, poorly governed countries will always be breeding grounds for trafficking. "Until the causes disappear, all we in the international aid community can do is fight the symptoms," she says.

"In order to really get rid of this problem," Beher continues, "you need political stability and a strong civil society, which in turn leads to the rule of law and stronger law enforcement. You know, there's a reason why there aren't a lot of Finnish people being trafficked."

But Calvert of the American Anti-Slavery Group says governments and international organizations could virtually shut down the trade in human beings if they wanted to. "The international community is in a state of denial and lacks the commitment to fight this," he says. "Look at Britain: They had whole fleets of ships devoted to stopping the slave trade on the high seas, and it worked."

Calvert says the United Nations and other international groups should be more aggressive and uncompromising in combating slavery. "They had weapons inspectors didn't they?" he asks. "Well that's what we need to fight this. We need that kind of action."

Pakistani Minister for Education Zobaida Jalal and U.S. Deputy Under Secretary of State Thomas Moorhead sign an agreement in Islamabad on Jan. 23, 2002, calling for the U.S. to provide $5 million to help educate working children in Pakistan.

Slavery and Forced Labor

Slavery today bears little resemblance to earlier forms of bondage. For instance, 150 years ago in the American South, a healthy slave was a valuable piece of property, worth up to $40,000 in today's dollars, according to Free the Slaves.[36] By contrast, slaves today are often worth less than $100, giving slaveholders little incentive to care for them.

Although slavery exists nearly everywhere, it is most prevalent in the poorer parts of South Asia, where an estimated 15 million to 20 million people are in bonded labor in India, Pakistan, Bangladesh and Nepal.

Bonded labor usually begins when someone borrows money from someone else and agrees to work for that person until the debt is paid. In most cases, the debt is never paid and the borrower and his immediate family become virtual slaves, working in exchange for basic amenities like food and shelter.

"Often you see a whole family in bondage for three or four generations because once someone borrows a small amount of money you're trapped," says Callahan of Free the Slaves. "You don't pay off the principal of the loan, you just keep paying off the interest."

Bonded laborers work at jobs ranging from making bricks in Pakistan to farming, cigarette rolling and carpet making in India. In the western Indian state of Gujarat, some 30,000 bonded families harvest salt in the marshes. The glare from the salt makes them color-blind. When they die, the laborers cannot even be cremated, according to Hindu custom, because their bodies have absorbed too much salt to burn properly.[37]

Slavery is also widespread in sub-Saharan Africa, where the Anti-Slavery Group estimates that at least 200,000 people are in bondage. Besides Sudan, the largest concentration of African slaves is in Mauritania. For hundreds of years, Mauritania's lighter-skinned ruling elite kept their darker compatriots in a system of chattel slavery, with generations being born into servitude. Although the country formally outlawed slavery in 1980, the practice is thought to still be widespread.

"For the thousands of slaves who were legally freed in 1980, life did not change at all," Bales writes. "No one bothered to tell the slaves about it. Some have never learned of their legal freedom, some did so years later, and for most legal freedom was never translated into actual freedom." Today, slaves are still "everywhere" in Mauritania "doing every job that is hard, onerous and dirty."[38]

Slaves also pick cotton in Egypt and Benin, harvest cocoa and other crops in Ivory Coast and mine diamonds in Sierra Leone.

In addition, hundreds of youngsters are abducted each year and forced to become soldiers for rebel fighters in war zones like Uganda and Congo.

Child soldiers often are made to do horrible things. A girl in Uganda who was kidnapped at 13 was forced to kill and abduct other children during her five years in captivity.[39]

But slavery also flourishes beyond the developing world. Although the problem is not as widespread, forced labor and servitude also occur in Europe and the United States—in brothels, farms and sweatshops. "It's amazing, but there are slaves in the United States doing all kinds of things," says Miller of the Office to Combat Trafficking. "Recently authorities found a group of Mexican [agricultural workers] who had been trafficked to work for no pay in Florida. It's unbelievable."

Moreover, slavery is not confined to just seedy brothels or plantations. In upscale American neighborhoods too, people, usually from other countries, have been enslaved, often as domestics. Last year, for instance, a suburban Maryland couple was convicted of forced labor for coercing an illegal alien from Ghana to work seven days a week as a domestic servant without pay. And from time to time, foreign diplomats are found to be harboring unpaid domestic workers from their home countries who cannot leave to work for someone else because the diplomats hold their visas.[40]

OUTLOOK

Impact of Globalization

The increasing ease of travel and communication brought about by globalization has helped many industries, including illegal ones like trafficking and slavery.

"Globalization has certainly made trafficking and slavery easier, but it is a double-edged sword," says Jacobson of Christian Freedom International. "It has also helped us to more quickly and effectively shine a spotlight on the evil thugs who are doing these bad things."

Moreover, Jacobson says, as globalization improves the general standard of living in the developing world, it becomes harder for traffickers to prey on innocents. "When the boats are rising for everyone, poverty and despair are alleviated," he says. "When someone gets a job and education and health care, they are much less susceptible to being abused."

The Polaris Project's Chon is also optimistic, although for different reasons. "I'm very upbeat about all of this, because tackling these problems is a matter of political will, and I think the world is slowly beginning to pay more attention to these issues," she says. "I feel as though we're at the same point as the [American] abolitionist movement at the beginning of the 19th century, in that things are slowly beginning to move in the right direction."

Rep. Smith agrees. "There's a fever all over the world to enact new, tough policies to deal with this," he says. "Because the U.S. is out front on this, a lot of countries are beginning to follow suit."

Moreover, the optimists note, victims themselves are increasingly fighting for their rights. "There is a silent revolution going on right now, in places like India, where people are literally freeing themselves from slavery," says Callahan of Free the Slaves, referring to thousands of quarry slaves in northern India who recently have left their bondage and begun new lives. "If this kind of thing keeps up, in a few decades these problems will be blips on the radar screen compared to what they are today."

But Beher of the United Methodist Committee on Relief sees little change ahead because of continuing poverty and societal dysfunction. "The problems that lead to trafficking and slavery are very complicated, and there are no easy fixes," she says. "We need to build up the economies and the civil society of the places where these things happen in order to get rid of this once and for all. And I'm afraid that that is going to take many decades."

Indeed, "Things could get a lot worse before they get better," warns Young of the Women's Commission for Refugee Women and Children, comparing trafficking to the drug trade.

"It's so profitable, and there is so little risk in getting caught that it seems like there will be plenty of this kind of thing going on for the foreseeable future."

NOTES

1. See www.freetheslaves.net/slavery_today/index.html.
2. Figure cited in "2003 Trafficking in Persons Report," U.S. Department of State, p. 7.
3. Frank Trejo, "Event Underscores Scope, Toll of Human Trafficking," *Dallas Morning News*, March 4, 2003, p. 3B.
4. Richard Mertens, "Smuggler's Prey: Poor Women of Eastern Europe," *The Christian Science Monitor*, Sept. 22, 2002, p. A7.
5. Quoted in *ibid*.
6. "Trafficking in Persons Report," *op. cit.*, p. 6.
7. The entire text of President Bush's speech can be found at www.whitehouse.gov/news/releases/2003/09/20030923-4.html.
8. "IPEC Action Against Child Labour: 2002-2003," International Labour Organization, January 2004, p. 15; see also ILO, "Investing in Every Child," December 2003, p. 32.
9. Figure cited in Davan Maharaj, "Panel Frowns on Efforts to Buy Sudan Slaves' Freedom," *Los Angeles Times*, May 28, 2002, p. A3.
10. Quoted from "60 Minutes II," May 15, 2002.
11. Nicholas D. Kristof, "Bargaining For Freedom," *The New York Times*, Jan 21, 2004, p. A27.
12. Figure cited at "UNICEF Oral Report on the Global Challenge of Child Trafficking," January 2004, at: www.unicef.org/about/TraffickingOralreport.pdf.
13. Full text of the law is at: www.state.gov/documents/organization/10492.pdf. The law was reauthorized in December 2003.
14. Figures cited at www.state.gov/g/tip/rls/fs/28548.htm.
15. Richard Mertens, "In Turkey, Childhoods Vanish in Weary Harvests," *The Christian Science Monitor*, May 8, 2003, p. 7.
16. ILO, *op. cit.*
17. See Brian Hansen, "Children in Crisis," *The CQ Researcher*, Aug. 31, 2001, p. 657.
18. See: www.ilo.org/public/english/standards/ipec/ratify_govern.pdf.
19. ILO, *op. cit.*, January 2004, p. 37.
20. "With a Little U.S. Help, ILO Targets Child Labour," *Indian Express*, March 3, 2004.
21. Hugh Thomas, *World History: The Story of Mankind from Prehistory to the Present* (1996), pp. 54-55.
22. *Ibid.*, pp. 105-107.
23. Quoted in Michael Grant, *The World of Rome* (1960), p. 116.
24. Thomas, *op. cit.*, pp. 107-110.
25. Figures cited in *ibid.*, p. 279.

26. John Hope Franklin and Alfred A Moss, Jr., *From Slavery to Freedom: A History of African-Americans* (2000), p. 100.

27. *Ibid.*, p. 94.

28. From a speech before the Congress of Angostura in 1819. See http://www.fordham.edu/halsall/mod/1819bolivar.html.

29. Franklin and Moss, *op. cit.*, p. 244.

30. The full text of the convention can be found at www.unicri.it/1926%20slavery%20convention.pdf.

31. Quoted at www.un.org/Overview/rights. html.

32. A complete list of those countries that have signed and ratified the protocol are at www.unodc.org/unodc/en/crime_cicp_signatures_trafficking.html.

33. Sylvie Briand, "Sold into Slavery: Ukrainian Girls Tricked into Sex Trade," Agence France Presse, Jan. 28, 2004.

34. Peter Landesman, "The Girls Next Door, *The New York Times Magazine*, Jan. 25, 2004, p. 30.

35. "Trafficking in Person's Report," *op. cit.*, p. 107.

36. See www.freetheslaves.net/slavery_today/ index.html.

37. Christopher Kremmer, "With a Handful of Salt," *The Boston Globe*, Nov. 28, 1999.

38. Kevin Bales, *Disposable People: The New Slavery in the Global Economy* (1999), p. 81.

39. Thomas Wagner, "Study Documents Trauma of Child Soldiers," Associated Press Online, March 11, 2004.

40. Ruben Castaneda, "Couple Enslaved Woman," *The Washington Post*, June 10, 2003, p. B1.

BIBLIOGRAPHY

Books

Bales, Kevin, *Disposable People: New Slavery in the Global Economy*, University of California Press, 1999.
The president of Free the Slaves and a leading expert on slavery offers strategies to end the practice.

Bok, Francis, *Escape From Slavery: The True Story of My Ten Years In Captivity and My Journey to Freedom in America*, St. Martin's Press, 2003.
A former slave in Sudan tells the gripping story of his ordeal and eventual journey to the United States.

Franklin, John Hope, and, Alfred Moss Jr., *From Slavery to Freedom: A History of African Americans*, McGraw-Hill, 2000.
Franklin, a renowned professor emeritus of history at Duke University and Moss, an associate professor at the University of Maryland, discuss the slave trade and slavery in the United States up to the Civil War.

Articles

Bales, Kevin, "The Social Psychology of Modern Slavery," *Scientific American*, April 2002, p. 68.
A leading expert on slavery examines the psychological underpinnings that may drive both traffickers and slaveholders as well as their victims.

"A Cargo of Exploitable Souls," *The Economist*, June 1, 2002.
The article examines human trafficking of prostitutes and forced laborers into the United States.

Cockburn, Andrew, "Hidden in Plain Sight: The World's 27 Million Slaves," *National Geographic*, Sept. 2003, p. 2.
A correspondent for London's *Independent* takes a hard look at slavery; includes chilling photographs of victims.

Hansen, Brian, "Children in Crisis," *The CQ Researcher*, Aug. 31, 2001, pp. 657-688.
Hansen examines the exploitation of children around the world, including sexual slaves and forced laborers.

Kristof, Nicolas D., "Bargaining For Freedom," *The New York Times*, Jan. 21, 2004, p. A27.
The veteran columnist describes how he "bought" and freed two sex slaves in Cambodia. The article is part of Kristof's series on his experiences in Southeast Asia.

Landesman, Peter, "The Girls Next Door," *The New York Times Magazine*, Jan. 25, 2004, p. 30.
Landesman's detailed exposé of trafficking focuses on the importation of young girls into the U.S. for prostitution.

Maharaj, Davan, "Panel Frowns on Efforts to Buy Sudan Slaves Freedom," *Los Angeles Times*, May 28, 2002, p. 3.
The article details the controversy surrounding the practice of slave redemption in Sudan.

Mertens, Richard, "Smugglers' Prey: Poor Women of Eastern Europe," *The Christian Science Monitor,* **Sept. 25, 2002, p. 7.**
The article examines the plight of Eastern European women trafficked into sexual slavery who manage to escape.

Miller, John, R., "Slavery in 2004," *The Washington Post,* **Jan. 1, 2004, p. A25.**
The director of the State Department's Office to Monitor and Combat Trafficking in Persons argues that the Trafficking Victims Protection Act has prodded other countries to act.

Power, Carla, *et al.,* **"Preying on Children,"** *Newsweek,* **Nov. 17, 2003, p. 34.**
The number of children being trafficked into Western Europe is rising, helped by more porous borders and the demand for young prostitutes.

Vaknin, Sam, "The Morality of Child Labor," United Press International, Oct. 4, 2002.
UPI's senior business correspondent argues that organizations opposed to most forms of child labor impose unrealistic, rich-world standards on the poorest countries.

Reports

"Investing in Every Child: An Economic Study of the Costs and Benefits of Eliminating Child Labor," International Labour Organization, December 2003.
The ILO contends that ending child labor would improve economic growth in the developing world.

"IPEC Action Against Child Labor: 2002-2003," International Labour Organization, January 2004.
The report charts the progress made by the ILO's International Program on the Elimination of Child Labor (IPEC), which funds anti-child labor initiatives around the world.

"Trafficking in Persons Report," U.S. Department of State, June 2003.
The annual report required by the Trafficking Victims Protection Act assesses global anti-trafficking efforts.

For More Information

American Anti-Slavery Group, 198 Tremont St., Suite 421, Boston, MA 02116; (800) 884-0719; www.iabolish.com.

Casa Alianza, 346 West 17th St., New York, N.Y. 10011; (212) 727-4000; www.casa-alianza.org. A San Jose, Costa Rica, group that aids street children in Latin America.

Christian Children's Fund, 2821 Emerywood Parkway, Richmond, VA 23294; (800) 776-6767; www.christianchildrensfund.org. CCF works in 28 countries on critical children's issues.

Christian Freedom International, P.O. Box 535, Front Royal, VA 22630; (800) 323-CARE (2273); (540) 636-8907; www.christianfreedom.org. An interdenominational human rights organization that combines advocacy with humanitarian assistance for persecuted Christians.

Christian Solidarity International, Zelglistrasse 64, CH-8122 Binz, Zurich, Switzerland; www.csi-int.ch/index.html. Works to redeem slaves in Sudan.

Defence for Children International, 1 Rue de Varembé, P.O. Box 88, CH 1211, Geneva 20, Switzerland; (+41 22) 734-0558; www.defence-for-children.org. Investigates sexual exploitation of children and other abuses.

Free the Children, 233 Carlton St., Toronto, Ontario M5A 2L2, Canada; (905) 760-9382; www.freethechildren.org. This group encourages youth to help exploited children.

Free the Slaves, 1326 14th St., N.W., Washington, DC 20005; (202) 588-1865; www.freetheslaves.net. International organization that works to eradicate slavery.

Human Rights Watch, 350 Fifth Ave., New York, NY 10118; (212) 290-4700; www.hrw.org. Investigates abuses worldwide.

International Labour Organization, 4, route des Morillons, CH-1211, Geneva 22, Switzerland; (+41 22) 799-6111; www.ilo.org. Sets and enforces worldwide labor standards.

Polaris Project, P.O. Box 77892, Washington, DC 20013; (202) 547-7909; www.polarisproject.org. Grass-roots organization fighting trafficking.

United Methodist Committee On Relief, 475 Riverside Dr., New York, NY 10115; (800) 554-8583; gbgm-umc.org. Worldwide humanitarian group.

United Nations Children's Fund (UNICEF), 3 United Nations Plaza, New York, NY 10017; (212) 326-7000; www.unicef.org. Helps poor children in 160 countries.

Women's Commission on Refugee Women and Children, 122 East 42nd St., 12th Floor, New York, NY 10168-1289; (212) 551-3088; www.womenscommission.org. Aids trafficking victims in the developing world.

World Vision International, 800 West Chestnut Ave., Monrovia, Calif. 91016; (626) 303-8811; www.wvi.org. A Christian relief and development organization established in 1950.

13

Ethics of War

David Masci and Kenneth Lukas

U.N. Secretary General Kofi Annan visits the Mulire Memorial honoring the estimated 1 million Tutsis and other Rwandans who were killed in the African country's 1994 genocide. Genocides and brutal civil wars in recent years have focused new attention on the wartime fate of civilians and captured combatants.

From *The CQ Researcher*,
December 13, 2002 (Revised September 2004).

Londoner Zumrati Juma had not heard from her 22-year-old son Feroz Abbasi for more than a year. After checking with the local police, and even the mosque where he worshipped, she began to think the worst.[1]

But in January 2002 she was stunned to learn that Feroz, a British citizen, was being held incommunicado by the United States. He had been transported, hooded and in chains, to the U.S. Naval Station at Guantanamo Bay, Cuba, where he remains. The Justice Department said he was a member of Al Qaeda, the global terrorist group headed by Saudi exile Osama bin Laden.[2]

Feroz is one of approximately 585 detainees at Guantanamo captured since the U.S.-led campaign launched against Al Qaeda and Afghanistan's ruling Taliban regime following the Sept. 11, 2001, terrorist attacks on New York City and the Pentagon.[3] The detainees have been interrogated for information that might help prevent future terrorist attacks or aid in the capture of bin Laden and other terrorists.

Classifying the detainees as "unlawful combatants," the Bush administration has refused to grant them access to either lawyers or U.S. courts. It contends that since the detainees are foreign nationals being held outside the United States, they do not warrant such rights.

"Are we supposed to read [terror suspects] their Miranda rights, hire a flamboyant defense lawyer, bring them back to the United States to create a new cable network of 'Osama TV,' provide a worldwide platform for propaganda?" Attorney General John D. Ashcroft asked the Senate Judiciary Committee on Dec. 6, 2001.

But lawyers representing Feroz and 16 other detainees sued in federal court, arguing the Bush administration has unlawfully denied the

273

A Century of War Atrocities

More people died in violent conflicts during the 20th century than in any previous century—including millions killed through genocide. Several factors fed the bloodshed, including the rise of state-supported racism, population growth, the destructive power of modern weapons, competition for dwindling natural resources and the emergence of unstable states. Major contemporary atrocities cited by historians include:

The Armenian Genocide—From 1915-1923, an estimated 1.5 million ethnic Armenian Christians were killed in forced marches and executions carried out by the "Young Turk" government of the Ottoman Empire. The Turkish government continues to challenge the veracity of some facts surrounding the atrocity.

Ukraine's Forced Famine—In an attempt to subordinate the Ukrainian republic, the Soviet leader Josef Stalin induced a famine in the Ukraine from 1932-1933 that killed an estimated 5 million people. While some organizations do not recognize famine as genocide, the Russian government has denounced Stalin's campaign as genocide.

The Rape of Nanking—When Japanese military forces sacked the Chinese city in 1937, they raped 20,000 women, killed over 200,000 people and imprisoned thousands more in one of history's bloodiest rampages.

The Holocaust—Under Adolf Hitler's Nazi regime in Germany, an estimated 6 million Jews were systematically killed in an attempt to eliminate the Jewish race. Gypsies, dissidents, homosexuals and others were also persecuted, with estimates of the number killed ranging from thousands to 5 million.

Cambodia's "Killing Fields"—The communist Khmer Rouge took control of Cambodia in 1975 and systematically forced most of the people into labor camps, where they starved or were worked to death. Vietnamese nationals, Chinese, Muslims, intellectuals and Buddhist monks were also "cleansed" from Cambodian society. An estimated 1.5 to 2 million people died during Pol Pot's Khmer Rouge reign, which ended in 1979.

Bosnia—Bosnian Serbs in the former Yugoslavia began a murderous campaign of "ethnic cleansing" against Muslims and Croats in 1992, killing hundreds of thousands of men, women and children by execution, imprisonment and torture.

Rwanda—Ethnic Hutus slaughtered an estimated 800,000 members of the Tutsi ethnic minority and suspected Hutu collaborators between April and July 1994. Millions of Hutus and Tutsis fled the country.

Sources: The Campaign to End Genocide, http://www.endgenocide.org/genocide/20thcen.htm; Aryeh Neier, *War Crimes,* Times Books, 1998; Human Rights Watch

Joe Margulies, of the Center for Constitutional Rights, one of the lawyers.[4] "The government says no court in the world may hear from my clients. Guantanamo is unique. It is utterly outside the law."[5]

But a June 2004 Supreme Court decision that detainees have a right to contest their detentions in a legal setting has raised the prospect that the detainees may ultimately have their status resolved in regular U.S. courts. (See p. 281)

The treatment of soldiers captured in warfare is one of the seminal issues addressed by the 1949 Geneva Convention and other treaties on the conduct of war.

These rules were developed in the 19th and 20th centuries, at the same time that new, more deadly weapons were being created. "War at its inception was a wholly barbaric business," says Paul Stevens, a former legal adviser to the National Security Council. "But as our ability to inflict mayhem increased, we began to recognize the need to find ways to stop or control the violence."

But while the rules of international humanitarian law only were developed over the past 150 years, efforts to regulate warfare date back to ancient times.

Indeed, three centuries after the rise of Christianity, the religion's first great political theorist, St. Augustine of Hippo, set out the conditions that needed to be met before a state could go to war. His theory of the "just war," later refined by St. Thomas Aquinas and others, mandates that war must be fought only for a good or just cause, by a legitimate authority and only as a last resort.

While the U.S. action in Afghanistan—dubbed Operation Enduring Freedom—was widely seen as ethi-

Guantanamo prisoners their legal rights. "Intelligence gathering may go forward, detentions at Guantanamo Bay may go forward, but [not] without process of law," said

cally and politically defensible, many theologians and other observers had said that U.S. action against Iraq would not meet the just-war test. They argued that although Iraqi leader Saddam Hussein was a brutal dictator who may indeed have had biological and chemical weapons, there was no evidence that he directly posed an imminent threat to the United States.

"Before we justify going to war, we need to see that Iraq poses a clear and present danger, and I just don't see it," said Bob Edgar, general secretary of the National Council of Churches, which represents 50 million Christians. Edgar advocated the continued use of the weapons-inspection process and other non-violent means to bring Iraq into compliance with U.N. disarmament resolutions.

But others had supported the administration's contention that Iraq directly threatened the United States and its allies, as indicated by the failure of the decade-long, non-violent effort to disarm the oil-rich nation. In addition, war supporters had pointed out, Hussein had repeatedly used weapons of mass destruction and was likely to do so again in the future.[6]

"If attacking Iraq doesn't meet the just-war threshold in some people's minds, nothing ever will," said Keith Pavlischek, director of the Civitas citizenship program at the Christian-based Center for Public Justice, in Annapolis, MD.

Ethical issues also surround the U.S. refusal to join the International Criminal Court (ICC), established in July 2002 to investigate war crimes.

Temporary war-crimes tribunals were used after World War II, when defeated German and Japanese leaders were tried for crimes against humanity. Currently, temporary tribunals in the Netherlands and Tanzania are prosecuting Yugoslavs and Hutus accused of committing atrocities during brutal conflicts in the former Yugoslavia and Rwanda.[7]

The United States has refused to support the ICC, arguing that it could become politicized and ultimately be used by unfriendly states to target U.S. soldiers and officials, even when engaged in peacekeeping missions. "[One cannot] answer with confidence whether the United States would now be accused of war crimes for legitimate but controversial uses of force to protect world peace," says John R. Bolton, under secretary for arms control and international security at the State Department.

But human-rights activists and other supporters of the ICC counter that the administration's concerns are overblown and that a permanent judicial body will bet-

U.N. weapons inspectors examine equipment on Dec. 9, 2002, at a factory near Baghdad that once produced chemical and biological weapons. The Bush administration had contended that if Iraqi leader Saddam Hussein didn't dismantle his alleged arsenal of weapons of mass destruction, an attack on Iraq would constitute a "just war" because the oil-rich nation poses an imminent threat to U.S. security.

AFP Photo/Karim Sahib

ter enable the international community to hold mass murderers accountable for their genocidal crimes.

While experts disagree about the ICC, many on both sides accept the contention that future conflicts may prove even more brutal and unregulated than past wars. Powerful countries, they predict, will find themselves fighting rebels or non-governmental entities like Al Qaeda, which are disinclined to follow generally accepted rules of humane warfare.

But human-rights activists argue that even though Al Qaeda and Taliban soldiers do not entirely fit the image or definition of traditional fighters, they still should be granted prisoner-of-war status when captured by the United States or other coalition forces. They point out that the Geneva Convention requires countries capturing combatants to presume they are POWs unless a legitimate tribunal decides otherwise.

The administration argues that the detainees do not warrant POW treatment because they have none of the trappings of regular soldiers, like uniforms and insignias.[8]

"The whole idea behind awarding someone POW status is that they look and act like soldiers, which means they behave differently than civilians," says David Rivkin, a former Justice Department official

Civilians Bear the Brunt of Warfare

Despite several treaties and international agreements designed to protect them, civilians bear the brunt of most fighting around the world.

Indeed, since World War II, non-combatants have made up 90 percent of all war-related casualties.[1] And academics estimate that between 1900 and 1987, a staggering 169 million civilians and unarmed soldiers were killed during conflicts, compared with the 34 million soldiers killed in combat.[2]

In the past, armies often were expected to "live off the land," pillaging and killing innocents as they moved from one area to another. In some conflicts, such as the religiously motivated Thirty Years' War (1618–1648), civilians were the targets of military aggression, as Protestant and Catholic armies attacked non-combatants to stamp out "heresy."

Civilians were constantly targeted during World War II. All sides bombed civilian areas, sometimes to destroy vital industries but sometimes to "demoralize" enemy populations, like the German V-2 rocket bombing of London, the U.S. fire-bombing of Dresden or even the atomic bombing of Hiroshima and Nagasaki by the United States. The Germans and the Japanese took the brutality a step further, wiping out entire towns and cities, and, in Germany's case, establishing concentration camps to exterminate whole races and groups of people.

The war's horrors prompted the International Committee on the Red Cross (ICRC) to recommend an international conference in Geneva, Switzerland, to regulate conduct during war. One of the four articles of the 1949 Geneva Convention specifically seeks to protect civilians and their property. The rules were refined and expanded in 1977 to protect civilians from the growing threat of terrorism.

"The civilian population, as such, as well as individual civilians, shall not be the object of attack," states Protocol I, from 1977. The protocol also outlaws terrorism during war: "Acts or threats of violence, the primary purpose of which is to spread terror among the civilian population [are] prohibited."[3]

In addition, the Geneva rules prohibit the kinds of attacks, such as carpet-bombing, most likely to cause excessive civilian casualties. They also prohibit armies from using civilians as human shields to advance strategic objectives.

The Geneva code does not *prohibit* attacks against legitimate military targets that may or are expected to cause so-called collateral damage and produce civilian casualties. But in these cases, commanders must do all they can to avoid hurting civilians.

Although the rules governing the treatment of civilians are clear and have been ratified by most nations, conditions for non-combatants have, if anything, gotten worse since World War II, because the Geneva rules are, essentially, unenforceable.

"While we have this nice-looking piece of paper that says all the right things, states feel free to ignore it and to act in what they see as their best interest because there's no enforcement mechanism, no way to hold them accountable," says Thomas Lynch, an attorney at the International Human Rights Law Group in Washington, D.C. "So protecting civilians comes down to a matter of convenience."

In addition, many conflicts of the last 60 years have taken place in the developing world, where armies are often disorganized, and non-uniformed soldiers blend in with the

---

[1] "The First Casualty," *The Economist*, Aug. 25, 2001.

[2] Eric Deggans, "A history of man's inhumanity," *The St. Petersburg* [Fla.] *Times*, April 4, 2002, p. 2B.

[3] Quoted in Roy Gutman and David Rieff, eds., *Crimes of War: What the Public Should Know* (1999), p. 85.

---

under former Presidents Ronald Reagan and George Bush. "These guys were no different than other men in Afghanistan, where everyone is armed and dresses in the same way."[9]

As policymakers and ethicists from the United States and other countries seek to apply the moral standards for warfare to today's terrorism, here are some of the questions being asked:

Would an invasion of Iraq be a "just war"?

All the major religious traditions contain teachings on war, including Islam. Western views are influenced by

civilian population, a combination that often leads to the killing of many innocents.

In some recent wars, civilians have been specifically targeted. During the civil war in Bosnia in the former Yugoslavia, all sides, especially the Serbs, targeted non-combatants—often in an attempt to "ethnically cleanse" an area. Serb soldiers executed thousands of civilians and raped enemy women as a form of torture.

In Chechnya, a breakaway Russian province, up to 160,000 people, mostly civilians, have died since Russia sought to put down the uprising in 1994.[4] Russian troops have been accused of everything from indiscriminately shelling Chechen villages to routinely torturing and executing suspected rebel sympathizers.

African conflicts have been especially hard on civilians. Over the last 40 years, civil wars in Angola, Sudan, Mozambique, Nigeria and elsewhere have left millions of innocents dead. In Sierra Leone, an entire generation has been maimed by machete-wielding soldiers who cut off the hands and feet of suspected enemy sympathizers or their children.

AFP Photo/Georges Gobet

One of the thousands of civilians deliberately maimed by rebels during Sierra Leone's brutal 10-year civil war casts his ballot in presidential elections in May 2002. Although the Geneva Convention prohibits attacks on non-combatants, 90 percent of the casualties in recent wars have been civilians.

Even the United States is not immune from allegations that it has indiscriminately killed civilians. During the Vietnam War, for instance, American planes carpet-bombed targets in Vietnam and Cambodia. Recently, scholars have unearthed evidence suggesting that American officers ordered pilots to bomb defenseless Korean refugees, killing hundreds.[5]

In a break from past atrocities, some recent mass killings of civilians, specifically in Bosnia and Rwanda, have led to prosecutions of some of the alleged perpetrators.

"The idea of individual responsibility is novel," Lynch says. "I can't say, but maybe it will begin to deter some people in the future from committing atrocities."

In fact, several potential atrocities have been prevented or at least mitigated by humanitarian intervention. For example, in Kosovo in 1999, a U.S.-led bombing campaign prevented Serbian attempts to ethnically cleanse the province of its Albanian majority. Likewise, the same year, the presence of Australian troops likely prevented mass killing in East Timor, an Indonesian province that became independent in May 2002.

---

[4]Sabrina Tavernise, "Chechnya is Caught in Grip of Russia's Anti-Terror Wrath," *The New York Times*, Nov. 12, 2002, p. A1.

[5]"The First Casualty," *op. cit.*

---

the Christian notion of the "just war," conceived nearly 2,000 years ago by St. Augustine of Hippo. According to generally accepted principles, a "just war," should be:

- based on clear, legitimate or just aims;
- undertaken by a legitimate authority—such as a recognized government;
- not undertaken out of hate, greed or other base motives;
- prosecuted only as a last resort; and,
- likely to succeed.

Many U.S. church leaders are among those who contended that war with Iraq would not have met most "just-war" tests, mainly because they said justification for an attack was absent. (The leaders of some religious groups, like the Baptists, said it met the test.)

"Is there clear and adequate evidence of direct connection between Iraq and the attacks of Sept. 11 or clear and adequate evidence of an imminent attack of a grave nature?" asked Bishop Wilton Gregory, president of the U.S. Catholic Conference of Bishops, in a Sept. 13, 2002, letter to President Bush.

Gregory and others said "no," adding that preempting threats that may or may not materialize sometime in the future doesn't constitute adequate justification. "Iraq has chemical and biological weapons and the ability to deliver them up to 400 miles," said Edgar of the National Council of Churches. "But Saddam Hussein hasn't used them for more than a decade, and it seems that the most likely way he will use them is by being backed into a corner by us—when we invade—and he has nothing to lose."

In addition, some church leaders had said, an invasion of Iraq, at least at this point, also would not have been a measure of last resort. "No one is trying to defend Saddam Hussein, because he's a dreadful person who has done dreadful things," said James E. Winkler, general secretary of the United Methodist Church. "But we have other ways to pursue our goal of disarming him." Among those, he said, are the U.N. weapons inspectors searching for weapons of mass destruction in Iraq.

Winkler also questioned the likelihood that invading Iraq would be successful. "I'm sure we can beat them militarily, but what happens afterward?" he asked. "Everyone knows that this will seriously threaten the peace and stability of the Middle East, because so many people would be unhappy with the United States going in and killing a lot of Iraqis."

But others countered that striking Iraq would have clearly met the just-war test, since Iraq had both the desire and capability to do great harm to the United States then or in the near future.

"It's clear that there is a case for just war here," said David Davenport, a research fellow at the Hoover Institution and past president of Pepperdine University, in Malibu, Calif. "If Saddam has weapons of mass destruction—and it's pretty clear from the evidence that he does—and there is a likelihood of his using them—and, again, it seems clear that he very well might, since

he already has—then you have a just cause for going to war."*

Even if Iraq is not yet a direct threat to the United States, it could endanger important U.S. allies, said supporters of an invasion. "Israel and our Arab allies in the region are already in danger," said Pavlischek of the Center for Public Justice.

In addition, Pavlischek said, an attack against Hussein would not be premature because he had been given chances to disarm and had thwarted all of them so far. "I'm not sure what we're supposed to do if Iraq doesn't disarm," Pavlischek said. "Do they need to be marching down Broadway before we do something?"

"In an era when we face the threat from weapons of mass destruction, the idea of last resort takes on a new meaning," Davenport said. "Sure, we can try to keep putting pressure on Saddam to accept inspections and disarmament, but my guess is that this may be one of the last chances we have to go in and really address this issue."

But Edgar questioned why, after more than a decade of sanctions and international isolation, Iraq was suddenly perceived as a great threat that must immediately be destroyed.

"There's been little evidence that Saddam Hussein has moved out of the box we put him in after the Gulf War," he said. "In fact, the last time he used those weapons was in the late 1980s, which was when we were supporting him. What makes him such a threat right now, and makes it so urgent that we go to war?"

Are the detainees at Guantanamo Bay entitled to prisoner-of-war status?

Traditional warfare features enemy combatants wearing uniforms and fighting for a specific country. Under the Geneva Convention, when such soldiers are captured they are supposed to be declared prisoners of war, treated humanely and repatriated when the fighting ends.

---

*After the March 2003 invasion of Iraq, Saddam Hussein's WMD programs were found to be essentially defunct, although he retained a knowledge base capable of restarting weapons programs in the future. No stockpiles of the outlawed weapons were found. A government investigation concluded that Iraq rebuffed requests for an alliance from Al Qaeda and played no role in the Sept. 11 attacks. See Barton Gellman, "Iraq's Arsenal Was Only on Paper," *The Washington Post,* Jan. 7, 2004, p. A1, and Philip Shenon and Christopher Marquis, "Panel Finds No Qaeda-Iraq Tie; Describes a Wider Plot for 9/11," *The New York Times,* June 17, 2004, p. A1.

But in the war against terrorism, the United States has been fighting a very different enemy. Al Qaeda is an organization, not a country, and those who fight for it come from many nations. In the case of the Taliban, the United States and nearly all other countries refused to recognize it as the legitimate government of Afghanistan. In fact, some Taliban soldiers are not even from Afghanistan but from the same states that supplied fighters for Al Qaeda.

The Bush administration has argued that the Taliban and Al Qaeda fighters held at Guantanamo are, in practice, receiving many POW rights, even though the administration says they do not qualify as POWs under the Geneva Convention. In addition, declaring them prisoners of war would require their release once the conflict ended, something administration officials argue could prove dangerous, since many are alleged terrorists who could attack the United States again if freed. Instead, the government has opted to classify them as "unlawful combatants" and to hold them indefinitely.

But civil liberties advocates argue that President Bush has no right to unilaterally declare that the Afghan war captives are not POWs, noting that the Geneva Convention specifies that soldiers captured during a conflict are presumed to be prisoners of war until otherwise judged differently.

"It's quite clear under the Geneva Convention that the U.S. has an obligation to declare all of these people at Guantanamo prisoners of war," says Vienna Colucci, director of the International Law Program at Amnesty International, a human-rights advocacy group based in London. "Under the treaty, there is a presumption that someone captured on the battlefield is a prisoner of war until a court decides otherwise."

But the administration and its supporters argue that the Geneva Convention covers the treatment of lawful combatants, but the Guantanamo prisoners are unlawful combatants. "People don't seem to think that the term 'unlawful combatant' is legitimate, but it is," says former National Security Council adviser Stevens, pointing out that international law recognizes that some fighters are not covered under the 1949 treaty.

Indeed, administration supporters dispute the notion that battlefield prisoners automatically deserve POW status until proven otherwise. "This presumption is only the case when you appear to qualify for POW status but something puts such a qualification into doubt," says for-

mer Justice Department official Rivkin. "So if you're captured and your uniform is hard to recognize because it's been so damaged in battle, then the presumption exists until we clarify your status."

But the Taliban and Al Qaeda detainees did not meet the criteria for POW status, according to Rivkin and Stevens. "These guys are not part of a regular armed force, with uniforms and insignias and other trappings of a real army," Stevens says. "Even the Taliban didn't wear uniforms, were not all from Afghanistan and were virtually interchangeable with Al Qaeda, who fought alongside them."

"The Taliban and Al Qaeda were indistinguishable from all other Afghanis," Rivkin says. "They're supposed to wear uniforms because we're not supposed to shoot civilians."

In addition, Rivkin says, the detainees meet none of the other criteria for POW status, such as having a discernable chain of command. "Between [Taliban leader] Mullah Omar and the regional commanders and everyone else, there doesn't seem to be a hierarchy," Rivkin says. "As for Al Qaeda, we don't know what their chain of command is."

Finally, POWs must represent a military that itself follows the rules of war. "Both groups have completely ignored the rules of war," Rivkin says, pointing out that they committed human-rights abuses against noncombatants before and during the war.

Stevens agrees, adding that the detainees at Guantanamo were not soldiers but terrorists. "All of these people were part of a huge terrorist network, and I'm sorry, you don't treat terrorists the same way you treat men in uniform who are part of a real army."

But administration critics contend the detainees in Guantanamo meet the test. "The Taliban were the de facto government of Afghanistan because they controlled over 90 percent of the country, so the Taliban soldiers are soldiers for the government of a nation state and should be treated that way," Amnesty International's Colucci says. Even Al Qaeda troops meet the definition of POWs, she and others say.

"The Geneva Convention recognizes that you have irregular armies and makes allowances for that," says Jamie Felner, director of U.S. programs at Human Rights Watch. "The Al Qaeda might not have all the trappings of a modern military, but we have declared

CHRONOLOGY

Before 1800s *Vague notions of the need to regulate war begin to take shape.*

4th Century St. Augustine of Hippo argues that countries should only go to war for good or just reasons.

13th Century St. Thomas Aquinas says states must have good intentions when waging war.

17th Century Dutch scholar Hugo Grotius sets out basic principles for the rules of war.

19th Century *The rise of mass media brings home the horrors of war and leads to international efforts to codify rules.*

1854-1856 The barbarity of the Crimean War shocks Europe.

1863 Reports from the front during the Civil War prompt President Abraham Lincoln to ask for military rules governing the conduct of the Army. Swiss banker Jean-Henry Dunant founds the International Committee of the Red Cross (ICRC) in Geneva, Switzerland.

1864 The ICRC sets out humane principles for dealing with the sick and wounded in battle.

1899 A second international convention on war is convened in The Hague, Netherlands.

1900-1999 *Unprecedented brutality and genocide lead to stronger rules of war and war-crimes tribunals.*

1929 ICRC adopts rules for humane treatment of prisoners.

1939-1945 Millions of civilians in Europe and Asia die during World War II.

1945 Nazi and Japanese leaders face war-crimes tribunals.

1948 U.N. adopts Genocide Convention.

1949 Geneva Convention sets protocols for the treatment of civilians, prisoners and the sick and wounded.

1977 Protocols to the 1949 Geneva Convention protect civilians against terrorism and other acts of violence. U.S. refuses to sign, citing a reluctance to legitimize terrorists.

1992 Civil war begins in the Yugoslav Republic of Bosnia.

1994 Rampaging Hutus in Rwanda kill up to 1 million ethnic Tutsis and moderate Hutus.

1995 Tribunal in The Hague begins trials of war criminals accused of atrocities in the former Yugoslavia.

1997 The first war-crimes trial against an alleged perpetrator of the Rwandan genocide begins in Arusha, Tanzania.

July 17, 1998 A U.N. conference adopts the Rome Treaty, setting the stage for creation of the International Criminal Court (ICC).

1999 American-led bombing halts Serbian ethnic cleansing in Kosovo; Australian-led forces stop violence in East Timor.

2000-Present *U.S. confronted with new threats.*

Dec. 31, 2000 President Bill Clinton signs the Rome Treaty.

January 2002 The first prisoners from Afghanistan arrive at the U.S. Naval Station at Guantanamo Bay, Cuba.

February 2002 War-crimes trial of former Yugoslav leader Slobodan Milosevic begins.

April 11, 2002 The ICC comes into existence in The Hague, Netherlands, after 76 nations ratify the Rome Treaty.

May 6, 2002 President Bush nullifies U.S. approval of the Rome Treaty.

March 19, 2003 U.S. invasion of Iraq begins.

June 28, 2004 Supreme Court rules that prisoners at Guantanamo must be allowed to contest their detention.

June 23, 2004 U.S. diplomats abandon efforts to renew exemption of U.S. citizens serving as UN peacekeepers from ICC.

July 30, 2004 Tribunals to review status of Guantanamo detainees begin.

war on them and should treat them as if we are at war with them."

"Al Qaeda forces were fighting alongside the Taliban to defend Afghanistan," Colucci adds. "They were part of their force structure and deserve POW status as well."

In June 2004, the Supreme Court ruled that U.S. courts' jurisdiction does extend to Guantanamo and the detainees have a right to contest their detention before U.S. courts or other "neutral decision-makers."[10] The Pentagon has initiated review tribunals staffed by military officers for all the detainees in an effort to comply with the Supreme Court's decision; the tribunals will assess whether the accused are actually unlawful enemy combatants and subject to detention.

However, lawyers for the detainees have denounced the proceedings as flawed and intend to pursue their cases in federal courts. Many legal experts expect that the tribunals will fail to satisfy the Supreme Court's judgment, and the detainees will be able ultimately to challenge their detention before regular U.S. courts.[11] As of Sept. 8, 2004, 30 detainees had completed the process and 29 had been confirmed as enemy combatants by the tribunals. The one detainee determined not to be an enemy combatant, held since January 2002, will be sent home.

While praising the action, executive director of the American Civil Liberties Union Anthony Romero remained critical of the government's behavior. "It should not take more than two years for the U.S. military to determine that we were holding someone who is apparently not an enemy combatant."[12]

On Aug. 24, 2004, preliminary hearings began in the trials of detainees charged with specific offenses, such as conspiring to commit war crimes. Four detainees have appeared in court so far, with another 11 selected as candidates for trials, including Feroz Abbasi.

Defense lawyers and human rights observers complain that due-process standards are not being met and hope that federal courts will also invalidate these trials. "These cases are headed straight to federal court," said Navy Lt. Cmdr. Charles Swift, appointed as one of the defense attorneys.[13]

BACKGROUND

Ancient Rules of War

Attempts to regulate war probably are as old as warfare itself. The ancients, most notably the philosophically minded Greeks, were known to have debated the morality of going to war or killing civilians.

But such exercises were the exception, not the rule. Weak neighbors typically were legitimate targets, and civilian populations and prisoners of war were often treated with great brutality.

The advent of Christianity, with its elements of pacifism, brought forth new doctrines on warfare. St. Augustine of Hippo (354–430), the first great Christian theologian to tackle political matters, theorized that war could be justified under certain limited conditions. In what became known as the "just-war" theory, Augustine argued that war was legitimate if it was fought by a proper authority and for what was then considered a good cause, which in those days might have meant a Christian kingdom prosecuting a crusade against non-Christians.

During the Middle Ages, theologian and philosopher St. Thomas Aquinas refined Augustine's theory, adding the requirement that "belligerents should have a rightful intention, so that they intend the advancement of good, or the avoidance of evil."[14]

In the 17th century, the Dutch scholar Hugo Grotius used the just-war theory to broaden the code for regulating conflict. Grotius set down rules of war that would become standard in the ensuing centuries, including the humane treatment of prisoners and non-combatants. "I saw in the whole Christian world a license of fighting at which even barbarous nations might blush," he wrote in 1625, explaining his desire to set down rules of warfare. "Wars were begun on trifling pretexts or none at all, and carried on without any reference of law, Divine or human."[15]

It was not until the 19th century, however, that efforts to regulate war really gathered steam. The invention of the telegraph and the development of industrial printing processes in the first half of the 1800s made on-the-scene reportage and widespread dissemination of information from the battlefield possible for the first time.

First in the Crimean War pitting Britain and France against Russia in the 1850s and then in the U.S. Civil War a decade later, war correspondents depicted the horror and cruelty of battle, shocking both officials and civilians back on the home front. The disturbing dispatches prompted President Abraham Lincoln to order the War Department to draft rules governing the army's conduct during wartime. Issued in 1863, the rules mandated humane treatment of prisoners of war and the

The near-total devastation of Hiroshima, Japan, remains evident three years after the United States dropped the first atomic bomb on the city on Aug. 6, 1945, killing 140,000 people. Three days later, a second atomic bomb killed 74,000 people in Nagasaki. Both sides bombed cities and other civilian targets during World War II.

wounded. Historians consider it the first attempt by an army to regulate itself.[16]

The same year, the International Committee of the Red Cross (ICRC) was founded by Jean-Henry Dunant, a Geneva banker who had been "seized with horror and pity" by what he witnessed at the Battle of Solferino in 1859, during the war for Italian unification. Tens of thousands had died, mostly from untreated wounds. Dunant resolved to find a way to prevent similar tragedies in the future.

In 1864, the ICRC held its inaugural conference in Geneva, Switzerland, and adopted the "Convention for the Amelioration of the Wounded and Sick in the Armies in the Field," calling on all states to care for the wounded and sick on the battlefield—even if they had fought for the enemy—and not to attack medical personnel.

In 1899 and 1907, delegates from several countries met in The Hague, the Netherlands, to build on the foundation set down in Geneva in 1864. Under the "Geneva Codes" passed by these two conferences, armies were charged not to unnecessarily kill civilians or destroy or confiscate civilian property. Prisoners of war were to be treated with respect.

World Wars

Only a handful of countries ever ratified any of the three treaties, and during the subsequent global wars the con-

ventions were largely ignored by all sides, including the allies.

During World War I, all sides used gas and other new weapons to kill and maim millions. And in World War II, German bomb and rocket attacks destroyed much of London, and allied forces targeted and killed hundreds of thousands of civilians in bombing raids over German and Japanese cities.

But it was German and Japanese atrocities committed during World War II that prompted the nations to meet again in 1949 to try to mitigate the ravages of future wars. The world had been stunned by Japanese brutality in East Asia and China—including the so-called Rape of Nanking—and by Germany's genocidal efforts during the Holocaust to exterminate entire populations of Jews, Gypsies (the Roma) and others it deemed "undesirable."[17]

Delegates to the Geneva Convention of 1949 produced what is considered the most significant and comprehensive document on the laws of war. Its four parts, ultimately ratified by 188 states, mandated countries involved in hostilities to treat the sick and wounded, prisoners of war and civilian non-combatants humanely and with respect.[18] They also prohibited attacks on civilian targets or the use of methods of warfare likely to lead to high levels of civilian casualties, such as so-called carpet-bombing.[19]

The horrors of World War II also led to the first formal, well-regulated war crimes trials for defeated Nazi and Japanese leaders held responsible for genocide and other mass attacks against civilians. Throughout military history, victors often executed enemy leaders and even regular soldiers and civilians without a trial. Only after the allied victory in 1945 did the notion of trying the leaders of defeated enemies fully take shape.

While ad hoc war-crimes tribunals had occasionally been convened after past wars, even in the Middle Ages, the tribunals at Nuremberg, Germany, and Tokyo set the standard by which subsequent war crimes trials have operated. Notably, the trials were the first instance where individuals were prosecuted for "crimes against humanity"—atrocities against non-combatants on a large scale.

Beginning in November 1945, in Nuremberg, 21 top Nazis—including Luftwaffe head Hermann Goering, armaments minister Albert Speer and Deputy Fuehrer Rudolf Hess—were tried for crimes against humanity, for their part in the murder of millions of Jews and others

Atrocities Lead to Rules of War

Since ancient times, man has tried to impose ethical rules on wartime behavior, spelling out morally acceptable reasons for waging war and rules for how they are fought and how prisoners and civilians treated. The modern movement to regulate war began gathering steam in the 19th century, after such innovations as the telegraph, photography and, later, radio and television, brought the starkness of the battlefield into people's living rooms. Major contemporary efforts to regulate war include the following treaties:

Instructions for the Government Armies of the United States in the Field, April 24, 1863—Prompted by descriptions of the horrors of the Civil War, President Abraham Lincoln ordered the War Department to create rules of conduct mandating humane treatment of prisoners during wartime. The so-called Lieber Code was drafted by Francis Lieber, a law professor at Columbia College, and revised by a board of Army officers.

Convention for the Amelioration of the Condition of the Wounded in Armies in the Field, Geneva, Switzerland, Aug. 22, 1864—The first Geneva Convention—drafted by the fledgling International Committee of the Red Cross after the brutality of the Crimean War—called on all nations to care for the wounded, including those of their foes, and not to attack medical personnel treating soldiers.

Convention II with Respect to the Laws and Customs of War on Land and its Annex: Regulation Concerning the Laws and Customs of War on Land, The Hague, July 29, 1899—The first Additional Protocol built on the 1864 Geneva agreement by setting down rules prohibiting the mistreatment of captive combatants or those disabled by sickness, injury or other means.

Convention for the Amelioration of the Condition of the Wounded and Sick in Armies in the Field, Geneva,

July 6, 1906—The 1906 Geneva Convention replaced the 1864 Geneva agreement and used more precise language to define the rights of wounded combatants and non-combatants. Rights of voluntary aid organizations were expressly recognized for the first time, and rules were established for the burial of dead combatants.

Convention on the Prevention and Punishment of the Crime of Genocide, United Nations, Dec. 9, 1948—Created in response to the atrocities of World War II, the so-called Genocide Convention outlawed abuse "committed with intent to destroy, in whole or in part, a national, ethnical, racial or religious group."

Geneva Convention, Aug. 12, 1949—Four conventions adopted in 1949 are the most significant and comprehensive efforts to codify the laws of war. Ultimately ratified by 188 nations, the conventions mandate humane treatment of sick and wounded ground and sea forces, prisoners of war and civilian non-combatants. They also prohibit attacks on civilian targets or methods of warfare that would injure civilians.

Additional Protocols to the Geneva Convention, June 8, 1977—Two Additional Protocols expanded the scope of the 1949 Geneva Convention to cover modern weapons and victims of internal conflicts and terrorism.

Rome Statute of the International Criminal Court, July 17, 1998—This treaty called for the creation of the International Criminal Court (ICC) to investigate crimes against humanity and serve as a permanent war-crimes court. Seventy-six nations have ratified the treaty, but on May 6, 2002, the Bush administration withdrew earlier U.S. approval by the Clinton administration. The court is expected to go into operation in 2003.

Sources: Aryeh Neier, *War Crimes* (Times Books, 1998); International Committee of the Red Cross, http://www.icrc.org

---

during the war. All but two were convicted, and 11 were executed. Similar trials occurred in Tokyo against Japanese leaders for their roles in massacres in China and elsewhere, including Prime Minister Hideki Tojo, who ordered the attack on Pearl Harbor. He was convicted as a war criminal and executed in 1948.

The United Nations Genocide Convention of 1948 was an outgrowth of the trials. It outlawed genocide,

defined as a premeditated attempt "to destroy, in whole or in part, a national, ethnical, racial or religious group."[20]

Since World War II, international affairs have been largely driven by the competition between the capitalist United States and the communist Soviet Union and—to a lesser degree—by the struggle for independence by European colonies in Africa, Asia and elsewhere. Both factors sparked horrific conflicts around

Defiant former Yugoslav President Slobodan Milosevic makes his first appearance before the U.N. War Crimes Tribunal in The Hague, Netherlands, in July 2001. Milosevic is charged with crimes against humanity for his alleged role in atrocities committed in Bosnia, Croatia and Kosovo during the civil wars in the 1990s that broke up Yugoslavia.

the globe, most of which were fought with little adherence to the Geneva Convention or any other humanitarian code or treaty. In conflicts from Cambodia, India and Pakistan to Afghanistan and Nigeria, civilians and combatants have been subjected to unimaginable brutality, and even genocide.[21]

Still, in some violent conflicts in the early 1990s, notably in Rwanda and Bosnia, the laws of war actually came into play in a meaningful way, even if only after the genocidal killing stopped. In both cases, some of the alleged perpetrators have been brought to trial and in some cases convicted and sentenced to prison.[22]

CURRENT SITUATION

International Court

Since the Nuremberg and Tokyo trials, several tribunals have been established to deal with horrific acts committed during war, often by soldiers. Currently, in The Hague, former Serbian leader Slobodan Milosevic is defending himself against charges that he deliberately ordered Serbia's military and paramilitary forces to commit genocide and other crimes against Muslims in Bosnia, Croatia and Kosovo. The international tribunal trying Milosevic was created in 1993 by the U.N. Security Council specifically to prosecute alleged war crimes associated with the war in Bosnia.

Besides Milosevic, more than 100 others also have been indicted and are either being tried or have had their cases resolved. As of Sept. 12, 2004, 52 trials have been completed, with two acquittals and three guilty verdicts overturned on appeal.[23]

Meanwhile, in Arusha, Tanzania, dozens of Rwandans are facing charges stemming from the 1994 genocide—perpetrated by ethnic Hutus and largely directed against members of the Tutsi ethnic group—that killed up to 1 million people in Rwanda. The tribunal has worked more slowly than its counterpart in the Netherlands, trying only 23 people and convicting 20 as of Aug. 30, 2004.

The Yugoslav and Rwandan tribunals inspired the creation of a permanent war-crimes court. On July 17, 1998, a United Nations-sponsored conference in Rome established the International Criminal Court (ICC), effective in July 2002.

Of the 127 countries at the conference, the United States was among the seven to vote against the treaty. In the ensuing years, U.S. opposition to the court has only grown stronger. A temporary compromise was worked out exempting U.S. troops working as U.N. peacekeepers for a year, and renewed in 2003. However, in June 2004 American diplomats failed to pass a resolution extending the exemption for another year.[24]

In addition, the United States has been pursuing bilateral agreements with individual countries to prevent American troops or officials from being extradited to the court from their jurisdictions; by September 2004, 92 nations had signed these so-called "Article 98" agreements.[25]

The administration is concerned that American soldiers and even civilian policymakers could be summoned before the tribunal by prosecutors and judges with political or anti-American agendas. They argue that even top American officials could be indicted, pointing to persistent efforts by human-rights activists and some judges in Europe to bring former Secretary of State Henry A. Kissinger to court for his alleged role in the bombing of Vietnam and Cambodia during the Vietnam War in the

Is President Bush's opposition to the International Criminal Court justified?

YES
John R. Bolton
Under Secretary for Arms Control and International Security

From remarks to the Aspen Institute, Berlin, Sept. 16, 2002

The International Criminal Court (ICC) has unacceptable consequences for our national sovereignty. [Its] precepts go against fundamental American notions of sovereignty, checks and balances and national independence. [It] is harmful to the national interests of the United States and harmful to our presence abroad.

The United States will regard as illegitimate any attempts to bring American citizens under its jurisdiction. The ICC does not fit into a coherent international "constitutional" design that delineates clearly how laws are made, adjudicated or enforced, subject to popular accountability and structured to protect liberty. . . . Requiring the United States to be bound by this treaty, with its unaccountable prosecutor, is clearly inconsistent with American standards of constitutionalism. . . .

The ICC's authority is vague and excessively elastic, and the court's discretion ranges far beyond normal . . . judicial responsibilities, giving it broad and unacceptable powers. . . . This is most emphatically not a court of limited jurisdiction. Crimes can be added subsequently that go beyond those included in the [authorizing] statute. Parties to the statute are subject to these subsequently added crimes only if they affirmatively accept them, but the statute purports automatically to bind non-parties—such as the United States—to [those] new crimes . . . [which] is neither reasonable nor fair.

Numerous prospective "crimes" were suggested and commanded wide support from participating nations, . . . such as the crime of "aggression," which was included in the statute, but was not defined. . . . There seems little doubt that Israel will be the target of a complaint in the ICC concerning conditions and practices by the Israeli military in the West Bank and Gaza. Moreover, one cannot answer with confidence whether the United States would now be accused of war crimes for legitimate but controversial uses of force to protect world peace.

Our concern goes beyond the possibility that the prosecutor will indict the isolated U.S. soldier who violates our own laws and values by allegedly committing a war crime. Our principal concern is for our country's top civilian and military leaders—those responsible for our defense and foreign policy. They are the ones potentially at risk at the hands of the ICC's politically unaccountable prosecutor. . . .

The prosecutor will answer to no superior executive power, elected or unelected. Nor is there any legislature anywhere in sight, elected or unelected. . . . The Europeans may be comfortable with such a system, but Americans are not.

NO
Heather B. Hamilton
Director of Programs, World Federalist Association, and Coordinator, Washington Working Group on the ICC

Written for the CQ Researcher, December 2002

Holding tyrants and war criminals accountable for their crimes not only serves America's national interest but also extends the legacy of U.S. moral leadership since Nuremberg. The International Criminal Court (ICC) is a response to the horrors of the 20th century, which demonstrated the incapacity of nation states alone to ensure justice for genocide, egregious war crimes or crimes against humanity.

America has little to fear from the ICC. The crimes covered by the court closely follow U.S. military law and were largely crafted by American military negotiators. U.S. soldiers and leaders need not fear the court, because they already play by its rules. Bill of Rights protections are guaranteed to suspects. . . . Without a Security Council referral, the limited jurisdiction of the court extends only to atrocities committed on the territory of—or by nationals of—countries that have accepted its jurisdiction (thereby ruling out cases against Israel, which is not a signatory).

Countries like the United States, with a functioning, independent judiciary will not see their nationals brought before the court, which is blocked from acting when a domestic court is willing and able.

The ICC is the "Court of the Democracies." Joining it means accepting its jurisdiction, where the vast majority of participating countries already respect the rule of law. Of the 85 states that are parties to the treaty, 65 percent are ranked by Freedom House as "totally free," and another 29 percent are "partly free." These democracies make up an oversight body that will elect (and can dismiss) judges and prosecutors, provide the budget and ensure accountability for the court's actions.

The administration's war on the ICC does not ensure protections from illusory threats, but only promotes the perception that America sees itself as above the rule of law and as uninterested in justice for genocide victims. Joining the ICC would allow the United States to oversee the election of U.S. judges and prosecutors, influence the workings of the court and hold accountable tyrants in Sudan, Iraq and other critical areas of concern.

But even without U.S. ratification, the United States would best be served by engaging with the court to ensure that it follows the carefully built-in safeguards and focuses on those cases—like Congo, Sudan, Burma—where justice is desperately needed.

Bosnian prisoners held by Serbs in the squalid Ternopolje prison camp in Prijedor, Bosnia, in the early 1990s show signs of starvation. International humanitarian law prohibits the mistreatment of civilians, but brutality toward non-combatants has been commonplace in recent conflicts throughout the world.

1970s and the toppling of Chile's left-wing President Salvador Allende.[26]

"The administration's concerns are fully justified," says Ted Galen Carpenter, vice president for foreign policy and defense studies at the Cato Institute, a libertarian think tank. "This looks like a highly politicized body, and I could see them pursuing a politically motivated prosecution of U.S. officials."

More important, the ICC lacks many fundamental due-process guarantees provided in the U.S. Constitution and in American courts, he says, "things like unanimous verdicts, the right to confront witnesses and protection against double jeopardy."

But supporters of the new court counter that administration concerns about politicization are overblown. "If you look at European countries like Spain and Belgium, where the courts have wide jurisdictional latitude to indict anyone they want, you'll find that none of them have ever indicted U.S. officials," says Todd Howland, director of the Robert F. Kennedy Center for Human Rights. "Given the power and influence of the United States, it seems unlikely that the ICC would be hauling in an American official unless it had a very good case against that person."

In addition, Howland says, while the ICC may not offer every protection afforded by a U.S. court, it basically follows the successful procedures used by the current war-crimes tribunals in the Netherlands and Tanzania, which

the U.S. supports. "Look, no court is going to ever be perfect, and the ICC is going to have problems here and there," he says. "But this system has been successful so far, and that's why it's internationally accepted."

Even though the United States opposes the ICC, it supports ad hoc war-crimes tribunals to prosecute crimes associated with specific atrocities, like those in Rwanda and the former Yugoslavia. However, the United States has agreed that Saddam Hussein, captured in December 2003 and declared a POW by the Pentagon, will be tried by an Iraqi tribunal, with support from the American government and perhaps some international experts in advisory roles. Citing the will of the Iraqi people, and perhaps mindful of former Serbian leader Slobodan Milosevic's ability to drag out his own trial and use it as a political platform, U.S. officials have ruled out an international or U.N. court. The Iraqi court will try Saddam and 11 of his closest associates, probably beginning before January 2005, according to interim Iraqi Prime Minister Ayad Allawi.

These plans have come under fierce criticism from international legal experts and human rights advocates, who describe the plan as another effort by the Bush administration to snub the international community. "The Bush administration pursued this route out of its antipathy to internationalized forms of justice," said Richard Dicker of Human Rights Watch.[27] International critics contend the Arab world will see any trial dominated by the U.S. and its Iraqi allies as victor's justice; they also say only an international court can provide a truly fair trial devoid of political influence.

OUTLOOK

More Brutal Wars?

In his 2002 bestseller, *Warrior Politics, Atlantic Monthly* correspondent Robert D. Kaplan predicts that future wars will be more chaotic and vicious, and less regulated.

While international law likely will grow in significance because of its role in trade organizations and human-rights tribunals, Kaplan writes, it will play less of a role in the conduct of future wars because "war will increasingly be unconventional and undeclared, and fought within states rather than between them."[28]

Moreover, Kaplan predicts that wartime justice in future conflicts will not depend on international humanitarian law but on "the moral fiber of military commanders themselves." In other words, every army will be as humane or inhumane as its leader.

Former Justice Department official Rivkin agrees that warfare will become more anarchic. But he says the efforts to regulate war are not keeping pace with the new reality that Kaplan and others envision.

While adversaries like Al Qaeda or the Bosnian Serbs don't generally obey international norms, new and more restrictive rules and limits are being imposed on the United States and other "war-fighting countries" like Britain, Israel and Australia, Rivkin says. "We've lost control of the process," he says, because the rules now are being made by humanitarian organizations like Amnesty International and international law professors. "These people are confining us more and more and giving our enemies more and more of a free hand."

Whether it is U.S. troops in Afghanistan or Israeli soldiers in the West Bank, the armies of the developed world are held to increasingly high standards while their adversaries brook no standards at all, he says. For example, Rivkin says, international human-rights activists are far more outspoken about civilian deaths due to Israeli incursions into Palestinian refugee camps than they are about Israeli civilian deaths due to Palestinian suicide bombers.[29]

"The pendulum needs to swing back a bit," Rivkin says. "We need to say: 'If you don't comply with the rules of war, we're going to take the gloves off.' "

The Hoover Institution's Davenport agrees that the rules of war "need to change to fit new realities. We're living in an age of terrorism, and my sense is that we're still acting defensively because we feel constrained by these rules."

But Howland of the Robert F. Kennedy Center for Human Rights says that ignoring the rules will simply make warfare more violent and horrific. "This idea that we should 'take off the gloves' is simply ridiculous," he says. "Doing that merely makes the conflict more brutal."

The solution is to bring everyone, even non-state entities, into the rulemaking process, Howland says. "This is a structural problem, not a problem with the rules themselves," he says. "You have these rebel groups and others who see the laws of war as Western constructs. We need to bring them in as parties to the process. We need to make the laws of war apply to everyone, not set a bad example by ignoring them ourselves."

NOTES

1. Glenn Frankel, "Road to Son's Freedom Paved With Anguish," *The Washington Post,* Nov. 30, 2002, p. A16.

2. *Ibid.*

3. For background, see David Masci and Kenneth Jost, "War on Terrorism," *The CQ Researcher,* Oct. 12, 2001, pp. 817-848, and Kenneth Jost, "Rebuilding Afghanistan," *The CQ Researcher,* Dec. 21, 2001, pp. 1041-1064.

4. Quoted in Neely Tucker, "Detainees Seek Access to Courts," *The Washington Post,* Dec. 3, 2002, p. A22.

5. For background, see David Masci and Patrick Marshall, "Civil Liberties in Wartime," *The CQ Researcher,* Dec. 14, 2001, pp. 1017-1040.

6. For background, see Mary H. Cooper, "Weapons of Mass Destruction," *The CQ Researcher,* March 8, 2002, pp. 193-216.

7. For background, see Kenneth Jost, "War Crimes," *The CQ Researcher,* July 7, 1995, pp. 585-608.

8. For a thorough defense of the Bush administration's position, see Lee A. Casey, David B. Rivkin Jr. and Darin R. Bartram, "The Laws of War: They Aren't POWs," *The Washington Post,* March 3, 2002, p. B3.

9. Anthony Dworkin, "British Court Attacks U.S. Policy on Detainees," crimesofwar.org., Nov. 7, 2002.

10. Linda Greenhouse, "Access to Courts," *The New York Times,* June 29, 2004, p. A1.

11. Neil. A. Lewis, "Scrutiny of Review Tribunals as War Crimes Trials Open," *The New York Times,* Aug. 24, 2004, p. A12.

12. Josh White, "Suspect Is Freed From Guantanamo," *The Washington Post,* Sept. 9, 2004, p. A3.

13. Scott Higham, "Hearings Open With Challenge to Tribunals," *The Washington Post,* Aug. 29, 2004, p. A12, and John Hendren, "Trials and Errors at Guantanamo," *Los Angeles Times,* Aug. 29, 2004, p. A1.

14. Quoted in Bill Broadway, "Challenges to Waging a 'Just War,' " *The Washington Post,* Oct. 13, 2001, p. B9.

15. Quoted at www.orst.edu/instruct/phl302/philoso phers/grotius.html; the Oregon State University Philosophy Web site.

16. Aryeh Neier, *War Crimes: Brutality, Genocide, Terror, and the Struggle for Justice* (1998), p. 14.

17. For background, see Kenneth Jost, "Holocaust Reparations," *The CQ Researcher,* March 26, 1999, pp. 257-290.

18. International Committee of the Red Cross, www. icrc.org.

19. *Ibid.*

20. Quoted in "Convention on the Prevention and Punishment of the Crime of Genocide," 78 U.N.T.S. 277, Article II.

21. For background, see Mary H. Cooper, "Women and Human Rights," *The CQ Researcher,* April 30, 1999, pp. 353-376.

22. For additional information, see Sarah Glazer, "Stopping Genocide," *The CQ Researcher,* Aug. 27, 2004, pp. 685-708.

23. United Nations tribunals for Yugoslavia (www.un.org/icty/) and Rwanda (www.ictr.org).

24. Maggie Farley, "U.S. Ends Bid to Exempt Troops From Global Court," *Los Angeles Times,* June 24, 2004, p. A1.

25. U.S. Department of State, www.state.gov/t/pm/art98/.

26. For background, see "Harry Dunphy, 'Incisive and Controversial, A Statesman Returns,'" The Associated Press, Nov. 28, 2002.

27. Peter Landesman, "Who V. Saddam?" *The New York Times Magazine,* July 11, 2004, p. 34.

28. Robert D. Kaplan, *Warrior Politics* (2002), p. 118.

29. For background, see Mary H. Cooper, "Global Refugee Crisis," *The CQ Researcher,* July 7, 1999, pp. 569-592.

BIBLIOGRAPHY

Books

Gutman, Roy, and David Rieff, eds., Crimes of War: What the Public Should Know, W. W. Norton, 1999.
An encyclopedia with 140 entries concerning war crimes, including Bosnia, civilian immunity, genocide and prisoners of war.

Johnson, James Turner, Morality and Contemporary Warfare, Yale University Press, 2000.
A professor of religion at Rutgers University argues that "just-war" theory is not essentially a pacifist doctrine, as some theologians and others see it.

Neier, Aryeh, War Crimes: Brutality, Genocide, Terror and the Struggle for Justice, Times Books, 1998.
A Holocaust survivor and president of the Open Society Institute chronicles efforts to bring war criminals to justice, focusing on recent atrocities in the former Yugoslavia and Rwanda.

Reisman, W. Michael, and Chris T. Antoniou, eds., The Laws of War: A Comprehensive Collection of Primary Documents on International Laws Governing Armed Conflict, Vintage Books, 1994.
An excellent primer on international humanitarian law (IHL), including excerpts from the Geneva and Hague Conventions and U.N. Charter.

Walzer, Michael, Just and Unjust Wars: A Moral Argument with Historical Illustrations, Basic Books, 2000.
A professor of social science at Princeton University considers the moral implications of making war, using examples from ancient times to the 20th century.

Articles

Frankel, Glen, "Road to Son's Freedom Paved With Anguish," The Washington Post, Nov. 30, 2002, p. A16.
Frankel explores lawyers' efforts to secure trials for the detainees from Afghanistan at Guantanamo Bay.

"Judging Genocide: Prosecuting War Crimes," The Economist, June 16, 2001.
An excellent overview of the war crimes trials dealing with alleged atrocities in the former Yugoslavia and Bosnia and what the new International Criminal Court can learn from their successes and mistakes.

Kagan, Robert, "Europeans Courting International Disaster," June 30, 2002, p. B7.
A senior associate at the Carnegie Endowment for International Peace defends the administration's concerns

about U.S. soldiers and officials being hauled before the International Criminal Court.

Lattin, Don, "Clerics Question Whether Pre-Emptive Iraq Strike Would be Just Wars," *The San Francisco Chronicle*, Oct. 12, 2002, p. A16.

Lattin provides an overview of religious leaders' opinions on whether a U.S. attack on Iraq would meet the "just-war" test.

Pavlischek, Keith J., "The Justice in Just War," First Things, May 2000, pp. 43–47.

A fellow at the Center for Public Justice contends many theologians mistakenly think that just-war theory is essentially a pacifist doctrine.

"The Prisoners Dilemma," The Economist, Jan. 24, 2002.

The article looks at the dispute over the rights of the Taliban and Al Qaeda prisoners at Guantanamo Bay.

Slevin, Peter, "U.S. Would Seek to Try Hussein for War Crimes," *The Washington Post*, Oct. 30, 2002, p. A1.

Slevin details administration plans to establish an ad hoc war-crimes tribunal to try Iraqi President Saddam Hussein and his inner circle for crimes against humanity, including gassing his own people.

Sprague, Joseph C., "We Must Say 'No' to War with Iraq," *Chicago Tribune*, Oct. 21, 2002, p. 16.

A United Methodist bishop argues that an attack on Iraq would not meet "just-war" criteria.

Tammeus, Bill, "Viewing War Through the Lens of Theology," *The Kansas City Star*, Oct. 13, 2002.

Tammeus goes back to the ancient roots of just-war theory and explains how it is being applied differently in today's global conflicts.

Reports

"Myths and Realities about the International Criminal Court," Washington Working Group on the International Criminal Court, www.wfa.org/issues/wicc/factsheets/myths.html.

The report argues the International Criminal Court (ICC) contains adequate due-process protections and will not become a "star chamber."

"The U.S. Response to the International Criminal Court: What Next?" *The Federalist Society*, May 2002.

Papers and documents outline U.S. concerns over how the ICC could mistreat U.S. soldiers and officials.

For More Information

American Non-Governmental Organizations Coalition for the International Criminal Court, (AMICC), United Nations Association, 801 Second Ave., 2nd Floor, New York, NY 10017-4706; www.amicc.org. The coalition supports U.S. approval of the International Criminal Court (ICC).

American Red Cross, 2025 E St., N.W., Washington, DC 20006; (202) 303-4498; www.redcross.org. The nation's leading humanitarian organization prepares and disseminates information on international humanitarian law.

Amnesty International USA, 322 8th Ave., New York, NY 10001; (212) 807-8400; www.amnestyusa.org. U.S. branch of the worldwide organization that promotes human rights.

Cato Institute, 1000 Massachusetts Ave., N.W., Washington, DC 20001; (202) 842-0200; www.cato.org. A public-policy research organization that advocates limited government and individual liberty.

Center for Public Justice, 2444 Solomons Island Rd., Suite 201, Annapolis, MD 21401; (410) 571-6300; www.cpjustice.org. A public-policy think tank that looks at issues from a Christian perspective.

Crimes of War Project, 1205 Lamont St., N.W., Washington, DC 20010; (202) 494-3834; www.crimesofwar.org. A collaboration of journalists, lawyers and scholars dedicated to raising public awareness of the laws of war.

The Federalist Society, 1015 18th St., N.W., Suite 425, Washington DC 20036; (202) 822-8138; www.fed-soc.org. Promotes conservative and libertarian views in the legal profession.

Hoover Institution, Stanford University, Stanford, CA 94305; (650) 723-1754; www.hoover.org. A conservative think tank devoted to the study of politics, economics and international affairs.

Human Rights Watch, 350 Fifth Ave., 34th Floor, New York, NY 10118-3299; (212) 290-4700; www.hrw.org. An advocacy group that investigates and documents human-rights abuses around the world.

International Committee of the Red Cross, Washington Delegation, 2100 Pennsylvania Ave N.W., Suite 545, Washington, DC 20037; (202) 293-9430; www.icrc.org. From its Geneva headquarters, the ICRC promotes more humane wartime behavior.

International Institute of Humanitarian Law, La Voie Creuse 16, 1202 Geneva, Switzerland; 41 22 9197930; www.iihl.org. A private, nonprofit organization founded in 1970 to develop and disseminate the principles of international humanitarian law.

National Council of Churches, 475 Riverside Dr., Suite 880, New York, NY 11080; (212) 870-2227; www.ncccusa.org. A coalition of 39 Christian denominations in the United States.

The Robert F. Kennedy Memorial, 1367 Connecticut Ave., N.W., Suite 200, Washington, DC 20036; (202) 463-7575; www.rfkmemorial.org. A charitable organization that works for a peaceful and just world through domestic and international programs that help the disadvantaged and oppressed.

14

Bush and the Environment

Mary H. Cooper

Smog envelops downtown Los Angeles shortly after sunrise in early September. President Bush's Clear Skies Initiative would cut by 70 percent power-plant emissions of three major air pollutants that contribute to smog and acid rain and cause respiratory and cardiovascular diseases. Bush would use market incentives—not current EPA-set mandates—to encourage utility operators to reduce emissions. Critics say the approach favors industry.

Getty Images/David McNew

From *The CQ Researcher,*
October 25, 2002 (Revised September 2004).

President Bush had barely hung his Stetson on the White House hat rack before he launched into a series of controversial environmental policy changes.

In one of his first moves, he froze 175 executive orders and regulations that President Bill Clinton had issued just before leaving office in January 2001. Since then, the Bush administration has implemented many other environmental policies that critics say favor oil producers, loggers, electric utilities and other industries.

In another early action, Bush sought to lower the arsenic levels permitted in drinking water, but the administration later bowed to widespread protests and restored Clinton's stricter standards. Still, the pace of Bush's regulatory "rollbacks" has since picked up.

In 2002, for example, the administration lifted a ban on new oil and gas drilling in the Rocky Mountains, eased tough air-conditioner efficiency standards and formally designated Nevada's Yucca Mountain as a nuclear-waste repository—despite lingering safety concerns. In June of that year, Bush announced a plan that critics said would weaken enforcement of Clean Air Act pollution limits. In August, the administration opposed a sweeping proposal by the World Summit on Sustainable Development to increase the use of solar power and other forms of renewable energy. The president also unveiled a controversial plan to reduce wildfire damage in national forests by waiving limits on logging.

In addition to rewriting regulations, Bush has made other controversial environmental decisions. Within weeks of taking office, he reversed a campaign pledge to push for limits on industrial emissions of carbon dioxide and other "greenhouse gases," which most scientists believe are causing a potentially catastrophic warming of

Air Quality Has Improved

The Clean Air Act has significantly reduced industrial emissions that contribute to smog and acid rain and cause respiratory and cardio-vascular diseases. From 1982-2001, for example, the required intro-duction of lead-free gas eliminated more than 90 percent of the lead in the air, and particulate matter dropped by half. Only carbon monoxide increased, largely due to the popularity of gas-guzzling sport-utility ve-hicles. President Bush's new Clear Skies Initiative adds mercury emis-sions to the list of targeted pollutants.

Major air pollutants affected by Clean Air Act	1982-2001	1992-2001
	(percentage increase or reduction)	
Nitrogen dioxide (NO_2)	+9%	-3%
Volatile organic compounds (form ground-level ozone)	-16	-8
Sulfur dioxide (SO_2)	-25	-24
Particulate matter	-51	-13
Carbon monoxide (CO)	0	+6
Lead	-93	-5

Source: Environmental Protection Agency, "Latest Findings on national Air Quality: 2001 Status and Trends," September 2002

Earth's atmosphere.[1] Bush also renounced the Kyoto Protocol, an international treaty calling for mandatory carbon emission reductions designed to slow global warming.*

Environmentalists say Bush's approach constitutes an unprecedented assault on the nation's commitment to protect the environment. "The Bush administration has the worst record of any presidential administration ever," said Gregory Wetstone, director of programs at the Natural Resources Defense Council (NRDC), an envi-ronmental advocacy group in New York City. "I don't think we've ever seen a more sweeping or potent assault on our bedrock environmental laws."

Conservatives, on the other hand, extol Bush's policies as innovative alternatives to bureaucratic red tape. "The

Bush administration wants to em-phasize the next generation of en-vironmental policy," said Steven F. Hayward, a resident scholar at the American Enterprise Institute (AEI), a conservative think tank. That policy will produce "less of the old-style, command-and-control regulation" from Washington, he explained, and more use of markets, incentives and regulatory flexibility to enable companies "to get around some of the rigidities in the way we've implemented environmental laws for the last 30 years."

Environmentalists point out that those environmental laws—among them the Clean Air Act, the Clean Water Act and the National En-vironmental Policy Act (NEPA)—have produced cleaner air and water, reduced the public's expo-sure to toxic waste and rescued many species from the brink of extinction. Most of the laws were enacted in the early 1970s, after a nationwide grass-roots movement persuaded Congress to clean up pollution generated by decades of unregulated industrial development and to protect the environment from future damage.[2]

But environmentalists say the progress made so far—such as banning the pesticide DDT, installing "scrubbers" on coal-burning smokestacks and halting the discharge of industrial waste into waterways—was the easy part. They concede the second generation of environmental improvements—preventing "runoff" from farms and city streets into streams, saving endangered species indigenous to prime real estate and slowing global warming—will cost more and be politically harder to accomplish.

Conservatives complain that environmentalists ignore the escalating costs of complying with environmental reg-ulations. Cost considerations are especially critical when considering such sweeping issues as global warming, they point out. For instance, the United States is the world's leading source of industrial greenhouse-gas emissions. In order to reduce emissions of those gases, America must

---

*Most scientists agree that industrial emissions of carbon dioxide and a few other gases act like the glass in a greenhouse, trapping heat within Earth's atmosphere, a process that over time could melt glaciers, raise sea levels and radically alter the world's ecosystems.

shift away from fossil fuels—oil, coal and natural gas—thought to be the main source of those emissions.

"If the environmentalists wanted to argue that addressing global warming would require us to get rid of fossil fuels, that would be an honest debate," said Jerry Taylor, director of natural resources studies at the Cato Institute, a libertarian think tank. "But to argue that it won't have major economic dislocations or dramatically change a number of aspects of our economy is silly. The main reason we don't use renewable-energy sources today is that it's too expensive and it's not very useful for most purposes."

However, environmentalists contend that cost-effective energy-saving alternatives already exist but policymakers refuse to support them. "We can get carbon-dioxide reduction that would be significant at an acceptable cost," said Michael Oppenheimer, a professor of geosciences and international affairs at Princeton University and an expert on climate change. "The quickest, most effective thing that could be done in the United States is to improve the fuel economy of motor vehicles," which he said would produce immediate emissions reductions without being "inordinately expensive."

In fact, Oppenheimer said, improving fuel economy would help the economy by generating "efficiencies that would ripple through industry," as individual producers figure out the cheapest way to implement the caps. Instead, the Bush administration wants to increase domestic production of fossil fuels, he pointed out.

Of course, not all the administration's actions can be said to favor business interests in environmental disputes. In December 2001, for example, the Environmental Protection Agency (EPA) ordered General Electric Co. to pay nearly $500 million to dredge deadly polychlorinated biphenyls (PCBs) from the Hudson River. The

U.S. Leads in Greenhouse Gas Pollution

The United States emitted more greenhouse gases—which are believed to cause global warming—in 1999 than the total emissions from 151 developing nations. Texas was the leading U.S. polluter. President Bush's Clean Skies Initiative does not regulate carbon dioxide—the main greenhouse gas and a major component of emissions from coal-fired power plants. Instead, the Bush plan depends on voluntary industry participation. Critics of the Kyoto Protocol on global warming, which Bush rejected, say it gives overly favorable treatment to developing countries by exempting them from the first round of required carbon-dioxide emission cuts. But Kyoto supporters say developing nations produce relatively few carbon emissions.

State/ Pollution Rank in U.S.	1999 Emissions (mmtce*)	Population (in millions)	No. of developing countries with lower combined emissions	Combined population of these developing countries (in millions)
Texas/1	166.6	21.8	119	1,000.0
California/2	94.8	35.1	109	791.1
Ohio/3	69.8	11.4	103	736.6
Penn./4	64.0	12.3	101	733.6
Florida/5	60.8	16.8	100	714.2
U.S. Total	1,526.1	288.2	151	2,631.0

* mmtce = million metric tons of carbon equivalent. The two biggest sources of mmtce are electric utilities and transportation.

Source: "First in Emissions, Behind in Solutions: Global Warming Pollution from U.S. States Compared to More Than 150 Developing Countries," National Environmental Trust, 2002

decision ended a lengthy struggle with the company, which had dumped 150,000 pounds of the toxic chemical into the river over several decades.[3]

And in October 2002 the EPA ordered the permanent shutdown and cleanup of Marine Shale Processors Inc., a hazardous-waste incinerator in rural Louisiana that had claimed it produced harmless recycled material for construction. Environmentalists said the plant was responsible for an outbreak of cancer among nearby residents in the 1980s.[4]

But on the most controversial issues—those with the biggest potential environmental and economic impacts—environmentalists say Bush has come down squarely on the side of industry. For example, following the reversal of

Key Bush Officials' Ties to Industry

President Bush has filled several key policy positions with people who have strong ties to industries opposed to environmental-protection laws. Some of the appointees even advocated the repeal or weakening of the very laws they were hired to enforce.

Bush himself is a former executive with Harken Energy Corp., a Texas oil-drilling firm. He chose fellow oilman Dick Cheney, then CEO of the oil-services firm Halliburton Corp., as his running mate in his successful bid for the White House in 2000. He then picked many of his administration's other top officials from the energy, mining and timber industries, all of which have chafed under regulations designed to curb pollution.

Topping the list of appointees hostile to existing environmental-protection programs is Energy Secretary Spencer Abraham, a former U.S. senator from Michigan who in 1999 actually proposed abolishing the department he was picked to head barely two years later. Abraham—whose home state is the center of the U.S. automobile industry—also voted against stronger fuel-efficiency standards for cars and trucks and for cuts to federal funding aimed at spurring the development of less-polluting renewable-energy sources.

Abraham helped craft the administration's national energy policy, presented last year, which calls for increased domestic production of fossil fuels—oil, coal and natural gas—which when burned produce gases and other air pollutants thought to contribute to global warming. The plan also calls for opening more public land, including 2,000 acres of the Arctic National Wildlife Refuge (ANWR), to drilling and mining operations. The energy plan is currently in limbo in Congress, where Democrats have refused to go along with drilling in ANWR. Abraham's lifetime environmental voting record earned a low 5 percent rating this year from the League of Conservation Voters.[1]

Meanwhile, oil and gas exploration and production is proceeding apace on other federal lands, especially in the Intermountain West, thanks to rulemaking changes backed by Interior Secretary Gale Norton. Norton came from the Denver-based Mountain States Legal Foundation, a conservative property-rights advocacy group headed by James Watt, President Ronald Reagan's controversial Interior secretary (1981–83). The foundation supports opening public lands to logging and mining and recently announced plans to file a suit to block the proposed new listing of a rare mouse under the Endangered Species Act, a law Norton is responsible for implementing.[2]

As Colorado's attorney general, Norton cut her agency's budget for enforcing environmental laws by a third. Since taking office, she has overseen a massive expansion of drilling for oil, gas and coal-bed methane in the Rockies, including on some national monuments. She withdrew a report from the Interior Department's Fish and Wildlife Service that was critical of mountaintop removal. The controversial coal-mining technique pollutes downstream water in much of Appalachia. Norton later delayed completion of a study on the technique's environmental impact.[3]

The records of other key Bush officials are less blatantly anti-environmental. Agriculture Secretary Ann Veneman, whose domain includes the Forest Service and such environmental issues as pesticide regulations and genetically modified food, worked for a law firm that fought President Clinton's proposed moratorium on road building in national forests. But she has won praise from environmentalists for supporting farm-conservation programs, though to little avail. This year's farm bill actually

---

[1]League of Conservation Voters, "Presidential Report Card," January 2002. Information in this section is based on this report unless otherwise noted.

[2]"Group Threatens Lawsuit to Keep Mouse Off Endangered List," Associated Press Newswires, Aug. 1, 2002.

[3]See John Raby, "Mining Study Not Expected Until February," Associated Press Newswires, Aug. 2, 2002.

---

national policy on global warming, strongly supported by energy producers, the president announced two major policy shifts that pit business interests against environmental-protection advocates.

The Clear Skies Initiative, which Bush proposed in February 2002, would no longer require owners of older, coal-fired electric utilities and other plants to install modern pollution controls when they expand their facilities. Although Congress rejected the proposal, the administration accomplished one of its central goals, weakening the requirement that plants install scrubbers when they upgrade, through regulatory changes. In August 2002, after one of the most devastating wildfire seasons in U.S. history, Bush announced plans to let log-

cut some of those pro-grams.[4] And Fran Mainella, director of the National Park Service, another Interior Department agency, won conservationists' praise for her management of Florida's state park system. Yet she also went along with Norton in reversing a Clinton ban on recreational snowmobiling in Yellowstone and Grand Teton national parks in 2002.[5]

The Bush administration officials with the most visible role in environmental policy

Conservationists have been critical of Interior Secretary Gale A. Norton, left, and, until she resigned in 2003, EPA Administrator Christine Todd Whitman.

enforcement have been Christine Todd Whitman, Bush's first head of the independent Environmental Protection Agency, and her successor, former Utah Gov. Michael O. Leavitt. As governor of New Jersey, Whitman had a mixed record on environmental issues. A strong supporter of so-called smart growth, she set up a program to save open space and discourage suburban sprawl. But she also loosened rules requiring industries to report their use and release of toxic chemicals. As EPA administrator, Whitman garnered mixed reviews from environmentalists, who welcomed some of her decisions, including one forcing General Electric to clean up its deposits of deadly dioxin from the Hudson River. But she was faulted for defending the Bush administration's loosening of rules requiring older power plants to install modern anti-pollution equipment.[6] After two years in office, Whitman resigned, and Leavitt took

over the EPA in the fall of 2003.

It is at lower echelons of government that less visible political appointees with industry ties are making some of the most sweeping changes to environmental policies through the rule-making process. Agriculture Undersecretary Mark Rey, for example, was a longtime timber-company lobbyist before becoming the administration's top forestry official. Rey helped shape the president's Healthy Forests Initiative, which would let his former clients harvest more large, commercially valuable trees in national forests in exchange for agreeing to clear them of fire-prone undergrowth. Only about half the changes called for under the plan require congressional approval.

Deputy Interior Secretary J. Steven Griles was a mining and energy industry lobbyist before joining the department that oversees both industries' access to public lands. He has come under scrutiny for potential conflict of interest stemming from his alleged interest in firms that stand to benefit from such department decisions as the issuance of permits for mining and mountaintop removal.[7]

[4]See Jake Thompson, "Farm-State Lawmakers Rip USDA Officials," *Omaha World-Herald*, Sept. 24, 2002.

[5]See Michael Kilian, "Park Service Tweaks Snowmobile Policy; New Guidelines to Avert Total Ban," *Chicago Tribune*, June 27, 2002.

[6]See H. Josef Hebert, "Bid to Ease Pollution Standards Under Fire," *Houston Chronicle*, Sept. 4, 2002.

[7]See Eric Pianin, "Official's Lobbying Ties Decried," *The Washington Post*, April 25, 2002; and "Boxer Seeks Conflict Probe in Mine Ruling," *Los Angeles Times*, Oct. 5, 2002.

gers harvest large trees in fire-prone national forests in exchange for clearing highly flammable brush and small trees. To expedite the process, the president's Healthy Forests Initiative, which he signed into law in December 2003, would relax the public-comment requirements spelled out in NEPA and make it harder to use the courts to block timber-clearing projects.

As lawmakers consider changes to environmental policy, these are some of the issues they are considering:

Should basic environmental laws be revised to reflect economic priorities?

Among the environmental-protection laws passed in the early days of the conservation movement, NEPA ranks as

Controversy Surrounds Use of Public Lands

The federal government owns more than one-quarter of the total U.S. land area—including more than three-quarters of Nevada and two-thirds of Alaska. Policies governing the use of public lands for recreation and industry—mainly logging, mining and grazing—are highly controversial. President Bill Clinton's ban on snowmobiles in Yellowstone and Grand Teton national parks was among 175 regulations that President Bush put on hold after taking office. Clinton's ban on new road building on 60 million acres of national forests was blocked by a federal judge in Idaho to prevent "irreparable harm" to the timber industry.

Percentages of Federally Owned Land

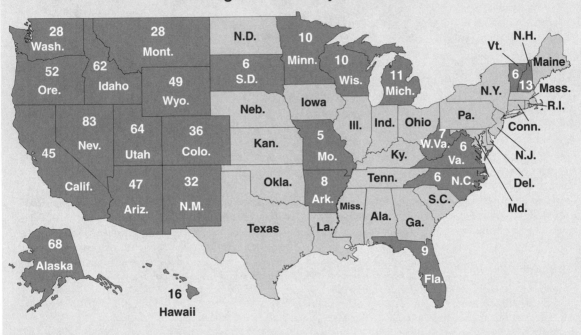

Note: States without percentages are 4 percent federally owned, or less.

Sources: www.anwr.org; Statistical Abstract of the United States

the most far-reaching, the cornerstone of environmental protection. A recent *New York Times* editorial called it "the Magna Carta of environmental protection and perhaps the most important of all the environmental statutes signed into law by Richard Nixon three decades ago."[5]

Designed to ensure public access to environmental policymaking, the 1970 law requires the government to carefully study the environmental impacts that likely would result from a federal project; consider the impact of alternatives; and take public comments into account before moving forward. A variety of federal projects, including roads and dams, have been changed or halted as a result of NEPA-mandated environmental-impact statements.

But critics say NEPA has caused needless, costly delays of projects and discouraged well-designed policy initiatives. "Because of the straitjacket of a lot of environmental policy, the rulemaking process often leaves administrators in an either-or situation, where you're either going to apply a very tough rule or you decide to waive the rule for certain parties or get rid of the rule completely," said AEI's Hayward. "That results in mistakes like the Bush administration's arsenic decision, which was a complete political disaster."

Other critics say that by emphasizing public oversight, NEPA discourages the scientific assessment of environmental issues. "The law is overreaching and unconstitutional," said Taylor of the Cato Institute. "It makes environmental determinations based not on science or the public interest but on political gain. Anybody who thinks that the exercise of federal power in the environment is based on anything other than a political calculation about what will most appeal to the swing voter is living in a make-believe country."

In May 2002, the Bush administration ordered the White House Council on Environmental Quality to conduct a review of NEPA, essentially inviting agencies to point out flaws in the law and suggest alternative language that may open the way for formal proposals to amend it. The council's task force completed its study of the environmental-impact statement process that September and released a report listing ways federal agencies could streamline the drafting of new regulations.

"Laws get static over time," said Agriculture Undersecretary Mark Rey, who plays a key role in setting the Bush administration's public lands policy. While he recognizes the need for continued public involvement in policymaking, Rey said agencies need to meet that broad goal "by exploring new ways to involve the public in a good-faith and interactive effort." As the administration's top forestry official, Rey helped shape Bush's new forest-thinning plan, which waives NEPA requirements for public input.

While the review process continues, the administration is using its executive power to make a broad array of changes to environmental policy with little public notice. "Rewriting laws requires a public process and an open debate," said the NRDC's Wetstone. "What we're seeing now is an effort to leave the laws largely on the books but render them for the most part empty words on paper, with little relevance for what polluters, mining companies and logging companies have to do in the real world."

Environmental laws set goals, such as keeping river, lake or ocean water safe for fishing and swimming. It is then up to executive branch agencies—such as the Interior Department or the EPA—to write regulations to enforce those goals. For instance, the EPA may set standards for maximum levels of water pollutants in a particular river. NEPA and the 1946 Administrative Procedures Act ensure a certain degree of public access to this rulemaking

President Bush wants to spur domestic energy production by allowing more oil and gas drilling on public lands, including 2,000 acres in Alaska's vast Arctic National Wildlife Refuge (ANWR), above. Environmentalists say the United States should try to save energy by improving auto fuel efficiency, developing alternative fuels and reducing the burning of fossil fuels.

process, by requiring public hearings before any new regulations are adopted.

But the laws do not prevent agencies from making significant policy changes by simply issuing "guidance" on regulatory matters, without oversight. Critics say the Bush administration is purposely using this mechanism to avoid exposure to public scrutiny.

"We've seen big changes in forest policy and policy on snowmobiles in national parks that weren't even [advertised as] rulemakings," said Wetsone, who cited more than 100 separate actions by six federal agencies and the White House that were taken outside the rulemaking process in Bush's first 18 months. "Rulemaking requires a public process, while guidance can happen with almost no public process."

Critics of the current regulatory system say Bush has not gone far enough to change it. "The environmental regulatory state is pretty much on autopilot, a fact that most observers miss," said Taylor of the Cato Institute. "Environmentalists have every incentive to tell the public that every little squiggle in the regulatory process is a huge threat to the environment."

Will the administration's proposed clean-air measures improve air quality?

On Feb. 14, 2002, President Bush announced his new Clear Skies Initiative, which he said would greatly improve

Why Bush Backtracked on Kyoto

During the 2000 presidential campaign, then-Texas Gov. George W. Bush promised to set limits on the pollutant that most scientists say is mainly responsible for global warming.

But in one of his first acts after entering the White House, Bush abandoned that pledge, saying the scientific evidence linking carbon-dioxide emissions from fossil-fuel combustion was outweighed by the economic cost of curtailing fossil-fuel use throughout the U.S. economy.

Later, Bush announced he would not submit the Kyoto Protocol to the U.S. Senate for ratification. The United Nations agreement to cap carbon emissions that cause global warming had been signed by President Bill Clinton in 1997, along with the leaders of 175 other countries.

Bush's rejection of Kyoto was not surprising. Even Clinton never submitted it for Senate ratification because he knew he would be unable to garner the required two-thirds majority. U.S. industry has always been adamantly opposed to the protocol's terms, which set tougher carbon-dioxide emission targets for the United States—the world's largest source of greenhouse-gas emissions—than for any other industrialized country.

Critics say that achieving the treaty's emission targets would require a massive shift to non-fossil fuels, imposing unacceptable costs on the U.S. economy. They also oppose the protocol's favorable treatment of developing countries, which would be exempted from the first round of required carbon-dioxide emission cuts.

Finally, despite the consensus of hundreds of scientists from around the world who advised the United Nations on the threat of climate change, critics continue to say the evidence linking global warming to fossil-fuel use is not strong enough to warrant the economically disruptive remedies called for under Kyoto.

"Everyone accepts the fact that the planet's surface has warmed by about a degree Fahrenheit over the last 100 years," said Jerry Taylor, director of natural-resource studies at the libertarian Cato Institute. "But it turns out that the warming is quite a bit below what the computer models say should have occurred by now. What it means is that on a January evening in Yellowknife, Canada, instead of being 28 degrees below zero it might be 25 degrees below zero. It's very hard to spin disaster stories around that."

President Bush has acknowledged that global warming poses a threat, but he agrees with Kyoto critics that the protocol's remedies are too drastic. In February 2002, as part of his new Clear Skies Initiative to combat air pollution, he submitted an alternative plan for dealing with global warming. In place of the established limits on carbon-dioxide emissions set by the protocol, the Bush plan would seek an 18 percent reduction over the next 10 years in the United States' "greenhouse-gas intensity"—the amount of carbon dioxide emitted per dollar of gross domestic product. This change, he said, would come as technological advances enabled industry to emit less carbon dioxide without jeopardizing economic growth.

"This will set America on a path to slow the growth of our greenhouse-gas emissions and, as science justifies, to stop and then reverse the growth of emissions," he said. "This is the common-sense way to measure progress. Our nation must have growth. Growth is what pays for investments in clean technologies, increased conservation and energy efficiency." The president predicted that the plan would achieve the equivalent of "taking 70 million cars off the road."[1]

Supporters of the Kyoto process are dismayed by the administration's repudiation of the protocol. "Every other industrialized country, with the possible exception of Australia, has announced its intention to ratify and implement the Kyoto Protocol," said Michael Oppenheimer, a professor of geosciences and international affairs at Princeton University and an expert on climate change. "We have a situation where on the most significant environmental problem of this century the United States not only

---

[1] Bush announced his Clear Skies Initiative Feb. 14, 2002, in a speech at the National Oceanic and Atmospheric Administration in Silver Spring, Md.

has abdicated leadership but also has essentially no plan for dealing with the problem. That will have the effect of significantly diluting global efforts to deal with the problem, and that inevitably means more global warming."

Bush made another major policy change affecting the global environment during his first weeks in office. In January 2001, he reinstated a ban on U.S. funding of international population programs that provide abortion services or counseling. The so-called "Mexico City" policy, strongly supported by anti-abortion activists, was first imposed by President Ronald Reagan and continued by the president's father, President George Bush senior. Critics charged that family-planning services are needed to slow the rapid growth of population in developing countries, where high population density poses threats to the environment and public health.

President Clinton resumed funding of population programs, but not of organizations that provide abortion services. For example, at the 1994 International Conference on Population and Development in Cairo, Egypt, the United States and other nations pledged to provide $17 billion a year on maternal-health programs.

Bush's action reversed that decision. In July, the Bush's administration withheld $34 million in funds from

U.S. Greenhouse Gases Increased

Total greenhouse-gas emissions—implicated in global warming—have risen 14.2 percent since 1990, according to the EPA. The dominant gas emitted was carbon dioxide, mostly from fossil-fuel combustion.

Increase in U.S. Greenhouse-Gas Emissions

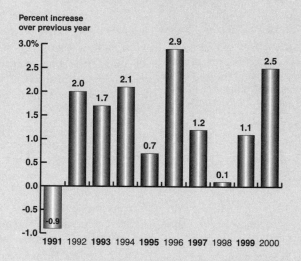

Percent increase over previous year

Source: "The U.S. Greenhouse Gas Inventory," Environmental Protection Agency, April 2002

the U.N. family-planning organization because it works with Chinese authorities who are alleged to coerce women into undergoing abortions and sterilizations. Today, U.S. funding of maternal-health programs stands at about $500 million.[2]

On the other hand, Bush has continued another international environmental initiative supported by his predecessor. In 2001, then-EPA Administrator Christine Todd Whitman signed a treaty, negotiated by the Clinton administration, that calls for the global phaseout of 12 persistent organic pollutants (POPs). The pollutants—including dioxin, PCBs and DDT—break down slowly, can travel long distances and have been linked to cancer and birth defects.

The 50-nation Stockholm Treaty on Persistent Organic Pollutants would allow for the addition to the list of new chemicals. But the enabling legislation Bush presented to the Senate for ratification in May lacks that provision.[3]

[2]See John Donnelly, "Maternal Health Survey Faults Cutbacks," *The Boston Globe,* Sept. 26, 2002.

[3]See Scott Lindlaw, "President Asks Senate to Ratify Treaty on Toxic Releases; Democrats Say His Plan Falls Short," Associated Press Newswires, May 7, 2002.

President Bush approved Yucca Mountain in the Nevada desert as the nation's repository for waste from nuclear-power plants. Environmentalists and Nevada officials had tried to block the site on health and environmental grounds. Pending approval by the Nuclear Regulatory Commission, more than 70,000 metric tons of nuclear waste will be shipped here beginning in 2010.

U.S. air quality and reduce the threat of global warming. "This new approach will harness the power of markets [and] the creativity of entrepreneurs and draw upon the best scientific research," Bush said. "And it will make possible a new partnership with the developing world to meet our common environmental and economic goals."[6]

The plan aims to cut by 70 percent power-plant emissions of three major air pollutants—nitrogen oxides, sulfur dioxide and mercury—that contribute to smog and acid rain and cause respiratory, cardiovascular and neurological disorders. But rather than relying on current EPA-set mandates, Bush would use market incentives to encourage utility operators to reduce emissions of the three pollutants. Bush's plan emulates an innovative program set up under 1990 amendments to the Clean Air Act that has successfully reduced acid rain in the Midwest and Northeast. The president's proposed "cap-and-trade" system would create markets in which less-polluting utilities could sell their pollution "credits" (based on the amount of pollution below the permitted maximum that they emit) to plants that exceed the caps but are unable or unwilling to invest in costly smokestack filters and other equipment to reduce their emissions.

"President Bush has a strong commitment to environmental protection, and this bill will not only accelerate the already improving air quality of our nation but begin key reforms to regulatory programs which have hindered

progress and impeded technological innovation," said Rep. Joe Barton, R-Texas, on introducing the legislation in the House on July 29, 2002. Congress rejected the measure. Environmentalists see the Bush plan as an attempt to get around existing law. "The Clear Skies Initiative is a legislative effort to weaken the Clear Air Act," Wetstone said. If the proposal goes forward, it "could be very damaging and have a dramatic impact on levels of pollution."

Especially troubling to environmental advocates is the plan's impact on so-called New Source Review (NSR) provisions in the Clean Air Act. Those measures required 17,000 older power plants, oil refineries and other facilities that were exempted from emission caps to comply with the caps if they modernize or expand their facilities, creating a new source of pollutants. Although Congress has not passed Bush's plan, rule changes have eliminated the NSR requirements in all but the most flagrant cases of air pollution.

"New Source Review can and should be reformed to make it less bureaucratic," said Sen. John Edwards, D-N.C., chairman of the Senate Health, Education, Labor and Pensions Subcommittee on Public Health, at a hearing on Sept. 3, 2002. "But the need for reform should not be an excuse so that polluters can send more deadly pollution into the air without cleaning up. That's exactly what's happening here."

Industry has been so opposed to the NSR program that utilities were not expected to support the rest of the Clear Skies Initiative—the 70 percent reduction target and the cap-and-trade program—unless the review program was weakened.

"This is a very aggressive proposal to restructure environmental regulations," said A. Denny Ellerman, executive director of the Massachusetts Institute of Technology's Center for Energy and Environmental Policy Research. "The very ambitious targets for the three pollutants are clearly linked with relief from New Source Review."

Ellerman said Bush's market approach is a better way to reduce air pollution than the current hands-on, "command-and-control" system. "Instead of getting into this endless nitpicking over how exactly you're supposed to reach emission targets, the plan defines the general objective within the acceptable parameters and then lets the market or individual firms figure that out," he said.

The existing system assumes that the regulator knows how to reduce emissions most cheaply, which is never the case, he said. Under a cap-and-trade system, he added, "Essentially we don't care what you do, just so you have a permit for whatever emissions you emit, and that's an inviolable rule. A market-based system would cost much less and in the end produce better environmental performance."

However, carbon dioxide—considered the main greenhouse gas and a major component of emissions from coal-fired power plants—is conspicuously missing from the list of air pollutants regulated by the Bush plan.

During the presidential campaign, Bush had promised to set carbon-dioxide emission limits. However, once elected, he backed off from that promise, saying it would hurt the economy. Indeed, since 2002, for the first time in six years, EPA's annual report on air-quality trends has contained no mention of carbon dioxide among the major pollutants.[7]

As an alternative to the carbon-dioxide emissions cuts mandated by the Kyoto Protocol, the Bush plan aims to reduce America's "greenhouse-gas intensity"—the amount of emissions created per million dollars of gross domestic product—from the current level of 183 metric tons to 151 metric tons by 2012. Industry participation in the effort would be voluntary.

"The approach taken under the Kyoto Protocol would have required the United States to make deep and immediate cuts in our economy to meet an arbitrary target," Bush said.[8] "It would have cost our economy up to $400 billion, and we would have lost 4.9 million jobs. As president of the United States, charged with safeguarding the welfare of the American people and American workers, I will not commit our nation to an unsound international treaty that will throw millions of our citizens out of work. Yet we recognize our international responsibilities. So in addition to acting here at home, the United States will actively help developing nations grow along a more efficient, more environmentally responsible path."

Supporters of international efforts to combat global warming say Bush's new policy will have little impact on carbon emissions in the United States—the world's largest source of industrial greenhouse gas output. "The plan to reduce slightly the carbon-dioxide emissions intensity of the U.S. economy effectively doesn't change anything," said Princeton geoscientist Oppenheimer. "On the whole, it appears that the Bush administration has effectively no policy on climate change—except to do nothing."

Would giving timber companies greater access to national forests help reduce wildfire damage?

In one of the worst wildfire seasons on record, 20 firefighters died in the summer of 2002 battling fires that scorched 6.5 million acres of national forests in the Western United States and destroyed hundreds of homes. To prevent similar outbreaks in the future, President Bush proposed encouraging logging companies to clear highly flammable brush and small trees from 10 million acres of national forests that are especially prone to wildfires.

Scientists agree on the need for changes in longstanding fire-prevention strategies. For most of the 20th century, forestry officials tried to suppress all types of fire in the nation's forests. Visitors were constantly warned to put out campfires and extinguish cigarettes. Billboards nationwide featured the Forest Service's mascot, Smokey Bear, admonishing the public, "Only YOU can prevent forest fires."

But total fire suppression, it turns out, literally added fuel to the problem, by preventing the relatively small natural fires needed periodically to burn off undergrowth and allow tall-tree seedlings to mature. Abundant brushy vegetation, combined with the drought conditions of recent summers, set the stage for wildfires that quickly turned into unmanageable infernos engulfing vast tracts of forests, as well as the houses that have proliferated in them in the fast-growing Western states.

"The growth of [vegetation] on these stands of trees over the last 30 years has increased exponentially," said Undersecretary Rey. "As a consequence of substantial fire suppression, when a fire ignites in these stands it becomes cataclysmic, burning much more hotly and intensely."

Complicating the problem, he points out, is the fact that the five fastest-growing states are in the Intermountain West. "Everyone wants to build their homes out in the forests," he said, forcing firefighters to concentrate on saving human life and property instead of the kinds of "prescribed burns" that normally are set to clear small tracts of underbrush before they can cause uncontrollable fires.

That August, as several large forest fires still raged, Bush unveiled a new plan to combat highly destructive wildfires. The Healthy Forests Initiative would waive NEPA-mandated environmental-impact statements for tree-thinning projects on 10 million acres of fire-prone federal land that is either near homes or watersheds or is infested by disease or insects. The plan would bar challenges to these projects through the Forest Service's normal administrative process or through the courts.

CHRONOLOGY

1970s *A grass-roots movement spurs environmental-protection legislation.*

1970 Congress passes Clean Air Act to curb industrial pollution. President Richard M. Nixon establishes Environmental Protection Agency (EPA) and signs National Environmental Policy Act (NEPA) ensuring public participation in the regulatory process.

1972 Clean Water Act requires industries and water-treatment facilities to stop dumping pollutants into rivers.

1973 Endangered Species Act authorizes EPA to list plants and animals threatened with extinction by habitat destruction or pollution.

1974 Safe Drinking Water Act authorizes EPA to set water-purity standards.

1977 Congress amends Clean Air Act to include the New Source Review (NSR) program, requiring companies to install state-of-the-art pollution-control equipment when they build a major new facility or upgrade an existing plant.

1980s *Anti-regulatory sentiment focuses on the costs of environmental protection.*

1980 Congress passes Comprehensive Environmental Response, Compensation and Liability Act—the Superfund law—requiring polluters to clean up toxic-waste sites.

1990s *The pace of new environmental laws slows.*

1990 Amendments to Clean Air Act require polluted cities to use oxygenated gasoline in winter and re-formulated gasoline in summer to curb auto emissions; amendments also set up an innovative, market-based program to reduce acid rain by allowing cleaner industries to sell "pollution credits" to heavy polluters.

December 1997 United States and 175 other nations agree in Kyoto, Japan, to take steps to reduce emissions of carbon dioxide and other gases believed to cause global warming.

Nov. 12, 1998 Clinton administration signs Kyoto Protocol, committing the U.S. to cut its carbon emissions by 7 percent below 1990 levels by 2012.

February 1999 President Bill Clinton places an 18-month moratorium on new logging roads in national forests.

2000s *President Bush begins a rollback of environmental protections.*

January 2001 Upon taking office, Bush puts on hold some 175 Clinton administration environmental regulations.

May 17, 2001 Bush unveils plan to open Alaska National Wildlife Refuge to drilling and mining to boost domestic production of fossil fuels.

Jan. 11, 2002 Bush signs Small Business Liability Relief and Brownfields Revitalization Act encouraging private investment in redeveloping less-polluted waste sites by limiting developers' liability for future claims of injury.

Feb. 14, 2002 Bush announces Clear Skies Initiative to amend Clean Air Act and cut power-plant emissions of sulfur dioxide, nitrogen oxide and mercury by 70 percent by letting individual companies trade pollution credits. The administration later announces plans to let plants avoid installing pollution-control equipment when they modernize; plan does not address carbon dioxide, the main greenhouse gas implicated in global warming.

May 2002 Bush launches review of Clinton's moratorium on road building on 60 million acres of national forests.

June 2002 Administration reverses Clinton-era ban on recreational snowmobiling in Yellowstone and Grand Teton national parks. Interior Secretary Gale Norton halts Clinton administration plan to reintroduce grizzly bears to Rocky Mountains.

July 2002 Bush signs congressional resolution naming Nevada's Yucca Mountain as the nation's central repository for radioactive waste from nuclear power plants.

December 2002 Bush signs into law the Healthy Forests Restoration Act, based on his plan to allow loggers to harvest more trees from national forests in exchange for clearing brush. The administration opposes proposal by World Summit on Sustainable Development to increase the use of renewable energy.

The initiative also would relax regulations for forest-thinning projects on public land outside the 10 million high-risk acres. A judge asked to halt a particular logging project, for example, would have to consider potential wildfire damage if the tract were not logged, as well as the immediate environmental impact. Finally, the plan would allow the Agriculture and Interior departments to enter into long-term "stewardship" agreements with logging companies and other private entities to harvest and sell large trees from public land, in exchange for clearing brush to reduce fire hazards. This provision, Rey said, also will help create markets for small trees that otherwise would have no commercial value.

For example, by allowing the government to sign longer-term tree-thinning contracts covering larger tracts of forest, the plan would allow companies to harvest enough three- to six-inch diameter trees to profitably turn them into laminated veneer. "If Congress will give us that authority to make that kind of transaction work," he said, "then over time much of that now valueless material will gain commercial value."

Environmental advocates express dismay over Bush's plan. "The Healthy Forests Initiative is going to be hugely damaging," said Wetstone of the NRDC. "We don't have that much old-growth forest left to protect, and to turn it over in a taxpayer-subsidized giveaway to logging companies is just tragic."

But conservatives argue that environmentalists forget that logging has always played a prominent role in the national forest system. "The Forest Service was created in 1898 for the purpose of supplying lumber to American business," said Michael Hardiman, legislative director of the American Land Rights Association, in Battle Ground, Wash., which opposes federal efforts to expand public land. "The Bush administration has seized on this forest-fire crisis to explain to the average person that chopping down trees in the national forests not only doesn't hurt the forests, but is actually a good idea."

Although many Democratic lawmakers were torn between the need to prevent a replay of this year's devastating wildfires and reluctance to approve a measure that they said would weaken environmental protection, enough signed on to the measure to ensure its passage. But even if Congress hadn't acted, said Rey, the administration could have accomplished about half of the plan's provisions by simply rewriting regulations that currently "bog the system down interminably."

Gale A. Norton, who as secretary of the Interior oversees most public land programs outside the Agriculture Department's Forest Service, echoed that theme in *The Washington Post*. "The program is a common-sense approach to reducing fuel loads in forests," she wrote. "The continuing threat to both people and wildlife is real. We must cut the red tape and restore the health of our forests."[9]

BACKGROUND

Status Report

The boom in heavy industry that began after World War II enabled the United States to become the world's leading economic power. Mining, steel, automaking, oil production and electricity generation fueled unparalleled economic growth. But they also took a heavy toll on the environment—polluting the air and water and releasing toxic waste that killed plant and animal life.

By the late 1960s, public concern over widespread pollution had sparked an environmental movement that would generate sweeping laws requiring industries to curb harmful emissions. The laws, and the regulations promulgated to enforce them, have had mixed results. Many environmental threats have been significantly reduced, but serious problems remain.

The following status report looks at the main environmental concerns addressed in the early laws and the Bush administration's actions since taking office in January 2001.

Air Quality

The 1970 Clean Air Act, one of the first major environmental-protection measures, set emissions standards for almost 200 pollutants that contribute to smog. The law required factory and power-plant owners to install smokestack "scrubbers" to curb the release of small particles, known as particulate matter, and to reduce sulfur dioxide emissions, a product of fossil-fuel combustion that causes acid rain. Oil companies had to remove lead—which causes degradation of intelligence and the nervous system in children—from gasoline, and automakers were required to install catalytic converters in cars to reduce tailpipe emissions.

In 1977, Congress amended the Clean Air Act to include the New Source Review (NSR) program, designed to reduce emissions from older power plants,

Glacial ice crashes into Alaska's Prince William Sound. Most scientists say industrial emissions of "greenhouse gases" are heating the atmosphere and eventually will melt glaciers and cause global flooding. President Bush contends his new Clear Skies Initiative would improve U.S. air quality and reduce global warming using voluntary market forces instead of regulatory mandates.

emissions-trading program, which have succeeded in reducing emissions of sulfur dioxide and nitrogen oxide.[11] The amendments also authorized the EPA to address regional air-pollution sources, such as Midwestern power-plant emissions that contribute to smog and acid rain in Northeastern cities and forests.

Since 1970, the United States has seen a 25 percent drop in emissions of the six main air pollutants—nitrogen dioxide, ozone, sulfur dioxide, particulate matter, carbon monoxide and lead.[12] However, rapidly growing metropolitan areas, like Los Angeles, Houston and the Northeastern corridor, continue to experience unhealthy levels of air pollution. Moreover, the Clean Air Act's goal of eliminating air pollution from 158 national parks and wilderness areas has fallen far short of expectations. Ozone levels in Great Smoky Mountains National Park, for example, now rival those of Los Angeles during the summer months, according to a recent study by the National Parks Conservation Association.[13]

The Clinton administration blamed much of the continuing air pollution on industrial facilities that refused to comply with emissions standards. It sued 51 power plants for violating NSR rules by making major improvements without installing modern smokestack scrubbers. Taking the opposite tack, the Bush administration charged in June 2001 that NSR requirements discouraged utilities and factories from modernizing and announced plans to review the program.

On Feb. 14, 2002, Bush announced his initiative to amend the Clean Air Act and cut power-plant emissions of sulfur dioxide, nitrogen oxide and mercury by 70 percent. Bush's plan would let individual companies trade pollution credits in a nationwide emissions-trading system. By allowing companies to decide which plants to clean up, critics said the plan would weaken current provisions that protect air quality in national parks and curb cross-boundary air pollution.

Although Congress did not approve the measure, the administration later relaxed NSR rules so that modernizing or expanding plants could avoid installing pollution-control equipment.

Although the Bush administration has overturned several rules introduced by President Clinton, it has retained a regulation calling for a 97 percent cut in sulfur levels in diesel fuel and a 95 percent cut in harmful emissions by diesel-powered trucks and buses. The EPA also proposed a rule to extend the diesel standards to off-

refineries and other industrial facilities that had been exempted from the stringent emission standards established for new plants. The NSR program required companies to install state-of-the-art pollution-control equipment when they built a major, new facility or modified an existing plant in ways that resulted in a significant rise in emissions.

Amendments enacted in 1990 strengthened the act by requiring oil companies to sell oxygenated gasoline in the winter to curb carbon-monoxide emissions and switch to reformulated gasoline in the summer to reduce ozone pollution in the most heavily polluted cities.[10] The amendments also strengthened emission standards for power plants and introduced a novel market-based

How Mercury Pollution Harms Humans

When U.S. power plants burn coal, they produce dangerous mercury vapors. Oxidants in the atmosphere turn vaporized mercury into water-soluble compounds. Rain and snow return the mercury compounds to lakes and streams, where they mix with bacteria to produce organic mercury (methylmercury)—which can cause brain and liver damage and heart problems; pregnant women, fetuses, children and subsistence fisherman are especially vulnerable. In the United States, coal-fired plants cause a third of all mercury emissions. President Bush's Clear Skies Initiative aims to cut by 70 percent the power-plant emissions of mercury, as well as other pollutants that contribute to smog and acid rain and cause respiratory and cardiovascular diseases.

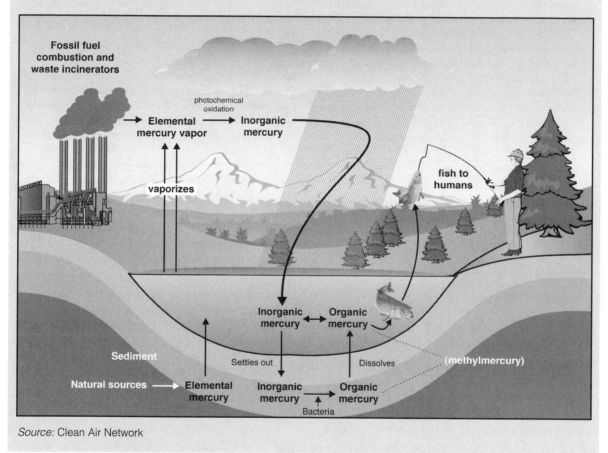

Source: Clean Air Network

road vehicles, such as bulldozers and tractors. Diesel emissions cause lung cancer and asthma.[14]

Water Quality

For most of the country's history, factory owners built their plants next to rivers, which provided hydropower, ease of shipping and a handy repository for waste. Towns and cities also grew up along waterways, which also used them to dispose of sewage and other waste. By the 1960s, many lakes and rivers were too polluted to support fish and aquatic plants. In 1969, an especially foul, debris-laden section of Cleveland's oil- and chemical-choked Cuyahoga River actually caught fire, sparking indignant calls for the government to clean up the nation's waterways.

The Hidden Power of Federal Regulations

Most federal policymaking involves both the legislative and executive branches of government. Congress passes the laws that lay out policy objectives, such as clean air. Then the executive branch, through its departments and agencies, sets the specific rules and regulations aimed at carrying out those objectives, such as the maximum allowable levels of air pollutants that power plants may emit without incurring sanctions. The third branch of government, the judiciary, comes into play when individuals or groups file suits alleging non-compliance with federal laws and regulations.

The rulemaking process itself can be highly complex. The 1946 Administrative Procedures Act required rulemaking agencies to publish a notice in the *Federal Register* describing the proposed rule; allow the public to comment in writing on it; and give notice of the final rule and its effective date.*

The act also authorized the courts to review any rule that was challenged as illegal.[1] Subsequent laws have expanded the public's right to participate in the rulemaking process.

Presidents exercise considerable control over the regulatory system. They have the power to appoint like-minded individuals to head the departments and agencies that write the rules. Presidents also can effectively boost or curtail the effectiveness of regulatory enforcement by allocating more or less money to relevant agencies in their annual budget requests to Congress.

They also can issue directives to the regulatory agencies in the form of executive orders. President Ronald Reagan, for example, issued executive orders requiring all proposed regulations to undergo a cost-benefit analysis. No federal regulation could be adopted if it cost more to implement than the value of the benefits it would provide to society. President Bill Clinton reversed that policy with his own executive order.

By their nature, environmental-protection laws involve a large array of regulations. The 1970 Clean Air Act and the 1972 Clean Water Act, for example, rely on specific limits on the release of pollutants into the air and water. As a result, the Environmental Protection Agency (EPA)—created by President Richard M. Nixon in 1970 by executive order—uses regulations as a primary vehicle for administering these laws. According to one study, the EPA, with an enforcement budget of $4.2 billion in fiscal 2002,

---

*The Federal Register is published by the federal government every workday and is the legal document for recording and communicating the rules and regulations established by the executive branch. Executive agencies are required to publish in the Register in advance some types of proposed regulations.

[1] For a detailed description and history of the regulatory process, see *Congressional Quarterly*'s Federal Regulatory Directory, 1999.

Congress responded with the 1972 Clean Water Act, which required factories, utilities and sewage-treatment plants to reduce toxic-waste discharges into waterways. Since then, water pollution from these easily identifiable sources has diminished, fish and wildlife have returned to many once-lifeless waterways and 60 percent of the nation's waters are clean enough to support fishing and swimming.

But runoff of fertilizers, pesticides and other toxic chemicals continues to pollute the remaining 40 percent of U.S. streams, rivers, lakes and coastal areas. The sources of these pollutants are widespread and hard to identify, including farms, suburban lawns and city streets and storm sewers. To reduce such so-called non-source pollution, the EPA has proposed a water-quality trading policy

similar to the administration's cap-and-trade policy for air emissions. It would allow states, private companies and farmers to trade or sell unused pollution-reduction credits to heavier polluters.

On May 3, 2002, the administration issued rules allowing coal companies to dump the rubble from mountaintop mining operations into surrounding streams, a practice the Clinton administration had barred. Critics of mountaintop removal, prevalent in Kentucky and West Virginia, say it exposes miles of Appalachian waterways to pollution from heavy metals and other toxic materials. A U.S. district judge had agreed with the Clinton administration's position and blocked the U.S. Army Corps of Engineers from issuing new permits for mountaintop removal.[15] In September 2004,

now spends more than any other agency to enforce federal regulations, accounting for a fifth of the total.[2]

Until recent decades, regulations played a relatively small part in government operations. Once confined to the field of commerce, such as the establishment of businesses and the rates they charged, regulations grew in scope and number as lawmakers created programs seeking broader social objectives, including environmental protection. By the late 1970s, the growth of regulations had sparked a heated debate between those who said they were necessary to force industries to stop polluting the environment, and others who blamed them for retarding economic growth.

President Reagan echoed the anti-regulatory message with his call to "get the government off our backs." His successor, President George Bush senior, oversaw a revival in regulatory activity following the passage of such laws as the Clean Air Act amendments of 1990. But he also set up a new office, the Council on Competitiveness, chaired by Vice President Dan Quayle, with a mandate to seek relief for American businesses from the growing number of regulations. Critics accused the council of engaging in "backdoor rulemaking" by failing to publicize its changes in regulations, as required by the 1946 Administrative Procedures Act.

Following President Clinton's election in 1992, anti-regulatory sentiment grew, helping the Republicans to gain control of the House in 1995. Central to the goal of the self-described Republican revolutionaries led by the House majority leader, Rep. Newt Gingrich, R-Ga., was the dismantling of environmental and other regulations. Clinton, too, joined the effort. His Executive Order 12866, "Regulatory Planning and Review," aimed to reduce existing rules by half and improve interagency coordination to reduce "red tape."

But after the 2000 election ensured Clinton's succession by an openly anti-regulatory administration, Clinton used his executive power to write scores of new environmental regulations during the closing days of his presidency.

Upon taking office, President Bush blocked most of Clinton's regulations while they were still in the public-comment phase. Although he later allowed some to take effect, critics say his administration is exploiting the relative obscurity of the rulemaking process to drastically weaken environmental-protection laws without public scrutiny.

"I think there's been an effort to avoid the public process," said Gregory Wetstone, director of programs at the Natural Resources Defense Council, an environmental advocacy group in New York City.

But supporters of Bush's extensive use of rulemaking to shape environmental policy say he is only responding to the need for a new approach. "The old way of doing things, with rulemaking from the EPA, has played itself out," said Steven F. Hayward, a resident scholar at the American Enterprise Institute. "We need to think of new ways of getting things done."

---

[2]See Clyde Wayne Crews Jr., "Ten Thousand Commandments: An Annual Snapshot of the Federal Regulatory State," Cato Institute, 2002, p. 19.

---

however, West Virginia regulators relaxed the Clinton-era regulation.

The Clean Water Act also provides protection for wetlands, which nurture the growth of new aquatic wildlife, filter pollutants and help prevent flooding. But development has destroyed more than half of U.S. wetlands, especially in coastal areas. Further destruction of wetlands seemed likely in the wake of the U.S. Supreme Court's January 2001 ruling that the law, which refers to "navigable waters," does not cover isolated bogs, pools and other bodies of water contained within a single state. The first Bush administration had adopted a policy of "no net loss of wetlands," requiring developers who drain and fill wetlands to build or protect additional wetlands. Conservationists charged that the new wetland rules announced by the Corps of Engineers in 2001 undermined that policy, and in December 2003 the Bush administration dropped plans to weaken wetland and stream protections.

The Clinton administration launched a plan to restore the Florida Everglades, the country's largest wetland, which has been greatly reduced in size and polluted by runoff from surrounding cities and farms. The plan, the most comprehensive wetlands-restoration effort ever attempted in the United States, received the support of President Bush, whose brother, Jeb, is Florida's Republican governor. In January 2002, the two brothers signed an agreement that ensures adequate water supplies to support the $7.8 billion, 30-year Comprehensive Everglades Restoration Plan, which the president says he will continue to support.[16]

The nation's other main water-quality statute, the 1974 Safe Drinking Water Act, called on the EPA to set national standards for the purity of tap water provided by public water systems. Amendments enacted in 1996 require states to monitor the quality of groundwater, the source of most of the country's drinking water.

In 1999, however, the National Research Council reported that high levels of arsenic in drinking water put Americans at risk for cancer and urged the EPA to strengthen its standards for this dangerous pollutant. After setting aside a Clinton administration regulation tightening the arsenic standard, the Bush administration faced a storm of criticism and in October 2001 announced it would adopt the Clinton standard after all.

Since the Sept. 11 terrorist attacks, the Bush administration has focused on protecting the nation's 168,000 public drinking-water and 16,000 public wastewater systems from attack. On June 12, 2002, the president signed the 2002 Public Health Security and Bioterrorism Response Act, which includes measures to protect water supplies.

Meanwhile, then-EPA Administrator Whitman warned on Sept. 30, 2002, that the gains in water quality over the past 30 years were being jeopardized by delays in maintaining and replacing deteriorating water-treatment systems. As a result, the agency reported an increase in the number of estuaries, lakes, streams and rivers classified as "impaired" over the previous two years. But many state and local governments, facing growing budget deficits, are asking the federal government to assume some of the financial responsibility for maintaining their water and wastewater-treatment systems.[17]

Toxic Waste

After addressing air and water quality, lawmakers turned to another major source of pollution: toxic-waste disposal sites. The 1980 Comprehensive Environmental Response, Compensation and Liability Act (CERCLA)—better known as the Superfund law—required the EPA to force the cleanup of toxic-waste sites. Under the "polluter pays" principle inherent in the law, industries that created toxic dumps must clean them up. To clean up sites where the polluter is unknown or unable to pay, the law created a Superfund, financed with a special corporate tax.

As it turned out, almost a third of all sites were "orphans," for which the polluter could not be identified, and Superfund came under intense scrutiny as the cost of running the program ballooned to an average of $30 million per cleanup. As a result, Congress has not reauthorized the corporate tax imposed to fund Superfund activities since 1995, and insufficient financing has delayed cleanup operations.

Despite the setbacks, Superfund has begun to pay off. A 2001 study found that more than half the nation's 1,300 most-toxic waste dumps had either been cleaned up or no longer posed a threat to human health or the environment. The same study predicted, however, that the list of Superfund sites would grow by up to 50 sites each year over the next decade.[18]

Nonetheless, the administration has not sought an extension of the Superfund trust-fund tax. It also reduced by half the number of sites to be cleaned up, a decision critics cited as another example of the Bush administration's desire to help industry shirk its legal responsibility.[19] Bush requested $1.3 billion—similar to spending levels since 1995—to help cover program costs in fiscal 2003. By fiscal 2004, the program faced a shortfall of $250 million, delaying cleanups at dozens of polluted sites. See "Not-So-Superfund," editorial, *Sarasota Herald-Tribune* (Fla.), Aug. 29, 2004.

Under the aegis of the Superfund law, the EPA runs a special cleanup program for about 500,000 less-hazardous toxic-waste sites known as "brownfields." Because many of the sites occupy prime, urban real estate, businesses pressed the agency to relax its regulations barring their redevelopment. Fulfilling a campaign pledge, President Bush signed the Small Business Liability Relief and Brownfields Revitalization Act, on Jan. 11, 2002. The law encourages private investment in cleaning up and redeveloping brownfields, in part by limiting developers' liability for future claims of damages stemming from exposure to toxic materials on the sites.

Radioactive waste, chiefly spent fuel from nuclear power plants, is treated separately. For decades, utilities have stored radioactive waste on site, pending the creation of a permanent, central repository that the Energy Department promised to open by January 1998. Technical obstacles, safety concerns and political opposition slowed construction of the chosen site, a deep underground vault at Yucca Mountain in the Nevada desert 90 miles from Las Vegas.

Overriding the opposition of Nevada officials, who tried to block the site designation on health and environmental grounds, President Bush signed a resolution passed by Congress in July 2002 naming the site as the sole repository for high-level nuclear waste. Pending approval by the Nuclear Regulatory Commission, Yucca Mountain is expected to begin accepting the waste, which now exceeds 70,000 metric tons, in 2010.[20]

Public Land

Since President Theodore Roosevelt oversaw the creation of the first national parks, the nation's inventory of public land has grown to include more than one-quarter of the total U.S. land area. Most of this land is in the West, where policy governing its use fuels an ongoing debate. Public land has long been open to a variety of industrial and agricultural uses, including logging, mining and livestock grazing. The 1872 Mining Law, for example, still allows mining companies to drill for hard-rock minerals on federal land for $5 an acre.

As the pace of residential and industrial development in the West quickened, however, policymakers began taking steps to protect public land. The 1964 Wilderness Act created the National Wilderness Preservation System to set aside some of the country's quickly disappearing pristine areas from all industrial use. Recreational uses of public lands also were restricted amid concerns that snowmobiles and other motorized vehicles were harming wildlife, causing erosion and polluting the air. Beginning in 1972, presidents have used executive orders prohibiting recreational snowmobile use in some national parks.

As one of his last environmental acts, President Clinton banned snowmobiles in Yellowstone and Grand Teton national parks. It was among the 175 regulations Bush put on hold after taking office. The administration later announced it would not block the ban, due to take effect in late 2003. But the National Park Service subsequently announced it would continue to allow snowmobilers into the two parks "with very strict limitations." In September 2002 the EPA required the makers of snowmobiles and other off-road vehicles to reduce their products' emissions. Conservationists say the new standards are too lax.[21]

Another Clinton initiative, a ban on road building on 60 million acres of national forests, has drawn strong criticism from the timber industry, which builds roads to reach remote stands of harvestable trees. Bush, who criticized the plan as detrimental to loggers, initiated a review of the ban in May 2002. Shortly thereafter, a federal judge in Idaho blocked the road-building ban, saying it would cause "irreparable harm" to the timber industry.

Bush's energy plan, announced in 2001, has fed pressure to open more public lands to drilling for oil and natural gas. His proposal to open a small part of the Arctic National Wildlife Refuge (ANWR) to drilling as a way to reduce growing U.S. dependence on foreign oil is stalled in the Senate.

Meanwhile, environmentalists have challenged thousands of leases to drill for coal-bed methane in Wyoming's Powder River Basin and other parts of the Rocky Mountain West managed by the Bureau of Land Management (BLM), charging that the agency granted permits in violation of NEPA.[22]

Rapid population growth, especially in the West, is sharpening a longstanding controversy over what kinds of recreational activities should be permitted on ecologically sensitive public land. Under the 1964 Wilderness Act, federal regulations prohibit "mechanized" activity in protected wilderness areas, barring not only off-road motorized vehicles but also mountain bikes and allowing only hikers and horseback riders. As demand for access to backcountry recreation grows, conservationists are trying to protect more land as wilderness. Bush has endorsed the addition of 530,000 acres to the 106 million acres of currently designated wilderness areas, the least of any president since President Lyndon B. Johnson signed the bill. See Bill Becher, "Landmark Wilderness Ruling Four Decades Old," *Daily News of Los Angeles*, Sept. 16, 2004.

Endangered Species

In 1962, Rachel Carson's bestseller, *Silent Spring*, chronicled the devastating toll the popular pesticide DDT had taken on dozens of species of large birds, focusing public attention on the power that pollution had to drive vulnerable animals and plants to extinction. The 1973 Endangered Species Act addressed that concern by mandating the protection of threatened or endangered plants and animals.

Almost from the beginning, the law emerged as a lightning rod for an often-hostile debate between environmentalists, who invoked it to protect vulnerable habitat, and loggers, ranchers and other users of the land, who claimed such action would cost them their livelihoods.

More recently, the Defense Department added its voice to the critics of the law, arguing that it made it difficult to conduct vital training. Exercises involving naval sonar equipment have been linked to the death and injury of scores of whales and dolphins.[24] In 2003 Congress approved the Pentagon's request to relax the law's application to naval operations. See Brad Knickerbocker, "Military Gets Break from Environmental Rules," Christian Science Monitor, Nov. 24, 2003.

The Bush administration has come under attack from environmentalists over its handling of water allocation in the Klamath River basin of Northern and Southern California, home to several endangered salmon species. Thousands of salmon died after the administration acceded to farmers' demands for more irrigation water in 2002, leaving insufficient water in the river to sustain the fish. Similar policies jeopardize salmon spawning areas in Idaho's Snake River.[25]

In the late 1980s, conservationists sought to halt logging in the Pacific Northwest's old-growth forests in order to save the northern spotted owl from extinction. Since then, most controversies over the Endangered Species Act have centered on the Western states.[26] Some Western lawmakers, for example, opposed a Clinton plan to reintroduce 25 threatened grizzly bears into a 1.4 million-acre wilderness area of Idaho and Montana.

Although the plan resulted from a compromise among local residents, timber workers and environmentalists, Gov. Kirk Kempthorne, R-Idaho, denounced it as a way to force "massive, flesh-eating carnivores into Idaho" and filed suit to halt its implementation. In June 2002, Interior Secretary Norton halted the reintroduction program.

CURRENT SITUATION

Energy Strategy

Despite calls to shift to less-polluting energy sources, the United States continues to rely overwhelmingly on fossil fuels to drive the economy. Oil-derived gasoline and diesel fuel power the nation's cars and trucks, and coal-fired power plants supply most of the electricity, while natural gas—the least polluting fossil fuel of all—heats a growing portion of houses and offices.

Domestic supplies of coal—the dirtiest fuel—are plentiful, and domestic and Canadian suppliers meet most of the demand for natural gas. But North American reserves of oil, the fuel in heaviest demand, are rapidly shrinking. For several years, the United States has had to import about 60 percent of the oil it consumes, largely from the politically unstable Middle East. As domestic oil supplies continue to dwindle, that portion can only increase over time.[27]

President Bush's solution to the country's energy needs is to spur domestic production. His energy plan, announced on May 17, 2001, would allow more oil and gas drilling on public lands, including 2,000 acres in Alaska's ANWR and wilderness areas in the Rocky Mountains, currently off-limits to industrial use. The plan also calls for greater reliance on coal and nuclear power.[28]

Environmentalists demanded that Vice President Dick Cheney, who headed the task force that produced the Bush energy plan, reveal records of the group's meeting with energy-business representatives while formulating the plan. Before taking office, Cheney was the chief executive of the Halliburton Co., an oil-services firm. The General Accounting Office, Congress' watchdog agency, sued to obtain the documents, but Cheney rejected the demands, saying the agency had no right to such sensitive information from the executive branch.[29]

In 2002 the Republican-dominated House and the Democratic Senate produced different versions of energy legislation that conferees were unable to merge into a compromise measure. In an effort to promote cleaner energy sources, a Senate proposal would have required large utilities to use wind and other renewable energy sources to generate 10 percent of their electricity output. Another Senate plan would have tripled the use of ethanol, a corn product, as an additive to gasoline over the next 10 years. Conferees also rejected the administration-backed proposal to allow oil drilling in ANWR and a Democratic proposal to require companies to disclose their emissions of greenhouse gases. Even after the 2002 elections produced a Republican majority in both houses, lawmakers have failed to agree on an energy plan.

Meanwhile, the Bush administration is trying to advance another part of its energy plan—construction of new natural gas pipelines—by having all 10 federal departments and agencies involved in pipeline construction conduct simultaneous environmental reviews.[30]

Initiatives in Congress

Congress' focus on homeland defense and the ongoing war with Iraq has given lawmakers little incentive to consider the president's main environmental proposals. Legislation embodying the Clear Skies Initiative was introduced in 2002 but failed to garner enough support to ensure its passage. Congressional Democrats are focusing their criticism of the Republican clean-air proposal on its omission of any effort to curb carbon emissions. A Senate bill co-authored by James Jeffords, I-Vt., chairman of the Environment Public Works Committee, and Sen. Joseph Lieberman, D-Conn., would impose mandatory caps on carbon-dioxide emissions as well as the three pollutants targeted by the Clear Skies Initiative. But that proposal has fared no better than the president's plan. The president's main legislative success on the environmental-policy front remains the Healthy Forests Initiative. Many Democratic lawmakers from the fire-stricken West heeded their constituents' calls for protection from future fires and joined Republicans to approve the Bush plan, despite their environmentalist supporters' strong opposition to the measure.[31]

Even before lawmakers approved the 2003 Healthy Forests Restoration Act, many of its provisions to speed the regulatory process and curb the public's ability to halt individual logging projects began to take effect through the rule-making process. Because so much of the plan is likely to take effect outside the legislative process, environmental advocates who want to curb commercial logging in the national forests appear resigned to defeat. "These are ecosystems, and they're not going to just grow back," said Wetstone of the Natural Resources Defense Council. "It takes hundreds of years and the right kinds of conditions. We've already lost so much of our old growth on this continent that it's really a shame to see it frittered away. Healthy Forests is really about healthy tree stumps, because I think, sadly, that's what we're going to be left with."

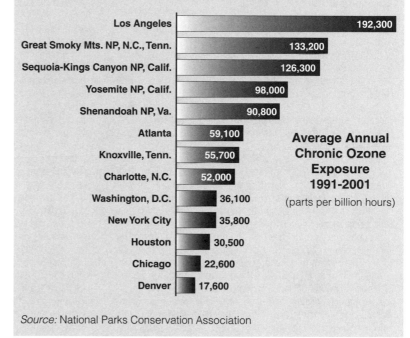

Some Parks More Polluted Than Cities

Ozone levels in four national parks were higher than in several major metropolitan areas, according to the National Parks Conservation Association. Since the 1970 Clean Air Act, the United States has seen a 25 percent drop in emissions of ozone and other major air pollutants. However, the act's goal of eliminating air pollution from 158 national parks and wilderness areas has fallen far short of expectations. Ozone levels in Great Smoky Mountains National Park, for example, now rival those in Los Angeles in the summer.

Los Angeles	192,300
Great Smoky Mts. NP, N.C., Tenn.	133,200
Sequoia-Kings Canyon NP, Calif.	126,300
Yosemite NP, Calif.	98,000
Shenandoah NP, Va.	90,800
Atlanta	59,100
Knoxville, Tenn.	55,700
Charlotte, N.C.	52,000
Washington, D.C.	36,100
New York City	35,800
Houston	30,500
Chicago	22,600
Denver	17,600

Average Annual Chronic Ozone Exposure 1991-2001

(parts per billion hours)

Source: National Parks Conservation Association

Regulatory Review

Bush administration officials are not relying solely on Congress to change environmental policy. In September 2002, the president issued an executive order to speed the NEPA-mandated environmental-impact statement process for transportation projects that the administration deems high priority.

In addition, Congress is considering a bill introduced by Rep. Don Young, R-Alaska, that would "streamline" the environmental-impact statement process for specific projects, such as the expansion of runways at Chicago's O'Hare Airport and an electric utility in Arizona. The bill also would give environmental agencies and organizations only 30 days to comment on the environmental impacts of transportation projects.

Should the government relax emissions rules on older power plants?

YES   Jeffrey Holmstead
Assistant Administrator, Environmental Protection Agency

From testimony before the Senate Health, Education, Labor and Pensions Subcommittee on Public Health, Sept. 3, 2002

There has been longstanding agreement among virtually all interested parties that the New Source Review program for existing [pollution] sources can and should be improved. For well over 10 years, representatives of industry, state and local agencies and environmental groups have worked closely with the Environmental Protection Agency (EPA) to make the program work better. In 1996, the EPA proposed rules to amend several key elements of the program [and since then] the EPA has had countless discussions with stakeholders and has invested substantial resources in developing final revisions to the program. . . .

EPA issued a report to President Bush on June 13 in which we concluded that the New Source Review program does, in fact, adversely affect or discourage some projects at existing facilities that would maintain or improve reliability, efficiency and safety of existing energy capacity. . . .

We now believe that it is time to finish the task of improving and reforming the New Source Review program. [When] we submitted our report to the president, we published a set of recommended reforms that we intend to make to the program. These reforms are designed to remove barriers to environmentally beneficial projects; provide incentives for companies to install good controls and reduce actual emissions; provide greater specificity regarding New Source Review applicability; and streamline and simplify several key New Source Review provisions.

To increase environmental protection and promote the implementation of routine repair and replacement projects, the EPA will propose a new definition of routine repairs. New Source Review excludes [routine] repairs and maintenance activities, but a multi-factored, case-by-case determination must be made regarding what repairs meet that standard. This has deterred some companies from conducting certain repairs because they are not sure whether they would need to go through New Source Review. The EPA is proposing guidelines for particular industries, to more clearly establish what activities meet this standard. . . .

Overall, our reforms will [enable] industry . . . to make improvements to their plants that will result in greater environmental protection without needing to go through a lengthy permitting process. Our actions are completely consistent with key provisions of the Clean Air Act designed to protect human health and the environment from . . . air pollution.

NO   Carol M. Browner
Former Administrator, Environmental Protection Agency (1993-2001)

From testimony before the Senate Health, Education, Labor and Pensions Subcommittee on Public Health, Sept. 3, 2002

The administration's recent announcement of final and proposed changes to the New Source Review program abandons the concept of steady air-quality improvements promised in the Clean Air Act. Some have suggested that the administration's announced changes [were supported by] the Clinton administration. Nothing could be further from the truth.

There is no guarantee, and more importantly, no evidence or disclosure demonstrating that the administration's announced final or proposed changes will make the air cleaner. In fact, they will allow the air to become dirtier. The administration owes the American people a full analysis of the public-health and air-quality consequences of their announced final changes—not just an explanation of the flexibilities they are giving industry.

Since 1977, a key provision of the Clean Air Act has been New Source Review. It is an important and reasonable means of achieving pollution reductions—a recognition that older plants, if and when they modernize and increase their emissions, should be held to the same pollution standards as new plants. New Source Review thus tailors the technology requirements for individual facilities to the public health-based ambient air-quality standards—providing a backstop that a facility will not exacerbate pollution problems—and guarantees that facilities will employ state-of-the-art pollution controls when they are built or rebuilt.

Thus, New Source Review requires existing power plants, refineries and other industrial facilities to install modern pollution-control equipment only when they make a "major modification" to their facility and increase the emissions of the most commonly found air pollutants—nitrogen oxide, sulfur dioxide and volatile organic compounds—[which] contribute to significant public health and environmental problems, [ranging] from premature death to worsening asthma attacks and acid rain.

Not every change to a facility triggers a requirement to install pollution-control equipment. EPA regulations provide exemptions from New Source Review for routine maintenance, repairs and increases in operating hours or production rates. . . .

Older facilities that do not meet modern air-pollution standards continue to be a huge pollution problem for this nation. Seventy to 80 percent of all power-plant emissions come from facilities built before 1977. Compared to modern or updated plants, old power plants emit four to 10 times more pollution for every megawatt produced, creating dramatic, adverse health consequences. . . .

Is U.S. environmental policy on the right track?

YES President George W. Bush

From remarks on Earth Day, April 22, 2002, in Wilmington, N.Y.

I firmly believe that 32 years after [the first] Earth Day, America understands our obligation much more than in years past: That we must be careful of our actions. Good stewardship is a personal responsibility of all of us. And that's what's important for Americans to understand—that each of us has a responsibility, and it's a part of our value system in our country to assume that responsibility. . . .

Not only do people have responsibility, but so does your government. And the federal government has a big responsibility. And I accept [those] responsibilities. For three decades, we've acted with clear purpose to prevent needless and, at times, reckless disregard of the air, water, soil and wildlife. This commitment has yielded tremendous progress. Our lakes and rivers are much cleaner than they were on the first Earth Day. Limits on toxic emissions have greatly improved the quality of the air we breathe. The Clean Air Act has helped reduce acid rain and urban air pollution. We've done all this at a time when our economy and population grew dramatically . . . [showing] that we can expand our economy for the good of all of us, while also being good and conscientious stewards of the environment.

Some of the biggest sources of air pollution are power plants, which send tons of emissions into our air. Therefore we have set a goal: With Clear Skies legislation, America will do more to reduce power-plant emissions than ever before in our history.

We will reach [this] ambitious goal through a market-based approach that rewards innovation, reduces cost and, most importantly, guarantees results. Mine is a results-oriented administration. When we say we expect results, we mean it.

We will set mandatory limits on air pollution, with firm deadlines, while giving companies the flexibility to find the best ways to meet the mandatory limits. Clear Skies legislation [would] significantly reduce smog and mercury emissions, [and] stop acid rain. It will put more money into programs to reduce pollution . . . and less money into the pockets of lawyers and regulators. . . .

Americans have reached a great consensus about the protection of the environment: We understand that the success of a generation is not defined by wealth alone. We want to be remembered for our material progress . . . but we also want to be remembered for the respect we give to our natural world. This Earth Day finds us on the right path, gaining in appreciation for the world in our care.

NO Tom Daschle, D-S.D.
Senate Majority Leader

From a speech to the League of Conservation Voters, Sept. 19, 2002?

Beginning with visionary leaders like Teddy Roosevelt and closing with a renewed recognition of our impact on the world around us, the 20th century was truly America's century of conservation.

As a new century unfolds, the question facing us is whether we will have the courage . . . to confront and defeat the threats to our global environment. For the first time, the answer to that question doesn't depend on science. The science on environmental issues and impacts is overwhelming, unequivocal and accepted. . . .

The answer hinges on one thing: leadership. Unfortunately, we haven't seen that leadership—at least not yet—from this White House. . . .

In the Senate, we've tried to use our majority to bring greater moral clarity to these moral issues. When they proposed opening the Arctic [National Wildlife] Refuge (ANWR) for drilling, we stopped them. We passed an energy bill that doesn't allow drilling in ANWR but does increase the amount of our energy we get from alternative and renewable fuels. When the administration tried to avoid issuing a strong rule to reduce arsenic in drinking water, we forced them to make that rule the law of the land. When they tried to cut the EPA's enforcement budget, we restored that money. . . .

We also believe that it is unacceptable for America to abdicate its responsibility to lead on the issue of global warming. Today, roughly 160 million Americans are breathing unhealthy air. In the space of five years, my part of the county has seen historic flooding and now a historic drought—something we can expect more of if we don't take steps to reduce the accumulation of greenhouse gases. [And] America is on the verge of a boom in power-plant construction. . . .

These things could be either a toxic combination or a historic opportunity. I choose to see this as an opportunity to lead—and that's why we're going to fight to enforce New Source Review requirements for power plants.

I believe we should go even further. I believe that we need to dramatically reduce the worst pollutants—sulfur dioxide, nitrogen oxides, mercury and carbon dioxide. So today, I want to make this pledge: If I have the privilege of serving as majority leader in the 108th Congress, we will put the environment back at the center of the national agenda, and a "four pollutants" bill will be high on my list of leadership priorities.

AP Photo/Nati Harnik

Bison and snowmobilers share a trail in Yellowstone National Park last January. President Clinton banned snowmobiles in Yellowstone and Grand Teton parks, but in June the National Park Service said it would continue to allow snowmobiles. The Environmental Protection Agency has since required manufacturers to reduce snowmobile emissions, but conservationists say the new standards are too lax.

"This bill would seriously undermine public health, endangered species and threatened wetlands by weakening natural resource laws," said Fred Krupp, executive director of Environmental Defense, an advocacy organization in New York City. "It makes the transportation objective paramount over natural-resource agencies' missions to protect public health and the environment."[32]

Even some conservative experts say that the move away from command-and-control regulations toward a market-based approach to environmental policy can only go so far. "The market approach works neatly for electric-utility plants, but after that it gets a lot harder," said Hayward of the American Enterprise Institute. "You'll never completely replace the regulatory system because there are a lot of environmental problems for which a market approach is very, very difficult to make work at all. I think the model that is going to evolve is not either pure markets or pure regulation, but some mix of the two."

Hayward predicted that the next major effort to change the regulatory system would focus on water quality. "We've pretty much done the big stuff with regulating pipes coming out of factories," he said. "Now what we're trying to get after is the much bigger problem of runoff from farm fields and streets." These "non-point"

sources of water pollution are hard to identify, making it all but impossible for EPA regulators to enforce Clean Water Act limits on specific pollutants.

Meanwhile, the EPA is experimenting with market-based alternatives to water-quality regulations. When water pollution exceeded acceptable limits in North Carolina's Tar-Pamlico basin, EPA officials convened community leaders and farmers and agreed to assist them in finding ways to reduce runoff from fields and storm sewers. Although runoff pollution levels remain high in the basin, the effort has resulted in a slight improvement in water quality.

A similar effort is taking place along the Charles River in Massachusetts. "This approach is neither purely market nor purely regulatory," Hayward said. "I think that's the way the world is going, no matter what kind of administration we have."

Environmentalists insist that the regulatory system continues to offer the best means of ensuring water quality. They are especially troubled by Bush administration plans to review the Clean Water Act to determine which waters the law covers and which are exempt from its regulatory oversight. "I haven't heard any indication that the American public is up in arms looking for ways to reduce the coverage of the Clean Water Act because our waters are too clean," Wetstone said. "The reality is, this is one of the most popular and successful laws ever, but there's still a long way to go."

OUTLOOK

Election Impact

Environmental issues often figure prominently in campaign debates. But this year, as in 2002, counterterrorism efforts and the Bush administration's war on Iraq are likely to dominate.

"Environmental issues will be a very high priority in some areas, such as the Intermountain West and South Florida, where recreational access to public lands and private-property rights are a local concern," said Hardiman of the American Land Rights Association during the 2002 campaign. But in most of the country, he said, "The war talk has pushed everything else further down the ladder, from health care to wilderness areas." The same concerns dominated the presidential campaign of 2004.

Some analysts say the Bush administration, rather than simply siding with industry on environmental issues, is actually vying for the support of voters who are open to new approaches to environmental protection.

"The environment has become a motherhood issue," said Ellerman of MIT. " Bush is playing for the environmental vote of the middle class—the soccer moms, the people who want to bring emissions levels down but who also want to get out of this system where you get into all these lawsuits. The Clear Skies Initiative has enabled them to inoculate themselves against Democrats' charges that they aren't doing anything on the environment."

Conservative analysts say the Democratic presidential nominee, Sen. John Kerry of Massachusetts, and other Democratic candidates who support vigorous environmental-protection policies face an uphill struggle to get the attention of voters this year, as they did in 2002. "Environmental policy has the best chance of corralling votes when virtually nothing else is on the political agenda," said Taylor of the Cato Institute. In the wake of the Sept. 11 terrorist attacks, he said, "Voters probably care much more right now about security issues and the economy than they do about the environment."

Critics of Bush's environmental initiatives are hoping that voters will catch on to what they see as a quiet but deliberate assault on environmental regulations carried out while the public is preoccupied by the Sept. 11 attacks and their aftermath.

"With the distraction of the war on terrorism, I think [the administration] felt emboldened," said Wetstone of the NRDC. "There clearly has been an effort to try to keep this below the public radar screen, but the Bush administration's environmental initiatives are unpopular, and voters do care," he said.

"History shows that people do have a way of catching on."

NOTES

1. For background, see Mary H. Cooper, "Global Warming Treaty," Jan. 26, 2001, *The CQ Researcher,* pp. 41-64.

2. For background, see Mary H. Cooper, "Setting Environmental Priorities," *The CQ Researcher,* May 21, 1999, pp. 425-448; Mary H. Cooper, "Water Quality," *The CQ Researcher,* Nov. 24, 2000, pp. 953-976, and Mary H. Cooper, "New Air Quality Standards," *The CQ Researcher,* March 7, 1997, pp. 193-216.

3. See Eric Pianin and Michael Powell, "General Electric Ordered to Pay for Cleanup of Hudson," *The Washington Post,* Dec. 5, 2001.

4. See "EPA Orders Marine Shale Closed for Good," Associated Press Newswires, Oct. 7, 2002.

5. "Undermining Environmental Law," *The New York Times,* Sept. 30, 2002.

6. Bush presented his plan in a speech to the National Oceanic and Atmospheric Administration in Silver Spring, MD.

7. U.S. Environmental Protection Agency, "Latest Findings on National Air Quality," September 2002. See Andrew C. Revkin, "With White House Approval, E.P.A. Pollution Report Omits Global Warming Section," *The New York Times,* Sept. 15, 2002.

8. From Bush's Feb, 14, 2002, speech at NOAA.

9. Gale A. Norton, "A Better Plan for the Forests," *The Washington Post,* Sept. 17, 2002.

10. For background, see Mary H. Cooper, "Ozone Depletion," *The CQ Researcher,* April 3, 1992, pp. 289-312.

11. In U.S. Environmental Protection Agency, "Progress Report on the EPA Acid Rain Program," November 1999.

12. U.S. Environmental Protection Agency, *op. cit.*

13. National Parks Conservation Association, "Code Red: America's Five Most Polluted National Parks," Sept. 24, 2002.

14. See Eric Pianin, "EPA Links Lung Cancer, Diesel Exhaust," *The Washington Post,* Sept. 4, 2002, p. A4.

15. See Francis X. Clines, "Judge Takes on the White House on Mountaintop Mining," *The New York Times,* May 19, 2002.

16. See Michael Grunwald, "Plan to Revive Everglades Brings Renewed Dispute," *The Washington Post,* Dec. 29, 2001.

17. See "Whitman Says Water Treatment Needs Outstrip Funding," *The Washington Post,* Oct. 1,

2002. See also U.S. Environmental Protection Agency, "The Clean Water and Drinking Water Infrastructure Gap Analysis," September 2002.

18. Katherine N. Probst, David M. Konisky, Robert Hersh, Michael B. Batz and Katherine D. Walker, "Superfund's Future: What Will It Cost?" Resources for the Future, July 2001.

19. See Eric Pianin, "Democrats Assail Shift in Superfund Cleanup," *The Washington Post,* April 11, 2002.

20. For background, see Brian Hansen, "Nuclear Waste," *The CQ Researcher,* pp. 489-504.

21. See John Heilprin, "Interior Department Originally Backed Tighter Snowmobile Emissions Rules, Letter Says," Associated Press Newswires, Sept. 25, 2002.

22. See "BLM to Re-Examine Thousands of CBM Leases," Associated Press Newswires, Aug. 31, 2002.

23. See "Mountain Bikers Up Against Calif. Conservationists," *The Washington Post,* Oct. 2, 2002.

24. For background, see Mary H. Cooper, "Threatened Fisheries," *The CQ Researcher,* Aug. 2, 2002, pp. 617-648.

25. See Brad Knickerbocker, "For Bush, Dollars and Cents Drive Land-Use Policies," *The Christian Science Monitor,* Oct. 2, 2002.

26. For background, see Mary H. Cooper, "Endangered Species Act," *The CQ Researcher,* Oct. 1, 1999, pp. 849-872.

27. For background, see Mary H. Cooper, "Energy Security," *The CQ Researcher,* Feb. 1, 2002, pp. 73-96.

28. For background, see Mary H. Cooper, "Energy Policy," *The CQ Researcher,* May 25, 2001, pp. 441-464.

29. See Neely Tucker, "Cheney-GAO Showdown Goes to Court," *The Washington Post,* Sept. 28, 2002.

30. See "USA: Bush Admin Will Speed Up Natgas Pipeline Permits," Reuters English News Service, Oct. 2, 2002.

31. See Eric Pianin and Juliet Eilperin, "At Loggerheads Over Forest Plan," *The Washington Post,* Oct. 9, 2002.

32. Environmental Defense, "Groups Criticize Bill to Limit Environmental Reviews of Highway Projects," Sept. 30, 2002.

BIBLIOGRAPHY

Books

Wilson, Edward Osborne, The Future of Life, Knopf, 2002.
An eminent Harvard naturalist makes an impassioned plea for a global strategy to protect Earth's natural resources using the best tools that science and technology can provide.

Articles

Adams, Rebecca, "Democrats Decry Bush's Clean Air Plan As Favoring Industry Over Environment," CQ Weekly, Aug. 3, 2002, pp. 2119-2120.
President Buhs's market-based proposal would allow industrial polluters to buy and sell pollution credits to each other.

Arrandale, Tom, "The Pollution Puzzle," Governing, August 2002, pp. 22-26.
As federal environmental laws fail to achieve the desired results, some states are trying to improve environmental quality on their own.

Easterbrook, Gregg, "Hostile Environment," The New York Times Magazine, Aug. 19, 2002, pp. 40-44.
Among President Bush's top policymakers, Environmental Protection Agency (EPA) Administrator Christine Todd Whitman is the lone champion of basic environmental laws.

Goodell, Jeff, "Blasts from the Past," The New York Times Magazine, July 22, 2001, pp. 30-64.
Mountaintop mining, a controversial technique that pollutes water downstream, is likely to proceed because of the Bush administration's support of increased coal production.

Norton, Gale A., "A Better Plan for the Forests," The Washington Post, Sept. 17, 2002.
The Interior Secretary defends President Bush's Healthy Forests Initiative, a plan to speed removal of brush from fire-prone national forests by waiving public-comment and judicial-appeal procedures called for by the National Environmental Policy Act.

Speth, James Gustave, "Recycling Environmentalism" Foreign Policy, July-August 2002, pp. 74-76.

International efforts to protect the global environment have failed to slow the pace of deforestation and other threats.

Weinstein, Michael M., and Steve Charnovitz, "The Greening of the WTO," Foreign Affairs, November-December 2001, pp. 147-156.
Despite the criticism of "greens" who say globalization is accelerating environmental degradation, the authors document a series of World Trade Organization rulings suggesting that trade does not impede effective environmental regulation.

Wuerthner, George, "Out of the Ashes," National Parks, September-October 2002, pp. 18-25.
Since 2000, forest fires have devastated vast tracts of Western national forests. The author examines the pros and cons of fire suppression and the role of drought in wildfires.

Reports and Studies

Hayward, Steven F., and Julie Majeres, "Index of Leading Environmental Indicators," Pacific Research Institute, April 17, 2002.
A conservative think tank documents improvements in air quality, energy supplies, water quality and land conservation.

H. John Heinz III Center for Science, Economics and the Environment, "The State of the Nation's Ecosystems," Sept. 24, 2002.
The first of a series of reports on the nation's environmental health offers data on land, water and natural resources.

League of Conservation Voters, "Presidential Report Card," January 2002.
The nonprofit watchdog group examines the environmental record of Bush and his department heads after one year in office.

National Parks Conservation Association, "Code Red: America's Five Most Polluted National Parks," Sept. 24, 2002.
An advocacy group that seeks to protect national parks reports that air quality in several parks continues to deteriorate, rivaling in some cases smog levels of heavily polluted cities.

Natural Resources Defense Council, "Rewriting the Rules: The Bush Administration's Assault on the Environment," April 2002.
A leading advocacy group criticizes the administration for using regulatory changes to undermine environmental laws and examines its record since January 2000.

U.S. Environmental Protection Agency, "Latest Findings on National Air Quality: 2001 Status and Trends," September 2002.
EPA's periodic report on air quality departs from recent reports by failing to include among major pollutants carbon dioxide, the main "greenhouse" gas most scientists agree causes global warming.

For More Information

American Land Rights Association, P.O. Box 400, Battle Ground, WA 98604; (360) 687-3087; www.landrights.org. A conservative advocacy group that supports private-property rights and opposes federal efforts to limit access to public lands.

Cato Institute, 1000 Massachusetts Ave., N.W., Washington, DC 20001-5403; (202) 842-0200; www.cato.org. A libertarian think tank that supports efforts to relax environmental regulations, seen as costly and counterproductive.

Center for Energy and Environmental Policy Research, Massachusetts Institute of Technology, MIT E40-279, 77 Massachusetts Ave., Cambridge, MA 02139-4307; (617) 253-3551; web.mit.edu/ceepr/www. The center conducts economic analyses of corporate and public-policy issues involving environmental protection and energy production.

Environmental Defense, 257 Park Ave. South, New York, NY 10010; (212) 505-2100; www.environmentaldefense.org. A national nonprofit group dedicated to protecting access to clean air and water, healthy and nourishing food and a flourishing ecosystem.

League of Conservation Voters, 1920 L St., N.W., Suite 800, Washington, DC 20036; (202) 785-8683; www.lcv.org. An advocacy group that tracks administration policies and law-makers' voting records on environmental issues.

Natural Resources Defense Council, 40 West 20th St., New York, NY 10011; (212) 727-2700; www.nrdc.org. A national advocacy group that studies and provides information on a wide array of environmental issues and policies.

Sierra Club, 85 Second St., 2nd Floor, San Francisco, CA 94105; (415) 977-5500; www.sierraclub.org. A leading environmental advocacy group that provides information on a wide array of current issues.

U.S. Environmental Protection Agency, 1200 Pennsylvania Ave., N.W., Washington, DC 20460; (202) 564-4700; www.epa.gov. Administers federal environmental policies and regulations and provides information on environmental issues.

U.S. Interior Department, 1849 C St., N.W., #6156, Washington, DC 20240; (202) 208-7351; www.doi.gov. As the main federal agency involved in conservation, manages most public land, except national forests, which are managed by the Agriculture Department.

15

Water Shortages

Mary H. Cooper

Imagine trying to sip water through a straw from a glass across the room. That's essentially what is being proposed to quench the growing thirst of the bustling Colorado cities on the eastern slope of the Rocky Mountains.

The "Big Straw" project would take water from the Colorado River in western Colorado and pump it 300 miles to Denver and its sprawling suburbs, tunneling through the 10,000-foot-high Continental Divide.

Environmental advocates have pounced on the massive project as yet another water boondoggle. "I've never heard anyone tell me with a straight face that the Big Straw can be built in a way that is economically viable," says Carrie Doyle, Denver program manager for the League of Conservation Voters, an environmental advocacy group. She says the project, and other shorter "straws" also under consideration in Colorado, would wreak havoc on the state's environment and vital tourist economy. "One of the main reasons why people choose to visit and live in Colorado is that we like our mountains, and that includes mountains with water running in streams."

Even supporters of the project have doubts about the Big Straw's prospects. "Technologically, it's feasible," says Peter Binney, director of utilities for Aurora, a Denver suburb. "But I've got major questions in my mind about whether it's practical or environmentally and economically feasible."

The impetus for eastern Colorado's desperate effort to find new sources of fresh water, of course, is a three-year drought that has parched most of the region. While droughts are common in that part of the country, this one is being exacerbated by a rapid population increase that has left communities with chronic water shortages.[1]

Rafters ride the Arkansas River near Salida, Colo. Efforts by Denver and other eastern Colorado cities to divert more of the river's waters have been criticized by environmentalists and local whitewater-rafting outfitters, who warn that depleting the river further will threaten the mountain river ecosystem.

From *The CQ Researcher*, August 1, 2003.

Water Shortages Expected to Spread

Water shortages are expected to affect up to 40 nations — mostly in Africa and western Asia — in 2025, compared with 25 nations in 2000. However, because world population growth is slowing significantly — largely due to greater use of family planning — future water shortages are expected to be less severe than earlier projections.

Water Scarcity in 2000 and 2025

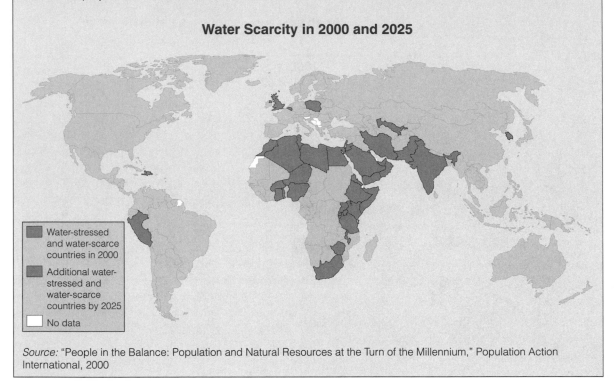

Water-stressed and water-scarce countries in 2000

Additional water-stressed and water-scarce countries by 2025

No data

Source: "People in the Balance: Population and Natural Resources at the Turn of the Millennium," Population Action International, 2000

"Last year was the worst year of drought in 300 years," says John Keys, commissioner of the Bureau of Reclamation, the U.S. Interior Department agency that manages water projects in the West.

The drought has intensified an ongoing struggle between thirsty cities and the ranchers and rural communities that oppose efforts to tap into their pristine rivers. The Interior Department recently issued a report identifying several dozen areas, including regions along the Mexican and Canadian borders, where water disputes could spark local, interstate and international crises over the next 25 years.[2]

As serious as they are, water shortages in the Western United States pale in comparison with problems facing other parts of the world. According to the United Nations, 1.1 billion people worldwide lack access to safe drinking water. Lack of sanitation makes matters worse by polluting existing sources of potable water. "Forty percent of the world's population—that's 2.4 billion people—lack access to sanitation services, which leads to hundreds of millions of cases every year of water-related diseases," says Peter H. Gleick, president of the Pacific Institute for Studies in Development, Environment and Security. "The world's biggest problem today is our failure to meet the basic need for water for billions of people."

Moreover, water shortages are bound to increase in coming years unless major changes are made in how water is provided and disposed of, experts say. Humans already extract 54 percent of all the accessible fresh water contained in rivers, lakes and underground aquifers, according to the United Nations. The U.N. predicts that if per-capita water consumption continues to rise at current rates, humans will take more than 90 percent of all available fresh water by 2025, leaving just 10 percent for all other animals and plants.[3]

At the same time, the number of people without adequate access to fresh water is expected to grow from 434 million today to between 2.6 billion and 3.1 billion by 2025, according to Population Action International, a nonprofit group that studies global population growth. Correspondingly, the number of countries afflicted with poor access to water is expected to grow from 25 today to between 36 and 40 by 2025.

Water scarcity may seem unlikely for a planet that, viewed from space, looks like a cloud-swept blue ball. Indeed, with water covering nearly three-quarters of Earth's surface, it's easy to take water supplies for granted. But while water is the most abundant substance on Earth, 97.5 percent of it is salt water, virtually useless for most human needs. Two-thirds of the fresh water, furthermore, is locked up in glaciers and permanent snow cover. That leaves barely 1 percent of all the water on Earth available for human use.[4]

Population growth and economic development have placed increasing stress on available water supplies in many parts of the world. The global population has more than doubled over the past half-century to more than 6 billion people. In addition to consuming more water directly for household use, growing populations also require more water to grow food and produce manufactured goods. Almost 70 percent of all water taken for human consumption is used to irrigate crops. Population growth and development also produce water pollution, which further diminishes available water supplies.

"Water problems around the world are more than just shortages," Gleick says. "There are problems with water

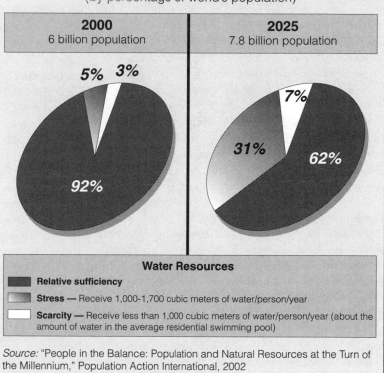

More People to Face Shortages

Nearly 40 percent of the world's population — about 3 billion people — will face shortages of fresh water by 2025 — six times the number who experienced shortages in 2000. Most of the shortfall will be in areas with high population growth and limited rainfall.

Fresh Water Availability in 2000 and 2025
(by percentage of world's population)

2000 6 billion population	**2025** 7.8 billion population
5% 3% 92%	7% 31% 62%

Water Resources

Relative sufficiency

Stress — Receive 1,000-1,700 cubic meters of water/person/year

Scarcity — Receive less than 1,000 cubic meters of water/person/year (about the amount of water in the average residential swimming pool)

Source: "People in the Balance: Population and Natural Resources at the Turn of the Millennium," Population Action International, 2002

quality; physical shortages, where there just isn't enough; economic shortages, where people can't get to the water resources they need; and there are political shortages, where water is denied to people. There are many different pieces to this puzzle."

Although last year's severe, almost nationwide, drought has disappeared in the East and Midwest, thanks to abundant rainfall, its persistence in the West and desert Southwest is forcing residents to change their water-consumption habits. Many local governments have restricted car washing and lawn watering, and some encourage homeowners to replace their grass with less thirsty native plants.[5]

"The drought is an acute problem, but it's finally getting people to start realizing that we've got a more chronic problem out here," utilities Director Binney says. "There now is a consciousness that water is a fixed resource and that we have to be more mindful of how we're using it."

The scarcity of water throughout the West has prompted lawmakers to consider strengthening the federal government's role in managing water supplies, traditionally a matter of state and local responsibility. A bill before Congress would create a new National Water Commission to coordinate state and local water policy.

Finding solutions to water shortages is complicated by the fact that many past solutions are no longer viable. For example, for decades the World Bank and other international lenders built scores of large dams around the world to store water and generate electricity, as did the U.S. Bureau of Reclamation in the Western United States. But most of the rivers deemed suitable for large water projects already have been dammed, and critics complain that dams damage the environment. Instead, environmentalists say, improving conservation is a cheaper, more sustainable way to ensure adequate supplies.

International institutions are raising the alarm over the world's dwindling water supply—a problem that has historically taken a backseat to arms control, peacekeeping, trade and other thorny international matters. The United Nations declared 2003 as the "International Year of Freshwater" and sponsored a recent conference in Kyoto, Japan, to identify effective approaches to improving access to safe water. Proposals include broader privatization of water utilities and more investment in technologies to turn seawater and glaciers into usable fresh water. But both solutions are controversial. Critics of privatization defend access to free water as a human right, and many environmental advocates say conservation would increase water supplies far more efficiently than any technological fix.

"The world is lumbering toward solutions to water scarcity," says Robert Engelman, vice president for research at Population Action International. "Governments are rather ham-handed in their efforts, but at least their intentions are good. They increasingly are recognizing that solving the water-scarcity problem is fundamental to the future of economic and human development in the 21st century."

As scientists and policymakers seek to increase access to water, these are some of the questions they are asking:

Does privatization help the world's poor gain access to water supplies?

Unlike the vast majority of natural resources, water often is seen as a free commodity, akin to the air we breathe. "Water is free in much of the world, where you can just dig a well and pull it out of the ground," says Engelman of Population Action International. "Even where utilities provide the water, in many countries—including until recently the United Kingdom—you may pay an annual fee to be plugged into the system, but it doesn't matter how much water you use."

Based on that experience, non-governmental organizations and citizens' groups around the world have declared that free access to clean water is a basic human right and condemned efforts to charge fees for water as the "commodification" of a basic natural resource. The debate intensified last October during the World Summit on Sustainable Development, held in Johannesburg, South Africa. In addition, activists bearing banners that read "World Water Mafia" and "Water Is a Human Right" stormed the stage at the Third World Water Forum in Kyoto in June.[6]

Most experts contend that providing water free to all users is not a viable expectation in the face of today's dwindling supplies. "There is wisdom to pricing water because it's a well-known human trait that we don't conserve things that are free," Engelman says. "Social activists at Johannesburg called for free water for the poor, saying there's more than enough water for everybody. On the other hand, the World Bank and its member governments argued that unless people conserve, there won't be enough for everybody. Unfortunately, that's where the debate stands today."

The Pacific Institute's Gleick says a key fact that often goes unrecognized in the pricing debate is the cost of maintaining the very utility systems that ensure people's access to safe water. "I think of water not as a commodity, but as an economic good, so there are certain economic principles that ought to be applied in managing water systems," he says. "Water services shouldn't be free. If people don't pay for it, then there's no money to operate and maintain high-quality systems. Those things cost money."

In recent decades, many countries have started charging people for the water they use. A study of industrial countries found that prices vary widely, reflecting the cost of storing, treating and transporting water to customers—from $1.91 per cubic meter in highly urbanized Germany to 51 cents in the United States and just 40 cents in Canada, whose vast water resources serve a relatively small population.[7] (*See table, p. 325.*)

The issue of who should control water resources is even more contentious.[8] For centuries, governments traditionally have had responsibility for providing water. But increasingly, they are handing over at least part of the job to private companies. Some of these are large multinational corporations, such as France's Ondeo, which provides water to more than 110 million people in 130 countries, and Britain's Thames Water, which has some 70 million customers in 46 countries.

But critics of privatization say corporate mismanagement and corruption have transformed some private water-development projects into poster children for the anti-privatization movement. The Lesotho Highlands Water Project, a multi-dam system in the small, impoverished country adjoining South Africa, is often cited as a case in point. The largest project of its kind in Africa, it being built and managed by a consortium of foreign companies to collect water in Lesotho and transport it to South Africa. The reservoirs created by its dams displaced more than 30,000 people, and promises to use part of the project's profits to help them relocate have not been honored. After repeated allegations of corruption and mismanagement, courts in Lesotho convicted Canadian and German firms involved in the project of bribing government officials.

"The local people where the water has been diverted have been severely impoverished as a result of this project," says Korinna Horta, senior economist at Environmental Defense, a U.S. advocacy group. "There's all this water flowing out of their country, but they themselves have no access to it."

In Horta's view, privatization threatens proper management of water resources. "Since private companies need to make profits, often the poorer people who can't afford to pay for the new water simply won't get it anymore," she says. And, because most privatization efforts have been implemented without adequate regulations or government oversight, the water may no longer be available to all. "Private companies have no incentive to go into remote, rural areas unless they are forced to," she says.

But the fight against privatization appears to be an uphill battle. "Privatization has been around for a long time in various forms," says Gleick, who points out that France has had private water companies for 100 years,

The controversial Lesotho Highlands Water Project will carry water from impoverished Lesotho to neighboring South Africa via tunnels. The foreign consortium that built the system did not resettle the 30,000 people its dams displaced. Courts in Lesotho convicted two of the firms of bribing government officials.

and 15 percent of Americans get their water from private utilities.[9] "There is private involvement in the water sector now, and there always will be," he says. "But it's being applied improperly."

In a report issued last year, Gleick and his colleagues listed several principles they say should be in place before any government turns over water supplies to private companies, including proper pricing, subsidies for the poor and strong government oversight.[10]

Governments that do not exercise oversight or ensure citizens' continued access to adequate water often doom utility privatization from the outset. When Bolivia invited a subsidiary of San Francisco-based Bechtel Corp. to take over water management in the city of Cochabamba, it failed to protect its poorest citizens from prohibitive water charges. Street demonstrations sparked by the high prices injured dozens of people and killed a young boy. Bechtel recently abandoned the project but sued the Bolivian government for $25 million, claiming the loss of its expected profits amounted to an "expropriated investment." A decision in the case is pending.[11]

Bolivia's experience offers a lesson for governments contemplating water privatization. "Private companies can operate and maintain water systems, but they should never own the water," Gleick says. "Water is an economic good, but it's also a social good, and private companies will not protect social goods without strong government encouragement."

Can technological advances ensure adequate water supplies?

Historically, technology has played the dominant role in expanding water supplies, from simple irrigation channels to the massive hydroelectric dams that exemplified the predominant 20th-century approach to water management, including the recently completed Three Gorges Dam in China. However, most of the economically feasible locations for big dams have now been developed.

Massive water projects also have fallen out of favor because of their record of huge cost overruns and failure to help needy populations. "In general, the megaprojects have not done much to improve water access for poor people," says Horta of Environmental Defense. "Indeed, the people most directly affected through displacement have actually suffered." Citing the Lesotho Highlands Water Project, Horta says, "Cost overruns are typical of these projects, but in this case they're so large that it's unclear if they will halt construction altogether."

While megaprojects generally are no longer being built in the United States, the Bureau of Reclamation still provides water to 30 million people and 10 million acres of irrigated land that produces 60 percent of U.S. vegetables and a quarter of its fruit. It also manages 58 power plants that generate enough electricity for 9 million people, and numerous marinas and other recreational facilities surrounding the reservoirs created by those dams. "We still have a definite mission in the world of water resources," says Commissioner Keys.

However, there are alternatives to big dams for enhancing water supplies. Because salt water accounts for more than 97 percent of the Earth's available water, desalination technology sometimes offers a viable solution. Many countries with limited fresh water and access to seawater—including the United States, South Africa and Israel—have built desalination plants.[12] But because of its high cost, the technology is used primarily to produce drinking water alone.

"Desalination is capital-, labor- and energy-intensive," Engelman says. "While in theory there are lots of possibilities for desalination, particularly for wealthy seacoast towns, it's not the answer to water scarcity in much of Africa or the Middle East because many of the places where water is scarce are simply too far from the sea. Also, these places typically don't have the resources to desalinate and transport the water they need."

Japan has taken the lead in researching new freshwater technology. It is building a combination desalination and electricity-generating plant in the Pacific island nation of Palau.[13] Low-lying islands like Palau are especially vulnerable to rising sea levels caused by global warming: Saltwater contaminates underground aquifers and encroaches on coastal settlements. (*See sidebar, p. 326.*)

More-fanciful technologies to increase water supplies are being developed, including breaking off huge chunks of polar ice and towing them to thirsty parts of the world and even probing space for new water sources.

Many experts contend, however, that conservation offers greater promise than any new technology for ensuring adequate supplies of water. In Gleick's view, industries and commercial buildings could save 40 percent of the water they use just by adopting existing technologies. "The most effective solution to water problems in the United States is water conservation and efficiency," Gleick says. "It's the cheapest, fastest and cleanest way of meeting our needs for water."

Moreover, Gleick says, the government could encourage conservation simply by eliminating water subsidies for irrigation, hydropower and household use that were introduced in the early 20th century to encourage settlement of the West. Today, as retirees and others migrate to Phoenix, Albuquerque and other burgeoning cities in the desert Southwest—threatening to overwhelm the region's water supply—the need for incentives is gone, he says. Most of the areas where the Interior Department says water conflicts are likely to arise by 2025 are located in this region.

But meaningful conservation programs will require overturning longstanding practices. "The 20th century was really a century of water engineering," Gleick explains. "Water planners and managers are trained to think like engineers. From an engineering point of view, it's much easier to build a dam to [serve] 100,000 people than to deal with the individual water uses of 100,000 people. That's a harder thing, and it requires a different set of tools and skills."

Should the federal government play a bigger role in U.S. water policy?

In the United States, water-supply policymaking primarily falls within state and local jurisdiction (*see p. 327*).

The federal government's most direct role involves the Bureau of Reclamation's construction and management of major water-storage facilities in the West. The other federal agency involved in water-use policy, the U.S. Army Corps of Engineers, focuses mainly on construction of navigation and flood-control projects throughout the country.[14]

The federal government also influences freshwater accessibility through its enforcement of the 1974 Safe Drinking Water Act and the 1977 Clean Water Act. It also can halt or alter environmentally destructive water projects under the 1973 Endangered Species Act. Finally, the federal government is responsible for honoring treaties with Canada and Mexico involving trans-border water flows.

Recent droughts and predictions of coming water shortages, especially in the West, have prompted reconsideration of the federal government's oversight of the nation's water supplies. In June, an Interior Department report warned of coming water conflicts in many parts of the West unless innovative steps are taken to augment the region's supplies. The "Water 2025" report recommended that states set up voluntary "water banks" that would enable growers to rent their excess water to municipalities or other users during droughts.

But the report stopped short of advocating a major federal role in such endeavors, beyond helping pay for research into water-saving technologies. "There's no one-size-fits-all policy for water," said Interior Secretary Gale Norton in releasing the report.[15]

Although 35 states have begun developing long-term drought-preparedness plans in recent years, some experts say the threat of water scarcity is too critical to leave water policy to an ad-hoc, state-by-state approach. "There has never been a lead federal agency dealing with drought, and that is part of the problem both from a response and a planning perspective," says Don Wilhite, director of the National Drought Mitigation Center at the University of Nebraska, Lincoln, which develops plans for drought preparedness and tracks precipitation trends for the federal government.[16] "What one state does with water is going to affect multiple other states, and interstate compacts now in place are continuously being challenged in the courts. Drought is a regional phenomenon; it doesn't confine itself to national, much less state, boundaries, so there is a problem with overlapping authorities."

Water Prices Vary

Among developed countries, Canada has the cheapest water and Germany the costliest.

Water Prices in Developed Countries

Country	$/cubic meter
Germany	$1.91
Belgium	1.54
Netherlands	1.25
France	1.23
United Kingdom	1.18
Italy	0.76
United States	0.51
Australia	0.50
South Africa	0.47
Canada	0.40

Source: "Water for People, Water for Life," United Nations World Water Development Report, March 2003

Some lawmakers agree that greater federal oversight is in order, especially with regard to drought preparedness. Sens. Max Baucus, D-Mont., and Pete V. Domenici, R-N.M., plan to reintroduce this year a bill they cosponsored last year, the National Drought Preparedness Act, which would establish a national drought council within the Federal Emergency Management Agency (FEMA) to develop a nationwide drought policy. Another bill, the 21st Century Water Commission Act, introduced this year by Rep. John Linder, R-Ga., would create a national water commission to coordinate water management and encourage the development of a comprehensive water policy to avoid future shortages. (*See "At Issue," p. 334.*)

Linder and other supporters of an enhanced federal oversight of water policy say they have no intention of infringing on the states' control over water. But efforts to strengthen the federal government's water policy decision-making powers may spark resistance at the state and local levels, especially in the West, where water rights and the authority to write water law are jealously guarded assets.

Global Warming Threatens Water Supplies

For more than a decade, scientists have observed a gradual rise in Earth's average surface temperature.[1] There is wide—though not unanimous—agreement that the main source of global warming is the burning of fossil fuels—oil, coal and natural gas—to run vehicles, power industry, generate electricity and heat buildings. Burning fossil fuels releases carbon dioxide and several other so-called greenhouse gases, which trap the sun's heat inside Earth's atmosphere, much as glass traps heat inside a greenhouse.

While the rise in temperature—estimated at about 3 to 6 degrees Fahrenheit by the end of the century—may seem insignificant, scientists warn it could have a dramatic and possibly catastrophic effect on the global environment. One of the biggest impacts could be on the world's supply of fresh water.

Rising surface temperatures melt glaciers and permanent snow cover in the polar regions and on high mountaintops. As polar ice melts into the oceans, sea levels rise, threatening to flood coastal areas and islands. Seawater already is beginning to encroach on fresh water aquifers on some Pacific islands, such as Palau and Samoa, while the Netherlands, much of it below sea level, is bracing for new assaults on its legendary system of dikes.[2]

Melting of glaciers also is beginning to threaten water supplies. As Himalayan snow and ice disappears, so does the high-altitude vegetation needed to slow runoff to the Ganges and other rivers of the Indian subcontinent. That, in turn, leads to recurrent cycles of flooding and low water levels in downstream areas of India and Bangladesh.[3] Similarly erratic water-supply patterns are being observed in regions along South America's Andes range and the Rocky Mountains in the United States and Canada.[4]

Global warming also is altering the world's precipitation patterns, scientists say. The tropics and subtropics are expected to receive lower and more erratic rainfall in coming decades, while the United States and other temperate zones are expected to experience more rain and snow. Warming is also expected to increase the frequency of extreme weather events, such as floods, droughts, typhoons and hurricanes. At times of drought, stream water may diminish and carry higher concentrations of pollutants, reducing still further the amount of usable fresh water.

On the positive side, rising temperatures may increase the amount of land that can be used for food production in the future by warming well-watered regions in northern Canada and Siberia that currently are too cold for agriculture. But at the same time there already are signs that warmer temperatures are accelerating drought and desertification in food-producing regions of Africa.[5] Indeed, the overall impact of global warming on water supplies is expected to be negative. The United Nations predicts that climate change alone will account for about 20 percent of the expected increase in global water scarcity.[6]

Climate experts say the combination of climate change and increased global demand for water makes it all the more urgent to find ways to improve access to clean water.

"There's more and more concern that future climate patterns may not reflect what we've seen in the past," says Don Wilhite, director of the National Drought Mitigation Center in Lincoln, Neb. "We really need to be looking at some other scenarios of future climate, which may include more extreme weather events and more variability. With more and more of us trying to live on finite water resources, climate change amounts to a double whammy for future water resources."

---

[1] For background, see Mary H. Cooper, "Global Warming Treaty," *The CQ Researcher*, Jan. 26, 2001, pp. 41-64.

[2] See William C. G. Burns, "Pacific Island Developing Country Water Resources and Climate Change," in Peter Gleick *et al.*, *The World's Water* (2002), pp. 113-131.

[3] See "The Ganges: Troubled Waters," *BBC News*, June 27, 2000.

[4] See Juan Forero, "As Andean Glaciers Shrink, Water Worries Grow," *The New York Times*, Nov. 24, 2002, p. A3; and Dan Vergano, "Global

Warming May Leave West in the Dust," *USA Today*, Nov. 21, 2002, p. D9.

[5] See Michael Grunwald, "Bizarre Weather Ravages Africa's Crops," *The Washington Post*, Jan. 7, 2003, p. A1.

[6] United Nations, "Water for People, Water for Life," *World Water Development Report*, executive summary, p. 10.

Indeed, states have long resisted the existing federal role in water issues, especially when federal enforcement of the Endangered Species Act has reduced localities' access to water. On June 12, the 10th U.S. Circuit Court of Appeals ruled that the Bureau of Reclamation must consider the effect on the endangered silvery minnow when it releases water from its San Juan-Chama Diversion Project, which supplies water to Albuquerque. The ruling prompted city officials to vow to fight the ruling, saying it would endanger the city's right to water it already has purchased. The city buys the rights to water piped from the Colorado River basin through the project's pipeline for municipal use. Sen. Domenici subsequently introduced legislation to block the taking of water from cities and farmers to protect the fish, as required under the Endangered Species Act.[17]

Similarly heated debates are taking place in the Pacific Northwest, where more than 20,000 salmon died during last summer's drought after the Bureau of Reclamation diverted Klamath River water to irrigate fields in Oregon and California.[18]

Efforts to better coordinate drought preparedness and create policies to improve water supplies may encounter similar obstacles if they are seen as infringing on traditional water rights.

"We own the water rights, we own the revenue stream and we own the facilities that move the water out here, so we're the ones who should be solving the problem," says Aurora, Colo., utilities Director Binney. "We're already actively involved with the federal government through the Bureau of Reclamation and in the implementation of the Endangered Species Act, which has a big impact on water development.

"I think the next generation of water projects will be developed at the local level," he continues, "and the state and federal governments will act more as regulators or facilitators."

BACKGROUND

Key to Civilization

Modern human history often boils down to the struggle for access to clean water. Archeological discoveries record evidence of this quest beginning some 20,000 years ago. Even before the invention of pottery, hunter-gatherers fashioned water containers out of ostrich eggshells or wood in order to reach hunting grounds far from streams and lakes.[19]

Civilization developed as a direct result of new advances in water management. Settlement of major river valleys such as the Tigris and Euphrates in Iraq and the Nile in Egypt occurred after humans discovered they could cultivate cereals and domesticate animals close to waterways and channel the flow into irrigation ditches to ensure a steady food supply without leaving home. Permanent settlement gave rise to an increasingly complex division of labor that would evolve into modern nation-states and political systems.

From eggshell canteens to today's massive hydroelectric dams, advances in water technology have driven human progress, primarily in boom-bust cycles. For instance, ancient Persians' discovery of a way to tap desert groundwater and deliver it to settlements through underground tunnels prompted a jump in population that eventually overwhelmed both the supply and quality of available water, resulting in sickness and famine.

This seemingly relentless cycle is the central paradox of water management. "[W]ater shortages have been an engine of human innovations: propelling, motivating and prodding societies to devise, accept and perpetuate solutions to water scarcity," wrote Fekri A. Hassan, an archeologist at University College, in London. "Water is thus the mainspring of civilization. However, . . . relief mechanisms always entailed . . . greater demands for water than what is available."[20]

Because it is essential to life, water also has been a target and even a weapon in military conflicts. As early as 596 BC, the Babylonian king Nebuchadnezzar conquered the Phoenician city of Tyre by breaching the city's aqueduct. In 1938, Gen. Chiang Kai-shek ordered the dismantling of dikes on China's Yellow River to flood areas threatened by invading Japanese forces—slowing the invasion but killing hundreds of thousands of Chinese in the process. U.S. forces bombed many dikes during the Vietnam War, causing floods and starvation that Vietnam claims killed up to 3 million people.[21]

Agriculture, industrialization and population growth have intensified water use over the millennia. Indeed, about 70 percent of all available fresh water today is used for irrigation. Food products vary widely in the amount of water needed to grow, ranging from just one cubic meter per kilo of potatoes, for example, to 15 cubic meters to produce a kilo of beef. Because livestock production

CHRONOLOGY

1900s-1920s *Federal government builds dams and reservoirs in the West to attract settlers.*

1902 Reclamation Act authorizes the Interior secretary to construct dams and other water-storage facilities to encourage farmers to "reclaim" and settle the drought-prone West.

1922 Colorado River Compact allocates water rights among seven states.

1930s-1960s *Most of the world's 45,000 large dams are built.*

1935 In an early U.S. water dispute, Arizona orders National Guard units to the California border to protest construction of the Parker Dam, built to divert water from the Colorado River to the booming city of Los Angeles.

1958 Federal Water Resources Council is created to assess the adequacy of water resources around the country and coordinate federal water policy.

1970s *Major environmental legislation affecting water quality goes into effect.*

1970 The National Environmental Policy Act slows new dam construction by requiring all federal agencies to conduct environmental-impact studies.

1973 Endangered Species Act requires federal agencies to protect threatened or endangered plants and animals, affecting future decisions on allocation of irrigation and municipal water supplies.

1974 Safe Drinking Water Act allows the Environmental Protection Agency (EPA) to regulate the level of contaminants in drinking water.

1977 The first United Nations conference on water, held at Mar del Plata, Argentina, calls for a global inventory of freshwater. Clean Water Act authorizes the EPA to implement pollution-control programs, including setting wastewater standards for industry.

1978 President Jimmy Carter declares that affordability and environmental sustainability will be the top priorities for federal water policy.

1980s *As freshwater availability continues to dwindle in the developing world, the U.N. declares the "International Drinking Water and Sanitation Decade."*

Sept. 17, 1981 President Ronald Reagan abolishes the Water Resources Council, diminishing the federal role in water policy.

1990s *The world's population surpasses 5 billion, doubling in less than 40 years.*

1992 An international water conference in Dublin, Ireland, concludes that water "should be recognized as an economic good," a principle hotly debated at a U.N. conference that year in Rio de Janeiro, Brazil.

1998 Amid mounting criticism of costly "megaprojects," the U.N. World Commission on Dams is established to assess the damage caused by massive water projects and consider alternative ways to make water accessible.

2000s *Water scarcity looms for much of the world.*

September 2002 More than 20,000 endangered salmon die in the Klamath River after the Bureau of Reclamation diverts river water, already depleted by drought, for irrigation.

June 12, 2003 The 10th U.S. Circuit Court of Appeals rules that the Bureau of Reclamation must consider the effect on the endangered silvery minnow when it releases water from the San Juan-Chama Diversion Project for irrigation or municipal uses, opening the way for new challenges to water transfers based on the Endangered Species Act.

2025 The number of people with inadequate access to fresh water is expected to reach 2.6-3.1 billion, up from 434 million in 2003, according to Population Action International. The number of countries experiencing these conditions is expected to grow from 25 to 36-40 over the same period.

consumes far more water per unit than cereals or produce, the growing consumption of meat that has helped
improve nutrition in developing countries has also contributed to their water-supply problems. Industrial technologies also consume varying amounts of water. Some
basic manufacturing sectors, such as the steel industry,
have developed methods to reduce their water usage, but
newer industries—such as manufacturers of computer
chips—require prodigious amounts of water, partially
offsetting other conservation efforts.

Not only do agriculture and industry consume water,
they also cause water pollution. As industrialization
spreads, water pollution is becoming a growing threat to
water supplies, especially in the developing world, where
70 percent of industrial wastes are dumped untreated
into rivers and lakes.[22] Some 2 million tons of human
waste, fertilizers, pesticides and chemical and industrial
wastes are released into waterways each day, according to
the United Nations.

Finite Resource

Although the amount of fresh water on Earth is finite,
most of it is considered a renewable resource because it
constantly circulates in a pattern known as the hydro-
logic cycle. Water vapor in clouds condenses and falls as
rain or snow, which then flows into streams, rivers, lakes
and wetlands until it reaches the sea. Along the way,
much of the water is taken up by plants and soil and
evaporates into the atmosphere, forming clouds and
starting the cycle all over again.

Some of the water also seeps into underground
aquifers. But because many aquifers take decades to
recharge, groundwater in many parts of the world is not
considered a renewable resource.[23]

Humans have learned to manage water to their
advantage by intervening in the cycle between the points
where precipitation reaches the ground and fresh water
empties into the sea. Over the millennia, they have built
dikes to prevent flooding, dams to store precious water,
canals to transport it to dry regions, irrigation systems to
divert natural flows onto croplands, and myriad ways to
collect and store rainwater and tap into aquifers.[24]

But growing population and improving living standards contribute to the world's steady decrease in freshwater supplies. In 1950, there were 2.5 billion people in
the world. Today, there are 6.3 billion, and the United
Nations predicts Earth's population will reach 8.9 billion

by 2050.[25] As the number of water users skyrockets, the
amount of water each person uses also increases. Both
industrial and personal water use grows with the advent
of indoor plumbing and other amenities.

Along with industrialization comes urbanization, as
people move to cities to find industrial employment.
Urbanization further depletes usable water supplies,
because it concentrates waste in waterways in towns
where sanitation and plumbing are lacking. Ironically,
those who use the least amount of water are exposed to
the most water pollution. Fully half the populations of
developing countries are exposed to polluted water, the
U.N. estimates.[26]

Pollution not only reduces the volume of accessible
fresh water but also causes sickness and death to those

Dead salmon line the banks of the Klamath River near Klamath,
Calif., last September. More than 20,000 salmon died during last
summer's drought after the Bureau of Reclamation diverted river
water to irrigate fields in Oregon and California.

Controversies Growing Over Water Transfers

In the arid Southwestern United States, thirsty cities acquire more and more of their water from distant rural areas where rivers and streams contain more water than residents consume for agriculture, ranching and commercial or household use. These so-called interbasin transfers involve the use of pumping stations and conduits, occasionally tunneling through miles of mountainous terrain.

At a time of growing water scarcity, transfers are becoming increasingly common—and controversial. Along the highway that runs beside the headwaters of the Arkansas River in central Colorado, signs protest efforts by Denver and other Front Range cities along the Rocky Mountains' eastern slope to divert more of the region's pristine waters. In the summer tourist season, local whitewater-rafting outfitters rely on high water, and environmental advocates warn that depleting the river further will threaten the mountain-river ecosystem.[1]

"Transfers are very controversial because our future economic development, our agricultural and ranching heritage—not to mention a rapidly growing tourist economy—all need water," says Carrie Doyle, program manager of the League of Conservation Voters in Denver. "That all this could be lost or diminished in order to water lawns on the Front Range is something that doesn't sit well with Western Slope folks."

But Peter Binney, utilities director in Aurora, a Denver suburb that has long depended on water transfers to fuel its rapid growth, says they are beneficial for both parties. "Water rights are one of the most valuable assets farmers who are moving away from cropping possess," he says. "If they decide to market those rights, we will agree to revegetate those fallow fields with native grasses, which use a third of the water needed to grow crops, and transfer the excess two-thirds of the water to the city for municipal use."

As fast-growing cities outstrip their water resources, controversies over water transfers are spreading beyond the Southwest. Atlanta Mayor Bob Young recently told a House subcommittee how communities in Georgia's Savannah River basin fought off efforts to transfer Savannah River water to the adjacent Chattahoochee River basin, where fast-growing Atlanta was running short of water. "The premise of interbasin transfers is that a watershed with excess supply will be tapped to subsidize a shortage of water in a neighboring watershed," Young said. "Such an approach penalizes regions that apply good planning and smart-growth principles and rewards communities that grow and expand without regard to whether existing water supplies will support the development."[2]

The Savannah River dispute was resolved when Atlanta dropped its water-permit application, and the Georgia General Assembly sought to avert future disputes by passing a bill discouraging future interbasin transfers and limiting such transfers to counties adjacent to the watershed in question. But Young warned that state legislatures are powerless to resolve disputes over watersheds that cross state lines. "Cross-border communities are virtually helpless when it comes to influencing the legislative and administration process in another state," he said.

A case in point is the ongoing dispute between Virginia and Maryland over rights to water flowing in the Potomac River, which separates the two states. When Virginia proposed moving a water-intake pipe farther toward the middle of the river to provide more drinking water for its share of the rapidly expanding Washington, D.C., suburbs, Maryland refused to allow the move, citing a 1632 grant by England's King Charles I giving it sole control over the Potomac. Citing subsequent U.S. Supreme Court rulings granting Virginia a share of the river's water, Virginia sued, and the Supreme Court is once again considering the dispute.[3]

---

[1] For a detailed account of Colorado water transfers, see Todd Hartman, "Dividing the Waters," *Rocky Mountain News*, July 11, 2003, p. 1W.

[2] Young testified before the House Transportation and Infrastructure Subcommittee on Water Resources and Environment on June 4, 2003.

[3] See Fred Bayles, "Living in a State of Uncertainty," *USA Today*, July 21, 2003, p. 3A; also Douglas Jehl, "A New Frontier in Water Wars Emerges in East," *The New York Times*, March 3, 2003, p. A1.

---

forced to use polluted water. Water-related illness is one of the most common causes of disease and death, chiefly in developing countries. Diarrhea, schistosomiasis and other preventable diseases caused by contaminated water killed more than 2 million people in 2000, most of them children under five. "In the vicious poverty/ill-health cycle, inadequate water supply and sanitation are both underlying cause and outcome," the U.N. reports. "Invariably, those who lack adequate and affordable water supplies are the poorest in society."[27]

Megaproject Heyday

The remains of dams built in the Middle East in 3000 BC reveal that humans have been storing water for millennia. But large-scale dam construction for water storage and hydroelectric power came of age in the 20th century. Often funded by the World Bank and other international lending and aid agencies, so-called megaprojects once were thought to be the key to propelling many poor countries into the modern age. Large hydroelectric dams would help control flooding and provide the electrical power needed to run factories and light homes, ensure reliable sources of water for irrigation and consumption in areas with sporadic rainfall.

From the 1930s to the '60s—the heyday of the megaprojects—dam construction accelerated, producing many of today's 45,000 large dams—a $2 trillion investment. At the time, the benefits were widely considered to be well worth the enormous investment. Dam construction provided jobs; roads and bridges were built to access the dam sites; farmers gained reliable irrigation water and remote rural areas received electrical power. Indeed, dams currently generate about a fifth of the world's electricity, and supply more than a third of all the world's irrigation water.[28]

But the hopes placed on dams as vehicles of development often fell short of expectations. Megaprojects in the 21st century displaced as many as 80 million people, many of whom encountered worse living conditions in their new villages. The dams changed the courses of more than half of the world's rivers, disrupted natural habitats and caused irreparable environmental damage.

AFP Photo/Joel Robine

AP Photo/Anung

Drought's Devastation

Drought in Ethiopia caused widespread famine and killed thousands of cattle and other animals in recent years (top). Population growth in Ethiopia and other African nations is steadily reducing water flows in the Nile River, raising protests from Egypt. If water becomes scarcer, such disputes over access could escalate into conflict.

Indonesian children collect water from a spring in a dry riverbed in West Java (bottom). The island was hit hard by drought last year, forcing villagers to walk miles to find drinking water. More than 1 billion people in developing nations lack access to safe drinking water, according to the U.N.

And widespread corruption meant that the promised electrification often failed to extend beyond large towns and cities.

As the controversy over dam construction mounted in the 1990s, the World Bank began to scale back its support of megaprojects, withdrawing altogether from some of the more controversial projects, such as the vast Three Gorges Dam on China's Yangtze River.* In 1998, the international World Commission on Dams was established to assess the damage caused by massive water projects and consider alternatives.

The debate over megaprojects has produced a growing consensus on the need for smaller, less costly projects designed to meet the needs of local communities. Such projects emphasize reducing water consumption by fixing leaky conduits and pipes, covering open-air channels and conserving water with such low-technology methods as drip irrigation and public-education campaigns.

Making consumers pay for the water they use also increases water supplies, because it encourages conservation. This approach, even if it is coupled with government subsidies for the poor, has sparked criticism from many who consider free access to safe water a basic human right. Supply-side alternatives to dam building include desalination and reuse of treated water for irrigation, clothes washing and uses other than drinking.

Renewed Attention

The failure of large dam projects to solve water-shortage problems around the world also sparked renewed international attention to the issue. Over the past three decades, some 20 major international conferences have focused on clean water and sanitation.

The United Nations convened its first conference on water in 1977 at Mar del Plata, Argentina, which called for the creation of a global inventory of freshwater availability. In a further effort to focus wealthy nations' attention to the rapidly declining availability of fresh water in the developing world, the U.N. declared the 1980s the "International Drinking Water and Sanitation Decade." Another water conference, held in 1992 in Dublin, Ireland, concluded that water "should be recognized as an economic good," a principle that was hotly debated at the U.N. Conference on Environment and Development, also known as the UNCED Earth Summit, held later that year in Rio de Janeiro, Brazil.

In 2000, the United Nations included as part of its Millennium Declaration a commitment "to halve, by the year 2015 . . . the proportion of people who are unable to reach or to afford safe drinking water."

The debate over water as a human right and privatization of utilities intensified at the World Summit on Sustainable Development, held last October in Johannesburg, South Africa.[29] Most recently, in June, the Third World Water Forum, held in Kyoto, Japan, issued the World Water Development Report, a massive document spelling out the major impediments to global access to clean water. To call attention to the progressive dwindling of global water supplies, the United Nations also named 2003 the International Year of Freshwater.

U.S. Water Puzzle

As a whole, the United States possesses abundant water supplies. For most of its history, the federal government—through the Army Corps of Engineers and the Bureau of Reclamation—has developed dams and flood-control projects that provide electricity and water storage for irrigation, industrial use and household consumption. Traditionally, the Corps has focused on building and maintaining projects for navigation, flood control and power generation, while the Bureau's main goal has been to store water for irrigation.[30]

Most municipal water systems are built and maintained by local governments in accordance with state water laws. Because they apply to a moving resource that crosses state boundaries in rivers, streams and underground aquifers, state water laws have sparked numerous lawsuits and interstate quarrels, especially in parts of the West where water is scarce.[31] In 1935, for example, Arizona ordered National Guard units to the California border to protest construction of the Parker Dam, which would divert water from the Colorado River to Imperial Valley farms as well as Los Angeles itself. That "water war," like myriad others, was settled in court.*

---

* China has continued the $25 billion project—the world's largest hydroelectric facility. On June 1, the dam's gates were shut, and the giant reservoir began filling.

* The Supreme Court agreed with Arizona that the Bureau of Reclamation lacked authority to build Parker Dam, but Congress quickly authorized the project, forcing Arizona to join the Colorado River Compact to preserve its right to a portion of the river's water.

Some of the country's most heated water conflicts involve the Colorado River, which flows from the Rocky Mountains of Colorado and Wyoming (via the Green River, a Colorado River tributary) through some of the country's most arid and populous regions before crossing into Mexico and emptying into the Gulf of California. Under the 1922 Colorado River Compact, seven states agreed to evenly split rights to the river's annual flow—then at 15 million acre-feet—between the upstream states of Wyoming, Colorado, New Mexico and Utah and the downstream states of Arizona, Nevada and California. The agreement specified that the downstream states would always have the right to their allocated 7.5 million acre-feet, leaving the upstream states to use any surplus that might occur in wet years but use less than their allocated right in dry years. Because it was later discovered that 1922 was a wet year, the upstream states have frequently had to make do with less river water than they have a legal right to, igniting frequent interstate quarrels.[32]

Two decades before the compact was signed, the bureau was already beginning to build large water-supply projects in the West. The 1902 Reclamation Act authorized the Interior secretary to construct dams and other water-storage facilities to encourage farmers to "reclaim" and settle the arid region, which receives only one-third to one-half the precipitation that falls on Eastern states. Reclamation projects went up rapidly from the 1930s until the early '70s, and today the bureau operates about 350 reservoirs and 250 dams. Two of the dams, Hoover on the Colorado River and Grand Coulee on the Columbia, are among the largest in the world.

With most suitable waterways already developed, additional major projects were prohibitively expensive, and as a result construction slowed in the early 1970s. Meanwhile, the nascent environmental movement advanced different priorities for the West's waterways, such as recreational use and conservation to protect fish and wildlife habitats. The 1970 National Environmental Policy Act further slowed new dam construction by requiring all federal agencies to conduct environmental-impact studies before embarking on new projects and by subjecting federal projects to greater public scrutiny. President Jimmy Carter declared in 1978 that affordability and environmental sustainability would be the top priorities for federal water policy.

President Ronald Reagan continued to oppose large water projects, and new construction of federal projects

Two-thirds of Earth's fresh water is locked up in permanent snow cover and ice like Norway's Briksdal Glacier (above). Global warming threatens to seriously reduce supplies of fresh water. As polar ice and glaciers melt, sea levels rise and cause coastal flooding that contaminates freshwater aquifers. Some Pacific islands already have been affected.

nearly ceased. Consistent with his desire to transfer many federal powers to the states, Reagan also abolished the Water Resources Council, a federal agency created in 1968 to assess the adequacy of the nation's water resources and coordinate interstate water policy.

Since the early 1990s, lawsuits brought under the 1973 Endangered Species Act increasingly have forced the Corps of Engineers and the Bureau of Reclamation to mitigate or prevent environmental damage caused by their projects. The law requires agencies to take necessary action to protect plants and animals threatened with extinction. Many of the bureau's efforts have focused on ways to restore populations of endangered salmon on the Columbia and Snake rivers, where bureau-operated dams impede the return of fish to upstream spawning grounds.

CURRENT SITUATION

U.S. Drought Response

The drought of 2002 was one of the worst in U.S. history. East Coast cities shut down fountains, crops shriveled in the fields and suburban homeowners under watering restrictions watched their lawns and gardens

Should federal water policy focus on increasing water supplies?

YES Rep. John Linder, R-Ga.
Sponsor, 21st Century Water Policy Commission Act

From a statement posted at linder.house.gov

Water-resources managers will be faced with unavoidable, life-threatening challenges in the 21st century, and we must prepare for these challenges now through extensive research and coordination of objectives among all levels of water management—federal, state, local and the private sector. In the 107th Congress, I introduced legislation to begin this process and have introduced similar legislation in the 108th Congress.

All humans, plants and animals depend on clean, fresh water for survival, yet 97 percent of the Earth's water is saline. Two-thirds of Earth's fresh water is frozen in glaciers and polar ice caps, leaving only 1 percent to serve all human beings and plant and animal needs. Projections of future population growth and the resulting demand for increased water resources forecast imminent water shortages. The United States' water resources will be appropriated to their fullest capacity in the coming decades, and current water supplies will prove inadequate.

While floods plague some regions of the country, droughts in other regions affect the lives of countless Americans. We have limited the amount of water allowed to circulate through our toilets. We have restricted outdoor water usage to specific days and times. Given these current restrictions, we must begin a coordinated effort to prepare for future water shortages now, before we are forced to limit our showers to three per week and to prohibitively restrict the water required to feed our nation.

The traditional methods of capturing and distributing fresh water within the United States will not be sufficient 20 years from now. Currently, roughly 50 trillion gallons of water fall on Georgia each year, yet our lakes are growing dangerously low, our citizens are subject to stringent water restrictions and our aquifers are being pumped dry. Why? Because we do not effectively capture Georgia's rainfall before it evaporates or runs off into the ocean. We must research new technologies, such as aquifer recharge, desalination, efficient irrigation techniques, recycled wastewater, wetlands creation and more in order to capture and store water for future usage. . . .

The engineering expertise exists to ensure future Americans access to fresh water. However, we need a comprehensive strategy . . . to implement this expertise. The 21st Century Water Policy Commission Act" is fundamental to meeting these objectives. We must no longer be reactive when faced with water emergencies. We must act now to face future emergencies proactively. Providing all Americans with fresh water is not a partisan issue. It is a matter of life and death.

NO Peter H. Gleick
President, Pacific Institute, Oakland, Calif.

From Testimony Before the House Resources Subcommittee on Water and Power, April 1, 2003

As we enter the 21st century, pressures on U.S. and international water resources are growing, and conflicts among water users are worsening. . . . Globally, the realization is growing that the failure to meet basic human and environmental needs for water is the greatest development disaster of the 20th century. Millions of people, mostly young children, die annually from preventable water-related diseases. Climate change is increasingly threatening our own water systems and water resources abroad. Controversy is developing over the proper role of expensive dams and infrastructure, private corporations and local communities in managing water. Yet the United States has not offered adequate leadership . . . to address these problems.

Here at home, municipalities are faced with billions of dollars of infrastructure needs and growing disputes over the role of public and private water management. Arguments among Western states over allocations of shared rivers are rising, as are tensions between cities and farmers over water rights. The U.S. and Mexico have unresolved disagreements over the Colorado and Rio Grande/Rio Bravo rivers, and our Canadian neighbors are concerned about proposals to divert Great Lakes or Canadian water for U.S. use. Communities are facing new challenges in meeting water-quality standards and ensuring that safe drinking water is available for all. . . .

I strongly support creation of a national [water] commission. I believe, however, that [Rep. Linder's] bill, as written, will not meet the needs of the nation. In particular, the "findings" of this bill are somewhat misdirected. . . .

In particular, the findings emphasize the need "to increase water supplies in every region of the country." Overall water supply is not a problem, with some regional exceptions. And even in these regions, increasing supplies does not appear to be the most efficient, cost-effective and timely response. The greatest water problems facing the United States are not shortages, but inefficient use, inappropriate water allocations, water pollution and ecological destruction. Indeed, water use in the United States has decreased in the past 20 years, reducing pressure on overall supply. On a per-person basis, this decrease is substantial. . . . Per-capita use in the U.S. has decreased 20 percent since 1980—a remarkable change. . . . [T]otal economic growth in the U.S. has continued, even as overall water use has leveled off and even declined. Moreover, where the problem is "shortage," the fastest, cheapest and most environmentally acceptable solution will not be an increase in "supply" but a reallocation of existing uses and improvements in efficiency

dry up. Although abundant rains have eliminated water shortages in most of the East this year, many state and local governments are taking steps to be better prepared the next time drought strikes.

But the drought has lingered in the fast-growing Southwest. "In some cases we're in the fifth or sixth straight year of drought," says the Bureau of Reclamation's Keys.

As water-supply concerns mount, more and more states—35 to date—are adopting plans to prepare for future droughts. "In recent years states [have been] more proactive," says Wilhite of the National Drought Mitigation Center. "They're moving from response planning, which is how you deal with a drought once you have one, to drought-mitigation planning, which is identifying and addressing your biggest vulnerabilities and putting in place comprehensive, early-warning systems. That enables states to reduce their risk to drought when it comes, rather than after it's here."

So far, the federal government's role in drought planning is limited to jawboning. "The federal government has said it wants the states to prepare," Wilhite says, "but there hasn't been a lot of national authority."

After failing to win congressional approval last year, the National Drought Preparedness Act, reintroduced on July 24 by Sens. Domenici and Jeff Bingaman, D-N.M., may fare better this year. With little drought relief in sight, the Western Governors' Association has thrown its support behind the bill, and Wilhite predicts it would face little opposition.

"The Western governors, as well as the National Governors' Association, are now going beyond water management to emphasize the importance of drought planning," he says. "I'm confident that the bill eventually is going to pass."

Meanwhile, the federal government is promoting the more-efficient transfer of water in the 17 Western states where the Bureau of Reclamation has authority over water supplies. The agency is encouraging the spread of "water banks," which would enable irrigation districts and other holders of capacity in its reservoirs to sell excess water to cities or other entities. Several reclamation water banks are already in operation, including one serving an irrigation district in southern Idaho that supplies water downstream in the Columbia River when it is needed to facilitate the salmon runs.

"Spaceholders have contracts that give them so much storage space in our reservoirs," Commissioner Keys explains. "If there is more water in their spaces than they need, they can put that into the water bank and sell it without affecting their contract or their state water rights."

> ## "One of the things that we've learned in the last three decades is that there is no one solution to water problems. What works in southern India may not work at all in sub-Saharan Africa."
>
> **— Peter H. Gleick**
> President, Pacific Institute for Studies in Development, Environment and Security

International Trends

Reflecting commitments enumerated in the 2000 Millennium Declaration, efforts are under way to halve by 2015 the number of people in the developing world who lack access to clean water and sanitation. "Today, more than in the past, there is an effort at the international level to try to meet those needs now," says Gleick of the Pacific Institute.

Africa and Southern Asia face the most severe lack of water, but Gleick argues that the solutions vary across regions. "One of the things that we've learned in the last three decades is that there is no one solution to water problems," he says. "What works in southern India may not work at all in sub-Saharan Africa."

As the number of approaches to water crises has grown, so too has the number of agencies and companies involved in mitigating the shortages. While the World Bank once took the lead role, today there are hundreds of non-governmental organizations (NGOs) working at the village level, international engineering companies working at the dam-construction and water-treatment level, and private companies trying to get involved—though somewhat controversially. "The U.N. is very heavily involved," Gleick says. "The principal international financial institutions—the World Bank, Asian Development Bank and International Monetary Fund—are supposed to be lending more in this area, though they actually haven't been."

The era of huge hydro projects appears to be coming to an end as there are fewer and fewer waterways available to dam. But there are still some holdouts for the big-dam approach. The World Bank-funded Lesotho Highlands project continues, and although the bank pulled out of the massive Three Gorges Yangtze River dam due to international complaints about its severe environmental and social cost, the Chinese government has continued building it and recently began filling its massive reservoir.[33]

Pressure is mounting to encourage the lending institutions to play a bigger role in small-scale water projects as they move away from megaprojects. The African Development Bank's president, Oman Kabbaj, recently called for spending $10 billion over the next seven years to help fund "sustainable" water supply and sanitation in rural Africa, with the overall goal of providing freshwater access to all Africans by 2025. "This will be done by adopting a program approach—as opposed to single projects—and using technologies that are appropriate to local skills and knowledge," Kabbaj said.[34]

In fact, many water projects now under way in the developing world focus on smaller-scale solutions. In southern India, for example, NGOs are helping villagers resurrect rooftop rainwater-collection tanks, an ancient technique that was all but abandoned when underground plumbing systems were built. But plumbing failed to reach the neediest households, so collection tanks are beginning to fill the gap.

"To me, this is pretty exciting technology," says Engelman of Population Action International. "It's very much community-based and helps solve the problem of water access at the household level."

Another promising approach is the use of "gray water"—water that already has been used for washing—for purposes other than drinking. Japan and Singapore, which have long contended with limited water supplies, have installed parallel water systems that supply households with clean water for drinking and cooking and gray water for gardens and toilets. "Why should we flush toilets with water that's been made potable?" Engelman asks. "That doesn't make any sense, especially where water is in short supply."

OUTLOOK

Water Wars?

The Interior Department warns that 10 areas in seven Western states have a "substantial" to "highly likely" potential to erupt in conflict over water accessibility during the next quarter-century.[35] They include virtually all of the Southwest's major metropolitan areas—Los Angeles, San Diego, San Francisco, Sacramento, Fresno, Las Vegas, Albuquerque, Santa Fe, Salt Lake City, Denver, Houston, Phoenix and Tucson—home to 40 million people.[36] Two of these hot spots—a 400-mile stretch of the Rio Grande and the point where the Colorado River flows from the California-Arizona border into Mexico—would involve international disputes with Mexico.

To avert future water wars, the Bureau of Reclamation wants Western states to improve conservation and continue developing water sales and transfers to move water from farms to the cities. To that end, the agency announced on July 3 that it would reduce California's allocation of Colorado River water to Imperial Valley farmers, leaving more for thirsty San Diego. Although the agency also promises to work cooperatively with water districts to settle disputes, the decision has sparked a heated debate among the state's water districts.[37]

"If we don't do something along the lines of our proposals in 'Water 2025,' those conflicts will be there, and they will multiply upon themselves," warns Commissioner Keys. "If we can get folks working together and collaborating on solutions, we think that we can get by without crises or conflicts. So it depends on what we do."

Gleick of the Pacific Institute hopes Americans will be able to conserve their way out of that grim scenario. "The United States is actually using less total water today than we used 20 years ago," he says. "Per capita water consumption has gone down 20 percent. So we're already becoming more efficient." The shift away from water-intensive manufacturing industries to less wasteful service industries has helped that trend, Gleick says. "We're producing more dollars per gallon of water used. This shows our potential to do more with less water, and that potential has just barely been tapped."

Much more potentially violent conflicts may erupt in scores of countries around the world where water is a far scarcer commodity. Access to water is a rarely mentioned but central source of tension in the Israeli-Palestinian conflict, as Israel controls most of the water supplies on which

Palestinians depend. Turkey's plans to dam the Tigris and Euphrates rivers have sparked charges by Syria and Iraq that Turkey is depriving them of water. Population growth in Sudan and Ethiopia is steadily reducing water flows in the Nile, raising protests from Egypt. The Ganges River is so depleted and polluted that its waters are barely usable by the time they reach Bangladesh.[38]

If water becomes scarcer, these and numerous other disputes could escalate into conflict, adding water to the list of reasons societies go to war. "Though there has been violence over water throughout history, there have not been wars over water to date," Gleick says. "But the potential for political and even military conflicts over water is growing. I also think the potential for cooperation over water is growing. The challenge is figuring out how to reduce the risks of conflict."

Population Is Key

A wild card in the water-scarcity equation is population growth. If the world's population continues to grow at the current rate, humans will consume 70 percent of all available fresh water by 2025, up from 54 percent today, according to the United Nations. Under this scenario, areas where water is already scarce would be ripe for conflict within the next two decades.

But recent population trends may yet save the world from thirst. "Demographers have been surprised by how rapidly the average human family is shrinking and how much later in their lives women tend to bear children compared with 30 years ago," says Engelman of Population Action International. "Both of these trends are contributing to slower population growth in every part of the world, including many where water is particularly scarce."

If the slowdown continues, population growth will actually halt around the middle of this century, Engelman says, reducing pressure on water supplies. "Population—more than water policy or technology—offers real hope for the future of water supply," he says. "It's going to get worse before it gets better, but there's a good chance that all we have to do is get through this window where population and economic growth are contributing to more and more usage of water.

"If we can better manage the water supply that we currently have," he adds, "[and] if we can learn how to use water much more efficiently, there's a good chance that we have all the water we need on this planet forever."

NOTES

1. For information on the Western drought, see Connie A. Woodhouse, Jeffrey J. Lukas and Peter M. Brown, "Drought in the Western Great Plains, 1845-56: Impacts and Implications," *Bulletin of the American Meteorological Society*, October 2002, pp. 1485-1493.

2. The areas at highest risk include California's Central Valley, Salt Lake City, Utah, and vast stretches of the Rio Grande. U.S. Department of the Interior, "Water 2025: Preventing Crises and Conflict in the West," June 2003.

3. See United Nations Educational, Scientific and Cultural Organization (UNESCO), www.wateryear 2003.org.

4. See United Nations, World Water Development Report, "Water for People: Water for Life," March 22, 2003.

5. See "Don't Drop Commitment to Conservation," *Fort Collins Coloradoan*, June 15, 2003, p. 6B.

6. See Erica Hartman, "Tidal Wave: International Movement Takes on the Water Industry," *In These Times*, June 23, 2003.

7. United Nations Water Development Report, *op. cit.*, p. 27.

8. For a critical view of privatization, see Center for Public Integrity, "The Water Barons," Feb. 3, 2003, www.icij.org. For the other side, see "Bogged Down," *The Economist*, March 20, 2003.

9. See National Research Council, "Privatization of Water Services in the United States," 2002.

10. Peter Gleick, *et al.*, "The World's Water 2002-2003: The Biennial Report on Freshwater Resources," July 23, 2002.

11. See Lisa Davis, "It's a Bechtel World," *San Francisco Weekly*, June 18, 2003.

12. See John Ritter, "Cities Look to Sea for Fresh Water," *USA Today*, Nov. 22, 2002, p. A3.

13. See "Japanese Technology May Help Islands Reap Pacific's Waters," *The New York Times*, March 23, 2003, p. A9.

14. For background on the Corps, see David Hosansky, "Reforming the Corps," *The CQ Researcher*, May 30, 2003, pp. 497-520.

15. See John Tierney, "Trying for Balance at the Interior Dept.," *The New York Times*, June 9, 2003, p. A26.

16. The center's national drought map is updated weekly at http://www.drought.unl.edu/dm/monitor.html.

17. See Thomas Hargrove, "Fish Case Raises New Squabble Over Water," *Albuquerque Tribune*, July 23, 2003, p. A4.

18. See Blaine Harden, "Judge Rules Plan Is Insufficient to Save Salmon," *The Washington Post*, May 8, 2003, p. A3; and Eric Bailey, "U.S. Denies Blame for Salmon Die-Off," *Los Angeles Times*, Oct. 3, 2002, p. B1.

19. Unless otherwise noted, material in this section is based on Fekri A. Hassan, "Water Management and Early Civilizations: From Cooperation to Conflict," UNESCO (United Nations Educational, Scientific and Cultural Organization), 2003.

20. *Ibid*, p. 2.

21. UNESCO, *op. cit.*

22. See "Water and Industry," UNESCO, *www.unesco.org*.

23. For information on aquifer depletion in the U.S. Great Plains, see Brian Hansen, "Crisis on the Plains," *The CQ Researcher*, May 9, 2003, pp. 434-435.

24. U.N. World Water Development Report, *op. cit.*

25. United Nations, "World Population Prospects: The 2002 Revision" (2003), http://esa.un.org/unpp.

26. U.N., *op. cit.*

27. *Ibid*, p. 11.

28. World Commission on Dams, "Dams and Development: A New Framework for Decision-Making," Nov. 16, 2000.

29. See "To Talk about Jobs, Not Birds," *The Economist*, Aug. 24, 2002, p. 38.

30. Unless otherwise noted, information in this section is based on Betsy A. Cody and Pervaze A. Sheikh, "Western Water Resource Issues," *Issue Brief for Congress*, Congressional Research Service, Oct. 25, 2002.

31. For background on U.S. water law, see Mary H. Cooper, "Global Water Shortages," *The CQ Researcher*, Dec. 15, 1995, p. 1124.

32. See, for example, Ed Quillen, "What Our Water Is Doing on Their Sand," *The Denver Post*, March 2, 2003, p. E6.

33. See Jonathan Finer, "World Bank Focused on Fighting Corruption," *The Washington Post*, July 4, 2003, p. E1.

34. "Africa Needs $10 Billion for Water, Sanitation," Deutsche Press-Agentur, June 4, 2003.

35. Interior Department, *op. cit.*

36. See J. J. Johnson, "Water 2025: The Coming War on the Western Front," July 11, 2003, *The Sierra Times* (www.sierratimes.com).

37. "A Thirsty, Ornery Gorilla," *Los Angeless Times*, July 24 2003, p. A14.

38. See "World Water Crisis," BBC, news.bbc.co.uk.

BIBLIOGRAPHY

Books

Gleick, Peter, *et al.*, *The World's Water 2002-2003: The Biennial Report on Freshwater Resources*, Island Press, 2002.
The president of the Pacific Institute for Studies in Development, Environment and Security describes a "soft path" to ending water scarcity, which focuses on improving efficiency and increasing conservation rather than building new large water projects.

Reisner, Marc, *Cadillac Desert: The American West and Its Disappearing Water*, Penguin, 2003.
This revised edition of a classic account of Western water policy by a noted environmental journalist describes the development of Los Angeles, Las Vegas and other cities that owe their existence to U.S. Bureau of Reclamation dams and reservoirs and the steady depletion of water supplies that has ensued.

Ward, Diane Raines, *Water Wars: Drought, Folly, and the Politics of Thirst*, Riverhead Books, 2002.
A comprehensive analysis of global water supplies that reviews numerous proposals to increase fresh water availability, including desalination and transporting glacial ice to parched southern regions.

Articles

Conte, Christopher, "Dry Spell," *Governing*, March 2003, pp. 20-24.
Last year's drought has prompted a re-examination of water policies, especially in the parched Southwest, where rapidly growing cities are trying to augment their supplies through water transfers from rural areas.

Curtis, Wayne, "The Iceberg Wars," *The Atlantic Monthly*, March 2002, pp. 76-78.
Towing icebergs to the Middle East and other thirsty regions, once dismissed as prohibitively expensive, is returning to the policy agenda as water shortages reach the critical point.

Hinrichsen, Don, "A Human Thirst," *Worldwatch*, January/February 2003, pp. 12-18.
Humans already use more than half of the world's available fresh water, but increasing demand from agriculture, industry and a growing population are rapidly depleting water resources.

"Priceless: A Survey of Water," *The Economist*, July 19, 2003, 16 pp.
This special report summarizes recent trends in global water management, including a report card on the world's largest dams, changing views on the need to set realistic prices for water and privatization of water utilities.

Tagliabue, John, "As Multinationals Run the Taps, Anger Rises Over Water for Profit," *The New York Times*, Aug. 26, 2002, p. A17.
Privatization of water utilities is emerging as one of the most controversial proposals for slowing the depletion of world water supplies.

Reports and Studies

American Rivers, "America's Most Endangered Rivers of 2003," April 2003.
The conservation group's most recent annual survey identifies 10 rivers threatened with diminished water flow and water quality due to overuse.

Engelman, Robert, *et al.*, "People in the Balance: Population and Natural Resources at the Turn of the Millennium," Population Action International, 2000.
Depending on population growt, the number of people who lack ready access to fresh water could increase from 505 million in 2000 to between 2.4 billion and 3.2 billion by 2025.

Rosengrant, Mark W., Ximing Cai and Sarah A. Cline, "Global Water Outlook to 2025," International Food Policy Research Institute, September 2002.
Failure to adopt water-saving technologies and policy reforms could result in "a breakdown in domestic water service for hundreds of millions of people, devastating loss of wetlands, serious reductions in food production and skyrocketing food prices . . ." by 2025, the authors conclude.

United Nations, "Water for People, Water for Life," World Water Development Report, March 2003.
This exhaustive report on global water supplies was released at the Third World Water Forum, held this year in Kyoto, Japan.

U.S. Department of the Interior, "Water 2025: Preventing Crises and Conflict in the West," June 2003.
This report identifies numerous areas in the 17 Western states where the Bureau of Reclamation manages water projects that face increasing tension over allocation of precious water resources unless steps are taken to improve efficiency and conservation.

World Panel on Financing Water Infrastructure, "Financing Water for All," March 2003.
Michel Camdessus, former managing director of the International Monetary Fund, chaired a panel that suggests that some $180 billion a year must be invested in water systems in poor countries to overcome chronic water scarcity.

For More Information

Bureau of Reclamation, U.S. Department of the Interior, 1849 C St., N.W., Washington, DC 20240; (202) 513-0575; www.usbr.gov. Government agency responsible for maintaining water projects in 17 Western states. Its recent report, "Water 2025," warns that water scarcity could heighten tensions in numerous Western communities unless they take steps to improve conservation and efficiency.

Environmental Defense, 257 Park Ave. South, New York, NY 10010; (212) 505-2100; www.edf.org. Studies the impact of climate change and large dam construction on water supplies.

National Drought Mitigation Center, University of Nebraska, Lincoln, 239 L.W. Chase Hall, P.O. Box 830749, Lincoln, NE 68583; (402) 472-6707; www.drought.unl.edu. Maintains the national drought map and provides extensive information on drought patterns.

Pacific Institute for Studies in Development, Environment and Security, 654 13th St., Preservation Park, Oakland, CA 94612; (510) 251-1600; www.pacinst.org. A valuable source of information on global fresh water supplies and efforts to augment them.

Population Action International, 1300 19th St., N.W., Second floor, Washington, DC 20036; (202) 557-3400; www.populationaction.org. Studies the impact of population growth on natural resources, including fresh water.

16

Fighting SARS

Mary H. Cooper

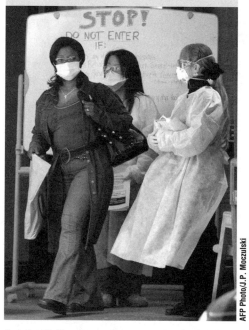

A visitor (left) passes nurses screening for SARS as she leaves Toronto General Hospital on June 11. SARS is the latest in a series of infectious-disease outbreaks that have appeared recently, such as West Nile virus. Since SARS hit China last fall, the pneumonia-like disease has killed some 800 people in 32 countries. In the United States, some health experts call SARS a wake-up call about underfunding of the public-health system.

From *The CQ Researcher*,
June 20, 2003.

O n March 7, a 63-year-old man went to the emergency room at Toronto's Scarborough Grace Hospital to get help when his chronic heart ailment flared up. What he got instead was a deadly infection from a patient in the next bed.

Nine days later, the man—officials only identify him as Mr. P— developed a rasping cough and high fever. When his wife took him back to the hospital, nurses whisked him into isolation while she went to handle the paperwork for her husband's admission.

Several weeks later, Mr. P and his wife had died, and 13 other people who had been in the hospital's admissions area with Mrs. P were seriously ill. Between them, the couple had spread their disease to 33 people.

As the world soon learned, Toronto was the epicenter of the outbreak in North America of a deadly, new disease now known as severe acute respiratory syndrome, or SARS. But at the time, the highly infectious disease had not been officially named or recognized.

By mid-June, health officials around the world had calculated SARS had sickened 8,464 people and killed 799 in 32 countries since it erupted the previous fall in China.

As it turned out, Mr. P had had the bad luck to be placed in a hospital bed next to the son of Canada's first recognized case of SARS—a 78-year-old woman who died from SARS shortly after returning to Toronto from Hong Kong.

SARS is the latest in a series of so-called emerging infectious diseases that have either appeared for the first time or occurred outside their endemic areas in recent decades, such as West Nile virus, Lyme disease and Legionnaire's disease.[1] Like Ebola hemorrhagic fever, which has killed about two-thirds of its 1,500 victims since first

SARS Death Toll Approaching 800

Since severe acute respiratory syndrome (SARS) first appeared in China last fall, at least 8,464 people have been infected, and 799 of them have died. Most cases occurred in China; cases elsewhere have been linked to persons who had recently traveled to Asia.

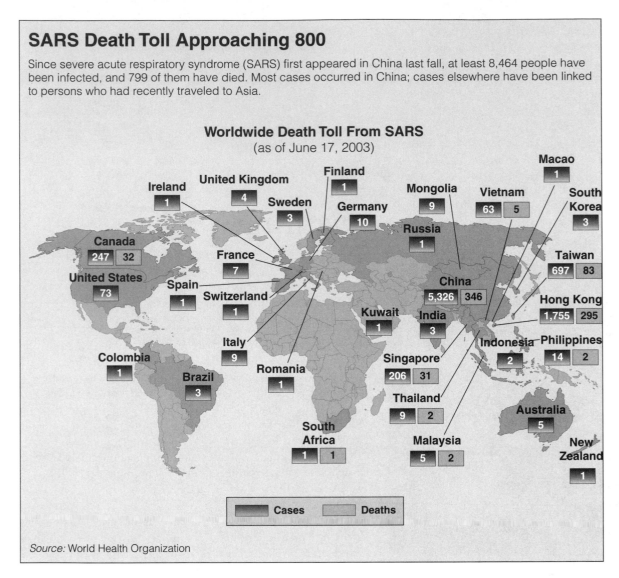

Worldwide Death Toll From SARS
(as of June 17, 2003)

Source: World Health Organization

erupting in Sudan and Zaire in 1976, SARS is a new disease with no known vaccine or cure.

Public-health experts, who have long complained about inadequate funding in the United States, see the SARS outbreak as a wake-up call. "Public health is being asked to do more with less," Georges Benjamin, executive director of the American Public Health Association (APHA), told a congressional subcommittee in May.

Benjamin notes the Bush administration's proposed budget for fiscal 2004 would cut funding for the Centers for Disease Control and Prevention (CDC) by 8.5 per-

cent from its current level of $7.1 billion. "We believe that far more significant investments in public health will need to occur if we are to prepare the nation's public-health system to protect us from the leading causes of death, prepare us for bioterrorism and chemical terrorism and respond to the public-health crises of the day," Benjamin said. "We will always be one plane ride away, one infected person away and one epidemic away from a global tragedy."[2]

In addition, health experts worry that Americans may not be willing to accept quarantines and other drastic measures needed to stop a SARS epidemic in the United States. Some also say the World Health Organization (WHO) should have the power to intervene in any country that fails to take appropriate action in an infectious outbreak.

The main symptoms of SARS—initially a low-grade fever, followed by a dry cough and difficulty breathing—are also typical of pneumonia, making it difficult to diagnose quickly. On average, SARS kills about 15 percent of the people who contract it, but the fatality rate varies greatly by age: While children tend to have mild symptoms, SARS kills most of its victims over 60.

The disease is extremely contagious, especially in patients like Mr. P, known as "superspreaders." Mr. P and several highly contagious patients have infected far more people than is typical of other respiratory infections. "It's astounding that we don't have 80,000 or 800,000 cases of SARS, instead of 8,000," says Anthony S. Fauci, director of the National Institute of Allergy and Infectious Diseases in Bethesda, Md.

The SARS epidemic demonstrates both the best and the worst of the state of global public health. In China, where most cases have occurred, a precious opportunity to contain SARS was lost when health officials ignored for months reports that a virulent form of pneumonia was spreading in the southern province of Guangdong. By the time news of the outbreak reached infectious-disease agencies in other countries and WHO, which tracks global disease outbreaks, SARS had spread far beyond China's borders.*

"Clearly, the initial response in China left much to be desired," Benjamin says. "No one really knows what their motives were, but it certainly did not help at all and in some ways limited the capacity to contain this thing early on."

---

* Proposals to prevent a repeat of China's inaction on SARS were on the agenda for a WHO-sponsored global SARS conference scheduled for June 17-18 in Malaysia.

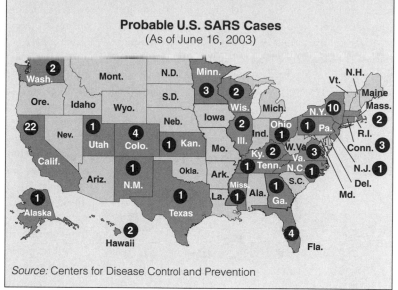

U.S. Has Had 73 SARS Cases, No Deaths

No one has died among the 73 people in the United States who have been infected with SARS, mostly recent visitors to Asia or Toronto. California has reported the highest number of cases.

Probable U.S. SARS Cases
(As of June 16, 2003)

Source: Centers for Disease Control and Prevention

On the positive side, the international scientific community—aided by the Internet, advances in medical research and an increasingly collaborative worldwide network of laboratories—quickly began trying to identify the new microbe and searching for diagnostic tests, vaccines and treatments. WHO and disease-control agencies around the world, including the U.S. Centers for Disease Control and Prevention (CDC) and National Institutes of Health (NIH), have taken the lead role in coordinating the assault on the disease.

"There are, from our perspective in Toronto, almost no good things to be said about SARS," said Allison McGeer, director of infection control at Toronto's Mt. Sinai Hospital. "The one good thing to be said about it is the phenomenal degree of collaboration and willingness to help among clinicians, epidemiologists and researchers around the world."[3]

Once they had determined that SARS was a distinct, new disease, scientists took just two weeks to identify the microbe as a novel form of coronavirus—similar to two relatively benign microbes that cause the common cold—and another two weeks to sequence its genome. By comparison, in the mid-1980s it took more than two years for scientists to identify the human immuno-deficiency virus (HIV), the microbe that causes AIDS, and more than two years to sequence its genome.

"Think about how long it took us to figure out the AIDS virus, or for that matter legionella in 1976 and the hantavirus outbreak in New Mexico and Arizona just a couple of years ago," says Murray Lumpkin, principal associate commissioner of the Food and Drug Administration (FDA). "Once people began working on SARS, they came up with the coronavirus in a matter of weeks. The technology and the epidemiology were absolutely wonderful."

SARS actually has given U.S. health officials another reason to be pleased: There have been only 73 probable SARS cases in the United States—and no SARS-related deaths. "Toronto could just as easily have been Los Angeles or Chicago," Lumpkin says. "It just happened that Toronto is where the infected people landed." Thirty-two people have died from SARS in Canada so far.

While luck may help explain why the U.S. was spared a major SARS outbreak, experts also credit a heightened awareness of the infectious-disease threat in U.S. hospitals since the anthrax attacks that killed five people in the fall of 2001.

"Bioterrorism has been a catalyst for many different efforts in public health that are critical to diagnosing and catching all types of emerging conditions, whether they are introduced intentionally or not," says James G. Hodge Jr., deputy director of the Center for Law and the Public's Health at Johns Hopkins and Georgetown universities. "One of the things about SARS that is very consistent with a bioterrorist attack is that we don't know when it's going to happen. Also, we can't predict exactly how it's going to spread until we know more about the disease. In any event, the tools that we would use during a bioterrorist attack are the same ones that we'd use in response to SARS."

But heightened preparedness hasn't made the United States invulnerable to a deadly outbreak by a previously unknown agent like SARS. "I can imagine someone sitting for eight hours in an ER [emergency room] at a hospital before anybody figures out that they have a pneumonia that could really cause havoc," says Barry R. Bloom, dean of Harvard University's School of Public Health. "I would hope that that possibility is much reduced, but it's not out of the question."

Some public-health experts say the attention given to SARS is overblown, especially in light of a recent decline in the number of new cases worldwide. Compared with the world's big killers, SARS is a blip on the radar screen that distracts attention and precious resources from more lethal threats, they argue. "Our zero-sum approach to infectious-disease control means that resources are drawn away from big killers that do not rock international markets or inconvenience tourist itineraries," wrote Paul Farmer, a professor of medical anthropology at Harvard Medical School, noting that tuberculosis, AIDS and malaria kill 6 million people a year in the developing world.[4]

But those involved in the fight against SARS reject such criticism. "A blip on the radar screen is 25 cases of Ebola in Africa that go nowhere," says Fauci of the National Institute of Allergy and Infectious Diseases. "We don't know how bad SARS is going to get. How well we'll be able to control it will depend on public-health mea-

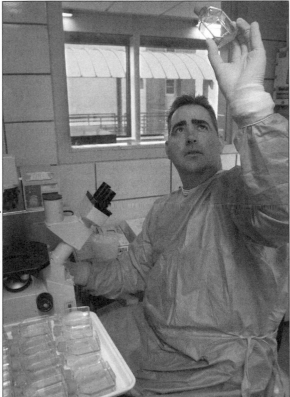

A Centers for Disease Control worker examines a container used in SARS research. Researchers think the virus originated in civets and raccoon dogs—wild animals considered delicacies in southern China—and jumped to humans working in live-animal markets.

sures, luck and the development of vaccines and drugs. Thirty countries involved with 8,000 cases is not a blip on the radar screen. This is an international epidemic."

Fauci and many infectious-disease experts who gathered on May 30 for an NIH-sponsored conference on SARS research worry that the recent decline of new cases may be temporary, and that SARS may become an endemic seasonal disease, like influenza, that will return with a vengeance this winter.

As lawmakers hold hearings to determine how to prepare for a possible SARS outbreak in the United States, these are some of the questions they are asking:

Should WHO intervene in countries that fail to halt the spread of infectious diseases?

In 1948, soon after the United Nations itself was created, it established WHO to improve public health throughout the world. Based in Geneva, Switzerland, WHO monitors infectious diseases and helps national health agencies combat epidemics. The agency also issues travel advisories to areas with active infectious-disease outbreaks, as it did at the height of the SARS epidemics in China, Taiwan and Canada.

But WHO lacks enforcement powers, so it cannot dispatch health professionals to the site of potential public-health threats without the consent of the host country.

"WHO [can] monitor situations and put political pressure on countries to engage in responsible behavior, like they've done with China," says Hodge of the Center for Law and the Public's Health. "What they can't do—and what U.S. public-health authorities can do in the states— is go into a country like China and implement their own protective measures. They have no enforcement powers whatsoever." For many years, WHO's limited authority wasn't a big problem. Advances in medical technology, including the widespread use of vaccines and antibiotics— as well as improved sanitation and education in much of the world—helped the agency carry out its mission.

But globalization has brought changes that threaten WHO's ability to protect public health. While the expansion of world trade and international air travel, for example, has boosted economies worldwide, it also has greatly expanded the reach of potentially virulent microbes. Germs that once may have existed harmlessly in remote areas can now reach new habitats oceans away aboard container ships or in the blood of seemingly healthy travelers. Consequently, some critics of the global public-health sys-

tem say a more aggressive approach is needed to halt the spread of infectious diseases like SARS.[5]

"We live in an age where we're just not used to infectious diseases anymore," says David Gratzer, a Toronto physician and senior fellow at the Manhattan Institute, a conservative think tank in New York City. "If there is an outbreak in Asia today, it is very relevant to North America. Based on the SARS experience in Toronto, the best bet is to prevent the damned virus from crossing the Pacific in the first place. As soon as there's an outbreak, the overwhelming concern should be to see that the virus [does] not come here."

But, Gratzer says, WHO is not up to that task because not all of its members are willing to accept the economic and political consequences of owning up to a major disease outbreak in their own backyard. Leading health officials in China and Taiwan were fired for trying to cover up their SARS outbreaks, and all countries with significant SARS cases are paying a heavy price in lost trade and tourism revenues. (*See sidebar, p. 352.*)

"Countries have to reliably and honestly report [outbreaks]," Gratzer says. "WHO simply has too much of an honor-based system, and there's just no honor to be found in countries like China and scores of others."

That makes it imperative, he adds, for the government to "aggressively screen passengers for disease symptoms in our airports and theirs," ensuring that the screening is "up to our standards."

Some health experts say a new international treaty is needed to empower WHO to intervene in countries that don't report potential threats to global public health. A strengthened WHO could send teams of epidemiologists and clinicians to isolate and eradicate a disease outbreak before it spreads, just as weapons inspectors from the International Atomic Energy Agency investigate allegations that a member country has violated arms-control agreements. "Currently, the WHO can rely only on moral suasion," wrote Jerome Groopman, a professor of medicine at Harvard Medical School. "This is not a dependable lever to consistently move authoritarian governments. We need new agreements around public health similar to those [involving] nuclear, chemical and biological weapons."[6]

Under Groopman's proposal, countries that provided timely data on a communicable disease and unrestrained access for health inspectors would receive financial and logistical aid to stem the outbreak. Those that covered up an outbreak or blocked efforts to halt it would be held liable for the resulting economic and human costs.[7]

Hodge is among the experts who say a treaty to strengthen WHO would be rejected as a threat to national sovereignty, and not only by authoritarian governments like China. "Imagine WHO coming into a state out West and making decisions for the state authorities there," says Hodge of the Center for Law and the Public's Health. "I don't think that's going to fly in the United States, and if it won't fly here, how should we expect it to fly in less-developed countries?"

Gratzer also places little hope on the ability of a treaty to enhance WHO's authority. "Most international treaty negotiations stall," he says. In the absence of such a treaty, Gratzer calls for a "coalition of the healthy"—named after the "coalition of the willing" that joined the United States in its recent war against Iraq—to take matters into their own hands. "We need a coalition of the healthy who simply state that if you don't disclose early and effectively and honestly your outbreak to the relevant authorities, you're going to be slapped with huge sanctions, and you're going to bleed economically."

Would Americans accept draconian measures to stop the spread of a deadly epidemic?

Once China acknowledged the scope of the SARS outbreak, the government—and other affected countries—imposed rigorous measures to contain the virus, including quarantining and isolating thousands of people.

Isolation, a less-drastic measure, involves separating infected patients from healthy people and other patients in a hospital setting. With highly infectious diseases like SARS, patients ideally should be placed in rooms with negative airflow to prevent the spread of the virus on airborne droplets released when a patient coughs. Doctors and nurses—who have proved especially vulnerable to infection from SARS patients—should be gowned and masked at all times.

Quarantine, a more radical—and controversial—measure, isolates healthy people who may have been exposed to an infectious disease during its incubation period (the time from exposure to onset of the disease)—10 days, on average, for SARS. Authoritarian governments may encounter little resistance to quarantine, which generally requires individuals to stay at home. Indeed, Vietnam won praise for quickly suppressing its SARS outbreak last month, largely through rigorous isolation and quarantine.

"In [authoritarian] regimes, it's not that big a leap for a government to isolate and quarantine people," says Abraham Verghese, director of the Center for Medical Humanities and Ethics at the University of Texas Health Science Center in San Antonio. "People expect the government to be heavy-handed."

Even in more open societies, like Canada, public outcry over mandatory quarantines to contain SARS has been minimal. But some experts are concerned about how Americans would react to tough measures.

"Canadians are a lot less combative and a lot more civil about these sorts of things," says Toronto physician Gratzer. Even so, he recalls that enough Canadians broke quarantine during a smallpox outbreak in Montreal during the 1880s to spark an epidemic that killed 6,000 of the city's 100,000 inhabitants. Some Canadians also reportedly broke their SARS quarantine in recent weeks.[8] And Toronto authorities warned potential violators they would, if necessary, be "chained to a bed" to keep them away from the community.[9]

"Even when you have civic-minded people like Canadians, quarantine and isolation are pretty weak and blunt instruments to use," Gratzer says. In the United States, he predicted, "There's going to be one person who will use his right to go to the shopping mall and infect everyone there."

Exercising that right can have catastrophic results. In 1915, Irish immigrant Mary Mallon broke quarantine to return to work in New York City, only to be arrested and imprisoned.[10] Typhoid Mary, as she was better known, was blamed for spreading typhoid fever to household members where she worked as a cook.

"Quarantine has always been problematic because it takes away individual rights for the larger benefit of the community," Verghese says. "But if there is a major outbreak in this country, people will understand, even though those being quarantined will have a hard time with it." A recent poll supports that view.[11]

Scores of Americans, in fact, already have undergone voluntary quarantine in the 25 states with reported SARS cases. (*See map, p. 343.*) "Every identified case of SARS has gone through some level of isolation, and contacts of those persons have gone through some level of quarantine, and the response that most Americans provide in relation to these measures is very positive," says Hodge of the Center for Law and the Public's Health. "People are rational, and they recognize that isolation

U.S. Privacy Rules Hide SARS Details

When a Canadian man was discharged June 3 from an Arkansas hospital after recovering from possible SARS, the state health department refused to identify the city, county or even the region of the state where the hospital was located—or the man's whereabouts before he got sick.

Officials would say only that they had contacted health agencies in areas where the man may have been before he checked into the hospital on May 22 and that those agencies were responsible for investigating any potential exposures to the deadly respiratory disease.[1]

In contrast, the names, gender, ages and hometowns of many SARS victims in Canada, Asia and elsewhere are common knowledge. Strict new U.S. patient-privacy rules account for the difference. The new rules—enacted as part of the 1996 Health Insurance Portability and Accountability Act, or HIPAA—went into effect on April 14, just as SARS cases began appearing in the United States.

Patient-privacy rights became a prominent issue in the United States in the 1980s, when the AIDS epidemic sparked such widespread panic that infected children were barred from school, and HIV-positive adults suffered discrimination, even after it was found that the virus was not transmissible through casual contact.

The HIPAA rules prohibit hospitals, doctors' offices, health plans and other entities that have access to individuals' health records from disclosing information in those records to anyone without that person's permission. Only public-health agencies have the right to the protected information in case of outbreaks of infectious diseases like tuberculosis, influenza and SARS.

But some state health agencies have interpreted HIPAA's mandate more strictly than others. For example, while Colorado, Massachusetts and Florida have released the age and gender of suspected SARS cases, and their counties of residence, others—including South Carolina and Arkansas—have not. Some concerned citizens argue that the secrecy violates their right to protect themselves and their families. "I'd like to see more information . . . to take every precaution to prevent it if possible," said Sam Turner, a resident of Greer, S.C. "Currently, it is possible my family has been exposed, and I wouldn't know because of information being withheld."[2]

But defenders of the new rules say they serve a dual purpose. "It's ethical to preserve patient anonymity, and it's ethical to not foster panic by not naming a city or locale," says Abraham Verghese, director of the Center for Medical Humanities and Ethics at the University of Texas Health Science Center in San Antonio.

Nevertheless, he adds, "I imagine that if a hospital in a given city had a major spread of the disease, that would not be something that they could or would keep quiet."

---

[1] See Greg Giuffrida, "Probable SARS Patient Recovered, Discharged," The Associated Press State and Local Wire, June 4, 2003.

[2] See Liv Osby, "State's SARS Secrecy Angers Some," *The Greenville* [South Carolina] *News,* April 27, 2003, p. 15A.

---

and quarantine, so long as it's as minimal as necessary and responsibly enforced in a way that's as non-intrusive as possible, will protect their families and friends from potential exposure, which is important to most people." Because people in quarantine receive close monitoring for possible signs of disease, Hodge says, "They also recognize that it's protecting themselves."

Hodge acknowledges that some Americans have resisted quarantine, including a Wisconsin man who balked at being questioned about his possible contacts with a SARS patient. "The authorities did have to call him in and basically sit him down and ask some critical questions of him," Hodge says. "So enforcement could be implemented very strongly if necessary to prevent a threat to the public's health. But in 99 percent of the cases, people adhere to isolation and quarantine measures because they know it's important for their own good to do so."

To deal with the 1 percent of Americans who might resist quarantine, President Bush recently signed an executive order authorizing immigration and customs agents at U.S. international airports to detain arriving passengers with SARS symptoms. In addition, federal and state laws authorize public-health officials to enforce isolation and quarantine. Even today, tuberculosis patients are routinely hospitalized against their will when they resist isolation and quarantine orders.

"It happens frequently enough that every health officer probably has experienced it," the APHA's Benjamin says. Nonetheless, he cautions that quarantine measures alone are unlikely to stop a massive SARS outbreak. "Apart from cabin fever, people break quarantine and isolation because provisions haven't been made for them to pick up their kids from school, deal with their job or shop for food," he says. "A social-support system must go with any kind of quarantine activity."

Can the public-health system protect Americans from infectious diseases?

Seventy-three people in half the states have contracted SARS—but no one has died from the disease. Health officials credit the zero-fatality rate to prompt medical attention. Moreover, officials say the United States has thus far escaped a full-blown SARS epidemic because rigorous isolation and quarantine measures were implemented.

Experts say the nation's brush with bioterrorism in 2001—when a series of anthrax-laden letters killed five Americans—helped prepare the country for SARS. "We are much more prepared than ever before about odd things walking into the ER," says Bloom of the Harvard School of Public Health. "There have been rehearsals, and there's been training on all the major bioterrorism agents, so the docs who work at the front line are looking for things."

Indeed, Bloom says, the anthrax letters turned traditional clinical training on its head. "The theory used to be that if you hear hoofbeats, don't think zebras," he says, citing a recent line by bioterrorism expert Margaret Hamburg, vice president for biological programs at the Nuclear Threat Initiative. "Now the thinking is, If you hear hoof-beats, first rule out zebras. That's a complete change in mentality, and while I regret that it took bioterrorism to force it upon us, it's paying off today in the face of SARS."

Bloom worries, however, that the public-health system is being stretched thin, especially the CDC. "They have up to 500 people running all around the world working on SARS," he says. But that means 500 fewer people are working on other potential disease threats, he notes, because they have been reassigned to the SARS epidemic. To make matters worse, Congress cut the CDC's current budget for most infectious diseases by $10.5 million, he complains.

"That's just crazy," Bloom says. "At a time when we're worried about bioterrorism and emerging infections—as we ought to be—that's not the place the government should be saving money."

A recent Institute of Medicine report supports Bloom's concerns about U.S. preparedness. "The prevention and control of infectious diseases are fundamental to individual, national and global security," the report concluded. "Failure to recognize—and act on—this essential truth will surely lead to disaster. We must therefore continue to trumpet a message of urgency and concern."[12]

The General Accounting Office (GAO) also has found that preparedness for a major outbreak varies dramatically across the country. "[M]ost hospitals across the country lack the capacity to respond to large-scale infectious-disease outbreaks," the GAO reported. "Most emergency departments have experienced some degree of crowding and therefore in some cases may not be able to handle a large influx of patients during a potential SARS or other infectious-disease outbreak."[13]

Experts say the public-health system suffers primarily from inadequate funding. Last year, Congress allocated $940 million to help local health departments cope with emerging threats, including bioterrorism and naturally occurring infectious-disease outbreaks.[14] But essential public-health agencies have seen their budgets cut: The Bush administration would cut the CDC's funding by 8.5 percent in fiscal 2004.

"We can achieve a lot more in public health if we're willing to pay for it," Hodge says. "But right now, we're not, and as a nation we've suffered the consequences." Heart disease and cancer, for example, kill far more people in the United States than infectious diseases, Hodge points out. "We deal with chronic diseases in the United States as if these were acceptable outcomes," he says, "because the public health community just is not equipped with the financial resources to prevent preventable causes of morbidity and mortality."

The lack of universal health insurance also undermines the public-health system, health advocates say, because it puts the nation's 41 million uninsured people at greatest risk if a deadly epidemic broke out in the United States.

"People are now beginning to recognize that the lack of universal health-care coverage is a major security issue in this country," says Benjamin of the APHA. "If you have insurance and you think you have SARS, you can call your doctor, who will arrange for the hospital to get you into an isolation room. But if you don't have health insurance and you show up unannounced at the ER, they won't be prepared for you, and they won't want you there because you're terribly contagious.

"This is not about not having the money," Benjamin concludes. "This is about priorities. We're now the only industrialized nation in the world without universal coverage."

BACKGROUND

Early Response

Infectious diseases have been a major scourge throughout human history and today account for about one in five deaths around the world. Early in the history of the United States, periodic epidemics of cholera, smallpox, yellow fever and other microbial diseases left tens of thousands of victims in their wake.

Before scientists discovered how germs spread disease, poor sanitary conditions in rapidly growing cities provided fertile breeding grounds for bacteria and viruses; animals also spread disease, like the mosquito that carries yellow fever.

Early Americans realized that epidemics tended to break out at ports of entry, where arriving slave ships introduced smallpox and yellow fever to North America. In 1796, New York passed the nation's first state public-health statute, which authorized offshore quarantine of passengers and crew aboard infected ships and on-shore "pest houses" to isolate the sick. Following a yellow-fever outbreak, Congress followed suit in 1798 by creating the U.S. Marine Health Service to extend port-quarantine authority throughout the country.[15]

The American public readily accepted quarantine—usually imposed on newly arrived immigrants and the urban poor—but it balked at mass immunization. In 1796, Edward Jenner, an English physician, discovered that exposing healthy individuals to material from cowpox pustules protected them from deadly smallpox.[16]

But the nation's first compulsory-vaccination law did not pass until 1850, when Providence, R.I., required all schoolchildren to receive smallpox inoculations. And resistance to vaccines persisted in the United States, even after 1905, when the U.S. Supreme Court ruled in *Jacobson v. Massachusetts* that the need to protect the public health outweighed the rights of individuals to reject a medical procedure.[17]

The link between then-invisible germs and disease—first advanced by France's Louis Pasteur in 1862—prompted slow but measurable improvements in public health, as communities across the United States adopted sanitation measures to prevent the spread of disease. But advances in public health faced several lasting obstacles during the 19th century. Unlike most other industrializing nations, where central governments assumed leading roles in health care, public health in the United States evolved primarily as a local or state responsibility.

Meanwhile, the U.S. medical establishment jealously guarded the primacy of the individual doctor's role in health care to a greater extent than in Europe, resulting in a greater focus on treating individuals than on government policies aimed at improving health conditions of the public as a whole. Today's absence of national health insurance, a basic benefit in other industrial nations, grew out of that fundamental difference in focus.

"Friction between healers and preventers, between . . . independent doctors and government regulators would form [a] lasting theme of American public health," wrote journalist Laurie Garrett in a history of public health. "Not only was there no genuine federal leadership in public health in 19th-century America, few states had laws and policies that extended to all of their counties and cities."[18]

Fueled by the Industrial Revolution, the U.S. economy grew rapidly, bringing notable improvements in public health, as communities drained mosquito-infested swamps, built sewers, improved drinking water and cleaned streets of sewage and rubbish. As a result, death rates from such major killers as yellow fever, smallpox and cholera fell.

As immigration increased rapidly in the late 19th century, the federal government also expanded its public-health role to include the processing of immigrants at Ellis Island and other facilities. In recognition of its growing role, which also included supervising national quarantines and investigating epidemics, the old Marine Health Service was renamed the Public Health Service in 1912.[19]

But public-health advances had some unintended consequences. Clean water deprived infants of small immunizing doses of the virus that causes polio, leaving the population unprotected when the crippling microbe infected water supplies during several hot summers in the early 1900s. In 1916 polio, or infantile paralysis, erupted in the first of a series of epidemics that would continue until effective vaccines appeared in the early 1950s.

But the most alarming sign that the public was still vulnerable to deadly microbes despite advances in public health came in 1918: The first of three waves of Spanish

CHRONOLOGY

1900s-1920s *U.S. public-health system emerges.*

1905 U.S. Supreme Court rules in *Jacobson v. Massachusetts* that protecting public health outweighs the rights of individuals to reject a medical procedure.

1915 Mary Mallon—"Typhoid Mary"—is imprisoned after breaking quarantine in New York City and spreading typhoid fever.

1918-20 Spanish influenza sweeps the globe, killing 20-50 million people, including 675,000 in the United States.

1925 Geneva Protocol bans the use of chemical and bacteriological weapons.

1930s-1970s *Antibiotics and vaccines advance the war against infectious diseases.*

1932 Scottish scientist Alexander Fleming discovers penicillin, the first of a new class of drugs called antibiotics, which kill a vast range of microbes that cause such scourges as tuberculosis and syphilis.

1946 U.S. Communicable Disease Center (CDC) is set up in Atlanta to combat malaria, then prevalent in the South.

April 7, 1948 U. N. affiliated World Health Organization (WHO) is founded in Geneva, Switzerland.

1951 U.S. schoolchildren receive polio vaccine developed by American researcher Jonas Salk. After 200 kids develop polio from a faulty batch of vaccine, a safer oral vaccine developed by American Albert Sabin is adopted in 1961.

1963 Measles vaccine is introduced and later (1969) combined with vaccines against rubella and mumps.

1968 Outbreak of Hong Kong flu, the latest in a series of periodic influenza epidemics, prompts the development of annual flu vaccines.

Jan. 22, 1975 President Gerald R. Ford ratifies the 1925 Geneva Protocol and the 1972 Biological and Toxin Weapons Convention.

1976 Ebola hemorrhagic fever, a deadly emerging viral disease, breaks out in Sudan and Zaire. Another new microbe causes Legionnaire's disease in the United States.

1980s-2000s *Emerging infectious diseases defy modern medicine.*

1980 CDC is renamed the Centers for Disease Control.

June 15, 1981 CDC reports the appearance of what will later be identified as acquired immunodeficiency syndrome—AIDS—a new disease that will kill more than 20 million people by the end of the century.

1992 CDC is renamed the Centers for Disease Control and Prevention.

2000 Fatal brain disorder is linked to the consumption of tainted British beef. "Mad cow disease" kills more than 130 people, mainly in Britain, before it is contained.

October 2001 Anonymous letters containing anthrax spores kill five people in the United States a month after the Sept. 11 terrorist attacks.

Nov. 16, 2002 First known case of severe acute respiratory syndrome—SARS—is reported in Guangdong Province, in southern China, but health authorities cover up the new disease.

January 2003 President Bush announces Project Bioshield, calling for spending $5.6 billion over 10 years on tests, drugs and vaccines to defend against bioterrorism.

March 5, 2003 An elderly Toronto woman dies of SARS after returning from Hong Kong, unleashing the disease's biggest outbreak outside Asia.

March 25, 2003 CDC tentatively identifies the microbe responsible for SARS as similar to the coronavirus that causes the common cold.

May 22, 2003 Toronto suffers a second SARS outbreak.

June 17-18, 2003 WHO holds the first global conference on SARS, in Malaysia.

influenza swept the globe in a three-year pandemic that killed 20-50 million people—675,000 in the United States. From the first cases, which appeared at Camp Funston, an Army base in Kansas, the highly contagious flu traveled to Europe aboard vessels carrying American soldiers to World War I battlefields, to Spain where the flu's high death rate gave the disease its name, and throughout most of the rest of the world.

Although Spanish flu's fatality rate was only 2.5 percent—low for a major killer—the disease's near-global reach made it the deadliest plague in history.[20]

Technology Prevails

The first half of the 20th century saw rapid advances in the battle against infectious diseases with the exception of a resurgence related to poverty during the Great Depression of the 1930s. The discovery of penicillin in 1932 by Scottish scientist Alexander Fleming introduced antibiotics, a new class of drugs that kill bacteria—a vast range of microbes that cause such scourges as tuberculosis, syphilis, streptococcal pneumonia and typhoid fever.

Thanks to some 36,000 antibiotic products developed by the early 1950s, the incidence of tuberculosis plummeted by 91 percent between 1944 and 1970, while the death rate from pneumonia dropped 40 percent from 1936 to 1945.[21]

The broad support for multilateral institutions that arose from the ashes of World War II encompassed not only economic policy (the creation of the World Bank and the International Monetary Fund) and international relations (the U.N.) but also public health. On April 7, 1948, the U.N.'s World Health Organization was created to achieve the best health standards "for every human being without distinction of race, religion, political belief or economic or social condition." The organization's constitution went on to warn that "unequal development in the promotion of health and control of disease" is a "common danger" for all.

In 1946, a new U.S. Public Health Service agency was created, the Communicable Disease Center. (It was renamed the Centers for Disease Control in 1980 and the Centers for Disease Control and Prevention in 1992.) The Atlanta-based CDC was charged with helping states and localities combat malaria, then prevalent in the South.

But the expansion of the Public Health Service masked an unseen problem. While the antibiotics revolution brought dramatic improvements in public health,

Workers in Beijing disinfect the waiting room of a deserted railway station in the fight against SARS, on May 25. The disease reportedly has decimated tourism in China, where more than half of the 8,500 SARS cases have occurred.

it undermined, ironically, the public-health sector itself, at least in the United States. Armed with pills to cure infectious diseases, private practitioners and hospitals came to dominate the field of medicine, relegating preventive medicine to secondary status.

"The bacteriological revolution had played itself out in the organization of public services, and soon the introduction of antibiotics and other drugs would enable private physicians to reclaim some of their functions, like the treatment of venereal disease and tuberculosis," wrote sociologist Paul Starr. "Yet it had been clear, long before, that public health in America was to be relegated to a secondary status: less prestigious than clinical medicine, less amply financed and blocked from assuming the higher-level functions of coordination and direction that might have developed had it not been banished from medical care."[22]

Viruses—much smaller than bacteria and harder to identify and combat—were unaffected by antibiotic "magic bullets" like penicillin. Such viral killers as polio, measles and influenza continued unchecked until vaccines made from attenuated live viruses or killed viruses were developed.*

In 1955, schoolchildren across the country received the first polio vaccine developed by Jonas Salk, an American

---

* Vaccines introduce just enough viral material into the body to trigger the production of antibodies to the targeted disease. The antibodies recognize and kill the virus during subsequent exposure.

SARS Sickens Global Economy

The SARS epidemic appears to be on the wane, but it continues to afflict the global economy. China, where more than half of the 8,460 SARS cases have occurred, has been especially hard hit.

Tourism and exports of consumer goods, the mainstay of China's economy, reportedly have plummeted, although few reliable statistics are available. Likewise, imports of electronics and other consumer goods have declined as fearful Chinese consumers have shunned shopping centers where such items normally are sold.

The falloff in Chinese sales has prompted cell-phone makers, like Finland's Nokia Corp. and Motorola Inc. of Illinois, to downgrade their growth forecasts.[1]

But SARS has given a lift to some economic sectors in China. Auto and bicycle retailers, for example, have enjoyed a small boom in sales from consumers wishing to avoid crowded trains and buses.[2]

SARS dominated the agenda at the 21-nation Asia-Pacific Economic Cooperation (APEC) conference in Thailand this month. The hardest-hit places outside China reportedly are nearby Hong Kong, Singapore and Taiwan, whose tourism- and export-driven economies are expected to shrink by 1-2 percentage points this year.[3] Retail sales in Hong Kong have dropped by 15 percent from last year, as residents have stayed away from shops and their jobs, and tourists have avoided the island altogether.

Even Australia—which has reported only five cases and no deaths from SARS—reported an 8 percent drop in export earnings in April, as tourists from SARS-affected Asian countries stayed home.

Beyond Asia, Canada has suffered the greatest economic fallout from SARS. In Toronto, where nearly all Canada's cases have occurred, nearly empty hotels and restaurants are slashing prices to lure tourists back.

"We usually get a lot of American tourists over Memorial Day—a holiday for you but not for us—but not this year," says David Gratzer, a Toronto physician. "The hotels are now running at about 20 percent capacity."

But, again, some industries stand to turn a profit from the outbreak. Drug and biotechnology firms are scurrying to be the first to develop diagnostic tests, vaccines and treatments for the new disease. Even before the World Health Organization confirmed that a novel coronavirus causes SARS, Artus GmbH—a small German biotechnology start-up—began supplying the first commercial test for the virus.[4]

Public and private laboratories, meanwhile, are rushing to patent the SARS virus. A private company could use such a patent to claim ownership of the virus itself and its component parts—assets that could produce a windfall if the disease spreads. The U.S. Centers for Disease Control and Prevention (CDC) itself is seeking the patent in order to keep the virus in the public domain. "The whole purpose of the patent is to prevent folks from controlling the technology," said CDC spokesman Llelwyn Grant. "This is being done to give the industry and other researchers reasonable access to the samples."[5]

Like other dread diseases, SARS has already ignited a flurry of hoaxes and folk remedies to ward off infection. In remote areas of China, people have set off firecrackers to fend off infection, and markets abound with herbs and roots said to confer immunity from SARS.

In the United States, the Food and Drug Administration (FDA) has warned at least eight individuals to halt false advertising for remedies they claim will protect against SARS. "We've been going after people who are out there touting all kinds of fraudulent products as protection from SARS," says Murray Lumpkin, the FDA's principal associate commissioner. "Their claims are totally unsubstantiated. It's nothing less than health fraud."

[1] See "Nokia Issues Sales Warning as SARS Impacts Industry," *The Wall Street Journal Online,* June 10, 2003.

[2] See "Economic Impact of New Disease, from Near Outbreak to Far Away," *The New York Times,* May 18, 2003, p. A12.

[3] See Jenny Paris, "APEC Will Focus on Impact of Disease on Flow of Goods," *Dow Jones Newswires,* June 2, 2003.

[4] See Vanessa Fuhrmans, "Agile Artus Sees Profit in Test to Detect SARS," *The Wall Street Journal Online,* June 10, 2003.

[5] Quoted in "SARS: Race to Patent Virus Renews Debate over 'Patents on Life'," NewsRx.com.

researcher. After 220 children contracted the disease through faulty vaccine production—Salk's vaccine used a killed virus vaccine, but the manufacturing lab failed to kill the viruses—a safer oral vaccine developed in 1961 by Albert Sabin, another American, became the standard polio vaccine.

Within the next couple of decades, some of the most dreaded childhood diseases virtually disappeared from the industrial world. By 1990, vaccines for measles (introduced in 1963) and rubella and mumps (1969) had helped reduce the incidence of vaccine-preventable childhood diseases to 0.1 percent of all deaths in the United States, Western Europe and Japan.[23]

Meanwhile, despite the persistence of influenza epidemics—such as the 1957 Asian flu and the 1968 Hong Kong flu—the development of annual flu vaccines kept up with the virus' rapid mutation rate and reduced the disease's impact.

As microbes played a decreasing role in illness and death in the industrial world, the medical establishment virtually declared victory over infectious diseases and turned its attention to such chronic killers as cancer and heart disease.

New Diseases

Technology's seeming triumph over infectious diseases proved illusory. On June 15, 1981, the CDC's weekly report of global disease patterns reported the appearance of a mysterious illness that would become the leading infectious scourge of the late 20th century. Two years later, scientists identified the human immunodeficiency virus (HIV) as the cause of acquired immune deficiency syndrome, or AIDS.

But despite a multimillion-dollar research effort and the development of advanced antiviral drugs, modern

Basic Facts About SARS

Symptoms

- Fever greater than 100.4° F
- Headache
- Overall feeling of discomfort
- Body aches
- Mild respiratory symptoms
- Dry cough, trouble breathing

Timeline

- After seven days of illness, patients tend either to get better or have increasingly severe respiratory stress; death occurs after four or five weeks in 15 percent of patients. The disease kills more than half of its victims over 60.
- Virus can survive outside the body on ordinary surfaces for 16 days.

Who's at Risk?

- Travelers returning from countries where SARS has been reported.
- Health-care workers and family-caregivers in close contact with SARS patients.

How to Avoid SARS

- In SARS-affected areas, wash hands frequently and avoid close contact with large numbers of people.
- Avoid non-essential travel to China, Hong Kong, Taiwan or Singapore; observe precautions when traveling to Hanoi and Toronto.
- Family members caring for SARS patients should follow strict precautions for 10 days after symptoms have passed. Recovered patients should avoid school, work and other public areas for the same period.

Source: U.S. Centers for Disease Control and Prevention.

medicine found no magic bullets to eradicate AIDS. By the late 1990s, the virus had killed nearly 20 million people worldwide—mostly in Africa—and become the leading cause of death among Americans ages 22-45.

Costly drug treatments have since helped prolong the lives of HIV-positive individuals in the developed world, but AIDS remains a leading killer in the Third World, particularly in Africa. While there are recent signs that the AIDS pandemic may be slowing, it is expected to continue devastating Africa, where more than 29 million people have HIV.[24]

Other new diseases—whether through first-time human exposure to existing microbes, new contacts with microbes that have caused disease outbreaks in the past or mutations of those germs—have cropped up at a rate of one a year since the 1960s.[25] Some of the more recent outbreaks in the United States include Legionnaires' disease, tick-borne Lyme disease, hantavirus pulmonary syndrome and mosquito-borne West Nile virus.

Rapid population growth has also brought humans into contact with some particularly lethal microbes. For instance, Ebola and other lethal viruses that cause rapid hemorrhaging and death have broken out in Congo, Gabon and other African countries. Meanwhile, excessive antibiotic use over several decades began to take its toll, as many bacteria—including those that cause tuberculosis and food poisoning—have developed resistance to successive generations of antibiotics.[26]

Modern agricultural practices also have spawned new diseases, some of which have jumped the species barrier, passing from animal hosts to humans. In the mid-1980s, an anomalous form of a naturally occurring particle known as a prion began infecting and killing British cattle that had been fed beef byproducts. The resultant sickness, called mad cow disease, later infected and killed nearly 140 consumers of infected beef, mostly in Britain.[27] Industrial agricultural practices, such as crowding animals in feedlots and aviaries, have also caused periodic animal-to-human flu epidemics, including a 1997 outbreak of avian, or bird, flu in Hong Kong and a new variant that recently erupted in the Netherlands, Belgium and Germany.[28]

At the same time, several old diseases continue to take a heavy toll, especially in the poorest countries. Plague, which killed millions in Europe during the Middle Ages, erupted in India in 1994, killing 50 people. And despite the successful eradication of disease-bearing mosquitoes in much of the world, malaria continues to kill at least 1 million Africans each year, 90 percent of them children under age 5.[29]

Threat of Bioterrorism

Germ warfare, once a staple of warring nations, waned during the 20th century. Appalled at Germany's use of biological and chemical weapons during World War I, the United States and many other countries endorsed the 1925 Geneva Protocol banning the military use of chemical and bacteriological weapons. Concerned that the treaty would limit the wartime use of riot-control agents and pesticides, however, the U.S. Senate deferred action.

Nonetheless, over the next several decades, many countries, including the United States, continued to develop lethal microbes. President Richard M. Nixon unilaterally disbanded the U.S. bioweapons program in 1969, and later signed the 1972 Biological and Toxin Weapons Convention banning the production, stockpiling and use of microbes as weapons. President Gerald R. Ford then proposed that the Senate consider both the Geneva Protocol and the Biological Weapons Convention. The Senate unanimously approved both treaties, which Ford ratified on Jan. 22, 1975.[30]

Evidence that Iraq, Israel, Syria and other countries continued to develop bioweapons in violation of the convention prompted recent efforts to strengthen the bioweapons treaty. But the United States and other industrial countries have balked, saying proposals to enforce the ban through inspections could reveal drug companies' commercial secrets.[31]

In any event, the treaties have failed to prevent nongovernmental belligerents from using deadly germs. In October 2001, just weeks after the Sept. 11, 2001, terrorist attacks on the World Trade Center and the Pentagon, the United States came under another nonconventional attack, this time from envelopes containing deadly anthrax spores. Mailed from a source that continues to elude authorities, the anthrax bacteria killed five people and sickened 13 others.

The Bush administration responded to the anthrax attacks with improvements in the CDC's disease-surveillance and emergency-response systems, while states and localities introduced federally funded programs to improve health-care workers' ability to quickly identify symptoms of rare diseases that could be caused by bioweapons.

CURRENT SITUATION

SARS Outbreak

Many of the factors that caused the resurgence of infectious diseases over the past decades converged when the SARS virus emerged last November.[32] The first person known to have contracted the disease was a man in Foshan, a city in China's Guangdong Province. Five more people died in that initial outbreak.

At that point, public-health experts say, the outbreak could have been contained by imposing isolation and quarantine at the source and alerting WHO and other global public-health agencies.

But China's authoritarian political system discourages the dissemination of bad news; indeed, a 1996 law decreed that highly infectious diseases should be classified top secret.[33] As a result, the outbreak went unacknowledged for months, eliminating the opportunity to isolate and eradicate the infection. It was not until Feb. 10, 2003, that WHO learned of the new disease from Promed, an online service that reports on outbreaks throughout the world. Thus, China not only caused the spread of SARS but also suffered its greatest impact—5,326 infections, including 346 deaths, as of June 17.

On Feb. 21, an infected Chinese doctor, 63-year-old Liu Jianlun, carried the virus to neighboring Hong Kong, where he attended a wedding and spread it to several other visitors at the Metropole Hotel; some of them later carried it to Vietnam, Singapore and Canada. One of the ironies of the SARS epidemic is that a physician was one of the deadliest carriers of the new disease—a so-called superspreader, like Toronto's Mr. P. WHO traces more than half the total number of SARS cases worldwide to Liu, who died in early March. Partly because local authorities failed to initiate isolation and quarantine measures for two weeks after Liu was hospitalized, Hong Kong has had 1,755 SARS cases, including 295 deaths.[34]

Esther Mok, a 26-year-old former flight attendant, was one of three Singaporean women to develop SARS after staying at the Metropole. Most of the other 205 cases in Singapore, including 31 deaths, contracted the illness from Mok, who recovered. Singaporean authorities rapidly quarantined hundreds of people possibly exposed to SARS, enabling them to contain the disease.

Another Metropole visitor, American Johnny Chen, is believed to have spread SARS to Vietnam in late February. Before he died on March 13, Chen spread SARS to 62 people, mostly health-care workers who had treated him at the Hanoi French Hospital; five of them died. Nonetheless, the government's aggressive quarantine measures made Vietnam the first country to contain a SARS outbreak, according to WHO.

Sui-chu Kwan, 78, another Metropole visitor, carried SARS to Canada and became the first SARS death in North America when she died in Toronto on March 5. Her 43-year-old son and caregiver, Chi Kwai Tse, died of SARS on March 13 and is believed to have been the source of most early Canadian cases.

Meanwhile, on March 30, an elderly man died of SARS in Malaysia at Kuala Lumpur Hospital after returning from a vacation in Guangdong. A 26-year-old tour operator, who died on April 22 after visiting China and Thailand, was Malaysia's only other SARS death.

The first person to identify SARS as a distinct disease was Carlo Urbani, 46, a WHO physician hospitalized in Bangkok on March 11 after arriving from Hanoi, where he had been studying Chen's case. Urbani died in Bangkok, one of only two SARS fatalities in Thailand.

SARS returned from North America to Asia with Adela Catalon, 46, a Philippine nursing assistant who flew home from her job at a Toronto retirement home to care for her sick father. Both later died at a Manila hospital.

Taiwan reported its first SARS fatality on April 26, when a 56-year-old man died after visiting his brother in Hong Kong. Since then, 697 people have contracted SARS in Taiwan, and 83 have died. Taiwan blames its high SARS mortality rate on China, which continues to block Taiwan's membership in WHO, because the Chinese say it would be an implicit recognition of the island's independence. The Taiwanese say if Taiwan had been a member of WHO, the health agency could have intervened aggressively to help stop the spread of SARS. But critics blame the Taiwan authorities themselves for failing to control the infection.[35]

SARS Update

By the end of April, after placing some 10,000 people in quarantine, Toronto health officials announced they had contained the outbreak. On April 30, WHO lifted its advisory against travel to Toronto. But two weeks later, city officials announced SARS had returned, perhaps after lying dormant in four local hospitals. Once again, thousands of people were quarantined, and WHO put Toronto back on its list of SARS sites.

"Toronto has been very fortunate in that we've never had a community outbreak," says Gratzer, the Toronto doctor whose hospital has escaped infection with SARS. "It's existed almost entirely in the hospital system. But even though we've been so lucky, it takes a lot to contain a virus like this."

Indeed, besides placing thousands of people under quarantine at once, Toronto health officials shut down two hospitals and discontinued outpatient services for the rest. The outbreak's economic costs, especially to Toronto's tourism industry, are expected to reduce

356 HEALTH AND THE ENVIRONMENT

Canada's second-quarter economic growth by fully 1 percent.

"What we're seeing in Toronto is how a single case can wreak havoc," Gratzer says. "So while we've had it relatively easy, we're finding out how, in an age of jet travel, a problem in Guangdong is a problem in downtown Toronto."

Indeed, on May 22 Toronto suffered yet another SARS outbreak, apparently spread unnoticed before it was known that the virus can survive more than two weeks on surfaces like bedding or doorknobs. On June 10, Canadian health authorities closed a hospital to new patients in Whitby, Ontario, because of a possible new cluster of SARS cases there, the first outside Toronto.

Canada, site of the largest SARS outbreak to take place outside Asia, has reported 247 cases and 32 deaths from the disease.

U.S. Reprieve

The United States, meanwhile, continues to be relatively free of SARS, aside from a few suspected cases in hospital settings. Hospitals and clinics around the country are taking advantage of the reprieve to prepare for a potential future outbreak. Indeed, Benjamin of the American Public Health Association says the global epidemic, coming on the heels of the anthrax and Sept. 11 attacks, provided a needed wake-up call among U.S. health-care workers. "We're better prepared than we were two years ago, though we still have some work to do," he says. "There are some places that have done a lot, others that are just beginning and probably some that still haven't done anything" to prepare for a major disease outbreak.

While many urban hospitals are at the forefront of infectious-disease preparedness, Benjamin says city-dwellers should not necessarily expect to receive better care than those in small towns. "What matters in community preparedness is whether the people at the hospital 'get it' or not," he says. "Before the anthrax attacks, when I talked to health-care professionals about biological terrorism, they thought I was a nice guy but a little wacko. Today there's a lot more interest."

The nation's blood supply is also vulnerable to infectious diseases. Before scientists discovered HIV, the virus infected numerous people who had received transfusions of tainted blood. A less catastrophic contamination occurred last summer, when blood from donors with West Nile virus entered the blood supply.

"We don't know if SARS is blood-borne, but it is a virus, and a lot of viruses are," says Lumpkin of the FDA. To ensure that SARS does not infect the nation's blood supply, the FDA is screening donors for physical symptoms of the disease and questioning them about any recent travel to SARS-affected areas. "If you've been to a SARS-endemic area, you are not allowed to donate blood for 14 days after leaving that area," Lumpkin says. "If you've actually had a diagnosis of SARS, you're required to wait for 28 days after being declared free of the disease."

The FDA also is responsible for ensuring that hospitals have enough medical supplies to cope with a major disease outbreak. "When it comes to fluids, standard drugs and respirators, we're in pretty good shape," Lumpkin says. But some are concerned, he says, that there may not be enough N95 masks—which can block the small SARS viral particles—because there is such a high demand for them in Asia.

Fortunately, the number of SARS cases has continued to decline in most affected countries, though WHO continues to post warnings against unnecessary travel to Taiwan, where a new cluster of cases has occurred in a hospital, as well as Beijing and three other areas in China.

"There's very good news that the SARS epidemic is over its peak," said Henk Bekedam, WHO's representative in China. "Our conclusion is that SARS can be contained, [even though] we don't have a test, treatment or cure."[36]

Bush Response

At the top of the Bush administration's public-health agenda is the threat of bioterrorism. Last December, Bush announced plans to vaccinate about 500,000 health workers against smallpox. Thanks to a global effort to stamp out smallpox, the deadly viral disease no longer occurs naturally, but there is concern that bioterrorists may gain access to lab strains and deliberately release them, causing a global smallpox pandemic.

So far, however, the administration has failed to convince health workers that the risk of bioterrorism outweighs the risk of occasionally severe side effects from the smallpox vaccine. Only about 36,000 people have received the vaccine.[37]

"This is a beautiful example of the perception of risk," says Lumpkin of the FDA. "People feel that there's no real risk of getting smallpox. If you had an outbreak of SARS in this country, however, that perception would be very different."

Can the U.S. public-health system protect America from SARS?

YES   Jerry Hauer
Acting Assistant Secretary for Public Health Emergency Preparedness, Department of Health and Human Services

From testimony before the House Energy And Commerce Subcommittee On Oversight and Investigations, May 7, 2003

The Department of Health and Human Services continues to work vigorously to ensure that the nation is ready to respond to terrorism and other public-health emergencies. As we strengthen our public-health infrastructure against bioterrorism, we are simultaneously enhancing our ability to respond to emerging public-health threats. . . .

Despite the seriousness of the virus' impact worldwide, we have reason to be encouraged by the response to SARS, for several reasons. First, the identification of the agent that causes the disease was completed in record time. In contrast to diseases, including HIV, legionnella and Lyme disease, which took over a year or even longer to pinpoint, we have and continue to have daily videoconferences to share information, map the response and coordinate our activities. . . .

We are partnering with industry to organize a full-court press on vaccine development. We are taking maximum advantage of technology to facilitate information sharing. The map of the SARS genome was published on the Internet soon after it was successfully sequenced by an international team of laboratories led by [the Centers for Disease Control and Prevention] and Health Canada. Improvements in laboratory capacity and coordination that were made recently as part of our enhancing of our overall public-health emergency preparedness have contributed to the speed and accuracy with which we've responded to SARS. . . .

Although the situation in Canada appears to be coming under control, it is critical that we are prepared to confront an outbreak of SARS on U.S. soil. Our recent efforts to enhance the nation's preparedness to respond to a smallpox outbreak have laid the foundation for managing a potential SARS event in cities throughout the country. . . .

The bioterrorism-preparedness funding has made a material difference at the state and local levels. Over 90 percent of the 50 states and three municipalities that have been awarded funds have developed systems for 24/7 notification or activation of their public-health emergency-response plans. And 87 percent of these grantees have developed interim plans. . . .

These are truly challenging times for our department. I believe that we are up to the task, and we look forward to working closely with Congress to ensure that the nation is prepared to respond to bioterrorism and other public-health emergencies such as the SARS virus.

NO   Dr. Georges Benjamin
Executive Director, American Public Health Association

From testimony before the House Energy And Commerce Subcommittee On Oversight and Investigations, May 7, 2003

The SARS outbreak and others, including anthrax and West Nile, have . . . exposed gaps in our own public-health system in the United States. We are at a critical juncture in public health. For many years, experts have been warning us that our nation's public-health infrastructure is in disarray. Recent preparedness funding has provided for improvements in the public-health preparedness infrastructure; however, gaps remain. There still is a lack of adequate personnel and training [and] laboratory-surge capacity, and there are still holes in our communications networks. There remain serious gaps in our disease-surveillance systems. . . .

Perhaps never before has it been so important to shore up our public-health system. This system is being asked to support our response to some of the most threatening emerging diseases of our time and to prepare for diseases yet unknown. In this age when biological and chemical terrorism is added to the portfolio of public-health threats, we need to be assured that the system works, and works well. . . .

In the absence of a robust public-health system with built-in surge capacity, every crisis "du jour" also forces trade-offs—attention to one infectious disease at the expense of another, infectious-disease prevention at the expense of chronic-disease prevention and other public-health responsibilities. . . . public-health is being asked to do more with less. Unless we start supporting our public-health base in a more holistic way, we are going to continue to need to come to Congress for special emergency requests for funds as each new threat emerges. Funding public-health outbreak by outbreak is not an effective way to ensure either preparedness or accountability. . . .

It is time to think more strategically about the future of our nation's public-health system. . . . Because of their impact on society, a coordinated strategy is necessary to understand, detect, control and ultimately prevent infectious diseases. We believe that far more significant investments in public health will need to occur if we are to prepare the nation's public-health system to protect us from the leading causes of death, prepare us for bioterrorism and chemical terrorism and respond to the public-health crises of the day.

I hope we all recognize that this SARS event is not over, and that we still have a ways to go to ensure containment. In the future, we will always be one plane ride away, one infected person away and one epidemic away from a global tragedy. We cannot lower our guard, not today, not tomorrow.

Bush's focus on bioterrorism has shaped the administration's priorities for public-health spending as well. Since Sept. 11, 2001, Congress has approved administration requests for $1.1 billion in federal funds to help states improve communications and lab capacity as well as hospital preparedness for massive casualties in a bioterrorist attack.

In his January 2003 State of the Union address, Bush also announced Project Bioshield, a plan to spend $5.6 billion over 10 years to buy an arsenal of tests, drugs and vaccines to defend against bioterrorism.[38]

At the same time, the administration has called for cuts in public-health agency budgets that critics say will hamper the nation's ability to ward off infectious disease, whether intentional or, like SARS, naturally occurring. After increasing the National Institutes of Health's budget by around 15 percent in the past two years, the administration has called for an increase of only 2 percent in fiscal 2004, to $27.9 billion.[39]

The CDC has fared so poorly under the Bush administration that it has had to solicit funds from private donors to carry out its mission. The agency would suffer an actual reduction in funding in 2004 under the current budget request; its Center for Infectious Disease would see its budget fall from $343 million to about $332 million.[40]

"The administration's emphasis on bioterrorism has unquestionably strengthened our capacity to respond to terrorist threats, has left us a lot better prepared than we were two years ago and is paying off with SARS," says Bloom of the Harvard School of Public Health. "Having said that, how they can cut infectious diseases and the CDC budget is beyond my comprehension."

OUTLOOK

Promising Research

Researchers around the world took only a matter of weeks to identify the SARS coronavirus and sequence its genome. They have found that the virus probably originated in masked palm civets and raccoon dogs—wild animals considered delicacies in southern China, where the virus apparently jumped to humans working in live-animal markets.

Interestingly, there have been no reports of transmission to or between children. Researchers at the recent NIH conference on SARS suggested that children might

be at least partially immune to the disease, or get milder symptoms than adults, just as they do with chicken pox and some other infectious diseases common in childhood.

Anecdotal evidence also indicates that immunosuppressed individuals, such as those with AIDS or undergoing chemotherapy, may also be less susceptible to SARS—suggesting the possibility that it is the individual's own immune response to the infection, and not the virus itself, that causes the severe and often fatal pneumonia-like symptoms.

But these are just hypotheses, and SARS remains largely a mystery. "We need a vaccine, and we need a better way to diagnose," says Fauci of the NIH. Currently, specimens from suspected SARS patients must be sent away for testing—a time-consuming process. "We need to get the next generation of user-friendly diagnostics that are readily available in the setting of the local hospital," Fauci says. "We have to see if drugs that we already have can be used to treat SARS. And there will be a whole array of vaccine initiatives aimed at preventing the disease."

The FDA is enlisting the drug industry to invest quickly in research to produce SARS tests, therapies and vaccines by streamlining its rules for drug testing and approval. "Obviously, this is not something we would do for every product," Lumpkin says. "But for true public-health emergencies like this—for serious and life-threatening illnesses that don't have good therapies available—absolutely. That's the way we do business, and SARS clearly fits into that category."

SARS Prognosis

As scientists search for diagnostics and therapies to test for and treat SARS, they also are working on a vaccine to prevent contagion in the first place. But vaccine research is notoriously slow and probably won't produce results for several years. "If we're really lucky and are able to rush it through, we may be able to have a big enough clinical trial in three years to get some reliable answers," Fauci says. "It could be three years, or it could just as easily be seven."

While the focus today is on SARS, Fauci and many other infectious-disease experts are more concerned about the potential for a deadly new influenza outbreak in the future. "We have our annual [flu] epidemics, which are bad enough," said Klaus Stohr, project leader for WHO's global influenza program. "More than a million people are dying every year from influenza."

In the industrial world, annual flu vaccinations help protect against major disease, but the world is past due for a major mutation of the flu virus that could render the vaccine useless, experts say.

"This vaccine, which we are producing now, will not be effective when the pandemic comes, and the pandemic will travel around the world within three to six months," Stohr warned. "Up to 50 percent of the population will be affected. Millions of people will die. This is something which we have seen in the past and, what is worse, it is going to lead certainly to a global health emergency because of the burden to the health-care system and to hospitals."[41]

One of the best defenses against such a pandemic would be an effective early-warning system that might enable health-care workers to isolate any new microbe before it escapes into the global community.

"Infectious diseases don't respect national boundaries," says Harvard's Bloom. "My lesson from the SARS epidemic is that if we want to protect ourselves, we need an early-warning system, whether it's a new global-surveillance network or upgrading the competence of national and regional labs, that can tell us what's happening anywhere in the world."

NOTES

1. For background, see Mary H. Cooper, "Combating Infectious Diseases," *The CQ Researcher*, June 9, 1995, pp. 489-512.

2. Benjamin testified before the House Energy and Commerce Subcommittee on Oversight and Investigations, on May 7, 2003.

3. McGeer spoke at a SARS conference held on May 30, 2003, at the National Institutes of Health in Bethesda, Md.

4. Paul Farmer, "SARS and Inequality," *The Nation*, May 26, 2003, p. 6.

5. See Rob Stein, "SARS Prompts WHO to Seek More Power to Fight Disease," *The Washington Post*, May 18, 2003, p. A10.

6. Jerome Groopman, "Global Warning," *The Wall Street Journal*, April 23, 2003, p. A22.

7. *Ibid.*

8. See "SARS Kills Man Who Broke Quarantine, Went to Work at Ont. Plant," *Canadian Press Newswire*, May 29, 2003.

9. See " 'Bed chains' for Canada SARS Violators," *BBC News*, June 1, 2003.

10. See Judith Walzer Leavitt, *Typhoid Mary* (1997).

11. The poll, conducted by Robert J. Blendon, professor of health polity and political analysis at the Harvard School of Public Health, was released May 21, 2003.

12. Institute of Medicine, "Microbial Threats to Health: Emergence, Detection and Response," March 2003, p. 7.

13. General Accounting Office, "Bioterrorism: Preparedness Varied Across State and Local Jurisdictions," April 7, 2003.

14. See Chris Conte, "Deadly Strains," *Governing*, June 2003, pp. 20-24.

15. Unless otherwise noted, information on the public-health system's history is based on Laurie Garrett, *Betrayal of Trust* (2000), pp. 268-485.

16. For background, see David Masci, "Smallpox Threat," *The CQ Researcher*, Feb.7, 2003, pp. 105-128.

17. For background, see Kathy Koch, "Vaccine Controversies," *The CQ Researcher*, Aug. 25, 2000, pp. 641-672.

18. Garrett, *op. cit.*, p. 291.

19. For more information on the Public Health Service's development, see www.nlm.nih.gov.

20. See Ronald Kotulak and Peter Gorner, "After SARS, What Might Come Next?" *The Chicago Tribune*, April 27, 2003, p. A1.

21. Garrett, *op. cit.*, pp. 326-327.

22. Paul Starr, *The Social Transformation of American Medicine* (1984), cited in Garrett, *op. cit.*, p. 309.

23. Garrett, *op. cit.*, p. 334.

24. For background, see David Masci, "Global AIDS Crisis," *The CQ Researcher*, Oct. 13, 2000, pp. 809-832.

25. Kotulak and Gorner, *op. cit.*

26. For background, see Adriel Bettelheim, "Drug-Resistant Bacteria," *The CQ Researcher*, June 4, 1999, pp. 473-496.

27. For background, see Mary H. Cooper, "Mad Cow Disease," *The CQ Researcher*, March 2, 2001, pp. 161-184.

28. See Vanessa Fuhrmans, "Europe Struggles to Contain Outbreak of a Bird Flu Virus," *The Wall Street Journal*, May 16, 2003, p. A5.

29. See "Four Horsemen of the Apocalypse?" *The Economist*, May 3, 2003, pp. 73-74.

30. For background, see *Congress and the Nation*, Vo. IV, 1973-1976, p. 863, and http://dosfan.lib.uic.edu/acda/treaties and click on geneva 1 or bwc1.

31. For background, see Mary H. Cooper, "Weapons of Mass Destruction," *The CQ Researcher*, March 8, 2002, pp. 193-216.

32. The following account is based on a chronology that is continuously updated in *The Wall Street Journal Online*.

33. See Jonathan Mirsky, "How the Chinese Spread SARS," *The New York Review of Books*, May 29, 2003, p. 42.

34. See Ellen Nakashima, "SARS Signals Missed in Hong Kong," *The Washington Post*, May 20, 2003, p. A1.

35. See Jason Dean and Matt Pottinger, "Complacency in Taiwan Led to Revival of Spread of SARS," *The Wall Street Journal*, May 19, 2003, p. B6.

36. Quoted by Elisabeth Rosenthal, "SARS Epidemic Winding Down, Health Officials Say," *The New York Times*, June 5, 2003, p. A10.

37. See "Missing the Smallpox Goal," *The New York Times* (editorial), May 12, 2003, p. A24.

38. See Michael Barbaro, "Biodefense Plan Greeted with Caution," *The Washington Post*, May 2, 2003, p. E1.

39. See Ted Agres, "Funding 2004," *The Scientist*, Feb. 4, 2003.

40. See Peter Gosselin, "CDC Turns to Private Aid to Stay Healthy," *Los Angeles Times*, April 25, 2003, p. A1.

41. Stohr was interviewed on CNN's "In the Money," on June 8, 2003.

BIBLIOGRAPHY

Books

Garrett, Laurie, *Betrayal of Trust: The Collapse of Global Public Health*, Hyperion, 2000.
A journalist describes how underfunding has undermined the public-health system's ability to cope with human disease throughout the world, including the United States. Garrett won a Pulitzer Prize for her book *The Coming Plague*, about emerging infectious diseases.

Articles

Bloom, Barry R., "Lessons from SARS," *Science*, May 2, 2003, p. 701.
The dean of the Harvard School of Public Health calls on the United States to help strengthen the global public-health system to prevent the spread of infectious diseases like SARS.

"China Wakes Up," *The Economist*, April 24, 2003.
China is coming under fire for covering up the SARS outbreak and allowing the deadly disease to spread beyond its borders.

Conte, Christopher, "Deadly Strains," *Governing*, June 2003, pp. 20-24.
Seattle's public-health department is struggling to protect residents from infectious-disease threats in the face of dwindling federal support.

Donnelly, Christl A., et al., "Epidemiological Determinants of Spread of Causal Agent of Severe Acute Respiratory Syndrome in Hong Kong," *The Lancet*, May 5, 2003, pp. 1-6.
The authors helped define SARS' average incubation period, course and fatality rate by studying 1,425 SARS cases in Hong Kong. They found the fatality rate rises with patient age.

Gerberding, Julie Louise, "Faster . . . But Fast Enough?" *The New England Journal of Medicine*, May 15, 2003, p. 2030.
The director of the U.S. Centers for Disease Control and Prevention (CDC) calls on researchers to move as quickly in seeking vaccines and drugs to combat SARS as they did in discovering the virus that causes the disease.

Gratzer, David, "SARS 101," *National Review Online*, May 19, 2003.
Pointing to China's SARS cover-up, a Toronto physician urges the CDC and its Canadian counterpart, Health Canada, to require airports around the world to adopt exit screening.

Kristof, Nicholas D., "Lock 'Em Up," *The New York Times*, May 2, 2003, p. A35.
This column calling for strict isolation of anyone suspected of harboring a deadly infection sparked numerous

letters to the editor. "If you disagree," Kristof writes, "how about if I visit your neighborhood the next time I'm back from an Ebola outbreak in Congo and feeling feverish?"

Lemonick, Michael D., and Alice Park, "The Truth about SARS," *Time,* **May 5, 2002, pp. 48-57.**
Fear of the deadly SARS virus has kept people away from markets in Asia and prompted travelers to cancel their vacation plans, causing a downturn in the global tourist trade

McNeil, Donald G. Jr., "Help! I'm Stuck in Quarantine and I Can't Get Out!" *The New York Times,* **June 1, 2003, p. D7.**
A New York City resident who may have been exposed to SARS during a recent visit to Taiwan describes the difficulty of maintaining his 10-day voluntary quarantine.

Mirsky, Jonathan, "How the Chinese Spread SARS," *The New York Review of Books,* **April 30, 2003, p. 42.**
China's oppressive political system, in particular its 1996 law classifying highly infectious diseases as top secret, caused health workers to deny the SARS outbreak for four months and enable its spread.

Shute, Nancy, "SARS Hits Home," *U.S. News & World Report,* **May 5, 2003, pp. 38-44.**
The deadly disease's arrival in Toronto is cause for concern in the United States.

Reports and Studies

General Accounting Office, *Bioterrorism: Preparedness Varied across State and Local Jurisdictions,* **April 7, 2003.**
The investigative arm of Congress found that most hospitals it studied "lack the capacity to respond to large-scale infectious-disease outbreaks."

Institute of Medicine, *The Future of the Public's Health in the 21st Century,* **Nov. 11, 2002.**
The U.S. public-health system is ill prepared to deal with both chronic and emerging diseases, the IOM says.

__, *Microbial Threats to Health: Emergence, Detection and Response,* **March 18, 2003.**
Released on the eve of the recent SARS outbreak, this IOM report calls for heightened preparedness in the United States and overseas to quickly detect and eradicate infectious diseases.

For More Information

American Public Health Association, 800 I St., N.W., Washington, DC 20001; (202) 777-2436; www.apha.org. The largest organization of public-health professionals in the world represents 50,000 members from 50 related occupations.

Center for Law and the Public's Health, Johns Hopkins and Georgetown universities, 624 North Broadway, Baltimore, MD 21205; (410) 955-7624 (Hopkins); 600 New Jersey Ave. N.W., Washington, DC 20001; (202) 662-9373 (Georgetown); www.publichealthlaw.net. The center was founded in 2000 with support from the Centers for Disease Control and Prevention as a primary, national resource on public health law, ethics and policy.

Center for Medical Humanities and Ethics, University of Texas Health Science Center, 7703 Floyd Curl Dr., San Antonio, TX 78229-3900; (210) 567-0795; www. texashumanities.org. The center uses literature, drama and the visual arts to integrate the humanities into medical education.

Centers for Disease Control and Prevention, 1600 Clifton Rd., Atlanta, GA 30333; (404) 639-3311; www.cdc.gov. The CDC is the lead federal public-health agency.

Food and Drug Administration, 5600 Fishers Lane, Rockville, MD 20857; (301) 827-5709; www.fda.gov.

National Institute of Allergy and Infectious Diseases, 9000 Rockville Pike, Bethesda, MD 20892; (301) 496-2263; www.nih.gov.

Nuclear Threat Initiative, 1747 Pennsylvania Ave., N.W., 7th Floor, Washington DC 20006; (202) 296-4810; www.nti.org. NTI seeks to reduce the risk of nuclear, biological and chemical weapons.

World Health Organization, Avenue Appia 20, 1211 Geneva 27, Switzerland; (41-22) 791-2111; www.who.int. The U.N. agency monitors infectious-disease outbreaks.